EVERYMAN'S LIBRARY
EDITED BY ERNEST RHYS

HISTORY

HISTORY OF THE
BYZANTINE EMPIRE
· BY GEORGE FINLAY ·
WITH AN INTRODUCTION BY V. R. R.

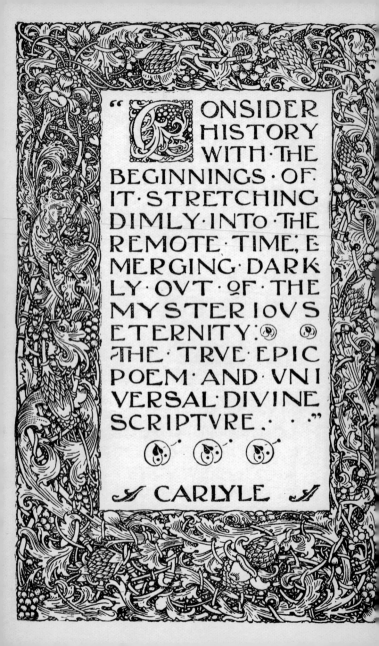

"CONSIDER HISTORY WITH·THE BEGINNINGS·OF·IT·STRETCHING DIMLY·INTO·THE REMOTE·TIME; E·MERGING·DARKLY·OVT·OF·THE MYSTERIOVS ETERNITY: THE·TRVE·EPIC POEM·AND·VNIVERSAL·DIVINE SCRIPTVRE·.·."

CARLYLE

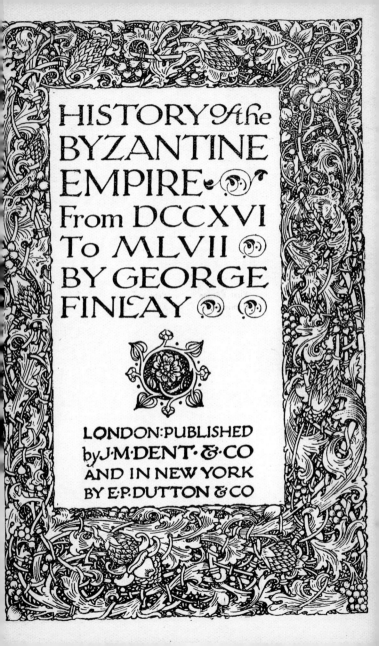

HISTORY of the BYZANTINE EMPIRE
From DCCXVI To MLVII
BY GEORGE FINLAY

LONDON: PUBLISHED
by J·M·DENT·&·CO
AND IN NEW YORK
BY E·P·DUTTON & CO

First Edition . . February 1906
Reprinted . . . April 1906

PLYMOUTH : WILLIAM BRENDON AND SON, LTD,
PRINTERS

EDITOR'S INTRODUCTION

" I WOULD rather," said a former president of Harvard University, Professor Felton, " be the author of your histories than Prime Minister of England." This was said in a letter to Finlay, reassuring and solacing him in his day of dejection. So Atticus once comforted Cicero ; but it is to be feared that Finlay's case was one of another order, less consolable. His misgivings were due to a sense of disillusion over that very cause, the renaissance of a new Greece, to which he had devoted his life with unswerving mind and singleness of purpose. And even that was not all. For his disappointment coincided with the beginning of his own physical decline, and with the apparent signs too, for so he read them, that his services to his day and generation had been in vain.

Now, we who look back along the steadfast line of his achievement, recognise how eminent it was, and how true was the prophecy of his friend Felton, uttered almost fifty years ago. We see the continuing effects of his labour, forty years long, as an historian, and the heroic difficulty of his work as an active and practical Philhellene. To gain an estimate of its force and quality, it is almost enough to read the books of his Byzantine history that follow ; but they ought to be read with the radiant hope of Finlay's youth and his first great ardour in the Hellenic cause gleaming upon the page.

Finlay, who died in Athens in 1875, was born at Faversham, Kent, in 1799 ; that is a few months before Macaulay, a very different master of history. His early circumstances were hardly such as to foster his special qualities. He went to no university until he was twenty, and had spent some months in a writer's office at Glasgow ; and of his schooldays, three years in a Liverpool boarding-school were, on his own showing, a lost and useless period.

But he was fortunate in having a mother who both loved history herself and had the art of making it alive to the imagination of her boy. When, then, Finlay went from Glasgow to Göttingen to study Roman law, he was better primed than the mere chart of his early years would seem to show. Moreover, he reached Germany at a time when the promise of the new awakening of Greece was bright, and he breathed the air of its revolt in a kind of intellectual ecstasy. He drank in eagerly every word he could of the news of the Greek cause, made friends with the one Greek student at the college ; and at length, in the autumn of 1823, very shortly after the news of Lord Byron's departure for Greece had been announced, he too set off thither. He reached Cephalonia in November, and met the poet ; went on to Athens, and then to Missolonghi. Probably it was there that he, like Lord Byron, laid the seeds of the fever that afterwards seriously threatened him. It was in April, 1824, that Byron died. Finlay had gone on meanwhile to Italy, where and in Sicily he spent some time, returning to Scotland to pass his examination in civil law. But that accomplished, he felt the power and the hope of Greece all dominant in his mind. He could not resist the unsated desire he felt to return and be in the very midst of the struggle. He left again for its shores in 1825, there to remain for the rest of his life, nearly half a century in all, with the intermission only of a few visits home. In 1829 Greece was able to declare her independence— thanks to the aid of many enthusiastic adherents, who, like Byron and Finlay, had been ready to give all they had to her cause. Alas ! Finlay lost nearly all he possessed, and often felt that he had given his days as well as his wealth in vain in this sacrifice.

But Finlay, if he doubted at times, and felt that all he had done and spent and written had been of no real avail, could never have echoed Byron's plaint in " Childe Harold " for the companion country :

> There is the moral of all human tales ;
> 'Tis but the same rehearsal of the past,
> First Freedom, and then Glory—when that fails,
> Wealth, vice, corruption,—barbarism at last.
> And History, with all her volumes vast,
> Hath but one page ! . . . .

Long afterwards, it is true, in 1855, Finlay wrote in the retrospect :—

" Had the hopes with which I joined the cause of Greece in 1823 been fulfilled, it is not probable that I should have abandoned the active duties of life, and the noble task of labouring to improve the land, for the sterile task of recording its misfortunes."

But Finlay was a philosopher in essence, if not always able to be philosophical in the common sense about the discrepancy that exists between human and ideal effort and sheer achievement. We turn back now to the record of his " sterile task "—his writing of Greek history. Its first results appeared in 1836, when his book on the " Hellenic Kingdom and the Greek Nation," was published. Then in 1844, his "Greece under the Romans" followed in two volumes. His History of the Byzantine and Greek Empires was completed in 1854. Two years later came the volumes dealing with the Ottoman and Venetian Domination ; and in 1861, his History of the Greek Revolution. If his life-work then seemed complete, he still did great service by his letters and articles contributed to the "Athenæum," the "Times," "Saturday Review," and other papers and reviews. We have seen already that his own feeling in these later years was one of much discouragement. He had seen the light of a new and regenerate Greece wax, and then wane : and the decline was a more serious one, viewed under his gravely human, philosophical estimate, than the outer world could perceive. Then his own stock of vitality was beginning to run low, and his faith in the validity of his life-work— considered purely as a literary and scholarly accomplishment and apart from the good or evil fortune of his chosen and adopted country—had been weakened, in spite of the encouragements of his peers and fellow-scholars—men like the President of Harvard and Professor Müller. Probably, living away in Athens as he did, he did not realise the full measure of his influence. But his was an order of work that could not hope to attain a great vogue. Sound and slow, without the surface brilliancy that made a Macaulay enormously popular, it has power to affect the circle of scholars and men who were the inner public of the time. It is not readily to be known, however, if this has been achieved, and, at any rate, the signs were not so deciphered by Finlay from his watch-tower at Athens.

But of the total value of his historical work there is, there can be, no question. He was the pioneer of the new movement which in England led at last to the re-writing of history with an eye to human development and social and economic change, as it was re-written for us by Green in his "History of the English People." But Finlay, long before Green, had come to the same sense of the true function of history. One passage, and a very remarkable one it is, may be quoted to show how he confronted his great task :—

"The vicissitudes which the great masses of the nations of the earth have undergone in past ages have hitherto received very little attention from historians, who have adorned their pages with the records of kings, and the personal exploits of princes and great men, or attached their narrative to the fortunes of the dominant classes, without noticing the fate of the people. History, however, continually repeats the lesson that powers, numbers, and the highest civilisation of an aristocracy are, even when united, insufficient to ensure national prosperity, and establish the power of the rulers on so firm and permanent a basis as shall guarantee the dominant class from annihilation. . . . It is that portion only of mankind, which eats bread raised from the soil by the sweat of its brow, that can form the basis of a permanent material existence."

In this passage we have Finlay's idea of the philosophy of history, and of the historian's exemplification of it in practice. It was an idea that was present and that was most devotedly pursued to the end in Finlay's own books. The test of a man's performance in this, as in other forms of literature, is in the reading ; and Finlay's readers, here and in other pages of his, will decide what his final place is in the common ground where literature and history meet.

We might have added a word from the tribute paid to him by a Greek contemporary on his death, who spoke of him as only Byron among foreigners had been spoken of previously. But more to the purpose here is that of the "Athenæum," to which he had contributed for some thirty-six years in all, at his death. In its obituary notice, it spoke of the great loss caused to history and to English literature by the death of this last of the old generation of Philhellenes who had followed Byron's lead. And the loss to Greece itself, it pointed out, was none the less, since the people needed a Mentor so much and so unwillingly endured one.

"To Finlay," continued the writer in the "Athenæum," his researches taught "the practical lesson that the regeneration of Greece was not to be sought in the reproduction of classic forms, but in the rational development of the people as they are. . . . It was with this view that he contributed to the 'Times' a remarkable series of letters from Greece . . . which appear to have produced a revolution in the Greek mind."

What, we cannot but ask, would Finlay have said had he witnessed the melancholy sequel of the last Greek war, with its exhibition of even deeper infirmities,—with evidence of a far graver disorder of state and people, than those he knew and those he anticipated?

Finlay's last publication was an edition, printed in Paris, of the journal kept by Brue, interpreter to the French embassy, who accompanied the Grand Vizier, Ali, in the Morean campaign of 1715. Finlay had purchased the MS. in 1843, and had drawn from it freely in his "Greece under the Ottoman and Venetian Domination."

Another passage from the poet who helped to kindle and inspire his Hellenic ardour is the best epilogue both to Finlay's sanguine first hopes and his last troubled decline. It occurs in "The Siege of Corinth":—

> The waters murmured of their name ;
> The woods were peopled with their fame.
> The silent pillar, lone and grey,
> Claimed kindred with their sacred clay ;
> Their spirits wrapped the dusky mountain,
> Their memory sparkled o'er the fountain ;
> The meanest rill, the mightiest river,
> Rolled mingling with their fame for ever.
> Despite of every yoke she bears
> That land is Glory's still and theirs !
> 'Tis still a watchword to the earth :
> When man would do a deed of worth
> He points to Greece. . . .

V. R. R.

———————

The following is a list of the published works of George Finlay (1799–1875):—

The Hellenic Kingdom and the Greek Nation, 1836. *Remarks on the Topography of Oropia and Diacria*, 1838. Ἐπιστολη προς τους Ἀθηναιους (and other pamphlets on Greek Finance), 1844. *Greece under the Romans*, 1844. *On the Site of the Holy Sepulchre*, 1847. *Greece to its Conquest by the Turks*, 1851. *Greece under Ottoman and Venetian Dominion*, 1856. *The Greek Revolution*, 1861. Ἀντικειμενα εὑρεθεντα εν Ἑλλαδι, 1869. παρατηρησεις ἐπι της ἐν Ἑλβετιᾳ, etc., 1869. *The French Narrative of Benjamin Brue*, 1870. *A History of Greece from its Conquest by the Romans to the Present Time*, B.C. 146–A.D. 1864 ; 1877 [Clarendon Press reissue of his History, revised by himself, and edited by Tozer].

Finlay also contributed to the "Times" (1864–70), "Athenæum," and "Saturday Review."

CONTENTS

BOOK I

THE CONTEST WITH THE ICONOCLASTS
A.D. 717–867

Contents

BOOK II

BASILIAN DYNASTY—PERIOD OF THE POWER AND GLORY OF THE BYZANTINE EMPIRE
A.D. 867–1057

CHAPTER I

THE ISAURIAN DYNASTY. A.D. 717-797

Section I

CHARACTERISTICS OF BYZANTINE HISTORY—ITS DIVISIONS—
EXTENT AND ADMINISTRATIVE DIVISIONS OF THE EMPIRE

THE institutions of Imperial Rome had long thwarted the great law of man's existence which impels him to better his condition, when the accession of Leo the Isaurian to the throne of Constantinople suddenly opened a new era in the history of the Eastern Empire. Both the material and intellectual progress of society had been deliberately opposed by the imperial legislation. A spirit of conservatism persuaded the legislators of the Roman empire that its power could not decline, if each order and profession of its citizens was fixed irrevocably in the sphere of their own peculiar duties by hereditary succession. An attempt was really made to divide the population into castes. But the political laws which were adopted to maintain mankind in a state of stationary prosperity by these trammels, depopulated and impoverished the empire, and threatened to dissolve the very elements of society. The Western Empire, under their operation, fell a prey to small tribes of northern nations; the Eastern was so depopulated that it was placed on the eve of being repeopled by Sclavonian colonists, and conquered by Saracen invaders.

Leo III. mounted the throne, and under his government the empire not only ceased to decline, but even began to regain much of its early vigour. Reformed modifications of the old Roman authority developed new energy in the empire. Great political reforms, and still greater changes in the condition of the people, mark the eighth century as an epoch of transition in Roman history, though the improved condition of the mass of the population is in some degree concealed by the prominence given to the disputes concerning image-worship in the records of this period. But the increased strength of the empire, and the energy infused into the administration, are forcibly displayed by the fact, that the Byzantine armies began from this time to oppose a firm barrier to the progress of the invaders of the empire.

When Leo III. was proclaimed Emperor, it seemed as if no human power could save Constantinople from falling as Rome had fallen. The Saracens considered the sovereignty of every land, in which any remains of Roman civilisation survived, as within their grasp. Leo, an Isaurian, and an Iconoclast, consequently a foreigner and a heretic, ascended the throne of Constantine, and arrested the victorious career of the Mohammedans. He then reorganised the whole administration so completely in accordance with the new exigencies of Eastern society, that the reformed empire outlived for many centuries every government contemporary with its establishment.

The Eastern Roman Empire, thus reformed, is called by modern historians the Byzantine Empire; and the term is well devised to mark the changes effected in the government, after the extinction of the last traces of the military monarchy of ancient Rome. The social condition of the inhabitants of the Eastern Empire had already undergone a considerable change during the century which elapsed from the accession of Heraclius to that of Leo, from the influence of causes to be noticed in the following pages; and this change in society created a new phase in the Roman empire. The gradual progress of this change has led some writers to date the commencement of the Byzantine Empire as early as the reigns of Zeno and Anastasius, and others to descend so late as the times of Maurice and Heraclius.[1] But as the Byzantine Empire was only a continuation of the Roman government under a reformed system, it seems most correct to date its commencement from the period when the new social and political modifications produced a visible effect on the fate of the Eastern Empire. This period is marked by the accession of Leo the Isaurian.

The administrative system of Rome, as modified by Constantine, continued in operation, though subjected to frequent reforms, until Constantinople was stormed by the Crusaders, and the Greek church enslaved by papal domination. The

---

[1] Clinton, *Fasti Romani*, Int. xiii. says, "The empire of Rome, properly so called, ends at A.D. 476," which is the third year of Zeno. Numismatists place the commencement of the Byzantine empire in the reign of Anastasius I.—Saulcy, *Essai de Classification des Suites Monétaires Byzantines*. Gibbon tells us, "Tiberius by the Arabs, and Maurice by the Italians, are distinguished as the first of the Greek Cæsars, as the founders of a new dynasty and empire. The silent revolution was accomplished before the death of Heraclius."—*Decline and Fall*, vol. x. chap. liii. p. 154.

General Council of Nicæa, and the dedication of the imperial city, with their concomitant legislative, administrative, and judicial institutions, engendered a succession of political measures, whose direct relations were uninterrupted until terminated by foreign conquest. The government of Great Britain has undergone greater changes during the last three centuries than that of the Eastern Empire during the nine centuries which elapsed from the foundation of Constantinople in 330, to its conquest in 1204.

Yet Leo III. has strong claims to be regarded as the first of a new series of emperors. He was the founder of a dynasty, the saviour of Constantinople, and the reformer of the church and state. He was the first Christian sovereign who arrested the torrent of Mohammedan conquest; he improved the condition of his subjects; he attempted to purify their religion from the superstitious reminiscences of Hellenism, with which it was still debased, and to stop the development of a quasi-idolatry in the orthodox church. Nothing can prove more decidedly the right of his empire to assume a new name than the contrast presented by the condition of its inhabitants to that of the subjects of the preceding dynasty. Under the successors of Heraclius, the Roman Empire presents the spectacle of a declining society, and its thinly-peopled provinces were exposed to the intrusion of foreign colonists and hostile invaders. But, under Leo, society offers an aspect of improvement and prosperity; the old population revives from its lethargy, and soon increases, both in number and strength, to such a degree as to drive back all intruders on its territories. In the records of human civilisation, Leo the Isaurian must always occupy a high position, as a type of what the central power in a state can effect even in a declining empire.

Before reviewing the history of Leo's reign, and recording his brilliant exploits, it is necessary to sketch the condition to which the Roman administrative system had reduced the empire. It would be an instructive lesson to trace the progress of the moral and mental decline of the Greeks, from the age of Plato and Aristotle to the time of the sixth ecumenical council, in the reign of Justinian II.; for the moral evils nourished in Greek society degraded the nation, before the oppressive government of the Romans impoverished and depopulated Greece. When the imperial authority was fully established, we easily trace the manner in which the inter-communication of different provinces and orders of society became gradually restricted to the operations of material interests, and how the limitation of ideas arose from this want of communication, until at length civilisation decayed. Good roads and commodious passage-boats have a more direct connection with the development of popular education, as we see it reflected in the works of Phidias and the writings of Sophocles, than is generally believed. Under the jealous system of the imperial government, the isolation of place and class became so complete, that even the highest members of the aristocracy received their ideas from the inferior domestics with whom they habitually associated in their own households —not from the transitory intercourse they held with able and experienced men of their own class, or with philosophic and religious teachers. Nurses and slaves implanted their ignorant superstitions in the households where the rulers of the empire and the provinces were reared; and no public assemblies existed, where discussion could efface such prejudices. Family education became a more influential feature in society than public instruction; and though family education, from the fourth to the seventh century, appears to have improved the morality of the population, it certainly increased their superstition and limited their understandings. Emperors, senators, landlords, and merchants, were alike educated under these influences; and though the church and the law opened a more enlarged circle of ideas, from creating a deeper sense of responsibility, still the prejudices of early education circumscribed the sense of duty more and more in each successive generation. The military class, which was the most powerful in society, consisted almost entirely of mere barbarians. The mental degradation, resulting from superstition, bigotry, and ignorance, which forms the marked social feature of the period between the reigns of Justinian I. and Leo III., brought the Eastern Empire to the state of depopulation and weakness that had delivered the Western a prey to small tribes of invaders.

The fiscal causes of the depopulation of the Roman empire have been noticed in a prior volume, as well as the extent to which immigrants had intruded themselves on the soil of Greece.[1] The corruption of the ancient language took place at the same time, and arose out of the causes which disseminated ignorance. At the accession of Leo, the disorder in

[1] *Greece under the Romans*, 60, 70, 238.

of society were annually drawn into the coffers of the state, leaving the inhabitants only a bare sufficiency for perpetuating the race of tax-payers. History, indeed, shows that the agricultural classes, from the labourer to the landlord, were unable to retain possession of the savings required to replace that depreciation which time is constantly producing in all vested capital, and that their numbers gradually diminished.

After the accession of Leo III., a new condition of society is soon apparent; and though many old political evils continued to exist, it becomes evident that a greater degree of personal liberty, as well as greater security for property, was henceforth guaranteed to the mass of the inhabitants of the empire. Indeed, no other government of which history has preserved the records, unless it be that of China, has secured equal advantages to its subjects for so long a period. The empires of the caliphs and of Charlemagne, though historians have celebrated their praises loudly, cannot, in their best days, compete with the administration organised by Leo on this point; and both sank into ruin while the Byzantine empire continued to flourish in full vigour. It must be confessed that eminent historians present a totally different picture of Byzantine history to their readers. Voltaire speaks of it as a worthless repertory of declamation and miracles, disgraceful to the human mind.[1] Even the sagacious Gibbon, after enumerating with just pride the extent of his labours, adds, " From these considerations, I should have abandoned without regret the Greek slaves and their servile historians, had I not reflected that the fate of the Byzantine monarchy is passively connected with the most splendid and important revolutions which have changed the state of the world."[2] The views of Byzantine history, unfolded in the following pages, are frequently

difference of price at Siout and Alexandria, less the expense of transport, or it can constitute itself the sole master of the transport on the Nile, and make a monopoly both of the right of purchase and of freight. The expense of transport is trifling, as the stream carries a loaded boat steadily down the river, while the north wind drives an empty one up against the current, almost with the regularity of a locomotive engine. The Nile offers, in this manner, all the advantages of a railway, nature having constructed the road, and supplied the locomotive power; while a monopoly of their use is vested in the hands of every tyrant who rules the country. Mehemet Ali, not content with this, created an almost universal monopoly in favour of his government. The whole produce of the country was purchased at a tariff price, the cultivator being only allowed to retain the means of perpetuating his class. The number of towns and the density of population in the Byzantine empire arose from the immense amount of capital which ages of security had expended in improving the soil, and from its cultivation as garden-land with the spade and mattock. Both these facts are easily proved.

[1] *Le Pyrrhonisme de l'Histoire*, chap. xv. note l. With this remark, the records of an empire, which witnessed the rise and fall of the Caliphs and the Carlovingians, are dismissed by one who exclaimed, " *J'ôterai aux nations le bandeau de l'erreur.*"

[2] *Decline and Fall*, chap. xlviii.

in direct opposition to these great authorities. The defects and vices of the political system will be carefully noticed, but the splendid achievements of the emperors, and the great merits of the judicial and ecclesiastical establishments, will be contrasted with their faults.

The history of the Byzantine empire divides itself into three periods, strongly marked by distinct characteristics.

The first period commences with the reign of Leo III. in 716, and terminates with that of Michael III. in 867. It comprises the whole history of the predominance of the Iconoclasts in the established church, and of the reaction which reinstated the orthodox in power. It opens with the efforts by which Leo and the people of the empire saved the Roman law and the Christian religion from the conquering Saracens. It embraces a long and violent struggle between the government and the people, the emperors seeking to increase the central power by annihilating every local franchise, and even the right of private opinion, among their subjects. The contest concerning image-worship, from the prevalence of ecclesiastical ideas, became the expression of this struggle. Its object was as much to consolidate the supremacy of the imperial authority, as to purify the practice of the church. The emperors wished to constitute themselves the fountains of ecclesiastical as completely as of civil legislation.

The long and bloody wars of this period, and the vehement character of the sovereigns who filled the throne, attract the attention of those who love to dwell on the romantic facts of history. Unfortunately, the biographical sketches and individual characters of the heroes of these ages lie concealed in the dullest chronicles. But the true historical feature of this memorable period is the aspect of a declining empire, saved by the moral vigour developed in society, and of the central authority struggling to restore national prosperity. Never was such a succession of able sovereigns seen following one another on any other throne. The stern Iconoclast, Leo the Isaurian, opens the line as the second founder of the Eastern Empire. His son, the fiery Constantine, who was said to prefer the odour of the stable to the perfumes of his palaces, replanted the Christian standards on the banks of the Euphrates. Irene, the beautiful Athenian, presents a strange combination of talent, heartlessness, and orthodoxy. The finance minister, Nicephoras, perishes on the field of battle like an old Roman. The Armenian Leo falls at the altar of his private chapel, murdered as he is singing psalms with his deep voice, before day-dawn. Michael the Amorian, who stammered Greek with his native Phrygian accent, became the founder of an imperial dynasty, destined to be extinguished by a Sclavonian groom. The accomplished Theophilus lived in an age of romance, both in action and literature. His son, Michael, the last of the Amorian family, was the only contemptible prince of this period, and he was certainly the most despicable buffoon that ever occupied a throne.

The second period commences with the reign of Basil I. in 867, and terminates with the deposition of Michael VI. in 1057. During these two centuries the imperial sceptre was retained by members of the Basilian family, or held by those who shared their throne as guardians or husbands. At this time the Byzantine empire attained its highest pitch of external power and internal prosperity. The Saracens were pursued into the plains of Syria. Antioch and Edessa were reunited to the empire. The Bulgarian monarchy was conquered, and the Danube became again the northern frontier. The Sclavonians in Greece were almost exterminated. Byzantine commerce filled the whole Mediterranean, and legitimated the claim of the emperor of Constantinople to the title of Autocrat of the Mediterranean sea.[1] But the real glory of this period consists in the power of the law. Respect for the administration of justice pervaded society more generally than it had ever done at any preceding period of the history of the world—a fact which our greatest historians have overlooked, though it is all-important in the history of human civilisation.

The third period extends from the accession of Isaac I. (Comnenus) in 1057, to the conquest of the Byzantine empire by the Crusaders, in 1204. This is the true period of the decline and fall of the Eastern Empire. It commenced by a rebellion of the great nobles of Asia, who effected an internal revolution in the Byzantine empire by wrenching the administration out of the hands of well-trained officials, and destroying the responsibility created by systematic procedure. A despotism supported by personal influence soon ruined the scientific fabric which had previously upheld the imperial power. The people were ground to the earth by a fiscal rapacity, over which the splendour of the house of Comnenus

---

[1] Constant. Porphyr. *De Them.* ii. 27—Διὰ τὸ τὸν Αὐτοκράτορα κωνσταντινουπόλεως θαλασσοκρατεῖν μέχρι τῶν Ἡρακλέος στηλῶν καὶ πάσης ὁμοῦ τῆς ὧδε θαλάσσης.

throws a thin veil.   The wealth of the empire was dissipated, its prosperity destroyed, the administration of justice corrupted, and the central authority lost all control over the population, when a band of 20,000 adventurers, masked as crusaders, put an end to the Roman empire of the East.

In the eighth and ninth centuries the Byzantine empire continued to embrace many nations differing from the Greeks in language and manners.   Even in religion there was a strong tendency to separation, and many of the heresies noticed in history assumed a national character, while the orthodox church circumscribed itself more and more within the nationality of the Greeks, and forfeited its ecumenical characteristics. The empire still included within its limits Romans, Greeks, Armenians, Isaurians, Lycaonians, Phrygians, Syrians, and Gallo-Grecians.   But the great Thracian race, which had once been inferior in number only to the Indian, and which, in the first century of our era, had excited the attention of Vespasian by the extent of the territory it occupied, was now extermi- nated.[1]   The country it had formerly inhabited was peopled by Sclavonian tribes, a diminished Roman and Greek popula- tion only retaining possession of the towns, and the Bulgarians, a Turkish tribe, ruling as the dominant race from Mount Hemus to the Danube.   The range of Mount Hemus gener- ally formed the Byzantine frontier to the north, and its moun- tain passes were guarded by imperial garrisons.[2]   Sclavonian colonies had established themselves over all the European provinces, and had even penetrated into the Peloponnesus. The military government of Strymon, above the passes in the plain of Heraclea Sintica, was formed to prevent the country to the south of Mounts Orbelos and Skomios from becoming an independent Sclavonian province.

The provincial divisions of the Roman Empire had fallen into oblivion.   A new geographical arrangement into Themes appears to have been established by Heraclius, when he recov- ered the Asiatic provinces from the Persians : it was reorganised by Leo, and endured as long as the Byzantine government.[3] The number of themes varied at different periods.   The

---

[1] Herodotus, v. 3.   Eustathius Thess., *Comm. in Dionys. Periegetem*, v. 323.

[2] The country within Mount Hemus, called Zagora, was only ceded to the Bulgarians in the reign of Michael III.   Cont., *Scrip. post Theoph.*, 102. Symeon Log., 440. Cedrenus, i. 446; ii. 541.

[3] The term *thema* was first applied to the Roman legion.   The military districts, garrisoned by legions, were then called *themata*, and ultimately the word was used merely to indicate geographical administrative divisions.—Ducange, *Glossarium med. et inf. Græcitatis.*

Emperor Constantine Porphyrogenitus, writing about the middle of the tenth century, counts sixteen in the Asiatic portion of the empire, and twelve in the European.

Seven great themes are particularly prominent in Asia Minor,[1] Optimaton, Opsikion, the Thrakesian, the Anatolic, the Bukellarian, the Kibyrraiot, and the Armeniac. In each of these a large military force was permanently maintained, under the command of a general of the province ; and in Opsikion, the Thrakesian, and the Kibyrraiot, a naval force was likewise stationed under its own officers. The commanders of the troops were called Strategoi, those of the navy Drungarioi. Several subordinate territorial divisions existed, called Tourms, and separate military commands were frequently established for the defence of important passes, traversed by great lines of communication, called Kleisouras. Several of the ancient nations in Asia Minor still continued to preserve their national peculiarities, and this circumstance has induced the Byzantine writers frequently to mention their country as recognised geographical divisions of the empire.

The European provinces were divided into eight continental and five insular or transmarine themes, until the loss of the exarchate of Ravenna reduced the number to twelve. Venice and Naples, though they acknowledged the suzerainty of the Eastern Empire, acted generally as independent cities. Sardinia was lost about the time of Leo's accession, and the circumstances attending its conquest by the Saracens are unknown.

The ecclesiastical divisions of the empire underwent frequent

---

[1] The Asiatic themes were—1. *Anatolikon*, including parts of Phrygia, Lycaonia, Isauria, Pamphylia, and Pisidia. 2. *The Armeniac*, including Pontus and Cappadocia. 3. *The Thrakesian*, part of Phrygia, Lydia, and Ionia. 4. *Opsikion*, Mysia, and part of Bithynia and Phrygia. 5. *Optimaton*, the part of Bithynia towards the Bosphorus. 6. *Bukellarion*, Galatia. 7. *Paphlagonia*. 8. *Chaldia*, the country about Trebizond. 9. *Mesopotamia*, the trifling possessions of the empire on the Mesopotamian frontier. 10. *Koloneia*, the country between Pontus and Armenia Minor, through which the Lycus flows, near Neocæsarea. 11. *Sebasteia*, the second Armenia.—*Scrip. post Theoph.* 112. 12. *Lycandos*, a theme formed by Leo VI. (the Wise) on the borders of Armenia. 13. *The Kibyrraiot*, Caria, Lycia, and the coast of Cilicia. 14. *Cyprus*. 15. *Samos*. 16. *The Ægean*. Cappadocia is mentioned as a theme.—*Scrip. post. Theoph.* 112; and Charsiania, *Genesius*, 46. They had formed part of the Armeniac theme.

The twelve European themes were—1. *Thrace*. 2. *Macedonia*.. 3. *Strymon*. 4. *Thessalonica*. 5. *Hellas*. 6. *Peloponnesus*. 7. *Cephallenia*. 8. *Nicopolis*. 9. *Dyrrachium*. 10. *Sicily*. 11. *Longibardia* (Calabria.) 12. *Cherson*. The islands of the Archipelago, which formed the 16th Asiatic theme, were the usual station of the European naval squadron, under the command of a *Drungarias*. They are often called *Dodekannesos*, and their admiral was an officer of consideration at the end of the eighth century.—*Theophanes*, 383. The list of the themes given by Constantine Porphyrogenitus is a traditional, not an official document. Cyprus and Sicily had been conquered by the Arabs long before he wrote.

modifications; but after the provinces of Epirus, Greece, and Sicily were withdrawn from the jurisdiction of the Pope, and placed under that of the Patriarch of Constantinople by Leo III., that patriarchate embraced the whole Byzantine empire. It was then divided into 52 metropolitan dioceses, which were subdivided into 649 suffragan bishopricks, and 13 archbishopricks, in which the prelates were independent, (αὐτοκέφαλοι,) but without any suffragans. There were, moreover, 34 titular archbishops.[1]

SECTION II

REIGN OF LEO III. (THE ISAURIAN,) A.D. 717–741 [2]

Saracen war—Siege of Constantinople—Circumstances favourable to Leo's reforms—Fables concerning Leo—Military, financial, and legal reforms—Ecclesiastical policy—Rebellion in Greece—Papal opposition —Physical phenomena.

When Leo was raised to the throne, the empire was threatened with immediate ruin. Six emperors had been dethroned within the space of twenty-one years. Four perished by the hand of the public executioner,[3] one died in obscurity, after being deprived of sight,[4] and the other was only allowed to end his days peacefully in a monastery, because Leo felt the imperial sceptre firmly fixed in his own grasp.[5] Every army assembled to encounter the Saracens had broken out into rebellion. The Bulgarians and Sclavonians wasted Europe up to the walls of Constantinople; the Saracens ravaged the whole of Asia Minor to the shores of the Bosphorus.

Amorium was the principal city of the theme Anatolikon.[6] The Caliph Suleiman had sent his brother, Moslemah, with a numerous army, to complete the conquest of the Roman empire, which appeared to be an enterprise of no extraordinary difficulty, and Amorium was besieged by the Saracens. Leo, who commanded the Byzantine troops, required some time to concert the operations by which he hoped to raise the siege. To gain the necessary delay, he opened negotiations

---

[1] Compare Codinus, *Notitiæ Græcorum Episcopatum*, with the index to the first volume of Lequien, *Oriens Christianus*.

[2] The most complete work on the history of the Iconoclast period is that of Schlosser, *Geschichte der Bilderstürmenden Kaiser*, 1812. It is a work of learning and original research.

[3] Leontius, Tiberius III., (Apsimar.) Justinian II., Philippicus.

[4] Anastasius II.   [5] Theodosius III.

[6] Amorium was at the ruins called Hergan Kaleh.—Hamilton, *Researches in Asia Minor*, i. 452. Leake's *Tour in Asia Minor*, 86.

with the invaders, and, under the pretext of hastening the conclusion of the treaty, he visited the Saracen general engaged in the siege with an escort of only 500 horse. The Saracens were invited to suspend their attacks until the decision of Moslemah—who was at the head of another division of the Mohammedan army—could be known. In an interview which took place with the bishop and principal inhabitants of the Amorium, relating to the proffered terms, Leo contrived to exhort them to continue their defence, and assured them of speedy succour. The besiegers, nevertheless, pressed forward their approaches. Leo, after his interview with the Amorians, proposed that the Saracen general should accompany him to the headquarters of Moslemah. The Saracen readily agreed to an arrangement which would enable him to deliver so important a hostage to the commander-in-chief. The wary Isaurian, who well knew that he would be closely watched, had made his plan of escape. On reaching a narrow defile, from which a cross road led to the advanced posts of his own army, Leo suddenly drew his sabre and attacked the Saracens about his person; while his guards, who were prepared for the signal, easily opened a way through the two thousand hostile cavalry of the escort, and all reached the Byzantine camp in safety. Leo's subsequent military dispositions and diplomatic negotiations induced the enemy to raise the siege of Amorium, and the grateful inhabitants united with the army in saluting him Emperor of the Romans. But in his arrangements with Moslemah, he is accused by his enemies of having agreed to conditions which facilitated the further progress of the Mohammedans, in order to secure his own march to Constantinople. On this march he was met by the son of Theodosius III., whom he defeated. Theodosius resigned his crown, and retired into a monastery;[1] while Leo made his triumphal entry into the capital by the Golden Gate, and was crowned by the Patriarch in the church of St. Sophia on the 25th of March, 717.

The position of Leo continued to be one of extreme difficulty. The Caliph Suleiman, who had seen one private adventurer succeed the other in quick succession on the imperial throne, deemed the moment favourable for the final conquest of the Christians; and, reinforcing his brother's army,

---

[1] Theodosius ended his life at Ephesus, where he was buried in the church of St. Philip. He ordered that his tombstone should bear no inscription but the word ΥΓΕΙΑ—"Health."

he ordered him to lay siege to Constantinople. The Saracen empire had now reached its greatest extent. From the banks of the Sihun and the Indus to the shores of the Atlantic in Mauretania and Spain, the orders of Suleiman were implicitly obeyed. The recent conquests of Spain in the West, and of Fergana, Cashgar, and Sind in the East, had animated the confidence of the Mohammedans to such a degree that no enterprise appeared difficult. The army Moslemah led against Constantinople was the best appointed that had ever attacked the Christians: it consisted of eighty thousand fighting men. The caliph announced his intention of taking the field in person with additional forces, should the capital of the Christians offer a protracted resistance to the arms of Islam. The whole expedition is said to have employed one hundred and eighty thousand; and the number does not appear to be greatly exaggerated, if it be supposed to include the sailors of the fleet, and the reinforcements which reached the camp before Constantinople.[1]

Moslemah, after capturing Pergamus, marched to Abydos, where he was joined by the Saracen fleet. He then transported his army across the Hellespont, and, marching along the shore of the Propontis, invested Leo in his capital both by land and sea. The strong walls of Constantinople, the engines of defence with which Roman and Greek art had covered the ramparts, and the skill of the Byzantine engineers, rendered every attempt to carry the place by assault hopeless, so that the Saracens were compelled to trust to the effect of a strict blockade for gaining possession of the city. They surrounded their camp with a deep ditch, and strengthened it with a strong dyke. Moslemah then sent out large detachments to collect forage and destroy the provisions, which might otherwise find their way into the besieged city. The presence of an active enemy and a populous city required constant vigilance on the part of a great portion of his land forces.

The Saracen fleet consisted of eighteen hundred vessels of war and transports. In order to form the blockade, it was divided into two squadrons: one was stationed on the Asiatic

---

[1] Compare Constantine Porphyrogenitus, *De Adm. Imp.* chap. 21, p. 74, with Weil, *Geschichte der Chalifen*, i. 566, 571, note, and Price, *Mahommedan Empire*, i. 518. These numbers enable us to estimate the credit due to the Western chronicles concerning the plundering expedition of Abd-el-Rahman into France, which was defeated by Charles Martel. Paulus Diaconus, lib. vi. chap. 47, says, that three hundred thousand Saracens perished during the siege of Constantinople.

coast, in the ports of Eutropius[1] and Anthimus, to prevent supplies arriving from the Archipelago; the other occupied the bays in the European shore of the Bosphorus above the point of Galata, in order to cut off all communication with the Black Sea and the cities of Cherson and Trebizond. The first naval engagement took place as the fleet was taking up its position within the Bosphorus. The current, rendered impetuous by a change of wind, threw the heavy ships and transports into confusion. The besieged directed some fire-ships against the crowded vessels, and succeeded in burning several, and driving others on shore under the walls of Constantinople. The Saracen admiral, Suleiman, confident in the number of his remaining ships of war, resolved to avenge his partial defeat by a complete victory. He placed one hundred chosen Arabs, in complete armour, in each of his best vessels, and, advancing to the walls of Constantinople, made a vigorous attempt to enter the place by assault, as it was entered long after by Doge Dandolo. Leo was well prepared to repulse the attack, and, under his experienced guidance, the Arabs were completely defeated. A number of the Saracen ships were burned by the Greek fire which the besieged launched from their walls.[2] After this defeat, Suleiman withdrew the European squadron of his fleet into the Sosthenian bay.

The besiegers encamped before Constantinople on the 15th August, 717. The Caliph Suleiman died before he was able to send any reinforcements to his brother. The winter proved unusually severe. The country all round Constantinople remained covered with deep snow for many weeks.[3] The greater part of the horses and camels in the camp of Moslemah perished; numbers of the best soldiers, accustomed to the mild winters of Syria, died from having neglected to take the requisite precautions against a northern climate. The difficulty of procuring food ruined the discipline of the troops. These misfortunes were increased by the untimely death of the admiral, Suleiman. In the mean time, Leo and the inhabitants of Constantinople, having made the necessary

---

[1] Mundi Burnou.

[2] On the subject of Greek fire, see *Du Feu Gregois*, par Reinaud et Favé, chap. iii., Paris, 1845; and *Mémoire sur la Découverte très-ancienne en Asie de la Poudre à Canon et des Armes à Feu*, par Paravey, Paris, 1850. The efficacity of Greek fire arose from the circumstance of the combatants being compelled to bring large masses into more rapid and direct collision than in modern tactics.

[3] Theophanes, 332, and Nicephorus, Pat. 35, with the ordinary love of the marvellous, say the snow covered the ground for a hundred days.

preparations for a long siege, passed the winter in security. A fleet, fitted out at Alexandria, brought supplies to Moslemah in spring. Four hundred transports, escorted by men-of-war, sailed past Constantinople, and, entering the Bosphorus, took up their station at Kalos Agros.[1]   Another fleet, almost equally numerous, arrived soon after from Africa, and anchored in the bays on the Bithynian coast.[2]   These positions rendered the current a protection against the fire-ships of the garrison of Constantinople. The crews of the new transports were in great part composed of Christians, and the weak condition of Moslemah's army filled them with fear. Many conspired to desert. Seizing the boats of their respective vessels during the night, numbers escaped to Con-stantinople, where they informed the emperor of the exact disposition of the whole Saracen force. Leo lost no time in taking advantage of the enemy's embarrassments. Fireships were sent with a favourable wind among the transports, while ships of war, furnished with engines for throwing Greek fire, increased the confusion. This bold attack was successful, and a part of the naval force of the Saracens was destroyed. Some ships fell a prey to the flames, some were driven on shore, and some were captured by the Byzantine squadron. The blockade was now at an end, for Moslemah's troops were dying from want, while the besieged were living in plenty ; but the Saracen obstinately persisted in maintaining posses-sion of his camp in Europe. It was not until his foraging parties were repeatedly cut off, and all the beasts of burden were consumed as food, that he consented to allow the standard of the Prophet to retreat before the Christians. The remains of his army were embarked in the relics of the fleet, and on the 15th August, 718, Moslemah raised the siege, after ruining one of the finest armies the Saracens ever assembled, by obstinately persisting in a hopeless under-taking.[3]   The troops were landed at Proconnesus, and marched back to Damascus, through Asia Minor ; but the fleet encountered a violent storm in passing through the Archipelago. The dispersed ships were pursued by the Greeks

---

[1] Buyuk-deré, and not a place in Bithynia, as Lebeau, xii. 118, and Schlosser, 151, infer from Nicephoru , Pat. 35. See Ducange, *Const. Christ.* 177 ; and Gyllius, *De Bosph. Thrac.* ii. chap. xviii. p. 301.

[2] Theophanes, 332, says this fleet consisted of 360 transports. It anchored at Saty-ros, Bryas, and Kartalimen.

[3] Theophanes, 334. Nicephorus, Pat. 35, however, says the siege lasted thirteen months. The Mohammedan accounts report, that of the one hundred and eighty thousand men who composed the expedition, only thirty thousand returned.

of the islands, and so many were lost or captured, that only five of the Syrian squadron returned home.

Few military details concerning Leo's defence of Constantinople have been preserved, but there can be no doubt that it was one of the most brilliant exploits of a warlike age. The Byzantine army was superior to every other in the art of defending fortresses. The Roman arsenals, in their best days, could probably have supplied no scientific or mechanical contrivance unknown to the corps of engineers of Leo's army, for we must recollect that the education, discipline, and practice of these engineers had been perpetuated in uninterrupted succession from the times of Trajan and Constantine. We are not to estimate the decline of mechanical science by the degradation of art, nor by the decay of military power in the field.[1] The depopulation of Europe rendered soldiers rare and dear, and a considerable part of the Byzantine armies was composed of foreign mercenaries. The army of Leo, though far inferior in number to that of Moslemah, was its equal in discipline and military skill; while the walls of Constantinople were garnished with engines from the ancient arsenals of the city, far exceeding in power and number any with which the Arabs had been in the habit of contending. The vanity of Gallic writers has magnified the success of Charles Martel over a plundering expedition of the Spanish Arabs into a marvellous victory, and attributed the deliverance of Europe from the Saracen yoke to the valour of the Franks. A veil has been thrown over the talents and courage of Leo, a soldier of fortune, just seated on the imperial throne, who defeated the long-planned schemes of conquest of the caliphs Welid and Suleiman. It is unfortunate that we have no Isaurian literature.

The catastrophe of Moslemah's army, and the state of the caliphate during the reigns of Omar II. and Yesid II., relieved the empire from all immediate danger, and Leo was enabled to pursue his schemes for reorganising the army and defending his dominions against future invasions. The war was languidly carried on for some years, and the Saracens were gradually expelled from most of their conquests beyond Mount Taurus. In the year 726, Leo was embarrassed by seditions and rebellions, caused by his decrees against image-

---

[1] It was in the time of Constantius, A.D. 357, that the largest obelisk at Rome was transported from Alexandria. It stands at St. John Lateran, and is said to weigh 445 tons. (?) Sir Gardner Wilkinson makes the great obelisk at Karnak weigh less than three hundred tons.—*Modern Egypt and Thebes*, ii. 145.

worship. Hescham seized the opportunity, and sent two powerful armies to invade the empire. Cæsarea was taken by Moslemah; while another army, under Moawyah, pushing forward, laid siege to Nicæa. Leo was well pleased to see the Saracens consume their resources in attacking a distant fortress; but though they were repulsed before Nicæa, they retreated without serious loss, carrying off immense plunder. The plundering excursions of the Arabs were frequently renewed by land and sea. In one of these expeditions, the celebrated Sid-al-Battal carried off an individual who was set up by the Saracens as a pretender to the Byzantine throne, under the pretext that he was Tiberius, the son of Justinian II. Two sons of the caliph appeared more than once at the head of the invading armies. In the year 739, the Saracen forces poured into Asia Minor in immense numbers, with all their early energy. Leo, who had taken the command of the Byzantine army, accompanied by his son Constantine, marched to meet Sid-al-Battal, whose great fame rendered him the most dangerous enemy. A battle took place at Acroïnon, in the Anatolic theme, in which the Saracens were totally defeated. The valiant Sid, the most renowned champion of Islamism, perished on the field; but the fame of his exploits has filled many volumes of Moslem romance, and furnished some of the tales that have adorned the memory of the Cid of Spain, three hundred years after the victory of Leo.[1] The Western Christians have robbed the Byzantine empire of its glory in every way. After this defeat the Saracen power ceased to be formidable to the empire, until the energy of the caliphate was revived by the vigorous administration of the Abassides.

Leo's victories over the Mohammedans were an indispensable step to the establishment of his personal authority. But the measures of administrative wisdom which rendered his reign a new era in Roman history, are its most important feature in the annals of the human race. His military exploits were the result of ordinary virtues, and of talents common in every age; but the ability to reform the internal government of an empire, in accordance with the exigencies of society, can

---

[1] Acroïnon was doubtless at Sid-el-Ghazi, nine hours to the south of Eskishehr, Dorylæum,) where the tomb of Sid-al-Battal-el-Ghazi is still shown.—Leake, *Asia Minor*, 21. Weil, *Geschichte der Chalifen*, i. 638, calls the hero Abd Allah; while d'Herbelot, *Bibliothèque Orientale*, voce "Batthal," calls him Abu Mohammed. Theophanes, 345, calls him simply Βατάλ. See also Hammer, *Histoire de l'Empire Ottoman*, par Hellert, i. 60, 372.

only be appreciated by those who have made the causes and the progress of national revolutions the object of long thought. The intellectual superiority of Leo may be estimated by the incompetence of sovereigns in the present century to meet new exigencies of society. Leo judiciously availed himself of many circumstances that favoured his reforms. The inherent vigour which is nourished by parochial and municipal responsibilities, bound together the remnants of the free population in the eastern Roman empire, and operated powerfully in resisting foreign domination. The universal respect felt for the administration of justice, and the general deference paid to the ecclesiastical establishment, inspired the inhabitants with energies wanting in the West. Civilisation was so generally diffused, that the necessity of upholding the civil and ecclesiastical tribunals, and defending the channels of commercial intercourse, reunited a powerful body of the people in every province to the central administration, by the strongest ties of interest and feeling.

The oppressive authority of the court of Constantinople had been much weakened by the anarchy that prevailed throughout the empire in the latter part of the seventh century. The government had been no longer able to inundate the provinces with those bands of officials who had previously consumed the wealth of the *curiæ ;* and the cities had been everywhere compelled to provide for their own defence by assuming powers hitherto reserved to the imperial officers. These new duties had inspired the people with new vigour, and developed unexpected talents. The destructive responsibility of fiscal guarantees and personal services, imposed by the administration of imperial Rome as a burden on every class of its subjects, from the senator to the ticket-porter, was lightened when the Western Empire fell a prey to foreign conquerors, and when the Eastern was filled with foreign colonists.[1] The curiales and the corporations at last relieved themselves from the attempt of the Roman government to fix society in a stationary condition, and the relief was followed by immediate improvement. Troubled times had also made the clergy more anxious to conciliate public opinion than official favour. A better and more popular class of bishops replaced the worldly priest satirised by Gregory Nazianzenos.[2] The influence of this change was very great, for the bishop, as the defender of

---

[1] Compare *Cod. Theod.* vi. 11,—*De Senatoribus,* and xiv. xxii. *De Saccariis.*
[2] *Carmen, De Episcopis,* v. 150.

the curia, and the real head of the people in the municipality, enjoyed extensive authority over the corporations of artisans and the mass of the labouring population. From a judge he gradually acquired the power of a civil governor, and the curia became his senate. The ordinary judicial tribunals being cut off from direct communication with the supreme courts, peculiar local usages gained force, and a customary law arose in many provinces restricting the application of the code of Justinian. The orthodox church alone preserved its unity of character, and its priests continued to be guided by principles of centralisation, which preserved their connection with the seat of the patriarchate at Constantinople, without injuring the energetic spirit of their local resistance to the progress of the Mohammedan power. Throughout the wide extent of the Eastern Empire, the priesthood served as a bond to connect the local feelings of the parish with the general interests of the orthodox church. Its authority was, moreover, endeared to a large body of the population from its language being Greek, and from its holy legends embodying national feelings and prejudices. Repulsive as the lives of the saints now appear to our taste, they were the delight of millions for many centuries.

From the earliest period to the present hour, the wealth of most of the cities in the East has been derived from their importance as points of commercial communication. The insane fury of the Emperor Justinian II., in devastating the flourishing cities of Ravenna and Cherson, failed to ruin these places, because they were then the greatest commercial entrepôts of the trade between India and Europe. But the alarm felt for the ruin of commerce throughout the Christian world, during the anarchy that existed in the last years of the seventh, and early years of the eighth centuries, contributed much to render men contented with the firm government of Leo, even though they may have considered him a heretic. On the other hand, the prevailing anarchy had relieved commerce both from much fiscal oppression and many official monopolies. The moment the financial burdens of the commercial classes were lightened, they experienced all the advantage of possessing a systematic administration of justice, enforced by a fixed legal procedure, and consequently they very naturally became warm partisans of the imperial authority, as, in their opinion, the personal influence of the emperor constituted the true fountain of legal order and judicial impartiality. A fixed legislation saved society from dissolution during many years of anarchy.

The obscure records of the eighth century allow us to discern through their dim atmosphere a considerable increase of power in popular feelings, and they even afford some glimpses of the causes of this new energy. The fermentation which then pervaded Christian society marks the commencement of modern civilisation, as contrasted with ancient times. Its force arose out of the general diminution of slave labour. The middle classes in the towns were no longer rich enough to be purchasers of slaves, consequently the slave population henceforward became a minority in the Eastern Empire; and those democratic ideas which exist among free labourers replaced the aristocratic caution, inseparable from the necessity of watching a numerous population of slaves. The general attention was directed to the equal administration of justice. The emperor alone appeared to be removed above the influence of partiality and bribery; under his powerful protection the masses hoped to escape official and aristocratic oppression, by the systematic observance of the rules of Roman law. The prosperity of commerce seemed as directly connected with the imperial supremacy as judicial equity itself, for the power of the emperor alone could enforce one uniform system of customs from Cherson to Ravenna. Every trader, and indeed every citizen, felt that the apparatus of the imperial government was necessary to secure financial and legal unity. Above all, Leo, the conqueror of the hitherto victorious Saracens, seemed the only individual who possessed the civil as well as the military talents necessary for averting the ruin of the empire. Leo converted the strong attachment to the laws of Rome prevalent in society into a lever of political power, and rendered the devotion felt for the personal authority of the sovereign the means of increasing the centralisation of power in the reformed fabric of the Roman administration. The laws of Rome, therefore, saved Christianity from Saracen domination more than the armies. The victories of Leo enabled him to consolidate his power, and constitute the Byzantine empire, in defiance of the Greek nation and the orthodox church; but the law supplied him with this moral power over society.

As long as Mohammedanism was only placed in collision with the fiscality of the Roman government and the intolerance of the orthodox church, the Saracens were everywhere victorious, and found everywhere Christian allies in the provinces they invaded. But when anarchy and misfortune had de-

stroyed the fiscal power of the state, and weakened the
ecclesiastical intolerance of the clergy, a new point of comparison between the governments of the emperors and the
caliphs presented itself to the attention. The question, how
justice was administered in the ordinary relations of life,
became of vital interest. The code of Justinian was compared with that of the Koran. The courts presided over by
judges and bishops were compared with those of the Moolahs.
The convictions which arose in the breasts of the subjects of
the Byzantine emperors changed the current of events. The
torrent of Mohammedan conquest was arrested, and as long as
the Roman law was cultivated in the empire, and administered
under proper control in the provinces, the invaders of the
Byzantine territory were everywhere unsuccessful. The inhabitants boasted with a just pride, that they lived under
the systematic rule of the Roman law, and not under the
arbitrary sway of despotic power.[1]

Such was the state of the Roman empire when Leo commenced his reforms. We must now proceed to examine what
history has recorded concerning this great reformer. Some
fables concerning his life and fortunes owe their existence to
the aversion with which his religious opinions were regarded
by the Greeks, and they supply us with the means of forming
a correcter view of the popular mind than of the emperor's
life. At the same time, it must be recollected that they embody the opinions of only a portion of his subjects, adopted
towards the close of his reign.

Leo was born at Germanicia, a city of Armenia Minor, in
the mountains near the borders of Cappadocia and Syria.[2]
Germanicia was taken by the Saracens, and the parents of
Leo emigrated with their son to Mesembria in Thrace. They
were persons of sufficient wealth to make the Emperor
Justinian II. a present of five hundred sheep, as he was advancing to regain possession of his throne with the assistance

---

[1] Every emperor was bound to make a confession of faith in a certain formula,
κατὰ τὸ ἐθιμόν.—Genesius, ii. Compare the coronation oath in Codinus, *De Officiis
Conpl.* chap. xvii., with *Corpus Juris Civ.* Cod. i. xiv. 4 and 5; *Basilica*, ii. vi. 9 and
10 ; see also Constantine Porphyrogenitus, *De Adm. Imp.* p. 64, edit. Band ; iii. 84,
edit. Bonn, and the Ecloga of Leo III. Leunclavius and Freher, *Jus Græco-Romanum*,
i. 178, ii. 83, tit. ii. § 4.

[2] The family of Leo, being neither Greek nor Roman, was regarded by these nations
as foreign. The Isaurians appear to have been the subjects of the empire who had retained the greatest share of their original nationality. The Armenians and Syrians,
though numerous, were always regarded as strangers rather than hereditary subjects.
Theophanes, 327, 330, and Anastasius, *Hist.* 128, called Leo a Syrian. He seems to
have considered himself an Armenian, and he married his daughter to an Armenian.

of the Bulgarians. This well-timed gift gained young Leo the
rank of spatharios, the personal favour of the tyrant, and a
high command on the Lazian frontier. His prudence and
courage raised him, during the reign of Anastasius II., to
the command of the Anatolic theme.

But another history of his life, unknown to the early
historians, Theophanes and Nicephorus, though both these
orthodox writers were his bitter enemies and detractors, became current in after times, and deserves notice as presenting
us with a specimen of the tales which then fed the mental
appetite of the Greeks.[1] Prodigies, prophecies, and miracles
were universally believed. Restricted communications and
neglected education were conducting society to an infantine
dotage. Every unusual event was said to have been predicted
by some prophetic revelation; and as the belief in the pre-
science of futurity was universal, public deceivers and self-
deceivers were always found acting the part of prophets. It is
said to have been foretold to Leontius that he should ascend
the throne, by two monks and an abbot.[2] The restoration of
Justinian II. had been announced to him while he was in
exile by a hermit of Cappadocia.[3] Philippicus had it revealed
in a dream, that he was to become emperor; and he was
banished by Tiberius II., (Apsimar,) when this vision became
publicly known.[4] It is not, therefore, wonderful that Leo
should have been honoured with communications from the
other world; though, as might have been expected from his
heretical opinions, and the orthodoxy of his historians, these
communications are represented to have been made by agents
from the lower rather than the higher regions.

A circumstance which it was believed had happened to the
Caliph Yezid I., proved most satisfactorily to the Greeks that
Satan often transacted business publicly by means of his agents
on earth. Two Jews—for Jews are generally selected by the
orthodox as the fittest agents of the demon—presented themselves to the caliph claiming the gift of prophecy. They
announced that, if he should put an end to the idolatrous
worship of images throughout his dominions, fate had predes-
tined him to reign for forty years over a rich and flourishing
empire. Yezid was a man of pleasure and a bigot, so that the
prophecy was peculiarly adapted to flatter his passions. The

---

[1] Compare Theophanes, 336, who has no objections to calumniate Leo, with the later
writers, Cedrenus, 450; Zonaras, ii. 103; Const. Manasses, 86; Glycas, 280; Leo
Gramm., 173, edit. Bonn. [2] Theophanes, 307. Nicephorus, Pat. 25.
[3] Theophanes, 313. [4] *Ib.* 311, 319.

images and pictures which adorned the Christian churches were torn down and destroyed throughout the caliph's dominions. But Yezid was occupied carrying his decree into execution when he died. His son, Moawyah II., sought the Jewish prophets in vain. The prince of darkness concealed them from his search, and transported them into the heart of Asia Minor, where they had new services to perform.

A young man named Conon, who had quitted his native mountains of Isauria, to gain his living as a pedlar in the wealthier plains, drove his ass, laden with merchandise, to a grove of evergreen oaks near a bubbling fountain, to seek rest during the heat of the day, and count his recent gains. The ass was turned loose to pasture in the little meadow formed by the stream of the fountain, and Conon sat down in the shade, by the chapel of St. Theodore, to eat his frugal meal. He soon perceived two travellers resting like himself, and enjoying their noontide repast. These travellers entered into conversation with young Conon, who was a lad of remarkable strength, beauty, and intelligence. They allowed the fact to transpire that they were Jews, prophets and astrologers, who had recently quitted the court of the caliph at Damascus, which very naturally awakened in the mind of the young pedlar a wish to know his future fortune, for he may have aspired at becoming a great post-contractor or a rich banker. The two Jews readily satisfied his curiosity, and, to his utter astonishment, informed him that he was destined to rule the Roman empire. As a proof of their veracity, the prophets declared that they sought neither wealth nor honours for themselves, but they conjured Conon to promise solemnly that, when he ascended the throne, he would put an end to the idolatry which disgraced Christianity in the East. If he engaged to do this, they assured him that his fulfilling the will of Heaven would bring prosperity to himself and to the empire. Young Conon, believing that the prophets had revealed the will of God, pledged himself to purify the Christian Church; and he kept this promise, when he ascended the throne as Leo the Isaurian. But as the prophets had made no stipulation for the free exercise of their own creed, and their interest in Christianity pointed out the true faith, Leo did not consider himself guilty of ingratitude, when, as emperor, he persecuted the Jewish religion with the greatest severity.

Such is the fable by which the later Byzantine historians explain Leo's hostility to image-worship. This adventure appeared to them a probable origin of the ecclesiastical reforms which characterise Leo's domestic policy. In the bright days of Hellenic genius, such materials would have been woven into an immortal tale; the chapel of St. Theodore, its fountain, and its evergreen oaks, Conon driving his ass with the two unearthly Jews reclining in the shade, would have formed a picture immortal in the minds of millions; but in the hands of ignorant monks and purblind chroniclers, it sinks into a dull and improbable narrative.

Unfortunately, it is almost as difficult to ascertain the precise legislative and executive acts by which Leo reformed the military, financial, and legal administration, as it is to obtain an impartial account of his ecclesiastical measures.

The military establishment of the empire had gradually lost its national character, from the impossibility of recruiting the army from among Roman citizens. In vain the soldier's son was fettered to his father's profession, as the artisan was bound to his corporation, and the proprietor to his estate.[1] Yet the superiority of the Roman armies seems to have suffered little from the loss of national spirit, as long as strict discipline was maintained in their ranks. For many centuries the majority of the imperial forces consisted of conscripts drawn from the lowest ranks of society, from the rude mountaineers of almost independent provinces, or from foreigners hired as mercenaries; yet the armies of all invaders, from the Goths to the Saracens, were repeatedly defeated in pitched battles. The state maxims which separated the servants of the emperor from the people, survived in the Eastern provinces after the loss of the Western, and served as the basis of the military policy of the Byzantine empire, when reformed by Leo. The conditions of soldier and citizen were deemed incompatible. The law prevented the citizen from assuming the position of a soldier, and watched with jealousy any attempt of the soldier to acquire the rights and feelings of a citizen. An impassable barrier was placed between the proprietor of the soil, who was the tax-payer, and the defender of the state, who was an agent of the imperial power.[2] It is true that, after

---

[1] The tendency of Roman despotism to reduce society to caste is remarkable.—*Cod. Theod.* vii. xxii. 8. This feeling may be traced to the last days of the Byzantine power. Gemistos Plethon, in the projects of reform at the beginning of the fifteenth century, by which he hoped to save the Peloponnesus from the Turks, insists on the separation of the classes of soldiers and taxpayers. See his memorial on the State of the Peloponnesus, addressed to the despot Theodore, at the end of two books of Stobæus, published by Canter, printed by Christopher Plantin, Antwerp, 1575, folio, page 222.

[2] A fixed number of conscripts was drawn from each province after the time of Constantine; and the proprietors, who were prohibited from serving in person, had to

the loss of the Western provinces, the Roman armies were recruited from the native subjects of the empire to a much greater degree than formerly; and that, after the time of Heraclius, it became impossible to enforce the fiscal arrangements to which the separation of the citizen from the soldier owed its origin, at least with the previous strictness.[1] Still the old imperial maxims were cherished in the reign of Leo, and the numerous colonies of Sclavonians, and other foreigners, established in the empire, owed their foundation to the supposed necessity of seeking for recruits as little as possible from among the native population of agriculturists. These colonies were governed by peculiar regulations, and their most important service was supplying a number of troops for the imperial army. Isauria and other mountainous districts, where it was difficult to collect any revenue by a land-tax, also supplied a fixed military contingent.[2]

Whatever modifications Leo made in the military system, and however great were the reforms he effected in the organisation of the army and the discipline of the troops, the mass of the population continued in the Byzantine empire to be excluded from the use of arms, as they had been in the Roman times; and this circumstance was the cause of that unwarlike disposition, which is made a standing reproach from the days of the Goths to those of the Crusaders. The state of society engendered by this policy opened the Western Empire to the northern nations, and the empire of Charlemagne to the Normans. Leo's great merit was, that without any violent

---

furnish conscripts. They were allowed to hire any freeman, beggar, or barbarian, with youth and strength. When the recruitment became still more difficult, on account of the diminished population, the Emperor Valens commuted the conscription for a payment of thirty-six solidi for each conscript.—*Cod. Theod.* vii. xiii. 7.

[1] For the Roman legislation relating to the army, see *Cod. Just.* x. 32, 17; xi. 48, 18; xii. 33, 2, 4. *Dig.* xlix. 16, 9 and 13. Colons and serfs were prohibited from entering the army even at those periods of public calamity which compelled the government to admit slaves as recruits. The views of Gibbon, vol. iii. chap. xvii. p. 65, require to be modified.

[2] An anecdote of the time of Theodosius II., A.D. 448, gives a correct idea of the condition of the Greek population of the Eastern Empire, at least until the time of the anarchy under Phocas. Priscus, the envoy of Theodosius II. to Attila, mentions that, in the Scythian territory, he was addressed in Greek by a man in the dress of the country—a circumstance which surprised him, as Latin was the customary language of communication with foreigners, and few strangers, except the slaves brought from Thrace and the coast of Illyria, ever spoke Greek. The man proved to be a Greek who was living among the Huns. He contrasted his past condition, as a citizen under the Roman emperors, with his present position as a freeman under Attila. The Roman citizen, he said, was compelled to trust for defence to the arms of others, because the Roman despotism prohibited the use of arms to the citizen. In the time of war, consequently, he was a prey either to the enemy or to the mercenary troops of the emperor, while in the time of peace his life was rendered intolerable by fiscal oppression and official injustice.—*Exc. e Prisci Historia*, 190. *Corpus Scrip. Hist. Byz.* pars i., edit. Bonn.

political change he infused new energy into the Byzantine military establishment, and organised a force that for five centuries defended the empire without acquiring the power of domineering in the state. As the army was destitute of patriotic feeling, it was necessary to lessen the influence of its commanders. This was done by dividing the provinces into themes, appointing a general of division for each theme, and grouping together in different stations the various corps of conscripts, subject nations, and hired mercenaries.[1] The adoption likewise of different arms, armour, and manœuvres in the various corps, and their seclusion from close inter-communication with the native legions, guarded against the danger of those rebellious movements which in reality destroyed the Western Empire. As much caution was displayed in the Byzantine empire to prevent the army from endangering the government by its seditions, as to render it formidable to the enemy by its strength.

The finances are soon felt to be the basis of government in all civilised states. Augustus experienced the truth of this as much as Louis XIV. The progress of society and the accumulation of wealth have a tendency to sink governments into the position of brokers of human intelligence, wealth, and labour; and the finances form the symbol indicating the quantity of these which the central authority can command. The reforms, therefore, which it was in the power of Leo III. to effect in the financial administration, must have proceeded from the force of circumstances rather than from the mind of the emperor. To this cause we must attribute the durability of the fabric he constructed. He confined himself to arranging prudently the materials accumulated to his hand. But no sovereign, and indeed no central executive authority, can form a correct estimate of the taxable capacity of the people. Want of knowledge increases the insatiable covetousness suggested by their position; and the wisest statesman is as likely to impose ruinous burdens on the people, if vested with despotic power, as the most rapacious tyrant. The people alone can find ways of levying on themselves an amount of taxation exceeding any burdens that the boldest despot could hope to impose; for the people can perceive what taxes will have the least effect in arresting the increase of the national wealth.

---

[1] Leo is said to have had a body of Frank mercenaries in his service during the siege of Constantinople. The authority is too modern to be implicitly relied on.— Abulpharagius, *Ch. Arab.* 130.

Leo, who felt the importance of the financial administration as deeply as Augustus, reserved to himself the immediate superintendence of the treasury; and this special control over the finances was retained by his successors, so that, during the whole duration of the Byzantine empire, the emperors may be regarded as their own ministers of finance. The grand Logothetes, who was the official minister, was in reality nothing more than the emperor's private secretary for the department. Leo unquestionably improved the central administration, while the invasions of the Saracens and Bulgarians made him extremely cautious in imposing heavy fiscal burdens on the distant cities and provinces of his dominions. But his reforms were certainly intended to circumscribe the authority of municipal and provincial institutions. The free cities and municipalities which had once been entrusted with the duty of apportioning their quota of the land-tax, and collecting the public burdens of their district, were now deprived of this authority. All fiscal business was transferred to the imperial officers. Each province had its own collectors of the revenue, its own officials charged to complete the registers of the public burdens, and to verify all statistical details. The traditions of imperial Rome still required that this mass of information should be regularly transmitted to the cabinet of the Byzantine emperors, as at the birth of our Saviour.[1]

The financial acts of Leo's reign, though they show that he increased the direct amount of taxation levied from his subjects, prove nevertheless, by the general improvement which took place in the condition of the people, that his reformed system of financial administration really lightened the weight of the public burdens. Still, there can be no doubt that the stringency of the measures adopted in Greece and Italy, for rendering the census more productive, was one of the causes of the rebellions in those countries, for which his Iconoclastic decrees served as a more honourable war-cry. In Calabria and Sicily he added one-third to the capitation; he confiscated to the profit of the treasury a tribute of three talents and a half of gold which had been remitted annually to Rome, and at the same time he ordered a correct register to be kept of all the males born in his dominions. This last

---

[1] Luke, chap. ii. v. 1. Novel iii. of John Comnenus in Leunclavius, *Jus Græco-Romanum*, 147. Novel vi. of Manuel, i. 156. Montreuil, *Histoire du Droit Byzantin*, iii. 107.

regulation excites a burst of indignation from the orthodox historian and confessor Theophanes, who allows neither his reason nor his memory to restrain his bigotry when recording the acts of the first Iconoclast emperor. He likens Leo's edict to Pharaoh's conduct to the children of Israel, and adds that the Saracens, Leo's teachers in wickedness, had never exercised the like oppression—forgetting, in his zeal against taxation, that the Caliph Abdelmelik had established the haratch or capitation of Christians as early as the commencement of the reign of Justinian II., A.D, 692.[1]

An earthquake that ruined the walls of Constantinople, and many cities in Thrace and Bithynia, induced Leo to adopt measures for supplying the treasury with a special fund for restoring them, and keeping their fortifications constantly in a state to resist the Bulgarians and Saracens. The municipal revenues which had once served for this purpose had been encroached upon by Justinian I., and the policy of Leo led him to diminish in every way the sphere of action of all local authorities.

The care of the fortifications was undoubtedly a duty to which the central government required to give its direct attention ; and to meet the extraordinary expenditure caused by the calamitous earthquake of 740, an addition of one-twelfth was made to the census. This tax was called the *dikeraton*, because the payment appears to have been generally made in the silver coins called keratia, two of which were equal to a miliaresion, the coin which represented one-twelfth of the nomisma, or gold Byzant.[2] Thus a calamity which diminished the public resources increased the public

---

[1] Theophanes, 343.

[2] Theophanes, 345. Constan. Manasses, 93. Glycas, 286, and the words φόλα and κεράτιον in Ducange's *Glossarium Med. et Infimæ Græcitatis.* It is very difficult to determine which is the miliaresion, and which the keration, among the coins of the Lower Empire we possess. I possess a medallion of Heraclius, and Heraclius Constantine, A.D. 613-641, which weighs 100 grains ; another of Constantine IV., (Pogonatus,) in bad preservation, which weighs only 88. These would seem to be miliaresia, of which twelve were reckoned to a gold nomisma. Yet some think the silver coin of a smaller size is the miliaresion. Of these I possess two, well preserved, of John I., Zimiskes, and of Basil II., and Constantine VIII., A.D. 970-1025, weighing each 44 grains. If the keration was the half of this piece, from being once the commonest silver coin, it has now become the rarest. Of twenty-five gold nomismata in my possession, the heaviest is one of Manuel I., A.D. 1143-1180. The next is a solidus of Aelia Verina, A.D. 457-474, in fine preservation, but which weighs only 68½ grains. Seventy-two or seventy-four nomismata were coined out of the pound weight of gold, which contained 5256 English grains. Compare the observations of Pinder and Friedläuder in their excellent dissertation, *Die Münzen Justinians,* p. 12, with Const. Porphyr., *De Ceremoniis Aulæ Byzantinæ,* i. 459 ; ii. 497, edit. Bonn. The present rarity of Byzantine silver is no proof of its being rare formerly. It has been consumed in ornaments and base coin. The gold was preserved by its value as a circulating medium from Scandinavia to India.

burdens. In such a contingency it seems that a paternal government and a wise despot ought to have felt the necessity of diminishing the pomp of the court, of curtailing the expenses of ecclesiastical pageants, and of reforming the extravagance of the popular amusements of the hippodrome, before imposing new burdens on the suffering population of the empire. Courtiers, saints, and charioteers ought to have been shorn of their splendour, before the groans of the provinces were increased. Yet Leo was neither a luxurious nor an avaricious prince; but, as has been said already, no despotic monarch can wisely measure the burden of taxation.

The influence of the provincial spirit on the legislation of the empire is strongly marked in the history of jurisprudence during Leo's reign. The anarchy which had long interrupted the official communications between the provinces and the capital lent an increased authority to local usages, and threw obstacles in the way of the regular administration of justice, according to the strict letter of the voluminous laws of Justinian. The consequence was, that various local abridgments of the law were used as guide-books, both by lawyers and judges, in the provincial tribunals, where the great expense of procuring a copy of the Justinianean collection prevented its use. Leo published a Greek manual of law, which by its official sanction became the primary authority in all the courts of the empire. This imperial abridgment is called the Ecloga: it affords some evidence concerning the state of society and the classes of the people for which it was prepared. Little notice is taken of the rights of the agriculturists; the various modes of acquiring property and constituting servitudes are omitted. The Ecloga has been censured for its imperfections by Basil I., the founder of a legislative dynasty, who speaks of it as an insult to the earlier legislators; yet the orthodox lawgiver, while he pretended to reject every act of the heretical Isaurian, servilely imitated all his political plans. The brevity and precision of Leo's Ecloga were highly appreciated both by the courts of law and the people, in spite of the heterodox opinions of its promulgator. It so judiciously supplied a want long felt by a large portion of society, that neither the attempt of Basil I. to supplant it by a new official manual, nor the publication of the great code of the Basilika in Greek, deprived it of value among the jurisconsults of the Byzantine empire.[1]

---

[1] See the works of Zacharias, whose enlightened criticism has shed light on this obscure period of history.—*Historiæ Juris Græco-Romani Delineatio, auct. C. E. Zachariæ*, 14.41. Ο‘ πρόχειρος νόμος, Heidelb., 1837, 8vo, p. xviii. &c.

The legislative labours of Leo were not circumscribed to the publication of the Ecloga. He seems to have sanctioned various minor codes, by which the regulations in use relating to military, agricultural, and maritime law were reduced into systematic order. The collections which are attached to the copies of the Ecloga, under the heads of military, agricultural, and Rhodian laws, cannot, however, be considered as official acts of his reign ; still, they are supposed to afford us a correct idea of the originals he published. Some abstract of the provisions contained in the Roman legislation on military affairs, was rendered necessary by the practice of maintaining corps of foreign mercenaries in the capital. A military code was likewise rendered necessary, in consequence of the changes that took place in the old system, as the Asiatic provinces were gradually cleared of the invading bands of Saracens.[1] The agricultural laws appear to be a tolerably exact copy of the enactments of Leo. The work bears the impress of the condition of society in his time, and it is not surprising that the title which perpetuated the merits and the memory of the heterodox Leo was suppressed by orthodox bigotry. The maritime laws are extremely interesting, from affording a picture of the state of commercial legislation in the eighth century, at the time when commerce and law saved the Roman empire. The exact date of the collection we possess is not ascertained. That Leo protected commerce, we may infer from its reviving under his government ; whether he promulgated a code to sanction or enforce his reforms, or whether the task was completed by one of his successors, is doubtful.

The whole policy of Leo's reign has been estimated by his ecclesiastical reforms. These have been severely judged by all historians, and they appear to have encountered a violent opposition from a large portion of his subjects. The general dissatisfaction has preserved sufficient authentic information to allow of a candid examination of the merits and errors of his policy. Theophanes considers the aversion of Leo to the adoration of images as originating in an impious attachment to the unitarianism of the Arabs. His own pages, however, refute some of his calumnies, for he records that Leo persecuted the unitarianism of the Jews, and the tendency to it in the Montanists.[2] Indeed, all those who differed from the most

---

[1] Montreuil, *Histoire du Droit Byzantin*, i. 393.
[2] Theophanes, 336, 343. Montreuil, in his *Histoire du Droit Byzantin*, i. 348, cites the law against the Jews and Montanists from Bonefidius, *Juris Orientalis Libri Tres*,

orthodox acknowledgment of the Trinity, received very little Christian charity at the hands of the Isaurian, who placed the cross on the reverse of many of his gold, silver, and copper coins, and over the gates of his palace, as a symbol for universal adoration. In his Iconoclast opinions, Leo is merely a type of the more enlightened laymen of his age. A strong reaction against the superstitions introduced into the Christian religion by the increasing ignorance of the people, pervaded the educated classes, who were anxious to put a stop to what might be considered a revival of the ideas and feelings of paganism. The Asiatic Christians, who were brought into frequent collision with the followers of Mahomet, Zoroaster, and Moses, were compelled to observe that the worship of the common people among themselves was sensual, when compared with the devotion of the infidels. The worship of God was neglected, and his service transferred to some human symbol. The favourite saint was usually one whose faults were found to bear some analogy to the vices of his worshipper, and thus pardon was supposed to be obtained for sin on easier terms than accords with Divine justice, and vice was consequently rendered more prevalent. The clergy had yielded to the popular ignorance; the walls of churches were covered with pictures which were reported to have wrought miraculous cures; their shrines were enriched by paintings not made with hands;[1] the superstitions of the people were increased, and the doctrines of Christianity were neglected. Pope Gregory II., in a letter to Leo, mentions the fact, that men expended their estates to have the sacred histories represented in paintings.[2]

In a time of general reform, and in a government where ecclesiastics acted as administrative officials of the central authority, it was impossible for Leo to permit the church to remain quite independent in ecclesiastical affairs, unless he was prepared for the clergy assuming a gradual supremacy in the state. The clergy, being the only class in the administration of public affairs connected with the people by interest

and refers to Cedrenus. But most of the laws cited by Bonefidius from Cedrenus will be found in Theophanes and the older Byzantine writers, not published when Bonefidius made his compilation; and reference ought to be made to these authorities. In this case, what is called a law seems to have been a series of edicts. Theophanes says that the Jews submitted to baptism and mocked the sacraments; the more conscientious Montanists burned themselves in their places of worship.

[1] Ἀχειροποίητα. Nothing can better prove the extent to which superstition had contaminated religion than the assertion of the Patriarch Germanos, that miracles were daily wrought by the images of Christ and the saints, and that balsam distilled from the painted hand of an image of the Virgin Mary.—Neander, *History of the Christian Religion and Church*, (Torrey's translation,) iii. 206.   [2] Neander, iii. 212.

and feelings, was always sure of a powerful popular support. It appeared, therefore, necessary to the emperor to secure them as sincere instruments in carrying out all his reforms, otherwise there was some reason to fear that they might constitute themselves the leaders of the people in Greece and Asia, as they had already done at Rome, and control the imperial administration throughout the whole Eastern Empire, as completely as they did in the Byzantine possessions in central Italy.

Leo commenced his ecclesiastical reforms in the year 726, by an edict ordering all pictures in churches to be placed so high as to prevent the people from kissing them, and prohibiting prostration before these symbols, or any act of public worship being addressed to them. Against this moderate edict of the emperor, the Patriarch Germanos and the Pope Gregory II. made strong representations. The opposition of interest which reigned between the church and the state impelled the two bodies to a contest for supremacy which it required centuries to decide, and both Germanos and Gregory were sincere supporters of image-worship. To the ablest writer of the time,—the celebrated John Damascenus, who dwelt under the protection of the caliph at Damascus, among Mohammedans and Jews,—this edict seemed to mark a relapse to Judaism, or a tendency to Islamism. He felt himself called upon to combat such feelings with all the eloquence and power of argument he possessed. The empire was thrown into a ferment; the lower clergy and the whole Greek nation declared in favour of image-worship. The professors of the university of Constantinople, an institution of a Greek character, likewise declared their opposition to the edict. Liberty of conscience was the watchword against the imperial authority. The Pope and the Patriarch denied the right of the civil power to interfere with the doctrines of the church; the monks everywhere echoed the words of John Damascenus, " It is not the business of the emperor to make laws for the church. Apostles preached the gospel; the welfare of the state is the monarch's care; pastors and teachers attend to that of the church."[1] The despotic principles of Leo's administration, and the severe measures of centralisation which he enforced as the means of reorganising the public service, created many additional enemies to his government.

The rebellion of the inhabitants of Greece, which occurred

[1] John Damascenus, *Orat.* ii. § 12, quoted in Neander's *History*, iii. 209.

in the year 727, seems to have originated in a dissatisfaction with the fiscal and administrative reforms of Leo, to which local circumstances, unnoticed by historians, gave peculiar violence, and which the edict against image-worship fanned into a flame. The unanimity of all classes, and the violence of the popular zeal in favour of their local privileges and superstitions, suggested the hope of dethroning Leo, and placing a Greek on the throne of Constantinople. A naval expedition, composed of the imperial fleet in the Cyclades, and attended by an army from the continent, was fitted out to attack the capital. Agallianos, who commanded the imperial forces destined to watch the Sclavonians settled in Greece, was placed at the head of the army destined to assail the conqueror of the Saracens. The name of the new emperor was Kosmas. In the month of April the Greek fleet appeared before Constantinople. It soon appeared that the Greeks, confiding in the goodness of their cause, had greatly overrated their own valour and strength, or strangely overlooked the resources of the Iconoclasts. Leo met the fleet as it approached his capital, and completely defeated it. Agallianos, with the spirit of a hero, when he saw the utter ruin of the enterprise, plunged fully armed into the sea rather than surrender. Kosmas was taken prisoner, with another leader, and immediately beheaded. Leo, however, treated the mass of the prisoners with mildness.[1]

Even if we admit that the Greeks displayed considerable presumption in attacking the Isaurian emperor, still we must accept the fact as a proof of the populous condition of the cities and islands of Greece, and of the flourishing condition of their trade, at a period generally represented as one of wretchedness and poverty. Though the Peloponnesus was filled with Sclavonian emigrants, and the Greek peasantry were in many districts excluded from the cultivation of the land in the seats of their ancestors, nevertheless their cities then contained the mercantile wealth and influence, which passed some centuries later into the possession of Venice, Amalfi, Genoa, and Pisa.

The opposition Leo encountered only confirmed him in his persuasion that it was indispensably necessary to increase the power of the central government in the provinces. As he was

---

[1] Theophanes, 339, calls the insurgents *Helladikoi*, and Cedrenus, i. 454, copies the scornful expression. Had the insurrection been believed to have originated in religious feeling, surely the orthodox confessor Theophanes would have regarded the sufferers as martyrs.

sincerely attached to the opinions of the Iconoclasts, he was led to connect his ecclesiastical reforms with his political measures, and to pursue both with additional zeal. In order to secure the active support of all the officers of the administration, and exclude all image-worshippers from power, he convoked an assembly, called a silention, consisting of the senators and the highest functionaries in the church and state. In this solemn manner it was decreed that images were to be removed from all the churches throughout the empire. In the capital the change met with no serious opposition. The population of Constantinople, at every period of its history, has consisted of a mixed multitude of different nations; nor has the majority ever been purely Greek for any great length of time. Nicetas, speaking of a time when the Byzantine empire was at the height of its power, and when the capital was more a Greek city than at any preceding or subsequent period, declares that its population was composed of various races.[1] The cause of image-worship was, however, generally the popular cause, and the Patriarch Germanos steadily resisted every change in the actual practice of the church until that change should be sanctioned by a general council.[2]

The turn now given to the dispute put an end to the power of the Eastern emperors in central Italy. The Latin provinces of the Roman empire, even before their conquest by the barbarians, had sunk into deeper ignorance than the Eastern. Civilisation had penetrated farther into society among the Greeks, Armenians, and Syrians, than among the Italians, Gauls, and Spaniards. Italy was already dissatisfied with the Constantinopolitan domination, when Leo's fiscal and religious reforms roused local interests and national prejudices to unite in opposing his government. The Pope of Rome had long been regarded by orthodox Christians as the head of the church; even the Greeks admitted his right of inspection over the whole body of the clergy, in virtue of the superior dignity of the Roman see.[3] From being the heads of the church, the popes became the defenders of the liberties of the people. In this character, as leaders of a lawful opposition to the tyranny of the imperial administration, they grew up to the possession of immense influence in the state. This power, having its basis in democratic feelings and energies,

---

[1] Nicetas. Alexius, ii. 152.
[2] Nicephorus, Pat. 38, ἄνευ οἰκουμενικῆς συνόδου ἔγγραφον πίστιν οὐκ ἐκτίθεμαι.
[3] Sozomen, Hist. Eccles. iii. chap. 8.

alarmed the emperors, and many attempts were made to circumscribe the papal authority. But the popes themselves did more to diminish their own influence than their enemies, for instead of remaining the protectors of the people, they aimed at making themselves their masters. Gregory II., who occupied the papal chair at the commencement of the contest with Leo, was a man of sound judgment, as well as an able and zealous priest. He availed himself of all the advantages of his position, as political chief of the Latin race, with prudence and moderation ; nor did he neglect the power he derived from the circumstance that Rome was the fountain of religious instruction for all western Europe. Both his political and ecclesiastical position entitled him to make a direct opposition to any oppressive measure of the emperor of Constantinople, when the edicts of Leo III. concerning image-worship prompted him to commence the contest, which soon ended in separating central Italy from the Byzantine empire.

The possessions of the Eastern emperors in Italy were still considerable. Venice, Rome, Ravenna, Naples, Bari, and Tarentum were all capitals of well-peopled and wealthy districts. The province embracing Venice and Rome was governed by an imperial viceroy or exarch who resided at Ravenna, and hence the Byzantine possessions in central Italy were called the Exarchate of Ravenna. Under the orders of the exarch, three governors or dukes commanded the troops in Ravenna, Rome, and Venice. As the native militia enrolled to defend the province from the Lombards formed a considerable portion of the military force, the popular feelings of the Italians exercised some influence over the soldiery. The Constantinopolitan governor was generally disliked, on account of the fiscal rapacity of which he was the agent ; and nothing but the dread of greater oppression on the part of the Lombards, whom the Italians had not the courage to encounter without the assistance of the Byzantine troops, preserved the people of central Italy in their allegiance. They hated the Greeks, but they feared the Lombards.

Gregory II. sent Leo strong representations against his first edicts on the subject of image-worship, and after the silention he repeated these representations, and entered on a more decided course of opposition to the emperor's ecclesiastical reforms, being then convinced that there was no hope of Leo abandoning his heretical opinions. It seems that Italy, like the rest of the empire, had escaped in some degree from the oppressive burden of imperial taxation during the anarchy that preceded Leo's election. But the defeat of the Saracens before Constantinople had been followed by the establishment of the fiscal system. To overcome the opposition made to the financial and ecclesiastical reforms, the exarch Paul was ordered to march to Rome and support Marinus, the duke, who found himself unable to contend against the papal influence.[1] The whole of central Italy burst into rebellion at this demonstration against its civil and religious interests. The exarch was compelled to shut himself up in Ravenna; for the cities of Italy, instead of obeying the imperial officers, elected magistrates of their own, on whom they conferred, in some cases, the title of duke.[2] Assemblies were held, and the project of electing an emperor of the West was adopted; but the unfortunate result of the rebellion of Greece damped the courage of the Italians; and though a rebel, named Tiberius Petasius, really assumed the purple in Tuscany, he was easily defeated and slain by Eutychius, who succeeded Paul as exarch of Ravenna. Luitprand, king of the Lombards, taking advantage of these dissensions, invaded the imperial territory, and gained possession of Ravenna; but Gregory, who saw the necessity of saving the country from the Lombards and from anarchy, wrote to Ursus, the duke of Venice, one of his warm partisans, and persuaded him to join Eutychius. The Lombards were defeated by the Byzantine troops, Ravenna was recovered, and Eutychius entered Rome with a victorious army.[3] Gregory died in 731. Though he excited the Italian cities to resist the imperial power, and approved of the measures they adopted for stopping the remittance of their taxes to Constantinople,[4] he does not appear to have adopted any measures for declaring Rome independent. That he contemplated the possibility of events taking a turn that might ultimately lead him to throw off his allegiance to the Emperor Leo, is nevertheless evident, from one of his letters to that emperor, in which he boasts very significantly that the eyes of the West were fixed on his humility, and that if Leo attempted to injure the Pope, he would find the West ready to defend him, and even to attack Constantinople. The allusion to the protection of the king of the Lombards and Charles Martel was certainly,

---

[1] The Latins accused Leo of ordering Marinus to assassinate the pope.
[2] Anastasius, *De Vit. Pont. Rom.* 69.
[3] Baronii, *Ann. Eccles.* xii. 343, No. xxvii. [4] Theophanes, 338.

in this case, a treasonable threat on the part of the Bishop of Rome to his sovereign.[1] Besides this, Gregory II. excommunicated the exarch Paul, and all the enemies of imageworship who were acting under the orders of the emperor, pretending to avoid the guilt of treason by not expressly naming the Emperor Leo in his anathema.[2] On the other hand, when we consider that Leo was striving to extend the bounds of the imperial authority in an arbitrary manner, and that his object was to sweep away every barrier against the exercise of despotism in the church and the state, we must acknowledge that the opposition of Gregory was founded in justice, and that he was entitled to defend the municipal institutions and local usages of Italy, and the constitution of the Romish church, even at the price of declaring himself a rebel.

The election of Gregory III. to the papal chair was confirmed by the Emperor Leo in the usual form; nor was that pope consecrated until the mandate from Constantinople reached Rome. This was the last time the emperors of the East were solicited to confirm the election of a pope. Meanwhile Leo steadily pursued his schemes of ecclesiastical reform, and the opposition to his measures gathered strength. Gregory III. assembled a council in Rome, at which the municipal authorities, whose power Leo was endeavouring to circumscribe, were present along with the nobles; and in this council the whole body of the Iconoclasts were excommunicated. Leo now felt that force alone could maintain Rome and its bishops in their allegiance. With his usual energy, he despatched an expedition under the command of Manes, the general of the Kibyrraiot theme, with orders to send the pope a prisoner to Constantinople, to be tried for his treasonable conduct. A storm in the Adriatic, the lukewarm conduct of the Greeks in the imperial service, and the courage of the people of Ravenna, whose municipal institutions enabled them to act in an organised manner, caused the complete overthrow of Manes. Leo revenged himself for this loss by confiscating all the estates of the papal see in the eastern provinces of his empire, and by separating the ecclesiastical government of southern Italy, Sicily, Greece, Illyria, and Macedonia, from the papal jurisdiction, and placing these countries under the immediate authority of the Patriarch of Constantinople.

---

[1] *Histoire des Souverains Pontifes Romains*, par le Chev. Artaud de Montor, i. 438. This work is more remarkable for popish bigotry than for historical accuracy. Two epistles of Gregory II. are preserved among the acts of the second council of Nicæa, viii. 651, 674.   [2] Theophanes, 342. Anastasius, *De Vit. Pont. Rom.* 69.

From this time, A.D. 733, the city of Rome enjoyed political independence under the guidance and protection of the popes;[1] but the officers of the Byzantine emperors were allowed to reside in the city, justice was publicly administered by Byzantine judges, and the supremacy of the Eastern Empire was still recognised. So completely, however, had Gregory III. thrown off his allegiance, that he entered into negotiations with Charles Martel, in order to induce that powerful prince to take an active part in the affairs of Italy.[2] The pope was now a much more powerful personage than the Exarch of Ravenna, for the cities of central Italy, which had assumed the control of their local government, intrusted the conduct of their external political relations to the care of Gregory, who thus held the balance of power between the Eastern emperor and the Lombard king.[3] In the year 742, while Constantine V., the son of Leo, was engaged with a civil war, the Lombards were on the eve of conquering Ravenna, but Pope Zacharias threw the whole of the Latin influence into the Byzantine scale, and enabled the exarch to maintain his position until the year 751, when Astolph, king of the Lombards, captured Ravenna.[4] The exarch retired to Naples, and the authority of the Byzantine emperors in central Italy ended.

The physical history of our globe is so intimately connected with the condition of its inhabitants, that it is well to record those remarkable variations from the ordinary course of nature which strongly affected the minds of contemporaries. The influence of famine and pestilence, during the tenth and eleventh centuries, in accelerating the extinction of slavery, has been pointed out by several recent writers on the subject, though that effect was not observed by the people who lived at the time. The importance of the late famine in Ireland, as a political cause, must be felt by any one who attempts to trace the origin of that course of social improvement on which the Irish seem about to enter. The severity of the winter of 717 aided Leo in defeating the Saracens at Constantinople. In the year 726, a terrific irruption of the dormant submarine volcano at the island of Thera (Santorin) in the Archipelago, was regarded by the bigoted image-worshippers as a manifesta-

---

[1] Anastasius, *De Vit. Pont. Rom* 74.
[2] Bossuet, *Défens Cler. Gallic.* ii. vi. chap. xviii.
[3] Paulus Diaconus, vi. chap. 54.
[4] The exarchate is usually said to have terminated in 752, after existing 184 years; but there is an act of Astolph, dated at Ravenna, 4th July, 751.—Fantucci, *Monumenti Ravennati*, tom. v. p. xiii. and cciii. Muratori, *Ant. Ital.* v. 689,

tion of divine wrath against Leo's reforms. For several days the sea between Thera and Therasia boiled up with great violence, vomiting forth flames, and enveloping the neighbouring islands in clouds of vapour and smoke. The flames were followed by showers of dust and pumice-stone, which covered the surface of the sea, and were carried by the waves to the shores of Asia Minor and Macedonia.[1] At last a new island rose out of the sea, and gradually extended itself until it joined the older rocky islet called Hieron.[2]

In the year 740, a terrible earthquake destroyed great part of the walls of Constantinople. The statue of Arcadius, on the Theodosian column in Xerolophon, and the statue of Theodosius over the golden gate, were both thrown down.[3] Churches, monasteries, and private buildings were ruined : the walls of many cities in Thrace and Bithynia, particularly Nicomedia, Prænetus, and Nicæa, were so injured as to require immediate restoration. This great earthquake caused the imposition of the tax already alluded to, termed the dikeration.

Leo has been accused as a persecutor of learning. It is by no means impossible that his Asiatic education and puritanical opinions rendered him hostile to the legendary literature and ecclesiastical art then cultivated by the Greeks ; but the circumstance usually brought forward in support of his barbarism is one of the calumnies invented by his enemies, and re-echoed by orthodox bigotry. He is said to have ordered a library consisting of 33,000 volumes, in the neighbourhood of St. Sophia's, to be burned, and the professors of the university to be thrown into the flames. A valuable collection of books seems to have fallen accidentally a prey to the flames during his reign, and neither his liberality nor the public spirit of the Greeks induced them to display any activity in replacing the loss.[4]

---

[1] Pumice-stone is sometimes found floating in the Archipelago at the present day, and there is generally a good deal on the shore of Attica, near Cape Zoster, washed thither from Santorin.

[2] Theophanes, 339. Nicephorus, Pat. 37. This addition to Hieron (Palaia Raïmené) may still be traced, *Histoire et Phénomènes du Volcan de Santorin*, par l'Abbé Pégues, 136. Ross, *Reisen auf den Griechischen Inseln*. i. 89. The author is reminded by this note of the pleasure he derived from a visit to Santorin in company with Professor Ross of Halle, a most accomplished and profound scholar, and Professor C. Ritter, the great geographer of Berlin, in 1837.

[3] Ducange, *Constantinopolis Christiana*, 78, 81. Scarlatos Byzantios, Η Κωνσταντινούπολις, i. 289. The latter is a work of more pretension than value.

[4] 1. Constant. Manasses, 87. Schlosser, *Geschichte der bilderstürmenden Kaiser*, 163. Spanheim, *Historia Imaginum Restituta*, 115. Maimbourg (*Histoire de l'Heresie des Iconoclastes*, i. 58) believes and magnifies the accounts of the later Byzantine chronicles, in spite of the silence of Leo's earlier enemies. According to Ephræmius, v. 1007, a library of 120,000 volumes had been destroyed by fire in the reign of Zeno, in

Leo III. died in the year 741. He had crowned his son Constantine emperor in the year 720, and married him to Irene, the daughter of the Khan of the Khazars, in 733.

SECTION III

CONSTANTINE V., (COPRONYMUS,) A.D. 741–775

Character of Constantine V.—Rebellion of Artavasdos—Saracen War—
Bulgarian War—Internal condition of the empire—Policy regarding
image-worship—Physical phenomena—Plague at Constantinople.

Constantine V., called Copronymus,[1] ascended the throne at the age of twenty-two, but he had already borne the title of emperor as his father's colleague one and twenty years, for the Byzantine empire preserved so strictly the elective type of the Roman imperial dignity, that the only mode of securing the hereditary transmission of the empire was for the reigning emperor to obtain his son's election during his own lifetime. Historians tell us that Constantine was a man possessing every vice disgraceful to humanity, combined with habits and tastes which must have rendered his company disgusting and his person contemptible. Yet they record facts proving that he possessed great talents, and that, even when his fortunes appeared desperate, he found many devoted friends. The obloquy heaped on his name must therefore be ascribed to the blind passion inspired by religious bigotry. The age was not one of forbearance and charity. The wisest generally considered freedom of opinion a species of anarchy incompatible with religious feeling, moral duty, and good government; consequently, both iconoclasts and image-worshippers approved of persecution, and practised calumny in favour of what each considered the good cause. Constantine tortured the image-worshippers—they revenged themselves by defaming the emperor. But the persecutions which rendered Constantine a monster in the eyes of the Greeks and Italians, elevated him to the rank of a saint in the opinion of a large body of the population of the empire, who regarded the worship of pictures as a species of idolatry abhorrent to Christianity. His religious zeal, political success, courage, military talents,

which was the MS. of the Iliad and Odyssey, written with letters of gold on serpents'
skin. This MS. was 120 feet long.
[1] Constantine received his name of Copronymus from having defiled the baptismal
font when the Patriarch plunged him into the water according to the usage of the
Greek Church.

together with the prosperity that attended his government, all conspired to make him the idol of the Iconoclasts, who regarded his tomb as a sacred shrine until it was destroyed by Michael the orthodox drunkard.[1]

Constantine was able, prudent, active, and brave; but he was not more tender of human suffering than monarchs generally are. The Patriarch Nicephorus justly accuses him of driving monks from their monasteries, and converting sacred buildings into barracks. In modern times, orthodox papist sovereigns have frequently done the same thing, without exciting much ecclesiastical indignation. But when the Patriarch assures us that the emperor's mind was as filthy as his name, we may be allowed to suspect that his pen is guided by orthodoxy instead of truth; and when we find grave historians recording that he loved the odour of horse-dung, and carried on amours with old maids, we are reminded of the Byzantine love of calumny which could delight in the anecdotes of Procopius, and believe that the Emperor Justinian was a man of such diabolical principles, that he was not ashamed to walk about his palace for many hours of the night without his head.[2] An account of the reign of Constantine by an intelligent Iconoclast, even if he represented the emperor as a saint, would be one of the most valuable illustrations of the history of the eighth century which time could have spared. He was accused of rejecting the practice of invoking the intercession of the Virgin Mary, though it is admitted he called her the Mother of God. He was also said to have denied the right of any man to be called a saint; and he had even the audacity to maintain, that though the martyrs benefited themselves by their sufferings, their merit, however great it might be, was not a quality that could be transferred to others. His enemies regarded these opinions as damnable crimes.[3] Few reputations, however, have passed through such an ordeal of malice as that of Constantine, and preserved so many undeniable virtues.

Shortly after his succession, Constantine lost possession of Constantinople through the treachery of his brother-in-law Artavasdos, who assumed the title of emperor, and kept possession of the throne for two years. Artavasdos was an Armenian noble who had commanded the troops of the

[1] *Scriptores post Theophanem.* Symeon Log., 449. Georg. Mon., 541.
[2] Nicephorus, Pat. 88. Suidas, v. Κωνσταντίνος, Procopius. *Historia Arcana*, iii, 80, edit. Bonn.
[3] Neander, *History of the Christian Religion*, ii. 218.

Armeniac theme in the reign of Theodosius III., and aided Leo to mount the throne. He was rewarded with the hand of Anna, the Isaurian's only daughter, and with the dignity of caropalates, second only to that of Cæsar, a rank then usually reserved for the imperial blood. Artavasdos had increased his influence by favouring the orthodox; his long services in the highest administrative offices had enabled him to attach many partisans to his personal cause in every branch of the public service. The manner in which Constantine was engaged in a civil war with his brother-in-law reflected no dishonour on the character of the young emperor.

The Saracens had pushed their incursions into the Opsikian theme, where the imperial guards, under the command of Artavasdos, were stationed. Constantine took the field in person to oppose the enemy, and advanced to the plains of Krasos. Here he ordered Artavasdos, who was at Dorylæum, to join him with the troops of the Opsikian theme. The order alarmed Artavasdos, who seems to have been already engaged in treasonable intrigues. Instead of obeying, he assumed the title of emperor, and attacked Constantine so unexpectedly, that the imperial army was easily dispersed, and the young emperor could only avoid being taken prisoner by galloping off alone. When his own horse sank from fatigue, Constantine was compelled to seize a post-horse, which he happened to find ready saddled, in order to continue his flight. He was fortunate enough to reach Amorium in safety.[1]

Artavasdos marched to Constantinople, where, it appears from coins, he affected for some time to act as the colleague of Constantine; and it is possible that some treaty may have been concluded between the brothers-in-law.[2] The usurper, however, soon considered himself strong enough, with the support of the orthodox, to set Constantine aside. The pope acknowledged him as emperor, pictures were replaced in the churches, a strong body of Armenian troops was collected, and Nicephorus, the eldest son of Artavasdos, was crowned as his father's colleague; while Niketas, the second, took the command of the Armeniac theme, where the family possessed great influence. All persons suspected of favouring Constantine were persecuted as heretics hostile to picture-worship.

In the following year (742) Constantine assembled an army composed chiefly of the troops of the Thrakesian and Anatolic

1 Theophanes, 347. Nicephorus, Pat. 38. Saint Martin, (*Lebeau*, xii. 190.) Krasos was a town of Phrygia Pacatiana.
2 De Saulcy, *Essai de Classification des Suites Monétaires Byzantines*, 156.

themes. With this force he marched to Chrysopolis, (Scutari,) hoping that a party in Constantinople would declare in his favour; but, being disappointed, he was compelled to withdraw to Amorium, where he passed the winter. In spring, Artavasdos marched to dislodge him, ordering his son Niketas to bring up the Armenian troops to operate on the right flank of the young emperor. All the country in the usurper's line of march was ravaged, as if it was a territory he never hoped to govern. Constantine, whose military genius had been cultivated by his father, formed a daring plan of campaign, and executed it in the most brilliant manner. While his enemies believed that they were advancing to attack him with superior forces, he resolved to move forward with such celerity as to become the attacking party, before they could approach near enough to combine any simultaneous movements. His first attack was directed against Artavasdos, whose numerous army was inferior in discipline to that of Niketas, and over which he expected an easier victory. A general engagement took place near Sardis, on quitting the Kelvian plain, watered by the Kaister. The victory was complete. The usurper was closely pursued to Cyzicus, from whence he escaped by sea to Constantinople. Constantine then moved forward to meet Niketas, who was defeated in a bloody battle fought at Modrina, in the Boukellarian theme, to the east of the Sangarius. The Armenian auxiliaries and the troops of the Armeniac theme sustained their high reputation, and long disputed the victory.

The emperor then marched to invest Constantinople, crossing the Bosphorus with one division of his army, and sending another, under the command of Sisinnios, the general of the Thrakesian theme, to cross the Hellespont at Abydos, and reduce the cities on the shores of the Propontis. The fleet of the Kibyrraiot theme was ordered to blockade the capital by sea. All communications with Greece, one of the strongholds of the image-worshippers, were thus cut off. Constantine repulsed every sally by land, and famine quickly made frightful ravages in the dense population of the capital, where no preparations had been made for a siege. Constantine acted on this occasion in a very different manner from Artavasdos during the campaign in Asia Minor. He felt that the people suddenly besieged were his own subjects; and his enemies record that he allowed all the starving population to seek refuge in his camp.[1]

[1] Nicephorus, Pat. 40. Theophanes, 352.

Niketas quickly reassembled the fugitives of his own and his father's army, and made an attempt to cut off Constantine's communications in Bithynia; but the emperor left the camp before Constantinople, and, putting himself at the head of the troops in Asia, again defeated Niketas near Nicomedia. Niketas and the orthodox archbishop of Gangra were both taken prisoners. The belligerent prelate was immediately beheaded as a traitor; but Niketas was carried to Constantinople, where he was exhibited before the walls laden with fetters. Artavasdos still rejected all terms of capitulation, and Constantine at last ordered a general assault, by which he captured the city on the 2nd November, 743. Artavasdos escaped by sea to a fortress called Pyzanitis, in the Opsikian theme, where he was soon after taken prisoner. His eyes, and those of his sons, Nicephorus and Niketas, were put out; and in this condition they were exhibited as a triumphal spectacle to the inhabitants of Constantinople, at the chariot races given by the emperor to celebrate his re-establishment on the throne. His brother-in-law and nephews were then immured in a monastery. Some of their principal adherents were beheaded. The head of Vaktageios, the principal minister of the usurper, was exhibited for three days in the Augusteon—a custom perpetuated by the Ottoman emperors in similar circumstances until our own times, the heads of rebel viziers having adorned the gate of the Serail during the reign of the late sultan. The Patriarch Anastasios was pardoned, and allowed to remain in possession of his dignity; yet Theophanes says that his eyes were put out, and he was exhibited in the circus, mounted on an ass, and exposed to the scorn of the mob.[1] Sisinnios, who had commanded one division of the emperor's army, was soon found to be engaged in treasonable intrigues, and lost his eyes forty days after he entered the capital in triumph with his sovereign.

Constantine no sooner found himself firmly established on the throne, than he devoted his attention to completing the organisation of the empire traced out by his father. The constant attacks of the Saracens and Bulgarians called him

---

[1] Theophanes, 353. The Patriarch Nicephorus, who, in a fragment preserved by Photius, (page 86,) has recapitulated all the misdeeds of Constantine with orthodox exaggeration, makes no mention of this treatment of his predecessor. Anastasios continued to occupy the patriarchal throne ten years after the taking of Constantinople, and died A.D. 753. There appears to be some accidental mistake in what Theophanes says with regard to Anastasios, for both he and Nicephorus recount similar circumstances as accompanying the deposition and death of the successor of Anastasios, Constantinos II.—Theophanes, 372. Niceph., Pat. 48.

frequently to the head of his armies, for the state of society rendered it dangerous to intrust large forces to the command of a subject. In the Byzantine empire few individuals had any scruple of violating the political constitution of their country, if by so doing they could increase their own power.

The incursions of the Saracens first required to be repressed. The empire of the caliphs was already distracted by the civil wars which preceded the fall of the Ommiad dynasty. Constantine took advantage of these troubles. He reconquered Germanicia and Doliche, and occupied for a time a considerable part of Commagene; but as he found it impossible to retain possession of the country, he removed the Christian population to Thrace, where he founded several flourishing colonies, long distinguished by their religious opinions from the surrounding population, A.D. 746.[1] The Saracens attempted to indemnify themselves for these losses by the conquest of Cyprus. This island appears to have been reconquered by Leo III., for it had been abandoned to the Mohammedans by Justinian II. The fleet of the caliph sailed from Alexandria, and landed an army at the port of Kerameia; but the fleet of the Kibyrraiot theme arrived in time to blockade the enemy's ships, and of a thousand Mohammedan vessels three only escaped, A.D. 748. The war was continued. In 752 the imperial armies took the cities of Melitene and Theodosiopolis, but some years later the caliph Mansour recovered Melitene and Germanicia: he seems, however, to have considered the tenure of the last so insecure, that he transported the inhabitants into Palestine. The Saracens invaded the empire almost every summer, but these incursions led to no permanent conquests. The agricultural population along the frontiers of the two empires must have been greatly diminished during these successive ravages; for farm-buildings and fruit-trees were constantly destroyed, and slaves formed the most valuable booty of the soldiers. The mildness and tolerant government of the emperor of Romania (for that name began now to be applied to the part of Asia Minor belonging to the Byzantine empire[2]) was so celebrated in the East, in spite of his persecution of the image-worshippers at Constantinople, that many Christians escaped by sea from the dominions of the Caliph Al Mansour to settle in those of Constantine.[3] In the year

---

[1] Theophanes, 354, mentions that these colonists retained in his time the heretical addition to the Trisaghion of Peter the Fuller—"O holy God! O holy Almighty! O holy Eternal, who was crucified for us!"—Mosheim. Murdock's *Trans.*, Soames's edit., i. 494.　　[2] Theophanes uses Romania frequently in this sense.　　[3] Theophanes, 376.

769 an exchange of prisoners took place, but without interrupting the course of hostilities, which were continued almost incessantly on the frontiers of the two empires.[1]

The vicinity of the Bulgarians to Constantinople rendered them more dangerous enemies than the Saracens, though their power was much inferior. The Bulgarians were a people who looked on war as the most honourable means of acquiring wealth, and they had long pursued it with profit: for as long as the Byzantine frontiers were populous, they obtained booty and slaves by their incursions: while, as soon as it became depopulated by their ravages, they were enabled to occupy new districts with their own pastoral hordes, and thus increase their numbers and strength. To resist their incursions, Constantine gradually repaired all the fortifications of the towns on the northern frontier, and then commenced fortifying the passes, until the Bulgarians found their predatory incursions attended with loss instead of gain. Their king was now compelled to make the cause of the predatory bands a national question, and an embassy was sent to Constantinople to demand payment of an annual tribute, under the pretext that some of the fortifications erected to guard the passes were situated in the Bulgarian territory, but, in reality, to replace the loss of the plunder which had enabled many of the warlike Bulgarians to live in idleness and luxury. The demands of the king were rejected, and he immediately invaded the empire with a powerful army. The Bulgarians carried their ravages up to the long wall; but though they derived assistance from the numerous Sclavonian colonies settled in Thrace, they were defeated, and driven back into their own territory with great slaughter, A.D. 757.

Constantine carried on a series of campaigns, systematically planned, for the purpose of weakening the Bulgarian power. Instead of allowing his enemy to make any incursions into the empire, he was always ready to carry the war into their territory. The difficulties of his enterprise were great, and he suffered several defeats; but his military talents and persevering energy prevented the Bulgarians from profiting by any partial success they obtained, and he soon regained the superiority. In the campaigns of 760, 763, and 765, Constantine marched far into Bulgaria, and carried off immense booty. In the year 766 he intended to complete the conquest of the country, by opening the campaign at the commence-

---

[1] Theophanes, 374.

ment of spring. His fleet, which consisted of two thousand six hundred vessels, in which he had embarked a considerable body of infantry in order to enter the Danube, was assailed by one of those furious storms that often sweep the Euxine. The force which the emperor expected would soon render him master of Bulgaria was suddenly ruined. The shores of the Black Sea were covered with the wrecks of his ships and the bodies of his soldiers. Constantine immediately abandoned all thought of continuing the campaign, and employed his whole army in alleviating the calamity to the survivors, and in securing Christian burial and funeral honours to the dead. A truce was concluded with the enemy, and the Roman army beheld the emperor as eager to employ their services in the cause of humanity and religion, as he had ever been to lead them to the field of glory and conquest. His conduct on this occasion gained him as much popularity with the people of Constantinople as with the troops.[1]

In the year 774 he again assembled an army of eighty thousand men, accompanied by a fleet of two thousand transports, and invaded Bulgaria. The Bulgarian monarch concluded a treaty of peace—which, however, was broken as soon as Constantine returned to his capital. But the emperor was not unprepared, and the moment he heard that the enemy had laid siege to Verzetia, one of the fortresses he had constructed to defend the frontier, he quitted Constantinople in the month of October, and, falling suddenly on the besiegers, routed their army with great slaughter. The following year his army was again ready to take the field; but as Constantine was on his way to join it he was attacked by a mortal illness, which compelled him to retrace his steps. Having embarked at Selymbria, in order to reach Constantinople with as little fatigue as possible, he died on board the vessel at the castle of Strongyle, just as he reached the walls of his capital, on the 23rd September, 775.[2]

The long war with the Bulgarians was carried on rather with the object of securing tranquillity to the northern pro-

---

[1] Nicephorus, Pat. 47. Theophanes, 368. The great services and victories of Constantine in the Bulgarian war were acknowledged by posterity. Leo Diaconus, 104, edit. Bonn.

[2] Strongyle is the same with the Cyclobion or Seven Towers.—Banduri, *Imp. Orient.* ii. 530, edit. Ven. Ducange, *Const. Christ.* 45, 102. Magnaura was the western point of Constantinople, Zonaras, ii. 89; though the authority of Theophanes, 294, would place it at the Hebdomon. Another passage, however, corrects this, (p. 331,) and proves that both Magnaura and Cyclobion were without the chain which closed the port at the points of the triangle towards the Propontis.—Ducange, *Const. Christ.* 127. Gyllius seems wrong—*De Topog. Const.* lib. iv. chap. 4.

vinces of the empire, than from any desire of a barren
conquest. The necessity of reducing the Sclavonian colonies
in Thrace and Macedonia to complete obedience to the
central administration, and of secluding them from all political
communication with one another, or with their countrymen in
Bulgaria, Servia, and Dalmatia, imposed on the emperor the
necessity of maintaining strong bodies of troops, and suggested
the policy of forming a line of Greek towns and Asiatic
colonies along the northern frontier of the empire. When
this was done, Constantine began to root out the brigandage,
which had greatly extended itself during the anarchy which
preceded his father's election, and which Leo had never been
able to exterminate. Numerous bands lived by plunder, in a
state of independence, within the bounds of the empire. They
were called Skamars, and, like the Bagauds of Gaul, formed
organised confederacies of outlaws, originally consisting of
men driven to despair by the intolerable burden of taxation,
and the severity of the fiscal legislation.[1] When the incursions
of the Bulgarians had wasted the fields of the cultivator, the
government still called upon him to pay the full amount of
taxation imposed on his estate in prosperous times: his
produce, his cattle, his slaves, and his seed-corn were carried
away by the imperial officers. He could then only live by
plundering his fellow-subjects, who had hitherto escaped the
calamities by which he had been ruined; and thus the oppression of the imperial government was avenged on the society
that submitted to it without striving to reform its evils   Constantine rooted out these bands. A celebrated chief of the
Skamars was publicly executed at Constantinople with the
greatest barbarity, his living body being dissected by surgeons
after the amputation of his hands and feet. The habitual
barbarity of legal punishments in the Byzantine empire can
hardly relieve the memory of Constantine from the reproach
of cruelty, which this punishment proves he was ready to
employ against the enemies of his authority, whether brigands
or image-worshippers. His error, therefore, was not only
passing laws against liberty of conscience—which was a fault
in accordance with the spirit of the age—but in carrying
these laws into execution with a cruelty offensive to human
feelings. Yet on many occasions Constantine gave proofs of
humanity, as well as of a desire to protect his subjects. The

---

[1] Compare Ducange, *Glossarium Med. et Infin. Latinitatis*, voce *Bagaudæ*, with
Wallon, *Histoire de l'Esclavage dans l'Antiquité*, iii. 287.

Sclavonians on the coast of Thrace, having fitted out some piratical vessels, carried off many of the inhabitants of Tenedos, Imbros, and Samothrace, to sell them as slaves. The emperor on this occasion ransomed two thousand five hundred of his subjects, preferring to lower his own dignity, by paying a tribute to the pirates, rather than allow those who looked to him for protection to pine away their lives in hopeless misery. No act of his reign shows so much real greatness of mind as this. He also concluded the convention with the Saracens for an exchange of prisoners, which has been already mentioned—one of the earliest examples of the exchanges between the Mohammedans and the Christians, which afterwards became frequent on the Byzantine frontiers. Man was exchanged for man, woman for woman, and child for child.[1] These conventions tended to save the lives of innumerable prisoners, and rendered the future wars between the Saracens and Romans less barbarous.

Constantine was active in his internal administration, and his schemes for improving the condition of the inhabitants of his empire were carried out on a far more gigantic scale than modern governments have considered practicable. One of his plans for reviving agriculture in uncultivated districts was by re-peopling them with colonies of emigrants, to whom he secured favourable conditions and efficient protection. On the banks of the Artanas in Bithynia, a colony of two hundred thousand Sclavonians was formed.[2] The Christian population of Germanicia, Doliche, Melitene, and Theodosiopolis was established in Thrace, to watch and restrain the rude Sclavonians settled in that province; and these Asiatic colonists long continued to flourish and multiply.[3] They are even accused of spreading the heretical opinions which they had brought from the East throughout great part of western Europe, by the extent of their commercial relations and the example of their prosperity and honesty.[4] It is not to be supposed that the measures of Constantine's administration, however great his political abilities

---

[1] Theophanes, 374. At this time the slave-trade was very active, and the Venetians carried on a flourishing commerce in Christian slaves with the Mohammedans.—Anastasius, *De Vit. Pont. Rom.* 79. *Epist. Hadriani*, i. ep. xii. Even during the anarchy that prevailed in western Europe at the end of the seventh century, Roman slave-merchants imported slaves from Britain, as we know from the anecdote of St. Gregory, repeated by all our historians.

[2] Nicephorus, Pat. 44. Theophanes, 364.

[3] Nicephorus, Pat. 43. Theophanes, 354, 360.

[4] How far the Albigenses were indebted for their doctrines to these colonies is still a question. See Schmidt, *Histoire et Doctrine de la Secte des Cathares ou Albigeois*, 2 vols. 1849.

might be, were competent to remove many of the social evils of his age. Agriculture was still carried on in the rudest manner; and as communications were difficult and insecure, and transport expensive, capital could hardly be laid out on land to any extent with much profit. As usual under such circumstances, we find years of famine and plenty alternating in close succession. Yet the bitterest enemy of Constantine, the abbot Theophanes, confesses that his reign was one of general abundance. It is true, he reproaches him with loading the husbandmen with taxes; but he also accuses him of being a new Midas, who made gold so common in the hands of all that it became cheap. The abbot's political economy, it must be confessed, is not so orthodox as his calumny. If the Patriarch Nicephorus, another enemy of Constantine, is to be believed, grain was so abundant, or gold so rare, that sixty measures of wheat, or seventy measures of barley, were sold for a nomisma, or gold Byzant.[1] To guard against severe drought in the capital, and supply the gardens in its immediate vicinity with water, Constantine repaired the great aqueduct of Valens. The flourishing condition of the towns in Greece at the time is attested by the fact, that the best workmen in cement were sought in the Hellenic cities and the islands of the Archipelago.[2]

The time and attention of Constantine, during his whole reign, were principally engaged in military occupations. In the eyes of his contemporaries, he was judged by his military conduct. His strategic abilities and indefatigable activity were the most striking characteristics of his administration. His campaigns, his financial measures, and the abundance they created, were known to all; but his ecclesiastical policy affected comparatively few. Yet by that policy his reign has been exclusively judged and condemned in modern times. The grounds of the condemnation are unjust. He has not, like his father, the merit of having saved an empire from ruin; but he may claim the honour of perfecting the reforms planned by his father, and of re-establishing the military power of the Roman empire on a basis that perpetuated Byzantine supremacy for several centuries. Hitherto historians have

1 Nicephorus, Pat. 48. Theophanes, 373. As a contrast to this cheapness, Theophanes, 352, mentions that a measure of barley was sold for twelve nomismata while Artavasdos was besieged in Constantinople.

2 Theophanes, 371. Six thousand nine hundred workmen were employed. One thousand masons and two hundred plasterers were brought from Asia Minor and Pontus; five hundred workers in cement from Greece and the islands of the Archipelago; five thousand labourers from Thrace, with two hundred potters.

treated the events of his reign as an accidental assemblage of facts; but surely, if he is to be rendered responsible for the persecution of the image-worshippers, in which he took comparatively little part, he deserves credit for his military successes and prosperous administration, since these were the result of his constant personal occupation. The history of his ecclesiastical measures, however, really possesses a deep interest, for they reflect with accuracy the feelings and ideas of millions of his subjects, as well as of the emperor.

Constantine was a sincere enemy of image-worship, and in his age sincerity implied bigotry, for persecution was considered both lawful and meritorious. Yet with all his energy, he was prudent in his first attempts to carry out his father's policy. While he was struggling with Artavasdos, and labouring to restore the discipline of his troops, and re-establish the military superiority of the Byzantine arms, he left the religious controversy concerning image-worship to the two parties of the clergy who then disputed for pre-eminence in the church. But when his power was consolidated, he steadily pursued his father's plans for centralising the ecclesiastical administration of the empire. To prepare for the final decision of the question, which probably, in his mind, related as much to the right of the emperor to govern the church, as to the question whether pictures were to be worshipped or not, he ordered the metropolitans and archbishops to hold provincial synods, in order to discipline the people for the execution of the edicts he proposed to carry in a general council of the Eastern church.[1]

This general council was convoked at Constantinople in the year 754. It was attended by 338 bishops, forming the most numerous assembly of the Christian clergy which had ever been collected together for ecclesiastical legislation. Theodosius, metropolitan of Ephesus, son of the Emperor Tiberius III., presided, for the patriarchal chair had been kept vacant since the death of Anastasios in the preceding year. Neither the Pope nor the patriarchs of Antioch, Alexandria, and Jerusalem sent representatives to this council, which was solely composed of the Byzantine clergy, so that it had no right to assume the rank of an ecumenical council. Its decisions were all against image-worship, which it declared to be contrary to Scripture. It proclaimed the use of images

---

[1] Theophanes, 358, μελετῶν σιλέντια καθ' ἑκάστην πόλιν τὸν λαὸν ἔπειθε πρὸς τὸ ἴδιον φρόνημα δογίως ἕπεσθαι.

and pictures in churches to be a pagan and antichristian practice, the abolition of which was necessary to avoid leading Christians into temptation. Even the use of the crucifix was condemned, on the ground that the only true symbol of the incarnation was the bread and wine which Christ had commanded to be received for the remission of sins. In its opposition to the worship of pictures, the council was led into the display of some animosity against painting itself; and every attempt at embodying sacred subjects by what it styled the dead and accursed art, foolishly invented by the pagans, was strongly condemned. The common people were thus deprived of a source of ideas, which, though liable to abuse, tended in general to civilise their minds, and might awaken noble thoughts and religious aspirations. We may fully agree with the Iconoclasts in the religious importance of not worshipping images, and not allowing the people to prostrate themselves on the pavements of churches before pictures of saints, whether said to be painted by human artists or miraculous agency; while at the same time we think that the walls of the vestibules or porticoes of sacred edifices may with propriety be adorned with pictures representing those sacred subjects most likely to awaken feelings of Christian charity. It is by embodying and ennobling the expression of feelings common to all mankind, that modern artists can alone unite in their works that combination of truth with the glow of creative imagination which gives a divine stamp to many pagan works. There is nothing in the circle of human affairs so democratic as art. The council of 754, however, deemed that it was necessary to sacrifice art to the purity of religion. "The godless art of painting" was proscribed. All who manufactured crucifixes or sacred paintings for worship, in public or private, whether laymen or monks, were ordered to be excommunicated by the church and punished by the state. At the same time, in order to guard against the indiscriminate destruction of sacred buildings and shrines possessing valuable ornaments and rich plate and jewels, by Iconoclastic zeal, or under its pretext, the council commanded that no alteration was to be made in existing churches, without the special permission of the patriarch and the emperor —a regulation bearing strong marks of the fiscal rapacity of the central treasury of the Roman empire. The bigotry of the age was displayed in the anathema which this council pronounced against three of the most distinguished and virtuous advocates of image-worship, Germanos, the Patriarch of Constantinople, George of Cyprus, and John Damascenus, the last of the fathers of the Greek church.[1]

The ecclesiastical decisions of the council served as the basis for penal enactments by the civil power. The success of the emperor in restoring prosperity to the empire, induced many of his subjects to believe that he was destined to reform the church as well as the state, and few thinking men could doubt that corruption had entered deep into both. In many minds there was a contest between the superstitions of picture-worship and the feeling of respect for the emperor's administration ; but there were still in the Roman empire many persons of education, unconnected with the church, who regarded the superstitions of the people with aversion. To them the reverence paid by the ignorant to images said to have fallen from heaven, to pictures painted by St. Luke, to virgins who wept, and to saints who supplied the lamps burning before their effigies with a perpetual fountain of oil, appeared rank idolatry.[2] There were also still a few men of philosophic minds who exercised the right of private judgment on public questions, both civil and ecclesiastical, and who felt that the emperor was making popular superstition the pretext for rendering his power despotic in the church as in the state. His conduct appeared to these men a violation of those principles of Roman law and ecclesiastical legislation which rendered the systematic government of society in the Roman empire superior to the arbitrary rule of Mohammedan despotism, or the wild license of Gothic anarchy. The Greek church had not hitherto made it imperative on its members to worship images ;—it had only tolerated popular abuse in the reverence paid to these symbols—so that the ignorant monks who resisted the enlightened Iconoclasts might, by liberal-minded men, be considered as the true defenders of the right of private judgment, and as benefactors of mankind. There is positive evidence that such feelings really existed, and they could not exist without producing some influence on society generally. Less than forty years after the death of Constantine, the tolerant party was so numerous that it could

---

[1] The acts of this council are only known from the garbled portions preserved by its enemies in the acts of the second council of Nicæa and the hostile historians.—Coleti, *Acta S. Conciliorum*, tom. viii. 1457.

[2] At Athens is a church of the blessed Virgin Mary, which has a lamp that burns always, and never wants oil.—*The Travels of Sæwulf*, 32. *Early Travels in Palestine*, Bohn's edit.

struggle in the imperial cabinet to save heretics from persecution, on the ground that the church had no authority to ask that men should be condemned to death for matters of belief, as God may always turn the mind of the sinner to repentance. Theophanes has recorded the existence of these humane sentiments in his eagerness to blame them.[1]

Many of the clergy boldly resisted the edicts of Constantine to enforce the new ecclesiastical legislation against images and pictures. They held that all the acts of the council of Constantinople were void, for a general council could only be convoked by an orthodox emperor; and they took upon themselves to declare the opinions of Constantine heterodox. The monks engaged with eagerness in the controversy which arose. The Pope, the patriarchs of Antioch, Alexandria, and Jerusalem, replied to the excommunications of the council by condemning all its supporters to eternal perdition. The emperor, enraged at the opposition he met with, enforced the execution of his edicts with all the activity and energy of his character; his political as well as his religious views urged him to be a persecutor. It is evident that policy and passion were as much connected with his violence against the image-worshippers as religious feeling, for he treated many heretics with toleration who appeared to be quiet and inoffensive subjects, incapable of offering any opposition to his political and ecclesiastical schemes. The Theopaschites, the Paulicians, and the Monophysites enjoyed religious toleration during his whole reign.[2]

In the year 766 the edicts against image-worship were extended in their application, and enforced with additional rigour. The use of relics and the practice of praying to saints were prohibited. Many monks, and several members of the dignified clergy, were banished; stripes, loss of the eyes and of the tongue, were inflicted as legal punishments for prostration before a picture, or praying before a relic. Yet, even at this period of the greatest excitement, the emperor at times displayed great personal forbearance; when, however, either policy or passion prompted him to order punishment to be inflicted, it was done with fearful severity.[3]

Two cases may be mentioned as affording a correct elucida-

---

[1] Theophanes, 419, ἐδογμάτιζον δὲ ἀμαθῶς μὴ ἐξεῖναι ἱερεῦσιν ἀποφαίνεσθαι κατὰ ἀσεβῶν θάνατος.   [2] Theophanes, 354, 360.

[3] Theophanes, 370. Bonefidius (*Jus Orientale*, 4) quotes this edict against relics from Cedrenas. Mortreuil, i. 349.

tion of the personal conduct of Constantine. A hermit, named Andreas the Kalybite, presented himself before the emperor, and upbraided him for causing dissension in the church. "If thou art a Christian, why dost thou persecute Christians?" shouted the monk to his prince, with audacious orthodoxy. Constantine ordered him to be carried off to prison for insulting the imperial authority. He was then called upon to submit to the decisions of the general council; and when he refused to admit the validity of its canons, and to obey the edicts of the emperor, he was tried and condemned to death. After being scourged in the hippodrome, he was beheaded, and his body, according to the practice of the age, was cast into the sea.

Stephen, the abbot of a monastery near Nicomedia, was banished to the island of Proconnesus, on account of his firm opposition to the emperor's edicts; but his fame for piety drew numerous votaries to his place of banishment, who flocked thither to hear him preach. This assembly of seditious and pious persons roused the anger of the civil authorities, and Stephen was brought to Constantinople to be more strictly watched. His eloquence still drew crowds to the door of his prison; and the reverence shown to him by his followers vexed the emperor so much, that he gave vent to his mortification by exclaiming—"It seems, in truth, that this monk is really emperor, and I am nothing in the empire." This speech was heard by some of the officers of the imperial guard. Like that of Henry II. concerning Thomas à Becket, it caused the death of Stephen. He was dragged from his prison by some of the emperor's guard, and cruelly murdered. The soldiery and the people joined in dragging his body through the streets, and his unburied remains were left exposed in the place destined to receive those of the lowest criminals. Both Stephen and Andreas were declared martyrs, and rewarded with a place in the calendar of Greek saints.[1]

Orthodox zeal and party ambition combined to form a dangerous conspiracy against Constantine. Men of the highest rank engaged in the plot, and even the Patriarch Constantinos, though himself an Iconoclast, appears to have joined the conspirators. He was removed from the patriarchate, and the dignity was conferred on a Sclavonian prelate, named Niketas.[2]

[1] Their festival is celebrated on the 28th November, old style.—*Menologium Græcorum Jussu Basilii Imp.*, 3 tom. fol. Urbini, 1727, tom. i. 216.

[2] Glycas (284) has preserved an anecdote which affords an amusing illustration of the fact that the Greek element in society at Constantinople was not yet the all-pre-

The deposed Patriarch was brought to trial and condemned to death. Constantinos, after his condemnation, and apparently with the hope of having his life spared, signed a declaration that he believed the worship of images to be idolatry, that the decrees of the council of Constantinople contained the true doctrines of the orthodox church, and that the faith of the emperor was pure. This last article was added because the patriarch was accused of having countenanced reports charging the emperor with heterodox opinions concerning the Virgin. If Constantinos expected mercy by his pliancy, he was mistaken. His sentence was carried into execution in the cruellest manner. The head of the Greek church was placed on an ass, with his face towards the tail, and conducted through the streets of the capital, while the mob treated him with every insult. On reaching the amphitheatre his head was struck off. It may easily be supposed that, when the highest ecclesiastic in the empire was treated in this manner in the capital, the severity of the imperial agents in the distant provinces was often fearfully tyrannical.

The spirit of ecclesiastical bigotry which has so often led popes, princes, and Protestants to burn those who differed from them in matters of opinion, gave the image-worshippers as much fortitude to resist as it gave their opponents cruelty to persecute. The religious and political reforms of the Isaurian emperors were equally a subject of aversion to the Pope and the Italians ; and all the possessions of the emperors in central Italy had been rendered virtually independent, even before Constantine convoked the council of Constantinople. His struggle with the Saracens and Bulgarians had prevented his making any effort in Italy. At Rome, however, the Popes continued to acknowledge the civil and judicial supremacy of the emperor of the East, even after the Lombards had conquered the exarchate of Ravenna. But the impossibility of receiving any support from Constantine against the encroachments of the Lombards, induced Pope Stephen to apply to Pepin of France for assistance. Pope Paul afterwards carried his eagerness to create a quarrel between Pepin and Constantine so far, that he accused the emperor of hostile designs

dominant. The Patriarch Niketas may have spoken Latin better than Greek, for there was something far from Hellenic in his accent and ideas. One day, reading the New Testament, he pronounced the name of the evangelist Ματθάϊον, and not Ματθαῖον. One of his suite observed that the vowels of the diphthong were not to be separated. The Sclavonic patriarch, displeased at the correction, turned angrily round, and said, "Don't talk nonsense ; my soul utterly abhors diphthongs and triphthongs!"

against Italy, which he was well aware Constantine had little time or power to execute.[1] Pepin, who was anxious to gain the aid of papal authority in his projects of usurpation, made a donation of the exarchate of Ravenna to the papal see in the year 755, though he had not the smallest right to dispose of it. The donation, however, supplied the Pope with a pretext for laying claim to the sovereignty over the country; and there can be no doubt that the papal government was at this period very popular among the Italians, for it secured them the administration of justice according to the Roman law, guaranteed to them a considerable degree of municipal independence, and permitted them to maintain their commercial relations with the Byzantine empire. The political dependence of many of the cities in central Italy, which escaped the Lombard domination, was not absolutely withdrawn from the empire of the East until a new emperor of the West was created, on the assumption of the imperial crown by Charlemagne, to whom the allegiance of the Italians, who threw off Constantine's authority, was at last transferred.[2]

Some remarkable physical phenomena occurred during the reign of Constantine. An unnatural darkness obscured the sun from the 10th to the 15th of August in the year 746. It terrified the inhabitants of Constantinople at the time it occurred; and when the great pestilence broke out in the following year, it was regarded as a prognostic of that calamity. In the year 750, violent earthquakes destroyed whole towns in Syria. In the month of October, 763, a winter of singular severity commenced long before severe cold generally sets in at Constantinople. The Bosphorus was frozen over, and men passed on foot between Europe and Asia in several places. The Black Sea was covered with ice from the Palus Mæotic to Mesembria. When the thaw began in the month of February, 764, immense mountains of ice were driven through the Bosphorus, and dashed with such violence against the walls of Constantinople as to threaten them with ruin. These icebergs were seventy feet in thickness; and Theophanes mentions that, when a boy, he mounted on one of them with thirty of his young companions.[3]

One great calamity in the age of Constantine appears to have travelled over the whole habitable world; this was the great pestilence, which made its appearance in the Byzantine

---

[1] *Codex Carolinus*, ep. 34, 35. A.D. 758. Schlosser, 219.
[2] Anastasius, *De Vitis Pont. Rom.* 101, 102.   [3] Theophanes, 365.

empire as early as 745. It had previously carried off a considerable portion of the population of Syria, and the Caliph Yezid III. perished of the disease in 744. From Syria it visited Egypt and Africa, from whence it passed into Sicily. After making great ravages in Sicily and Calabria, it spread to Greece; and at last, in the year 749, it broke out with terrible violence in Constantinople, then probably the most populous city in the universe. It was supposed to have been introduced, and dispersed through Christian countries, by the Venetian and Greek ships employed in carrying on a contraband trade in slaves with the Mohammedan nations, and it spread wherever commerce extended. Monemvasia, one of the commercial cities at the time, received the contagion with the return of its trading vessels, and disseminated the disease over all Greece, and the islands of the Archipelago. On the continent, this plague threatened to exterminate the Hellenic race.

Historians have left us a vivid picture of the horrors of this fearful visitation, which show us that the terror it inspired disturbed the fabric of society. Strange superstitions preoccupied men's minds, and annihilated every sense of duty. Some appeared to be urged by a demoniacal impulse to commit heinous but useless crime, with the wildest recklessness. Small crosses of unctuous matter were supposed to appear suddenly, traced by an invisible hand on the clothes of persons as they were engaged in their ordinary pursuits; examples were narrated of their having appeared suddenly visible to the eyes of the assembled congregation on the vestments of the priest as he officiated at the altar. The individual thus marked out was invariably assailed by the disease on his return home, and soon died. Crosses were constantly found traced on the doors and outer walls of buildings; houses, palaces, huts, and monasteries were alike marked. This was considered as an intimation that some of the inmates were ordered to prepare for immediate death. In the delirium of fear and the first paroxysms of the plague, many declared that they beheld hideous spectres wandering about; these apparitions were seen flitting through the crowded streets of the city, at times questioning the passengers, at times walking into houses before the inmates, and then driving the proprietors from the door. At times it was said that these spectres had even attacked the citizens with naked swords. That these things were not reported solely on the delusion of the fancy of persons rendered insane by attacks of disease, is asserted by a historian who was born about ten years later, and who certainly passed his youth at Constantinople.[1] The testimony of Theophanes is confirmed by the records of similar diseases in other populous cities. The uncertainty of life offers additional chances of impunity to crime, and thus relaxes the power of the law, and weakens the bonds of moral restraint. Danger is generally what man fears little, when there are several chances of escape. The bold and wicked, deriding the general panic, frequently make periods of pestilence times of revelry and plunder; the very individuals charged as policemen to preserve order in society, finding themselves free from control, have been known to assume the disguise of demons, in order to plunder the terrified and superstitious with impunity. The predominant passions of all find full scope when the feeling of responsibility is removed; shame is thrown aside, the most unfeeling avarice and the wildest debauchery are displayed. But, at the same time, it is on such fearful occasions that we see examples of the noblest courage, the most devoted self-sacrifice and the purest charity. Boccaccio and Defoe, in describing the scenes which occurred at Florence in 1348, and at London in 1665, afford a correct picture of what happened at Constantinople in 747.

The number of dead was so great, that when the ordinary means of transporting the bodies to interment were insufficient, boxes were slung over the pack-saddles of mules, into which the dead were cast without distinction of rank. When the mules became insufficient, low chariots were constructed to receive piles of human bodies, and these frightful hearses were drawn through the streets to receive their loads, by a crowd of men who received a fixed sum of money with each body. Long trenches were prepared without the walls to serve as graves for hundreds of bodies, and into these the aged beggar and the youthful noble were precipitated side by side. When all the cemeteries around the capital were filled, and the panic kept the mass of the population shut up in their dwellings, bodies were interred in the fields and vineyards nearest to the city gates, or they were cast into vacant houses and empty cisterns. The disease prevailed for a year, and left whole houses tenantless, having exterminated many families.[2] We possess no record of the number of deaths it caused, but if we suppose the population of Constantinople at the time to have exceeded a million, we may form an estimate of the probable loss it

[1] Theophanes, 355.   He was born A.D. 758.   [2] Nicephorus, Pat. 43, 87.

sustained, by observing that, during the great plague at Milan, in 1630, about eighty-six thousand persons perished in the course of a year, in a population hardly exceeding one hundred and fifty thousand souls.[1]

After the plague had completely disappeared, the capital required an immense influx of new inhabitants. To fill up the void caused by the scourge, Constantine induced many Greek families from the continent and the islands to emigrate to Constantinople. These new citizens immediately occupied a well-defined social position; for whether artisans, tradesmen, merchants, or householders, they became members of established corporations, and knew how to act in their new relations of life without embarrassment. It was by the perfection of its corporate societies and police regulations, that the Byzantine empire effected the translocation of the inhabitants of whole cities and provinces, without misfortune or discontent. By modifying the fiscal severity of the Roman government, by relieving the members of the municipality from the ruinous obligation of mutual responsibility for the total amount of the land-tax, and by relaxing the laws that fettered children to the profession or handicraft of their parents, the Byzantine administration infused new energy into an enfeebled social system. It still preserved, as an inheritance from Rome, an intimate knowledge of the practical methods of regulating the relative supplies of labour, food, and population in the manner least likely to inconvenience the government, though undoubtedly with little reference to the measures best calculated to advance the happiness of the people.[2]

This memorable pestilence produced as great changes in the provinces as in the capital. While the population of Constantinople lost much of its Roman character and traditions by the infusion of a large number of Greek emigrants, Greece itself lost also much of its Hellenic character and ancient traditions, by the departure of a considerable portion of its native middle classes for Constantinople, and the destruction of a large part by the plague itself. The middle classes of the Hellenic cities flocked to Constantinople, while an inferior class from the villages crowded to supply their place, and thus a general translocation of the population was effected; and

[1] *La Peste di Milano del* 1630 *dal Canonico G. Ripamonti dal original Latino da Francesco Cusani.* Milano, 1841. At Florence, one hundred thousand are said to have died of the plague; at London, ninety thousand.

[2] For the Byzantine system of taxation, as far as direct payment by the individual is concerned, see Zonaras, ii. 24 ; Cedrenus, 706–723 ; Mortreuil, iii. 105.

though this emigration may have been confined principally to the Greek race, it must have tended greatly to separate the future traditions of the people from those of an earlier period. The Athenian or the Lacedemonian who settled at Constantinople, lost all local characteristics; and the emigrants from the islands, who supplied their place at Athens and Lacedemon, mingled their traditions and dialect with the Attic and Doric prejudices of their new homes; ancient traditions were thus consigned to oblivion. The depopulation on the continent and in the Peloponnesus was also so great that the Sclavonian population extended their settlements over the greater part of the open country; the Greeks crowded into the towns, or into the districts immediately under the protection of their walls. The Sclavonian colonies, which had been gradually increasing ever since the reign of Heraclius, attained at this time their greatest extension; and the depopulation caused by this pestilence is said by the Emperor Constantine Porphyrogenitus, who wrote two centuries later, to have been so great, that the Sclavonians occupied the whole of the open country in Greece and the Peloponnesus, and reduced it to a state of barbarism.[1] The emperor perhaps confounded in some degree the general translocation of the Greek population itself with the occupation of extensive districts, then abandoned to Sclavonian cultivators and herdsmen. It is certain, however, that from this time the oblivion of the ancient Hellenic names of villages, districts, rivers, and mountains became general; and the final extinction of those dialects, which marked a direct affiliation of the inhabitants of particular spots with the ancient Hellenic population of the same districts, was consummated. The new names which came into use, whether Sclavonian or Greek, equally mark the loss of ancient traditions.[2]

In closing the history of the reign of Constantine V., it is necessary to observe that he deserves praise for the care with which he educated his family. The most bigoted imageworshippers inform us that he was so mild in his domestic circle that he permitted his third wife to protect a nun named Anthusa, who was a most devoted worshipper of images; and one of the emperor's daughters received from this nun both her name and education. The Princess Anthusa was distinguished for her benevolence and piety; she is said to have

---

[1] *De Thematibus*, ii. 25.
[2] *Strabonis Epitome*, edit. Almeloven, 1251-1261. Edit. Coray, tom. iii. 373-386.

founded one of the first orphan asylums established in the Christian world; and her orthodox devotion to pictures obtained for her a place among the saints of the Greek church, an honour granted also to her godmother and teacher.[1]

SECTION IV

REIGNS OF LEO IV., (THE KHAZAR,) CONSTANTINE VI., AND IRENE, A.D. 775–802

Leo IV., A.D. 775–780—Irene regent for her son—Restores image-worship—Second council of Nicæa—Extinction of Byzantine authority at Rome—Constantine assumes the government—Divorces Maria, and marries Theodota—Opposition of monks—Persecution of Theodore Studita—Irene dethrones Constantine VI.—Policy of reigns of Constantine VI. and Irene—Saracen war—Bulgarian war.

Leo IV. succeeded his father at the age of twenty-five. His mother, Irene, was the daughter of the emperor or chagan of the Khazars, then a powerful people, through whose territories the greater part of the commercial intercourse between the Christians and the rich countries in eastern Asia was carried on. Leo inherited from his mother a mild and amiable disposition; nor does he appear to have been destitute of some portion of his father's talents, but the state of his health prevented him from displaying the same activity. His reign lasted four years and a half, and his administration was conducted in strict accordance with the policy of his father and grandfather; but the weak state of his health kept the public attention fixed on the question of the imperial succession. Constantine V. had selected an Athenian lady, of great beauty and accomplishments, named Irene, to be his son's wife, and Leo had a son named Constantine, who was born in the year 771. The indefinite nature of the imperial succession, and the infancy of Leo's child, gave the two half-brothers of the emperor, who had been invested by their father with the rank of Cæsar, some hope of ascending the throne on their brother's death. Leo conferred on his infant son the title of Emperor, in order to secure his succession; and this was done in a more popular manner than usual, at the express desire of the senate, in order to give the ceremony all the character of a popular election. The young emperor's five

---

[1] *Menologium Græcorum*, tom. iii. 60-183. The festival of Constantine's daughter was celebrated on the 17th April, and that of the nun Anthusa on the 27th July.

uncles—the two Cæsars, and the three who bore the title of Nobilissimi—were compelled to take the same oath of allegiance as the other subjects.[1] Yet, shortly after this, the Cæsar Nicephorus formed a conspiracy to render himself master of the government. Leo, who felt that he was rapidly sinking into the grave, referred the decision of his brother's guilt to a Silention, which condemned all the conspirators to death. Nicephorus was pardoned, but his partisans were scourged and banished to Cherson. The death of Leo IV. happened on the 8th of September, 780.[2]

Constantine was ten years old when his father died, so that the whole direction of the empire devolved on his mother, Irene, who had received the imperial crown from Constantine V.; for that emperor seems to have felt that the weak state of Leo's health would require the assistance of Irene's talents. The virtues Irene had displayed in a private station were insufficient to resist the corrupting influence of irresponsible power. Ambition took possession of her own soul, and it was the ambition of reigning alone, not of reigning well. The education of her son was neglected—perhaps as a means of securing her power; favour was avowedly a surer road to preferment than long service, so that the court became a scene of political intrigue, and personal motives decided most public acts. As no organ of public opinion possessed the power of awakening a sense of moral responsibility among the officers of state, the intrigues of the court ended in conspiracies, murder, and treason.

The parties struggling for power soon ranged themselves under the banners of the ecclesiastical factions that had long divided the empire. Little, probably, did many of the leaders care what party they espoused in the religious question; but it was necessary to proclaim themselves members of an ecclesiastical faction in order to secure a popular following. The

---

[1] Theophanes, 380. Zonaras, ii. 114, where the popular character of the assembly is expressly pointed out—Καὶ ὤμοσαν ἅπαντες οὐχ' οἱ τῆς Συγκλήτου βουλῆς καὶ οἱ τοῦ στρατεύματος μόνον, ἀλλὰ καὶ ὁ δημώδης ὄχλος καὶ ἔμποροι καὶ οἱ τῶν ἐργασηρίων προεστήκεσαν καὶ ἔγγραφα περὶ τούτων ἐξέθεντο. This mention of the corporation of artisans is curious.

[2] I doubt whether the authority of Cedrenus, 469, negatived by the silence of earlier zealots, can authorise our believing the anecdote that the Emperor Leo discovered pictures of saints under Irene's pillow, and quarrelled with her in consequence; nor do I think that the story of his having taken one of the crowns from the church of St. Sophia of any importance, since it could not have been the cause of his death. Divine vengeance certainly did not visit Leo with sudden death, whether he took the crown from St. Sophia's or not. See the turn Constantine Porphyrogenitus gives the anecdote, *De Adm. Imp.* 64.

Empress Irene was known to favour image-worship; as a woman and a Greek, this was natural; yet policy would have dictated to her to adopt that party as the most certain manner of securing support powerful enough to counterbalance the family influence of the Isaurian dynasty, which was now wielded by the uncles of the young emperor. The conflict between the image-worshippers and the Iconoclasts soon commenced. The Cæsar Nicephorus, who was as ambitious as his sister-in-law, was eager to drive her from the regency. He organised a conspiracy, in which several ministers and members of the senate took part. Irene obtained full proof of all its ramifications before the conspirators were prepared to act, seized her five brothers-in-law, and compelled them to enter the priesthood. In order to make it generally known that they had assumed the sacerdotal character, they were obliged to officiate during the Christmas ceremonies at the high altar of St. Sophia's, while the young emperor and his mother restored to the church the rich jewels of which it had been deprived by the Iconoclast emperors. The intendant-general of posts, the general of the Armeniac theme, the commander of the imperial guard, and the admiral of the Archipelago, who had all taken part in the conspiracy, were scourged, and immured as monks in distant monasteries. Helpidios, the governor of Sicily, assumed the title of emperor as soon as he found that his participation in the plot was known at court; but he was compelled to seek shelter among the Saracens, in whose armies he afterwards served. Nicephorus Doukas, another conspirator, fled also to the Mohammedans.[1] Some years later, when Constantine VI. had assumed the government into his own hands, a new conspiracy was formed by the partisans of his uncles (A.D. 792). The princes were then treated with great severity. The Cæsar Nicephorus was deprived of sight; and the tongues of the others were cut out, by the order of their nephew, not long before he lost his own eyes by the order of his mother.

The influence of the clergy in the ordinary administration of justice, and the great extent to which ecclesiastical legislation regulated civil rights, rendered councils of the church an important feature in those forms and usages that practically circumscribed the despotic power of the emperor by a frame-

[1] Theophanes, 383, 384. Theophylactos, son of Rhangabé, was the admiral of the Archipelago, or Drungarios of Dodekannesos. This is the earliest mention of the twelve islands as a geographical and administrative division of the empire. It was retained by the Crusaders when they conquered Greece.

work of customs, opinions, and convictions which he could with difficulty alter, and rarely oppose without danger. The political ambition of Irene, the national vanity of the Greeks, and the religious feelings of the orthodox, required the sanction of a constitutional public authority, before the laws against image-worship could be openly repealed. The Byzantine empire had at this time an ecclesiastical, though not a political constitution. The will of the sovereign was alone insufficient to change an organic law, forming part of the ecclesiastical administration of the empire. It was necessary to convoke a general council to legalise image-worship; and to render such a council a fit instrument for the proposed revolution, much arrangement was necessary. No person was ever endued with greater talents for removing opposition and conciliating personal support than the empress. The Patriarch Paul, a decided Iconoclast, was induced to resign, and declare that he repented of his hostility to image-worship, because it had cut off the church of Constantinople from communion with the rest of the Christian world. This declaration pointed out the necessity of holding a general council, in order to establish that communion. The crisis required a new Patriarch, of stainless character, great ability, and perfect acquaintance with the party connections and individual characters of the leading bishops. No person could be selected from among the dignitaries of the church, who had been generally appointed by Iconoclast emperors. The choice of Irene fell on a civilian. Tarasios, the chief secretary of the imperial cabinet —a man of noble birth, considerable popularity, and a high reputation for learning and probity—was suddenly elevated to be the head of the Greek church, and allowed to be not unworthy of the high rank. The orthodox would probably have raised a question concerning the legality of nominating a layman, had it not been evident that the objection would favour the interests of their opponents. The empress and her advisers were not bold enough to venture on an irretrievable declaration in favour of image-worship, until they had obtained a public assurance of popular support. An assembly of the inhabitants of the capital was convoked in the palace of Magnaura, in order to secure a majority pledged to the cause of Tarasios. The fact that such an assembly was considered necessary, is a strong proof that the strength of the rival parties was very nearly balanced, and that this manifestation of public opinion was required in order to relieve the empress from personal responsibility. Irene proposed to the assembly that Tarasios should be elected Patriarch, and the proposal was received with general acclamation. Tarasios, however, refused the dignity, declaring that he would not accept the Patriarchate unless a general council should be convoked for restoring unity to the church. The convocation of a council was adopted, and the nomination of Tarasios ratified. Though great care had been taken to fill this assembly with image-worshippers, nevertheless several dissentient voices made themselves heard, protesting against the proceedings as an attack on the existing legislation of the empire.[1]

The Iconoclasts were still strong in the capital, and the opposition of the soldiery was excited by the determination of Tarasios to re-establish image-worship. They openly declared that they would not allow a council of the church to be held, nor permit the ecclesiastics of their party to be unjustly treated by the court. More than one tumult warned the empress that no council could be held at Constantinople. It was found necessary to disperse the Iconoclastic soldiery in distant provinces, and form new cohorts of guards devoted to the court, before any steps could be publicly taken to change the laws of the church. The experience of Tarasios as a minister of state was more useful to Irene during the first period of his patriarchate than his theological learning. It required nearly three years to smooth the way for the meeting of the council, which was at length held at Nicæa, in September, 787. Three hundred and sixty-seven members attended, of whom, however, not a few were abbots and monks, who assumed the title of confessors from having been ejected from their monasteries by the decrees of the Iconoclast sovereigns. Some of the persons present deserve to be particularly mentioned, for they have individually conferred greater benefits on mankind by their learned labours, than they rendered to Christianity by their zealous advocacy of image-worship in this council. The secretary of the two commissioners who represented the imperial authority was Nicephorus the historian, subsequently Patriarch of Constantinople.[2] His sketch of the history of the empire, from the year 602 to 770, is a valuable work, and indicates that he was a man of judgment, whenever his perceptions were not obscured by theological and ecclesiastical prejudices. Two other eminent Byzantine

---

[1] Theophanes, 386. Coleti, *Acta S. Conciliorum*, viii. 677. Schlosser, 278.
[2] Nicephorus was Patriarch from 806 to 815; he died in 828.

writers were also present.   George, called Syncellus, from the office he held under the Patriarch Tarasios.   He has left us a chronological work, which has preserved the knowledge of many important facts recorded by no other ancient authority.[1] Theophanes, the friend and companion of the Syncellus, has continued this work; and his chronography of Roman and Byzantine history, with all its faults, forms the best picture of the condition of the empire that we possess for a long period. Theophanes enjoyed the honour of becoming, at a later day, a confessor in the cause of image-worship; he was exiled from a monastery which he had founded, and died in the island of Samothrace, A.D. 817.[2]

The second council of Nicæa had no better title than the Iconoclast council of Constantinople to be regarded as a general council of the church.   The Pope Hadrian, indeed, sent deputies from the Latin church; but the churches of Jerusalem, Alexandria, and Antioch, whose patriarchs were groaning under the government of the caliphs, did not dare to communicate with foreign authorities.   An attempt was nevertheless made to deceive the world into a belief that they were represented, by allowing two monks from Palestine to present themselves as the syncelli of these patriarchs, without scrutinising the validity of their credentials.   Pope Hadrian, though he sent deputies, wrote at the same time to Tarasios, making several demands tending to establish the ecclesiastical supremacy of the papal See, and complaining in strong terms that the Patriarch of Constantinople had no right to assume the title of ecumenic.   The hope of recovering the estates of the patrimony of St. Peter in the Byzantine provinces, which had been sequestrated by Leo III., and of re-establishing the supremacy of the See of Rome, made Hadrian overlook much that was offensive to papal pride.[3]

The second council of Nicæa authorised the worship of images as an orthodox practice.   Forged passages, pretending to be extracts from the earlier fathers, and genuine from the more modern, were quoted in favour of the practice.   Simony was already a prevailing evil in the Greek church.   Many of

---

[1] George Syncellus died in 800.   His chronography extends from Adam to Diocletian.

[2] The chronography of Theophanes extends from Diocletian, A.D. 285, to A.D. 813. It is the best authority for Byzantine history after the time of Leo III.   His life, by Theodorus, abbot of Studion in Constantinople, is prefixed to the editions of the chronography.

[3] Schlosser, 279.   Coleti, *Acta S. Conciliorum*, viii. 748.   Neander, iii. 228 (American translation).

the bishops had purchased their sees, and most of these naturally preferred doing violence to their opinions rather than lose their revenues. From this cause, unanimity was easily obtained by court influence. The council decided that not only was the cross an object of reverence, but also that the images of Christ, and the pictures of the Virgin Mary—of angels, saints, and holy men, whether painted in colours, or worked in embroidery in sacred ornaments, or formed in mosaic in the walls of churches—were all lawful objects of worship. At the same time, in order to guard against the accusation of idolatry, it was declared that the worship of an image, which is merely a sign of reverence, must not be confounded with the adoration due only to God. The council of Constantinople held in 754 was declared heretical, and all who maintained its doctrines, and condemned the use of images, were anathematised. The patriarchs Anastasios, Constantinos, and Niketas were especially doomed to eternal condemnation.

The Pope adopted the decrees of this council, but he refused to confirm them officially, because the empress delayed restoring the estates of St. Peter's patrimony. In the countries of western Europe which had formed parts of the Western Empire, the superstitions of the image-worshippers were viewed with as much dissatisfaction as the fanaticism of the Iconoclasts; and the council of Nicæa was as much condemned as that of Constantinople by a large body of enlightened ecclesiastics. The public mind in the West was almost as much divided as in the East; and if a general council of the Latin church had been assembled, its unbiassed decisions would probably have been at variance with those supported by the Pope and the council of Nicæa.

Charlemagne published a refutation of the doctrines of this council on the subject of image-worship. His work, called the Caroline Books, consists of four parts, and was certainly composed under his immediate personal superintendence, though he was doubtless incapable of writing it himself.[1] At all events, it was published as his composition. This work condemns the superstitious bigotry of the Greek image-worshippers in a decided manner, while at the same time it only

[1] The title of the first edition is—*Opus illust. viri Caroli Magni Regis Francorum ete contra Synodum quæ in Partibus Græci pro Adorandis Imaginibus Stalide sive Arroganter gesta est*, etc. 1549. 16mo. It was published by Jean du Tillet, (Eli Phili,) afterwards bishop of Meaux. There is an edition, with a learned preface, by Christopher A. Heumann. Hanover. 1731. 8vo. Alcuin, of course, deserves all the credit due to the literary and theological merits of the Caroline books.

blames the misguided zeal of the Iconoclasts. Altogether it is a very remarkable production, and gives a more correct idea of the extent to which Roman civilisation still survived in Western society, and counterbalanced ecclesiastical influence, than any other contemporary document.[1] In 794 Charlemagne assembled a council of three hundred bishops at Frankfort; and, in the presence of the papal legates, this council maintained that pictures ought to be placed in churches, but that they should not be worshipped, but only regarded with respect, as recalling more vividly to the mind the subjects represented.[2] The similarity existing at this time in the opinions of enlightened men throughout the whole Christian world must be noted as a proof that general communications and commercial intercourse still pervaded society with common sentiments. The dark night of medieval ignorance and local prejudices had not yet settled on the West; nor had feudal anarchy confined the ideas and wants of society to the narrow sphere of provincial interests. The aspect of public opinion alarmed Pope Hadrian, whose interests required that the relations of the West and East should not become friendly. His position, however, rendered him more suspicious of Constantine and Irene, in spite of their orthodoxy, than of Charlemagne, with all his heterodox ideas. The Frank monarch, though he differed in ecclesiastical opinions, was sure to be a political protector. The Pope consequently laboured to foment the jealousy that reigned between the Frank and Byzantine governments concerning Italy, where the commercial relations of the Greeks still counterbalanced the military influence of the Franks. When writing to Charlemagne, he accused the Greeks and their Italian partisans of every crime likely to arouse the hostility of the Franks. They were reproached, and not unjustly, with carrying on an extensive

[1] Charlemagne mentions that he had learned from his ambassadors, that though the Greeks expended large sums on decorations and paintings, they allowed their churches to fall to ruin; and he contrasts the magnificent endowments of the Frank churches with the meanness of the Greek. It is really surprising how few churches of any size appear to have been constructed in the Byzantine empire, when we remember that for many centuries it was the richest country in the world, and the one most occupied with ecclesiastical affairs and church ceremonies. Several small Byzantine churches at Athens are said to have been constructed by Irene; common tradition says twelve. A few exist; some were destroyed during the war of the Revolution; others were swept away by the Bavarian plans of the town.

[2] The council of Frankfort blames that of Nicæa for inculcating the worship of images; but the council really draws a distinction between the reverence it inculcates, τιμητικὴ προσκύνησις, and the devotion it condemns, λατρεία. This distinction, to which, of course, the people paid no attention, serves the Greek church as a defence against the accusation of idolatrous practice. For the opinions of the British clergy on the question, see Spelman, *Ad Concilia Magnæ Britanniæ*, i. 73.

trade in slaves, who were purchased in western Europe, and sold to the Saracens. The Pope knew well that this commerce was carried on in all the trading cities of the West, both by Greeks and Latins; for slaves then constituted the principal article of European export to Africa, Syria, and Egypt, in payment of the produce of the East, which was brought from those countries. The Pope seized and burned some Greek vessels at Centumcellæ, (Civita-Vecchia,) because the crews were accused of kidnapping the people of the neighbourhood. The violent expressions of Hadrian, in speaking of the Greeks, could not fail to produce a great effect in western Europe, where the letters of the Popes formed the literary productions most generally read and studied by all ranks.[1] His calumnies must have sunk deep into the public mind, and tended to impress on Western nations that aversion to the Greeks, which was subsequently increased by mercantile jealousy and religious strife.

The extinction of the last traces of the supremacy of the Eastern Empire at Rome was the most gratifying result of their machinations to the Popes. On Christmas-day, A.D. 800, Charlemagne revived the existence of the Western Empire, and received the imperial crown from Pope Leo III. in the church of St. Peter's. Hitherto the Frank monarch had acknowledged a titular supremacy in the Eastern Empire, and had borne the title of Patrician of the Roman empire, as a mark of dignity conferred on him by the emperors of Constantinople; but he now raised himself to an equality with the emperors of the East, by assuming the title of Emperor of the West. The assumption of the title of emperor of the Romans was not an act of idle vanity. Roman usages, Roman prejudices, and Roman law still exercised a powerful influence over the minds of the most numerous body of Charlemagne's subjects; and by all the clergy and lawyers throughout his dominions the rights and prerogatives of the Roman emperors of the West were held to be legally vested in his person by the fact of his election, such as it was, and his coronation by the Pope. The political allegiance of the Pope to the emperor, which was then undisputed, became thus transferred

---

[1] *Hadriani I. Epist.* 12, 13. "Nefandissimi Neapolitani et Deo odibiles Græci."—Schlosser, 262. Pope Stephen III. had given an example of national calumny. He wrote to Charlemagne—"Perfida et fœtentissimi Langobardorum gens—quæ in numero gentium nequaquam computatur, de cujus natione et leprosorum genus oriri certum est." It is a task of difficulty to extract impartial history from the records of an age when the head of the Christian church used such language.

from the emperor of the East to the emperor of the West as a matter of course; while the papal rights of administration over the former exarchate of Ravenna, the Pentapolis, and the dukedom of Rome, acquired, under the protection of the Franks, the character of a decided sovereignty. Many towns of Italy at this time acquired a degree of municipal independence which made them almost independent republics. The influence of Roman law in binding society together, the military weakness of the papal power, and the rapid decline of the central authority in the empire of the Franks, enabled these towns to perpetuate their peculiar constitutions and independent jurisdictions down to the French Revolution.[1]

A female regency in an absolute government must always render the conduct of public affairs liable to be directed by court intrigues. When Irene wished to gain Charlemagne as an ally, in order to deprive the Iconoclasts of any hope of foreign assistance, she had negotiated a treaty of marriage between her son and Rotrud, the eldest daughter of the Frank monarch, A.D. 781. But when the question of image-worship was settled, she began to fear that this alliance might become the means of excluding her from power, and she then broke off the treaty, and compelled her son to marry a Paphlagonian lady of the court named Maria, whom the young emperor soon regarded with aversion. Constantine, however, submitted quietly to his mother's domination until his twentieth year. He then began to display dissatisfaction at the state of tutelage in which he was held, and at his complete seclusion from public business. A plan was formed by many leading men in the administration to place him at the head of affairs, but it was discovered before it was ripe for execution. Irene on this occasion displayed unseemly violence, in her eagerness to retain a power she ought immediately to have resigned. The conspirators were seized, scourged, and banished. When her son was conducted into her presence, she struck him, and overwhelmed him with reproaches and insults. The young emperor was then confined so strictly in the palace that all communication with his friends was cut off.

This unprincipled conduct of the regent-mother became the object of general reprobation. The troops of the Armeniac theme refused to obey her orders, and marched to the capital to deliver Constantine. On the way they were joined by

---

[1] Niebuhr's *History of Rome, from the First Punic War to the Death of Constantine*, by L. Schmitz, i. 424.

other legions, and Irene found herself compelled to release her son, who immediately hastened to the advancing army. A total revolution was effected at court. The ministers and creatures of Irene were removed from office, and some who had displayed particular animosity against Constantine were scourged and beheaded.[1] Constantine ruled the empire for about six years, (A.D. 790-797). But his education had been neglected in a disgraceful manner, and his mind was perhaps naturally fickle. Though he displayed the courage of his family at the head of his army, his incapacity for business, and his inconstancy in his friendships, soon lost him the support of his most devoted partisans. He lost his popularity by putting out the eyes of his uncle, Nicephorus, and cutting out the tongues of his four uncles, who were accused of having taken part in the plots of their brother. He alienated the attachment of the Armenian troops by putting out the eyes of their general, Alexis Mouselen, who had been the means of delivering him from confinement. The folly of this last act was even greater than the ingratitude, for it was done to gratify the revengeful feelings of his mother. These acts of folly, cruelty, and ingratitude destroyed his influence, and induced his sincerest friends to make their peace with Irene, whom it was evident her son would ultimately allow to rule the empire.

The unhappy marriage into which Constantine had been forced by his mother, she at last converted into the cause of his ruin. The emperor fell in love with Theodota, one of his mother's maids of honour, and determined to divorce Maria in order to marry her. Irene, whose ambition induced her to stoop to the basest intrigues, flattered him in this project, as it seemed likely to increase her influence and ruin his reputation. The Empress Maria was induced to retire into a monastery, and the emperor expected to be able to celebrate his marriage with Theodota without difficulty. But the usage of the Byzantine empire required that the Patriarch should pronounce the sentence of divorce, and this Tarasios, who was a devoted partisan and active political agent of Irene, long refused to do. The imprudence of Constantine, and the insidious advice of Irene, soon involved the emperor in a dispute with the whole body of monks, who had an overwhelming influence in society. The Patriarch at last yielded to the influence of Irene, so far as to allow his catechist to give the veil to the Empress Maria, whom he pronounced

[1] Theophanes, 393.

divorced, and then to permit the celebration of the emperor's marriage with Theodota by Joseph, one of the principal clergy of the patriarchal chapter, and abbot of a monastery in the capital.[1]

In the Byzantine empire, at this time, constant religious discussions and pretensions to superior sanctity, had introduced a profound religious spirit into the highest ranks of society. Numbers of the wealthiest nobles founded monasteries, into which they retired. The manners, the extensive charity, and the pure morality of these abbots, secured them the love and admiration of the people, and tended to disseminate a higher standard of morality than had previously prevailed in Constantinople. This fact must not be overlooked in estimating the various causes which led to the regeneration of the Eastern Empire under the Iconoclast emperors. Security of life and property, and all the foundations of national prosperity, are more closely connected with moral purity than the ruling classes are inclined to allow. It may not be quite useless, as an illustration of the state of the Byzantine empire, to remind the reader of the violence, injustice, and debauchery which prevailed at the courts of the west of Europe, including that of Charlemagne. While the Pope winked at the disorders in the palace of Charlemagne, the monks of the East prepared the public mind for the dethronement of Constantine, because he obtained an illegal divorce, and formed a second marriage. The corruption of morals, and the irregularities prevalent in the monasteries of the West, contrast strongly with the condition of the Eastern monks.[2]

The habit of building monasteries as a place of retreat, from motives of piety, was also adopted by some as a mode of securing a portion of their wealth from confiscation, in case of their condemnation for political crimes, peculiar privileges being reserved in the monasteries so founded for members of the founder's family.[3] At this time Plato, abbot of the monastery of Sakkoudion, on Mount Olympus in

[1] Theophanes, 397.

[2] Mosheim, *Institutes of Ecclesiastical History*, (translated by Murdoch,) ii. 143, 193; Soames' edit. But not to wrong St. Eligius, see also Arnold, *Introductory Lectures on Modern History*, 102. Maitland (*The Dark Ages*, 102) makes the most of Mosheim's error. The times, however, were not better than Mosheim represents them.

[3] The abuse of fictitious donations to monasteries had become so great an evil in Western Europe, as to require numerous laws to restrain the practice. The Lombard law allowed the granters to reserve the faculty of revoking these donations during their lives, and they reserved possession on paying a small annual sum as rent to the monas-

Bithynia, and his nephew Theodore, who was a relation of
the new Empress Theodota, were the leaders of a powerful
party of monks possessing great influence in the church.
Theodore (who is known by the name Studita, from having
been afterwards appointed abbot of the celebrated monastery
of Studion) had founded a monastery on his own property,
in which he assembled his father, two brothers, and a young
sister, and, emancipating all his household and agricultural
slaves, established them as lay brethren on the farms. Most
of the abbots round Constantinople were men of family and
wealth, as well as learning and piety; but they repaid the
sincere respect with which they were regarded by the people,
by participating in popular prejudices, so that we cannot
be surprised to find them constantly acting the part of dema-
gogues.   Plato separated himself from all spiritual communion with the Patriarch Tarasios, whom he declared to
have violated the principles of Christianity in permitting the
adulterous marriage of the emperor. His views were warmly
supported by his nephew Theodore, and many monks began
openly to preach both against the Patriarch and the emperor.
Irene now saw that the movement was taking a turn favourable
to her ambition. She encouraged the monks, and prepared
Tarasios for quitting the party of his sovereign. Plato and
Theodore were dangerous enemies, from their great reputation and extensive political and ecclesiastical connections,
and into a personal contest with these men Constantine rashly
plunged.

Plato was arrested at his monastery, and placed in confinement under the wardship of the abbot Joseph, who had
celebrated the imperial marriage. Theodore was banished to
Thessalonica, whither he was conveyed by a detachment of
police soldiers. He has left us an account of his journey,
which proves that the orders of the emperor were not carried
into execution with undue severity.[1] Theodore and his
attendant monks were seized by the imperial officers at a
distance from the monastery, and compelled to commence

---

tery. Charlemagne declared all such donations irrevocable, in order to check the evil.
The abuse existed among the Anglo-Saxons—Lingard's *History of England*, i. 517.
The Empress Irene founded the monastery of St. Euphrosyne, where her son Constantine, his divorced wife Maria, and his two daughters were buried ; and also the monastery in Prince's Island, to which she was sent after her dethronement, and before her
banishment to Lesbos.

[1] *Theodori Studitæ Opp.* 230. Schlosser, 319. Some letters of Theodore Studita
are given by Baronius. I have extracted the account of the journey from Schlosser,
Geschichte der bilderstürmenden Kaiser, for I have not been able to supply myself
with the works of Theodore.

their journey on the first horses their escort could procure, instead of being permitted to send for their ambling mules. They were hurried forward for three days, resting during the night at Kathara in Liviana, Lefka, and Phyraion. At the last place they encountered a melancholy array of monks, driven from the great monastery of Sakkoudion after the arrest of Plato; but with these fellow-sufferers, though ranged along the road, Theodore was not allowed to communicate, except by bestowing on them his blessing as he rode past. He was then carried to Paula, from whence he wrote to Plato that he had seen his sister, with the venerable Sabas, abbot of the monastery of Studion. They had visited him secretly, but had been allowed by the guards to pass the evening in his society. Next night they reached Loupadion, where the exiles were kindly treated by their host. At Tilin they were joined by two abbots, Zacharias and Pionios, but they were not allowed to travel in company. The journey was continued by Alberiza, Anagegrammenos, Perperina, Parium, and Horkos, to Lampsacus. On the road, the bishops expressed the greatest sympathy and eagerness to serve them; but the bigoted Theodore declared that his conscience would not permit him to hold any communication with those who were so unchristian as to continue in communion with Tarasios and the emperor.

From Lampsacus the journey was prosecuted by sea. A pious governor received them at Abydos with great kindness, and they rested there eight days. At Eleaus there was again a detention of seven days, and from thence they sailed to Lemnos, where the bishop treated Theodore with so much attention that his bigotry was laid asleep. The passage from Lemnos to Thessalonica was not without danger from the piratical boats of the Sclavonians who dwelt on the coast of Thrace, and exercised the trades of robbers and pirates as well as herdsmen and shepherds. A favourable wind carried the exiles without accident to Kanastron, from whence they touched at Pallene before entering the harbour of Thessalonica, which they reached on the 25th March, 797. Here they were received by a guard, and conducted through the city to the residence of the governor. The people assembled in crowds to view the pious opponents of their emperor; while the governor received them with marks of personal respect, which showed him more anxious to conciliate the powerful monks than to uphold the dignity of the weak emperor. He conducted Theodore to the cathedral, that he might return thanks to God publicly for his safe arrival; he then waited on him to the palace of the archbishop, where he was treated to a bath, and entertained most hospitably. The exiles were, however, according to the tenor of the imperial orders, placed in separate places of confinement; and even Theodore and his brother were not permitted to dwell together. The day of their triumph was not far distant, and their banishment does not appear to have subjected them to much inconvenience. They were martyrs at a small cost.

As soon as Irene thought that her son had rendered himself unpopular throughout the empire, she formed her plot for dethroning him. The support of the principal officers in the palace was secured by liberal promises of wealth and advancement: a band of conspirators was then appointed to seize Constantine, but a timely warning enabled him to escape to Triton on the Propontis. He might easily have recovered possession of the capital, had he not wasted two months in idleness and folly. Abandoned at last by every friend, he was seized by his mother's emissaries and dragged to Constantinople. After being detained some time a prisoner in the porphyry apartment in which he was born, his eyes were put out on the 19th August, 797.[1] Constantine had given his cruel mother public marks of that affection which he appears really to have felt for her, and to which he had sacrificed his best friends. He had erected a statue of bronze to her honour, which long adorned the hippodrome of Constantinople.[2]

Irene was now publicly proclaimed sovereign of the empire. She had for some time been allowed by her careless son to direct the whole administration, and it was his confidence in her maternal affection which enabled her to work his ruin. She of course immediately released all the ecclesiastical opponents of her son from confinement, and restored them to their honours and offices. The Patriarch Tarasios was ordered to make his peace with the monks by excommunicating his creature, the abbot Joseph; and the closest alliance was formed between him and his former opponents, Plato and Theodore, the latter of whom was shortly after rewarded for his sufferings by being elevated to the dignity of abbot of the great monastery of Studion.

---

[1] Gibbon, ix. 33. The authorities which prove that Constantine did not die of the inhuman treatment he received, but was living when Nicephorus dethroned his mother, are, *Contin. Const. Porphyr. sc. p. Theoph.* 33. Leo Gramm. 202, edit. Bonn.

[2] Cordinus, *De Orig. Constantinop.* 62.

The Empress Irene reigned five years, during which her peace was disturbed by the political intrigues of her ministers. Her life offers a more interesting subject for biography than for history, for it is more striking by its personal details, than important in its political effects. But the records of private life in the age in which she lived, and of the state of society at Athens, among which she was educated, are so few, that it would require to be written by a novelist, who could combine the strange vicissitudes of her fortunes with a true portraiture of human feelings, coloured with a train of thought, and enriched with facts gleaned from contemporary lives and letters of Greek saints and monks.[1] Born in a private station, and in a provincial, though a wealthy and populous city, it must have required a rare combination of personal beauty, native grace, and mental superiority, to fill the rank of empress of the Romans, to which she was suddenly raised, at the court of a haughty sovereign like her father-in-law Constantine V., not only without embarrassment, but even with universal praise. Again, when vested with the regency, as widow of an Iconoclast emperor, it required no trifling talent, firmness of purpose, and conciliation of manner, to overthrow an ecclesiastical party which had ruled the church for more than half a century. On the other hand, the deliberate way in which she undermined the authority of her son, whose character she had corrupted by a bad education, and the callousness with which she gained his confidence in order to deprive him of his throne, and send him to pass his life as a blind monk in a secluded cell, proves that the beautiful empress, whose memory was cherished as an orthodox saint, was endowed with the thoughts and feelings of a demon. Strange to say, when the object of Irene's crimes was reached, she soon felt all the satiety of gratified ambition. She no longer took the interest she had previously taken in conducting the public business of the empire, and abandoned the exercise of her power to seven eunuchs, whom she selected to perform the duties of ministers of state. She forgot that her own elevation to the throne offered a tempting premium to successful treason. Nicephorus, the grand treasurer, cajoled her favourite eunuchs to join a plot, by which she was dethroned, and exiled to a monastery she had founded in Prince's Island; but she was soon after removed to Lesbos, where she died in

[1] There is a work on the life of Irene, by Abbé Mignot, *Histoire de l'Impératrice Irène*, Amst. 1662. It is inexact as history, and worthless as biography.

a few months, almost forgotten.[1] Her fate after her death was as singular as during her life. The unnatural mother was canonised by the Greeks as an orthodox saint, and at her native Athens several churches are still pointed out which she is said to have founded, though not on any certain authority.[2]

Under the government of Constantine VI. and Irene, the imperial policy, both in the civil administration and external relations, followed the course traced out by Leo the Isaurian. To reduce all the Sclavonian colonists who had formed settlements within the bounds of the empire to complete submission, was the first object of Irene's regency. The extension of these settlements, after the great plague in 747, began to alarm the government. Extensive districts in Thrace, Macedonia, and the Peloponnesus, had assumed the form of independent communities, and hardly acknowledged allegiance to the central administration at Constantinople. Irene naturally took more than ordinary interest in the state of Greece. She kept up the closest communications with her family at Athens, and shared the desire of every Greek to repress the presumption of the Sclavonians and restore the ascendancy of the Greek population in the rural districts. In the year 783 she sent Stavrakios at the head of a well-appointed army to Thessalonica, to reduce the Sclavonian tribes in Macedonia to direct dependence, and enforce the regular payment of tribute.[3] From Thessalonica, Stavrakios marched through Macedonia and Greece to the Peloponnesus, punishing the Sclavonians for the disorders they had committed, and carrying off a number of their able-bodied men to serve as soldiers or to be sold as slaves. In the following year Irene led the young Emperor Constantine to visit the Sclavonian settlements in the vicinity of Thessalonica, which had been reduced to absolute submission. Berrhoea, like several Greek cities, had fallen into ruins; it was now rebuilt, and received the name of Irenopolis. Strong garrisons were placed in Philippopolis and Auchialos, to cut off all communication between the Sclavonians in the empire, and their countrymen under the Bulgarian government. The Sclavonians in Thrace and

---

[1] Irene must have felt that there was some justice in the saying by which the Greeks characterised the hopeless demoralisation of her favourites : "If you have a eunuch, kill him ; if you haven't one, buy one, and kill him."

[2] It is to St. Irene the martyr, and not to the imperial saint, that the present cathedral of Athens is dedicated. The festival of the empress saint is on the 7th August.—*Menologium*, iii. 195.

[3] Stavrakios was one of Irene's favourite eunuchs.—Theophanes, 384.

Macedonia, though unable to maintain their provincial independence, still took advantage of their position, when removed from the eye of the local administration, to form bands of robbers and pirates, which rendered the communications with Constantinople and Thessalonica at times insecure both by land and sea.[1]

After Irene had dethroned her son, the Sclavonian population gave proofs of dangerous activity. A conspiracy was formed to place one of the sons of Constantine V. on the throne. Irene had banished her brothers-in-law to Athens, where they were sure of being carefully watched by her relations, who were strongly interested in supporting her cause. The project of the partisans of the exiled princes to seize Constantinople was discovered, and it was found that the chief reliance of the Isaurian party in Greece was placed in the assistance they expected to derive from the Sclavonian population. The chief of Velzetia was to have carried off the sons of Constantine V. from Athens, when the plan was discovered and frustrated by the vigilance of Irene's friends.[2] The four unfortunate princes, who had already lost their tongues, were now deprived of their sight, and exiled with their brother Nicephorus to Panormus, where they were again made tools of a conspiracy in the reign of Michael I.

The war with the Saracens was carried on with varied success during the reigns of Leo IV., Constantine VI., and Irene. The military talents of Leo III. and Constantine V. had formed an army that resisted the forces of the caliphs under the powerful government of Mansur; and even after the veterans had been disbanded by Irene, the celebrated Haroun Al Rashid was unable to make any permanent conquests, though the empire was engaged in war with the Saracens, the Bulgarians, and the troops of Charlemagne at the same time.

In the year 782, Haroun was sent by his father, the Caliph Mahdy, to invade the empire, at the head of one hundred thousand men, attended by Rabia and Jahja the Barmecid. The object of the Mohammedan prince was, however, rather directed to pillaging the country, and carrying off prisoners to

---

[1] See the danger to which Theodore Studita was exposed, at page 78.
[2] Theophanes, 400. It is difficult to fix the position of Velzetia. The geographical nomenclature of the Sclavonians gives us the same repetition of the same names, in widely-distant districts, that we find in our own colonies. Theophanes, 376, mentions Verzetia as a frontier district of Bulgaria. This passage is remarkable for containing the earliest mention of the Russians in Byzantine history.

supply the slave-markets of his father's dominions, than to effect permanent conquests. The absence of a considerable part of the Byzantine army, which was engaged in Sicily suppressing the rebellion of Helpidios, enabled Haroun to march through all Asia Minor to the shores of the Bosphorus, and from the hill above Sutari to gaze on Constantinople, which must then have presented a more imposing aspect than Bagdad. Irene was compelled to purchase peace, or rather to conclude a truce for three years, by paying an annual tribute of seventy thousand pieces of gold, and stipulating to allow the Saracen army to retire unmolested with all its plunder; for Haroun and his generals found that their advance had involved them in many difficulties, of which an active enemy might have taken advantage. Haroun Al Rashid is said to have commanded in person against the Byzantine empire in eight campaigns. Experience taught him to respect the valour and discipline of the Christian armies, whenever able officers enjoyed the confidence of the court of Constantinople; and when he ascended the throne, he deemed it necessary to form a permanent army along the Mesopotamian frontier, to strengthen the fortifications of the towns with additional works, and add to their means of defence by planting in them new colonies of Mohammedan inhabitants.[1] During the time Constantine VI. ruled the empire, he appeared several times at the head of the Byzantine armies, and his fickle character did not prevent his displaying firmness in the field. His popularity with the soldiers was viewed with jealousy by his mother, who laboured to retard his movements, and prevent him from obtaining any decided success. The Saracens acknowledged that the Greeks were their superiors in naval affairs; but in the year 792 they defeated the Byzantine fleet in the gulf of Attalia with great loss. The admiral, Theophilos, was taken prisoner, and solicited by the caliph to abjure Christianity and enter his service. The admiral refused to forsake his religion or serve against his country, and Haroun Al Rashid was mean enough to order him to be put to death.

When the Saracens heard that Constantine had been dethroned, and the empire was again ruled by a woman whom they had already compelled to pay tribute, they again plundered Asia Minor up to the walls of Ephesus. Irene, whose ministers were occupied with court intrigues, took no measures to resist

[1] Weil, *Geschichte der Chalifen*, ii. 155.

the enemy, and was once more obliged to pay tribute to the caliph.[1] The annual incursions of the Saracens into the Christian territory were made in great part for the purpose of carrying away slaves; and great numbers of Christians were sold throughout the caliph's dominions into hopeless slavery. Haroun, therefore, took the field in his wars with the Byzantine empire more as a slave-merchant than a conqueror. But this very circumstance, which made war a commercial speculation, introduced humanity into the hostile operations of the Christians and Mohammedans: the lower classes were spared, as they were immediately sold for the price they would bring in the first slave-market; while prisoners of the better class were retained, in order to draw from them a higher ransom than their value as slaves, or to exchange them for men of equal rank who had fallen into the hands of the enemy. This circumstance had at last brought about a regular exchange of prisoners as early as the reign of Constantine V., A.D. 769.[2] In the year 797, a new clause was inserted in a treaty for the exchange of prisoners, binding the contracting parties to release all supernumerary captives, on the payment of a fixed sum for each individual.[3] This arrangement enabled the Christians, who were generally the greatest sufferers, to save their friends from death or perpetual slavery, but it added to the inducements of the Saracens to invade the empire. The Byzantine, or, as they were still called, the Roman armies, were placed at a disadvantage in this species of warfare. Their discipline was adapted to defensive military operations, or to meet the enemy on the field of battle, but not to act with rapidity in plundering and carrying off slaves; while the state of society in Christian countries rendered the demand for slaves less constant than in countries where polygamy prevailed, and women were excluded from many of the duties of domestic service.

The war on the Bulgarian frontier was carried on simultaneously with that against the Mohammedans. In the year 788, a Bulgarian army surprised the general of Thrace, who had encamped carelessly on the banks of the Strymon, and destroyed him, with the greater part of the troops. In 791,

---

[1] Theophanes gives the Byzantine account of the Saracen war, which has been compared with the Arabian authorities by Weil, *Geschicte der Chalifen*, ii. 155.

[2] Theophanes, 374.

[3] Three thousand seven hundred prisoners were exchanged, exclusive of the additional individuals ransomed by the Christians. A similar treaty was concluded between Haroun and Nicephorus in 805.—*Notices et Extraits des MS.* viii. 193.

Constantine VI. took the field in person against Cardam, king
of the Bulgarians, but the campaign was without any result: in
the following year, however, the Emperor was defeated in a
pitched battle, in which several of the ablest generals of the
Roman armies were slain. Yet, in 796, Constantine again led
his troops against the Bulgarians: though victorious, he obtained
no success sufficient to compensate his former defeat. The
effects of the military organisation of the frontier by Constantine V. are visible in the superiority which the Byzantine
armies assumed, even after the loss of a battle, and the confidence with which they carried the war into the Bulgarian
territory.[1]

The Byzantine empire was at this period the country in
which there reigned a higher degree of order, and more justice,
than in any other. This is shown by the extensive emigration of Armenian Christians which took place in the year 787.
The Caliph Haroun Al Rashid, whose reputation among the
Mohammedans has arisen rather from his orthodoxy than his
virtues, persecuted his Christian subjects with great cruelty,
and at last his oppression induced twelve thousand Armenians
to quit their native country, and settle in the Byzantine
empire.[2] Some years later, in the reign of Michael III. the
drunkard, orthodoxy became the great feature in the Byzantine
administration; and, unfortunately, Christian orthodoxy strongly
resembled Mohammedanism in the spirit of persecution. The
Paulicians were then persecuted by the emperors, as the
Armenians had previously been by the caliphs, and fled for
toleration to the Mohammedans.

[1] Theophanes, 391-394. Constantine VI. and his grandfather, Constantine V., are
said to have been the only emperors before John I., Ziniskes, who defeated the Bulgarians in their own country.—Leo Diaconus, 104, edit. Bonn.
[2] Chamich, *History of Armenia*, ii. 393.

CHAPTER II

THE REIGNS OF NICEPHORUS I., MICHAEL I., AND LEO V. THE ARMENIAN. A.D. 802-820

SECTION I

NICEPHORUS I. 802-811

His family and character—Rebellion of Bardanes—Tolerant ecclesiastical policy—Oppressive fiscal administration—Relations with Charlemagne —Saracen war—Defeat of Sclavonians at Patras—Bulgarian war— Death of Nicephorus.

NICEPHORUS held the office of grand logathetes, or treasurer, when he dethroned Irene. He was born at Seleucia, in Pisidia, of a family which claimed descent from the Arabian kings. His ancestor Djaballah, the Christian monarch of Ghassan in the time of Heraclius, abjured the allegiance of the Roman empire, and embraced the Mohammedan religion. He carried among the stern and independent Moslems the monarchical pride and arrogance of a vassal court. As he was performing the religious rites of the pilgrimage in the mosque at Mecca, an Arab accidentally trod on his cloak; Djaballah, enraged that a king should be treated with so little respect, struck the careless Arab in the face, and knocked out some of his teeth. The justice of the Caliph Omar knew no distinction of persons, and the king of Ghassan was ordered to make satisfactory reparation to the injured Arab, or submit to the law of retaliation. The monarch's pride was so deeply wounded by this sentence that he fled to Constantinople, and renounced the Mohammedan religion.[1] From this king the Arabs, who paid the most minute attention to genealogy, allow that Nicephorus was lineally descended.[2]

The leading features of the reign of Nicephorus were political order and fiscal oppression. His character was said to be veiled in impenetrable hypocrisy; yet anecdotes are recounted

---

[1] Abulpharagius, *Chron. Syr.* 139. Oakley, *History of the Saracens*, i. 150. Eichhorn, *De Antiquiss. Hist. Arab Monumentis*, 171, gives an account of the same event from Ibn Kathaïba.

[2] *Conquête de l'Egypte*, par Wakedy, publiée par Hamaker, 66. Lebeau, *Histoire du Bas-Empire*, xiv. 393, note 2, edit. St. Martin.

which indicate that he made no secret of his avarice, and the other vices attributed to him. His orthodoxy was certainly suspicious, but, on the whole, he appears to have been an able and humane prince. He has certainly obtained a worse reputation in history than many emperors who have been guilty of greater crimes. Many anecdotes are recounted concerning his rapacity.

As soon as he received the imperial crown, he bethought himself of the treasures Irene had concealed, and resolved to gain possession of them. These treasures are conceived by the Byzantine historians to be a part of the immense sums Leo III. and Constantine V. were supposed to have accumulated. The abundance and low price of provisions which had prevailed, particularly in the reign of Constantine V., was ascribed to the rarity of specie caused by the hoards accumulated by these emperors. Irene was said to know where all this wealth was concealed; and though her administration had been marked by lavish expenditure and a diminution of the taxes, still she was believed to possess immense sums. If we believe the story of the chronicles, Nicephorus presented himself to Irene in a private garb, and assured her that he had only assumed the imperial crown to serve her and save her life. By flattery mingled with intimidation, he obtained possession of her treasures, and then, in violation of his promises, banished her to Lesbos.

The dethroned Constantine had been left by his mother in possession of great wealth. Nicephorus is accused of ingratiating himself into the confidence of the blind prince, gaining possession of these treasures, and then neglecting him. Loud complaints were made against the extortion of the tax-gatherers in the reigns of Constantine VI. and Irene, and Nicephorus established a court of review to revise the accounts of every public functionary. But his enemies accused him of converting this court into a means of confiscating the property of the guilty, instead of enabling the sufferers to recover their losses.

The accession of Nicephorus was an event unexpected both by the people and the army; and the success of a man whose name was previously almost unknown beyond the circle of the administration, held out a hope to every man of influence that an emperor, who owed his elevation to a conspiracy of eunuchs and a court intrigue, might easily be driven from the throne. Bardanes, whom Nicephorus appointed general of the troops of five Asiatic themes to march against the Saracens, instead of leading this army against Haroun Al Rashid, proclaimed himself emperor. He was supported by Thomas the Sclavonian,[1] as well as by Leo the Armenian and Michael the Armorian, who both subsequently mounted the throne. The crisis was one of extreme difficulty, but Nicephorus soon convinced the world that he was worthy of the throne. The rebel troops were discouraged by his preparations, and rendered ashamed of their conduct by his reproaches. Leo and Michael were gained over by a promise of promotion; and Bardanes, seeing his army rapidly dispersing, negotiated for his own pardon. He was allowed to retire to a monastery he had founded in the island of Prote, but his estates were confiscated. Shortly after, while Bardanes was living in seclusion as an humble monk, a band of Lycaonian brigands crossed over from the Asiatic coast and put out his eyes. As the perpetrators of this atrocity were evidently moved by personal vengeance, suspicion fell so strongly on the emperor, that he deemed it necessary to take a solemn oath in public that he had no knowledge of the crime, and never entertained a thought of violating the safe-conduct he had given to Bardanes. This safe-conduct, it must be observed, had received the ratification of the Patriarch and the senate. Bardanes himself did not appear to suspect the emperor; he showed the greatest resignation and piety; gave up the use of wheaten bread, wine, oil, and fish, living entirely on barley cakes, which he baked in the embers. In summer he wore a single leather garment, and in winter a mantle of hair-cloth. In this way he lived contentedly, and died during the reign of Leo the Armenian.

The civil transactions of the reign of Nicephorus present some interesting facts. Though a brave soldier, he was essentially a statesman, and his conviction that the finance department was the peculiar business of the sovereign, and the key of public affairs, can be traced in many significant events. He eagerly pursued the centralising policy of his Iconoclast predecessors, and strove to render the civil power supreme over the clergy and the Church. He forbade the Patriarch to hold any communications with the Pope, whom he considered as the Patriarch of Charlemagne; and this prudent measure has caused much of the virulence with which his memory has been attacked by ecclesiastical and orthodox

[1] Concerning Thomas, see page 106, note 1, and page 121, note 2.

historians.[1] The Patriarch Tarasios had shown himself no enemy to the supremacy of the emperor, and he was highly esteemed by Nicephorus as one of the heads of the party, both in the church and state, which the emperor was anxious to conciliate. When Tarasios died, A.D. 806, Nicephorus made a solemn display of his grief. The body, clad in the patriarchal robes, crowned with the mitre, and seated on the episcopal throne, according to the usage of the East, was transported to a monastery founded by the deceased Patriarch on the shores of the Bosphorus, where the funeral was performed with great pomp, the emperor assisting, embracing the body, and covering it with his purple robe.[2]

Nicephorus succeeded in finding an able and popular prelate, disposed to support his secular views, worthy to succeed Tarasios. This was the historian Nicephoros. He had already retired from public life, and was residing in a monastery he had founded, though he had not yet taken monastic vows. On his election, he entered the clergy, and took the monastic habit. This last step was rendered necessary by the usage of the Greek church, which now only admitted monks to the episcopal dignity. To give the ceremony additional splendour, Stavrakios, the son of the Emperor Nicephorus, who had received the imperial crown from his father, was deputed to be present at the tonsure.

The Patriarch Nicephoros was no sooner installed than the emperor began to execute his measures for establishing the supremacy of the civil power. Tarasios, after sanctioning the divorce of Constantine VI., and allowing the celebration of his second marriage, had yielded to the influence of Irene and the monks, and declared both acts illegal. The Emperor Nicephorus considered this a dangerous precedent, and resolved to obtain an affirmation of the validity of the second marriage. The new Patriarch assembled a synod, in which the marriage was declared valid, and the abbot Joseph, who had celebrated it, was absolved from all ecclesiastical censure. The monastic party, enraged at the emperor seeking emancipation from their authority, broke out into a furious opposition. Theodore Studita, their leader, calls this synod an assembly of adulterers and heretics, and reproached the Patriarch with sacrificing the interests of religion.[3] But Nicephorus having succeeded in bringing about this explosion

---

[1] Theophanes, 419.   [2] *Ibid.* 407.
[3] In a letter to the Pope—*Baronii Annales Eccles.* ix. 378, A.D. 806.

of monastic ire on a question in which he had no personal interest, the people, who now regarded the unfortunate Constantine VI. as hardly used on the subject of his marriage with Theodota, could not be persuaded to take any part in the dispute. Theodore's violence was also supposed to arise from his disappointment at not being elected Patriarch.

Public opinion became so favourable to the emperor's ecclesiastical views, that a synod assembled in 809 declared the Patriarch and bishops to possess the power of granting dispensations from rules of ecclesiastical law, and that the emperor was not bound by legislative provisions enacted for subjects. Nicephorus considered the time had now come for compelling the monks to obey his authority. He ordered Theodore Studita and Plato to take part in the ecclesiastical ceremonies with the Patriarch; and when these refractory abbots refused, he banished them to Prince's Island, and then deposed them. Had the monks now opposed the emperor on the reasonable ground that he was violating the principles on which the security of society depended, by setting up his individual will against the systematic rules of justice, the maxims of Roman law, the established usages of the empire, and the eternal rules of equity, they would have found a response in the hearts of the people. Such doctrines might have led to some political reform in the government, and to the establishment of some constitutional check on the exercise of arbitrary power; and the exclamation of Theodore, in one of his letters to the Pope, "Where now is the gospel for kings?" might then have revived the spirit of liberty among the Greeks.

At this time there existed a party which openly advocated the right of every man to the free exercise of his own religious opinions in private, and urged the policy of the government abstaining from every attempt to enforce unity. Some of this party probably indulged in as liberal speculations concerning the political rights of men, but such opinions were generally considered incompatible with social order.[1] The emperor, however, favoured the tolerant party, and gave its members a predominant influence in his cabinet. Greatly to the dissatisfaction of the Greek party, he refused to persecute the Paulicians, who had formed a considerable community in the eastern provinces of Asia Minor; and he tolerated the Athingans in Pisidia and Lycaonia, allowing them to exercise their

[1] Compare Theophanes, 413 and 419.

religion in peace, as long as they violated none of the laws of the empire.[1]

The financial administration of Nicephorus is justly accused of severity, and even of rapacity. He affords a good personification of the fiscal genius of the Roman empire, as described by the Emperor Justin II., upwards of three centuries earlier.[2] His thoughts were chiefly of tributes and taxes; and, unfortunately for his subjects, his intimate acquaintance with financial affairs enabled him to extort a great increase of revenue, without appearing to impose new taxes. But though he is justly accused of oppression, he does not merit the reproach of avarice often urged against him. When he considered expenditure necessary, he was liberal of the public money. He spared no expense to keep up numerous armies, and it was not from ill-judged economy, but from want of military talents, that his campaigns were unsuccessful.

Nicephorus restored the duties levied at the entrance of the Hellespont and the Bosphorus, which had been remitted by Irene to purchase popularity after her cruelty to her son.[3] He ordered all the provinces to furnish a stated number of ablebodied recruits for the army, drawn from among the poor, and obliged each district to pay the sum of eighteen nomismata a-head for their equipment—enforcing the old Roman principle of mutual responsibility for the payment of any taxes, in case the recruits should possess property liable to taxation.[4] One-twelfth was likewise added to the duty on public documents. An additional tax of two nomismata was imposed on all domestic slaves purchased beyond the Hellespont. The inhabitants of Asia Minor who engaged in commerce were compelled to purchase a certain quantity of landed property belonging to the fisc at a fixed valuation: and, what tended to blacken the emperor's reputation more than anything else, he extended the hearth-tax to the property of the church, to monasteries, and charitable institutions, which had hitherto been exempted from the burden; and he

---

[1] Theophanes, 413. For the Paulicians, see Gibbon, x. 169; Mosheim, ii. 255; Neander, iii. 244.

[2] "Die noctuque pro utilitate reipublicæ subtiliter cogitantes illa properamus renovare, quanta in locis opportunis sunt necessaria et maxime pro tributis atque reditibus, sine quibus impossibile est aliquid agere prosperum."—*Const. Justini et Tib.* vii. 2. *De Adscriptitiis et Colonis—Corp. Jur. Civ.* ii. 512, 4to edit. ster.

[3] Theophanes, 401.

[4] Eighteen nomismata is nearly £10. We see from this that the individual in the ranks was more expensive in ancient than in modern times. He acted also a more important part. Artillery was then inferior, and less expensive. We must not forget that, during the period embraced in this volume, the Byzantine army was the finest in the world.

enforced the payment of arrears from the commencement of his reign. The innumerable private monasteries, which it was the fashion to multiply, withdrew so much property from taxation that this measure was absolutely necessary to prevent frauds on the fisc; but though necessary, it was unpopular. Nicephorus, moreover, permitted the sale of gold and silver plate dedicated as holy offerings by private superstition; and, like many modern princes, he quartered troops in monasteries. It is also made an accusation against his government, that he furnished the merchants at Constantinople engaged in foreign trade with the sum of twelve pounds' weight of gold, for which they were compelled to pay twenty per cent interest. It is difficult, from the statements of the Byzantine writers concerning the legislative acts, to form a precise idea of the emperor's object in some cases, or the effects of the law in others. His enemies do not hesitate to enumerate among his crimes the exertions he made to establish military colonies in the waste districts on the Bulgarian frontier, secured by the line of fortresses constructed by Constantine V. His object was to cut off effectually all communication between the unruly Sclavonians in Thrace and the population to the north. There can be no doubt of his enforcing every claim of the government with rigour. He ordered a strict census of all agriculturists who were not natives to be made throughout the provinces, and the land they cultivated was declared to belong to the imperial domain. He then converted these cultivators into slaves of the fisc, by the application of an old law, which declared that all who had cultivated the same land for the space of thirty years consecutively, were restricted to the condition of *coloni*, or serfs attached to the soil.[1]

The conspiracies which were formed against Nicephorus cannot be admitted as evidence of his unpopularity, for the best of the Byzantine monarchs were as often victims of secret plots as the worst. The elective title to the empire rendered the prize to successful ambition one which overpowered the respect due to their country's laws in the breasts of the courtiers of Constantinople. It is only from popular insurrections that we can judge of the sovereign's unpopularity. The principles of humanity that rendered Nicephorus averse to religious persecution, caused him to treat conspirators with much less cruelty than most Byzantine emperors. Perhaps the historians

[1] Theophanes, 411, 413, 414. Cedrenus, ii. 480. *Cod. Justin.—De Agricolis et Censitis*, xi. 41-9.

hostile to his government have deceived posterity, giving considerable importance to insignificant plots, as we see modern diplomatists continually deceiving their courts by magnifying trifling expressions of dissatisfaction into dangerous presages of widespread discontent. In the year 808, however, a conspiracy was really formed to place Arsaber—a patrician, who held the office of questor, or minister of legislation—on the throne. Though Arsaber was of an Armenian family, many persons of rank were leagued with him; yet Nicephorus only confiscated his estates, and compelled him to embrace the monastic life.[1] An attempt was made to assassinate the emperor by a man who rushed into the palace, and seized the sword of one of the guards of the imperial chamber, severely wounding many persons before he was secured. The criminal was a monk, who was put to the torture, according to the cruel practice of the time; but Nicephorus, on learning that he was a maniac, ordered him to be placed in a lunatic asylum. Indeed, though historians accuse Nicephorus of inhumanity, the punishment of death, in cases of treason, was never carried into effect during his reign.

The relations of Nicephorus with Charlemagne were for a short time amicable. A treaty was concluded at Aix-la-Chapelle, in 803, regulating the frontiers of the two empires. In this treaty, the supremacy of the Eastern Empire over Venice, Istria, the maritime parts of Dalmatia, and the south of Italy, was acknowledged; while the authority of the Western Empire in Rome, the exarchate of Ravenna, and the Pentapolis, was recognised by Nicephorus.[2] The commerce of Venice with the East was already so important, and the Byzantine administration afforded so many guarantees for the security of property, that the Venetians, in spite of the menaces of Charlemagne, remained firm in their allegiance to Nicephorus. Istria, on the other hand, placed itself subsequently under the protection of the Frank emperor, and paid him a tribute of 354 marks. Pepin, king of Italy, was also charged by his father to render the Venetians, and the allies of the Byzantine empire in the north of Italy, tributary to

---

[1] Arsaber and Bardanes were both of Armenian descent. Chamich (or Tchamtchian) says, "In this age, three Armenians were elected at different periods to the imperial throne of the Greeks. Two of them, Vardan and Arshavir, only held that high post for a few days. The other, Levond, (Leo V.) an Arzunian, reigned seven years. Not long after, Prince Manuel, of the tribe of the Mamiconians, greatly distinguished himself at the court of the emperor (Theophilus) by his undaunted valour and skill in war."— *History of Armenia*, (translated by Avdall,) vol. i. 399.
[2] A. Dandolo. Muratori, *Scrip. Rer. Ital.* xii.

the Franks; but Nicephorus sent a fleet into the Adriatic, and effectually protected his friends. A body of people, called Orobiatæ, who maintained themselves as an independent community in the Apennines, pretending to preserve their allegiance to the emperor of Constantinople, plundered Populonium in Tuscany. They afford us proof how much easier Charlemagne found it to extend his conquests than to preserve order.[1] Venice, it is true, found itself in the end compelled to purchase peace with the Frank empire, by the payment of an annual tribute of thirty-six pounds of gold, in order to secure its commercial relations from interruption; and it was not released from this tribute until the time of Otho the Great.[2] It was during the reign of Nicephorus that the site of the present city of Venice became the seat of the Venetian government, Rivalto (Rialto) becoming the residence of the duke and the principal inhabitants, who retired from the continent to escape the attacks of Pepin. Heraclea had previously been the capital of the Venetian municipality. In 810, peace was again concluded between Nicephorus and Charlemagne, without making any change in frontier of the two empires.

The power of the caliphate was never more actively employed than under Haroun Al Rashid, but the reputation of that prince was by no means so great among his contemporaries as it became in after times. Nicephorus was no sooner seated on the throne, than he refused to pay the caliph the tribute imposed on Irene. The Arabian historians pretend that his refusal was communicated to Haroun in an insolent letter.[3] To resist the attacks of the Saracens, which he well knew would follow his refusal, he collected a powerful army in Asia Minor; but this army broke out into rebellion, and, as has been already mentioned, proclaimed Bardanes emperor. The caliph, availing himself of the defenceless state of the empire, laid waste Asia Minor; and when the rebellion of Bardanes was extinguished, Nicephorus, afraid to trust any of the veteran generals with the command of a large army, placed himself at the head of the troops in Asia, and was defeated in a great battle at Krasos in Phrygia.[4] After this victory the Saracens laid waste the country in every

---

[1] Eginhard, *Ann. Franc.* A.D. 809.
[2] Constantine Porphyr. *De Adm. Imp.* chap. 28, A.D. 962.
[3] Weil, *Geschichte der Chalifen*, ii. 159, gives the letter of the emperor and the answer of the caliph. I cannot suppose they are authentic.
[4] Theophanes, 406.

direction, until a rebellion in Chorasan compelled Haroun to withdraw his troops from the Byzantine frontier, and gave Nicephorus time to reassemble a new army. As soon as the affairs in the East were tranquillised, the caliph again invaded the Byzantine empire. Haroun himself fixed his headquarters at Tyana, where he built a mosque, to mark that he annexed that city to the Mohammedan empire. One division of his army, sixty thousand strong, took and destroyed Ancyra. Heraclea on Mount Taurus was also captured, and sixteen thousand prisoners were carried off in a single campaign,[1] A.D. 806. Nicephorus, unable to arrest these ravages, endeavoured to obtain peace; and in spite of the religious bigotry which is supposed to have envenomed the hostilities of Haroun, the imperial embassy consisted of the bishop of Synnada, the abbot of Gulaias, and the economos of Amastris. As winter was approaching, and the Saracens were averse to remain longer beyond Mount Taurus, the three ecclesiastical ambassadors succeeded in arranging a treaty; but Nicephorus was compelled to submit to severe and degrading conditions. He engaged not to rebuild the frontier fortifications which had been destroyed by the caliph's armies, and he consented to pay a tribute of thirty thousand pieces of gold annually, adding three additional pieces for himself, and three for his son and colleague Stavrakios, which we must suppose to have been medallions of superior size, since they were offered as a direct proof that the emperor of the Romans paid a personal tribute to the caliph.[2]

Nicephorus seems to have been sadly deficient in feelings of honour, for, the moment he conceived he could evade the stipulations of the treaty without danger, he commenced repairing the ruined fortifications. His subjects suffered for his conduct. The caliph again sent troops to invade the empire; Cyprus and Rhodes were ravaged; the bishop of Cyprus was compelled to pay one thousand dinars as his ransom; and many Christians were carried away from Asia Minor, and settled in Syria.

The death of Haroun, in 809, delivered the Christians from a barbarous enemy, who ruined their country like a brigand,

---

[1] Gibbon, x. 55, adopts the opinion that the Pontic Heraclea was taken in an earlier campaign: but St. Martin, in his notes to Lebeau, xii. 426, points out that this is not probable. Theophanes, 407. Schlosser, 350. Weil, ii. 160.

[2] If these tribute-pieces were medallions like the celebrated medal of Justinian I., which was stolen from the National Library at Paris, the sight of one would gladden the heart of a numismatist.—See Pinder and Friedländer, *Die Münzen Justinians*, plate ii.

without endeavouring to subdue it like a conqueror. Haroun's personal valour, his charity, his liberality to men of letters, and his religious zeal, have secured him interested panegyrics, which have drowned the voice of justice. The hero of the Arabian Tales and the ally of Charlemagne is vaunted as one of the greatest princes who ever occupied a throne. The disgraceful murder of the Barmecides, and many other acts of injustice and cruelty, give him a very different character in history. His plundering incursions into the Byzantine empire might have been glorious proofs of courage in some petty Syrian chieftain, but they degrade the ruler of the richest and most extensive empire on the earth into a mere slave-dealer.[1]

The Saracens continued their incursions, and in the year 811, Leo the Armenian, then lieutenant-governor of the Armeniac theme, left a sum of thirteen hundred pounds' weight of silver, which had been collected as taxes, at Euchaites, without a sufficient guard. A band of Saracens carried off this money; and for his negligence Leo was ordered to Constantinople, where the future emperor was scourged, and deprived of his command.[2]

The Sclavonian colonies in Greece were now so powerful that they formed the project of rendering themselves masters of the Peloponnesus, and expelling the Greek population. The Byzantine expedition, in the early part of the regency of Irene, had only subjected these intruders to tribute, without diminishing their numbers or breaking their power.[3] The troubled aspect of public affairs, after Nicephorus seized the throne, induced them to consider the moment favourable for gaining their independence. They assembled a numerous force under arms, and selected Patras as their first object of attack. The possession of a commercial port was necessary to their success, in order to enable them to supply their wants from abroad, and obtain a public revenue by the duties on the produce they exported. Patras was then the most flourishing harbour on the west coast of Greece, and its possession would have enabled the Sclavonians to establish direct communications with, and draw assistance from, the kindred race established on the shores of the Adriatic, and from the Saracen

---

[1] The story of the three apples in the Arabian Nights gives a correct idea of the violence and injustice of the celebrated caliph, whose hasty temper was well known. For the causes of Haroun's injustice to the Barmecides, see Weil, *Geschichte der Chalifen* ii. 137.

[2] Theophanes, 414. *Script. post Theoph. Anon. Cont.* 7. Genesius, 6.

[3] Theophanes, 385.

pirates, among whose followers the Saclavi, or Sclavonian captives and renegades, made a considerable figure.[1] The property of the Greeks beyond the protection of the walled towns was plundered, to supply the army destined to besiege Patras with provisions, and a communication was opened with a Saracen squadron of African pirates who blockaded the gulf.[2] Patras was kept closely invested, until want began to threaten the inhabitants with death, and compelled them to think of surrender.

The Byzantine government had no regular troops nearer than Corinth, which is three days' march from Patras. But the governor of the province who resided there was unable immediately to detach a force sufficient to attack the besieging army. In the mean time, as the inhabitants were anxiously waiting for relief, one of their scouts, stationed to announce the approach of succours from Cornith, accidentally gave the signal agreed upon. The enthusiasm of the Greeks was excited to the highest pitch by the hopes of speedy deliverance, and, eager for revenge on their enemies, they threw open the city gates and made a vigorous attack on the besiegers, whom they drove from their position with considerable loss.

The Byzantine general arrived three days after this victory. His jealousy of the military success of the armed citizens induced him to give currency to the popular accounts, which he found the superstition of the people had already circulated, that St. Andrew, the patron of Patras, had shown himself on the field of battle. The devastations committed by the Sclavonians, the victory of the Greeks, and the miraculous appearance of the apostle at the head of the besieged, were all announced to the Emperor Nicephorus, whose political views rendered him more willing to reward the church for St. Andrew's assistance, than to allow his subjects to perceive that their own valour was sufficient to defend their property : he feared they might discover that a well-constituted municipal government would always be able to protect them, while a distant central authority was often incapable, and generally indifferent. Nicephorus was too experienced a statesman, with the examples of Venice and Cherson before his eyes, not to fear that such a discovery among the Greek population in the Peloponnesus would tend to circumscribe the fiscal energy of the Constantinopolitan treasury. The church, and not the people, profited

---

[1] Reinaud, *Invasions des Sarrazins en France*, 237
[2] Constant. Porphyr. *De Adm. Imp.* chap. 49.

E

by the success of the Greeks: the imperial share of the spoil
taken from the Sclavonians, both property and slaves, was
bestowed on the church of St. Andrew; and the bishops of
Methone, Lacedemon, and Corone, were declared suffragans
of the metropolitan of Patras. This charter of Nicephorus
was ratified by Leo VI., the Wise, in a new and extended
act.[1]

The Bulgarians were always troublesome neighbours, as a
rude people generally proves to a wealthy population. Their
king, Crumn, was an able and warlike prince. For some time
after his accession, he was occupied by hostilities with the
Avars, but as soon as that war was terminated, he seized an
opportunity of plundering a Byzantine military chest, containing eleven hundred pounds of gold, destined for the payment
of the troops stationed on the banks of the Strymon. After
surprising the camp, dispersing the troops, murdering the
officers, and capturing the treasure, he extended his ravages
as far as Sardica, where he slew six thousand Roman soldiers.

Nicephorus immediately assembled a considerable army,
and marched to re-establish the security of his northern
frontier. The death of Haroun left so large a force at his
disposal that he contemplated the destruction of the Bulgarian
kingdom; but the Byzantine troops in Europe were in a disaffected state, and their indiscipline rendered the campaign
abortive. The resolution of Nicephorus remained, nevertheless, unshaken, though his life was in danger from the seditious conduct of the soldiery; and he was in the end compelled to escape from his own camp, and seek safety in
Constantinople.

In 811, a new army, consisting chiefly of conscripts and
raw recruits, was hastily assembled, and hurried into the field.
In preparing for the campaign, Nicephorus displayed extreme
financial severity, and ridiculed the timidity of those who
counselled delay with a degree of cynicism which paints well
the singular character of this bold financier. Having resolved
to tax monasteries, and levy an augmentation of the land-tax
from the nobility for the eight preceding years, his ministers
endeavoured to persuade him of the impolicy of his proceedings; but he only exclaimed, "What can you expect! God
has hardened my heart, and my subjects can expect nothing
else from me." The historian Theophanes says that these
words were repeated to him by Theodosios, the minister to

---

[1] Leunclavius, *Jus Græco-Romanum*, 278.   Lequien, *Oriens Christianus*, ii. 179.

whom they were addressed.[1] The energy of Nicephorus was equal to his rapacity, but it was not supported by a corresponding degree of military skill. He led his army so rapidly to Markelles, a fortress built by Constantine VI., within the line of the Bulgarian frontier, that Crumn, alarmed at his vigour, sent an embassy to solicit peace.[2] This proposal was rejected, and the emperor pushed forward and captured a residence of the Bulgarian monarch's near the frontiers, in which a considerable amount of treasure was found. Crumn, dispirited at this loss, offered to accept any terms of peace compatible with the existence of his independence, but Nicephorus would agree to no terms but absolute submission.

The only contemporary account of the following events is in the chronicle of Theophanes, and it leaves us in doubt whether the rashness of Nicephorus or the treason of his generals was the real cause of his disastrous defeat. Even if we give Crumn credit for great military skill, the success of the stratagem, by which he destroyed a Byzantine army greatly superior to his own, could not have been achieved without some treasonable co-operation in the enemy's camp. It is certain that an officer of the emperor's household had deserted at Markelles, carrying away the emperor's wardrobe and one hundred pounds' weight of gold, and that one of the ablest engineers in the Byzantine service had previously fled to Bulgaria. It seems not improbable, that by means of these officers treasonable communications were maintained with the disaffected in the Byzantine army.

When Nicephorus entered the Bulgarian territory, Crumn had a much larger force in his immediate vicinity than the emperor supposed. The Bulgarian troops, though defeated in the advance, were consequently allowed to watch the movements of the invaders, and intrench at no great distance without any attempt to dislodge them. It is even said that Crumn was allowed to work for two days, forming a strong palisade to circumscribe the operations of the imperial army, while Nicephorus was wasting his time collecting the booty found in the Bulgarian palace; and that, when the emperor saw the work finished, he exclaimed, "We have no chance of safety except by being transformed into birds!" Yet even in this

---

[1] Theophanes, 414. Cedrenus, ii. 481. Zonaras, ii. 124. Theodosios perished with his master, therefore these words were repeated while he was a favourite minister. It may thence be inferred that some misconstruction has been put on the circumstances by the prejudices of Theophanes. [2] Theophanes, 394.

desperate position the emperor is said to have neglected the usual precautions to secure his camp against a night attack. Much of this seems incredible.

Crumn made a grand nocturnal attack on the camp of Nicephorus, just six days after the emperor had invaded the Bulgarian kingdom. The Byzantine army was taken by surprise, and their camp entered on every side; the whole baggage and military chest were taken; the Emperor Nicephorus and six patricians, with many officers of the highest rank, were slain; and the Bulgarian king made a drinking-cup of the skull of the emperor of the Romans, in which the Sclavonian princes of the Bulgarian court pledged him in the richest wines of Greece when he celebrated his triumphal festivals.[1] The Bulgarians must have abandoned their strong palisade when they attacked the camp, for a considerable portion of the defeated army, with the Emperor Stavrakios, who was severely wounded, Stephen the general of the guard, and Theoctistos the master of the palace, reached Adrianople in safety. Stavrakios was immediately proclaimed his father's successor, and the army was able and willing to maintain him on the throne, had he possessed health and ability equal to the crisis. But the fiscal severity of his father had created a host of enemies to the existing system of government, and in the Byzantine empire a change of administration implied a change of the emperor. The numerous statesmen who expected to profit by a revolution declared in favour of Michael Rhangabé, an insignificant noble, who had married Procopia the daughter of Nicephorus. Stavrakios was compelled by his brother-in-law to retire into a monastery, where he soon died of his wounds. He had occupied the throne two months.

SECTION II

MICHAEL I., (RHANGABÉ), A.D. 812-813

Religious zeal of Michael—Bulgarian war—Defeat of Michael.

Michael I. was crowned by the Patriarch Nicephoros, after signing a written declaration that he would defend the church, protect the ministers of religion, and never put the orthodox to death. This election of a tool of the bigoted party in the Byzantine church was a reaction against the tolerant policy of

---

[1] Theophanes, 416. Nicephorus was slain on the 25th July, 811.

Nicephorus. The new emperor began his reign by remitting all the additional taxes imposed by his predecessor which had awakened clerical opposition. He was a weak, well-meaning man; but his wife Procopia was a lady of superior qualifications, who united to a virtuous and charitable disposition something of her father's vigour of mind. Michael's reign proved the necessity of always having a firm hand to guide that complicated administrative machine which the Byzantine sovereigns inherited from the empire of Rome.

Michael purchased popularity in the capital by the lavish manner in which he distributed the wealth left by Nicephorus in the imperial treasury. He bestowed large sums on monasteries, hospitals, poor-houses, and other charitable institutions, and he divided liberal gratuities among the leading members of the clergy, the chief dignitaries of the state, and the highest officers of the army.[1] His piety, as well as his party connections, induced him to admit several monks to a place in his council; and he made it an object of political importance to reconcile the Patriarch Nicephoros with Theodore Studita. But by abandoning the policy of his predecessor, after it had received the Patriarch's sanction and become the law of the church, Michael lost more in public opinion than he gained by the alliance of a troop of bigoted monks, who laboured to subject the power of the emperor and the policy of the state to their own narrow ideas. The abbot Joseph, who had celebrated the marriage of the Emperor Constantine VI., was again excommunicated, as the peace-offering which allowed the bigots to renew their communion with the Patriarch.

The counsels of Theodore Studita soon involved the government in fresh embarrassment. To signalise his zeal for orthodoxy, he persuaded the emperor to persecute the Iconoclasts, who during the preceding reign had been allowed to profess their opinions without molestation. It was also proposed, in an assembly of the senate, to put the leaders of the Paulicians and Athigans to death, in order to intimidate their followers and persuade them to become orthodox Christians. This method of converting men to the Greek church excited strong opposition on the part of the tolerant members of the senate; but the Patriarch and clergy having deserted the

---

[1] Theophanes, 418-19. The following sums are recorded in detail :—Fifty pounds' weight of gold to the Patriarch Nicephoros : twenty-five to the clergy, at the coronation ; five hundred lb. of gold to the widows of those who fell with Nicephorus ; one hundred lb. of gold, besides robes and ornaments, to the Patriarch and clergy, at the coronation of his son Theophylactus.

cause of humanity, the permanent interests of Christianity were sacrificed to the cause of orthodoxy.

While the emperor persecuted a large body of his subjects on the northern and eastern frontiers of his empire, he neglected to defend the provinces against the incursions of the Bulgarians, who ravaged great part of Thrace and Macedonia, and took several large and wealthy towns. The weight of taxation which fell on the mass of the population was not lightened when the emperor relieved the clergy and the nobility from the additional burdens imposed on them by Nicephorus. Discontent spread rapidly. A lunatic girl, placed in a prominent position, as the emperor passed through the streets of Constantinople, cried aloud—"Descend from thy seat! descend, and make room for another!" The continual disasters which were announced from the Bulgarian frontier made the people and the army remember with regret the prosperous days of Constantine V., when the slave-markets of the capital were filled with their enemies. Encouraged by the general dissatisfaction, the Iconoclasts formed a conspiracy to convey the sons of Constantine V., who were living, blind and mute, in their exile at Panormus, to the army. The plot was discovered, and Michael ordered the helpless princes to be conveyed to Aphinsa, a small island in the Propontis, where they could be closely guarded. One of the conspirators had his tongue cut out.

The wars of Mohammed Alemen and Almamun, the sons of Haroun al Rashid, relieved the empire from all serious danger on the side of the Saracens. But the Bulgarian war, to which Michael owed his throne, soon proved the cause of his ruin. The army and the people despised him, because he owed his elevation, not to his talents, but to the accident of his marriage, his popularity with the monks, and the weakness of his character, which made him an instrument in the hands of a party. Public opinion soon decided that he was unfit to rule the empire. The year after the death of Nicephorus, Crumn invaded the empire with a numerous army, and took the town of Develtos. Michael left the capital accompanied by the Empress Procopia, in order to place himself at the head of the troops in Thrace; but the soldiers showed so much dissatisfaction at the presence of a female court, that the emperor turned back to Constantinople from Tzourlou. The Bulgarian king took advantage of the disorder which ensued to capture Anchialos, Berrhoea, Nicæa, and Probaton in Thrace; and that province fell into such a state of anarchy, that many of the colonists established by Nicephorus in Philippopolis and on the banks of the Strymon abandoned their settlements and returned to Asia.

Crumn nevertheless offered peace to Michael, on the basis of a treaty concluded between the Emperor Theodosius III. and Cornesius, prior to the victories of the Iconoclast princes. These terms, fixing the frontier at Meleona, and regulating the duties to be paid on merchandise in the Bulgarian kingdom, would have been accepted by Michael, but Crumn availed himself of his success to demand that all deserters and refugees should be given up. As the Bulgarians were in the habit of ransoming the greater part of their captives at the end of each campaign, and of killing the remainder, or selling them as slaves, this clause was introduced into the treaty to enable Crumn to gratify his vengeance against a number of refugees whom his tyranny had caused to quit Bulgaria, and who had generally embraced Christianity. The emperor remitted the examination of these conditions to the imperial council, and in the discussion which ensued, he, the Patriarch Nicephoros, and several bishops, declared themselves in favour of the treaty, on the ground that it was necessary to sacrifice the refugees for the safety of the natives of the empire who were in slavery in Bulgaria, and to preserve the population from further suffering. But Theoctistos the master of the palace, the energetic Theodore Studita, and a majority of the senators, declared that such conduct would be an indelible stain to the Roman empire, and would only invite the Bulgarians to recommence hostilities by the fear shown in the concession. The civilians declared it would be an act of infamy to consign to death, or to a slavery worse than death, men who had been received as subjects; and Theodore pronounced that it was an act of impiety to think of delivering Christians into the hands of pagans, quoting St. John, "All that the Father giveth me shall come to me, and him that cometh to me I will in no wise cast out."[1] The emperor, from motives of piety, yielded to the advice of Theodore. Could he have adopted something of the firm character of the abbot, he would either have obtained peace on his own terms, or secured victory to his army.

While the emperor was debating at Constantinople, Crumn pushed forward the siege of Mesembria, which fell into his

---

[1] Gospel of St. John, vi. 37.

hands in November, 812. He acquired great booty, as the place was a commercial town of considerable importance; and he made himself master of twenty-six of the brazen tubes used for propelling Greek fire, with a quantity of the combustible material prepared for use in this artillery. Yet, even after this alarming news had reached Constantinople, the weak emperor continued to devote his attention to ecclesiastical affairs instead of military. He seems to have felt that he was utterly unfit to conduct the war in person; yet the Byzantine or Roman army demanded to be led by the emperor.

In the spring of 813, Michael had an army in the field prepared to resist the Bulgarians; and Crumn, finding that his troops were suffering from a severe epidemic, retreated. The Emperor, proud of his success, returned to his capital. The epidemic which had interrupted the operations of the enemy was ascribed to the intervention of Tarasios, who had been canonised for his services to orthodoxy; and the emperor, in order to mark his gratitude for his unexpected acquisition of military renown, covered the tomb of St. Tarasios with plates of silver weighing ninety-five lb., an act of piety which added to the contempt the army already felt for their sovereign's courage and capacity.

In the month of May, Michael again resumed the command of the army, but instead of listening to the advice of the experienced generals who commanded the troops, he allowed himself to be guided by civilians and priests, or he listened to the suggestions of his own timidity. There were at the time three able officers in the army—Leo the Armenian, the general of the Anatolic theme; Michael the Amorian, who commanded one wing of the army; and John Aplakes, the general of the Macedonian troops. Leo and Aplakes urged the emperor to attack the Bulgarians; but the Amorian, who was intriguing against Theoctistos the master of the palace, seems to have been disinclined to serve the emperor with sincerity. The Bulgarians were encamped at Bersinikia, about thirty miles from the Byzantine army; and Michael, after changing his plans more than once, resolved at last to risk a battle. Aplakes, who commanded the Macedonian and Thracian troops, consisting chiefly of hardy Sclavonian recruits, defeated the Bulgarian division opposed to him; but a panic seized a party of the Byzantine troops; and Leo, with the Asiatic troops, was accused of allowing Aplakes to be surrounded and slain, when he might have saved him. Leo certainly saved his own division, and made it the rallying-point for the fugitives; yet he does not appear to have been considered guilty of any neglect by the soldiers themselves. The emperor fled to Constantinople, while the defeated army retreated to Adrianople.

Michael assembled his ministers in the capital, and talked of resigning his crown; for he deemed his defeat a judgment for mounting the throne of his brother-in-law. Procopia and his courtiers easily persuaded him to abandon his half-formed resolution. The army in the mean time decided the fate of the Empire. Leo the Armenian appeared alone worthy of the crown. The defeated troops saluted him Emperor, and marched to Constantinople, where nobody felt inclined to support the weak Michael; so that Leo was acknowledged without opposition, and crowned in St. Sophia's on the 11th July, 813.

The dethroned emperor was compelled to embrace the monastic life, and lived unmolested in the island of Prote, where he died in 845. His eldest son, Theophylactus, who had been crowned as his colleague, was emasculated, as well as his brother Ignatius, and forced into a monastery. Ignatius became Patriarch of Constantinople in the reign of Michael III.[1]

SECTION III

LEO V., (THE ARMENIAN,) A.D.[2] 813–820

Policy of Leo—Treacherous attack on Crumn—Victory over Bulgarians—Affairs of Italy and Sicily—Moderation in ecclesiastical contests—Council favourable to Iconoclasts—Impartial administration of justice—Conspiracy against Leo—His assassination.

When Leo entered the capital, the Patriarch Nicephoros endeavoured to convert the precedent which Michael I. had given, of signing a written declaration of orthodoxy, into an established usage of the empire; but the new emperor excused himself from signing any document before his coronation, and afterwards he denied the right to require.[3] Leo was inclined

---

[1] Anonymous chronicle at the end of Theophanes, 431. Contin. Const. Porphyr., in the *Scriptores post Theophanem*, 13.

[2] Leo was the son of Bardas, a patrician of the distinguished Armenian family of the Ardzrounians. Genesius, 16. Chamich, i. 399.

[3] Theophanes, 426, says Leo gave the Patriarch a written assurance of his orthodoxy, and he is followed by the anonymous chronicle, page 431, by Leo Grammaticus, p. 445, by Symeon Mag. 402, and Georg. Mon. 499. But the anonymous history written by the order of Constantine Porphyrogenitus in the *Scriptores post Theophanem*, 18, and

to favour the Iconoclasts, but he was no bigot. The Asiatic party in the army and in the administration, which supported him, were both enemies to image-worship. To strengthen the influence of his friends was naturally the first step of his reign. Michael the Amorian, who had warmly supported his election, was made a patrician. Thomas, another general, who is said to have been descended from the Sclavonian colonists settled in Asia Minor, was appointed general of the federates.[1] Manuel, an Armenian of the noble race of the Mamiconians, received the command of the Armenian troops, and subsequently of the Anatolic theme.[2] At Christmas the title of Emperor was conferred on Sembat, the eldest son of Leo, who then changed his name to Constantine.

Leo was allowed little time to attend to civil business, for, six days after his coronation, Crumn appeared before the walls of Constantinople. The Bulgarian king encamped in the suburb of St. Mamas,[3] and extended his lines from the Blachernian to the Golden Gate; but he soon perceived that his army could not long maintain its position, and he allowed his troops to plunder and destroy the property of the citizens in every direction, in order to hasten the conclusion of a treaty of peace. Leo was anxious to save the possessions of his subjects from ruin, Crumn was eager to retreat without losing any of the plunder his army had collected. A treaty might have been concluded, had not Leo attempted to get rid of his enemy by an act of the basest treachery. A conference was appointed, to which the emperor and the king were to repair, attended only by a fixed number of guards. Leo laid a plot for assassinating Crumn at this meeting, and the Bulgarian monarch escaped with the greatest difficulty, leaving his chancellor dead, and most of his attendants captives. This infamous act was so generally approved by the perverted religious feelings of the Greek ecclesiastics, that the historian Theophanes, an abbot and holy confessor, in concluding his chronological record of the transactions of the Roman emperors, remarks that the empire was not permitted to witness

---

Genesius, ii., give the statement in the text, which is confirmed by Ignatius in his life of the Patriarch Nicephoros.—*Acta Sanct Mart.* 710. The authority of the Patriarch Ignatius far outweighs every other. Schlosser, 391. Neander, iii. 532. The Emperor Leo doubtless made the customary general declaration of orthodoxy contained in the coronation oath, which had appeared so vague as to require the written supplement signed by his predecessor.

[1] Genesius, 3-14. Contin. Const. Porphyr. 32. We must conclude that one of the parents of Thomas was a Sclavonian, the other an Armenian, (see p. 121 note 2).

[2] Cont. Const. Porphyr. 15-68.

[3] Between Eyoub and the walls of Constantinople.

the death of Crumn by this ambuscade, in consequence of the multitude of the people's sins.[1]

The Bulgarians avenged the emperor's treachery on the helpless inhabitants of the empire in a terrible manner. They began by destroying the suburb of St. Mamas; palaces, churches, public and private buildings were burnt to the ground; the lead was torn from the domes, which were fire-proof; the vessels taken at the head of the port were added to the conflagration; numerous beautiful works of art were destroyed, and many carried off, among which particular mention is made of a celebrated bronze lion, a bear, and a hydra.[2] The Bulgarians then quitted their lines before Constantinople, and marched to Selymbria, destroying on their way the immense stone bridge over the river Athyras, (Karason,) celebrated for the beauty of its construction.[3] Selymbria, Rhedestos, and Apres were sacked; the country round Ganas was ravaged, but Heraclea and Panion resisted the assaults of the invaders. Men were everywhere put to the sword, while the young women, children, and cattle were driven away to Bulgaria. Part of the army penetrated into the Thracian Chersonese, and laid waste the country, Adrianople was compelled to surrender by famine, and after it had been plundered, the barbarians retired unmolested with an incredible booty, and an innumerable train of slaves.

The success of this campaign induced a body of 30,000 Bulgarians to invade the empire during the winter. They captured Arcadiopolis; and though they were detained for a fortnight, during their retreat, by the swelling of the river Rheginas, (Bithyas,) Leo could not venture to attack them.[4] They regained the Bulgarian frontier, carrying away fifty thousand captives and immense booty, and leaving behind them a terrible scene of desolation.[5]

Emboldened by the apparent weakness of the empire, Crumn made preparations for besieging Constantinople, by collecting all the machines of war then in use.[6] Leo thought it necessary to construct a new wall beyond that in existence at the Blach-

1 Theophanes, 427.
2 Theophanes, 427. Leo Grammaticus, 446. Anonym., *De Ant. Const.*, No. 163, No. 246, Gyllius. Banduri, *Imp. Orient.* i. 416.
3 Steph. Byz. Ἀθύρας Plinii, H. N. iv. 11-18.
4 Erginus? Scylax, 28. Plinii, H. N., 11-18. Hierocles, 31, and Constant. Porphyr. *De Them.* ii. 2, mention Ganos.
5 The booty consisted of Armenian blankets, carpets, clothing, and brazen pans. Symeon Mag. 410. Contin. at the end of Theophanes, 434.
6 Contin. of Theophanes, 434, who gives a curious list of the ancient machines then in use.

ernian gate, and to add a deep ditch, for in this quarter the fortifications of the capital appeared weak. Crumn died before the opening of the campaign; and Leo, having by the greatest exertion at last collected an army capable of taking the field, marched to Mesembria. There he succeeded in surprising the Bulgarians by a night attack on their camp. The defeat was most sanguinary. The Bulgarian army was annihilated, and the place where the dead were buried was long called the Mountain of Leo, and avoided by the Bulgarians as a spot of evil augury. After this victory the emperor ininvaded Bulgaria, which he ravaged with as much cruelty as Crumn had ever shown in plundering the empire. At last a truce for thirty years was concluded with Montagon, the new king. The power of these dangerous neighbours was so weakened by the recent exertions they had made, and by the wealth they had acquired, that for many years they were disposed to remain at peace.

The influence of the Byzantine emperors in the West, though much diminished by the conquests of Charlemagne, the independence of the Popes, and the formation of two Saracen kingdoms in Africa and Spain, continued, nevertheless, to be very great, in consequence of the extensive mercantile connections of the Greeks, who then possessed the most lucrative part of the commerce of the Mediterranean.

At this time the Aglabites of Africa and the Ommiades of Spain ruled a rebellious and ill-organised society of Mohammedan chiefs of various races, which even arbitrary power could not bend to the habits of a settled administration. Both these states sent out piratical expeditions by sea, when their incursions by land were restrained by the warlike power of their neighbours. Michael I. had been compelled to send an army to Sicily, to protect it from the incursions of pirates both from Africa and Spain. Lampedosa had been occupied by Saracen corsairs, and many Greek ships captured, before the joint forces of the Dukes of Sicily and Naples, with the vessels from Amalfi and Venice, defeated the plunderers and cleared the sea for a while. The quarrels of the Aglabites and Ommiades induced the former to conclude a truce for ten years with Leo, and to join the naval forces of the Greeks and Venetians in attacking the Spanish Saracens.[1]

The disturbances which prevailed in the East during the caliphate of Almamun insured tranquillity to the Asiatic frontier

---

[1] Schlosser, 403. Pope Leo's Letter. Coletti. *Acta S. Concil.* ix. 157.

of the empire, and allowed Leo to devote his whole attention to the internal state of his dominions. The church was the only public institution immediately connected with the feelings of the whole population. By its conduct the people were directly interested in the proceedings of the imperial government. Ecclesiastical affairs, offering the only field for the expression of public opinion, became naturally the centre of all political ideas and party struggles. Even in an administrative point of view, the regular organisation of the clergy under parish priests, bishops, and provincial councils, gave the church a degree of power in the state which compelled the emperor to watch it attentively. The principles of ecclesiastical independence inculcated by Theodore Studita, and adopted by the monks, and that portion of the clergy which favoured image-worship, alarmed the emperor. This party inculcated a belief in contemporary miracles, and in the daily intervention of God in human affairs. All prudence, all exertion on the part of individuals, was as nothing compared to the favour of some image accidentally endowed with divine grace. That such images could at any time reveal the existence of a hidden treasure, or raise the possessor to high official rank, was the common conviction of the superstitious and enthusiastic, both among the laity and the clergy; and such doctrines were especially favoured by the monks, so that the people, under the guidance of these teachers, became negligent of moral duties and regular industry. The Iconoclasts themselves appealed to the decision of Heaven as favouring their cause, by pointing to the misfortunes of Constantine VI., Irene, Nicephorus, and Michael I., who had supported image-worship, and contrasting their reigns with the victories and peaceful end of Leo the Isaurian, Constantine V., and Leo IV., who were the steady opponents of idolatry.

Leo V., though averse to image-worship, possessed so much prudence and moderation, that he was inclined to rest satisfied with a direct acknowledgment that the civil power possessed the right of tolerating religious difference. But the army demanded the abolition of image-worship, and the monks the persecution of Iconoclasts. Leo's difficulties, in meddling with ecclesiastical affairs, gave his policy a dubious character, and obtained for him, among the Greeks, the name of the Chameleon. Several learned members of the clergy were opposed to image-worship; and of these the most eminent were the abbot John Hylilas, of the illustrious family of the

Morochorzanians, and Anthony, bishop of Syllæum. John, called, from his superior learning, the Grammarian, was accused by the ignorant of studying magic ; and the nickname of Lekanomantis was given him, because he was said to read the secrets of futurity in a brazen basin.[1] The Iconoclasts were also supported by Theodotos Kassiteras, son of the patrician Michael Melissenos, whose sister had been the third wife of Constantine V. These three endeavoured to persuade Leo to declare openly against image-worship. On the other hand, the majority of the Greek nation was firmly attached to image-worship ; and the cause was supported by the Patriarch, by Theodore Studita, and a host of monks. The emperor flattered himself that he should be able to bring about an amicable arrangement to insure general toleration, and commanded John Hylilas to draw up a report of the opinions expressed by the earliest fathers of the church on the subject of image-worship.

As soon as he was in possession of this report, he asked the Patriarch to make some concessions on the subject of pictures, in order to satisfy the army and preserve peace in the church. He wished that the pictures should be placed so high as to prevent the people making the gross display of superstitious worship constantly witnessed in the churches. But the Patriarch coldly pronounced himself in favour of images and pictures, whose worship, he declared, was authorised by immemorial tradition, and the foundation of the orthodox faith was formed according to the opinion of the church on tradition as well as on Holy Scripture. He added that the opinions of the church were inspired by the Holy Spirit as well as the Scriptures. The emperor then proposed a conference between the two parties, and the clergy was thrown into a state of the greatest excitement at this pro-position, which implied a doubt of their divine inspiration. The Patriarch summoned his partisans to pass the night in prayers for the safety of the church, in the cathedral of St. Sophia. The emperor had some reason to regard this as seditious, and he was alarmed at the disorders which must evidently arise from both parties appealing to popular support. He summoned the Patriarch to the palace, where the night was spent in controversy. Theodore Studita was one of those who attended the Patriarch on this occasion, and his steady assertion of ecclesiastical supremacy rendered him worthy,

[1] See note 3, p. 132

from his bold and uncompromising views, to have occupied the chair of St. Peter. He declared plainly to the emperor that he had no authority to interfere with the doctrines of the church, since his rule only extended over the civil and military government of the empire. The church had full authority to govern itself. Leo was enraged at this boldness, and dissatisfied with the conduct of the Patriarch, who anathematised Anthony, the bishop of Syllæum, who was viewed as the leader of the Iconoclasts; but for the present the clergy were only required to abstain from holding public assemblies.

The Iconoclasts, however, now began to remove images and pictures from the churches in possession of the clergy of their party, and the troops on several occasions insulted the image over the entrance of the imperial palace, which had been once removed by Leo the Isaurian, and replaced by Irene. The emperor now ordered it to be again removed, on the ground that this was necessary to avoid public disturbance. These acts induced Theodore Studita to call on the monks to subscribe a declaration that they adhered firmly to the doctrines of the church, with respect to image-worship, as then established. The emperor, alarmed at the danger of causing a new schism in the church, but feeling himself called upon to resist the attacks now made on his authority, determined to relieve the civil power from the necessity of engaging in a contest with the ecclesiastical, by assembling a general council of the church, and leaving the two parties in the priesthood to settle their own differences. As he was in doubt how to proceed, it happened that both the Patriarch and the abbot, John Hylilas, were officiating together in the Christmas ceremonies while Leo was present, and that John, in the performance of his duty, had to repeat the words of Isaiah, "To whom then will ye liken God? or what will ye compare unto him? The workman melteth a graven image, and the goldsmith spreadeth it over with gold, and casteth silver chains."[1] In pronouncing these words, he turned to the emperor, and uttered them in the most emphatic manner. A few days after this scene, a band of mutinous soldiers broke into the patriarchal palace and destroyed the pictures of the saints with which the building was adorned, and committing other disorders, until they were driven out by the regular guard. At length, in the month of April, 815, Leo ordered

[1] Isaiah, xl. 18, 19.

a provincial synod to assemble at Constantinople, and before this assembly the Patriarch Nicephoros was brought by force, for he denied its competency to take cognisance of his conduct. He was deposed, and confined in a monastery which he had founded, where he survived twelve years—a time which he passed more usefully for the world, in compiling the historical works we possess, than he could have passed them amidst the contests of the patriarchal dignity.[1]

The bigotry of both parties rendered the moderate policy of the emperor of no effect; and public attention became so exclusively absorbed by the state of the church, that it was impossible for him to remain any longer neuter. His first decided step was to nominate a new Patriarch hostile to image-worship; and he selected Theodotos Melissenos, a layman already mentioned, who held a high post in the imperial court. The example of the election of Tarasios prevented the votaries of image-worship disputing the legality of the election of a layman; but they refused to acknowledge Theodotos, on the ground that the deposition of Nicephoros was illegal, and that he was consequently still their lawful Patriarch. Theodotos was nevertheless ordained and consecrated, A.D. 815. He was a man of learning and ability, but his habits as a military man and a courtier were said to be visible in his manners, and he was accused of living with too great splendour, keeping a luxurious table, and indulging habitually in society of too worldly a character.

A general council of the church was now held at Constantinople, in which the new Patriarch, and Constantine the son of Leo, presided; for the emperor declined taking a personal part in the dispute, in order to allow the church to decide on questions of doctrine without any direct interference of the civil power. This council re-established the acts of that held in 754 by Constantine V., abolishing image-worship, and it anathematised the Patriarchs Tarasios and Nicephoros, and all image-worshippers. The clergy, therefore, who adhered to the principles of the image-worshippers were, in consequence, deprived of their ecclesiastical dignities, and sent into banishment; but the party revolutions that had frequently occurred

---

[1] Nicephoros died A.D. 828. His works are—*Breviarium Historicum de Rebus Gestis ab Obitu Mauricii ad Constantinum usque Copronymum*, in the Byzantine collection, and a Chronographia annexed to the work of Syncellus. The Patriarch Photius, in a letter to the Emperor Basil I., mentions that Leo treated the deposed Patriarch with indulgence. He enjoyed the use of his books and the society of his friends, as well as the possession of his private fortune.—*Photii Epistolæ*, 97, page 136, edit. Lond.

in the Greek church had introduced a dishonourable system of compliance with the reigning faction, and most of the clergy were readier to yield up their opinions than their benefices.[1] This habitual practice of falsehood received the mild name of arrangement, or economy, to soften the public aversion to such conduct.[2]

The Iconoclast party, on this occasion, used its victory with unusual mildness. They naturally drove their opponents from their ecclesiastical offices; and when some bold monks persisted in preaching against the acts of the council, they banished these non-conformists to distant monasteries; but it does not appear that the civil power was called upon to enforce conformity with the customary rigour.[3] The council had decided that images and pictures were to be removed from the churches, and if the people resisted their removal, or the clergy or monks replaced them, severe punishments were inflicted for this violation of the law. Cruelty was a feature in the Byzantine civil administration, without any impulse of religious fanaticism.

Theodore Studita, who feared neither patriarch nor emperor, and acknowledged no authority in ecclesiastical affairs but the church, while he recognised nothing as the church but what accorded with his own standard of orthodoxy, set the decrees of this council at defiance. He proceeded openly through the streets of the capital, followed by his monks in solemn procession, bearing aloft the pictures which had been removed from the churches, to give them a safe asylum within the walls of the monastery of Studion. For this display of contempt for the law he was banished by the emperor to Asia Minor; and his conduct in exile affords us a remarkable proof of the practical liberty the monks had acquired by their honest and steady resistance to the civil power. All eyes were fixed on Theodore as the leader of the monastic party; and so great was the power he exerted over public opinion, that the emperor did not venture to employ any illegal severity against the bold monk he had imprisoned. Indeed, the administration of justice in the Byzantine empire seems never to have been more regular and equitable than during the reign of Leo the Armenian.

---

[1] The historian Theophanes, author of the Chronography, which has been at times our only, and often our best, guide in the preceding pages, was a noble exception to the system of compliance. He was among those who were banished, and died shortly after in exile in Samothrace.

[2] Ὀικονομία was the word.—Neander, iii. 541.   [3] Photii Ep. 97.

Theodore from his prison corresponded not only with the most eminent bishops and monks of his party, and with ladies of piety and wealth, but also with the Pope, to whom, though now a foreign potentate, the bold abbot sent deputies, as if he were himself an independent Patriarch in the Eastern church.[1] His great object was to oppose the Iconoclasts in every way, and prevent all those over whose minds he exercised any influence from holding communion with those who conformed to their authority· One thing seems to have distressed and alarmed him, and he exerted all his eloquence to expose its fallacy. The Iconoclasts declared that no one could be a martyr for Christ's sake, who was only punished by the usual power for image-worship, since the question at issue had no connection with the truth of Christianity. Theodore argued that the night of heresy was darker than that of ignorance, and the merit of labouring to illuminate it was at least as great. The Emperor Leo was, however, too prudent to give any of Theodore's party the slightest hope of claiming the crown of martyrdom. He persisted in his policy of enforcing the decrees of the council with so much mildness, and balancing his own expressions of personal opinion with such a degree of impartiality that he excited the dissatisfaction of the violent of both parties.[2]

Even in a corrupted and factious society, most men appreciate the equitable administration of justice. Interest and ambition may indeed so far pervert the feelings of an administrative or aristocratic class, as to make the members of such privileged societies regard the equal distribution of justice to the mass of people as an infringement of their rights ; and the passions engendered by religious zeal may blind those under its influence to any injustice committed against men of different opinions. Hence it is that a government, to secure the administration of justice, must be established on a broader basis than administrative wisdom, aristocratic pre-eminence, or religious orthodoxy. In the Byzantine empire, public opinion found no home among the mass of the population, whose minds and actions were regulated and enslaved by

[1] He seems to have been the chief mover of the foundation of the monastery of St. Praxedes at Rome, in which the Greek monks who fled from persecution were established by Pope Paschal.—*Anastassi de Vitis Pont.* 150.

[2] The letters of Theodore Studita furnish information concerning the mildness of Leo's government. The fact that the banished abbot should carry on so extensive a correspondence, proves that the liberty guaranteed by the laws of the Roman empire, when these laws were equitably administered, was not an idle phrase at Constantinople under the Iconoclasts.

administrative influence, by the power of the wealthy, and by the authority of the clergy and the monks.[1] One result of this state of society is visible in the violence of party passion displayed concerning insignificant matters in the capital; and hence it arose at last that the political interests of the empire were frequently disconnected with the subjects that exercised the greatest influence on the fate of the government. The moderation of Leo, which, had public opinion possessed any vitality, ought to have rendered his administration popular with the majority of his subjects in the provinces, certainly rendered it unpopular in Constantinople. Crowds, seeking excitement, express the temporary feelings of the people before deliberation has fixed the public opinion. Leo was hated by the Greeks as an Armenian and an Iconoclast; and he was disliked by many of the highest officers in the state and the army for the severity of his judicial administration, and the strictness with which he maintained moral as well as military discipline, so that no inconsiderable number of the class who directed state affairs were disposed to welcome a revolution. Irene had governed the empire by eunuchs, who had put up everything for sale; Nicephorus had thought of those reforms only that tended to fill the treasury; Michael I. had been the tool of a bigoted faction. All these sovereigns had accumulated opposition to good government.

Leo undertook the task of purifying the administration, and he commenced his reforms by enforcing a stricter dispensation of justice. His enemies acknowledged that he put a stop to corruption with wonderful promptitude and ability. He restored the discipline of the army, he repressed bribery in the courts of justice, by strictly reviewing all judicial decisions, and he re-established an equitable system of collecting the revenue.[2] He repaired the fortresses destroyed by the Bulgarians, and placed all the frontiers of the empire in a respectable state of defence. All this, it was universally acknowledged, was due to his personal activity in watching over the proceedings of his ministers. Even the Patriarch

---

1 In the Byzantine, as in the Roman empire, the administration, including the emperor and all his servants, or, as the servants of the state were called, his household, formed a class apart from the inhabitants of the empire, governed by different laws, while the subjects under the civil laws of Rome were again separated into the rich and the poor, οἱ δυνατο and οἱ πένητες, whom usage more than legislation constituted into separate classes.

2 A case of his personal decision, where the prætor had refused justice against a senator, is reported as a proof of his rigid attention to the equal administration of the law.—Genesius, 8; Contin. Const. Porphyr. 19. Mortreuil, i. 355, gives it from Bonefidius, 7, who has extracted it from Cedrenus, ii. 491.

Nicephoros, whom he had deposed, gave testimony to his merits as an emperor. When he heard of Leo's assassination, he exclaimed, "The church is delivered from a dangerous enemy, but the empire has lost a useful sovereign."

The officers of the court, who expected to profit by a change of measures, formed a conspiracy to overthrow Leo's government, which was joined by Michael the Amorian, who had long been the emperor's most intimate friend. The ambition of this turbulent and unprincipled soldier led him to think that he had as good a right to the throne as Leo; and when he perceived that a general opposition was felt in Constantinople to the emperor's conduct, his ambition got the better of his gratitude, and he plotted to mount the throne. It was generally reported that Leo had refused to accept the Imperial crown, when proclaimed emperor by the army at Adrianople, from his knowledge of the difficulties with which he would have to contend, and that Michael forced him to yield his assent, by declaring that he must either accept the crown, or be put to death to make way for a new candidate. The turbulent character of Michael gave currency to this anecdote.

Michael's conduct had long been seditious, when at length his share in a conspiracy against the government was discovered, and he was tried, found guilty, and condemned to death. It is said by the chronicles that the court of justice left it to the emperor to order his execution in any way he might think proper, and that Leo condemned him to be immediately cast into the furnace used for heating the baths of the palace, and prepared to attend the execution in person. It is needless to say that, though cruelty was the vice of the Byzantine court, we must rank this story as a tale fitter for the legends of the saints than for the history of the empire. The event took place on Christmas-eve, when the empress, hearing what was about to happen, and moved with compassion for one who had long been her husband's intimate friend, hastened to Leo, and implored him to defer the execution until after Christmas-day. She urged the sin of participating in the holy communion with the cries of the dying companion of his youth echoing in his ear. Leo—who, though severe, was not personally cruel—yielded to his wife's entreaties, and consented with great reluctance to postpone the punishment, for his knowledge of the extent of the conspiracy gave him a presentiment of danger. After giving orders for staying the execution, he turned to the empress and said, "I grant your request: you think only of my eternal welfare; but you expose my life to the greatest peril, and your scruples may bring misfortune on you and on our children."

Michael was conducted back to his dungeon, and the key of his fetters was brought to Leo. It was afterwards told in Constantinople that during the night the emperor was unable to sleep. A sense of impending danger, disturbing his imagination, impelled him to rise from his bed, envelop himself in a mantle, and secretly visit the cell in which Michael was confined. There he found the door unlocked, and Michael stretched on the bed of his jailor, buried in profound sleep, while the jailor himself was lying on the criminal's bed on the floor. The emperor's alarm was increased at this spectacle. He withdrew to consider what measures he should take to watch both the prisoner and the jailor. But Michael had already many partisans within the walls of the palace, and one of these had, having observed the emperor's nocturnal visit to the criminal's cell, immediately awakened Michael. There was not a moment to lose. As a friendly confessor had been introduced into the palace to afford the condemned criminal the consolations of religion, this priest was sent to Theoctistos to announce that, unless a blow was instantly struck, Michael would at daylight purchase his own pardon by revealing the names of the principal conspirators. This message caused the conspirators to resolve on the immediate assassination of the emperor.

The imperial palace was a fortress separated from the city like the present seraï of the sultan. It was the practice of Leo to attend matins in his chapel, and as it was Christmas-day, a number of the best singers in Constantinople were that morning admitted at a postern-gate before daybreak, in order to join in the celebration of the service, whose solemn chant was then the admiration of the Christian world.[1] Leo, who was of a religious turn of mind, delighted in displaying his deep sonorous voice in the choir. He delayed his measures for securing Michael and the jailor to hasten to the chapel, and the conspirators availed themselves of his presence during the celebration of divine service to execute their plans. Disguised

---

[1] Charlemagne was profoundly affected by the solemn music of the Greek service. We may conclude that it bore a closer resemblance to the music of the Russian church of to-day than to the nasal melody of modern Greek psalmody. See the enthusiastic manner in which Joannes Cameniates speaks of Byzantine church-music in the tenth century, *De Excidio Thessalonicensi*, chap. x. ; *Scriptores post Theophanem*, p. 326.

as choristers, with daggers concealed in their clothes, they obtained admittance at the postern, and ranged themselves among the singers in the imperial chapel.

The morning was dark and cold, and both the emperor and the officiating chaplain were enveloped in furred mantles, which, with the thick bonnets they wore as a protection against the damp, effectually concealed their faces. But as soon as the powerful voice of Leo was heard in the solemn hymns, the assassins pressed forward to stab him. Some, however, mistaking the chaplain for the emperor, wounded the priest, whose cries revealed the mistake, and then all turned on Leo, who defended himself for some time with the crucifix which he snatched up. His hand was soon cut off, and he fell before the communion-table, where his body was hewed in pieces.

The assassins then hurried to the cell of Michael, whom they proclaimed emperor, and thus consummated the revolution for which he was under sentence of death. Few sovereigns of the Byzantine empire seem to have exerted themselves more sincerely than Leo V. to perform the duties of their station, yet few have received less praise for their good qualities; nor did his assassination create any reaction of public opinion in his favour. Though he died with the crucifix in his hand, he was condemned as if he had been a bigoted Iconoclast. His wife and children were compelled to adopt a monastic life.[1]

[1] For the reign of Leo V., see the anonymous author at the end of Theophanes; Leo Grammaticus, 445; the continuator of Theophanes, by order of Constantine Porphyrogenitus, in *Scriptores post Theophanem*; Symeon Log. et Mag. 411, and Georg. Mon. 500—both in the *Scriptores post Theoph.*; Genesius; Cedrenus, 487; Zonares, ii. 152; and the shorter chronicles.

CHAPTER III

THE AMORIAN DYNASTY, A.D. 820–867

SECTION I

MICHAEL II., (THE STAMMERER,) A.D. 820–829

Birth of Michael II.—Rebellion of Thomas—Loss of Crete and Sicily—
Michael's ecclesiastical policy—Marriage and death.

MICHAEL II. was proclaimed emperor with the fetters on his
limbs; and the first spectacle of his reign was the jailor
delivering him from a felon's bonds. When relieved from his
irons, he proceeded to the church of St. Sophia, where he was
crowned by the Patriarch.

Michael II. was born in the lowest rank of society. He
had entered the army as a private soldier in early youth, but
his attention to his duties, and his military talents, quickly
raised him to the rank of general. His influence over the
troops aided in placing Leo V. on the imperial throne.
Amorium was his birthplace—an important and wealthy city,
inhabited by a mixed population of various races and
languages, collected together by trading interests.[1] The
Phrygians, who formed the majority, still retained many
native usages, and some religious ideas adverse to Greek
prejudices. Many Jews had also been established in the city
for ages, and a sect called the Athingans, who held that the
touch of many things was a contamination, had numerous
votaries.[2]

The low origin of Michael, and the half-suppressed contempt he disclosed for Greek learning, Roman pride, and
ecclesiastical tradition, awakened some animosity in the
breasts of the pedants, the nobles, and the orthodox of
Constantinople.[3] It is not surprising, therefore, that the

---

[1] See page 14, note 6.

[2] The Athingans took their names from θιγγάνω, and the allusion is to Colossians,
ii, 21—" Touch not, taste not, handle not."

[3] Τὴν Ἑλληνικὴν παιδεύσιν διαπτύων, Contin. Const, Porphyr. Sc. post Theoph.
31. Abulpharagius (Ch. Syr. 150) says Michael was the son of a converted Jew.
Niketas, in his Life of Ignatius, (Concil. Labb. viii. 1183,) says he was of the Sabbatian
heresy. Some moderns wish to make both the emperor and the Athingans gypseys
without any reason.

historians who wrote under the patronage of the enemies of the Amorian dynasty should represent its founder as a horse-jockey, a heretic, and a stammerer. As he showed no particular favour to the Greek party in the Byzantine church, his orthodoxy was questioned by the great body of the clergy; and as he very probably expressed himself with hesitation in the Greek language, as spoken at court, any calumny would find credit with the Hellenic populace, who have always been jealous of strangers, and eager to avenge, by words, the compliance they have been compelled to yield by deeds to foreign masters.

Michael, however, had sagacity to observe the difficulties which the various parties in the church and court had the power of raising up against his administration. To gain time, he began by conciliating every party. The orthodox, headed by Theodore Studita and the exiled Patriarch Nicephoros, were the most powerful. He flattered these two ecclesiastics, by allowing them to return to the capital, and even permitted Theodore to resume his functions as abbot of Studion; but, on the other hand, he refused to adopt their suggestions for a reaction in favour of image-worship. He seems to have been naturally inclined to religious toleration, and he was anxious to repress all disputes within the pale of the church, as the best means of maintaining the public tranquillity. In order to give a public guarantee for the spirit of the civil power, which he desired should characterise his reign, he held a silention to announce toleration of private opinion in ecclesiastical questions; but it was declared that the existing laws against the exhibition of images and pictures in churches were to be strictly enforced.[1] The indifference of Michael to the ecclesiastical disputes which agitated a church, to many of whose doctrines he was at heart adverse, did not create so violent an opposition as the sincerer conduct of his predecessors, who banished images on religious grounds.

The elevation of a new emperor, who possessed few claims to distinction, awakened, as usual, the hopes of every ambitious general. A formidable rival appeared in the person of Thomas, the only officer of eminence who had remained faithful to the rebel Bardanes, when Leo and Michael deserted his standard. Thomas, as has been already mentioned, was appointed general of the federates by Leo V., but, owing to some circumstances which are not recorded, he had retired into the

---

[1] Pagi ad Baron, *Ann. Eccles.* A.D. 821, tom. xiv.

dominions of the caliph, and remained for some time on the borders of Armenia.[1] His origin, whether Sclavonian or Armenian, by separating him in an unusual degree from the ruling classes in the empire—for he was, like Michael, of a very low rank in society—caused him to be regarded as a friend of the people ; and all the subject races in the empire espoused his cause, which in many provinces took the form of an attack on the Roman administration, rather than of a revolution to place a new emperor on the throne.[2] This rebellion is remarkable for assuming more of the character of a social revolution than of an ordinary insurrection.[3] Thomas overran all Asia Minor without meeting with any serious opposition even on the part of the towns ; so that, with the exception of the Armeniac theme and Opsikion, his authority was universally acknowledged, and the administration was conducted by his officers. He concluded an alliance with the Saracens to enable him to visit Antioch, and receive the imperial crown from the hands of the Patriarch Job.[4] This alliance with the infidels tended to injure his popularity ; and when he returned accompanied by large bodies of mercenary troops, collected from the Mohammedan tribes on the frontier, the public enthusiasm for his cause became sensibly diminished. Thomas, too, feeling more confidence in the power of his army, began to show himself careless of the good-will of the people.

The only manner of putting an end to the war was by taking Constantinople, and this Thomas prepared to attempt. An immense fleet was assembled at Lesbos. Gregorios Pterotes, a relation of Leo V., who had been banished to Skyros by Michael, was sent into Thrace at the head of ten thousand men to prepare for the arrival of Thomas, who soon followed with the bulk of his army, and formed the siege of Constantinople. Michael had taken every precaution for sustaining a long siege, and Thomas seems to have committed a serious error in attacking so strong a city, while the troops of the Armeniac

---

[1] Schlosser, *Geschichte der bild. Kaiser*, 437. The letter of Michael to Louis le Debonnaire. *Baronii, Ann. Eccles.* xiv. 62. Fleury, *Hist. Eccles.* lib. xlviii. art. 2. 4.

[2] Compare Genesius, iii. 14, with continuator, (*Scrip. post Theoph.* 5,) who says Thomas was born at the lake Gazouras. The town of Gazouria, near the river Iris in Pontus, is mentioned by Strabo, lib. xii. chap. ii. § 15, p. 547. Hamilton, *Researches in Asia Minor*, i. 359. He is said to have lived long among the Saracens, and to have given himself out for Constantine VI. Some of the reports seem irreconcilable, and look as if the history of two persons had been confounded.

[3] Contin. *Scrip. post Theoph*, 4, ἐντεῦθεν καὶ δοῦλοι κατὰ δεσποτῶν καὶ στρατιώτης κατὰ ταξεώτου, καὶ λοχαγὸς κατὰ στρατηγέτου τὴν χεῖρα φονῶσαν καθώπλιζε.—κ. τ. λ.   [4] Contin. 35. Genesius, 15.

theme and of Opsikion were in sufficient strength to attack his communications with the centre of Asia Minor, and maintain a constant communication with the garrison of Constantinople from the coast of Bithynia. The army of Thomas, though very numerous, was in part composed of an undisciplined rabble, whose plundering propensities increased the difficulty of obtaining supplies. On the other hand, Constantinople, though closely invested, was well supplied with all kinds of provisions and stores, and the inhabitants displayed great firmness in opposing an enemy whom they saw bent on plunder, while Michael and his son Theophilus performed the duties of able generals. Two attempts were made to storm the fortifications, one during the winter, in 821, and the other in the spring of 822; and both were equally unsuccessful, and entailed considerable loss on the besiegers. In the mean time the partisans of Michael collected a fleet of 350 ships in the islands of the Archipelago and Greece; and this force, having gained a complete victory over the fleet of Thomas, cut off the besiegers from communication with Asia.

The Bulgarians, in order to profit by the civil war, invaded the empire, and plundered the country from which the rebels were compelled to draw their supplies. Thomas marched to oppose them with a part of his army, but was defeated, and lost the greater part of his baggage. He was so much weakened by this defeat that Michael sallied out from Constantinople, again routed him, and compelled the rebel army to retire to Arcadiopolis, where Thomas was soon closely besieged.[1] For five months the place was obstinately defended, but at last Thomas was delivered up by his own followers; and his adopted son, who had been invested with the title of Emperor, was captured shortly after in Byza. Both were hanged, after their limbs had been cut off.[2] This junction of a son with the reigning emperor as his successor, had become a rule of the Byzantine constitution, which was rarely neglected by any sovereign. Two chiefs attached to the party of Thomas continued for some time to defend the towns of Kabala and Saniana in Asia Minor, until the latter place was betrayed by one who bargained to be appointed archbishop of Neocesarea,

---

[1] Genesius, 19; Georg. Mon. *Script. post Theoph.* 384, mention Arcadiopolis. Contin. 31, and the later writers, Cedrenus and Zonares, say Adrianople. Schlosser, 446 note.

[2] Michael's own letter to Louis le Debonnaire is the authority for this cruelty, as well as the early historians. Baronius, xiv. 64.

a fact recorded in a satirical verse preserved by one of the Byzantine historians.[1]

This remarkable civil war lasted nearly three years, and is distinguished by some features of unusual occurrence from most of the great rebellions in the Byzantine empire. The large fleets collected on both sides prove that the population and wealth of the coasts and islands of the Archipelago had not declined under the administration of the Iconoclasts, though this part of the empire was likely to be least favoured by the central power, as having attempted to dethrone Leo III., and having always firmly supported the party of the image-worshippers.[2] The most numerous partisans of Thomas, and those who gave the strong revolutionary impulse to the rebellion at its commencement, were that body of the Asiatic population which national distinctions or religious opinions excluded from participation in public and local affairs, and to whom even the ecclesiastical courts were shut, on account of their heretical opinions; and to the ecclesiastical courts alone recourse could be had for the equitable administration of justice in some cases. The discontent of these classes, joined to the poverty created by excessive taxation, supplied the army of Thomas with those numerous bands of marauders, eager to seek revenge, who spread desolation far and wide, alarmed all men possessing property, and ultimately ruined his enterprise. The indiscipline of his troops, and his incapacity to apply any remedy to the financial oppression and religious intolerance against which the population of the Asiatic provinces had taken up arms, alienated the minds of all who expected to find in him an instrument for reforming the empire. But had Thomas really been a man of a powerful mind, he might have laid the foundation of a new state of society in the Eastern Empire, by lightening the burden of taxation, carrying out toleration for religious opinions, securing an impartial administration of justice even to heretics, and giving every class of subjects, without distinction of nationality or race, equal security for their lives and property. The spirit of the age was, however, averse to toleration, and the sense of justice was so defective that these equitable principles could only have been upheld by the power of a well-disciplined mercenary army.

---

[1] Saniana was in the mountains of the theme Charsianon.—Const. Porphyr. *De Them.*, lib. i. 6, page 11. *De Adm. Imp.* chap. 50. Cont. *Scrip. post Theoph.* 45.
[2] Contin. 40. Genesius, 18.

The necessity of adopting a general measure for improving the condition of the people was not felt by Michael II., even when this rebellion was suppressed; and though he saw that some reduction of taxation to the lower classes was required, he restricted the boon to the Armeniac theme and Opsikion, because these provinces had not joined Thomas in the civil war;[1] and even in them he only reduced the hearth-tax to one-half of the amount imposed by Nicephorus I. The rest of the empire was oppressed more than usual, as a punishment. It is certain that this unfortunate rebellion caused an immense destruction of property in Asia Minor, and was no inconsiderable cause of the accumulation of property in immense estates, which began to depopulate the country, and prepare it for the reception of a new race of inhabitants.

The state of society under every known government was at this period troubled by civil wars. The seeds of these convulsions may, therefore, be sought in some general cause affecting the relations of the various classes of men in the development of social progress, and so far it lay beyond the immediate influence of the political laws of the respective governments, whether Mohammedan or Christian. The frame of society in the Saracen and Frank empires betrayed as many signs of decay as in the Byzantine. One of the remarkable features of the age is the appearance of bands of men, so powerful as to set the existing governments everywhere at defiance. These bands consisted in great part of men of what may be called the middle and higher classes of society, driven by dissatisfaction with their prospects in life to seek their fortunes as brigands and pirates; and the extent to which slavery and the slave-trade prevailed, afforded them a ready means of recruiting their forces with daring and desperate men. The feeling which in our days impels nations to colonise new countries, and improve uncultivated lands, in the ninth century led the Saracens and Normans to ravage every country they could enter, destroy capital, and consequently diminish cultivation and population.

Crete and Sicily, two of the most valuable provinces of the Byzantine empire, inhabited almost exclusively by Greeks, and both in a high state of civilisation and prosperity, were conquered by the Saracens without offering the resistance that might have been expected from the wealth and numbers of the inhabitants. Indeed, we are compelled to infer that the

---

[1] Contin. *Scrip. post Theoph.* 34.   Theophanes, 411.

change from the orthodox sway of the emperors of Constantinople to the domination of the Mohammedans, was not considered by the majority of the Greeks of Crete and Sicily so severe a calamity as we generally believe. In almost every case in which the Saracens conquered Christian nations, history unfortunately reveals that they owed their success chiefly to the favour with which their progress was regarded by the mass of the people. To the disgrace of most Christian governments, it will be found that their administration was more oppressive than that of the Arabian conquerors. Oppression commenced when the rude tribes of the desert adopted the corruptions of a ruling class. The inhabitants of Syria welcomed the first followers of Mahomet; the Copts of Egypt contributed to place their country under the domination of the Arabs; the Christian Berbers aided in the conquest of Africa. All these nations were induced, by hatred of the government at Constantinople, to place themselves under the sway of the Mohammedans. The treachery of the nobles, and the indifference of the people, made Spain and the south of France an easy prey to the Saracens. The conquest of Crete and Sicily must be traced to the same causes, for if the mass of the people had not been indifferent to the change, the Byzantine government could easily have retained possession of these valuable islands. The same disgraceful characteristic of Christian monarchies is also apparent at a much later period. The conquest of the Greeks, Servians, and Vallachians by the Othoman Turks was effected rather by the voluntary submission of the mass of the Christians than by the power of the Mohammedans. This fact is rendered apparent by the effective resistance offered by the Albanians under Scanderbeg. Church and state must divide between them this blot on Christian society, for it is difficult to apportion the share due to the fiscal oppression of Roman centralisation, and to the unrelenting persecution of ecclesiastical orthodoxy.

Crete fell a prey to a band of pirates. The reign of Al Hakem, the Ommiade caliph of Spain, was disturbed by continual troubles; and some theological disputes having created a violent insurrection in the suburbs of Cordova, about 15,000 Spanish Arabs were compelled to emigrate in the year 815. The greater part of these desperadoes established themselves at Alexandria, where they soon took an active part in the civil wars of Egypt. The rebellion of Thomas, and the absence of the naval forces of the Byzantine empire from the Archipelago, left the island of Crete unprotected. The Andalusian Arabs in Alexandria availed themselves of this circumstance to invade the island, and establish a settlement on it, in the year 823.[1] Michael was unable to take any measures for expelling these invaders, and an event soon happened in Egypt which added greatly to the strength of this Saracen colony. The victories of the lieutenants of the Caliph Almamun compelled the remainder of the Andalusian Arabs to quit Alexandria; so that Abou Hafs, called by Greeks Apochaps, joined his countrymen in Crete with forty ships, determined to make the new settlement their permanent home. It is said by the Byzantine writers that they commenced their conquest of the island by destroying their fleet, and constructing a strong fortified camp, surrounded by an immense ditch, from which it received the name of Chandak, now corrupted by the Western nations into Candia.[2] The construction of the new city, as the capital of their conquests, was part of the Saracen system of establishing their domination. The foundation of Cairo, Cairowan, Fez, Cufa, and Bagdat, was the result of this policy. A new state of society, and new institutions, were introduced with greater facility in a new residence.

The Saracen pirates derived some facilities towards rendering their conquests permanent, from the circumstance that their bands generally consisted of young men, destitute of domestic ties, who were seeking family establishments as well as wealth. It was thus that they became real colonists, to a much greater extent than is usually the case with conquerors in civilised countries. The ease, moreover, with which the Saracens, even of the highest rank, formed marriages with the lower orders, and the equality which reigned among the followers of the Prophet, presented fewer barriers to the increase of their number than prevailed in the various orders and classes of Byzantine society. The native population of Crete was in a stationary, if not a declining condition, at the time of the arrival of the Saracens, while these new colonists were introduced into the country under circumstances extremely

---

[1] Contin. *Scrip. post Theoph.* 35, 47. Genesius, 21. The Saracens are said to have established themselves first at Suda.

[2] The favourable disposition of a portion of the Cretans is indicated by the tradition, that a native monk pointed out to the Saracens the site of Chandak; and the power of the islanders to have offered a more effectual resistance than they did, is shown by one district obtaining leave to preserve its own laws and usages, without any interference on the part of the Saracens. This was probably Sphakia. Contin. 48. Genesius, 21.

favourable to a rapid increase of their numbers. History, however, rarely enables us to mark, from age to age, the increase and decrease of the different classes, tribes, and nations concerning whose affairs it treats, though no fact is more important to enable us to form a correct estimate of the virtues and vices of society, to trace the progress of civilisation, and understand the foundations of political power.

The Emperor Michael II. was at length, by the defeat of Thomas, enabled to make some attempts to drive the invaders out of Crete. The first expedition was intrusted to the command of Photinos, general of the Anatolic theme, a man of high rank and family; it was also strengthened by a reinforcement under Damianos, count of the imperial stables and protospatharios; but this expedition was completely defeated. Damianos was slain, and Photinos escaped with a single galley to Dia. The second attack on the Saracens was commanded by Krateros, the general of the Kibyrraiot theme, who was accompanied by a fleet of seventy ships of war. The Byzantine historians pretend that their army was victorious in a battle on shore, but that the Saracens, rallying during the night, surprised the Christian camp, and captured the whole fleet. Krateros escaped in a merchant vessel, but was pursued and taken near Cos, where he was immediately crucified by the Saracens.

The Saracens, having established their sovereignty over the twenty-eight districts into which Crete was then divided, sent out piratical expeditions to plunder the islands of the Archipelago and the coasts of Greece. Michael, alarmed lest more of his subjects should prefer the Saracen to the Byzantine government, fitted out a well-appointed fleet to cruise in the Egean Sea, and named Oryphas to command it. A choice of the best soldiers in the empire was secured, by paying a bounty of forty byzants a man; and in this, a most effective squadron, with a body of experienced warriors on board, the Byzantine admiral scoured the Archipelago. [1] The Saracen pirates from Syria, Egypt, Africa, and Spain, who had been stimulated by the successes of their countrymen to plunder the Greeks, were pursued and destroyed; but Oryphas was

---

[1] It is remarkable, as a proof of the relative value of money, that the price of a substitute was fixed at 36 solidi by the Emperor Valens, A.D. 375.—*Cod. Theod.* vii. xiii. 7. This shows how little change four centuries and a half had made in the value of the circulating medium, and in the condition of the people throughout the Eastern Empire.—Genesius, 23. Undoubtedly gold and silver mines must have been worked to a considerable extent, in order to maintain this equilibrium.

MⅡ
827
831

unable to effect anything, when he attacked the Cretan colony on shore.[1] This fleet was subsequently neglected; and, in the first year of the reign of Theophilus, an imperial squadron was totally destroyed by the Saracens, in a naval engagement near Thasos, leaving the corsairs masters of the sea. The islands of the Archipelago were then plundered, and immense booty in property and slaves was carried off.[2] The Saracens retained possession of Crete for one hundred and thirty-five years.

The conquest of Sicily was facilitated by the treachery of Euphemios, a native Greek of high rank, who is said to have carried off a nun, and whom the emperor ordered to be punished by the loss of his nose; for though Michael himself espoused Euphrosyne, the daughter of Constantine VI., after she had taken the veil, he did not intend that any of his subjects should be allowed a similar license. Euphemios was informed of the emperor's order in time to save his nose, by exciting a sedition in Syracuse, his native city.[3] In this tumult, Gregoras the Byzantine governor was slain. Michael then deputed Photinos, whose unsuccessful expedition to Crete has been already mentioned, to supply the place of Gregoras, and carry on the war against the Saracens of Africa, whom Euphemios had already invited into Sicily, to distract the attention of the Byzantine military. Ziadet Allah, the Aglabite sovereign of Cairowan, had paid particular attention to his fleet, so that he was well prepared to carry on the war, and delighted to gain an entrance for his troops into Sicily. In June, 827, his admiral effected a junction with the ships of Euphemios, who had been driven out of Syracuse, and the Saracens landed at Mazara. Photinos was defeated in a battle near Platana, and retreated to Enna. The Saracens occupied Girgenti, but they were not strong enough to commence offensive operations until the Byzantine fleet was driven off the coast by the arrival of a squadron of ships from Spain, which joined the Aglabites, and enabled fresh reinforcements to arrive from Africa. The war was then carried on with activity: Messina was taken in 831; Palermo capitulated in the following year;

---

[1] Symeon, Mag. 414.   [2] Contin. 85.
[3] The story that Euphemios carried off a nun is not quite sure, and looks something like an invention of the orthodox, who wished to point out that the sin of Michael had been punished by a divine judgment. John the Deacon, in his history of the Bishops of Naples, only says that he fled to Africa with his wife and son.—Muratori, *Scrip. Rer. Italicarum*, i. pl. 2-313. Euphemios is said to have been killed before the walls of Syracuse, as he was inviting the inhabitants to throw off the oppressive government of the Byzantine emperors for the lighter yoke of the Saracens.—Cedrenus, ii. 512.

and Enna was besieged, for the first time, in 836. The war continued with various success, as the invaders received assistance from Africa, and the Christians from Constantinople. The Byzantine forces recovered possession of Messina, which was not permanently occupied by the Saracens until 843. The Emperor Theophilus was too much engaged by his military operations in Asia Minor to send effectual aid to the Sicilians;[1] while his father Michael II. had been too fond of his ease on the throne to devote the requisite attenton to the business of the distant provinces. Michael III. thought of nothing but his pleasures. At length, in the year 859, Enna was taken by the Saracens. Syracuse, in order to preserve its commerce from ruin, had purchased peace by paying a tribute of 50,000 byzants; and it was not until the reign of Basil I., in the year 878, that it was compelled to surrender, and the conquest of Sicily was completed by the Arabs.[2] Some districts, however, continued, either by treaty or by force of arms, to preserve their municipal independence, and the exclusive exercise of the Christian religion, within their territory, to a later period.[3]

The loss of Crete and Sicily seems to have been viewed with strange apathy by the court at Constantinople. The reason of this is probably to be attributed to the circumstance that the surplus revenue was comparatively small, and the defence of these distant possessions was found often to require a military force, which it was deemed might be more advantageously employed near the capital. These feelings of the statesmen at Constantinople were doubtless strengthened by the circumstance that a portion of the population, both in Crete and Sicily, had acquired a degree of municipal independence extremely adverse to the principles which guided the imperial cabinet.

The bold and indefatigable abbot, Theodore Studita, still struggled to establish the supremacy of the church over the emperor in religious and ecclesiastical affairs. He appears to deserve the credit of having discovered the necessity of

---

[1] Theophilus seems to have named his brother-in-law, Alexis Mousel, Strategos and Duke of Sicily, merely to send him into exile.—Symeon Mag. 418.

[2] *Chronicon Siculum. Bibliotheca Hist. Regni Siciliæ a Carusio*, 6. Symeon Mag. places the taking of Syracuse in the ninth year of Basil I., which would be nearly two years earlier.

[3] The authorities for the conquest of Sicily are reviewed by Schlosser, *Geschichte der bild. Kaiser*, 455; and Weil, *Geschichte der Chalifen*, ii. 249. The Byzantine writers who lived nearest to the time conceal the facts, as the ultimate loss of the island reflected disgrace on Basil I., the grandfather of their patron Constantine VII., (Porphyrogenitus).

F

creating a systematic restraint on the arbitrary authority of the sovereign; but his scheme for making the ecclesiastical legislation superior to the executive power was defective, inasmuch as it sought to confer on the church a more irresponsible and dangerous authority than that of which the emperor would have been deprived. Experience had not yet taught mankind that no irresponsible power, whether it be intrusted to king or priest, in a monarchy or a republic, can be exercised without abuse. Until the law is superior to the executive government there is no true liberty; but in the Byzantine empire the emperor was above the law, and the imperial officials and the clergy had a law of their own, and so the people were doubly oppressed.

The conduct of Michael in conducting ecclesiastical business indicates that he was not destitute of statesmanlike qualities, though he generally thought rather of enjoying his ease on the throne than of fulfilling the duties of his high station.[1] During the civil war he was anxious to secure the good-will of the monks and of the Greek party in the church. He recalled Theodore from banishment, and declared himself in favour of perfect toleration. This was far from satisfying the enthusiastic abbot, and the bigoted ecclesiastics of his party; and after the establishment of tranquillity they incited the image-worshippers to an open violation of the laws against presenting pictures to the adoration of the people. Theodore also engaged with fresh zeal in an extensive correspondence with all persons of influence whom he knew to be favourable to his party. The emperor ordered him to discontinue this correspondence, as of a seditious tendency; but the bold abbot ventured to argue the case with Michael himself in a long letter, which is preserved in his works.[2]

The policy of forming friendly relations with the western nations of Europe was every day becoming more apparent to the rulers of the Byzantine empire, as the political influence of the Popes extended itself, and the power of the western nations increased. Michael II., in order to prevent the discontented image-worshippers from receiving support from the Franks, opened negotiations with the Emperor Louis le Debonnaire, in the hope of obtaining a condemnation of image-worship similar to that of Charlemagne. In the year

---

[1] Constantine Porphyrogenitus accuses Michael of neglecting the interests of the empire in Dalmatia as much as in Sicily and Crete.—*De Adm. Imp.* chap. 29
[2] S. *Theod. Stud. Epist., et alia Scripta Dogmatica*, Paris, 1696, lib. ii. ep. 199.

824, an embassy, bearing a vainglorious and bombastical letter, announcing the defeat of Thomas, reached the court of Louis.[1] In this epistle Michael recapitulates the religious principles which ought to guide the emperors of the Romans in their ecclesiastical affairs. He alludes to the condemnation of image-worship by the council of Frankfort, and declares that he has not destroyed holy images and pictures, but only removed them to such an elevation as was necessary to prevent the abuses caused by popular superstition.[2] He considers the councils held for the condemnation of image-worship merely as local synods, and fully recognises the existence of a higher authority in general councils of the church, giving, at the same time, his own confession of faith, in terms which he knew would secure the assent of Louis and the Frank clergy. He then solicits the Frank emperor to induce the Pope to withdraw his protection from the rebellious image-worshippers who had fled from the Byzantine empire to Rome. A synod was convoked at Paris in consequence of this communication, which condemned the worship of images in the same terms as the Caroline Books, and blamed the second council of Nicæa for the superstitious reverence it had shown for images, but, at the same time, approved of the rebuke given to the Eastern emperors, for their rashness in removing and destroying images, by Pope Hadrian, A.D. 825. The Emperor Louis was also requested by the synod to forward a letter to Pope Eugenius, inviting him to write to the Emperor Michael, in order to re-establish peace and unity in the Christian church. But the Pope, the two emperors, and Theodore Studita, were all afraid of plunging into ecclesiastical discussions at this period; for public opinion had been so exercised in these polemics, that it was impossible to foresee the result of the contest. Matters were therefore allowed to go on during the reign of Michael without any open rupture. The imprisonment of Methodios, afterwards Patriarch of Constantinople, and the condemnation to death of Euthymios, bishop of Sardis, were the only acts of extreme severity with which the image-worshippers could reproach Michael; and these seem to have originated from political and party motives

---

[1] For this letter, see Barionus, tom. xiv. 66; *Colet. Concil.* ix. 642; *Mansi Concil.* xiv. 419.

[2] Pictures were sometimes made godfathers and godmothers at the baptism of children. The sacramental wine was mixed with paint scraped from the figures of saints, and the consecrated bread was placed on the hand of the image to make it co-partaker in the sacrament.—Neander, iii. 546.

rather than from religious opinions, though the zeal of these ecclesiastics rendered them eager to be considered as martyrs.[1]

The marriage of Michael with Euphrosyne, the daughter of Constantine VI., who had already taken the veil, was also made a ground for exciting public reprobation against the emperor. It is probable, however, that more importance is given to this marriage, as a violation of religion, by later writers, than it received among contemporaries. The Patriarch absolved Euphrosyne from her vows, and the senate repeatedly solicited the emperor to unite himself with the last scion of Leo the Isaurian, the second founder of the Eastern Empire. Michael affected to be averse to second marriages, and to yield only to the public wish. That the marriage of the emperor with a nun excited the animosity of the monks, who regarded marriage as an evil, and second marriages as a delict, is very natural; and it would, of course, supply a fertile source of calumnious gossip to the enemies of the Amorian dynasty.

Michael II. died in October, 829, and was buried in a sarcophagus of green Thessalian marble, in the sepulchral chapel erected by Justinian in the Church of the Holy Apostles.[2]

SECTION II

THEOPHILUS, A.D. 829–842

Anecdotes concerning the Emperor's love of justice—Concerning his marriage—Ecclesiastical persecution—Love of art—Colony on the Don—Saracen war—Theophilus destroys Zapetra—Motassem destroys Amorium—Death of Theophilus.

No emperor ever ascended the throne of Constantinople with greater personal and political advantages than Theophilus. His education had been the best the age could supply, and he possessed considerable talent and industry. The general direction of his education had been intrusted to John the Grammarian, one of the most accomplished as well as the most learned men of the time.[3] In arts and

[1] Contin. *Scrip. post Theoph.* 31. Genesius, 23.
[2] Contin. *Scrip. post Theoph.* 52.
[3] John Hylilas, as has been already mentioned, page 110, was called Lekanomant by the people, because he was said to use a polished basin for the purpose of divination. He was Patriarch of Constantinople from 832 to 842. He was a member of the distinguished family of the Morocharzanians.—Contin. 96. Cedrenus, 536. St. Martin conjectures that this family was of Armenian origin, and his brother's name was Arsaber, which, at least, is an Armenian name.—Contin. 97. Lebeau, xiii. 14.

arms, in law and theology, the emperor was equally well instructed: his taste made him a lover of poetry, music, and architecture; his courage rendered him a brave soldier, his sense of justice a sound legislator; but his theology made him a stern bigot; and a discontented temperament of mind prevented his accomplishments and virtues from producing a harmonious union. All acknowledged his merit, none seemed affectionately attached to his person; and in the midst of his power he was called the Unfortunate. During his father's lifetime he had been intrusted with an active share in the government, and had devoted particular attention to the ecclesiastical department. He embraced the party of the Iconoclasts with fervour; and though his father endeavoured to moderate his zeal, his influence seems to have produced the isolated acts of persecution during the reign of Michael, which were at variance with that emperor's general policy.

Theophilus observed that the population of the empire was everywhere suffering from the defects of the central government, and he was anxious to remedy the evil. He erroneously attributed the greatest part of the sufferings of the people to the corruption of the administration, instead of ascribing it to the fact that the central authorities assumed duties which they were unable to execute, and prevented local bodies, who could easily have performed these duties in an efficient manner, from attempting to undertake them. Theophilus, however, justly believed that a great reform might be effected by improving the administration of justice, and he set about the task with vigour; still many of his measures for enforcing equitable conduct on the part of the judges were so strongly marked with personality, that his severity, even when necessary, was stigmatised as cruel. He was in the habit of riding through the streets of Constantinople on a weekly visit to the church of St. Mary at Blachern, in order to afford his subjects a public opportunity of presenting such petitions as might otherwise never reach his hands.[1] The practice is perpetuated in the Othoman empire to this day. The sultan pays a public visit to one of the principal mosques of his capital weekly for the same purpose. In both cases it may be received as a proof of the want of a better and more systematic control over the judicial administration of a mighty empire. There was no emperor, in the reign of Theophilus,

---

[1] Contin. *Scrip. post Theoph.* 53.

to parade the streets of provincial towns, where control was most wanted; and there is no substitute for the sultan's procession to the mosque in the provincial cities of Turkey.

The first proof Theophilus gave of his love of justice was so strangely chosen, that it was represented as originating in the wish to get rid of some dangerous courtiers, rather than in a sense of equity. He assembled the senate, and, exhibiting to its astonished members the candelabrum of which one of the branches had been struck off at the assassination of Leo V., he demanded whether the laws of the empire and divine justice did not both call for the punishment of the men who had committed the double sacrilege of murdering their emperor, and shedding his blood before the altar. Some senators, prepared for the scene, suggested that, in order to avert the vengeance of Heaven, it was necessary to put the traitors to death. Theophilus immediately ordered the prefect of Constantinople to arrest every person concerned in Leo's assassination and bring them to trial, whether they belonged to the party of the image-worshippers or of the Greek ecclesiastics. They were all convicted, and executed in the Hippodrome, vainly protesting against the injustice of their sentence, since their deed had been ratified and pardoned by the Emperor Michael II., and the reigning emperor confirmed that ratification by enjoying the profit of their act.[1]

Other examples of the emperor's severity were less liable to suspicion. A poor widow accused Petronas, the emperor's brother-in-law, an officer of talents and courage, of having, in violation of law, raised his house so high as to render hers almost uninhabitable from want of air and light. The laws concerning the disposition of private buildings in Constantinople were always regarded as an important object of imperial legislation. Theophilus ordered the grievance to be redressed; but the complaint was subsequently reiterated, and the emperor discovered that his brother-in-law had disobeyed his decision. He now gave orders that the newly-built house should be levelled with the ground, and condemned Petronas to be scourged in the public highway.[2] Some time after this, Petronas was appointed to the high post

---

[1] Leo Grammaticus, 449, edit. Par.; 214, edit. Bonn.
[2] The law of Zeno, giving the rules to be followed in constructing private houses at Constantinople, is contained in the *Corpus Juris Civilis—Cod. Just.* viii. 10-12, *De Ædificiis Privatis.* Dirksen has published a memoir containing much information explanatory of this law, in the Transactions of the Berlin Academy for 1844: it is entitled, *Das Polizei-Gesetz des Kaisers Zeno über die bauliche Aulage der Privathäuser in Constantinople.*

of governor of Cherson, and during the reign of his nephew, Michael III., he defeated the Saracens in an important battle in Asia Minor, as will be hereafter related. This anecdote illustrates the state of society at the Byzantine court, by the contrast it presents between the servile feelings of the Romans and Greeks of Constantinople, and the independent spirit of the Franks and Germans of western Europe. In the Eastern Empire the shame of blows was nothing, and a bastinado inflicted on an emperor's brother-in-law, who retained his official rank, was not likely to be a very painful operation. The degradation of the punishment was effaced by the arbitrary nature of the power that inflicted it. The sense of justice inherent in mankind is always wounded by the infliction of arbitrary punishment; cruelty or caprice are supposed to dictate the sentence; the public attention is averted from the crime, and pity is often created when the sufferer really deserves to be branded with infamy.

On another occasion, as Theophilus rode through the streets, a man stepped forward, and, laying his hand on the horse the emperor was riding, exclaimed, "This horse is mine, O emperor!" On investigating the circumstances, it appeared that the horse had really been taken by force from its proprietor by an officer of rank, who wished to present it to the emperor on account of its beauty. This act of violence was also punished, and the proprietor received two pounds' weight of gold as an indemnity for the loss he had sustained. The horse was worth about one hundred byzants.[1]

Theophilus was also indefatigable in examining the police details of the capital, and looking into the state of the markets. It is true that the abundance of provisions, and their price at Constantinople, was a matter of great importance to the Byzantine government, which, like the Roman, too often sacrificed the prosperity of the provinces to the tranquillity of the capital; yet still the minute attention which Theophilus gave to performing the duties of a prefect, indicate that he was deficient in the grasp of intellect required for the clear perception of the duties of an emperor.

The reign of Theophilus was an age of anecdotes and tales. It had many poetic aspirations, smothered in chronicles and legends of saints. Volumes of tales were then current which would have given us a better insight into Byzantine manners

---

[1] Seventy-two or seventy-four byzants weighed a pound.—Leo Gramm. 454.

than the folios of the historians, who have preserved an outline of a few of these stories. Theophilus seems to have been a kind of Byzantine Haroun Al Rashid. Unfortunately the Iconoclasts appear to have embodied more of this species of literature in their habits than the orthodox, who delighted in silly legends concerning saints rather than in imaginative pictures of the deeds of men; and thus the mirror of truth has perished, while the fables that have been preserved are neglected from their unnatural stupidity.[1]

Theophilus was unmarried when he ascended the throne, and he found difficulty in choosing a wife.[2] At last he arranged with his stepmother, Euphrosyne, a project for enabling him to make a suitable selection, or at least to make his choice from a goodly collection. The empress-mother invited all the most beautiful and accomplished virgins at Constantinople to a fête in her private apartments. When the gaiety of the assembled beauties had removed their first shyness, Theophilus entered the rooms, and walked forward with a golden apple in his hand. Struck by the grace and beauty of Eikasia, with whose features he must have been already acquainted, and of whose accomplishments he had often heard, he stopped to address her. The proud beauty felt herself already an empress; but Theophilus commenced his conversation with the ungallant remark, "Woman is the source of evil;" to which the young lady too promptly replied, "But woman is also the cause of much good." The answer or the tone jarred on the captious mind of the emperor, and he walked on. His eye then fell on the modest features of the young Theodora, whose eyes were fixed on the ground. To her he gave the apple without risking a word. Eikasia, who for a moment had felt the throb of gratified ambition, could not recover from the shock. She retired into a monastery which she founded, and passed her life dividing her time between the practice of devotion and the cultivation of her mind. She composed some hymns, which continued long in use in the Greek church.[3] A short time after this, the Empress Euphrosyne retired into the monastery of Gastria,

---

[1] I presume few persons have now either time or opportunity to read much of the *Acta Sanctorum*, fifty-three volumes of which were published at Antwerp from 1643 to 1793. This only goes as far as the 14th of October; yet much of the social history of the middle ages can be sought for in no other source.

[2] It seems probable he was a widower, from the age of his daughters. See page 143, note 2.

[3] Zonaras, ii. 141. Codinus, *De Orig. Const.* 61, 104. Banduri, *Imp. Orientale*, ii. 717, ed. Par.; 527, ed. Ven.

an agreeable retreat, selected also by Theoctista, the mother
of Theodora, as her residence.[1]

Theodora herself is the heroine of another tale, illustrating
the corruption of the officials about the court, and the in-
flexible love of justice of the emperor. The courtiers in the
service of the imperial family had been in the habit of drawing large profits from evading the custom-duties to which
other traders were liable, by engaging the emperor-colleague
or the empress in commercial adventures. The revenue of
the state and the commerce of the honest merchant both
suffered by this aristocratic mode of trading. Theophilus,
who knew of the abuse, learned that the young empress had
been persuaded to lend her name to one of these trading
speculations, and that a ship, laden with a valuable cargo in
her name, was about to arrive at Constantinople. In order
to put an end to these frauds by a striking example, he took
care to be informed as this ship entered the port. When this
vessel arrived, it displayed the imperial standard, and stood
proudly towards the public warehouses with a fair wind.
Theophilus, who had led the court to a spot overlooking the
port, pretending to be struck by the gallant appearance of
the vessel, demanded with what military stores she was laden,
and whence she came. The truth was soon elicited, and
when he obtained a full confession of the nature of the cargo,
he ordered it to be landed and publicly burned; for he said,
it was never heard that a Roman emperor or empress turned
trader.[2]

The principles of toleration which had guided the imperial
administration during the preceding reigns were not entirely
laid aside by Theophilus, and though his religious bigotry was
strong, he preferred punishing the image-worshippers for disobedience to the civil laws to persecuting them for their
ecclesiastical opinions. The emperor's own prejudices in
favour of the divine right of kings were as intolerant as his
aversion to image-worship, so that he may really have acted
as much on political as religious grounds. His father had
not removed pictures from the walls of churches when they
were placed in elevated situations; and had Theophilus
followed his example, Iconoclasts and image - worshippers

---

[1] Contin. 56. Gastria was certainly not selected as a place of exile, as modern
writers have supposed, or Euphrosyne would, in all probability, have been sent back to
the monastery at Prince's Island, which she had quitted to ascend the throne.
[2] Contin. 55. Zonaras, ii. 143. The reference to Syria by Zonaras is, as Schlosser
observes, a mistake originating in the ἐξ οὐρίας of the elder historian.

might at last have accepted the compromise, and dwelt peaceably together in the Eastern church. The monks, too, had been wisely allowed considerable latitude within the walls of their monasteries, though they were forbidden to preach publicly to the people in favour of image-worship. Theophilus was inclined to imitate the policy of Leo the Isaurian, but he could not venture to dissolve the refractory monasteries and imprison the monks. The government of the earlier Iconoclasts reposed on an army organised by themselves, and ready to enforce all their orders; but in the time of Theophilus, the army neither possessed the same power over society, nor was it equally devoted to the emperor.

In the year 832, an edict was issued prohibiting every display of picture-worship, and commanding that the word *holy*, usually placed in letters of gold before the name of a saint, should be erased. This edict was at times carried into execution in an arbitrary and oppressive manner, and caused discontent and opposition.[1] A celebrated painter of ecclesiastical subjects, named Lazaros, who acquired great fame during the reign of Michael III., was imprisoned and scourged, but subsequently released from confinement at the intercession of Theodora.[2] Two monks, Theophanes the Singer and Theodore Graptos, were much more cruelly treated, for, in addition to other tortures, some verses were branded on the forehead of Theodore, who from that circumstance received his surname of Graptos.[3]

Some time after the publication of this edict against image-worship, John the Grammarian was elected Patriarch. Though a decided opponent of image-worship, he was a man of a larger intellect and more tolerant disposition than his imperial pupil, over whose mind, however, he fortunately retained considerable influence.[4] Still, when the emperor found his edict unavailing, he compelled the Patriarch to assemble a synod,

[1] Contin. 62. Cedrenus, 514.
[2] Lazaros painted a picture of St. John the Baptist while he was suffering from the stripes he received, which was reported to have performed many miraculous cures.
[3] Schlosser, *Geschichte der bild. Kaiser*, 553.
[4] The chronology of John's patriarchate presents some difficulties. Schlosser places his election in 833—see his note, page 486. Pagi and Banduri in 832.—*Imp. Orient*, ii. 908. The length of his patriarchate is given differently in the various lists we possess. Some fix it at nine years. Zonaras, ii. 153, says he was only six years Patriarch. Symeon Mag., 421, says he was elected the eighth year of Theophilus. These two writers consequently place his election in 837. The continuator (*Scrip post Theophanem*, 75) says he was elected on Sunday, 21st April. Now it appears from *L'Art de Vérifier les Dates* that Easter Sunday fell on the 21st of April in 832 and 838, and not in any intermediate year. The embassy of John to Bagdat preceded his election. It is placed by Symeon Mag., 419, in the fifth year of Theophilus. Weil, *Geschichte der Chalifen*, ii. 297, considers that it occurred at the end of the year 833.

which was induced to excommunicate all image-worshippers. As the Patriarch was averse to these violent proceedings, it can hardly be supposed that they produced much effect within the pale of the church; but they certainly tended to inflame the zeal of those marked out for persecution, and strengthened the minds of the orthodox to perform what they considered to be their duty, arming them with faith to resist the civil power. The spirit of religious strife was awakened, and the emperor was so imprudent as to engage personally in controversies with monks and priests. These discussions ruffled his temper and increased his severity, by exposing the lofty pretensions he entertained of his dignity and talents to be wounded by men who gloried in displaying their contempt for all earthly power. Theophilus sought revenge for his injured vanity. The monks who persisted in publicly displaying images and pictures were driven from their monasteries; and many members of the clergy, distinguished for learning and beloved for virtue, were imprisoned and scourged. Yet, even during the height of his resentment, the emperor winked at the superstition of those who kept their opinions private, tolerated the prejudices of the Empress Theodora, and at her request released Methodios, the future Patriarch of Constantinople, from prison.[1]

The wealth of the Byzantine empire was at this period very great, and its industry in the most flourishing condition. Theophilus, though engaged in expensive and disastrous wars, found the imperial revenue so much increased by the augmented commerce of his subjects, that he was able to indulge an inordinate passion for pomp and display. His love of art was gratified by the fantastic employment of rich materials in luxurious ornament, rather than by durable works of useful grandeur. His architectural taste alone took a direction at times advantageous to the public. The walls of Constantinople towards the sea were strengthened, and their height increased. He founded an hospital, which remained one of

---

[1] Gibbon, *Decline and Fall*, ix. 42, has exaggerated the cruelty of the punishments inflicted by Theophilus. Schlosser, 524, remarks that he has found no authority to authorise the reproaches of excessive tyranny. Even the Jesuit Maimbourg, *Histoire de l'Hérésie des Iconoclastes*, ii. 233, mentions the imprisonment of Methodios with a dead robber, and the branding verses on the foreheads of Theodore and Theophanes, (if the latter suffered this punishment,) as the most inhuman acts of Theophilus. Contin. 65.

The story that Theodora persuaded her husband to believe that some images of saints in her possession were only dolls for her children's amusement, is a popular anecdote more deserving of a place in the dull Legends of the Saints than in the Byzantine tales.

the most useful institutions of the city to the latest days of Byzantine history;[1] but, at the same time, he gratified his love of display in architecture, by constructing palaces, at an enormous expense, in no very durable manner. One of these, built in imitation of the great palace of the caliphs at Bagdat, was erected at Bryas, on the Asiatic shore.[2] The varied form, the peculiar arches, the coloured decorations, the mathematical tracery, and the rich gilding, had induced John the Grammarian, when he visited the Caliph Motassem as ambassador from Theophilus, to bring back drawings and plans of this building, which was totally different from the Byzantine style then in use. Other buildings constructed by Theophilus are described by historians in a way that indicates they must have been far superior in magnificence to the works of preceding or following emperors.[3]

Theophilus was also an enthusiastic admirer of music, and as church-music was in his time one of the principal amusements of persons of taste, musical science was devoted to add to the grandeur and solemnity of ecclesiastical ceremonies. In works of art, the emperor's taste appears not to have been very pure. A puerile vanity induced him to lavish enormous sums in fabricating gorgeous toys of jewellery. In these ornaments, singular mechanical contrivances were combined with rich figures to astonish the spectator. A golden plane-tree, covered with innumerable artificial birds, that warbled and fluttered their wings on its branches, vultures that screamed, and lions that roared, stood at the entrance of the hall of state. Invisible organs, that filled the ceilings of the apartments with soft melody, were among the strange things that Theophilus placed in the great palace of Constantinople. They doubtless formed the theme of many Byzantine tales, of which we still see a reflected image in the Arabian Nights.[4]

Two laws of Theophilus deserve especial notice: one exhibits him in the character of a capricious tyrant; the other reveals the extent to which elements adverse to Roman and Greek nationality pervaded Byzantine society. The first of these edicts ordered all the Romans—that is, all the subjects

---

[1] Codinus, *De Orig. Const.* 28. Banduri, *Imp. Orient.* ii. 648.
[2] Contin. 61. Ducange, *Const. Christ.* lib. iv. 177.
[3] Symeon Mag., 450, tells us that Leo, a great mathematician, invented a kind of telegraph, with a dial, in the palace of Theophilus in Constantinople, which reported the news transmitted from the Cilician frontier by fire-signals to the Bosphorus.
[4] Cont. 107; Leo Gramm. 450; Const. Manasses, 107; Glycas, 292; Cedrenus, Zonaras, and the later writers. Many of these works were executed under the direction of John Hylilas and Leo the Mathematician.—See *post.*

of the empire,—to wear their hair cropped short, under the pain of the bastinado. Theophilus pretended that he wished to restore old Roman fashions, but the world believed that the flowing locks of others rendered him ashamed of his own bald head. The other law declared that the marriage of Persians and Romans did in no way derogate from the rights of those who were citizens of the empire; and it shows that a very great emigration of Persian Christians from the dominions of the caliphs must have taken place, or such a law would not have become necessary. Theophobus, one of the most distinguished leaders of the Persians, who claimed descent from the Sassanides, married Helena, the emperor's sister.[1]

The wide extended frontiers of the empire required Theophilus to maintain relations with the sovereigns of a large portion of Asia and Europe. To secure allies against his great enemy, the Caliph of Bagdat, he renewed the ancient alliance of the emperors of Constantinople with the sovereign of the Khazars; but this people was now too much occupied in defending its own territories against a new race of intruders, called Patzinaks, to renew their invasions of the northern provinces of the Mohammedan empire. The progress of the Patzinaks alarmed Theophilus for the security of the Byzantine commerce with the northern nations, from which the imperial treasury drew immense duties; and he sent his brother-in-law Petronas (whom, as we have mentioned, he had condemned to be scourged) to Cherson, which was then a free city like Venice, with orders to construct a fortress on the banks of the Don. This commercial colony, called Sarkel, was used as the trading depot with the north.[2] A friendly intercourse was kept up with Louis le Debonnaire and his son Lothaire. The Venetians were invited to assist in the naval war for the defence of Sicily and southern Italy against the Saracens of Africa.[3] An embassy was sent to Abderrahman II., the caliph of Spain, to secure the commerce of the Greeks in the West from any interruption, and to excite the Ommiad caliph to hostilities against the Abassides of Bagdat.[4]

When Theophilus ascended the throne, the Byzantine and

---

[1] Contin. 67-70.
[2] Cherson was then governed by a president and senate, elected by the citizens, and no governor was sent from Constantinople. Theophilus succeeded in reducing it to complete dependence.—See *post*. Contin. 76. Constant. Porphyr. *De Adm. Imp.* ii. chap. 42. Now Bielaveja, near Tcherkask, the capital of the Don Cossacks. Lehrberg, *Untersuchungen zur erläuterung der ältern Geschichte Russlands.* Petersburg, 1816. Cedrenus, 415. [3] Dandolo, *Chron.* viii. 4-6.
[4] Murphy's *History of the Mohammedan Empire in Spain*, 93; A.D. 839.

Saracen empires enjoyed peace; but they were soon involved in a fierce contest, which bears some resemblance to the mortal combat between the Roman and Persian empires in the time of Heraclius. Almamun, who ruled the caliphate from 813 to 833, was a magnificent and liberal sovereign, distinguished for his love of science and literature, and eager to surpass the Greeks in knowledge and the Romans in arms. Though not himself a soldier, his armies were commanded by several celebrated generals. The want of a moral check on the highest officials of arbitrary governments usually prevents the existence of a sense of duty in political relations, and hence rebellions and civil wars become prevalent. In the reign of Almamun, the disturbances in Persia reduced the population, whether fire-worshippers or Christians, to despair; and a great number, unable to live in their native country, escaped into the Byzantine empire, and established themselves at Sinope. This immigration seems to have consisted chiefly of Christians, who feared equally the government of Almamun and the rebel Babek, who, though preaching the equality of all mankind, was accused of allowing every license to his own followers. The Persian troops at Sinope were placed under the command of Theophobos, and their number was increased by an addition of seven thousand men, when Afshin, the general of the Caliph Motassem, defeated Babek, and extinguished the civil war in Persia.[1]

The protection granted by Theophilus to refugees from the caliph's dominions, induced Almamun to invade the empire in the year 831; and the Saracen general, Abu Chazar, completely defeated the Byzantine army, commanded by Theophilus in person. The emperor repaired this disgrace in the following year by gaining a victory over the Saracens in Charsiana, which he celebrated with great pomp and vainglory in the hippodrome of Constantinople.[2] Almamun revenged the defeat of his generals by putting himself at the head of his army, ravaging Cappadocia, and capturing Heracleia.

[1] The Babek who is said by the Byzantine historians to have fled into the empire with seven thousand followers, was certainly a different person from the celebrated leader of the rebellion. The arrival of this refugee is placed before the commencement of the war between Theophilus and Almamun, A.D. 831. The great rebel Babek sustained an important defeat in 833, when many of his followers fled into Armenia and the Byzantine provinces, according to the Arabian historians; but he still continued the war in Adzerbijan.—Compare Contin. 70; Symeon Mag. 415; Cedrenus, ii. 523; and Weil, *Geschichte der Chalifen*, ii. 239.

[2] Constant. Porphyr. *De Ceremoniis Aulæ Byzantinæ*, 290, edit. Leich; tom. i. 503, edit. Bonn. Reiske considers that this account of the triumph of Theophilus refers to his return after the destruction of Zapetra.—Tom. ii. 590.

The armies of the Byzantine empire at this period consisted in great part of foreign mercenaries. Some secondary causes, connected with the development of society, which have escaped the notice of historians, operated to render the recruitment of armies more than usually difficult among the civilised portions of mankind, and caused all the powerful sovereigns of the age to exclude their native subjects as much as possible from the use of arms. In the Saracen empire this feeling led to the transference of all military power into the hands of Turkish mercenaries; and in the Frank empire it led to the exposure of the country, without defence, to the incursions of the Normans. It is true that jealousy of the Arab aristocracy in one case, and fear of the hostile disposition of the Romanised population in the other, had considerable influence on the conduct of the caliphs and the Western emperors. The Byzantine empire, though under the influence of similar tendencies, was saved from a similar fate by a higher degree of political civilisation. The distrust of Theophilus for his generals was shown by the severity with which he treated them. Manuel, one of the best officers of the empire, disgusted at his suspicions, fled to the Saracens, and served with distinction in their armies against the rebels of Chorasan.[1] Alexis Mousel, an Armenian, who received the favourite daughter of Theophilus in marriage, with the rank of Cæsar, was degraded and scourged in consequence of his father-in-law's suspicions.[2]

Immediately after the death of Almamun, the emperor sent John the Grammarian on an embassy to Motassem, who had succeeded his brother as caliph. The object of this embassy was to conclude a lasting peace, and at all events to persuade Manuel, whose fame in the war of Chorasan had reached the ears of Theophilus, to return home. With the caliph the negotiations appear not to have been as successful as the emperor expected, but with Manuel they succeeded perfectly. The magnificence of John on this occasion gave rise to many wonderful tales, and the Greeks were long amused by the

---

[1] See the romantic account of the exploits of Manuel, which, as they set chronology at defiance, cannot be received as historical.—Contin. 74; Cedrenus. ii. 527.

[2] It would seem that Theophilus had been married before his father's death. Maria the wife of Alexios was the youngest of five daughters, and her marriage, even according to Symeon Mag., who says she was the daughter of Theodora, took place in the third year of the reign of Theophilus, (417, 418). We must suppose that Theophilus had two wives named Theodora, and was a widower at his father's death, after which he married the second. But even then difficulties will be found, and the chronology of this period is singularly confused. Thekla, the eldest daughter of Theophilus, received the imperial title from her father before the birth of Michael III.

accounts of the marvellous wealth displayed by the priestly ambassador.

Not very long after this embassy, Theophilus, availing himself of the troubles occasioned in the caliph's dominions by the civil wars arising out of the heretical opinions concerning the human composition of the Koran, which had been favoured by Almamun, invaded the caliph's dominions. The Byzantine troops ravaged the country to the south of Melitene, anciently called Commagene, defeated the Saracens with great loss, captured Zapetra, and penetrated as far as Samosata, which Theophilus also took and destroyed. Zapetra, or Sosopetra, lay about two days' journey to the west of the road from Melitene to Samosata.[1] The Greeks pretended that it was the birthplace of Motassem, and that the caliph sent an embassy to the emperor entreating him to spare the town, which he offered to ransom at any price; but Theophilus dismissed the ambassadors and razed Zapetra to the ground.[2] This campaign seems to have been remarkable for the cruelty with which the Mohammedans were treated, and the wanton ravages committed by the Persian emigrants in the Byzantine service. The Saracens repeated one of the tales in connection with this expedition which was current among their countrymen, and applied, as occasion served, from the banks of the Guadalquivir to those of the Indus. In Spain it was told of Al Hakem, in Asia of Motassem. A female prisoner, when insulted by a Christian soldier, was reported to have exclaimed in her agony, "Oh, shame on Motassem!"[3] The circumstance was repeated to the caliph, who learned at the same time that the unfortunate woman was of the tribe of Hashem, and consequently, according to the clannish feelings of the Arabs, a member of his own family. Motassem swore by the Prophet he would do everything in his power to revenge her.

In the mean time Theophilus, proud of his easy victories, returned to Constantinople, and instead of strengthening his frontier, and placing strong garrisons near the mountain-passes, brought his best troops to Constantinople to attend on his own person. As he entered the hippodrome in a chariot

[1] Abulfeda, cited by Weil, ii. 309, note 2.
[2] Contin. 77. Genesius, 31, says it was the birthplace of Motassem's mother. Symeon Mag., 421, places the destruction of Zapetra in the seventh year of Theophilus.
[3] Gibbon, x. 68. The story, as told of Motassem, is given by Price, *Mohammedan History*, ii. 147; as told of Al Hakem, by Murphy, *History of the Mohammedan Empire in Spain*, 90.

drawn by four white horses, wearing the colours of the blue
faction, his happy return was hailed by the people with loud
shouts. His welcome was more like that of a successful
charioteer than of a victorious general.

The Persian mercenaries, whose number had now increased
to thirty thousand, were placed in winter-quarters at Sinope
and Amastris, where they began to display a seditious spirit;
for Theophilus could neither trust his generals nor acquire the
confidence of his soldiers. These mercenaries at last broke
out into rebellion, and resolved to form a Persian kingdom in
Pontus. They proclaimed their general Theophobus king;
but that officer had no ambition to insure the ruin of his
brother-in-law's empire by grasping a doubtful sceptre; and he
sent assurances to Theophilus that he would remain faithful to
his allegiance, and do everything in his power to put an end
to the rebellion. Without much difficulty, therefore, this army
of Persians was gradually dispersed through the different
themes, but tranquillity was obtained by sacrificing the
efficiency of one of the best armies in the empire.

Motassem, having also re-established tranquillity in the
interior of his dominions, turned his whole attention to
the war with the Byzantine empire. A well-appointed army
of veterans, composed of the troops who had suppressed the
rebellion of Babek, was assembled on the frontiers of Cilicia,
and the caliph placed himself at the head of the army, on the
banks of the Cydnus, in the year 838.[1] A second army
of thirty thousand men, under Afshin, advanced into the
empire at a considerable distance to the north-east of the
grand army, under the immediate orders of the caliph.
Afshin had suppressed the rebellion of Babek after it had
lasted twenty years, and was considered the ablest general of
the Saracens. On hearing that the army of Afshin had invaded Lykandos, Theophilus intrusted the defences of the
Cilician passes, by which the caliph proposed to advance,
to Aetios, the general of the Anatolic theme, and hastened to
stop the progress of Afshin, whose army, strengthened by
a strong body of Armenians under Sembat the native governor
of the country, and by ten thousand Turkish mercenaries, who
were then considered the best troops in Asia, was overrunning

---

[1] Contin. 78. Symeon Mag. 423. This last places the defeat of Theophilus and the
death of Manuel in the ninth year of Theophilus, and the taking of Amorium in
the tenth. The reign of Theophilus commenced in October 829. They evidently occurred in one campaign, and the Arabian historians give the 23rd September, 838, as the
date of the capture of Amorium.—Weil, ii. 315.

Cappadocia. Theophilus, apprehensive that this army might turn his flank, and alarmed lest the Armenians and Persians, of which it was part composed, might seduce those of the same nations in his service, was anxious to hasten an engagement. The battle was fought at Dasymon, where the Byzantine army, commanded by Theophobus and Manuel, under the immediate orders of Theophilus, attacked the Saracens. The field was fiercely contested, and for some time it seemed as if victory would favour the Christians; but the admirable discipline of the Turkish archers decided the fate of the day. In vain the emperor exposed his person with the greatest valour to recover the advantage he had lost; Manuel was compelled to make the most desperate efforts to save him, and induce him to retreat. The greater part of the Byzantine troops fled from the field, and the Persian mercenaries alone remained to guard the emperor's person. During the night, however, Theophilus was informed that the foreigners were negotiating with the Saracens to deliver him up a prisoner, and he was compelled to mount his horse, and ride almost unattended to Chiliokomon, where a portion of the native troops of the empire had rallied.[1] From thence he retired to Donylæum, where he endeavoured to assemble an army to defend Amorium. Manuel died of the wounds he received in saving the emperor.

While Theophilus was marching to his defeat, the advanced guard of the Caliph's army, under Ashnas[2] and Wassif, threaded the Cilician passes in the direction of Tyana; and Aetios, unable to resist their advance, allowed the main body of the Saracens to penetrate into the central plains of Asia Minor without opposition. Abandoning the whole of the Anatolic theme to the invaders, he concentrated his forces under the walls of Amorium. After ravaging Lycaonia and Pisidia, Motassem marched to besiege Amorium. The capture of this city, as the birthplace of the Amorian dynasty, had been announced by the caliph to be the object of the campaign; and it was said that 130,000 men had marched out of Tarsus with AMORIUM painted on their shields. Motassem expected to carry the place by assault, and the defeat of Theophilus by his lieutenants inspired him with the hope of carrying his arms to the shores of the Bosphorus, and

---

[1] Strabo, lib. xii. 561. North of Amasir, the native place of the geographer.
[2] Ashnas was a Turk. Motassem had collected at this time about 70,000 Turks in his service.—Weil, ii. 304.

plundering the Asiatic suburb of Constantinople. But all his attempts to storm Amorium, though repeated with fresh troops on three successive days, were defeated by Aetios, who had thrown himself into the city with the best soldiers in his army, and the caliph found himself obliged to commence a regular siege. Theophilus now sued for peace. The bishop of Amorium and the leading citizens offered to capitulate, for the numerous army within the walls soon exhausted the provisions. But Motassem declared that he would neither conclude a peace nor grant terms of capitulation; vengeance was what he sought, not victory. Amorium was valiantly defended for fifty-five days, but treachery at length enabled the caliph to gratify his passion, just as he was preparing to try the fortune of a fourth general assault. The traitor who sold his post and admitted the Saracens into the city was named Voiditzes. In this case both the Christian and Mohammedan accounts agree in ascribing the success of the besiegers to treason in the Christian ranks, and the defence appears to have been conducted by Aetios both with skill and valour.[1] The cruelty of Motassem far exceeded that of Theophilus. Thirty thousand persons were massacred, and the inhabitants who were spared were sold as slaves. The city of Amorium was burned to the ground, and the walls destroyed. The ambassadors sent by Theophilus to beg for peace had been detained by the caliph, to witness his conquest. They were now sent back with this answer, "Tell your master that I have at last discharged the debt contracted at Zapetra."

Motassem, however, perceived that a considerable change had taken place in the empire since the days in which the Saracens had besieged Constantinople. He did not even consider it prudent to attempt advancing to the shores of the Bosphorus, but returned to his own dominions, carrying with him Aetios and forty officers of rank captured in Amorium. For seven years these men were vainly urged to embrace the Mohammedan faith; at last they were put to death by Vathek, the son of Motassem, and they are regarded as martyrs by the orthodox church.[2] Theophilus is said to have offered the Caliph Motassem the sum of 2400 lb. of gold to purchase peace, and the deliverance of all the Christians who had been

---

[1] Continuator, 81.
[2] Their martyrdom is celebrated on 6th March. It occurred in 845.—*Menologium Græcorum*, iii. 7.

taken prisoner during the war; but the caliph demanded in addition that a Persian refugee named Naser, and Manuel, of whose death he appears not to have been assured, should also be given up. Theophilus refused to disgrace himself by delivering up Naser, and the treaty was broken off. Naser was shortly after killed in an engagement on the frontier.

The war was prosecuted for some years in a languid manner, and success rather inclined to the Byzantine arms. The port of Antioch, on the Orontes, was taken and plundered by a Greek fleet; the province of Melitene was ravaged as far as Marash; Abou Said, who had defeated and slain Naser, was in turn himself defeated and taken prisoner. At last a truce seems to have been concluded, but no exchange of prisoners took place.[1]

Theophilus never recovered from the wound his pride received at Amorium. The frequent defeats he sustained in those battles where he was personally engaged, contrasted with the success of his generals, rankled in his melancholy disposition. His sensitive temperament and the fatigues of his campaigns undermined his health. To divert his mind, he indulged his passion for building; and so great were the resources of the Byzantine treasury, that even at this period of misfortune he could lavish enormous sums in idle ornament. It would have been well, both for him and for the Christian world, had he employed some of this wealth at an earlier period in fortifying the frontier and diminishing the burden of the land-tax. He now erected a new chapel called Triconchos, a circus for public races, a staircase called Sigma, a whispering gallery called the Mystery, and a magnificent fountain called Phiala.[2] But the emperor's health continued to decline, and he perceived that his end was not very distant.

Theophilus prepared for death with prudence and courage, but with that suspicion which disgraced his character. A council of regency was named to assist Theodora. His habitual distrust induced him to exclude Theophobos from this council. He feared lest Theophobos might seize the throne by means of the army, or establish an independent kingdom in the Armeniac theme by means of the Persian mercenaries. The conspiracy on the night after the defeat at Dasymon had augmented the jealousy with which the emperor

[1] No exchange of prisoners took place until September, 845.—Weil, ii. 343.
[2] Contin. 62, 86. Symeon Mag. 424. An account of the buildings of Theophilus will be found in the *History of Art*, by Dr. Carl Schnaase.—*Geschichte der bildenden Künste im Mittelalter. Altchristliche und Mohammedanische Kunst.* i. 151.

regarded his brother-in-law ever after the rebellion of the
Persian troops at Sinope and Amastris. He now resolved to
secure his son's throne at the expense of his own conscience,
and ordered Theophobos to be beheaded. Recollecting the
fortune of his father, and the fate of Leo the Armenian, he
commanded the head of his brother-in-law to be brought to
his bedside. The agitation of the emperor's mind, after
issuing this order, greatly increased his malady; and when
the lifeless head of his former friend was placed before him,
he gazed long and steadily at its features, his mind doubtless
wandering over the memory of many a battle-field in which
they had fought together. At last he slowly exclaimed,
"Thou art no longer Theophobos, and I am no more Theophilus:" then, turning away his head, he sank on his pillow,
and never again opened his lips.

SECTION III

MICHAEL III., (THE DRUNKARD,) A.D. 842–867

Regency of Theodora—Moral and religious reaction—Restoration of
Image-worship—Rebellion of the Sclavonians in the Peloponnesus—
Saracen war—Persecution of the Paulicians—Personal conduct of
Michael III.—Wealth in the treasury—Bardas—Ignatios and Photius
Origin of papal authority in the church—General council in 861—
Bulgarian war—Saracen war—Victory of Petronas—Russians attack
Constantinople—State of the court—Assassinations—Origin of the
tale of Belisarius—Assassination of Michael III. by Basil the
Macedonian.

Michael the son of Theophilus was between three and four
years old when his father died. His mother Theodora, having
been crowned empress, was regent in her own right. The will
of her husband had joined with her, as a council of administration, Theoktistos, the ablest statesman in the empire;
Manuel, the uncle of the empress; and Bardas, her brother.[1]
Thekla, an elder sister of Michael, had also received the title
of Empress before her father's death.

The great struggle between the Iconoclasts and the image-
worshippers was terminated during the regency of Theodora,
and she is consequently regarded by the orthodox as a pattern
of excellence, though she countenanced the vices of her son,

---

[1] Theoktistos was a eunuch, and held the office of logothetes of the dromos,—a kind
of postmaster-general. He was made kanicleios, or keeper of the purple ink, with
which the emperor signed. The postmaster was a most important officer in the Saracen
as well as in the Byzantine empire at this time.

by being present at his most disgraceful scenes of debauchery. The most remarkable circumstance, at the termination of this long religious contest, is the immorality which invaded all ranks of society. The moral and religious sincerity and strictness which, during the government of the early Icono-clasts, had raised the empire from the verge of social dissolu-tion to dignity and strength, had subsequently been supplanted by a degree of cant and hypocrisy that became at last intolerable. The sincerity of both the ecclesiastical parties, in their early contests, obtained for them the respect of the people; but when the political question concerning the sub-jection of the ecclesiastical to the civil power became the principal object of dispute, official tyranny and priestly am-bition only used a hypocritical veil of religious phrases for the purpose of concealing their interested ends from popular scrutiny. As usual, the people saw much farther than their rulers supposed, and the consequence was that, both parties being suspected of hypocrisy, the influence of true religion was weakened, and the most sacred ties of society rent asunder. The Byzantine clergy showed themselves ready on all occasions to flatter the vices of the civil government: the monks were eager for popular distinction, and acted the part of dema-gogues; while servile prelates and seditious monks were both equally indifferent to alleviating the people's burdens.

Every rank of society at last proclaimed that it was weary of religious discussion and domestic strife. Indifference to the ecclesiastical questions so long predominant, produced indifference to religion itself, and the power of conscience became dormant; enjoyment was soon considered the object of life; and vice, under the name of pleasure, became the fashion of the day. In this state of society, of which the germs were visible in the reign of Theophilus, superstition was sure to be more powerful than religion. It was easier to pay adoration to a picture, to reverence a relic, or to observe a ceremony, than to regulate one's conduct in life by the principles of morality and the doctrines of religion. Pictures, images, relics, and ceremonies became consequently the great objects of veneration. The Greek population of the empire had identified its national feelings with traditional usages rather than with Christian doctrines, and its opposition to the Asiatic puritanism of the Isaurian, Armenian, and Amorian emperors, ingrafted the reverence for relics, the adoration of pictures and the worship of saints, into the religious fabric of the Eastern church, as essentials of Christian worship. Whatever the church has gained in this way, in the amount of popular devotion, seems to have been lost to popular morality.

The senate at this time possessed considerable influence in administrative business. It was called upon to ratify the will of Theophilus, and a majority of its members were gained over to the party of the empress, who was known to favour image-worship.[1] The people of Constantinople had always been of this party; and the Iconoclasts of the higher ranks, tired of the persecutions which had been the result of the ecclesiastical quarrel, desired peace and toleration more than victory. The Patriarch, John the Grammarian, and some of the highest dignitaries in the church, were, nevertheless, conscientiously opposed to a species of devotion which they thought too closely resembled idolatry, and from them no public compliance could be expected. Manuel, however, the only member of the regency who had been a fervent Inconoclast, suddenly abandoned the defence of his opinions; and his change was so unexpected that it was reported he had been converted by a miracle. A sudden illness brought him to the point of death, when the prayers and the images of the monks of Studion as suddenly restored him to health. Such was the belief of the people of Constantinople, and it must have been a belief extremely profitable to the monks.

It was necessary to hold a general council in order to effect the restoration of image-worship; but to do this as long as John the Grammarian remained Patriarch was evidently impossible. The regency, however, ordered him to convoke a synod, and invite to it all the bishops and abbots sequestered as image-worshippers, or else to resign the patriarchate. John refused both commands, and a disturbance occurred, in which he was wounded by the imperial guards. The court party spread a report that he had wounded himself in an attempt to commit suicide—the greatest crime a Christian could commit. The great mechanical knowledge of John, and his studies in natural philosophy, were already considered by the ignorant as criminal in an ecclesiastic; so that the calumnious accusation, like that already circulated of his magical powers, found ready credence among the orthodox Greeks. The court seized the opportunity of deposing him. He was first exiled to a monastery, and subsequently, on an accusation that he had picked out the eyes in a picture of a saint, he was scourged, and his own eyes were put out. His mental superiority was perhaps as much the cause of his persecution as his religious opinions.

Methodios, who had been released from imprisonment by Theophilus at the intercession of Theodora, was named Patriarch, and a council of the church was held at Constantinople in 842, to which all the exiled bishops, abbots, and monks who had distinguished themselves as confessors in the cause of image-worship were admitted. Those bishops who remained firm to their Iconoclastic opinions were expelled from their Sees, and replaced by the most eminent confessors. The practices and doctrines of the Iconoclasts were formally anathematised, and banished for ever from the orthodox church. A crowd of monks descended from the secluded monasteries of Olympus, Ida, and Athos, to revive the enthusiasm of the people in favour of images, pictures, and relics; and the last remains of traditional idolatry were carefully interwoven with the established religion in the form of the legendary history of the saints.[1]

A singular scene was enacted in this synod by the Empress Theodora. She presented herself to the assembled clergy, and asked for an act declaring that the church pardoned all the sins of her deceased husband, with a certificate that divine grace had effaced the record of his persecutions. When she saw dissatisfaction visible in the looks of a majority of the members, she threatened, with frank simplicity, that if they would not do her that favour, she would not employ her influence as empress and regent to give them the victory over the Iconoclasts, but would leave the affairs of the church in their actual situation. The Patriarch Methodios answered, that the church was bound to employ its influence in relieving the souls of orthodox princes from the pains of hell, but, unfortunately, the prayers of the church had no power to obtain forgiveness from God for those who died without the pale of orthodoxy. The church was only intrusted with the keys of heaven to open and shut the gates of salvation to the living—the dead were beyond its help. Theodora, however, determined to secure the services of the church for her deceased husband. She declared that in his last agony Theophilus had received and kissed an image she laid on his breast. Although it was more than probable that the agony had really passed before the occurrence happened, her

[1] Genesius, 39.

statement satisfied Methodios and the synod, who consented to absolve its dead emperor from excommunication as an Iconoclast, and admit him into the bosom of the orthodox church, declaring that, things having happened as the Empress Theodora certified in a written attestation, Theophilus had found pardon from God.[1]

The victory of the image-worshippers was celebrated by the installation of the long-banished pictures in the church of St. Sophia, on the 19th February, 842, just thirty days after the death of Theophilus. This festival continues to be observed in the Greek church as the feast of orthodoxy on the first Sunday in Lent.[2]

The first military expedition of the regency was to repress a rebellion of the Sclavonians in the Peloponnesus, which had commenced during the reign of Theophilus. On this occasion the mass of the Sclavonian colonists was reduced to complete submission, and subjected to the regular system of taxation; but two tribes settled on Mount Taygetus, the Ezerits and Melings, succeeded in retaining a certain degree of independence, governing themselves according to their own usages, and paying only a fixed annual tribute. For the Ezerits this tribute amounted to three hundred pieces of gold, and for the Melings to the trifling sum of sixty. The general who commanded the Byzantine troops on this occasion was Theoktistos Briennios, who held the office of protospatharios.[3]

In the mean time Theoktistos the regent, anxious to obtain that degree of power and influence which, in the Byzantine as in the Roman empire, was inseparable from military renown, took the command of a great expedition into Cholcis, to conquer the Abasges. His fleet was destroyed by a tempest, and his troops were defeated by the enemy. In order to regain the reputation he had lost, he made an attempt in the following year to reconquer the island of Crete from the Saracens. But while he was engaged in the siege of Chandax, (Candia,) the report of a revolution at Constantinople induced him to quit his army, in order to look after his personal interests and political intrigues. The troops suffered severely after they were

[1] Continuator, 95.
[2] Pagi ad Baron. xiv. 266, note xv. The Patriarch Methodios did not escape the calumny which had been employed by his partisans against his predecessor. An accusation of adultery was brought against him, but the Patriarch is said to have proved its falsity to the assembled clergy in a singular manner.—Continuator, 99.
[3] Constantine Porphyr. De Adm. Imp. chap. 50. This Theoktistos must not be confounded with the regent, who never returned successful from any expedition.—Contin. 126.

abandoned by their general, whom they were compelled at last to follow.[1]

The war with the caliph of Bagdat still continued, and the destruction of a Saracen fleet, consisting of four hundred galleys, by a tempest off Cape Chelidonia, in the Kibyrraiot theme, consoled the Byzantine government for its other losses. The caliph had expected, by means of this great naval force, to secure the command of the Archipelago, and assist the operations of his armies in Asia Minor. The hostilities on the Cilician frontier were prosecuted without any decided advantage to either party, until the unlucky Theoktistos placed himself at the head of the Byzantine troops. His incapacity brought on a general engagement, in which the imperial army was completely defeated, at a place called Mauropotamos, near the range of Mount Taurus.[2] After this battle, an officer of reputation, (Theophanes, from Ferganah,) disgusted with the severity and blunders of Theoktistos, deserted to the Saracens, and embraced Islamism. At a subsequent period, however, he again returned to the Byzantine service and the Christian religion.[3]

In the year 845, an exchange of prisoners was effected on the banks of the river Lamus, a day's journey to the west of Tarsus. This was the first that had taken place since the taking of Amorium. The frequent exchange of prisoners between the Christians and the Mussulmans always tended to soften the miseries of war; and the cruelty which inflicted martyrdom on the forty-two prisoners of rank taken at Amorium in the beginning of this year, seems to have been connected with the interruption of the negotiations which had previously so often facilitated these exchanges.[4]

A female regency was supposed by the barbarians to be of necessity a period of weakness. The Bulgarians, under this impression, threatened to commence hostilities unless the Byzantine government consented to pay them an annual subsidy. A firm answer on the part of Theodora, accompanied

---

1 Contin. 126. About this time Weil, ii. 343, mentions that a Cretan fleet threatened to blockade the Hellespont. 2 Georg. Mon. *Scrip. post Theoph.* 529.

3 Leo Gramm. 457, 461. Georg. Mon. 533. Guards from Fergana (φαργάνοι ἄνδρες) are mentioned as having been sent to Italy in the time of Romanus I., A.D. 935.—Constant. Porphyr. *De Ceremoniis Aulæ Byzantinæ*, 381, 434, edit. Leich. It must be observed, however, that there was a country called Fergunna, and Franganeo Civitates, among the Sclavonians in Polabia.—*Schafarik Slawische Alterthümer*, ii. 607, 630. So extensive were the relations of the Byzantine empire, that it is not easy to decide between the Sclavonians of the West and the Turks of the East.

4 Abulpharagius, *Ch. Arab.* 167. Constant. Porphyr. *De Cer. Aulæ Byzantinæ*, 329.

by the display of a considerable military force on the frontier, however, restrained the predatory disposition of King Bogoris and his subjects. Peace was re-established after some trifling hostilities, an exchange of prisoners took place, the commercial relations between the two states became closer; and many Bulgarians, who had lived so long in the Byzantine empire as to have acquired the arts of civilised life and a knowledge of Christianity, returning to their homes, prepared their countrymen for receiving a higher degree of social culture, and with it the Christian religion.

The disturbed state of the Saracen empire, under the Caliphs Vathek and Motawukel, would have enabled the regency to enjoy tranquillity, had religious zeal not impelled the orthodox to persecute the inhabitants of the empire in the south-eastern provinces of Asia Minor. The regency unfortunately followed the counsels of the bigoted party, which regarded the extinction of heresy as the most important duty of the rulers of the state. A numerous body of Christians were persecuted with so much cruelty that they were driven to rebellion, and compelled to solicit protection for their lives and property from the Saracens, who seized the opportunity of transporting hostilities within the Byzantine frontiers.

The Paulicians were the heretics who at this time irritated the orthodoxy of Constantinople. They were enemies of image-worship, and showed little respect to the authority of a church establishment, for their priests devoted themselves to the service of their fellow-creatures without forming themselves into a separate order of society, or attempting to establish a hierarchical organisation. Their social and political opinions were viewed with as much hatred and alarm by the ecclesiastical counsellors of Theodora, as the philanthropic principles of the early Christians had been by the pagan emperors of Rome. The same calumnies were circulated among the orthodox against the Paulicians, which had been propagated amongst the heathen against the Christians. The populace of Constantinople was taught to exult in the tortures of those accused of manicheanism, as the populace of Rome had been persuaded to delight in the cruelties committed on the early Christians as enemies of the human race.

From the time of Constantine V. the Paulicians had generally enjoyed some degree of toleration; but the regency of Theodora resolved to consummate the triumph of orthodoxy, by a cruel persecution of all who refused to conform to the ceremonies of the established church. Imperial commissioners were sent into the Paulician districts to enforce ecclesiastical union, and every individual who resisted the invitations of the clergy was either condemned to death or his property was confiscated. It is the boast of orthodox historians that ten thousand Paulicians perished in this manner. Far greater numbers, however, escaped into the province of Melitene, where the Saracen emir granted them protection, and assisted them to plan schemes of revenge.[1]

The cruelty of the Byzantine administration at last goaded the oppressed to resistance within the empire; and the injustice displayed by the officers of the government induced many, who were themselves indifferent on the religious question, to take up arms against oppression. Karbeas, one of the principal officers on the staff of Theodotos Melissenos, the general of the Anatolic theme, hearing that his father had been crucified for his adherence to the doctrines of the Paulicians, fled to the emir of Melitene, and collected a body of five thousand men, with which he invaded the empire.[2] The Paulician refugees were established, by the caliph's order, in two cities called Argaous, and Amara; but their number soon increased so much, by the arrival of fresh emigrants, that they formed a third establishment at a place called Tephrike, (Divreky,) in the district of Sebaste, (Sivas,) in a secluded country of difficult access, where they constructed a strong fortress, and dwelt in a state of independence.[3] Omar, the emir of Melitene, at the head of a Saracen army, and Karbeas with a strong body of Paulicians, ravaged the frontiers of the empire. They were opposed by Petronas, the brother of Theodora, then general of the Thrakesian theme. The Byzantine army confined its operations to defence; while Alim, the governor of Tarsus, having been defeated, and civil war breaking out in the Saracen dominions in consequence of the cruelties of the Caliph Motawukel, the incursions of the Paulicians were confined to mere plundering forays. In the mean time a considerable body of Paulicians continued to dwell in several provinces of the empire, escaping persecution by outward conformity to the Greek church, and by paying exactly all the

---

[1] Continuator, 103.   [2] Ibid., 103.
[3] St. Martin, Mémoires sur l'Arménie, i. 188. The secluded position of Divreky made it the seat of an almost independent band of Kurds when it was visited by Otter in 1743.—Voyage en Turquie et en Perse, ii. 306. It contains at present about two thousand houses, situated in a fertile valley amidst luxuriant gardens.—Ainsworth, Travels and Researches in Asia Minor, ii. 7.

dues levied on them by the Byzantine clergy. The whole force of the empire was not directed against the Paulicians until some years later, during the reign of Basil I.[1]

In the year 852, the regency revenged the losses inflicted by the Saracen pirates on the maritime districts of the empire, by invading Egypt. A Byzantine fleet landed a body of troops at Damietta, which was plundered and burned: the country round was ravaged, and six hundred female slaves were carried away.[2]

Theodora, like her female predecessor Irene, displayed considerable talents for government. She preserved the tranquillity of the empire, and increased its prosperity in spite of her persecuting policy; but, like Irene, she neglected her duty to her son in the most shameful manner. In the series of Byzantine sovereigns from Leo III. (the Isaurian) to Michael III., only two proved utterly unfit for the duties of their station, and both appear to have been corrupted by the education they received from their mothers. The unfeeling ambition of Irene, and the heartless vanity of Theodora, were the original causes of the folly of Constantine VI. and the vices of Michael III. The system of education generally adopted at the time seems to have been singularly well adapted to form men of ability, as we see in the instances of Constantine V., Leo IV., and Theophilus, who were all educated as princes and heirs to the empire. Even if we take the most extended view of Byzantine society, we shall find that the constant supply of great talents displayed in the public service must have been the result of careful cultivation and judicious systematic study. No monarchical government can produce such a long succession of able ministers and statesmen as conducted the Byzantine administration during the eighth, ninth, and tenth centuries. The remarkable deficiency of original genius during this period only adds an additional proof that the mind was disciplined by a rigid system of education.

Theodora abandoned the care of her child's education to her brother Bardas, of whose taste and talents she may have been a very incompetent judge, but of whose debauched manners she must have seen and heard too much. With the assistance of Theoktistos she arrogated to herself the sole

---

[1] Concerning the Paulicians, see Mosheim, Soames' edit. ii. 251. Neander, iii. 243. Gibbon, x. 168.

[2] We owe the knowledge of this expedition to the *Arabic Chronicle* of Abul-pharagius, p. 170.

direction of the public administration, and viewed with indifference the course of idleness and profligacy by which Bardas corrupted the principles of her son in his endeavour to secure a mastery over his mind. Both mother and uncle appear to have expected to profit by the young emperor's vices. Bardas soon became a prime favourite, as he not only afforded the young emperor every facility for gratifying his passions, but supported him in the disputes with the regency that originated on account of his lavish expenditure. Michael at last came to an open quarrel with his mother. He had fallen in love with Eudocia, the daughter of Inger, of the great family of the Martinakes, a connection which both Theodora and Theoktistos viewed with alarm, as likely to create a powerful opposition to their political influence.[1] To prevent a marriage, Theodora succeeded in compelling Michael, who was then in his sixteenth year, to marry another lady named Eudocia, the daughter of Dekapolitas. The young debauchee, however, made Eudocia Ingerina his mistress, and, towards the end of his reign, bestowed her in marriage on Basil the Macedonian as a mark of his favour. She became the mother of the Emperor Leo VI., the Wise.[2]

This forced marriage enabled Bardas to excite the animosity of Michael against the regency to such a degree that he was persuaded to sanction the murder of Theoktistos, whose able financial administration was so generally acknowledged that Bardas feared to contend openly with so honest a minister. Theoktistos was arrested by order of the young emperor, and murdered in prison. The majority of Michael III. was not immediately proclaimed, but Bardas was advanced to the office of Master of the Horse, and assumed the direction of the administration. He was consequently regarded as the real author of the murder of Theoktistos.[3]

Theodora, though her real power had ceased, continued to occupy her place as empress-regent; but in order to prepare for her approaching resignation, and at the same time prove the wisdom of her financial administration, and the value of

[1] A prophecy is said to have announced that this family should give the empire a longer succession of emperors than the Amorian dynasty.—Continuator, 75.

[2] There seems a doubt whether Eudocia Ingerina's first son, after her marriage with Basil, was named Constantine.—Symeon Mag. 449; Leo. Gramm. 472; or Leo George the Monk, 540; and Leo Grammaticus himself, at page 468, edit. Par. This child, whether the one or the other, was generally supposed to be the child of Michael III.

[3] Theophanes of Fergana, who had returned and become captain of the guard, was one of the murderers.—Symeon Mag. 435. George Mon. 533. The history of the murder is detailed in the Continuator, 105, and Genesius, 42.

the services of Theoktistos, by whose counsels she had been guided, she presented to the senate a statement of the condition of the imperial treasury. By this account it appeared that there was then an immense accumulation of specie in the coffers of the state. The sum is stated to have consisted of 109,000 lb. of gold, and 300,000 lb. of silver, besides immense stores of merchandise, jewels, and plate. The Empress Theodora was evidently anxious to guard against all responsibility, and prevent those calumnious accusations which she knew to be common at the Byzantine court. The immense treasure thus accumulated would probably have given immortal strength to Byzantine society, had it been left in the possession of the people, by a wise reduction in the amount of taxation, accompanied by a judicious expenditure for the defence of the frontiers, and for facilitating the conveyance of agricultural produce to distant markets.[1]

The Empress Theodora continued to live in the imperial palace, after the murder of Theoktistos, until her regency expired, on her son attaining the age of eighteen.[2] Her residence there was, however, rendered a torture to her mind by the unseemly exhibitions of the debauched associates of her son. The eagerness of Michael to be delivered from her presence at length caused him to send both his mother and his sisters to reside in the Carian Palace, and even to attempt persuading the Patriarch Ignatius to give them the veil. After her banishment from the imperial palace, Theodora still hoped to recover her influence with her son, if she could separate him from Bardas; and she engaged in intrigues with her brother's enemies, whose secret object was his assassination.[3] This conspiracy was discovered, and only tended to increase the power of Bardas. He was now raised to the dignity of curopalat. Theodora and the sisters of Michael were removed to the monastery of Gastria, the usual residence of the ladies of the imperial family who were secluded from

---

[1] Continuator, 108. Symeon Mag. 436. The gold may have equalled 3,250,000 sovereigns, and the silver 4,000,000 crown-pieces, equal perhaps in value to more than double that sum at Constantinople, and probably more valuable than four times that sum in the rest of Europe. But all comparisons of the value of money at different times must be mere conjecture. Coin travels along bad roads with greater difficulty than merchandise.

[2] He was more than three years old at his father's death.—Continuator, 92. He reigned with Theodora more than fourteen years.—Krug. *Chronologie der Byzantiner*, 3. Theoktistos was murdered in the thirteenth year of his reign.—Symeon Mag. 435. From the conclusion of Theodora's regency Michael reigned upwards of eleven years. —*S. Nicephori Chron. ad cal. Syncelli Chron.* 403. Many anecdotes confirm this chronology.—Schlosser, 572.   [3] Symeon Mag. 435. Georg. Mon. 534.

the world. After the death of Bardas, however, Theodora recovered some influence over her son; she was allowed to occupy apartments in the palace of St. Mamas, and it was at a party in her rural residence at the Anthemian Palace that Michael was assassinated.[1] Theodora died in the first year of the reign of Basil I.; and Thekla, the sister of Michael, who had received the imperial title, and was as debauched in her manners as her brother, continued her scandalous life during great part of Basil's reign;[2] yet Theodora is eulogised as a saint by the ecclesiastical writers of the Western as well as the Eastern church, and is honoured with a place in the Greek calendar.

Encouraged by the counsels and example of Bardas, Michael plunged into every vice. His orgies obtained for him the name of the Drunkard; but, in spite of his vicious conduct, his devotion to chariot-races and his love of festivals gave him considerable popularity among the people of Constantinople. The people were amused by his follies, and the citizens profited by his lavish expenditure. Many anecdotes concerning his vices have been preserved, but they are deserving of detailed notice only as proofs of the great demoralization then existing at Constantinople, for, as facts concerning Michael, it is probable they have received their colouring from the flatterers of the dynasty of his assassin. Michael's unworthy conduct, however, ultimately rendered him contemptible to all classes. Had the emperor confined himself to appearing as a charioteer in the Hippodrome, it would have been easily pardoned; but he carried his extravagance so far as to caricature the ceremonies of the orthodox church, and publicly to burlesque the religious processions of the clergy. The indifference of the people to this ribaldry seems doubly strange, when we reflect on the state of superstition into which the Constantinopolitans had fallen, and on the important place occupied by the Eastern church in Byzantine society. Perhaps, however, the endeavours which had been made, both by the church and the emperors, to render church ceremonies an attractive species of public amusement, had tended to prepare the public mind for this irreverent caricature. It is always imprudent to trifle with a serious subject, and more especially with religion and religious feelings. At this time, music, singing, eloquence, magnificence of costume,

---

[1] Symeon Mag. 451. Georg. Mon. 541. Leo Gramm. 468, edit. Par.; 250, edit. Bonn. [2] Georg. Mon. 545. Leo Gramm. 471.

and scenic effect, had all been carefully blended with architectural decoration of the richest kind in the splendid church of St. Sophia, to excite the admiration and engage the attention. The consequence was, that religion was the thing least thought of by the people, when they assembled together at ecclesiastical festivals. Their object was to enjoy the music, view the pageantry, and criticise the performers. Michael gratified the supercilious critics by his caricatures, and gave variety to the public entertainments by the introduction of comedy and farce. The necessity of this was felt in the Roman Catholic church, which authorised similar saturnalia, to prevent the ground being occupied by opponents. The Emperor Michael exhibited a clever but very irreverent caricature of the ecclesiastical processions of the Patriarch and clergy of Constantinople. The masquerade consisted of an excellent buffoon arrayed in the patriarchal robes, attended by eleven mimic metropolitan bishops in full costume, embroidered with gold, and followed by a crowd disguised as choristers and priests. This *cortège*, accompanied by the emperor in person, as if in a solemn procession, walked through the streets of the capital singing ridiculous songs to psalm tunes, and burlesque hymns in praise of debauchery, mingling the richest melodies of Oriental church-music with the most discordant nasal screams of Greek popular ballads. This disgraceful exhibition was frequently repeated, and on one occasion encountered the real Patriarch, whom the buffoon saluted with ribald courtesy, without exciting a burst of indignation from the pious Greeks.[1]

The depravity of society in all ranks had reached the most scandalous pitch. Bardas, when placed at the head of the public administration, took no care to conceal his vices; he was accused of an incestuous intercourse with his son's wife, while the young man held the high office of generalissimo of the European troops.[2] Ignatius the Patriarch was a man of the highest character, eager to obtain for the church in the East that moral supremacy which the papal power now arrogated to itself in the West. Disgusted with the vices of Bardas, he refused to administer the sacrament to him on Advent Sunday, when it was usual for all the great dignitaries

---

[1] Continuator, 124. If the fable of the female Pope Joanna proves anything, it may be received as evidence that the state of society in Rome was little better than at Constantinople. The imaginary female pope was supposed to be a contemporary of the real drunken emperor.

[2] Symeon Mag. 439; μονοστρατηγὸς τῶν δυτικῶν.

G

of the empire to receive the holy communion from the hands of the Patriarch, A.D. 857. Bardas, to revenge himself for this public mark of infamy, recalled to the memory of the young emperor the resistance Ignatius had made to Theodora's receiving the veil, and accused him of holding private communication with a monk who had given himself out to be a son of Theodora, born before her marriage with Theophilus. As this monk was known to be mad, and as many senators and bishops were attached to Ignatius, it would have been extremely difficult to convict the Patriarch of treason on such an accusation; and there appeared no possibility of framing any charge of heresy against him. Michael was, however, persuaded to arrest him on various charges of having committed acts of sedition, and to banish him to the island of Tenebinthos.

It was now necessary to look out for a new Patriarch, and the circumstances required that the successor of Ignatius should be a man of high character as well as talent, for the deposed Patriarch had occupied no ordinary position. His father and his maternal grandfather (Michael I. and Nicephorus I.) had both filled the throne of Constantinople; he was celebrated for his piety and his devotion to the cause of the church. But his party zeal had already raised up a strong opposition to his measures in the bosom of the church; and Bardas took advantage of these ecclesiastical dissensions to make the contest concerning the patriarchate a clerical struggle, without bringing the state into direct collision with the church, whose factious spirit did the work of its own degradation. Gregory, a son of the Emperor Leo V., the Armenian, was Bishop of Syracuse. He had been suspended by the Patriarch Methodios for consecrating a priest out of his diocese. During the patriarchate of Ignatius, the hereditary hostility of the sons of two rival emperors had perpetuated the quarrel, and Ignatius had probably availed himself with pleasure of the opportunity offered him of excommunicating Gregory as some revenge for the loss of the imperial throne. It was pretended that Gregory had a hereditary aversion to image-worship, and the suspicions of Methodios were magnified by the animosity of Ignatius into absolute heresy.[1] This dispute had been referred to Pope Benedict III., and his

---

[1] Genesius, 47. Symeon Mag. 443. Schlosser, p. 592, points out that Gregory, one of the sons of Leo the Armenian, was the same person with Gregory Asbestas, archbishop of Syracuse.—*Colet. Concil.* x. 698. Nicetas, *Vita Ignatii.*

decision in favour of Ignatius had induced Gregory and his partisans, who were numerous and powerful, to call in question the legality of the election of Ignatius. Bardas, availing himself of this ecclesiastical contest, employed threats, and strained the influence of the emperor to the utmost, to induce Ignatius to resign the patriarchate; but in vain. It was, therefore, decided that Photius should be elected Patriarch without obtaining a formal resignation of the office from Ignatius, whose election was declared null.

Photius, the chief secretary of state, who was thus suddenly raised to the head of the Eastern church, was a man of high rank, noble descent, profound learning, and great personal influence. If we believe his own declaration, publicly and frequently repeated, he was elected against his will; and there seems no doubt that he could not have opposed the selection of the emperor without forfeiting all rank at court, and perhaps incurring personal danger.[1] His popularity, his intimate acquaintance with civil and canon law, and his family alliance with the imperial house, gave him many advantages in his new rank. Like his celebrated predecessors, Tarasios and Nicephorus, he was a layman when his election took place. On the 20th December 857, he was consecrated a monk by Gregory, archbishop of Syracuse; on the following day he became an anagnostes; the day after, a sub-deacon; next day he was appointed deacon; and on the 24th he received priest's orders. He was then formally elected Patriarch in a synod, and on Christmas-day solemnly consecrated in the church of St. Sophia.[2]

The election of Photius, which was evidently illegal, only increased the dissensions already existing in the church; but they drew off the attention of the people in some degree from political abuses, and enabled Bardas to constitute the civil power judge in ecclesiastical matters. Ignatius and the leading men of his party were imprisoned and ill treated; but even the clergy of the party of Photius could not escape

---

[1] Photius was the grand-nephew of the Patriarch Tarasios, who like himself had been raised from the post of secretary of state to rule the church.—Letter of Photius to Pope Nicholas in *Histoire de Photius*, par l'Abbé Jager, 448;—a prejudiced and not very accurate work. Irene, sister of the Empress Theodora, was married to Sergius, the brother of Photius—Ducange, *Fam. Aug. Byz.* 135. Continuator, 109. Cedrenus, 545. The Abbé Jager says that Arsaber, who married another sister of Theodora, (Kalomeria,) was uncle to Photius.

[2] Baronius, *Annales Eccles.* xiv. ; Coleti, *Conciliorum Coll.* ix. and x; *Photii Epistolæ*, London, 1651, are the chief sources of ecclesiastical history for this period. The account of Photius in the work of Haukins, *De Byzantinarum Rerum Scriptoribus Græcis*, p. 269, deserves attention.

being insulted and carried before the ordinary tribunals, if they refused to comply with the iniquitous demands of the courtiers, or ventured to oppose the injustice of the government officials. Photius soon bitterly repented having rendered himself the agent of such men as Bardas and Michael; and as he knew their conduct and characters before his election, we may believe the assertion he makes in his letters to Bardas himself, and which he repeats to the Pope, that he was compelled to accept the patriarchate against his wish.[1]

In the mean time, Ignatius was allowed so much liberty by the crafty Bardas, who found Photius a less docile instrument than he had expected, that his partisans assembled a synod in the church of Irene for forty days. In this assembly Photius and his adherents were excommunicated. Bardas, however, declared in favour of Photius, and allowed him to hold a counter-synod in the Church of the Holy Apostles, in which the election of Ignatius was declared uncanonical, as having been made by the Empress Theodora in opposition to the protest of several bishops.[2] The persecution of Ignatius was renewed; he was exiled to Mitylene, and his property was sequestrated, in the hope that by these measures he would be induced to resign the patriarchal dignity. Photius, however, had the sense to see that this persecution only increased his rival's popularity, and strengthened his party; he therefore persuaded the emperor to recall him, and reinstate him in the possession of his private fortune. Photius must have felt that his own former intimacy with his debauched relation Bardas, and his toleration of the vices of Michael, had fixed a deep stain on his character in the eyes of all sincere Christians.

It was now necessary to legalise the election of Photius, and obtain the ratification of the deposition of Ignatius by a general council of the church; but no general council could be convoked without the sanction of the Pope. The Emperor Michael consequently despatched ambassadors to Rome, to invite Pope Nicholas I. to send legates to Constantinople, for the purpose of holding a general council, to put an end to the dissensions in the Eastern Church. Nicholas appointed two legates, Zacharias and Rodoald, who were instructed to examine into the disputes concerning the patriarchate, and

---

[1] *Photii Epistolæ*, iii. and vi. Schlosser, 602. The *Histoire de Photius*, by the Abbé Jager, gives a letter to Pope Nicholas confirming this unwillingness, pp. 34 and 433.
[2] Schlosser, 603.

also to demand the restitution of the estates belonging to the patrimony of St. Peter in Calabria and Sicily, of which the papal See had been deprived in the time of Leo III. The Pope, moreover, required the emperor to re-establish the papal jurisdiction over the Illyrian provinces, and recognise its right to appoint the archbishop of Syracuse, and confirm the election of all the bishops in the European provinces of the empire.

The Popes were how beginning to arrogate to themselves that temporal power over the whole church which had grown out of their new position as sovereign princes; but they based their temporal ambition on that spiritual power which they claimed as the rock of St. Peter, not on the donation of Charlemagne. The truth is, that the first Christian emperors had laid a firm foundation for the papal power, by constituting the Bishop of Rome a kind of secretary of state for Christian affairs. He was employed as a central authority for communicating with the bishops of the provinces; and out of this circumstance it very naturally arose that he acted for a considerable period as a minister of religion and public instruction in the imperial administration, which conferred immense power in a government so strictly centralised as that of the Roman empire.[1] The Christian emperors of the West, being placed in more direct collision with paganism than those of the East, vested more extensive powers, both of administration and police, in the Bishop of Rome, and the provincial bishops of the Western Church, than the clergy attained in the East. This authority of the bishops increased as the civil and military power of the Western Empire declined; and when the imperial city became a provincial city of the Eastern Empire, the popes became the political chiefs of Roman society, and inherited no small portion of the influence formerly exercised by the imperial administration over the provincial ecclesiastics. It is true, the Bishops of Rome could not exercise this power without control, but, in the opinion of a majority of the subjects of the barbarian conquerors in the West, the Pope was the legal representative of the civilisation of imperial Rome as well as the legitimate successor of St. Peter, and the guardian of the rock on which Christianity was founded. Unless the authority of the popes be traced back to their

---

[1] *Lex Theodosii et Valentiniani, apud Scriptores rerum Francic. et Gallic.* tom. . 768. See Thierry, *Historie de la Conquête de l'Angleterre; Notes et Pièces Just.*; *Cod. Theod.* xvi. tit. 2, *De Episcopis Ecclesiis et Clericis*; *Cod. Justin* i. 3, *De Episcopis et Clericis.*

original position as archbishops of Rome and patriarchs of the Western Empire, and the institutions of the papal church be viewed as they originally existed in connection with the imperial administration, the real value of the papal claims to universal domination, founded on traditional feelings, cannot be justly estimated. The popes only imitated the Roman emperors in their most exorbitant pretensions; and the vicious principles of Constantine, while he was still a pagan, continue to exert their corrupt influence over the ecclesiastical institutions of the greater part of Europe to the present day.

The popes early assumed that Constantine had conferred on the Bishop of Rome a supreme ecclesiastical jurisdiction over the three European divisions of his dominions, when he divided the empire into four prefectures.[1] There were, indeed, many facts which tended to support this claim. Africa, in so far as it belonged to the jurisdiction of the European prefectures, acknowledged the authority of the Bishop of Rome; and even after the final division of the empire, Dacia, Macedonia, Thessaly, Epirus, and Greece, though they were separated from the prefecture of Illyricum, and formed a new province of the Eastern Empire, continued to be dependent on the ecclesiastical jurisdiction of the Pope. The Patriarch of Antioch was considered the head of the church in the East. Egypt formed a peculiar district in the ecclesiastical, as it did in the civil administration of the Roman empire, and had its own head, the Patriarch of Alexandria. The Patriarchs of Jerusalem and Constantinople were modern creations. The bishop of Jerusalem, who had been dependent on the Patriarch of Antioch, received the honorary title of Patriarch at the council of Nicæa, and the Emperor Theodosius II. conferred on him an independent jurisdiction over the three Palestines, the two Phœnicias, and Arabia; but it was not until after the council of Chalcedon that his authority was acknowledged by the body of the church, and it was then restricted to the three Palestines, A.D. 451.

The bishop of Byzantium had been dependent on the metropolitan or exarch of Heraclea before the translation of the imperial residence to his See, and the foundation of Constantinople. In the council held at Constantinople in 381, he was first ranked as Patriarch, because he was the bishop of the capital of the Eastern Empire, and placed immediately after the Bishop of Rome in the ecclesiastical hierarchy. St. Chry-

[1] Zosimus, ii. 33.

sostom and his successors exercised the patriarchal jurisdiction, both in Europe and Asia, over the Eastern Empire, just as the popes of Rome exercised it in the Western, yielding merely a precedence in ecclesiastical honour to the representative of St. Peter.[1] In spite of the opposition of the bishops of old Rome, the bishops of new Rome thus attained an equality of power which made the popes tremble for their supremacy, and they regarded the Patriarchs of Constantinople rather as rivals than as joint rulers of the church. Their ambitious jealousy, joined to the aspiring arrogance of their rivals, caused all the evils they feared. The disputes between Ignatius and Photius now gave the Pope hopes of re-establishing the supremacy of Rome over the whole church, and of rendering the Patriarchs of the East merely vicegerents of the Roman See.

The Papal legates sent by Nicholas were present at a general council held at Constantinople in the year 861, which was attended by three hundred and eighteen bishops. Bardas and Photius had succeeded in securing the goodwill of the majority of the Eastern clergy. They also succeeded in gaining the support of the representatives of the Pope, if they did not purchase it. Ignatius, who was residing in his mother's palace of Posis, was required to present himself before the council. He was deposed, though he appealed to the Pope's legates, and persisted in protesting that the council did not possess a legal right to depose him. It is said that a pen was placed forcibly between his fingers, and a cross drawn with it, as his signature to the act of deposition. He was then ordered to read his abdication, on the day of Pentecost, in the Church of the Holy Apostles; but, to avoid this disgrace, he escaped in the disguise of a slave to the Prince's Islands, and concealed himself among the innumerable monks who had taken up their abode in these delicious retreats. Bardas sent Oryphas with six galleys to examine every one of the insular monasteries in succession, in order to arrest the fugitive; but the search was vain. After the termination of the council, Ignatius returned privately to his maternal palace, where he was allowed to remain unmolested.[2] The discussions of this council are

---

[1] Socrates, *Hist. Eccles.* vii. 28. *Cod. Theodosianus*, xvi. tom. 2. lib. 45. Council of Chalcedon, 9th, 17th, and 28th canons.

[2] He was said to have been indebted to an earthquake for this mild treatment. Bardas was frightened, and Photius was looked upon as impious for declaring from the pulpit that earthquakes were produced by physical causes acting upon the waters under the earth, and not from divine wrath to awaken mankind to a sense of their sins.— Symeon Mag. 445. Photius, like his predecessor, John the Grammarian, was too

said by its enemies to have been conducted in a very tumultuous manner; but as the majority was favoured by the Patriarch, the papal legates, and the imperial administration, it is not likely that any confusion was allowed within the walls of the council, even though the party of Ignatius was supported by the Empresses Theodora and Eudocia, and by the great body of the monks. The Emperor Michael, with great impartiality, refused to throw the whole weight of his authority in either scale. The truth is, that, being somewhat of a freethinker as well as a debauchee, he laughed at both parties, saying that Ignatius was the patriarch of the people, Photius the patriarch of Bardas, and Gryllos (the imperial buffoon) his own patriarch.[1] Nevertheless, Ignatius was deposed, and the acts of the council were ratified by the papal legates.[2]

The legates of the Pope certainly yielded to improper influence, for, besides approving the measures of the Byzantine government with reference to the patriarchate, they neglected to demand the recognition of the spiritual authority of the papal see in the terms prescribed by their instructions. They were consequently disavowed on their return to Rome. The party of Ignatius appealed to the Pope, who, seeing that no concessions could be gained from Michael, Bardas, or Photius, embraced the cause of the deposed Patriarch with warmth. A synod was convoked at Rome; Photius was excommunicated, in case he should dare to retain possession of the patriarchal chair, after receiving the papal decision in favour of Ignatius, A.D. 863. Gregory, the archbishop of Syracuse, who had ordained Photius, was anathematised, and declared a schismatic, as well as all those who held communion with him, if he continued to perform the sacerdotal functions. When the acts of this synod were communicated to Michael by papal letters, the indignation of the emperor was awakened by what he considered the insolent interference of a foreign priest in the affairs of the empire, and he replied in a violent and unbecoming letter. He told his Holiness that he had invited him to send legates to the general council at Constantinople, from a wish to maintain unity in the church,

learned for the populace, and his knowledge was attributed to personal intercourse with demons, who in that age were supposed to act as professors of Hellenic literature. Symeon gives some curious anecdotes to the disadvantage of Photius.

[1] Gryllos, whom the emperor had employed to enact the patriarch, received from the people the name of the hog, from his low debauchery.

[2] This council is called by the Greeks the first and second, from having been held in two separate series of sessions. It seems that it re-enacted the acts of the synod held by Photius in 857.

not because the participation of the Bishop of Rome was necessary to the validity of the acts of the Eastern Church. This was all very reasonable ; but he went on to treat the Pope and the Latin clergy as barbarians, because they were ignorant of Greek. For this insult, however, the emperor received a sharp and well-merited rebuke from Pope Nicholas, who asked him why he styled himself Emperor of the Romans, if he thought the language of the Roman empire and of the Roman church a barbarous one. It was a greater disgrace, in the opinion of the Pope, for the Roman emperor to be ignorant of the Roman language, than for the head of the Roman church to be ignorant of Greek.

Nicholas had nothing to fear from the power of Michael, so that he acted without the restraint imposed on Gregory II. in his contest with Leo the Isaurian. Indeed, the recent success of the Pope, in his dispute with Lothaire, king of Austrasia, gave him hopes of coming off victorious, even in a quarrel with the Eastern emperor. He did not sufficiently understand the effect of more advanced civilisation and extended education on Byzantine society. Nicholas, therefore, boldly called on Michael to cancel his insolent letter, declaring that it would otherwise be publicly burned by the Latin clergy ; and he summoned the rival Patriarchs of Constantinople to appear in person before the papal court, that he might hear and decide their differences.

This pretension of the Pope to make himself absolute master of the Christian church, awakened the spirit of resistance at Constantinople, and caused Photius to respond by advancing new claims for his See. He insisted that the Patriarchs of Constantinople were equal in rank and authority to the Popes of Rome. The disputes of the clergy being the only subject on which the government of the Eastern Empire allowed any expression of public opinion, the whole attention of society was soon directed to this ecclesiastical quarrel. Michael assembled a council of the church in 866, at which pretended representatives of the patriarchs of Antioch, Alexandria, and Jerusalem were present; and in this assembly Pope Nicholas was declared unworthy of his See, and excommunicated. There was no means of rendering this sentence of excommunication of any effect, unless Louis II., the emperor of the West, could be induced, by the hatred he bore to Nicholas, to put it in execution. Ambassadors were sent to urge him to depose the Pope, but the death of Michael suddenly put an end to the contest with Rome, for Basil I. embraced the party of Ignatius.

The contest between Rome and Constantinople was not merely a quarrel between Pope Nicholas and the Patriarch Photius. There were other causes of difference between the two Sees, in which Ignatius was as much opposed to papal pretensions as Photius. Not to mention the old claim of Rome to recover her jurisdiction over those provinces of the Byzantine empire which had been dissevered from her authority, a new conflict had arisen for supremacy over the church in Bulgaria. When the Bulgarian king Crumn invaded the empire, after the defeat of Michael I., he carried away so many prisoners that the Bulgarians, who had already made considerable advances in civilisation, were prepared, by their intercourse with these slaves, to receive Christianity. A Greek monk, Theodore Koupharas, who remained long a prisoner in Bulgaria, converted many by his preaching. During the invasion of Bulgaria by Leo V., a sister of King Bogoris was carried to Constantinople as a prisoner, and educated with care. The Empress Theodore exchanged this princess for Theodore Koupharas, and on her return she introduced the Christian religion into her brother's palace.

War subsequently broke out between the Bulgarian monarch and the empire, and Michael and Bardas made an expedition against the Bulgarians in the year 861.[1] The circumstances of the war are not detailed; but in the end the Bulgarian king embraced Christianity, receiving the name of Michael from the emperor, who became his sponsor. To purchase this peace, however, the Byzantine emperor ceded to the Bulgarians all the country along the range of Mount Hæmus, called by the Greeks Sideras, and by the Bulgarians Zagora, of which Debeltos is the chief town.[2] Michael pretended that the cession was made as a baptismal donation to the king. The change in the religion of the Bulgarian monarch caused some discontent among his subjects, but their opposition was soon vanquished with the assistance of Michael, and the most refractory were transported to Constantinople, where the wealth and civilisation of Byzantine society produced such an impression on their minds that they readily embraced Christianity.[3]

---

[1] Symeon Mag. 440. In the fourth year of Michael's sole government.

[2] The Continuator, 102, attributes this treaty to the Empress Theodora, but the date seems more precisely given by Symeon Magister, 440, Georg. Mon. 534. This district had been ceded to the Bulgarians by Justinian II., but recovered by Constantine V.

[3] Leo Gramm. 462. For the conversion of the Bulgarians, Contin. 101; Cedrenus, ii. 540; Zonaras, ii. 156.

The Bulgarian monarch, fearing lest the influence of the Byzantine clergy on his Christian subjects might render him in some degree dependent on the emperor, opened communications with Pope Nicholas for the purpose of balancing the power of the Greek clergy by placing the ecclesiastical affairs of his kingdom under the control of the Latins. He expected also to derive some political support for this alliance, when he saw the eagerness of the Pope to drive the Eastern clergy out of Bulgaria. Pope Nicholas appears to have thought that Photius would have made great concessions to the papal See, in order to receive the pallium from Rome; but when that Patriarch treated the question concerning the ecclesiastical jurisdiction of the Eastern church in Bulgaria as a political affair, and referred its decision to the imperial cabinet, the Pope sent legates into Bulgaria, and the churches of Rome and Constantinople were involved in a direct conflict for the ecclesiastical patronage of that extensive kingdom. At a later period, when Ignatius was re-established as Patriarch, and the general council of 869 was held to condemn the acts of Photius, Pope Hadrian found Ignatius as little inclined to make any concessions to the papal See in Bulgaria as his deposed rival, and this subject remained a permanent cause of quarrel between the two churches.

Michael, though a drunkard, was not naturally deficient in ability, activity, or ambition. Though he left the ordinary administration of public business in the hands of Bardas, on whom he conferred the title of Cæsar, which was then almost equivalent to a recognition of his title as heir-apparent to the empire, still he never allowed him to obtain the complete control over the whole administration, nor permitted him entirely to crush his opponents in the public service.[1] Hence many officers of rank continued to regard the emperor, with all his vices, as their protector in office. Like all the emperors of Constantinople, Michael felt himself constrained to appear frequently at the head of his armies. The tie between the emperor and the soldiers was perhaps strengthened by these visits, but it can hardly be supposed that the personal

[1] The nomination of Bardas as Cæsar took place in the year 862, at Easter, according to Genesius, 46. But Symeon Magister places it in the third year of Michael, or 860, while he places the victory of Petronas (which Genesius says preceded it) in the fifth, or 862. George the Monk and Leo Grammaticus follow the same order as Symeon; while the Continuator, 114, agrees with Genesius, and places the nomination of Bardas after the victory of Petronas. Yet the nomination of Bardas seems to be rightly fixed by Genesius, while the Arabian historians prove that the battle of Petronas occurred in 863.—See page 172, note 3.

presence of Michael added much to the efficiency of military operations.

The war on the frontiers of the Byzantine and Saracen empires was carried on by Omar, the emir of Melitene, without interruption, in a series of plundering incursions on a gigantic scale. These were at times revenged by daring exploits on the part of the Byzantine generals. In the year 856, Leo, the imperial commander-in-chief, invaded the dominions of the caliph. After taking Anazarba, he crossed the Euphrates at Samosata, and advanced with his army into Mesopotamia, ravaging the country as far as Amida. The Saracens revenged themselves by several plundering incursions into the different parts of the empire. To stop these attacks, Michael put himself at the head of the army, and laid siege to Samosata without effect. Bardas accompanied the emperor rather to watch over his own influence at court, than to assist his sovereign in obtaining military glory. The following year Michael was engaged in the campaign against the Bulgarians, of which the result has been already mentioned. In 860, he led an army of 40,000 European troops against Omar of Melitene, who had carried his plundering incursions up to the walls of Sinope.[1] A battle took place in the territory of Dasymon, near the spot which had witnessed the defeat of Theophilus, and the overthrow of Michael was as complete as that of his father. The same difficulties in the ground which had favoured the retreat of Theophilus enabled Manuel, one of the generals of Michael, to save the army.[2]

The war was still prosecuted with vigour on both sides. In 863, Omar entered the Armeniac theme with a large force, and took Amisus. Petronas, the emperor's uncle, who had now acquired considerable military experience and reputation as general of the Thrakesian theme, was placed at the head of the Byzantine army.[3] He collected his forces at Aghionoros,

---

[1] The Arabian historians pretend that Omar carried off 17,000 slaves, and Karbeas, with his Paulicians, 5000 in one expedition. Ali Ibu Yahia, governor of Tarsus, was equally successful. Abulpharagius (Bar Hebræus) says that in a previous campaign the Byzantine army had made 20,000 prisoners.—Weil, *Geschichte der Chalifen*, ii. 363, note 2, and 365. These devastations deserve notice, as causes of the depopulation of the country.

[2] Continuator, 110. Genesius, 44. It is evident that the details of the battle of Theophilus have been mixed up with those of this battle. The exploits attributed to the two Manuels are a mere transcript. There is so much confusion in the narrative and chronology of Michael's war with the Saracens, that it would occupy too much space to examine its details.—See Weil, ii., 365, note 1.

[3] For the date, see Abulfeda, *Annal. Muss.* ii. 209. Abulpharagius, *Ch.. Syr.* 171, 249th year of the Hegira, from 23d February 863 to 12th February 864. Also Weil, ii. 380, note 6.

near Ephesus, and when his army was reinforced by a strong body of Macedonian and Thracian troops, marched towards the frontier in several divisions, which he concentrated in such a manner as to cut off the retreat of Omar, and enclose him with an overwhelming force. The troops under Nasar, the general of the Boukellarian theme, strengthened by the Armeniac and Paphlagonian legions, and the troops of the theme Koloneia, enclosed the Saracens on the north. Petronas himself, with the Thrakesian, Macedonian, and Thracian legions, secured the passes and advanced from the west; while the troops of the Anatolic, Opsikian, and Cappadocian themes, with the divisions of the Kleisourarchs of Seleucia and Charsiana, having secured the passes to the south, cut off the direct line of Omar's retreat. An impassable range of rocky mountains, broken into precipices, rendered escape to the eastward impracticable. The headquarters of Petronas were established at Poson, a place situated on the frontiers of the Paphlagonian and Armeniac themes, near the river Lalakon, which flows from the north to south. Omar had encamped in a plain without suspecting the danger lurking in its rugged boundary to the east. He suddenly found himself enclosed by the simultaneous advance of the various divisions of the Byzantine army, and closely blockaded. He attempted to escape by attacking each division of the enemy in succession, but the strength of the positions selected by the imperial officers rendered all his attacks vain. Omar at last fell in the desperate struggle; and Petronas, leading fresh troops into the plain to attack the weary Saracens, completed the destruction of their army. The son of Omar contrived to escape from the field of battle, but he was pursued and taken prisoner by the Kleisourarch of Charsiana, after he had crossed the Halys.[1] When Petronas returned to Constantinople, he was allowed to celebrate his victory with great pomp and public rejoicings. The Byzantine writers estimated the army that was destroyed at 40,000, while the Arabian historians reduced their loss to only 2000 men. Public opinion in the empire of the caliph, however, considered the defeat as a great calamity; and its real importance may be ascertained from the fact, that alarm-

---

[1] It is not easy to determine the spot where this battle was fought. Genesius calls the place Abysianos, and says it was five hundred miles from Aminsos, page 46. A valley in the vicinity was called Gyris.—Continuator, 113. Edrisi, ii. 308, places the valley Merdj Aluskuf twenty-four miles north-west of Baranda, (Laranda), on the road from Tarsus to Abydos. This would place it in the Anatolic theme, among the Lycaonian counter-forts of Taurus, and would lead to the supposition that Omar was retreating to gain Tarsus, in order to place his booty in security.—See Weil, ii. 381.

ing seditions broke out against the government when the news reached Bagdat.[1] After this victory, too, the eastern frontier enjoyed tranquillity for some time.

In the year 865, a nation hitherto unknown made its first appearance in the history of the world, where it was destined to act no unimportant part. Its entrance into the political system of the European nations was marked by an attempt to take Constantinople, a project which it has often revived, and which the progress of Christian civilisation seems to indicate must now be realised at no very distant date, unless the revival of the Bulgarian kingdom to the south of the Danube create a new Sclavonian power in the east of Europe capable of arresting its progress. In the year 862, Rurik, a Scandinavian or Varangian chief, arrived at Novgorod, and laid the first foundation of the state which has grown into the Russian empire. The Russian people, under Varangian domination, rapidly increased in power, and reduced many of their neighbours to submission.[2] Oskold and Dir, the princes of Kiof, rendered themselves masters of the whole course of the Dnieper, and it would seem that either commercial jealousy or the rapacity of ambition produced some collision with the Byzantine settlements on the northern shores of the Black Sea; but from what particular circumstances the Russians were led to make their daring attack on Constantinople is not known.[3] The Emperor Michael had taken the command of an army to act against the Saracens, and Oryphas, admiral of the fleet, acted as governor of the capital during his absence. Before the Emperor had commenced his military operations, a fleet of two hundred Russian vessels of small size, taking advantage of a favourable wind, suddenly passed through the Bosphorus, and anchored at the mouth of the Black River in the Propontis, about eighteen miles from Constantinople.[4] This Russian expedition had already plundered the shores of the Black Sea, and from its station within the Bosphorus it ravaged the country about Constantinople, and plundered the Prince's Islands, pillaging the monasteries, and slaying the monks as well as the other inhabitants. The emperor, in-

---

[1] Weil, ii. 381.   [2] *Photii Epistolæ*, p. 58.
[3] *La Chronique de Nestor*, traduite par L. Paris, i. 22.
[4] Κόλπος μέλας is the bay at the mouth of the Athyras, Buyuk Tchekmadjé. The Russian vessels are called μονόξυλα; they must have been only decked boats, and twenty men to each will be an ample allowance. They cannot therefore have carried more than 4000 men when they passed the Bosphorus. The expedition seems not unlike those against which, about this time, Alfred had to contend in England, and Charles the Bald in France.

formed by Oryphas of the attack on his capital, hastened to its defence. Though a daring and cruel enemy, the Russians were by no means formidable to the strength and discipline of the Byzantine forces. It required no great exertions on the part of the imperial officers to equip a force sufficient to attack and put to flight these invaders; but the barbarous cruelty of the soldiers and sailors, and the wild daring of their Varangian leaders, made a profound impression on the people of Constantinople, suddenly rendered spectators of the miseries of war, in their most hideous form, in a moment of perfect security. We need not, therefore, be surprised to find that the sudden destruction of these dreaded enemies by the drunken emperor, of whom the citizens of the capital entertained probably even more contempt than he merited as a soldier, was ascribed to the miraculous interposition of the Virgin of the Blachern, rather than to the superior military tactics and overwhelming numbers of the imperial forces. How far this expedition of the Russians must be connected with the enterprising spirit of that vigorous band of warriors and pirates from Scandinavia, who, under the name of Danes, Normans, and Varangians, became the sovereigns of Normandy, Naples, Sicily, England, and Russia, is still a subject of learned discussion.[1]

About the same time a fleet, manned by the Saracens of Crete, plundered the Cyclades, and ravaged the coast of Asia Minor, carrying off great booty and a number of slaves.[2] It would seem that the absence of the Emperor Michael from Constantinople at the time of the Russian attack was connected with this movement of the Saracens.

Our conceptions of the manner in which the Byzantine empire was governed during Michael's reign, will become more precise if we enter into some details concerning the court intrigues and personal conduct of the rulers of the state. The crimes and assassinations, which figure as the prominent events of the age in the chronicles of the time, were not, it is true, the events which decided the fate of the

---

[1] Wilken, *Über die Verhältnisse der Russen zum Byzantinischen Reiche*, in the Transactions of the Academy of Berlin. *Hist. Philolog. Klasse*, 1829, p. 88. For the date of the expedition, see Bayer, *De Russorum Prima Expeditione Constantinopolitana.—(Commentarii Acad. Scient. Petropolitanæ*, tom. viii.) For the facts, Leo Gramm. 463; Georg. Mon. 535; the Life of the Patriarch Ignatius, by Niketas David, annexed to the acts of the eighth ecumenic council, and Nestor's *Russian Chronicle*.

[2] Continuator, 122. This fleet consisted of twenty κουμβαρίων, seven γαλέας, and some σατούρας; but it would perhaps be difficult to determine the size and class of these different vessels.

people; and they probably excited less interest among contemporaries who lived beyond the circle of court favour, than history would lead us to suppose. Each rank of society had its own robberies and murders to occupy its attention. The state of society at the court of Constantinople was not amenable to public opinion, for few knew much of what passed within the walls of the great palace; but yet the immense machinery of the imperial administration gave the emperors' power a solid basis, always opposed to the temporary vices of the courtiers. The order which rendered property secure, and enabled the industrious classes to prosper, through the equitable administration of the Roman law, nourished the vitality of the empire, when the madness of a Nero and the drunkenness of a Michael appeared to threaten political order with ruin. The people, carefully secluded from public business, and almost without any knowledge of the proceedings of their government, were in all probability little better acquainted with the intrigues and crimes of their day than we at present. They acted, therefore, when some real suffering or imaginary grievance brought oppression directly home to their interests or their feelings. Court murders were to them no more than a tragedy or a scene in the amphitheatre, at which they were not present.

Bardas had assassinated Theoktistos to obtain power; yet, with all his crimes, he had great natural talents and some literary taste. He had the reputation of being a good lawyer and a just judge; and after he obtained power, he devoted his attention to watch over the judicial department as the surest basis of popularity. Nevertheless, we find the government of Michael accused of persecuting the wealthy, merely for the purpose of filling the public treasury by the confiscation of their property. This was an old Roman fiscal resource, which had existed ever since the days of the republic, and whose exercise under the earlier emperors calls forth the bitterness of Tacitus in some of his most vigorous pages. After Bardas was elevated to the dignity of Cæsar, his mature age gave him a deeper interest in projects of ambition than in the wild debauchery of his nephew. He devoted more time to public business and grave society, and less to the wine-cup and the imperial feasts. New boon-companions assembled round Michael, and, to advance their own fortunes, strove to awaken some jealousy of the Cæsar in the breast of the emperor. They solicited the office of spies to watch the conduct of one who, they said, was aspiring to the crown. Michael, seeing Bardas devoted to improving the administration of justice, reforming abuses in the army, regulating the affairs of the church, and protecting learning, felt how much he himself neglected his duties, and naturally began to suspect his uncle. The reformation of the Cæsar was an act of sedition against the worthless emperor.

The favourite parasite of Michael at this time was a man named Basil, who from a simple groom had risen to the rank of lord chamberlain. Basil had attracted the attention of the emperor while still a stable-boy in the service of an officer of the court. The young groom had the good fortune to overcome a celebrated Bulgarian wrestler at a public wrestling-match. The impression produced by this victory over the foreigner, who had been long considered invincible, was increased by a wonderful display of his power in taming the wildest horses, for he possessed the singular natural gift of subduing horses by a whisper.[1] The emperor took him into his service as a groom; but Basil's skill as a sportsman soon made him a favourite and a companion of one who showed little discrimination in the choice of his associates. At the imperial orgies, Basil's perseverance as a boon-companion, and his devotion to all the whims of the emperor, raised him quickly to the highest offices of the court, and he was placed in constant attendance on his sovereign. These favours awakened the jealousy of Bardas, who suspected the Macedonian groom of the power of whispering to Michael as well as to horses. At the same time it secured Basil the support of all the Cæsar's enemies, who considered a drunken groom, even though he had risen to great power at court, as a person not likely to be their rival in ministerial offices.

Basil, however, soon received a very high mark of Michael's personal favour. He was ordered to divorce his wife and marry Eudocia Ingerina, who had long been the emperor's mistress; and it was said that the intercourse continued after she became the wife of the chamberlain.[2] Every ambitious and debauched officer about the court now looked to the fall of Bardas as the readiest means of promotion. Symbatios an

---

[1] Basil rendered an ungovernable horse belonging to the emperor *as tame as a sheep*, by stretching out his hand to its ear.—Leo Gramm. 458.

[2] The chronicles of Michael's reign accuse the emperor of encouraging a criminal intercourse between Basil and Thekla his elder sister, apparently as a recompense for his own intimacy with Eudocia Ingerina after she became Basil's wife.—Symeon Mag. 446. Georg. Mon. 536. Leo Gramm. 464. As a further illustration of the conduct of these ladies, see Leo Gramm. 471, 472; Georg. Mon. 545, sects. viii. and xii.

Armenian, a patrician and postmaster of the empire, who was the son-in-law of Bardas, dissatisfied with his father-in-law for refusing to gratify his inordinate ambition, joined Basil in accusing the Cæsar of plotting to mount the throne. The emperor, without much hesitation, authorised the two intriguers to assassinate his uncle.

An expedition for reconquering Crete from the Saracens was about to sail. The emperor, the Cæsar, and Basil all partook of the holy sacrament together before embarking in the fleet, which then proceeded along the coast of Asia Minor to Kepos in the Thrakesian theme.[1] Here the army remained encamped, under the pretext that a sufficient number of transports had not been assembled. Bardas expressed great dissatisfaction at this delay; and one day, while he was urging Michael to give orders for the immediate embarkation of the troops, he was suddenly attacked by Symbatios and Basil, and murdered at the emperor's feet. Basil, who, as chamberlain, had conducted him to the imperial tent, stabbed him in the back.

The accomplished but unprincipled Bardas being removed, the project of invading Crete was abandoned, and Michael returned to the capital. On entering Constantinople, however, it was evident that the assassination of his uncle had given universal dissatisfaction. Bardas, with all his faults, was the best of Michael's ministers, and the failure of the expedition against Crete was attributed to his death. As Michael passed through the streets, a monk greeted him with this bitter salutation: "All hail, emperor! all hail from your glorious campaign! You return covered with blood, and it is your own!" The imperial guards attempted in vain to arrest the fanatic; the people protected him, declaring he was mad.

The assassination of Bardas took place in spring 866; and on the 26th of May, Michael rewarded Basil by proclaiming him his colleague, with the title of Emperor.[2]

Symbatios expected that his participation in his father-in-law's murder would have secured him the title of Cæsar; but he soon perceived he had injured his own fortunes by his crime. He now sought to obtain by open force what he had failed to gain by private murder. He succeeded in drawing Peganes, who commanded the troops in the Opsikian theme, into his conspiracy. The two rebels took up arms, and proclaimed that their object was not to dethrone Michael, but to depose Basil. Though they drew together a considerable body of

---

[1] Probably near Halicarnassus or Cnidus.   [2] Continuator, 129.

troops, rendered themselves masters of a great extent of country, and captured many merchant-ships on their passage to Constantinople, they did not venture to attack the capital. Their plan was ill concerted, for before the end of the summer they had allowed themselves to be completely surrounded by the imperial troops. Peganes was taken prisoner at Kotaeion, and conducted to Constantinople, where his eyes were put out. He was then placed in the Milion, with a platter in his hand, to ask charity from the passers-by. Symbatios was subsequently captured at Keltzene. When he reached Constantinople, he was conducted before Michael. Peganes was brought out to meet him, with a censer of earthenware filled with burning sulphur instead of incense. Symbatios was then deprived of one of his eyes, and his right hand was cut off. In this condition he was placed before the palace of Lausus, with a dish on his knees, as a common beggar. After exhibiting his rebellious officers in this position for three days, Michael allowed them to be imprisoned in their own houses. When Basil mounted the throne, they were pardoned as men no longer dangerous.

The degrading punishment to which two men of the highest rank in the empire were subjected, made a deep impression on the people of Constantinople. The figure of Peganes—a soldier of high reputation—standing in the Milion, asking for an obolos, with a platter in his hand like a blind beggar, haunted their imagination, and, finding its way into the romances of the age, was borrowed to illustrate the greatest vicissitudes of court favour, and give colouring to the strongest pictures of the ingratitude of emperors. The fate of Peganes and Symbatios, woven into a tale called the Life of Belisarius, in which the interest of tragic sentiment was heightened by much historical and local truth, has gained immortality in European literature, and confounded the critical sagacity of eminent modern writers.[1]

One of the few acts which are recorded of the joint reign

[1] Compare Const. Porphyr. Basilius Macedo (*Scrip. post Theoph.* 150, 163,) with Symeon Mag. 449; Georg. Mon. 540; and Leo Gramm. 467; and for the resemblance with the fable of Belisarius, the anonymous author of *Antiquities of Constantinople*, in Banduri, *Imperium Orientale*, i. 7, and Joannis Tzetzæ. *Hist. Variarum Chiliades*, 94, edit. Kiesslingii; also Lord Mahon, *Life of Belisarius*, who tries to support the fable; and "Belisarius—was he blind?" in *Blackwood's Magazine* for May 1847, where the connection of the fable with history is pointed out. It may be worth mentioning, moreover, that Zacharias, *Historiæ Juris Græco-Romani Delineatio*, 58; and Mortreuil, *Histoire du Droit Byzantin*, ii. 499, have both fallen into an error in supposing this Symbatios, who had lost an eye and his right hand during the reign of Michael III., to be the same person as the Symbatios or Sabbatios who assisted Leo VI. in the revision of the Basilika.

of Michael and Basil was the desecration of the tomb of Constantine V. (Copronymus). This base act was perpetrated to flatter a powerful party in the church, of which the leading members were hostile to Bardas, on account of his persecution of Ignatius. The precarious position of Photius after the murder of his patron, and the inherent subserviency of the Greek ecclesiastical dignitaries, made him ready to countenance any display of orthodoxy, however bigoted, that pleased the populace. The memory of Constantine V. was still cherished by no inconsiderable number of Iconoclasts. Common report still boasted of the wealth and power to which the empire had attained under the just administration of the Iconoclast emperors, and their conduct served as a constant subject of reproach to Michael. The people, however, were easily persuaded that the great exploits of Constantine V., and the apparent prosperity of his reign, had been the work of the devil. The sarcophagus in which the body of this great emperor reposed was of green marble, and of the richest workmanship. By the order of the drunken Michael and the Sclavonian groom Basil, it was broken open, and the body, after having lain for upwards of ninety years in peace, was dragged into the circus, where the body of John the Grammarian, torn also from the tomb, was placed beside it. The remains of these great men were beaten with rods to amuse the vilest populace, and then burned in the Amastrianon— the filthiest quarter of the capital, and the place often used for the execution of malefactors.[1] The splendid sarcophagus of Constantine was cut in pieces by order of Michael, to form a balustrade in a new chapel he was constructing at Pharos.

The drunkenness of Michael brought on delirium tremens, and rendered him liable to fits of madness. He observed that Basil's desire to maintain the high position he had reached produced the same reformation in his conduct which had been visible in that of Bardas. The Emperor Basil became a very different man from Basil the groom. The change was observed by Michael, and it rendered him dissatisfied with his colleague. In one of his fits of madness he invested another of the companions of his orgies, named Basiliskian, with the imperial title.

---

[1] Georg. Mon. 540. Leo. Gramm. 467. The anonymous author of the *Ant. Constant.* (Banduri, *Imp. Orientale*, 20) says that the Amastrianon was a favourite resort of demons; see the notes to tom. ii. 558.

In such a court there could be little doubt that the three emperors, Michael, Basil, and Basiliskian, could not long hold joint sway. It was probably soon a race who should be the first murdered, and in such cases the ablest man is generally the most successful criminal. Basil, having reason to fear for his own safety, planned the assassination of his benefactor with the greatest deliberation. The murder was carried into execution after a supper-party given by Theodora to her son in the palace of Anthimos, where he had resolved to spend a day hunting on the Asiatic coast. Basil and his wife, Eudocia Ingerina, were invited by the empress-mother to meet her son, for all decency was banished from this most orthodox court. Michael, according to his usual habit, was carried from the supper-table in a state of intoxication, and Basil accompanied his colleague to his chamber, of which he had previously rendered the lock useless. Basiliskian, the third of this infamous trio, was sleeping, in a state of intoxication, on the bed placed in the imperial apartment for the chamberlain on duty. The chamberlain, on following his master, found the lock of the door useless and the bolts broken, but did not think of calling for assistance to secure the entrance in the palace of the empress-mother.

Basil soon returned, attended by John of Chaldia, a Persian officer named Apelates, a Bulgarian named Peter, Constantine Toxaras, his own father Bardas, his brother Marinos, and his cousin Ayleon. The chamberlain immediately guessed their purpose, and opposed their entry into the chamber. Michael, disturbed by the noise, rose from his drunken sleep, and was attacked by John of Chaldia, who cut off both his hands with a blow of his sabre. The emperor fell on the ground. Basiliskian was slain in the mean time by Apelates. Constantine Toxaras, with the relatives of Basil, guarded the door and the corridor leading to the apartment, lest the officers of the emperor or the servants of Theodora should be alarmed by the noise. The shouts of the chamberlain and the cries of Michael alarmed Basil and those in the chamber, and they rushed into the corridor to secure their retreat. But the tumult of debauchery had been often as loud, and the cries of murder produced no extraordinary sensation where Michael was known to be present. All remaining silent without, some of the conspirators expressed alarm lest Michael should not be mortally wounded. John of Chaldia, the boldest of the assassins, returned to make his work sure. Finding the emperor sitting on the floor uttering bitter lamentations, he plunged his sword into his heart, and then returned to assure Basil that all was finished.

The conspirators crossed over to Constantinople, and having secured their entrance into the imperial palace by means of two Persians, Eulogios and Artabasd, who were on guard, Basil was immediately proclaimed sole emperor, and the death of Michael III. was publicly announced. In the morning the body of Michael was interred in a monastery at Chrysopolis, near the palace of Anthimos. Theodora was allowed to direct the funeral ceremonies of the son whom her own neglect had conducted to an early and bloody death.

The people of Constantinople appear to have taken very little interest in this infamous assassination, by which a small band of mercenary adventurers transferred the empire of the Romans from the Amorian dynasty to a Macedonian groom, whose family reigned at Constantinople for two centuries, with greater power and glory than the Eastern Empire had attained since the days of Justinian.

CHAPTER IV

STATE OF THE BYZANTINE EMPIRE DURING THE ICONOCLAST PERIOD

SECTION I

PUBLIC ADMINISTRATION—DIPLOMATIC AND COMMERCIAL RELATIONS

Constantinople neither a Greek nor a Roman city—The Greek race not the dominant people in the empire—Circumstances which modified despotic power—Extent of the empire—Military strength—Loss of Italy, Sicily, and Crete—Embassy of John the Grammarian to Bagdat —Commercial policy—Wealth.

IN ancient times, when the civilisation of the Greek people had attained its highest degree of moral culture, the Hellenic race was assailed almost simultaneously by the Persians, Carthaginians, and Tyrrhenians. The victories obtained over these enemies are still regarded as the triumphs on which the political civilisation of Europe, and of the great dwelling-place of liberty beyond the Atlantic, is based. The age of Leo the Isaurian found the government of the Byzantine empire in a position not very dissimilar from that of the Greek race in the time of Miltiades. The Athenian people fought for the political progress of human civilisation on the plain of Marathon. Leo battled for the empire of law and administration behind the walls of Constantinople; the victory of Miltiades secured only one hundred and fifty years of liberty to the Greeks, that of the Iconoclast gave nearly five centuries of despotic power to a system hostile to the development of the human intellect. The voice of fame has conferred immortal glory on the doubtful virtues of the Athenian general, and treated with neglect the profound statesmanship of the stern Isaurian sovereign; and it has done so not unjustly, for the gratitude of all succeeding ages is due to those who extend the political ideas of mankind, whereas those who only preserve property must be satisfied with the applause of the proprietors. Nevertheless the Iconoclast period of Byzantine history presents a valuable study to the historian, both in what it did and what it left undone—in the greatness of the imperial administration, and the littleness of the people who were its subjects.

The Byzantine empire passed through a more dangerous ordeal than classic Greece, inasmuch as patriotism is a surer national bulwark than mechanical administration. The struggle for the preservation of Constantinople from the Saracens awakens no general feelings and noble aspirations; it only teaches those who examine history as political philosophers, what social and administrative tendencies a free people ought carefully to avoid. On this subject the scanty annals of the Greek people, as slaves of the Byzantine emperors, though far from an attractive chapter in history, are filled with much premonitory instruction for nations in an advanced social condition.

Neither the emperors of Constantinople, though they styled themselves Emperors of the Romans, nor their subjects, though calling themselves Roman citizens, sought at this period to identify themselves with the reminiscences of the earlier Roman Empire. The Romans of Italy and the Greeks of Hellas had both now fallen very low in public opinion.[1] Constantinople, as a Christian capital, claimed to be the mistress of a new world, and the emperors of the East considered themselves masters of all the territories of pagan Rome, because the dominion over all Christians was a right inherent in the emperor of the orthodox. But Constantinople was founded as an antagonist to old Rome, and this antagonism has always been a portion of its existence. As a Christian city, its church and its ecclesiastical language always stood in opposition to the church and ecclesiastical language of Rome. The thoughts of the one were never transferred in their pure conception to the mind of the other. For several centuries Latin was the language of the court, of the civil government, and of the higher ranks of society at Constantinople. In the time of Leo III., and during the Byzantine Empire, Greek was the language of the administration and the people, as well as of the church; but we are not to suppose, from that circumstance, that the inhabitants of the city considered themselves as Greeks by descent. Even by the populace the term would have been looked upon as one of reproach, applicable as a national appellation only to the

---

[1] See Pausanias, *Achaica*, xvii. 2, for the character the Greeks bore in the time of Vespasian; and the passage of Luitprand, *Scrip. Rer. Ital.* ii. pars i. 481, for that of the Romans. Gibbon says, " For the sins of Cato or Tully, Minos might have imposed as a fit penance the daily perusal of this barbarous passage."—ix. 143, note x.

lower orders of society in the Hellenic themes. The people of Constantinople, and of the Byzantine empire at large, in their civil capacity, were Romans, and in their religious, orthodox Christians; in no social relation, whether of race or nationality, did they consider themselves Greeks.

At the time of the succession of Leo III., the Hellenic race occupied a very subordinate position in the empire. The predominant influence in the political administration was in the hands of Asiatics, and particularly of Armenians, who filled the highest military commands. The family of Leo the Isaurian was said to be of Armenian descent; Nicephorus I. was descended from an Arabian family; Leo V. was an Armenian; Michael II., the founder of the Amorian dynasty, was of a Phrygian stock. So that for a century and a half, the Empress Irene appears to be the only sovereign of pure Greek blood who occupied the imperial throne, though it is possible that Michael Rhangabé was an Asiatic Greek. Of the numerous rebels who assumed the title of Emperor, the greater part were Armenians.[1] Indeed, Kosmas, who was elected by the Greeks when they attacked Constantinople in the year 727, was the only rebel of the Greek nation who attempted to occupy the throne for a century and a half. Artabasdos, who rebelled against his brother-in-law, Constantine V., was an Armenian. Alexis Mousel, strangled by order of Constantine VI. in the year 790; Bardan, called the Turk, who rebelled against Nicephorus I.; Arsaber, the father-in-law of Leo V., convicted of treason in 808; and Thomas, who revolted against Michael II., were all Asiatics, and most of them Armenians. Another Alexis Mousel, who married Maria, the favourite daughter of Theophilus; Theophobos, the brother-in-law of the same emperor; and Manuel, who became a member of the council of regency at his death, were likewise of foreign Asiatic descent. Many of the Armenians in the Byzantine empire at this time belonged to the oldest and most illustrious families of the Christian world, and their connection with the remains of Roman society at Constantinople, in which the pride of birth was cherished, is a proof that Asiatic influence had eclipsed Roman and Greek in the government of the empire. Before this happened, the Roman aristocracy transplanted to Constantinople must have

[1] See the conjectures of St. Martin on the Armenian origin of these officers, in his edition of Lebeau, *Histoire du Bas-Empire*, xii. 355, note 3; 4c4, note 3; 431, note 2; also, *The History of Armenia*, by Father Michael Chamich, translated by J. Avdall; Calcutta, 1827; vol. i. pp. 395, 399.

become nearly extinct. The names which appear as belonging to the aristocracy of Constantinople, when it became thoroughly Greek, make their first appearance under the Iconoclasts; and the earliest are those of Doukas, Skleros, and Melissenos.[1] The order introduced into society by the political and ecclesiastical reforms of Leo III., gave a permanence to high birth and great wealth, which constituted henceforth a claim to high office. A degree of certainty attended the transmission of all social advantages which never before existed in the Roman empire. This change would alone establish the fact that the reforms of Leo III. had rendered life and property more secure, and consequently circumscribed the arbitrary power of preceding emperors by stricter forms of administrative and legal procedure. An amusing instance of the influence of aristocratic and Asiatic prejudices at Constantinople, will appear in the eagerness displayed by Basil I., a Sclavonian groom from Macedonia, to claim descent from the Armenian royal family. The defence of this absurd pretension is given by his grandson, Constantine VII. (Porphyrogenitus.)[2]

It is difficult to draw an exact picture of the Byzantine government at this period, for facts can easily be collected, which, if viewed in perfect isolation, would, according to our modern ideas, warrant the conclusion, either that it was a tyrannical despotism, or a mild legal monarchy. The personal exercise of power by the emperor, in punishing his officers with death and stripes, without trial, and his constant interference with the administration of justice, contrast strongly with the boldness displayed by the monks and clergy in opposing his power. In order to form a correct estimate of the real position occupied by the Byzantine empire in the progressive improvement of the human race, it is necessary to compare it, on one hand, with the degraded Roman empire which it replaced; and on the other, with the arbitrary government of the Mohammedans, and the barbarous administration of the northern nations, which it resisted. The regularity of its civil, financial, and judicial administration, the defensive power of its military and naval establishments, are remarkable in an age of temporary measures and universal aggression. The state of education, and the moral position of the clergy, certainly offer favourable points of comparison, even with the

---

[1] Theophanes, *inc.* Contin. 428. *Script. Post Theoph.* 14.
[2] Const. Porphyr. *Vita Basilii*, 133.

brilliant empires of Haroun Al Rashid and Charlemagne. On the other hand, fiscal rapacity was the incurable canker of the Byzantine, as it had been of the Roman government. From it arose all those precautionary measures which reduced society to a stationary condition. No class of men was invested with a constitutional or legal authority to act as defenders of the people's rights against the fiscality of the imperial administration. Insurrection, rebellion, and revolution were the only means of obtaining either reform or justice, when the interests of the treasury were concerned. Yet even in this branch of its administration no other absolute government ever displayed equal prudence and honesty. Respect for the law was regarded by the emperors as self-respect; and the power possessed by the clergy, who in some degree participated in popular feelings, contributed to temper and restrain the exercise of arbitrary rule.

Yet the Byzantine empire, however superior it might be to contemporary governments, presents points of resemblance, which prove that the social condition of its population was in no inconsiderable degree affected by some general causes operating on the general progress of human civilisation in the East and the West. The seventh century was a period of disorganisation in the Eastern Empire, and of anarchy in all the kingdoms formed out of the provinces of the Western. Even throughout the dominions of the Saracens, in spite of the power and energy of the central administration of the caliphs, the nations under its rule were in a declining state.

The first step towards the constitution of modern society, which renders all equal in the eye of the law, was made at Constantinople about the commencement of the eighth century. The reign of Leo III. opens a new social era for mankind, as well as for the Eastern Empire; for when he reorganised the frame of Roman society, he gave it the seeds of the peculiar features of modern times. Much of this amelioration is, without doubt, to be attributed to the abilities of the Iconoclast emperors; but something may be traced to the infusion of new vigour into society from popular feelings, of which it is difficult to trace the causes or the development. The Byzantine empire, though it regained something of the old Roman vigour at the centre of its power, was unable to prevent the loss of several provinces; and Basil I. succeeded to an empire of smaller extent than Leo III., although to one that was far richer and more powerful. The exarchate of

Ravenna, Rome, Crete, and Sicily had passed under the dominion of hostile states. Venice had become completely independent. On the other hand, it must be remembered, that in 717 the Saracens occupied the greater part of Asia Minor and Cyprus, from both which they had been almost entirely expelled before 867. The only conquest of which the emperors of Constantinople could boast was the complete subjugation of the allied city of Cherson to the central administration. Cherson had hitherto enjoyed a certain degree of political independence which had for centuries secured its commercial prosperity. Its local freedom was destroyed in the time of Theophilus, who sent his brother-in-law Petronas to occupy it with an army, and govern it as an imperial province. The power of the emperor was, however, only momentarily increased by the destruction of the liberties of Cherson; the city fell rapidly from the degree of wealth and energy which had enabled it to afford military aid to Constantine the Great, and to resist the tyranny of Justinian II., and lost much of its commercial importance.

Historians generally speak of the Byzantine empire at this period as if it had been destitute of military power. Events as far removed from one another, in point of time, as our own misfortunes in India at the Black Hole of Calcutta, and the massacre of Cabul, are cited to prove that the Byzantine government was incapable, and the Byzantine army feeble and unwarlike. The truth is this, the Byzantine empire was a highly civilised society, and consequently its tendencies were essentially defensive when those of the rest of the world were aggressive. The Saracens, Franks, and Bulgarians were nations devoted to war, and yet the Byzantine empire effectually resisted and long outlived these empires of warriors. No contemporary government possessed a permanent military establishment so perfectly organised as the emperor of Constantinople, nor could any bring into the field, on a sudden exigency, a better appointed army. The caliphs had the power of deluging the frontier provinces with larger bodies of light troops than could be prevented from plundering the country, for the imperial armies were compelled to act on the defensive in order to secure the fortified towns, and defensive warfare can rarely protect all the assailable points of an extensive frontier. Whole provinces were therefore often laid waste and depopulated; yet, under the Iconoclast emperors, the Byzantine territories increased in prosperity.

The united attacks of the Saracens, Bulgarians, and Franks inflicted trifling evils on the Byzantine empire, compared with what the predatory incursions of small bands of Normans inflicted on the empire of the successors of Charlemagne, or the incessant rebellions and civil wars on the dominions of the caliphs.

The Saracens devoted all the immense wealth of their empire to their military establishment, and they were certainly more formidable enemies to the Byzantine emperors than the Parthians had been to the Romans; yet the emperors of Constantinople resisted these powerful enemies most successfully. The Saracen troops were no way inferior to the Byzantine in arms, discipline, artillery, and military science; their cavalry was mailed from head to foot, each horseman bearing a lance, a scimitar, and a bow slung over his shoulder. Their discipline was of the strictest kind, and their armies moved not only with catapultas and military engines for field service, but also with all the materials and machines requisite for besieging cities. Under Kassim a band of six thousand men ventured to invade India;[1] yet the caliphs never thought of encountering the Byzantine army unless with immense numbers of their chosen warriors; and they sustained more signal defeats from the emperors of Constantinople than from all the other enemies they encountered together. The bloody contests and hard-fought battles with the armies of the caliphs in Asia Minor, entitle the Byzantine army to rank for several centuries as one of the best the world has ever seen.

The Bulgarians were likewise dangerous enemies. Their continual wars gave them no mean knowledge of military science; and the individual soldiers, from their habits of life, possessed the greatest activity and powers of endurance. In the wars at the end of the eighth and the beginning of the ninth centuries they fought completely armed in steel, and possessed military engines of every kind then known. We have the testimony of a Byzantine writer, that the armies of Crumn were supplied with every warlike machine discovered by the engineering knowledge of the Romans.[2]

In all the scientific departments of war, in the application of mechanical and chemical skill to the art of destruction, and in the construction of engines for the attack and defence

---

[1] Elphinston's *History of the Mohammedans in India*, i. 512.

[2] The army of Crumn consisted of 30,000 ὁλοσίδηροι. See also the list of military engines. Theophanes, *Incent. Con.* 434.

of fortresses, there can be no doubt that the Byzantine engineers were no way inferior to the Roman; for in the arsenals of Constantinople, the workmen and the troops had been uninterruptedly employed from generation to generation in executing and improving the same works. Only one important invention seems to have been made, which changed, in some degree, the art of defence on shore, and of attack at sea: this was the discovery of Greek fire, and the method of launching it to a certain distance from brazen tubes.[1]

The aristocracy of the Byzantine empire, though not exclusively devoted to war, like the nobility of other contemporary nations, was still deeply imbued with the military spirit. No people can boast of a greater number of warlike sovereigns than the Byzantine empire, from the accession of Leo III. to the death of Michael III. During this period of a century and a half, not one of the emperors failed to appear at the head of the army; and Leo III., Constantine V., Leo V., Michael II., and Theophilus, were experienced generals; the careless Constantine VI. and the debauched Michael III. appeared to greater advantage in the camp than in the capital; and it was only the weak, religious persecutor, Michael Rhangabé, who was absolutely contemptible as a soldier.

Amidst this military energy, nothing seems more remarkable than the indifference with which the loss of central Italy, and the islands of Crete and Sicily, was viewed by the Byzantine government.[2] It would seem that the value of these distant provinces was estimated at Constantinople solely by the amount of revenue they produced to the imperial treasury, and that when the expenses of a province absorbed all its revenues, or its reconquest was found to entail a degree of outlay that was never likely to be repaid, the emperors were often indifferent at the loss.

The foundation of the Frank empire by Charles Martel very nearly corresponds with the organisation of the Byzantine by Leo III. The invasion of Italy by Pepin, A.D. 754, and the temporal authority conceded to the popes, compelled the

---

[1] *De Feu Grégois, des Feux de Guerre, et des Origines de la Poudre à Canon,* par Reinaud et Favé, 79. *Mémoire sur la Découverte Très-ancienne en Asie et dans l'Indo-Perse de la Poudre à Canon et des Armes à Feu,* par le Chev. de Paravey; Paris, 1850.

[2] The exarchate extended from the Po to Fermo, and included all the country between the Adriatic and the Apennines. The Pentapolis, now the Marca d'Ancona, comprised the country from Rimini to Fermo. The duchy of Rome embraced the patrimony of St. Peter and the Campagna. This territory, filled as it then was with cities, towns, and slaves, may have contained a population of 2,000,000 of inhabitants.

Byzantine emperors to enter into negotiations with Charlemagne on a footing of equality. The importance of maintaining friendly relations with Constantinople is said by Eginhard to have influenced Charlemagne in affecting to receive the imperial crown from the Pope by surprise; he wished to be able to plead that his election as emperor of the West was unsought on his part. Interest silenced pride on both sides, and diplomatic relations were established between the two emperors of the East and the West; embassies and presents were sent from Constantinople to Charlemagne and his successors, treaties were concluded, and the Byzantine government became in some degree connected with the international system of medieval Europe.[1] The superiority still held by the court of Constantinople in public opinion, is manifest in the Greek salutations with which the Pope flattered Charlemagne at the commencement of his letters; yet Greek official salutations had only lately supplanted Latin at Constantinople itself.[2]

The political alliances and diplomatic relations of the Byzantine court were very extensive; but the most important were those with the Khan of the Khazars, who ruled all the northern shores of the Caspian Sea, and with the Ommiad caliphs of Spain. Scandinavian ambassadors who had passed through Russia visited the splendid court of Theophilus; but their mission related rather to mercantile questions, or to the manner of furnishing recruits to the mercenary legions at Constantinople, than to political alliance.[3]

The remarkable embassy of John the Grammarian, who was sent by Theophilus as ambassador to the Caliph Motassem, deserves particular notice, as illustrating the external character of Byzantine diplomacy.[4] The avowed object of the mission

---

[1] Michael II. sent a copy of the works attributed to Dionysius the Areopagite to Louis le Débonnaire, as a valuable present, in 824. The regency of Theodora attached considerable importance to the embassies sent to Lothaire and Louis II.—Schlosser, 566.

[2] Constant. Porphyr. *De Ceremon. Aulæ Byzantinæ*, ii. 29.

[3] Schlosser, *Geschichte der Bilderstürmender Kaiser*, 483.

[4] There is some difficulty in fixing the precise date of this embassy. Weil, with great probability, places it at the end of 833, ii. 297. Compare Continuator, 60; Symeon Mag., 419; Genesius, 29; Leo Gramm. 452, edit. Par.; 218, edit. Bonn.; also note 4 at page 138 of this volume. The people of Constantinople regarded Leo, the archbishop of Thessalonica, as a necromancer or magician, as well as John, on account of the great mechanical works executed under his direction. This need not appear surprising, when we recollect that English tradition ascribes feats of magic to a hero so modern as Sir Francis Drake, for executing the aqueduct that supplies Plymouth with water. It was completed with wonderful celerity, and hence the people relate that Sir Francis made a contract with the devil, in virtue of which the water flowed after his horse's feet as he galloped from the spring to the town. Roger Bacon, on account of his rare knowledge as a natural philosopher, and Faustus as the first printer, were both supposed to have unlawful dealings with the other world.

was to conclude a treaty of peace, but the ambassador had secret instructions to employ every art of persuasion to induce Manuel, one of the ablest generals of the empire, who had distinguished himself greatly in the civil wars of the Saracens, to return to his allegiance. The personal qualities of John rendered him peculiarly well suited to this embassy. To great literary attainments he joined a degree of scientific knowledge, which gained him the reputation of a magician, and he was perfectly acquainted with the Arabic language. All these circumstances insured him a good reception at the court of Bagdat, which had been so lately and so long governed by the Caliph Almamun, one of the greatest encouragers of science and literature who ever occupied a throne. The Byzantine ambassador was equally celebrated for his knowledge of medicine, architecture, mechanics, mathematics, chemistry, astronomy, and astrology; and probably even the Caliph Motassem, though a free-thinker, and a disbeliever in the divine origin of the Koran, shared so much of the popular belief as to credit the tale that the learned Christian priest could read the secrets of futurity in a brazen basin, and felt great curiosity to converse with a man who possessed this rare gift of brazen magnetism.

On quitting Constantinople, John was furnished with the richest furniture, splendid carpets, damasked silk hangings, and plate chased and inlaid with the most beautiful ornaments, taken from the imperial palaces, to which was added 400 lb. of gold for the current expenses of the embassy.

According to the usage of the East, the ambassador was lodged at Bagdat in a palace furnished by the caliph. The magnificent style in which the diplomatic priest installed himself in the apartments he reserved for his own use made a sensation at the court of Motassem, though many then living had witnessed the splendour of Haroun Al Rashid. This lavish display of wealth was better adapted to gratify the vanity of Theophilus than to advance the conclusion of a lasting peace. If we could place implicit confidence in the stories recorded by the Byzantine writers, of various tricks to which the ambassador resorted in order to augment the wonder of the Saracen nobles at the enormous wealth of the Christians, we should be inclined to question the judgment of John himself. His conduct could only have originated in personal pride; and the course attributed to him would have been more likely to excite the Mohammedans to active warfare, where they had prospect of plundering so rich an enemy, than of persuading them to conclude a treaty of peace.

One anecdote, dwelt on with peculiar satisfaction, deserves to be recorded. John possessed a splendid golden basin and ewer, richly chased and ornamented with jewels, and of this he made a great display. Throughout the East, and in many parts of European Turkey at the present day, where knives and forks are not yet in use, it is the practice to wash the hands immediately before commencing a meal, and on rising from the table. A servant pours water from a ewer over the hands of the guest, while another holds a basin to receive it as it falls. This, being done by each guest in turn, would leave ample time for observing the magnificent golden utensils of John at the entertainments he was in the habit of giving to the leading men in Bagdat. At a grand entertainment given by the Byzantine ambassador to the principal nobility of the caliph's court, the slaves rushed into the hall where the guests were assembled, and informed John, in a state of great alarm, that his magnificent golden basin was not to be found. The Saracens eagerly suggested measures for its recovery; but John treated the affair with indifference, and calmly ordered his steward to give the slaves another. Soon two slaves appeared, one bearing in his hand a golden ewer, and the other a basin, larger and more valuable, if not more elegant, than that which it was supposed had been stolen. These had been hitherto kept concealed, on purpose to attract public attention by this pitiful trick.

John, however, gained the respect of the Saracens by his disinterested conduct, for he declined to receive any present of value for himself, even from the caliph. Motassem, therefore, presented him with a hundred Christian captives; but even then he sent immediately to Theophilus, to beg him to return a like number of Saracen prisoners to the caliph. No general exchange of prisoners, however, appears to have been effected at the time of this embassy, which, with other circumstances, affords a proof that the avowed object of the embassy totally failed. When John returned to Constantinople, he persuaded the Emperor Theophilus to construct the palace of Bryas in the varied style of Saracenic architecture, of which those who have seen the interior of the palaces at Damascus, or the work of Owen Jones on the Alhambra, can alone form an adequate idea.

The great wealth of the Byzantine government at this period

H

was derived from the commercial pre-eminence it then enjoyed among the nations of the earth. The commerce of Europe centred at Constantinople in the eighth and ninth centuries more completely than it has ever since done in any one city.[1] The principles of the government, which reprobated monopoly, and the moderation of its duties, which repudiated privileges, were favourable to the extension of trade. While Charlemagne ruined the internal trade of his dominions by fixing a maximum of prices, and destroyed foreign commerce under the persuasion that, by discouraging luxury, he could enable his subjects to accumulate treasures which he might afterwards extort or filch into his own treasury, Theophilus prohibited the persons about his court from engaging in mercantile speculations, lest by so doing they should injure the regular channels of commercial intercourse, by diminishing the profits of the individual dealer.[2] Theophilus proclaimed that commerce was the principal source of the wealth of his people, and that as many derived their means of subsistence from trade, and drew from it alone the funds for payment of the public burdens, any interference with the liberty of commerce was a public as well as a private injury. The political importance of the commercial classes induced Irene, when she usurped the empire, to purchase their favour by diminishing the duties levied at the passages of the Bosphorus and the Hellespont.[3]

During this period the western nations of Europe drew their supplies of Indian commodities from Constantinople, and the Byzantine empire supplied them with all the gold coin in circulation for several centuries.

The Greek navy, both mercantile and warlike, was the most numerous then in existence. Against the merchantships of the Greeks, the piratical enterprises of the Egyptian, African, and Spanish Arabs were principally directed. Unfortunately we possess no authentic details of the commercial state of the Byzantine empire, nor of the Greek population during the Iconoclast period, yet we may safely transfer to this time the records that exist proving the extent of the Greek commerce under the Basilian dynasty. Indeed, we may remember that, as the ignorance and poverty of western Europe was much

[1] The short reign of Theodosius III. was distinguished by the conclusion of a very important commercial treaty, which was taken as the basis of the fiscal stipulations for a long period.—Theophanes, 421, not. 665; or 113, edit. Ven.

[2] Compare the Capitularies of Charlemagne, A.D. 805, art. 5, with the conduct of Theophilus.—Continuator, 55.   [3] Theophanes, 401.

greater in the eleventh and twelfth centuries than in the eighth and ninth, we may conclude that Byzantine commerce was also greater.

The influence of the trade of the Arabians with the East Indies on the supply of the markets of western Europe has been overrated, and that of the Greeks generally lost sight of. This is, in some degree, to be attributed to the circumstance that the most westerly nations, in the times preceding the Crusades, were better acquainted with the commerce and the literature of the Arabs of Spain than with that of the Byzantine Greeks, and also to the preservation of an interesting account of the extensive voyages of the Arabs in the Indian seas during this very period, when we are deprived of all records of Byzantine commerce.[1] The Byzantine markets drew their supplies of Indian and Chinese productions from Central Asia, passing to the north of the caliph's dominions through the territory of the Khazars to the Black Sea. This route was long frequented by the Christians, to avoid the countries in the possession of the Mohammedans, and was the highway of European commerce for several centuries. Though it appears at present a far more difficult and expensive route than that by the Red Sea and the Indian Ocean, it was really safer, more rapid, and more economical, in the eighth, ninth, and tenth centuries. This requires no proof to those who are acquainted with caravan life in the East, and who reflect on the imperfections of ancient navigation, and the dangers which sailing vessels of any burden are exposed to in the Red Sea. When the Venetians and Genoese began to surpass the Greeks in commercial enterprise, they endeavoured to occupy this route; and we have some account of the line it followed, and the manner in which it was carried on, after the East had been thrown into confusion by the conquests of the Crusaders and Tartars, in the travels of Marco Polo.[2] For several centuries the numerous cities of the Byzantine empire supplied the majority of the European consumers with Indian wares, and it was in them alone that the necessary security of property existed to preserve large stores of merchandise. Constantinople was as much superior to every city in the civilised world, in wealth and commerce, as London now is to

[1] See *Relation des Voyages faits par les Arabes et Persans dans l'Inde et à la Chine dans le 9ème Siècle*, Traduction et Eclaircissements par Reinaud; Abulpharagius, *Hist. Dyn.* 284.
[2] *The Travels of Marco Polo*, greatly amended and enlarged, by Hugh Murray, F.R.S.E. Edinburgh, 1844.

the other European capitals. And it must also be borne in mind, that the countries of Central Asia were not then in the rude and barbarous condition into which they have now sunk, since nomade nations have subdued them. On many parts of the road traversed by the caravans, the merchants found a numerous and wealthy population ready to traffic in many articles sought after both in the East and West; and the single commodity of furs supplied the traders with the means of adding greatly to their profits.

Several circumstances contributed to turn the great highway of trade from the dominions of the caliphs to Constantinople. The Mohammedan law, which prohibited all loans at interest, and the arbitrary nature of the administration of justice, rendered all property, and particularly commercial property, insecure.[1] Again, the commercial route of the Eastern trade, by the way of Egypt and the Red Sea, was suddenly rendered both difficult and expensive, about the year 767, by the Caliph Al Mansur, who closed the canal connecting the Nile with the Red Sea. The harvests of Egypt, which had previously filled the coast of Arabia with plenty, could no longer be transported in quantity to the ports of the Red Sea; living became expensive; the population of Arabia declined; and the carrying trade was ruined by the additional expenditure required. The caliph certainly by this measure impoverished and depopulated the rebellious cities of Medina and Mecca to such a degree as to render their military and political power less dangerous to the central authority at Bagdat, but at the same time he ruined the commerce of Egypt with India and the eastern coast of Southern Africa. Since that period, this most important line of communication has never been restored, and the coarser articles of food, of which Egypt can produce inexhaustible stores, are deprived of their natural market in the arid regions of Arabia.[2] The hostile relations between the caliphs of Bagdat and Spain likewise

1 The picture presented by the Oriental historians of the oppressive rule of the caliphs shows how little security existed under the most powerful of the Abassides. Price has the following passage in the history of Al Mansur, and his testimony is confirmed by the recent excellent work of Weil, *Geschichte der Chalifen*: "But the sufferings of the inhabitants of Bagdat had reached that point beyond which there was no further endurance. A licentious banditti had re-established its sway in that unhappy city; the women, the slaves, the property of the inhabitants of every rank and description, had once more become the prey of robbers and outlaws, who regarded neither the authority of Mansur nor of any other person."—*History of the Mohammedan Empire*, ii. 132

2 The last mention of this canal by a European author is in Dicuil, who had heard a monk named Fidelis relate that he navigated on a branch of the Nile from Babylon (old Cairo) to the Red Sea.—Dicuili, *Liber de Mensura Orbis Terræ*, chap. vi. § iii. 6. *Récherches Géograph. et Critiques*, par Letronne, 23.

induced a considerable portion of the Mohammedan population on the shores of the Mediterranean to maintain close commercial relations with Constantinople.[1]

A remarkable proof of the great wealth of society at this period is to be found in the immense amount of specie in circulation. We have already noticed that the Byzantine empire furnished all the western nations of Europe with gold coin for several centuries; and when the hoards of the Mohammedan conquerors of India fell a prey to European invaders, it was found that the gold coins of the Byzantine emperors formed no small part of their treasures. The sums accumulated by Al Mansur and Theophilus were so great, that no extortion could have collected them unless the people had been wealthy, and great activity had existed in the commercial transactions of the age. It is true that the Caliph Al Mansur was remarkable for his extreme parsimony during twelve years of his reign. During this period he is said to have accumulated a treasure amounting to six hundred millions of dirhems in silver, (about £13,750,000,) and fourteen millions of dinars of gold, (£6,417,000,) or at the rate of £1,680,000 a-year.[2] The Emperor Theophilus, whose lavish expenditure in various ways has been recorded, left a large sum in the imperial treasury at his death, which, when increased by the prudent economy of the regency of Theodora, amounted to one thousand and ninety-nine centenaries of gold, three thousand centenaries of silver, besides plate and gold embroidery, that, on being melted down, yielded two hundred centenaries of gold. The gold may be estimated as equal to about four millions and a half of sovereigns, and the weight of silver as equal to £930,000, and the remainder of the treasure as equal to 800,000 sovereigns, making the whole equal to a metallic coinage of 5,230,000 sovereigns, and of course far exceeding that sum in its exchangeable value, from the comparative scarcity of the precious metals, and the more circumscribed circulation of money. There does not appear to be any

[1] Cardonne, *Histoire de l'Afrique et de l'Espagne sous la Domination des Arabes,* i. 340.
[2] The name of Abou Dowaneck (the Father of a Farthing) was given to Al Mansur on account of his avarice. Almamun is said to have expended 300,000 dinars in translating the works of the Greeks, (£137,500.) — Price, ii. 142. Weil, ii. 83, note 2, says that, according to *Cod. Goth.* f. 21, Al Mansur left 900,000,000 dinars, and 60,000,000 dirhems; and also that the treasure left by Haroun Al Rashid amounted to 900,000,000 dinars, and twice as many dirhems. — ii. 127, note 3. It is needless to say that either there must here be a fault of the copyist or gross exaggeration.

exaggeration in this account of the sums left in the Byzantine treasury at the termination of the regency of Theodora, for the historians who have transmitted it wrote under the government of the Basilian dynasty, and under circumstances which afforded access to official sources of information. The Emperor Constantine Porphyrogenitus, their patron, who lived in the third generation after Theodora, would not have authorised any misrepresentation on such a subject.[1]

Some further confirmation of the general wealth of the countries on the shores of the Mediterranean, in which commerce was allowed some degree of liberty, is found in the wealth of Abderrahman III., in Spain, who is said to have possessed an annual revenue of 5,480,000 dinars, though some historians have calculated the whole income of his treasury at 12,945,000, which would be equal to £5,500,000 sterling.[2] The poverty of Europe at a later period, when the isolation caused by the feudal system had annihilated commerce and prevented the circulation of the precious metals, cannot be used as an argument against the probability of this wealth having existed at the earlier period of which we are treating.[3]

In contrasting the state of commercial society in the Byzantine and Saracen empires, we must not overlook the existence of one social feature favourable to the Mohammedans. The higher classes of the Byzantine empire, imbued with the old Roman prejudices, looked on trade of every kind as a debasing pursuit, unsuitable to those who were called by birth or position to serve the state, while the Saracens still paid an outward respect to the antique maxims of Arabian wisdom, which inculcated industry as a source of independence even to men of the highest rank. In deference to this injunction, the Abassid caliphs were in the habit of learning some trade, and selling the produce of their manual labour, to be employed in purchasing the food they consumed.[4]

Perhaps we may also hazard the conjecture, that a considerable addition had, shortly before the reign of Theophilus, been made to the quantity of precious metals in existence by the discovery of new mines. We know, indeed, that the

---

[1] *Scrip. post Theoph.* Contin. 107. Symeon Mag. 436.

[2] Murphy's *Mohammedan Empire in Spain*, 303.

[3] After the conquests of Henry V. in France, the revenues of the crown of England in 1431 amounted only to £53,000 sterling annually.—Michelet, *Hist. de France*, iii. 658. edit. Brux.

[4] In ancient times a Roman citizen who became an artisan was expelled from his tribe. Οὐδενὶ γὰρ ἐξῆν ‘Ρωμαίων οὔτε κάπηλον οὔτε χειροτέχνην βίον ἔχειν.—Dion. Halicar. ix. 25.

Saracens in Spain worked mines of gold and silver to a considerable extent, and we may therefore infer that they did the same in many other portions of their vast dominions. At the same time, whatever was done with profit by the Saracens was sure to be attempted by the Christians under the Byzantine government. The abundance of Byzantine gold coins still in existence leads to the conclusion that gold was obtained in considerable quantities from mines within the circuit of the Eastern Empire.

SECTION II

STATE OF SOCIETY AMONG THE PEOPLE OF THE BYZANTINE EMPIRE IN THE EIGHTH AND NINTH CENTURIES

Decline of civilisation—Influence of the Greek church—Slavery—Theologic spirit of the people—State of science and art—Literature.

The wealth of nations depends in a great degree on their commerce, but the health and strength of a people is derived from its agricultural industry. The population which is pressed into large cities by commercial pursuits, or crowded into little space by manufacturing industry—even the wanderers with the caravan and the navigators of ships—rarely perpetuate their own numbers. All these hunters after riches require to be constantly recruited from the agricultural population of their respective countries. This constant change, which is going on in the population of cities, operates powerfully in altering the condition of society in each successive generation. Hence we find the nature of society in Constantinople strongly opposed to the principles of the Byzantine government. The imperial government, as has been already mentioned, inherited the conservative principles of Roman society, and, had it been possible, would have fettered the population to its actual condition, and reduced the people to castes. The laws of Providence opposed the laws of Rome, and society dwindled away. The ruling classes in the Western Empire had expired before their place was occupied by the conquering nations of the north. In the Eastern Empire, the change went on more gradually; the towns and cities were far more numerous, but many of them embraced within their own walls an agricultural population, which not only recruited the population engaged in trade, but also sent off continual colonies to maintain the great cities of the empire, and especially Constantinople. This great capital, recruited from distant towns, and from nations dissimilar in manners and language, was consequently always undergoing great changes, yet always preserving its peculiar type of a city destitute of any decided nationality, and of homogeneity in its society. It became in turn a Roman, an Asiatic, and a Greek city, as the Roman, the Asiatic, or the Greek aristocracy acquired the predominant influence in the administration. Under the Iconoclasts, it was decidedly more an Asiatic city than either a Greek or a Roman. Whether the Asiatics, the Greeks, or the Sclavonians formed the greater number of the inhabitants, cannot be ascertained. The aristocracy was certainly Asiatic, the middle classes and artisans were chiefly Greeks, but the lowest rabble, the day labourers, the porters, and the domestic servants, when not slaves, appear to have consisted principally of the Sclavonians of Thrace and Macedonia, who, like the Emperor Basil the Macedonian, entered the city with a wallet on their shoulder to seek their fortune. A similar condition of society exists to-day, and thousands of labourers may be seen weekly arriving at Constantinople in the steamers from the Asiatic coast of the Black Sea, and from the coasts between Smyrna, Thessalonica, and the capital.

The causes of decline in society throughout the Roman world have been already noticed, and the nature of the improvement which took place in the Eastern Empire during the reigns of Leo III. and his successors has been pointed out. It is now necessary to examine why the improvement of society so soon assumed a stationary aspect, and arrested the revival of civilisation. We must not forget that the empire was still Roman in its name, traditions, and prejudices. The trammels, binding the actions and even the thoughts of the various classes, were very slightly relaxed, and the permanent relaxation had been made in the interest of the government, not of the people. Men of every rank were confined within a restricted circle, and compelled to act in their individual spheres in one unvarying manner. Within the imperial palace the incessant ceremonial was regarded as the highest branch of human knowledge. It was multiplied into a code, and treated as a science. In the church, tradition, not gospel, was the guide, and the innumerable forms and ceremonies and liturgies were hostile to the exercise of thought and the use of reason. Among the people at large, though the curial system of castes had been broken down, still the trader was fettered to his corporation, and often to his quarter or his street, where he exercised his calling amidst men of the same profession. The education of the child, and the tendencies of society, both prevented the individual from acquiring more than the confined knowledge requisite for his position in the empire. No learning, no talent, and no virtue could conduct either to distinction or wealth, unless exercised according to the fixed formulas that governed the state and the church. Hence even the merchant, who travelled over all Asia, and who supported the system by the immense duties he furnished to government, supplied no new ideas to society, and perhaps passed through life without acquiring many.

This peculiar constitution of society affords us the explanation of the causes which have created some of the vices in the character of the Greeks of later times, which are erroneously supposed to be an inheritance of the days of liberty. The envy and jealousy produced by party contests, in small cities acting as independent governments, was certainly very great, and, we may add, quite natural, where men were violent from their sincerity, and political institutions rendered law imperfect. The envy and jealousy of modern times were baser feelings, and had their origin in meaner interests. Roman society crowded men of the same professions together, and in some measure excluded them from much intercourse with others. The consequence was, that a most violent struggle for wealth, and often for the means of existence, was created amongst those living in permanent personal contact. Every man was deeply interested in rendering himself superior to his nearest neighbour; and as the fixed condition of everything in the empire rendered individual progress unattainable, the only method of obtaining any superiority was by the depreciation of the moral or professional character of a rival, who was always a near neighbour. Envy and calumny were the feelings of the mind which Roman society under the emperors tended to develop with efficacy in every rank. The same cause produces the same effect in the Greek bazaar of every Turkish town of the present day, where tradesmen of the same profession are crowded into the same street. When it is impossible to depreciate the merit of the material and the workmanship, it is easy to calumniate the moral character of the workman.

The influence of the Greek church on the political fabric

of the empire had been long in operation, yet it had failed to infuse a sound moral spirit into either the administration or the people. Still it may be possible to trace some of the secondary causes which prepared the way for the reforms of Leo III. to the sense of justice, moral respect, and real religious faith, infused into the mass of the population by a comparison of the doctrines of Christianity with those of Mohammedanism. But the blindness of the age has concealed from our view many of the causes which impelled society to co-operate with the Iconoclast emperors in their career of improvement and re-organisation. That the moral condition of the people of the Byzantine empire under the Iconoclast emperors was superior to that of any equal number of the human race in any preceding period, can hardly be doubted. The bulk of society occupied a higher social position in the time of Constantine Copronymus than of Pericles; the masses had gained more by the decrease of slavery and the extension of free labour than the privileged citizens had lost. Public opinion, though occupied on meaner objects, had a more extended basis, and embraced a larger class. Perhaps, too, the war of opinions concerning ecclesiastical forms or subtleties tended to develop pure morality as much as the ambitious party-struggles of the Pnyx. When the merits and defects of each age are fairly weighed, both will be found to offer lessons of experience which the student of political history ought not to neglect.

There may be some difference of opinion concerning the respective merits of Hellenic, Roman, and Byzantine society, but there can be none concerning the superiority of Byzantine over that which existed in the contemporary empires of the Saracens and the Franks. There we find all moral restraints weakened, and privileged classes or conquering nations ruling an immense subject population, with very little reference to law, morality, or religion. Violence and injustice claimed at Bagdat an unbounded license, until the Turkish mercenaries extinguished the caliphate, and it was the Norman invaders who reformed the social condition of the Franks. Mohammedanism legalised polygamy with all its evils in the East. In the West, licentiousness was unbounded, in defiance of the precepts of Christianity. Charles Martel, Pepin, and Charlemagne are said all to have had two wives at a time, and a numerous household of concubines. But on turning to the Byzantine empire, we find that the Emperor Constantine VI.

prepared the way for his own ruin by divorcing his first wife and marrying a second, in what was considered an illegal manner. The laws of the Franks attest the frequency of female drunkenness; and the whole legislation of Western Europe, during the seventh and eighth centuries, indicates great immorality, and a degree of social anarchy, which explains more clearly than the political events recorded in history, the real cause of the fall of one government after another.[1] The superior moral tone of society in the Byzantine empire was one of the great causes of its long duration; it was its true conservative principle.

The authority exercised by the senate, the powers possessed by synods and general councils of the church, and the importance often attached by the emperors to the ratification of their laws by silentia and popular assemblies, mark a change in the Byzantine empire in strong contrast with the earlier military empire of the Romans. The highest power in the state had been transferred from the army to the laws of the empire—no inconsiderable step in the progress of political civilisation. The influence of those feelings of humanity which resulted from this change, are visible in the mild treatment of many unsuccessful usurpers and dethroned emperors. During the reign of Nicephorus I., the sons of Constantine V., Bardanes, and Arsaber, were all living in monasteries, though they had all attempted to occupy the throne. Constantine VI. and Michael I. lived unmolested by their successors.

The marked feature of ancient society was the division of mankind into two great classes—freemen and slaves. The proportion between these classes was liable to continual variation, and every considerable variation produced a corresponding alteration in the laws of society, which we are generally unable to follow. The progress of the mass of the population was, however, constantly retarded until the extinction of slavery. But towards that boon to mankind, great progress was made in the Byzantine empire during the eighth and ninth centuries. The causes that directly tended to render free labour more profitable than it had been hitherto, when applied to the cultivation of the soil, and which consequently operated more immediately in extinguishing predial slavery, and repressing the most extensive branch of the slave-trade, by supplying the cities with free emigrants, cannot be indicated with precision. It has been very generally asserted that we

[1] *Charlemagne*, par Capefigue, i. 54, 185,

ought to attribute the change to the influence of the Christian religion. If this be really true, cavillers might observe that so powerful a cause never in any other case produced its effects so tardily. Unfortunately, however, though ecclesiastical influence has exercised immense authority over the internal policy of European society, religious influence has always been comparatively small; and though Christianity has laboured to abolish slavery, it was often for the interest of the church to perpetuate the institution. Slavery had, in fact, ceased to exist in most European countries, while many Christians still upheld its legality and maintained that its existence was not at variance with the doctrines of their religion.[1]

The precise condition of slaves in the Byzantine empire at this period must be learned from a careful study of the imperial legislation of Rome, compared with later documents. As a proof of the improved philanthropy of enlightened men during the Iconoclast period, the testament of Theodore Studita deserves to be quoted. That bold and independent abbot says, "A monk ought not to possess a slave, neither for his own service, nor for the service of his monastery, nor for the culture of its lands; for a slave is a man made after the image of God;" but he derogates in some degree from his own merits, though he gives a correct picture of the feelings of his time, by adding, "and this, like marriage, is only allowable in those living a secular life."[2]

The foundation of numerous hospitals, and other charitable institutions, both by emperors and private individuals, is also a proof that feelings of philanthropy as well as religion had penetrated deeply into men's minds.

The theologic spirit which pervaded Byzantine society is to be attributed as much to material causes as to the intellectual condition of the Greek nation. Indeed, the Greeks had at times only a secondary share in the ecclesiastical controversies in the Eastern church, though the circumstance of those controversies having been carried on in the Greek language has made the nations of western Europe attribute them to a

---

[1] For the extent to which the slave-trade was carried on by the Latin Christians, see Marin. *Storia civile e politica del Commercio de' Veneziana*, ii. 52.

[2] *Sancti Theodori Studitæ Epistolæ aliaque Scripta Dogmatica*, in the fifth volume of *Sirmondi Opera Varia*, p. 66. On the subject of Roman and Byzantine slavery, see Blair, *An Inquiry into the State of Slavery amongst the Romans*; Biot, *De l'Abolition de l'Esclavage ancien en Occident*; Babington, *The Influence of Christianity in Promoting the Abolition of Slavery in Europe*; and Wallon, *Histoire de l'Esclavage dans l'Antiquité*, in 3 volumes. This last work is a valuable addition to our knowledge of society under the Roman emperors.

philosophic, speculative, and polemic spirit inherent in the Hellenic mind. A very slight examination of history is sufficient to prove, that several of the heresies which disturbed the Eastern church had their origin in the more profound religious ideas of the Oriental nations, and that many of the opinions called heretical were, in a great measure, expressions of the mental nationality of the Syrians, Armenians, Egyptians, and Persians, and had no connection whatever with the Greek mind.

Even the contest with the Iconoclasts was a dispute in which the ancient Oriental opinions concerning the operations of mind and matter were as much concerned, as the Greek contest between the necessity of artificial symbols of faith on the one hand, and the duty of developing the intellectual faculties by cultivating truth through the reason, not the imagination, on the other. The ablest writer on the Greek side of the question, John Damascenus, was a Syrian, and not a Greek. The political struggle to establish the centralisation of ecclesiastical and political power was likewise quite as important an element in the contest as the religious question; and as soon as it appeared firmly established, the emperors became much more inclined to yield to popular prejudices. The victory of the image-worshippers tended to exalt a party in the Eastern church devoted to ecclesiastical tradition, but little inclined to cultivate Hellenic literature or cherish Hellenic ideas, which it considered hostile to the legendary lore contained in the lives of the saints. From the victory of this party, accordingly, we find a more circumscribed circle of intellectual culture began to prevail in the Byzantine empire. John the Grammarian, Leo the Mathematician, and Photius, who acquired his vast literary attainments as a layman, were the last profound and enlightened Byzantine scholars; they left no successors, nor has any Greek of the same intellectual calibre since appeared in the world.

A greater similarity of thought and action may be traced throughout the Christian world in the eighth century than in subsequent ages. The same predominance of religious feeling and ecclesiastical ceremonials; the same passion for founding monasteries and raising discussions; the same disposition to make life subservient to religion, to make all amusements ecclesiastical, and to embody the enjoyment of music, painting, and poetry in the ceremonies of the church; the same abuse of the right of asylum to criminals by the ecclesiastical authorities, and the same antagonsim between the church and the state, is visible in the East and the West.[1]

The orthodox church was originally Greek; the seven general councils whose canons had fixed its doctrines were Greek; and the popes, when they rose into importance, could only adopt a scheme of theology already framed. The religious or theological portion of Popery, as a section of the Christian church, is really Greek; and it is only the ecclesiastical, political, and theocratic peculiarities of the fabric which can be considered as the work of the Latin church. The general unity of Christians was, however, prominent in good as well as evil, for if the missionary labours of Boniface among the Germans, at the commencement of the eighth century, reflect glory on the Latin church, the conversion of the Bulgarians in the middle of the ninth, by the ministry of Methodios and Kyrillos, is honourable to the Byzantine. These two monks, natives of Thessalonica, where they lived surrounded by a fierce tribe of Sclavonians, devoted themselves to study the language of these troublesome neighbours. Under the regency of the Empress Theodora, they rendered their knowledge of the Sclavonian dialect the means of propagating Christianity and advancing the cause of civilisation, by visiting Bulgaria in the character of missionaries. They are universally allowed to have conducted their mission in a Christian spirit, and to have merited the great success that attended their labours.[2]

The great improvement which took place in the administration of justice, and the legal reforms effected by Leo III. and Constantine V., have been already noticed. Leo V. and Theophilus also gained the greatest praise, even from their adversaries, for the strict control they established over the forms of proceeding and the decisions of the courts of law. The legal monuments of this period, however, by no means correspond with the extent of the administrative improvement which took place. The era of legislative greatness in the Byzantine empire was under the Basilian dynasty, but it was under the Iconoclast emperors that new vigour was infused into the system, and the improvements were made which laid

[1] The influence of the monks during the Iconoclast contest became so great that the monasteries on Olympus, Athos, and Ida formed themselves into small republics, and almost aspired at living independent of the civil power.—Genesius, 39. The Emperor Theophilus, a man by no means under the direct influence of the clergy, formed a new asylum for criminals at the silver tomb of his beloved daughter Maria.—Leo Gramm. 451.
[2] Mosheim, *Ecclesiastical History*, ii. 280—Soames. Neander, *History of the Christian Religion and Church*, iii. 307.—Torrey.

the foundation of the stability, wealth, and power of the Byzantine empire.

The scientific attainments of the educated class in the Byzantine empire were unquestionably very considerable. Many were invited to the court of the Caliph Almamun, and contributed far more than his own subjects to the reputation that sovereign has deservedly gained in the history of science. The accurate measurement of the earth's orbit in his time seems to show that astronomical and mathematical knowledge had at no previous period attained a greater height; and if the Byzantine authorities are to be credited, one of their learned men, Leo the Mathematician, who was afterwards archbishop of Thessalonica, was invited to the court of the caliph, because he was universally recognised to be superior to all the scientific men at Bagdat in mathematical and mechanical knowledge.[1] A proof that learning was still cultivated in the distant provinces of the Byzantine empire, and that schools of some eminence existed in Greece, is to be found in the fact that Leo, when a layman, retired to a college in the island of Andros to pursue his studies, and there laid the foundation of the scientific knowledge by which he acquired his reputation. After he was compelled, on account of his opposition to image-worship, to resign the archbishopric of Thessalonica, the general respect felt for his learning obtained for him from Bardas Cæsar the appointment of president of the new university, founded at Constantinople in the reign of Michael III., in which chairs of geometry and astronomy had been established, as well as the usual instruction in Greek literature.[2]

It was under the direction of Leo that several of those remarkable works of jewellery, combined with wonderful mechanical contrivances, were executed for the Emperor Theophilus, which have been already mentioned.[3] The perfection

---

[1] Almamun's astronomers calculated the length of the year at 365 days 5 hours 46 minutes and 30 seconds. The true length is 365 days 5 hours 48 minutes and 48 seconds. Niebuhr has pointed out the exactitude attained by the Etruscans in fixing the length of the solar year.—*Hist. of Rome*, i. 274. The Mexican calendar in use before the discovery of America was the most perfect before the Gregorian. Humboldt, *Vues des Cordillères et Monumens des Peuples Indigènes de l'Amerique*, 125. For the obligations of the Arabs to the Byzantines from the time of Mansur, see Weil, ii. 81, 84, 93. Greek physicians and Greek cooks are mentioned in the Arabian Nights. The Caliph Mansur was attended by Greek and Indian physicians.

[2] The history of Leo is given at length by the Continuator, 115. He was called the great philosopher, and it is said that Almamun wrote to Theophilus requesting him to send Leo to the court of Bagdat. Leo studied grammar and poetry at Constantinople; rhetoric, philosophy, and the pure sciences at Andros. In the year 869 he was present in the Church of the Virgin, called Sigma C, when it fell in consequence of the shock of an earthquake, and all the congregation, with the exception of Leo and a few others, perished.—Symeon Mag. 454.   [3] See page 140

of the telegraph by fire-signals, from the frontiers of the empire to the shores of the Bosphorus, and the machinery by which the signals were communicated to a dial placed in the imperial council-chamber, were also the work of Leo.[1] The fame which still attended distinguished artists and mechanicians at Constantinople shows us that the love of knowledge and art was not entirely extinct; and the relics of Byzantine jewellery, often found buried in the most distant regions of Europe, prove that a considerable trade was carried on in these works.

Even the art of statuary was not entirely neglected, for it has been noticed already that Constantine VI. erected a statue of bronze in honour of his mother Irene.[2] Painting, however, was more universally admired, and mosaics were easily adapted to private dwellings. There were many distinguished painters in the Byzantine empire at this time, and there is reason to think that some of their productions were wonderful displays of artistic skill, without giving credit to the miraculous powers of the works of Lazaros. The missionary Methodios is recorded to have awakened the terror of the King of the Bulgarians by a vivid representation of the tortures of the damned, in a painting combining the natural portraiture of frightful realities mixed with horrors supplied from a fertile imagination. The sombre character of Byzantine art was well adapted to the subject, and the fame Methodios acquired among his contemporaries, as well as from those in after times who saw his paintings, may be accepted as a proof that they possessed some touches of nature and truth. It would be unfair to decide peremptorily on the effect of larger works of art from the illuminated Byzantine manuscripts which still exist. Art is subject to strange vicissitudes in very short periods, as may be seen by any one who compares a guinea of the reign of George III. with a coin of Cromwell or even Queen Anne, or who looks at Whitehall and the National Gallery.[3]

The literature of the ancient world was never entirely neglected at Constantinople, so that the intellectual culture of each successive period must always be viewed in connection with the ages immediately preceding. The literary history of Constantinople consequently opens immediately a field of

---

[1] Continuator, 122. Symeon Mag. 450. Const. Manasses, 107.

[2] Codinus, *De Orig. Constpl.* 62.

[3] The MSS. of the works of St. Gregory of Nazianzus, in the National Library at Paris, and of the Menologium of Basil in the Library of the Vatican, with their rich decorations and miniatures, belong to the ninth century. The copy of the Menologium was prepared for the Emperor Basil I.

inquiry too wide to be entered on in the limited space assigned to this political history. The works of the classic writers of Hellas, of the legists of Rome, and of the fathers of Christian theology, all exercised a direct influence on Byzantine literature at every period of its existence, until Constantinople was conquered by the Turks. It has been too much the practice of the literary historians of Europe to underrate the positive knowledge of ancient literature possessed by the learned in the East during the eighth and ninth centuries. What has been often called the dawn of civilisation, even in the West, was nothing more than an acquaintance with the bad models transmitted from the last ages of ancient literature. It is as great an error as to suppose that the English of the present day are ignorant of sculpture, because they are occupied in adorning the new Houses of Parliament with deformed statues ; and of architecture, because they have built a gallery for their pictures ill suited to the desired object.[1]

The most eminent Byzantine writers of this period were George Syncellus, Theophanes, the Patriarch Nicephorus, and perhaps John Malalas, in history; John Damascenus (who perhaps may be considered as a Syrian) and Theodore Studita, in theology ; and Photius, in general literature.

During the middle ages the Greek scientific writers became generally known in western Europe by means of translations from Arabic versions, and this circumstance has induced many to draw the conclusion that these works were better known and more popular among the Arabs at Cordova, Cairo, and Bagdat, than among the Greeks at Constantinople. The Almagest of Ptolemy affords an example of this double translation and erroneous inference.

[1] M. Guizot, from not paying sufficient attention to this fact, has mistaken the sophistry of the second century for the rays of a supposed dawn of civilisation in the eighth. In his excellent *Histoire de la Civilisation en France*, ii. 183, he gives specimens of a *disputatio* between Alcuin and Pepin, the son of Charlemagne, which he considers as an example of the eager curiosity with which the human mind, while young and ignorant, views every unexpected combination of ideas. Unfortunately the work he thus characterises is a verbal translation from Secundus, an Athenian sophist of the time of Hadrian, or a transcript of part of an *altercatio* attributed to Hadrian and Epictetus.—See *Opuscula Græcorum Veterum Sententiosa et Moralia.* Orellius, i. 218.

HISTORY OF THE BYZANTINE EMPIRE

BOOK TWO

BASILIAN DYNASTY
PERIOD OF THE POWER AND GLORY
OF THE BYZANTINE EMPIRE
A.D. 867–1057

CHAPTER I

CONSOLIDATION OF BYZANTINE LEGISLATION AND DESPOTISM. A.D. 867-963

SECTION . I

REIGN OF BASIL I. (THE MACEDONIAN,) A.D. 867–886

Personal history of Basil—Ecclesiastical administration—Financial legis-
lation—Military administration—Paulician war—Campaigns in Asia
Minor—Saracens ravage Sicily and Italy—Court and character of
Basil I.

THE history of Basil I. has been transmitted to us by writers
who compiled their works under the eye of his grandson, the
Emperor Constantine VII., and by that grandson with his
own pen. Under such auspices, history is more likely to
conceal than to divulge the whole truth, and nothing but the
truth. One instance of falsification may be mentioned. The
imperial compilations would fain persuade us that the Sclavonian groom was a man of noble descent,[1] and that he
could trace that descent either through a line of paternal or
maternal ancestors to Constantine, to the Arsacidæ, and to
Alexander the Great, yet they allow that his father laboured
as a poor peasant in the neighbourhood of Adrianople, until
Basil himself, despising the cultivation of the paternal farm,
sought to improve his fortune by wandering to the capital.
We are told by other authorities that Basil was a Sclavonian,
and we know that the whole of Thrace and Macedonia was
at this period cultivated by Sclavonian colonists. His father's
family had been carried away captive into Bulgaria when
Basil was almost an infant, at the time Crumn took Adrianople, A.D. 813. During the reign of Theophilus, some of
the Byzantine captives succeeded in taking up arms and
marching off into the empire. Basil, who was among the

---

[1] The Armenian historians claim Basil as a countryman, but it seems they only
echo the genealogy invented at Constantinople to flatter the emperor.—Chamich,
History of Armenia, ii. 8. Lebeau, xiii. 180, 4, and 479. Gibbon, ix. 48. Hamsa of
Ispahan says he was of Sclavonian race.—Reiske, *Commentarii ad Constant. Porphyr.
de Ceremoniis Aulæ Byz.* tom. ii. p. 451, edit. Bonn. There is a confirmation of this
in the expression κατὰ πόδρεξαν,—Genesius, 52, according to Kopitar, *Glagolita*,
lxxi.—See Constant. Porphyr. *Basilius*, 138 ; and Ephræmius, 111.

number, after serving the governor of Macedonia for a time, resolved to seek his fortune in Constantinople.[1] He departed, carrying all his worldly wealth in a wallet on his shoulders, and reached the capital on a summer's evening without knowing where to seek a night's rest. Fatigued with his journey, he sat down in the portico of the church of St. Diomed, near the Adrianople gate, and slept there all night. In a short time he found employment as a groom in the service of a courtier named Theophilitzes, where his talent of taming unruly horses, his large head, tall figure, and great strength, rendered him remarkable; while his activity, zeal, and intelligence secured him particular notice from his master, and rapid promotion in his household.[2]

Theophilitzes was sent into the Peloponnesus on public business by the Empress Theodora, while she was regent; and Basil, who accompanied his master, fell sick at Patras with the fever, still so prevalent in the Morea. Here he was fortunate enough to acquire the protection of an old lady of immense wealth, whose extraordinary liberality to the unknown youth induces us to suppose that she was herself of Sclavonian race.[3] She made Basil a member of her family, by uniting him with her own son John, in those spiritual ties of fraternity which the Greek church sanctions by peculiar rites; and she bestowed on him considerable wealth when he was able to return to his master. It would appear that Basil had already acquired a position of some rank, for the widow Danielis furnished him with a train of thirty slaves. The riches Basil acquired by the generosity of his benefactress were employed in purchasing an estate in Macedonia, and in making liberal donations to his own relations. He still continued in the service of Theophilitzes, but his skill in wrestling and taming horses at last introduced him to the Emperor Michael, who immediately became his patron. His progress as boon-companion, friend, colleague, and murderer of this benefactor, has been already recounted.

The elevation of a man like Basil to the throne of Constantinople was a strange accident; but the fact that he reigned for nineteen years seems still more singular, when we recollect that he could neither boast of military service nor administrative knowledge. Nothing can prove more com-

---

[1] Symeon Mag. 434.   [2] Constant. Porphyr. *Basilius*, 144.
[3] Niketas, a Sclavonian of Peloponnesus, celebrated for his pride, was connected by marriage with Constantine Porphyrogenitus, the grandson of Basil.—See *infra*.

pletely the perfection of the governmental machine at the time of his accession, than the circumstance that a man without education could so easily be moulded into a tolerable emperor. Personally, he could have possessed no partisans either in the army or the administration; nor is it likely that he had many among the people. We are tempted to conjecture that he was allowed to establish himself on the throne, because less was known about him than about most of the other men of influence at court, and consequently less evil was laid to his charge, and less personal opposition was created by his election. He succeeded in maintaining his position by displaying unexpected talents for administration. Able and unprincipled, he seems to have pursued a line of conduct which prevented the factions of the court, the parties in the church, the feelings of the army, and the prejudices of the people, from ever uniting in opposition to his personal authority. His knowledge of the sentiments of the people rendered him aware that financial oppression was the most dangerous grievance both to the emperor and the empire; he therefore carefully avoided increasing the public burdens, and devoted his attention to the establishment of order in every branch of the public service.

The depravity and impiety of Michael III. had disgusted the people. Basil, in order to proclaim that his conduct was to be guided by different sentiments, seized the opportunity of his coronation in the Church of St. Sophia to make a public display of his piety. After the ceremony was concluded, he knelt down at the high altar and cried with a loud voice, "Lord, thou hast given me the crown; I deposit it at thy feet, and dedicate myself to thy service." The crimes and intrigues of courts are often kept so long secret in despotic governments, that it is possible few of those present who heard this declaration were aware that a few hours only had elapsed since the hypocritical devotee had buried his sword in the bosom of his sovereign and benefactor.

For two years Basil made no changes in the government of the church. Photius, the actual Patriarch, was unpopular from his connection with the family of the late emperor, and the toleration he had shown for the vices of the court, while Ignatius, his deposed predecessor, possessed a powerful body of partisans among the people and the monks. Basil attached this numerous and active party to his interest by reinstating Ignatius in the patriarchate; but at the same time he con-

trived to avoid exciting any violent opposition on the part of
Photius, by keeping up constant personal communications
with that accomplished and able ecclesiastic. Photius was
at the head of a party possessed of no inconsiderable weight
in the church and the public administration. The aristocratic classes, and the Asiatics generally, favoured his cause;
while the people of Constantinople and the Greeks of Europe
were warm supporters of Ignatius.

The arbitrary authority of the emperor over the church is
as strongly displayed in the treatment of Photius by Basil, as
in the persecution of Ignatius by Bardas and Michael.
Photius had occupied the patriarchal chair for ten years, and
though his election may have been irregular, his ecclesiastical
authority was completely established; and there appeared no
chance that anything would occur to disturb it, when Basil,
to gain a body of active political partisans, suddenly reinstated Ignatius. It is said that Photius reproached the emperor with the murder of his benefactor; but as that Patriarch
was allowed to remain in office for about two years, his deposition must be ascribed entirely to political motives. The
fact is, that Basil was anxious to secure the support of the
monks in the East, and of the Pope of Rome in the West,
yet he feared to quarrel with the party of Photius.[1]

The negotiations with the Pope had occupied some time,
but when they were brought to a conclusion, a general council
was held at Constantinople, which is called by the Latins the
eighth general council of the church. Only one hundred and
two bishops could be assembled on this occasion, for the
greater part of the dignified clergy had been consecrated by
Photius, and many adhered to his party.[2] Photius himself
was compelled to attend, but his calm and dignified attitude
deprived his enemies of the triumph they had expected.
The acts of the council of 861, by which Ignatius had been
deposed, were declared to be forgeries, and the consecration
of Photius as a priest was annulled. The accusation of
forgery was generally regarded as false, since it rested only on
some slight changes which had been made in the translation
of the Pope's letter to the emperor, and these changes had
been sanctioned by the papal legates who were present in the

---

[1] Photius baptised Stephen, the son of Basil, on Christmas-day, 868.—Symeon
Mag. 454. Georg. Mon. 544. Leo Gramm. 471.
[2] This council commenced on the 5th October, 869, and terminated on the 12th
February, 870. The entire acts are only preserved in the Latin translation of
Anastasius Bibliothecarius. A Greek abridgment exists.

council. The Latins, who expect the Greeks to tolerate them in lengthening the Creed, have made a violent outcry against the Greeks, on this occasion, for modifying a papal letter in a Greek translation. The compliancy of Basil, the reintegration of Ignatius, and the subservient disposition of the council of 869, induced the Pope to suppose that the time had arrived when it would be possible to regain possession of the estates belonging to the patrimony of St. Peter in the provinces of the Eastern Empire, which had been confiscated by Leo. III., and that the supremacy of the See of Rome over the kingdom of Bulgaria might now be firmly established. He even hoped to gain the power of controlling the ecclesiastical affairs of the Eastern church. Such pretensions, however, only required to be plainly revealed to insure unanimous opposition on the part of the emperor, the clergy, and the people throughout the Byzantine empire. Ignatius and Basil showed themselves as firm in resisting papal usurpation as Photius and Michael.

In the mean time, Photius was banished to the monastery of Skepés; and we possess several of his letters, written during the period of his disgrace, which give a more favourable view of his character than would be formed from his public life alone. They afford convincing proof of the falsity of some of the charges brought against him by his opponents. The real fault of Photius was, that the statesman, and not the Christian, was dominant in his conduct as Patriarch; but this has been a fault so general at Rome, at Constantinople, and at Canterbury, that he would have incurred little censure in the West had he not shown himself a devoted partisan of his national church, and a successful enemy of papal ambition. The majority of the Eastern bishops, in spite of his exile, remained attached to his cause, and it was soon evident to Basil that his restoration was the only means of restoring unity to the Greek church. Accordingly, when Ignatius died in the year 878, Photius was reinstated as Patriarch, and another general council was assembled at Constantinople. This council, which is called the eighth general council of the church by the Eastern Christians, was attended by three hundred and eighty-three bishops. The Emperor Basil, the Pope, and Photius, all resolved to temporise, and each played his own game of diplomacy and tergiversation, in the hope of ultimately succeeding. The Pope proved the greatest loser, for his legates were bribed—or at least the Latins say so—to yield up everything that Basil and Photius desired. They are even accused of having allowed a covert attack on the ortho-doxy of Rome, in lengthening the Creed, by the addition of the words "and the Son," to pass unchallenged.[1] The passion displayed by the clergy of the Greek and Latin churches, during the quarrels between Ignatius and Photius, makes it difficult to ascertain the truth. It appears, however, that Pope John VIII. would have restored the Nicene Creed to its original form, by expunging the clause which had been added, if he could have secured the concessions he required from the Eastern church and the Byzantine emperor to his political pretensions. Certainly this is to be implied from the letter addressed to Photius; but papal writers have since defended the consistency and infallibility of the popes, by asserting that the copy of the letter annexed to the acts of the council is a forgery. If either of the churches committed a tithe of the iniquities with which they charge one another, we must allow that Christianity exercised very little influence on the priestly character during the ninth century.

When the Emperor Leo VI. succeeded his father Basil, Photius was again banished, in order to make way for the emperor's brother Stephen to occupy the patriarchal throne. Photius was exiled to a monastery in Armenia, A.D. 886, and he died in this retirement in the year 891, leaving behind him the reputation of having been the most accomplished and learned man of his time, and one of the last enlightened scholars in the East. Even Leo treated him with respect; and in his letter to the Pope announcing his exile, he spoke of it as a voluntary resignation, which may, perhaps, be accounted a proof that it was the result of a political negotia-tion. As this distinguished man was one of the most dangerous opponents of papal ambition prior to the time of Luther, his conduct has been made the object of innumerable misrepre-sentations; and the writers of the Romish church even now can rarely discuss his conduct in moderate language, and with equitable feelings.[2]

The most interesting point of dispute to the heads of the Eastern and Western churches in their quarrels, for some time, was the supremacy over the church of the Bulgarians. This was a momentous political question to the Byzantine

[1] This council commenced in November, 879, and terminated 13th March, 880. Its acts are to be found in the collections of Hardouin and Coletti.

[2] The work of Abbé Jager may be cited as a proof—*Histoire de Photius*. It is violent in its opinions, and inaccurate in its facts.

emperors, independent of its ecclesiastical importance to the patriarchs of Constantinople, for papal influence was sure to be employed in a manner hostile to the Eastern Empire. Besides this, as the claim of Rome to supremacy over Bulgaria rested on the ancient subjection of the Danubian provinces to the archbishopric of Thessalonica, in the times when that archbishopric was immediately dependent on the papal See, the establishment of papal authority in Bulgaria would have afforded good ground for commencing a struggle for withdrawing Thessalonica itself from the jurisdiction of the Patriarch of Constantinople, and placing it under the control of the Pope of Rome. The conduct of the emperors of Constantinople in these ecclesiastical negotiations was therefore the result of sound policy, and it was marked with moderation and crowned with success.

The financial administration of Basil was, on the whole, honourable to his government. At his accession, he gave out that he found only 300 lb. of gold, and a small quantity of silver coin in the imperial treasury.[1] This served as a pretext for a partial resumption of some of the lavish grants of Michael to worthless favourites, and in this way Basil collected 30,000 lb. of gold without increasing the public burdens. With this supply in hand for immediate wants, he was enabled to take measures for effecting the economy necessary to make the ordinary revenues meet the demands of the public service. His personal experience of the real sufferings of the lower orders, and the prudence imposed by his doubtful position, prevented him, during the whole course of his reign, from augmenting the taxes; and the adoption of this policy insured to his government the power and popularity which constituted him the founder of the longest dynasty that ever occupied the throne of Constantinople. Though his successors were, on the whole, far inferior to his predecessors of the Iconoclast period in ability, still their moderation, in conforming to the financial system traced out by Basil, gave the Byzantine empire a degree of power it had not previously possessed.

The government of the Eastern Empire was always systematic and cautious. Reforms were slowly effected; but when the necessity was admitted, great changes were gradually completed. Generations, however, passed away without men

---

1 Symeon Mag., 436, says thirteen centenaries of gold and nine sacks of miliaresia, so that the ten may have been omitted by a copyist in the Life of Basil by Constantine Porphyrogenitus, 159.

noticing how far they had quitted the customs of their fathers, and entered on new paths leading to very different habits, thoughts, and institutions. The reign of no one emperor, if we except that of Leo the Isaurian, embraces a revolution in the institutions of the state, completed in a single generation; hence it is that Byzantine history loses the interest to be derived from individual biography. It steps over centuries, marking rather the movement of generations of mankind than the acts of individual emperors and statesmen, and it becomes a didactic essay on political progress instead of a living picture of man's actions. In the days of the liberty of Athens, the life of each leader embraces the history of many revolutions, and the mind of a single individual seems often to guide or modify their course; but in the years of Constantinopolitan servitude, emperors and people are borne slowly onward by a current of which we are not always certain that we can trace the origin or follow the direction. These observations receive their best development by a review of the legislative acts of the Basilian dynasty. It was reserved to Basil I. and his son Leo VI. to complete the reorganisation of the empire commenced by Leo III.; for the promulgation of a revised code of the laws of the empire, in the Greek language, was the accomplishment of an idea impressed on the Byzantine administration by the great Iconoclast reformer, and of which his own Ecloga or manual was the first imperfect expression.

The legal reforms of the early Iconoclast emperors were sufficient to supply the exigencies of the moment, in the state of anarchy, ignorance, and disorder to which the provinces of the empire were then reduced by the ravages of the Sclavonians, Bulgarians, and Saracens. But when the vigorous administration of the Isaurian dynasty had driven back these invaders, and re-established order and security of property, the rapid progress of society called for additional improvements, and for a systematic reform in the legislation of the empire. Enlarged views concerning the changes which it was necessary to make in the compilations of Justinian were gradually adopted. Nicephorus I. and Leo V. (the Armenian) seem to have confined their attention to practical reforms in the dispensation of justice, by improving the forms of procedure in the existing tribunals; but when Bardas was charged with the judicial department, during the reign of Michael III., the necessity of a thorough revision of the laws of the empire began to be deeply felt. Bardas was probably ambitious of the glory of effecting this reform as the surest step to the imperial throne. The legal school at Constantinople, which he encouraged, certainly prepared the materials for the great legislative work that forms the marked feature in consolidating the power of the Basilian dynasty.[1]

The legislative views of Basil I. were modelled in conformity to the policy impressed on the Byzantine empire by Leo III. They were directed to vest all legislative power in the hands of the emperor, and to constitute the person of the sovereign the centre of law as much as of financial authority and military power.[2] The senate had continued to act as a legislative council from time to time during the Iconoclast period, and the emperors had often invited it to discuss important laws, in order to give extraordinary solemnity to their sanction. Such a practice suggested the question whether the senate and the people did not still possess a right to share in the legislation of the empire, which opportunity might constitute into a permanent control over the imperial authority in this branch of government. The absolute centralisation of the legislative authority in the person of the emperor was the only point which prevented the government of the Byzantine empire from being theoretically an absolute despotism, when Basil I. ascended the throne, and he completed that centralisation. Though the senate consisted of persons selected by the sovereign, and though it acted generally as a subservient agent of the executive power, still, as some of the most powerful men in the empire were usually found among its members, its position as a legislative council invested it with a degree of political influence that might have checked the absolute power of the emperor. Basil deprived it of all participation in legislative functions, and restricted its duties solely to those of an administrative council.[3] At the same time, the privileges formerly possessed by the provincial proprietors, the remains of the Roman curiæ, or of the more recently formed municipalities that had grown up to replace them, were swept away as offensive to despotic power. Cherson had been robbed of its free institutions as early as the reign of Theo-

---

[1] Continuator, *Scrip. post Theoph.* 119. Zonaras, ii. 161. Καὶ τοὺς νόμους δὲ τοὺς πολιτικοὺς ἀνηβῆσαι πεποίηκε, φοιτῶν αὐτὸς εἰς τὰ δικαστήρια ἤδη καὶ τῆς τούτων γνώσεως σχεδὸν ἐκλελοιπυίας παντάπασιν. Ἡ μὲν οὖν τὰς ἐπιστήμας καὶ μαθήματα τοῦ Βάρδα σπουδὴ ἀξιέπαινος.

[2] Constant. Porphyr. *Basilius*, 161-163.

[3] *Leonis Novellæ*, lxxviii. *Corpus Juris Civilis.*

philus.[1] But the total abolition of municipal institutions by imperial edict was certainly rather theoretical than practical. The long series of progressive alterations in society, which had destroyed the efficacy of the older municipalities, had replaced them by new societies and corporations having confined and local objects, too far beneath the sphere of action of the central administration to excite any jealousy on the part of those deputed to exercise the imperial power. The bishops now lost their position of defenders of the people, for as they were chosen by the sovereign, the dignitaries of the Byzantine church were remarkable for their servility to the civil power.

The promulgation of the Basilika may be considered as marking the complete union of all legislative, executive, judicial, financial, and administrative power in the person of the emperor. The church had already been reduced to complete submission to the imperial authority. Basil, therefore, may claim to be the emperor who established arbitrary despotism as the constitution of the Roman empire. The divine right of the sovereign to rule as God might be pleased to enlighten his understanding and soften his heart, was henceforth the recognised organic law of the Byzantine empire.

The compilation of the laws of Justinian is one of the strangest examples of the manner in which sovereigns vitiate the most extensive and liberal reforms, by their conservative prejudices in practical details. Justinian reconstructed the legislation of the Roman empire, in order to adapt it to the wants of the people who spoke Greek; yet he restricted the benefit of his new code, by promulgating it in Latin, though that language had ceased to be in use among three quarters of his civilised subjects. The conservative principles of the imperial government, and the pride of the higher classes of Constantinople in their Roman origin, induced the emperor to cling to the use of the Latin language as marking their connection with past ages, and drawing a line of separation between the government and the mass of the people. Justinian himself pronounced the condemnation of his own conduct by publishing his latest laws in Greek, and thus leaving his legislation dispersed in sources promulgated in two different languages.

A Greek school of legists, founded long before the time of

[1] *Leonis Novellæ*, xlvi. xlvii. Continuator, 76.

Justinian, but which flourished during his reign, did much to remedy this defect, by translating the Latin body of the law. Greek translations of the Institutions, the Pandects, the Code, and the Edicts, as well as Greek commentaries on these works, soon replaced the original Latin texts, and became the authorities that guided the courts of law throughout the Eastern Empire. The decline of knowledge, and the anarchy that prevailed during the century in which the empire was ruled by the Heraclian dynasty, caused the translations of the larger works to be neglected, and the writings of commentators, who had published popular abridgments, to be generally consulted. The evil of this state of things was felt so strongly when Leo III. had restored some degree of order throughout the empire, that, as we have already mentioned, he promulgated an official handbook of the law, called the Ecloga. From that time the subject of legislative reform occupied the attention of the imperial government, as well as of those professionally engaged in the administration of justice; and it appears certain that Bardas had made considerable progress towards the execution of those legislative reforms which were promulgated by Basil I., and completed by Leo VI. Indeed, it appears probable that the project was conceived as early as the time of Theophilus, whose personal knowledge of the law was greater than was possessed by his successors, who have gained a high place in history as law reformers.

The precise share which the predecessors of Basil are entitled to claim in the legislative labours of the Basilian dynasty cannot be determined with exactitude, but that it is not inconsiderable, is evident from the internal evidence afforded by the works themselves. Certainly divine right to rule the state as emperor could never have rendered the Sclavonian groom, who had qualified for the throne as the boon-companion of Michael the Drunkard, a fit person to direct the progress of legislation. All that could be expected from him was, that he should learn to appreciate the importance of the subject, and adopt the labours of the jurisconsults who had assisted Bardas. It seems, therefore, probable that he envied the popularity the Cæsar had gained by his attention to legal business, and understood fully that there was no surer mode of acquiring the goodwill of all classes than by becoming himself a law reformer. Basil, however, though eager to obtain the glory of publishing a new code, remained utterly ignorant of legislation, and personally incapable of guiding the work. A consequence of his eagerness to obtain the desired end, and of his ignorance of what was necessary to the proper performance of the task, is apparent in the first legal work published by his authority, called the Procheiron, or manual of law. The primary object of this publication was to supplant the Ecloga of Leo III., in order to efface the memory of the reforms of the Iconoclasts.[1] The Procheiron appears to have been promulgated as early as the year 870, and it bears marks of having been hurried into premature publicity.[2] The first half of the work is executed in a completely different manner from the latter part. In the earlier titles, the texts borrowed from the Institutions, Pandects, Code, and Novels of Justinian, are arranged in regular order, and are followed by the modern laws; but this well-arranged plan is abandoned in the latter titles, apparently in consequence of a sudden determination having been adopted to hurry forward the publication. The much-abused Ecloga of Leo III. was then adopted as the most available guide-book, and, in conjunction with the Institutes and Novels, became the principal source consulted. The Pandects and the Code were neglected, because they required too much time and study for their arrangement.

This fact suggests the conclusion that a commission of jurisconsults had been named as revisers of the law, who had been sitting from the time of Bardas; and these lawyers had systematically proceeded to compile a manual of the law in forty titles, and a new civil code or revision of the old law in sixty books, in which they had made considerable progress, when Basil suddenly hurried forward the premature publication of the manual in the form it now bears. It is impossible that the same spirit can have directed the latter portion of the work which dictated the compilation of the earlier. The science of Bardas is visible in the one, the ignorance of Basil in the other. For many years Basil remained satisfied with his performance as a legislator, for he was unable to appreciate the legal wants of the empire; but the subject was again forced on his attention by the confusion that prevailed in the sources of the law, to which the tribunals were still compelled to refer.

At length, in the year 884, a new code, embracing the

---

[1] We must recollect that Basil was the colleague of Michael III., when the tomb of Constantine V., the saint, so to speak, of the Iconoclasts, was destroyed, and we must connect this with the violent manner in which the Ecloga is criticised in the Procheiron.

[2] For this date, see Mortreuil, *Histoire du Droit Byzantin*, ii. 29, 30.

whole legislation of the empire in one work, was published under the title of the Revision of the Old Law. The respect paid to the laws of Rome was so deeply implanted in the minds of the people, that new laws, however superior they might have been, could not have insured the same solid basis for their support, which was claimed by a legislation aspiring to be regarded merely as the legitimate representative of the Roman jurisprudence, clothed in a Greek dress. The code of Basil was nothing but a compilation formed from the Greek translations of Justinian's laws, and the commentaries on them which had received the sanction of the Byzantine tribunals and legal schools. But this revision of the old law was hurried forward to publicity on account of some special reason, suggested either by imperial vanity or accidental policy. In the Procheiron, Basil had announced that the revised code about to be promulgated consisted of sixty books, yet, when he published it, the work was divided into forty. This premature edition was, however, again revised by Leo VI.; and it is the new and more complete code published by that emperor in sixty books, as originally announced, which we now possess under the title of Basilika, or *imperial* laws; but no perfect manuscript has been preserved.[1]

The object proposed in the Basilian legislation was too simple not to have been long in agitation before the precise plan on which it was ultimately executed was adopted. The Basilika is merely a reunion, in one work, of all the sources of Roman law in vigour at the time, without any attempt to condense them into clearer and more precise rules. Every preceding law or maxim of jurisprudence actually in force, is arranged under its own head in a series of books and titles, distributed so as to facilitate their use in the courts of law and chambers of counsel.[2] Some modern commentaries have been added to the work as we possess it, which appear not to have formed part of the original text.

After the promulgation of the first edition of the Basilika, Basil published a second legal manual, to serve as an introduction to its study. It is called the Epanagogé, but it appears never to have attained the popularity of the Ecloga and the Procheiron.

The Basilika remained the law of the Byzantine empire

---

[1] A new edition of the Basilika, in the imperfect state in which it has reached us, has been lately published by Heimbach, in five quarto volumes.
[2] Leo's edict at the commencement of Heimbach's edition of the Basilika.

until its conquest by the Franks, and it continued in use as the national law of the Greeks at Nicæa, Constantinople, and Trebizond, and in the Morea, until they were conquered by the Ottomans. The want of a system of law growing up out of the social exigencies of the people, and interwoven in its creation with the national institutions, is a serious defect in Greek civilisation. Since the time of the Achaian league, the Greeks have not possessed a national government, and they have never possessed a national system of laws; hence their communal institutions and municipal rights have received only such protection as the church could afford them; and even the church was generally the subservient instrument of the Roman, Byzantine, and Turkish governments. The evil still exists— the spirit of Bavarian law and French centralisation have prevented an admirable basis for municipal liberties, which existed in the communal institutions, from receiving legislative development in the spirit of the nation. The pedantry of Phanariots, who cling to Byzantine prejudices, induced the rulers of liberated Greece to declare the Basilika, of which no perfect copy exists, to be the law of the new Greek kingdom.[1]

Basil found the army in a much better state than the financial administration; for, even amidst the disorders of Michael's reign, measures had been taken to maintain the discipline of the troops. Basil had, consequently, only to maintain the army on the footing on which he found it, without augmenting the power of the generals he intrusted with the command of large armies. Being personally without either military experience or scientific knowledge, Basil can only be considered responsible for the general direction of the military affairs of his reign; and in this he does not appear to have displayed much talent. He allowed the Saracens to take Syracuse, while he kept the marines of the imperial navy employed in digging the foundations of a new church, and the ships in transporting marbles and building materials for its construction.[2] Basil, indeed, like all his predecessors, appeared more than once at the head of his armies in the East; for this was a duty which no emperor of Constantinople since Leo III. had ventured to neglect. It is probable, however, that his presence was calculated rather to restrain than to excite the activity of his generals, who were sure to be rendered responsible for any

---

[1] On the subject of Byzantine legislation and law, see the able sketch of Zacharia, *Historiæ Juris Græco-Romani Delineatio*, and the valuable and learned work of Mortreuil, *Histoire du Droit Byzantin*, 3 vols.   [2] Leo Gramm. 472.

want of success, and to be deprived of every merit in case of victory; while any brilliant personal exploit, which eclipsed the glory of the emperor, might have the effect of making them objects of jealousy.

The principal military operation of Basil's reign was the war he carried on with the Paulicians. This sect first made its appearance in Armenia about the middle of the seventh century, in the reign of Constans II., and it was persecuted by that emperor. Constantine IV., (Pogonatus,) Justinian II., and Leo III., all endeavoured to extirpate the heresy as one which threatened the unity of the church; for unity in religious opinions was then regarded as the basis of the prosperity of the empire, and a portion of its political constitution.[1] Constantine V., after taking Melitene, transported numbers of Asiatic colonists into Thrace, many of whom were converts to the Paulician doctrines.[2] Under this emperor and his immediate successors they enjoyed toleration, and made many converts in Pontus, Cappadocia, Phrygia, and Pisidia.[3] Nicephorus allowed them all the rights of citizens, and they continued to be loyal subjects, until Michael I. commenced persecuting them in the most barbarous manner. This circumstance, though it affords the orthodox historian Theophanes great delight, ultimately prepared the way for the depopulation of Asia Minor.[4] These cruelties continued under Leo V., until some of the Paulicians, rising in rebellion, slew the bishop of Neocæsarea, and the imperial commissioners engaged in torturing them, and withdrew into the province of Melitene, under the protection of the caliph. From this period they are often found forming the vanguard of the Saracen invasions into the south-eastern provinces of the Byzantine empire. Under Michael II. and Theophilus some degree of religious toleration was restored, and the Paulicians within the bounds of the empire were allowed to hold their religious opinions in tranquillity. But their persecution recommenced during the regency of Theodora; and the cruelty with which they were treated drove such numbers into rebellion, that they were enabled to found an independent republic, as has been already mentioned.[5] If we believe the friends of the Paulicians, they were strict Christians, who reverenced the

---

[1] The Montanists, in the edict of Leo III., (Theophanes, 336,) are supposed by Baronius to be Manicheans, which was then often an epithet for Paulicians—*Notæ in Theophanem*, p. 72, edit. Ven. See page 33 of this volume.
[2] Theophanes, 354 and 360. See pages 48 and 57 of this volume.
[3] Theophanes, 413.   [4] *Ibid.* 419.   [5] See page 156 of this volume.

teaching of St. Paul, and proposed him as their sole guide and legislator; but if we credit their enemies, they were Manicheans, who merged Christianity in their heretical opinions.

The little republic founded by the Paulicians at Tephrike, against which the armies of the Emperor Michael III. had contended without any decided success, though it owed its foundation to religious opinion, soon became a place of refuge for all fugitives from the Byzantine empire; and its existence as a state, on the frontier of a bigoted and oppressive government, became a serious danger to the rulers of Constantinople. Chrysochir, the son of Karbeas, succeeded his father in the command of the armed bands of Tephrike, and supported his army by plundering the Byzantine provinces, as the Danes or Normans about the same time maintained themselves by their expeditions in France and England. The number of prisoners taken by the Paulicians was so great that Basil found himself compelled to send an embassy to Tephrike, for the purpose of ransoming his subjects. Petrus Siculus, the ambassador, remained at Tephrike about nine months, but was unable to effect any peaceable arrangement with Chrysochir. He has, however, left us a valuable account of the Paulician community.[1] During his residence at Tephrike, he discovered that the Paulicians had sent ambassadors into Bulgaria, to induce the king of that newly converted country to form an alliance with them, and missionaries to persuade the people to receive their doctrines, which were prevalent in some districts of Thrace. The ravages committed by the Paulician troops, the bad success of the embassy of Peter Siculus, and the danger of an increase of the power of Chryoschir by new alliances, determined Basil at length to make a powerful effort for the destruction of this alarming enemy. It was evident nothing short of extermination could put an end to their plundering expeditions.

In 871, Basil made his first attack on the Paulicians; but, after destroying some of their villages, he suffered a severe check, and lost a considerable portion of his army, he himself only escaping in consequence of the valour of Theophylactus, the father of the future emperor, Romanus I., who by this exploit brought himself forward in the army.[2] Fortunately

---

[1] *Petri Siculi Historia Manichæorum seu Paulicianorum,* Gr. and Lat. Gieseler. Gotting. 1846.
[2] For the first campaign against the Paulicians, see Symeon Mag. 455; Georg. Mon. 544; and Leo Gramm. 471; and for the second, compare Constant. Porphyr., *Basilius,* 166, and Cedrenus, 570.

for Basil, the repeated seditions of the Turkish mercenaries at Badgat had weakened the power of the caliphate; a succession of revolutions had caused the deposition and murder of several caliphs within the space of a few years, and some of the distant provinces of the immense empire of the Abassides had already established independent governments.[1] The Paulicians, therefore, at this period could obtain no very important aid from the Saracens, who, as we are informed by Basil's son, the Emperor Leo VI., in his work on military tactics, were regarded as the best soldiers in the world, and far superior both to the Bulgarians and Franks. Basil had found little difficulty in driving all the plundering bands of the Paulicians back into their own territory; but it was dangerous to attempt the siege of Tephrike as long as the enemy could assemble an army to attack the rear of the besiegers in the frontier towns of the caliph's dominions. The empires of Constantinople and Bagdat were at war, though hostilities had for some time been languidly carried on. Basil now resolved to capture or destroy the fortified towns which had afforded aid to the Paulicians. After ravaging the territory of Melitene, he sent his general, Christophoros, with a division of the army to capture Sozopetra and Samosata; while he himself crossed the Euphrates, and laid waste the country as far as the Asanias. On his return, the emperor fought a battle with the Emir of Melitene, who had succeeded in collecting an army to dispute his progress. The success of this battle was not so decided as to induce Basil to besiege either Melitene or Tephrike, and he returned to Constantinople leaving his general to prosecute the war. In the mean time, Chrysochir, unable to maintain his troops without plunder, invaded Cappadocia, but was overtaken by Christophoros at Agranes, where his movements were circumscribed by the superior military skill of the Byzantine general. Chrysochir found himself compelled to retreat, with an active enemy watching his march. Christophoros soon surprised the Paulician camp, and Chrysochir was slain in the battle. His head was sent to Constantinople, that the Emperor Basil might fulfil a vow he had made that he would pierce it with three arrows. Tephrike was taken not long after, and destroyed. The town of Catabatala, to which the Paulicians

---

1 From the year 861 to 870 the throne of Bagdat was occupied by five caliphs, three of whom were dethroned. Egypt and Chorasan rebelled during this period, and several independent dynasties arose.

retired after the loss of Tephrike, was captured in the succeeding campaign, and the Paulician troops, unable to continue their plundering expeditions, either retreated into Armenia or dispersed. Many found means of entering the Byzantine service, and were employed in southern Italy against the African Saracens.[1]

The war with the Saracens continued, though it was not prosecuted with vigour by either party. In the year 876, the Byzantine troops gained possession of the fortress of Lulu, the bulwark of Tarsus, which alarmed the Caliph Almutamid for the safety of his possessions in Cilicia to such a degree, that he intrusted their defence to his powerful vassal, Touloun, the viceroy of Egypt.[2] In the following year, the Emperor Basil, hoping to extend his conquests, again appeared at the head of the army of Asia, and established his headquarters at Cæsarea. His object was to drive the Saracens out of Cilicia, but he only succeeded in ravaging the country beyond the passes of Mount Taurus up to the suburbs of Germanicia, Adana, and Tarsus, without being able to gain possession of any of these cities.[3] After the emperor's return to Constantinople, the commander-in-chief of the army, Andrew the Sclavonian, continued to ravage the Saracen territory, and destroyed an army sent to oppose him on the banks of the river Podandos. This defeat was, however, soon avenged by the Mohammedans, who routed Stypiotes, the successor of Andrew, with great loss, as he was preparing to besiege Tarsus. In the thirteenth year of his reign, (780,) Basil again invaded the caliphate, but failed in an attempt to take Germanicia. The war was subsequently allowed to languish, though the Saracens made several plundering expeditions against the Christians, both by land and sea ; but the fortress of Lulu, and some other castles commanding the passes of Mount Taurus, remained in the possession of the Byzantine troops.

The Saracens of Africa had for some time past devastated the shores of every Christian country bordering on the Mediterranean, and plundered the islands of the Ionian Sea and the Archipelago as regularly as the Paulicians had ravaged Asia Minor. Basil was hardly seated on the throne before an embassy from the Sclavonians of Dalmatia arrived at Con-

---

1 Const. Porphyr. "Basil," 192.
2 *Ibid.*, 172. Weil, *Geschichte der Chalifen*, ii. 472.
3 Const. Porphyr. "Basil," 173. Symeon Mag. 456. Cedrenus, 574.

stantinople, to solicit his aid against these corsairs. A Saracen fleet of thirty-six ships had attacked Dalmatia, in which a few Roman cities still existed, maintaining a partial independence among the Sclavonian tribes, who had occupied all the country. Several towns were taken by the Saracens, and Ragusa, a place of considerable commercial importance, was closely besieged.[1] Basil lost no time in sending assistance to the inhabitants. A fleet of a hundred vessels, under the admiral Niketas Oryphas, was prepared for sea with all possible expedition : and the Saracens, hearing of his approach, hastily abandoned the siege of Ragusa, after they had invested it for fifteen months. The expedition of Oryphas re-established the imperial influence in the maritime districts of Dalmatia, and obtained from the Sclavonians a direct recognition of the emperor's sovereignty. They retained their own government, and elected their magistrates ; and their submission to the Byzantine empire was purchased by their being permitted to receive a regular tribute from several Roman cities, which, in consideration of this payment, were allowed to occupy districts on the mainland without the neighbouring Sclavonians exercising any jurisdiction over such property. The Roman inhabitants in the islands on the Dalmatian coast had preserved their allegiance to the Eastern emperors, and maintained themselves independent of the Sclavonians, who had conquered and colonised the mainland, receiving their governors and judges from the central authority at Constantinople.[2]

As early as the year 842, two rival princes, of Lombard race, who disputed the possession of the duchy of Beneventum, solicited assistance from the Saracens ; and the Infidels, indifferent to the claims of either, but eager for plunder, readily took part in the quarrel. A body of Saracens from Sicily, who had arrived for the purpose of assisting one of the Christian claimants, resolved to secure a firm establishment in Italy on their own account. To effect this they stormed the city of Bari, though it belonged to their own ally. At Bari they formed a camp for the purpose of ravaging Italy, and made it their station for plundering the possessions of the

---

1 Const. Porphyr. " Basil," 179. The towns taken by the Saracens were Boutuma, Rosa, and the lower Dekateras.—Const. Prophyr. *De Adm. Imp.* chap. 30.
2 Const. Porphyr. *De Adm. Imp.* chap. xxx. p. 146, edit. Bonn. The tribute paid by the Roman cities to the Sclavonians was as follows :—Aspalathus (Spalatro,) 200 nomismata or gold byzants; Tetrangurium, (Trau,) Opsara, Arbe, Bekla, each 100 ; Jadera, (near Zara,) 110; and Ragusa, for its rural district, 72

Frank and Byzantine empires on the coast of the Adriatic. In 846, other bands of Sicilian Saracens landed at the mouth of the Tiber, and plundered the churches of St. Peter and St. Paul, both then without the walls of Rome. Indeed, the "mistress of the world" was only saved from falling into the hands of the Mohammedans by the troops of the Emperor Louis II. (850). Shortly after, Pope Leo IV. fortified the suburb of the Vatican, and thus placed the church of St. Peter in security in the new quarter of the town called the Leonine city.[1] From this period the ravages of the Saracens in Italy were incessant, and the proprietors who dwelt in the country were compelled to build fortified towers, strong enough to resist any sudden attacks, and so high as to be beyond the reach of fire kindled at their base. The manners formed by this state of social insecurity coloured the history of Italy with dark stains for several centuries. In the year 867, the Emperor Louis II. exerted himself to restrain the ravages of the Saracens. He laid siege to Bari, and sent ambassadors to Constantinople to solicit the co-operation of a Byzantine fleet. The fleet of Oryphas, strengthened by the naval forces of the Dalmatian cities, was ordered to assist the operations of the Western emperor; but the pride of the court of Constantinople (more sensitive than usual), prevented the conclusion of a treaty with a sovereign who claimed to be treated as emperor of the West.[2] In February, 871, Louis carried the city of Bari by assault, and put the garrison to the sword. The Franks and Greeks disputed the honour of the conquest, and each attempted to turn it to their own profit, so that the war was continued in a desultory manner, without leading to any decided results; and the cultivators of the soil were in turn plundered by the Lombard princes, the Saracen corsairs, and the German and Byzantine emperors. The Saracens again attacked Rome, and compelled Pope John VIII. to purchase their retreat by engaging to pay an annual tribute of 25,000 merks of silver. The south of Italy was a scene of political confusion. The Dukes of Naples, Amalfi, and Salerno joined the Saracens in plundering the Roman terri-

---

[1] A.D. 852. Voltaire, *Annales de l'Empire*, A.D. 847. *Essai sur les Mœurs*, chap. xxviii.

[2] The naval force of the Sclavonians in the Adriatic was not inconsiderable. The Chrovatians alone had eighty galleys, (sagenas,) carrying each forty men, and one hundred konduras or boats, carrying twenty, besides merchant-ships. Though a commercial people, they then abstained from piracy, which we know, from Venetian history, all the Sclavonians in the Adriatic were addicted to at a later period.—Constant. Porphyr. *De Adm. Imp.* chap. 30, p. 150, edit. Bonn.

tory; but Pope John VIII., placing himself at the head of the Roman troops, fought both with Christians and Mohammedans, won battles, and cut off the heads of his prisoners, without the slightest reference to the canons of the church. The bishop of Naples, as bold a warrior as the Pope, dethroned his own brother, and put out his eyes, on the pretext that he had allied himself with the Infidels; yet, when the bishop had possessed himself of his brother's dukedom, he also kept up communications with the Saracens, and aided them in plundering the territory of Rome. This lawless state of affairs induced the Italians to turn for security to the Byzantine empire. The troops of Basil rendered themselves masters of Bari without difficulty, and the extent of the Byzantine province in southern Italy was greatly extended by a series of campaigns, in which Nicephorus Phokas, grandfather of the emperor of the same name, distinguished himself by his prudent conduct and able tactics.[1] The Saracens were at last expelled from all their possessions in Calabria. The Byzantine government formed its possessions into a province called the Theme of Longobardia, but this province was constantly liable to vary in its extent; and though Gaeta, Naples, Sorrento, and Amalfi acknowledged allegiance to the Emperor of Constantinople, his authority was often very little respected in these cities.

While Basil was successful in extending his power in Italy, the Saracens revenged themselves in Sicily by the conquest of Syracuse, which fell into their hands in 878, and placed them in possession of the whole island. The city, though besieged on the land side by the Saracens established in Sicily, and blockaded by a fleet from Africa, made a gallant defence, and might have been relieved had the emperor shown more activity, or intrusted the force prepared for its relief to a competent officer. The expedition he sent, though it was delayed until nothing could be effected without rapid movements, wasted two months in the port of Monemvasia, where it received the news of the fall of Syracuse. The loss of the last Greek city in Sicily was deeply felt by the people of the Byzantine empire, on account of its commercial importance; and it was reported that the news of so great a calamity to the Christian world was first made known to the inhabitants

[1] The Emperor Leo. VI., in his work on military tactics, cites the campaign of Nicephorus Phokas, in which he took Tarsus, as an example of able generalship.—*Institutions Militaires de l'Empereur Leon le Philosophe*, traduites par. M. Joly de Maizeroy, tom. ii., p. 75.

of Greece by an assembly of demons, who met in the forest of Helos, on the banks of the Eurotas, to rejoice in the event, where their revels were witnessed by a Laconian shepherd.[1] Basil, however, seems to have treated the ruin of a Greek city as a matter of less importance than did Satan. The daring with which the Saracens carried on their naval expeditions over the Mediterranean at this period is a remarkable feature in the state of society. The attacks of the Danes and Normans on the coasts of England and France were not more constant nor more terrible.

Some of these expeditions deserve to be noticed, in order to point out the great destruction of capital, and the disorganisation of society they caused. For some years they threatened the maritime districts of the Eastern Empire with as great a degree of insecurity as that from which society had been delivered by Leo III. In the year 881, the emir of Tarsus, with a fleet of thirty large ships, laid siege to Chalcis, on the Euripus; but Oiniates, the general of the theme of Hellas, having assembled the troops in his province, the emir was killed in an attempt to storm the place, and the Saracen expedition was completely defeated.[2] Shortly after this, the Saracens of Crete ravaged the islands of the Archipelago with a fleet of twenty-seven large ships and a number of smaller vessels.[3] Entering the Hellespont, they plundered the island of Proconnesus; but they were at last overtaken and defeated by the imperial fleet under Oryphas. Undismayed by their losses, they soon fitted out a new fleet, and recommenced their ravages, hoping to avoid the Byzantine admiral by doubling Cape Tænarus, and plundering the western shores of Greece. Niketas Oryphas, on visiting the port of Kenchrees, found that the corsairs were already cruising off the entrance of the Adriatic. He promptly ordered all his galleys to be transported over the isthmus of Corinth by the ancient tram-road, which had been often used for the same purpose in earlier times, and which was still kept in such a state of repair that all his vessels were conveyed from sea to sea in a single night.[4] The Saracens, surprised by this sudden arrival of a fleet from a quarter where they supposed there

---

[1] Constant. Porphyr. 'Basil," 191. Cedrenus, ii. 585.
[2] Constant. Porphyr "Basil," 184. Cedrenus, ii. 580.
[3] Constant. Porphyr. "Basil," 185.
[4] The breadth of the isthmus is about four geographical miles—5950 metres. Zonaras calls the vessels triremes, but they were certainly with only two banks of oars, and were probably the kind of galley called dromones.—ii. 171.

was no naval force, fought with less courage than usual, and lost their whole fleet. The cruelty with which the captives, especially the renegades, were treated, was to the last degree inhuman, and affords sad proof of the widespread misery and deep exasperation their previous atrocities had produced, as well as of the barbarity of the age. No torture was spared by the Byzantine authorities.[1] Shortly after this an African fleet of sixty vessels, of extraordinary size, laid waste Zante and Cephallenia. Nasar, the Byzantine admiral, who succeeded Niketas Oryphas, while in pursuit of this fleet, touched at Methone to re-victual; but at that port all his rowers deserted, and his ships were detained until the general of the Peloponnesian theme replaced them by a levy of Mardaïtes and other inhabitants of the peninsula.[2] The Byzantine naval force, even after this contrariety, was again victorious over the Saracens; and the war of pillage was transferred into Sicily, where the Greeks laid waste the neighbourhood of Palermo, and captured a number of valuable merchant-ships, with such an abundant supply of oil that it was sold at Constantinople for an obolos the litra.

During these wars, Basil recovered possession of the island of Cyprus, but was only able to retain possession of it for seven years, when the Saracens again reconquered it.[3]

Much of Basil's reputation as a wise sovereign is due to his judicious adoption of administrative reforms, called for by the disorders introduced into the government by the neglect of Michael III. His endeavours to lighten the burden of taxation, without decreasing the public revenues, was then a rare merit. But the eulogies which his grandson and other flatterers have heaped on his private virtues deserve but little credit. The court certainly maintained more outward decency than in the time of his predecessor, but there are many proofs that the reformation was merely external. Thekla, the sister of the Emperor Michael III., who had received the imperial crown from her father Theophilus, had been the concubine of Basil, with the consent of her brother. After Basil assassinated the brother, he neglected and probably feared the sister, but she consoled herself with other lovers. It happened that on some occasion a person employed in the household of Thekla waited on the emperor, who, with the

---

[1] Constant. Porphyr. "Basil," 186.
[2] Mardaïtes are mentioned by Constant. Porphyr. "Basil," 187, but whether they were so called because they were descendants of a Syrian colony is not certain.
[3] Constant. Porphyr. *De Thematibus*, i. § 15.

rude facetiousness he inherited from the stable-yard, asked the domestic, "Who lives with your mistress at present?" The individual (Neatokomites) was immediately named, for shame was out of the question in such society. But the jealousy of Basil was roused by this open installation of a successor in the favours of one who had once occupied a place on the throne he had usurped, and he ordered Neatokomites to be seized, scourged, and immured for life in a monastery. It is said that he was base enough to order Thekla to be ill-treated, and to confiscate great part of her private fortune.[1] The Empress Eudocia Ingerina avenged Thekla, by conducting herself on the throne in a manner more pardonable in the mistress of Michael the Drunkard than in the wife of Basil. When her amours were discovered, the emperor prudently avoided scandal, by compelling her lover to retire privately into a monastery.

The most interesting episode in the private history of Basil is the friendship of Danielis, the Greek lady of Patras. As she had laid the foundation of his wealth while he was only a servant of Theophilitzes, we may believe that she was eager to see him when she heard that he was seated on the imperial throne. But though she might boast of having been the first to perceive the merits of Basil, she must have doubted whether she would be regarded as a welcome visitor at court. Basil, however, was not ungrateful to those who had assisted him in his poverty, and he sent for the son of his benefactor, and raised him to the rank of protospatharios. The widow also received an invitation to visit Constantinople, and see her adopted son seated on the throne—which, it was said, she had long believed he was destined by heaven to fill; for it had been reported that, when Basil first entered the cathedral of St. Andrew at Patras, a monk was seized with a prophetic vision, and proclaimed that he was destined to become

---

[1] This same Joannes Neatokomites had of old been a rival of Basil, for he had attempted to put the Cæsar Bardas on his guard against the conspiracy by which he lost his life.—Leo. Gramm. 244, edit. Bonn. Thekla has been usually called the sister of Basil and the concubine of Michael III. Gibbon has adopted this view, for he says, "Basil was raised and supported by a disgraceful marriage with a royal concubine, (Eudocia,) and the dishonour of his sister, (Thekla,) who succeeded to her place."—Vol. ix. p. 51. Lebeau, xiii. 284, is more decided, and more detailed. Georg. Mon. 545, in recounting the anecdote, certainly calls Thekla the sister of the emperor, and from this it is inferred she must have been the sister of the reigning emperor Basil; but a comparison of Leo. Gramm. p. 242, edit. Bonn., and p. 256, (the Latin translation calls her the sister of Michael, without this being said in the Greek text, where a word has fallen out,) and especially Symeon Mag. 446, and Georg. Mon. 536, prove that she was the sister of Michael III.; and though she had been compelled to adopt the monastic dress, to deprive her of the title of Empress, by her brother, was by him bestowed on Basil.

emperor. This prophecy Danielis had heard and believed. The invitation must have afforded her the highest gratification, as a proof of her own discernment in selecting one who possessed affection and gratitude, as well as great talents and divine favour. The old lady was the possessor of a princely fortune, and her wealth indicates that the state of society in the Peloponnesus was not very dissimilar in the ninth century from what it had been in the first centuries of our era, under the Roman government, when Caius Antonius and Eurykles were proprietors of whole provinces, and Herodes Atticus possessed riches that an emperor might have envied.[1]

The lady Danielis set off from Patras in a litter or covered couch, carried on the shoulders of ten slaves; and the train which followed her, destined to relieve these litter-bearers, amounted to three hundred persons. When she reached Constantinople, she was lodged in the apartments of the palace of Magnaura appropriated for the reception of princely guests. The rich presents she had prepared for the emperor astonished the inhabitants of the capital, for no foreign monarch had ever offered gifts of equal value to a Byzantine sovereign. The slaves that bore the gifts were themselves a part of the present, and were all distinguished for their youth, beauty, and accomplishments. Four hundred young men, one hundred eunuchs, and one hundred maidens, formed the living portion of this magnificent offering. A hundred pieces of the richest coloured drapery, one hundred pieces of soft woollen cloth, two hundred pieces of linen, and one hundred of cambric, so fine that each piece could be enclosed in the joint of a reed. To all this a service of cups, dishes, and plates of gold and silver was added.[2] When Danielis reached Constantinople, she found that the emperor had constructed a magnificent church as an expiation for the murder of his benefactor, Michael III. She sent orders to the Peloponnesus to manufacture carpets of unusual size, in order to cover the whole floor, that they might protect the rich mosaic pavement, in which a peacock with outspread tail astonished every one who beheld it by the extreme brilliancy of its colouring. Before the widow quitted Constantinople, she settled a considerable portion of her estates in Greece on her son, the

[1] *Greece under the Romans*, 58.
[2] The Emperor Constantine Porphyrogenitus, who knew something about the matter, says that the old lady knew that eunuchs are collected about the court like blue-bottle flies round a sheep-fold.—P. 195. A curious dissertation might be written as a commentary on the presents.

protospatharios, and on her adopted child the emperor, in joint property.

After Basil's death, she again visited Constantinople; her own son was also dead, so she constituted the Emperor Leo VI. her sole heir. On quitting the capital for the last time, she desired that the protospathar Zenobios might be despatched to the Peloponnesus, for the purpose of preparing a register of her extensive estates and immense property. She died shortly after her return; and even the imperial officers were amazed at the amount of her wealth: the quantity of gold coin, gold and silver plate, works of art in bronze, furniture, rich stuffs in linen, cotton, wool, and silk, cattle and slaves, palaces and farms, formed an inheritance that enriched even an emperor of Constantinople. The slaves, of which the Emperor Leo became the proprietor, were so numerous that he ordered three thousand to be enfranchised and sent to the theme of Longobardia, as Apulia was then called, where they were put in possession of land, which they cultivated as serfs. After the payment of many legacies, and the division of a part of the landed property, according to the dispositions of the testament, the emperor remained possessor of eighty farms or villages. This narration furnishes a curious glimpse into the condition of society in Greece during the latter part of the ninth century, which is the period when the Greek race began to recover a numerical superiority, and prepare for the consolidation of its political ascendancy over the Sclavonian colonists in the Peloponnesus. Unfortunately, history supplies us with no contemporary facts that point out the precise causes of the diminution of the relative numbers of the Sclavonians, and the rapid increase in the absolute numbers of the Greek agricultural population. We are left to seek for explanations of these facts in the general laws which regulate the progress of population and the decline of society.

The steps by which Basil mounted the throne were never forgotten by the political and military adventurers, who considered the empire a fit reward for a successful conspirator. John Kurkuas, a patrician of great wealth, who commanded the Ikanates, expected to seize the crown as a lawful prize, and engaged sixty-six of the leading men in the public administration to participate in his design. The plot was revealed to Basil by some of the conspirators, who perceived they could gain more by a second treachery than by persisting in their first treason. Kurkuas was seized, and his eyes were put out: the other conspirators were scourged in the hippodrome; their heads were shaved, their beards burned off, and after being paraded through the capital they were exiled, and their estates confiscated. The clemency of Basil in inflicting these paternal punishments, instead of exacting the penalties imposed by the law of treason, is lauded by his interested historians. The fate of Kurkuas, however, only claims our notice, because he was the father of John Kurkuas, a general whom the Byzantine writers consider as a hero worthy to be compared with Trajan and Belisarius. Kurkuas was also the great-grandfather of the Emperor John Zimiskes, one of the ablest soldiers who ever occupied the throne of Constantinople.[1]

Though Basil founded the longest dynasty that ruled the Byzantine empire, the race proceeded from a corrupt source. Constantine, the son of Basil's first wife, Maria, was regarded with much affection by his father, and received the imperial crown in the year 868, but died about the year 879. The loss was severely felt by the emperor, who expressed an eager desire to be assured that his favourite child enjoyed eternal felicity. The abbot Theodoros Santabaren took advantage of this paternal solicitude to impose on the emperor's superstition and credulity. A phantom, which bore the likeness of Constantine, met the emperor while he was hunting, and galloped towards him, until it approached so near that Basil could perceive the happy expression of his son's face. It then faded from his sight; but the radiant aspect of the vision satisfied the father that his deceased son was received to grace.

Leo, the eldest child of Eudocia, was generally believed to be the son of Michael the Drunkard; and though Basil had conferred on him the imperial crown in his infancy, (A.D. 870,) he seems never to have regarded him with feelings of affection. It would seem he entertained the common opinion concerning the parentage of Leo. The latter years of Basil were clouded with suspicion of his heir, who he feared might avenge the murder of Michael, even at the risk of becoming a parricide. Whether truly or not, young Leo was accused of plotting against Basil's life before he was sixteen years of age.[2] The accusation was founded on the discovery of a dagger con-

---

[1] Const. Porphyr. "Basil," 172. Symeon Mag. 460.
[2] Georg. Mon. 541; Leo Gramm. 468; Zonaras, ii. 166, indicate that Leo was considered the son of Michael III.—Symeon Mag. 455. Georg. Mon., at page 544, and Leo Gramm., at page 471, (edit. Par.,) speak of Alexander as the legitimate child of Basil in opposition to Leo. Leo was crowned 6th January, 870.—Krug. 39.

cealed in the boot of the young prince, while he was in attendance on his father at a hunting-party, when Byzantine etiquette demanded that he should be unarmed. The historians who wrote under the eye of Leo's son, Constantine Porphyrogenitus, pretend that the abbot Theodoros Santabaren persuaded Leo to conceal the weapon for his own defence, and then informed Basil that his son was armed to attempt his assassination. The charge underwent a full examination, during which the young emperor was deprived of the insignia of the imperial rank; but the result of the investigation must have proved his innocence, for, in spite of the suspicions rooted in Basil's mind, he was restored to his rank as heir-apparent.[1]

The cruelty displayed by Basil in his latter days loosens the tongues of his servile historians, and indicates that he never entirely laid aside the vices of his earlier years. While engaged in hunting, to which he was passionately devoted, a stag that had been brought to bay rushed at him, and, striking its antlers into his girdle, dragged him from his horse. One of the attendants drew his hunting-knife, and, cutting the girdle, saved the emperor's life; but the suspicious despot, fearing an attempt at assassination, ordered his faithful servant to be immediately decapitated. The shock he received from the stag brought on a fever, which terminated his eventful life, and he ended his reign, as he had commenced it, by the murder of a benefactor. Though he was a judicious and able sovereign, he has been unduly praised, because he was one of the most orthodox emperors of Constantinople in the opinion of the Latin as well as of the Greek church.[2]

[1] The people of Thessalonica still show a tower, in which they say Leo was confined during the time he was deprived of the imperial title. I could not succeed in obtaining permission to visit it. Perhaps some Byzantine inscription in the walls has caused the tradition. A private English traveller, who has neither wealth nor titles, does not meet with the same facilities in literary researches as a foreigner.

[2] Basil's determination to keep on good terms with the Pope, his zeal in building churches, and his eagerness to baptize Jews, made him powerful friends in his own age, whose opinions have been reflected in modern history : but Zonaras represents him as an ignorant and superstitious bigot. It is needless to say that he cannot have composed the advice to his hopeful son, Leo the Philosopher, which appears in the Byzantine Collection as his work.

Character and court of Leo VI.—Ecclesiastical administration—Legislation—Saracen war—Taking of Thessalonica—Bulgarian war.

Leo the Philosopher gave countenance to the rumour that he was the son of Michael III. by one of the first acts of his reign. He ordered the body of the murdered emperor to be transported from Chrysopolis, where it had been interred by Theodora, and entombed it with great ceremony in the Church of the Holy Apostles.

In every characteristic of a sovereign Leo differed from Basil, and almost every point of difference was to the disadvantage of the philosopher. The ease with which the throne was retained by a man such as Basil had appeared before he became sole emperor, is explained, when we see a trifling pedant like Leo ruling the empire without difficulty. The energy which had re-established the Eastern Empire under the Iconoclasts was now dormant, and society had degenerated as much as the court. When the foundations of the Byzantine government were laid by Leo III., the mass of society was as eager to reform its own vices as the emperor was to improve the administration; but when Basil mounted the throne, the people were as eager to enjoy their wealth as the emperor to gratify his ambition. The emperors of Constantinople, as the throne was to a certain degree elective, are generally types of their age; and though Leo the Philosopher succeeded as the son and successor of Basil, no sovereign ever represented the character of his age better. He typifies the idle spirit of conservatism as correctly as Constantine VI. does the aggressive energy of progress.

Leo VI. was a man of learning and a lover of luxurious ease, a conceited pedant and an arbitrary but mild despot. Naturally of a confined intellect, he owes his title of "the Philosopher," or "the Learned," rather to the ignorance of the people, who attributed to him an acquaintance with the secrets of astrological science, than either to his own attainments, or to any remarkable patronage he bestowed on learned men.[1] His personal character, however, exercised even greater

---

[1] Leo's works consist of some poetical oracles and hymns, and a treatise on military tactics. The oracles are published at the end of Codinus, *De Antiquitatibus Constantinopolitanis*, and the Tactics in Lamé's edition of the works of Meursius, tom. vi. There is a French translation of the tactics by Joly de Maizeroy.

influence on the public administration of the empire than that of his predecessors, for the government was now so completely despotic that the court, rather than the cabinet, directed the business of the state. Hence it was that the empire met with disgraceful disasters at a period when its force was sufficient to have protected all its subjects. The last traces of the Roman constitution were now suppressed, and the trammels of an inviolable court ceremonial, and the invariable routine of administrators and lawyers, were all that was preserved of the institutions of an earlier and grander period. The extinction of the Roman empire, and complete consolidation of Byzantine despotism, is recorded in the edicts of Leo, suppressing the old municipal system, and abolishing senatus-consulta.[1] The language of legislation became as despotic as the acts of the emperor were abitrary. Two Patriarchs, Photius and Nikolaos, were removed from the government of the church by the emperor's order. Leo lived in open adultery on a throne from which Constantine VI. had been driven for venturing on a second marriage while his divorced wife was living. Yet Zoe, the fourth wife of Leo VI., gave birth to the future emperor, Constantine Porphyrogenitus, in the purple chamber of the imperial palace, before the marriage ceremony had been performed.[2] A Saracen renegade, named Samonas, was for years the prime favourite of the infatuated Leo, who raised him to the rank of patrician, and allowed him to stand god-father to his son Constantine, though great doubts were entertained of the orthodoxy, or perhaps of the Christianity, of this disreputable favourite.[3] The expenditure of the imperial household was greatly increased ; the revenue previously destined to the service of the empire was diverted to the gratification of the court, and corruption was introduced into every branch of the administration by the example of the emperor, who raised money by selling places. The Emperor Basil, like his predecessors, had been contented to make use of a galley, with a single bank of oars, in his visits to the country round Constantinople; but Leo never condescended to move unless in a dromon of two banks of oars, rowed by two hundred men—and two of these vessels were constantly maintained as imperial yachts.[4] Constantine Porphyrogenitus recounts an anecdote concerning the corruption of his father's

---

[1] *Leonis Novellæ.* Const. xlvi. lxxviii.   [2] Contin. Const. Porphyr. "Leo," 228.
[3] Continuator, 231.   Symeon Mag. 468.
[4] Const. Porphyr. *De Adm. Imp* chap. 51.

court, which deserves particular notice, as proving, on the best evidence, that the emperor encouraged the system by sharing in its profits. Ktenas, a rich man in holy orders, and the best public singer of the time, was extremely anxious to possess acknowledged rank at the imperial court. He secured the support of Samonas, the Saracen grand-chamberlain, and hoped to obtain the rank of protospatharios, by offering to make the emperor a present of forty pounds' weight of gold, the pay of the office amounting only to a pound of gold annually. The Emperor Leo refused, declaring, as his son tells us, that it was a transaction unworthy of the imperial dignity, and that it was a thing unheard of to appoint a clerk protospatharios. The old man, however, by the means of Samonas, increased his offers, adding to his first proposal a pair of earrings, worth ten pounds of gold, and a richly-chased table of silver gilt, also worth ten pounds of gold. This addition produced so great an effect on Leo's mind, that, according to his own declaration, he disgraced the imperial dignity, for he made a member of the clergy a protospatharios. Constantine then chuckles at his father's good fortune; for after receiving sixty pounds' weight of gold, the new protospatharios only lived to draw two years' pay.[1]

The strongest contrast between the administration of Leo and Basil was visible in the financial affairs of the empire. Though the direct taxes were not increased, the careless conduct of Leo, and his neglect to maintain the strict control over the tax-gatherers exercised by his father, allowed every species of abuse to creep into this branch of government, and the people were subject to the severest oppression.[2] Monopolies were also created in favour of the creatures of the court, which were the cause of great complaints, and one of these ultimately involved the empire in a most disastrous war with the Bulgarians.

The state of the church in the Byzantine empire was always

---

1 Const. Porphyr. *De Adm. Imp.* chap. 50, page 232, edit. Bonn.

2 Constantine Porphyrogenitus mentions the case of an illiterate man being appointed judge-admiral, a lawyer being joined with him as deputy to prepare the decisions. The administration of the kingdom of Greece was organised in a similar manner by Count Armansperg, under the especial protection of Great Britain : and King Otho has since been liberally calumniated for following a bad system, which he has been weak enough to persist in. A good picture of the abuses of authority in a civilised age, even in a country where the freedom of the press existed, is given by Sir Walter Scott.— *The Chronicles of the Canongate*—"The Surgeon's Daughter," chap. 21. Emigrants are said to fare often little better at Liverpool in the present day. Yet too much power ought not to be conferred on any central government, for if society cannot cure its own evils, they will continue to exist.

important, as ecclesiastical affairs afforded the only opportunity for the expression of public opinion. A considerable body of the clergy was more closely connected with the people, by feelings and interests, than with the court. At this time, however, all classes enjoyed a degree of sensual abundance that rendered society torpid, and few were inclined to take part in violent contests. The majority of the subjects of the Byzantine empire, perhaps, never felt greater aversion to the conduct of the government, both in civil and ecclesiastical matters; and we may attribute the parade Leo made of his divine right to govern both the state and the church, to the fact that he was fully aware of the popular feeling; but no class of men saw any probability of bettering their condition, either by revolution or change, so that a bad government began to be looked upon as one of the unavoidable evils of an advanced state of civilisation, and as one of the inevitable calamities which Heaven itself had interwoven in man's existence.

The Emperor Leo VI. deposed the Patriarch Photius without pretending any religious motive for the change. The object was to confer the dignity on his brother Stephen, who was then only eighteen years of age. Photius retired into a monastery, where, as has been already mentioned, he was treated with respect by Leo, who pretended that his resignation was a voluntary act. Photius survived his deposition about five years, more universally respected, and probably happier, than when he sate on the patriarchal throne, though he had been excommunicated by nine popes of Rome. Leo displayed a mean spirit in his eagerness to punish the abbot Theodoros Santabaren, whom he regarded as the author of his degradation and imprisonment during his father's reign. Failing to procure evidence to convict the abbot of any crime, he ordered him to be scourged and exiled to Athens. His eyes were subsequently put out by the emperor's order. But Leo, though a tyrant, was not implacable, and some years later Theodoros was recalled to Constantinople, and received a pension.

The predominance of ceremonial feelings in religion is shown in a remarkable manner by the legislative acts of the Byzantine government, relating to the observance of the Sabbath. As early as the reign of Constantine the Great, A.D. 321, there is a law commanding the suspension of all civil business on Sunday; and this enactment is enforced by a law of Theodosius I., in 386.[1] During the contests concerning image-worship, society was strict in all religious observances, and great attention was paid to Sunday. In the year 960, Leo the Philosopher, who was far from affecting the practice of piety, even while he made a parade of ecclesiastical observances, revoked all the exemptions which the law had hitherto made in favour of the performance of useful labour on Sunday, and forbade even necessary agricultural work, as dishonouring the Lord's day. Arguing with the bigotry of the predestinarian, that the arbitrary will of God, and not the fixed laws which he has revealed to man, gives abundant harvests to the earth, the emperor regards the diligence of the agriculturist as of no avail. Fate became the refuge of the human mind when the government of Rome had rendered the improvement of pagan society hopeless; superstition assumed its place among the Christians, and the stagnation in the Byzantine empire persuaded men that no prudence in the conduct of their affairs could better man's condition.

Ecclesiastical affairs gave Leo very little trouble during his reign, but towards its end he was involved in a dispute with the Patriarch Nikolaos the mystic. After the death of Leo's third wife, without male issue, the emperor, not wishing to violate openly the laws of the Eastern church, enforced by his own legislation, which forbade fourth marriages, installed the beautiful Zoe Carbonopsina, a grand-niece of the historian Theophanes, as his concubine in the palace.[2] Zoe gave birth to a son in the purple chamber, who was the celebrated emperor and author, Constantine VII. (Porphyrogenitus). The young prince was baptised in the Church of St. Sophia by the Patriarch Nikolaos, but that severe ecclesiastic only consented to officiate at the ceremony on receiving the emperor's promise that he would not live any longer with his concubine. Three days after the baptism of Constantine, the Emperor Leo celebrated his marriage with Zoe, and conferred on her the imperial title, thus keeping his promise to the Patriarch in one sense. But Nikolaos, indignant at having been paltered with in a double sense, degraded the priest who performed the nuptial ceremony, and interdicted the entry of the church to Leo. The emperor only thought it necessary to pay so much respect to the interdict as to attend the church

---

1 *Cod. Theod.* ii. tit. viii. 18, *De Feriis.*
2 Basil had prohibited fourth marriages.—Mortreuil, ii. 280; and Leo himself had subjected third marriages to ecclesiastical censure.—Const. xc.

ceremonies by a private door; and the people, caring little about the quarrel, laughed when they saw the imperial philosopher showing so much wit. Leo, however, took measures to gain the Pope's goodwill, and when assured of papal support, he deposed Nikolaos and appointed Euthymios the syncellus his successor. The new Patriarch, though he had been a monk on Mount Olympus, recognised the validity of the emperor's fourth marriage, on the pretext that the public good required the ecclesiastical laws to yield to the exigencies of the state. The populace, to excuse their Patriarch, believed a report that the emperor had threatened, in case the Patriarch refused to recognise the validity of his marriage with Zoe, to publish a law allowing every man to marry four wives at the same time. This rumour, notwithstanding its absurdity, affords strong proof of the power of the emperor, and of the credulity with which the Greeks received every rumour unfavourable to their rulers.[1]

The legislative labours of Leo's reign are more deserving of attention than his ecclesiastical skirmishes, though he only followed in the traces of his father, and made use of materials already prepared to his hand. We have already noticed that he published a revised edition of the Basilika, to which he added a considerable amount of supplementary legislation. Byzantine law, however, even after it had received all the improvements of Basil and Leo, was ill suited to serve as a practical guide to the population of the empire. The Basilika is an inspiration of imperial pride, not a work whose details follow the suggestions of public utility. Whole titles are filled with translations of imperial edicts, useless in the altered circumstances of the empire; and one of the consequences of the ill-devised measure of adopting an old code was, that no perfect copy of the Basilika has been preserved. Many books fell into neglect, and have been entirely lost. The sovereigns of the Byzantine empire, except while it was ruled by the Iconoclasts, felt that their power rested on the fabric of the Roman administration, not on their own strength.

The collection of the edicts or "novels" of Leo, inserted in the editions of the Corpus Juris Civilis, has rendered the legislation of Leo more generally known than his revised edition of the Byzantine code. These edicts were published for the purpose of modifying portions of the law, as pro-

[1] Georg. Mon. 559.

mulgated in the Basilika. The greater number are addressed
to Stylianos, who is supposed to have been the father of Zoe,
Leo's second wife, and it is thought they were published
between the years 887 and 893, while Stylianos was master
of the offices and logothetes.[1]

The military events of Leo's reign were marked by several
disgraceful defeats; but the strength of the empire was not
seriously affected by the losses sustained, though the people
often suffered the severest misery. The Asiatic frontier was
generally defended with success. Nicephorus Phokas, who
had distinguished himself in Italy during the reign of Basil,
acquired additional glory by his activity as general of the
Thrakesian theme. The Saracens, nevertheless, continued to
make destructive inroads into the empire, as it was found
impossible to watch every point where they could assemble an
army. In the year 887, the town of Hysela in Charsiana was
taken, and its inhabitants carried away into slavery.[2] In 888,
Samos was plundered, and the governor, with many of the
inhabitants, made prisoner. In 893, the fortress of Koron
in Cappadocia was taken.[3] In 901, reciprocal incursions were
made by the Christians and Mohammedans, but the Byzantine
troops were more successful than the Saracen, for they penetrated as far as the district of Aleppo, and carried off fifteen
thousand prisoners. This advantage was compensated by the
victories of the Saracen fleet, which took and plundered the
island of Lemnos.[4] The Saracen fleet also, in the year 902,
took and destroyed the city of Demetrias in Thessaly, where
all the inhabitants who could not be carried away, and sold
with profit as slaves, were murdered.[5] During these calamities,
Leo, in imitation of his father, employed the resources of the
state, which ought to have been devoted to putting the naval
forces of the empire in an efficient condition, in building
a new church, and in constructing a monastery for eunuchs.[6]
Before the end of Leo's reign, the isolated and independent
position assumed by several of the Saracen emirs on the
frontier, enabled the Byzantine generals to make some permanent conquests. Melias, an Armenian who had distinguished himself in the Bulgarian war, gained possession of the

---

[1] Zacharia, *Delineatio*, 50. As a proof of the mental movement throughout Europe,
it may be observed that the legislation of Alfred is contemporary with that of Leo VI.
Christian society was moved by some impulses which operated both in England and
Constantinople.   [2] Continuator, "Leo," 218.   [3] Symeon Mag. 462.

[4] Continuator, "Leo," 225. Symeon Mag. 463. Weil, ii. 492.
[5] Continuator, 224.   Symeon Mag. 463. Cameniates, *De Excidio Thessalonicensi*, 329.   [6] Georg. Mon. 556. Symeon Mag. 453.

country between Mount Amanus and the Euphrates, and this district was formed into a new theme called Lykandos.[1] The Saracens were also driven from the city of Theodosiopolis by Leo Katakalon, and the Araxes was constituted the boundary of the empire towards the Iberians.[2]

The ruinous effects of the piratical system of warfare pursued by the Saracen fleets, and the miseries it inflicted on thousands of Christian families in the Byzantine empire, deserves a record in the page of history. Fortunately we do not require, in describing what really happened, to indulge the imagination by painting what probably occurred, for time has spared the narrative of one of the sufferers, in which the author describes his own fate, and the calamities he witnessed, with the minute exactitude of truth and pedantry. Many severe blows were inflicted on the Byzantine empire by the daring enterprises of the Mohammedans, who took advantage of the neglected state of the imperial navy to plunder the richest cities of Greece. But the most terrible catastrophe the Christians suffered was the sack of Thessalonica, the second city of the empire in population and wealth. Of this event Johannes Cameniates, an ecclesiastic of the order of Readers, and a native of the place, has left us a full account. He shared all the dangers of the assault, and after the capture of his native city he was carried prisoner to Tarsus, in order to be exchanged at one of the exchanges of prisoners which took place between the Christians and Saracens from time to time in that city.[3]

Thessalonica is situated at the head of an inner basin terminating the long gulf stretching up to the northward, between the snowy peaks and rugged mountains of Olympus and Ossa to the west, and the rich shores of the Chalcidice and the peninsula of Cassandra to the east. The bay, on which the city looks down, affords a safe anchorage; and in the tenth century an ancient mole enclosed an inner port within its arms, where the largest vessels could land or receive their cargoes as in a modern dock. This port bounded the city on the south, and was separated from it by a wall about a mile in length running along the shore. Within, the houses

---

[1] Constant. Porphyr. *De Adm. Imp.* chap. 50, p. 228, edit. Bonn. *De Thematibus*, p. 32, edit. Bonn.

[2] Constant. Porphyr. *De Adm. Imp.* chap. 45, p. 201, edit. Bonn.

[3] Joannes Cameniates held the office of Kubuklesios or crozier-bearer to the Archbishop of Thessalonica. His narrative is contained in the volume of the Byzantine historians entitled *Scriptores post Theophanem.*

rose gradually, until the upper part of the city was crowned with an acropolis, separated from the hills behind by a rugged precipice. This citadel is now called the Seven Towers. Two ravines, running to the sea from the rocky base of the acropolis, serve as ditches to the western and eastern walls of the city, which to this day follow the same line, and present nearly the same aspect as in the reign of Leo the Philosopher. Their angles at the sea, where they join the wall along the port, are strengthened by towers of extraordinary size. The Egnatian Way, which for many centuries served as the high-road for the communications between Rome and Constanti-nople, formed a great street passing in a straight line through the centre of the city from its western to its eastern wall. This relic of Roman greatness, with its triumphal arches, still forms a marked feature of the Turkish city; but the moles of the ancient port have fallen to ruin, and the space between the sea-wall and the water is disfigured by a collection of filthy huts. Yet the admirable situation of Thessalonica, and the fertility of the surrounding country, watered by several noble rivers, still enables it to nourish a population of upwards of sixty thousand souls. Nature has made it the capital and seaport of a rich and extensive district, and under a good government it could not fail to become one of the largest and most flourishing cities on the shores of the Mediterranean.[1]

Leo of Tripolis was the most active, daring, and skilful of the Saracen admirals. He was born of Christian parents, at Attalia in Pamphylia, but became a renegade, and settled at Tripolis in Syria after he embraced the Mohammedan faith. In the year 904, Leo sailed from Tarsus with a fleet of fifty-four ships, each carrying two hundred men, besides their officers and a few chosen troops. The ablest corsairs in the East were assembled for this expedition, and a rumour of the unusual care that was shown in fitting out the fleet reached the court of the idle philosopher at Constantinople. He foresaw that some daring attack on his dominions would be made, and would fain have placed the imperial navy in a con-dition to defend the islands and shores of the Egean; but though the commerce of Greece could have supplied sailors to

[1] The population is said to have varied from 50,000 to 70,000 during the present century. Cameniates mentions that upwards of 22,000 young men, women, and children, selected either because they had wealthy relations to redeem them, or strength and beauty to command a good price in the slave-market, were carried away captive by the Saracens. Supposing that this was a tenth of the whole population—and when the state of society is considered, it may be doubted whether it formed a greater portion—the population of Thessalonica was then 220,000.—*De Excidio Thessal.* lxxiii.

man the largest force, the negligence and incapacity of the admiralty had been so great, that several years of misfortune were required to raise the Byzantine fleet to the condition from which it had fallen. The naval force that was now sent to defend the empire did not venture to encounter the Saracen fleet, but retired before it, seeking shelter within the Hellespont, and leaving the whole Archipelago unprotected. In the mean time fugitives reached Constantinople, who reported that the enemy proposed to attack Thessalonica.

The walls of Thessalonica had been originally of great strength, but the fortifications were in a neglected state, and the city was almost without a garrison of regular troops. The sea-wall was in want of repair, and parts were so low that it was not difficult to mount the battlements from the yards of the ships in the port. On the land side the floors of the towers that flanked the walls had in some places fallen into such a state of decay, that the communications of the defenders on the curtains were interrupted. The emperor, when informed of the defenceless state of the place, increased the confusion by his injudicious meddling. He sent a succession of officers from the capital with different instructions, fresh counsels, and new powers; and, as usually happens in similar cases, each of his deputies availed himself of his authority to alter the plan of defence adopted by his predecessor. As might be expected under such circumstances, the Saracens arrived before the fortifications were repaired, and before the arrangements for defence were completed.

The most alarming defect in the fortifications was the condition of the wall that ran along the border of the port. It was too low, without the necessary towers to afford a flanking defence, and in several places the depth of the water admitted ships to approach close to the quay that ran under its battlements. Petronas, the first officer sent by the emperor, thinking that there was not sufficient time to raise the wall or construct new towers, adopted measures for preventing the approach of the enemy's ships. To effect this, he transported to the port the sculptured sarcophagi, and immense blocks of marble that then adorned the Hellenic tombs on both sides of the Egnatian Way, without the western and eastern gates of the city, and commenced laying them in the sea at some distance from the quay. His object was to form a mole reaching within a few feet of the surface of the water, against which the enemy might run their ships, and leave them exposed, for some time, to the missiles and Greek fire of the defenders of the city. But the inhabitants of Thessalonica showed themselves insensible of danger before it approached, and incapable of defending themselves when it arrived. Their whole confidence was placed in St. Demetrius, who had never deceived them—not in their emperor, whose armies and fleets were every day defeated. They knew that Thessalonica had often repulsed the attacks of the Sclavonians in the seventh and eighth centuries; they boasted that it had never been taken by pagan or unbelievers; and they believed that, whenever it had been besieged, St. Demetrius had shown himself active in its defence: it was therefore the universal opinion, that as patron saint he would now defend a place in which he had a strong personal interest; for in no other spot on earth was he worshipped by so numerous, so wealthy, and so devoted a community.[1] The fate of Thessalonica proves the wisdom of Leo III. in endeavouring to exterminate the worship of images and saints.

Petronas had not made much progress with his work when he was superseded by an officer named Leo, who was appointed general of the theme of Thessalonica. Leo, finding that the wall towards the port was not higher than the immense stern-galleries of the ships then in use, ordered the undertaking of Petronas to be suspended, and every nerve to be strained to raise the wall. Reports became every day more alarming. At one time it was announced that the Saracen fleet had pursued the Byzantine admiral, Eustathios Argyros, up the Hellespont as far as Parium. Afterwards it became certain that it had quitted the Hellespont and reached Thasos. The people of the city would not, however, shake off their apathy, and their confidence in St. Demetrius. They showed little aptitude for building or for military discipline; the wall advanced slowly, and the militia did not seem likely to defend it with alacrity, even should it be completed. At this conjuncture a third officer arrived from Constantinople, named Niketas. His arrival was of itself sufficient to produce some disorder; but, unfortunately, an accident that happened shortly after threw everything into confusion. Leo and Niketas met on horseback to inspect the defences of the city; the horse of Leo reared, threw his rider, and injured his right thigh and side in such a manner that his life was in danger,

---

[1] J. Cameniates, *De Excidio Thessal*, chap. viii. Tafel, *De Thessalonica ejusqu Agro*, proleg. lviii. civ.

and for several days he was unable to move. This accident invested Niketas with the chief command.

Niketas seems to have had more military experience than his predecessor, and he felt that the citizens of Thessalonica, though they formed a numerous militia, were not to be depended on for defending the place. He therefore endeavoured to assemble a body of troops accustomed to war, by calling on the general of the theme of Strymon to send some of the federate Sclavonians from his government; but the envy or negligence of the general, and the avarice and ill-will of the Sclavonian leaders, prevented the arrival of any assistance from that quarter. Though Niketas threatened to report the misconduct of the general of Strymon to the emperor, he could obtain no addition to the garrison, except a few ill-equipped Sclavonian archers from the villages in the plains near the city. The generals seemed all to place too much confidence in human prudence; the people preferred relying on St. Demetrius and heaven. To secure the divine aid, a solemn procession of all the clergy and citizens, accompanied by every stranger residing in Thessalonica, headed by the archbishop and the civil and military authorities, visited the church of St. Demetrius. Public prayers were offered up day and night with great fervour; but long after, when Joannes Cameniates recorded that the intervention of St. Demetrius had proved unavailing, he acknowledged that God permitted the destruction of Thessalonica to show mankind that nothing renders the divine ear accessible to the intercession of the saints but pious life and good deeds.

The Saracens stopped a short time at Thasos to prepare engines for hurling stones, and other machines used in sieges. At last, as the inhabitants of Thessalonica were leaving their houses at daybreak, to attend morning prayer, on Sunday the 29th of July 904, a rumour arose that the enemy was already in the gulf, and only concealed from view by Cape Ekvolos. The unwarlike city was filled with lamentations, tumult, and alarm; but the citizens enrolled in the militia armed themselves, amidst the tears of their wives and children, and hastened to the battlements. The anxious crowd had not long to wait before fifty-four ships were seen rounding the cape in succession with all sail, set. The sea-breeze bore them rapidly forward, and before noon they were at anchor close to the city. The entrance of the port between the moles was shut by a chain; and to prevent this chain from being broken by hostile ships impelled by the strong sea-breezes of the summer months, several vessels had been sunk across the mouth. Leo of Tripolis immediately reconnoitred the fortifications, and examined the unfinished work of Petronas, in order to ascertain if it were still practicable to approach the wall beyond its junction with the mole. After this examination was completed a desultory attack was made on the place to occupy the attention of the garrison, and induced the besieged to show all their force and means of defence.

Next day the Saracens landed and attacked the gate Roma, which was situated in the eastern wall, and not far from the sea. Seven of the engines constructed at Thasos were placed in battery, and an attempt was made to plant scaling-ladders against the fortifications, under cover of a shower of stones, darts, and arrows; but a vigorous sally of the Byzantine troops repulsed the assault and captured the ladders. In the afternoon the plan of attack was changed. It was resolved to force an entrance by burning down two of the four gates in the eastern wall. The gate Roma and the gate Cassandra, on the Egnatian Way, were selected. Waggons filled with dry wood, pitch, and sulphur, were covered over by fishing-boats turned upside down, to prevent those on the wall from setting fire to the combustibles at a distance. Sheltered by these boats, the Saracen sailors pushed the waggons close to the gates, and when they had lighted their fires, they escaped to their companions with their shields over their heads, while the rising flames, the stones from the ballistæ, and the arrows of the archers, distracted the attention of the defenders of the wall. The iron plates on the doors were soon heated red-hot, and, the door-posts being consumed, the gates fell; but when the fire burned low, an inner gateway was seen closed with masonry, and well protected by flanking towers, so that the Saracens gained nothing by the success of this project. But the real object of the besiegers in all these preliminary operations had only been to draw off the attention of the Greeks from the point where most danger was to be apprehended. The second night of the siege was a sleepless one for both parties. The inhabitants, seriously alarmed at the daring courage and contempt of death displayed by the assailants, deemed it necessary to keep up a strict watch along the whole circuit of the fortifications, lest some unguarded spot should be found by the besiegers during the darkness. On board the fleet an incessant noise of hammers, and of Arabs and Ethiopians shouting, with a constant moving of lights, proclaimed that active preparation was going on for renewing the attack.

When Leo of Tripolis reconnoitred the fortifications, he had ascertained that his ships could approach the wall in several places, and he had carefully marked the spots. The interval had been employed in getting everything ready for an attack in this quarter, and now the night was devoted to complete the work, in order that the besieged might remain in ignorance of the design until the moment of its execution. It was necessary to form stages, in which the assailants could overlook the defenders of the place, and from which they could descend on the wall. The project was executed with ability and promptitude in a very simple manner. Two ships were bound firmly together by cables and chains, and the long yards of the immense lateen sails then in use were reversed, so as to extend far beyond the bows of the double ship. These yards were strong enough to support a framework of wood capable of containing a small body of men, who were protected by boards on the sides from missiles, while shrouds kept up a constant communication with the deck below. These cages, when swung aloft from the yards, could be elevated above the battlements where the sea-wall was lowest, and to the besieged looked like the tops of towers suddenly raised out of the sea. In the morning the double ships were rowed into their positions, and the fight commenced between the besiegers in their hanging towers and the defenders on the ramparts. Stones, arrows, pots filled with flaming combustibles, and fire launched from long brazen tubes, the composition of which had been at an earlier period a secret known only in the Byzantine arsenal, now came pouring down from above on the Greeks, who were soon driven from the battlements. The Ethiopians of the Alexandrian ships were the first to make good their footing on the wall, and as soon as they had cleared the whole line of the fortifications towards the sea from its defenders, they broke open the gates, and the crews of the other ships rushed into the city. The sailors employed to collect the booty entered with their drawn swords, wearing only their trousers, in order that no plunder might be abstracted secretly. The militia fled without a thought of further resistance : the Sclavonians escaped from a gate in the citadel, which they had secured as a means of retreat.

The Saracens divided themselves into bands, and commenced slaughtering every person they found in the streets, though they encountered crowds of women and children, who had rushed out of their houses to learn the cause of the unusual commotion. A number of the inhabitants endeavoured to escape by the Golden Gate, which formed the entrance of the Egnatian Way into the city from the west, but the crowd rendered it impossible to throw open the doors. A party of Ethiopians came upon the people as they were struggling to effect their purpose. Hundreds were crushed to death or suffocated, and the blacks stabbed the rest, without sparing age or sex. John Cameniates, his father, his uncle, and two brothers, fled towards the wall that separates the town from the citadel, intending to conceal themselves in a tower until the first fury of the assailants was assuaged. They had hardly ascended the wall when a band of Ethiopians reached the place in pursuit of a crowd of people, whom they murdered before the eyes of the terrified family. The Ethiopians then mounted the wall, but a tower was between them and Cameniates, of which the floor was in such a ruinous condition that it seemed dangerous to pass. As the enemy paused, John Cameniates deemed the moment favourable to implore mercy, and running quickly over a beam that remained unbroken, he threw himself at the feet of the black captain, promising that he would reveal where a treasure was hidden, in case his own life and that of his relations was spared. His confidence won the favour of the barbarians, one of whom understood Greek, and the family was taken under their protection; yet as they were marching through the streets, Cameniates received two wounds from an Ethiopian belonging to another band. On their way to the port the prisoners were carried into the convent of Akroullios, where they found the chief of the Ethiopians seated in the vestibule. After hearing the promises of old Cameniates, he rose and entered the church, in which about three hundred Christians had been collected. There, seating himself cross-legged on the altar, he made a signal to his followers, who immediately put all to death, leaving only the family of Cameniates. From this hideous spectacle they were conducted to the Saracen admiral.

After Leo of Tripolis had heard what Cameniates had to say, he sent a guard to convey the treasure to the port. Fortunately the hoard, which contained all the wealth of many members of the family, was found untouched, for had it not satisfied the avarice of the chiefs, the whole family would have been murdered, as happened in many other cases. This treasure was received by Leo only as a ransom for the lives of his prisoners, who were embarked in order to be exchanged at Tarsus for Saracens in captivity among the Christians. Cameniates found Leo, the general of the theme of Thessalonica, Niketas, the third envoy of the emperor, and Rodophyles, a eunuch of the imperial household, who had stopped as he was conveying a hundred pounds' weight of gold to the Byzantine army in Italy, all among the prisoners. Rodophyles was brought before the Saracen admiral, who had learned from the captives that he was intrusted with treasure. The eunuch boldly replied that he had performed his duty to the emperor, by sending away the gold to the general of the theme of Strymon as soon as the enemy approached; and when Leo of Tripolis found that this was true, he flew into a passion, and ordered Rodophyles to be beaten to death on the spot.[1]

Several days were spent in collecting the booty in the city, in releasing such of the captives as had friends in the neighbourhood able to purchase their liberty by the payment of a second ransom, and in negotiating the exchange of two hundred persons, for whom an officer of the emperor named Simeon engaged that an equal number of Saracen captives should be delivered up at Tarsus. When all other business was settled, the Saracens threatened to burn the city, and succeeded in forcing the general of Strymon to deliver up the gold for which Rodophyles had lost his life, in order to save the place from destruction. The hostile fleet quitted the harbour of Thessalonica ten days after the capture of the city. Cameniates was embarked in the ship of the Egyptian admiral, who served under Leo of Tripolis. The crew consisted of two hundred men and eight hundred captives; men, women, and children were crowded together on the lower deck. These unfortunate people, all of whom were of the higher ranks, suffered indescribable misery, and many died of hunger, thirst, and suffocation before they reached the island of Crete, where, after a fortnight's confinement, they were allowed to land for the first time. The fleet had deviated from its course in order

---

[1] Cameniates calls the sum intrusted to Rodophyles two talents, by which he of course means centners; other authors call it only one hundred pounds.—Continuator, "Leo," 226. Symeon Mag. 466. Georg. Mon. 558. Leo Gramm. 277, edit. Bonn. Concerning the variety of weight in ancient talents, see Hussey, *Essay on Ancient Weights and Money*, 28-42.

to avoid falling in with the Byzantine squadron, for it was impossible to fight when every ship was crowded with prisoners. It had therefore remained six days at Patmos and two at Naxos, which was then tributary to the Saracens at Crete.

The fleet anchored at Zontarion, a port opposite the island of Dia, which afforded better shelter than the harbour of Chandax, and where it could obtain the seclusion necessary for dividing the slaves and spoil among the different parties composing the expedition, in order that each might hasten home before the autumnal storms commenced. The whole of the captives were landed, and three days were spent by them in endeavouring to find their relations, and unite families that had been dispersed, many of which were again separated by the new division. As not only the fifty-four ships of Leo's fleet, but also several Byzantine men-of-war and merchantmen, taken in the port of Thessalonica, had been filled with prisoners, it is not surprising that the number, even after the loss sustained on the passage, still amounted to twenty-two thousand souls. Of these, with the exception of the small number reserved for exchange at Tarsus, all consisted of young men and women in the flower of their youth, or children remarkable for the bloom of their beauty: they had been saved from the slaughter of the older inhabitants, or selected from those seized in the houses, because they were sure of commanding a high price in the slave-markets of the East. When all the booty had been landed, the spoil was divided by lot, and then the fleet dispersed, the ships sailing from Crete directly to Alexandria, or to the different ports of Syria to which they belonged. Many of the unfortunate prisoners, exposed to sale in the slave-markets of Fostal, the capital of Egypt and Damascus, were transported to Ethiopia and Arabia, and even to the southern parts of Africa; the more fortunate were re-purchased from those to whose share they had fallen, by the Cretans, and by them re-sold to their friends.

The island of Crete had become a great slave-mart, in consequence of the extensive piracies of its Saracen population; and at this time the slave-trade was the most profitable branch of commerce in the Mediterranean![1] A large portion

---

[1] The prevalence of piracy on the coast of Attica, about the end of the twelfth century, after the Saracens had been long expelled from the Grecian seas, is proved by the Memorial of the Athenians to the Emperor Alexios III., A.D. 1195-1203, drawn up by their archbishop, Michael Akominatos.—Tafel, *Thessalonica*, p. 467, where τὴν λεηλασίαν τῶν θαλαττίων λῃστῶν, is spoken of.

of the Greek inhabitants of Crete having embraced Mohammedanism, and established communications with the Christian
slave-merchants in the Byzantine empire, carried on a regular
trade in purchasing Byzantine captives of wealthy families,
and arranging exchanges of prisoners with their relations. As
these exchanges were private speculations, and not, like those
at Tarsus, under the regulation of an official cartel, the
Christians were generally compelled to pay a considerable
sum as redemption-money, in order to deliver their relatives,
in addition to releasing a Saracen captive. After the buying
and selling of the captives from Thessalonica had been carried
on for several days, the Saracens embarked their prisoners for
their ultimate destination. The wife of one of the brothers of
Cameniates was purchased by a Cretan slave-merchant, but he
had the misery of seeing his mother, his wife, and two of his
children, (for the third had died during the voyage,) embarked
in a ship belonging to Sidon. Cameniates, with his father,
and the greater part of the captives set apart for the exchange
at Tarsus, were put on board a Byzantine man-of-war, the
upper deck of which was occupied by the Saracens, while
the Christians were crowded on the lower, in filth and darkness.

On the passage from Crete to Syria, an event happened
which shows that Leo, the Saracen admiral, was a man of
energy and courage, well fitted for his daring occupation, and
by no means so deaf to the calls of humanity, in the hour
of the most terrific danger, as his ferocious conduct after
the taking of Thessalonica might lead us to believe. A violent
storm threatened one of the smaller galleys with destruction,
for it broke in the middle—an accident to which ancient ships,
from their extreme length and want of beam, were very liable.
The Saracens on board were near the admiral's ship, and that
in which Cameniates was embarked, and they requested Leo
to order the crew of the Byzantine man-of-war to throw all the
captives overboard and receive them. The order was given,
allowing the crew to quit the sinking ship, but the violence of
the wind had driven the ship in which Cameniates was embarked to such a distance that the signals of the admiral were
unnoticed or unheeded. Leo, however, ordered his own ship
to be brought as near the galley as possible, and succeeded in
saving, not only the Saracen crew, but every Christian on
board, though the crews and captives of the two vessels
amounted to upwards of one thousand persons. The Byzan-

tine generals, Leo and Niketas, who were on board Leo's ship, recounted the circumstances to Cameniates, and declared that their ship was ill-calculated to contain so great a crowd, and was navigated with great difficulty. After refitting at Cyprus, the squadron reached Tripolis on the 14th of September. The father of Cameniates died there, before the prisoners were removed to Tarsus. While waiting at Tarsus, in fear of death from the unhealthiness of the place, Cameniates wrote the account of his sufferings, from which the preceding narrative has been extracted; and we must pardon what he calls the feebleness, but what others are more likely to term the inflation of his style, on account of the interesting matter embalmed in its verbosity. The worthy Anagnostes appears to have returned to his native city, and obtained the office of koubouklesios to the archbishop.

The taking of Thessalonica affords a sad lesson of the inefficiency of central governments, which deny the use of arms to the people, to defend the wealthy and unfortified cities of an extensive empire. The tendency of a court to expend the revenues of the state on the pageantry of power, on palaces, churches, and *fêtes* in the capital, without bestowing a thought on the destruction of a village or the loss of a parish, reveals to us one of the paths by which despotic power invariably tends to degrade the mass of human civilisation.

The wealth the Saracens had obtained at Thessalonica invited them to make fresh attacks on the empire, until at last the public sufferings compelled the Emperor Leo, in the last year of his reign, to make a vigorous attempt to put an end to the piracies of the Cretans, A.D. 912. Himerios, who had gained a naval victory over the Saracens in the year 909, was intrusted with the command of a powerful fleet, and commenced his operations by clearing the Archipelago of the Cretan pirates. His fleet consisted of forty dromons or war-galleys of the largest size, besides other vessels; and it was manned by twelve thousand native sailors, besides seven hundred Russians, who are considered worthy of especial enumeration. A powerful army, under the orders of Romanus the future emperor, was assembled at Samos for the purpose of besieging Chandax; but after eight months of insignificant demonstrations, the expedition was defeated with great loss by the Saracens, under the command of Leo of Tripolis and Damian, off the coast of Samos. Himerios escaped with difficulty to Mitylene, but Romanus saved the remains of the imperial force.[1]

In southern Italy, everything was in such a state of confusion that it is not worth while following the political changes it suffered. The dukes of Naples, Gaeta, Salerno and Amalfi were at times the willing subjects of the Byzantine emperor, and at times their personal ambition induced them to form alliances with the Saracens of Africa and Sicily, or, with the Pope and the Romans, to carry on war with the Byzantine generals of the theme of Longibardia (Apulia). The Italian population, as in ancient times, consisted of many nations living under different laws and usages, so that only a powerful central government, or a system of political equality, could preserve order in the discordant elements. The state of civilisation rendered the first difficult, the second impossible. The popes were always striving to increase their power, allying themselves alternately with the Franks and the Byzantines; the native Italian population in the cities was struggling for municipal independence; a powerful aristocracy, of Germanic origin, was contending for power; the Byzantine authorities were toiling to secure an increase of revenue, and the whole peninsula was exposed to the plundering incursions either of the Hungarians or of the Saracens. In this scene of confusion the Emperor Leo was suddenly compelled to take an active part by the loss of Bari, which was seized by the Duke of Beneventum. A Byzantine army regained possession of that city, and revenged the injury the Greeks had suffered by taking Beneventum, which, however, only remained in possession of the imperial troops for four years. The Byzantine fleet in Italy was subsequently defeated by the Sicilian Saracens in the Straits of Messina. In short, the administration of Leo the Philosopher in Italy was marked by his usual negligence and incapacity, and the weakness of his enemies alone preserved the Byzantine possessions.

The kingdom of Bulgaria had for a considerable period proved a quiet neighbour and useful ally. It formed a barrier against the Turkish tribes, whom the ruin of the

---

[1] Constantine Porphyrogenitus gives a curious account of the forces that composed this expedition.—*De Ceremon. Aulæ. Byzant.*, tom. i. 651. edit. Bonn. Contin. 232. Symeon Log. 470. The imperial fleet in the Egean Sea amounted usually to sixty dromons, of which seven were furnished by the islands of the Archipelago, ten by Samos and the islands depending on it, and ten by the continent of Greece: the rest were furnished from the coasts of Macedonia, Thrace, and Asia Minor. A dromon, complete for active service, carried two hundred and thirty rowers and sailors, and seventy soldiers or marines.

Khazar empire drove into Europe. Leo, however, allowed himself to be involved in hostilities with the Bulgarians by the avarice of his ministers. Stylianos, the father of his second wife Zoe, established a monopoly of the Bulgarian trade in favour of two Greek merchants. To conceal the extortions to which this monopoly gave rise, the depôt of the Bulgarian commerce was removed from Constantinople to Thessalonica.[1] The Bulgarians, whose interest suffered by this fraud, applied to their King Simeon for protection; and when the Emperor Leo, after repeated solicitations, took no steps to redress the injustice, the Bulgarian monarch declared war. An almost uninterrupted peace of seventy-four years had existed between the sovereigns of Constantinople and Bulgaria, for only temporary and trifling hostilities had occurred since the treaty between Leo V. and Mortagan in 814. Bogoris — called, after his baptism, Michael — had governed his kingdom with great prudence, and not only converted all his subjects to Christianity, but also augmented their means of education and wellbeing. His own religious views induced him to join the Eastern church, and he sent his second son Simeon to Constantinople for his education. Bogoris retired into a monastery, and left the throne to his eldest son Vladimir, about the year 885. The disorderly conduct of Vladimir drew his father from his retreat, who was compelled to dethrone and put out the eyes of this unworthy prince, before immuring him in a monastery. He then placed his second son Simeon on the throne, (A.D. 888,) and, retiring again to his cell, died a monk, A.D. 907.

Simeon proved an able and active monarch. His education at Constantinople had enlarged his mind, but inspired him with some contempt for the meanness and luxury of the Byzantine court, and for the pedantry and presumption of the Greek people. He was himself both a warrior and a scholar, but he followed the military system of the Bulgarians, and wrote in his native language.[2] The Bulgarian nation had now attained the position occupied some centuries before by the Avars. They were the most civilised and commercial of all the northern barbarians, and formed the medium for supply-

---

[1] At this time Theophano, the first wife of Leo, was still living, and Zoe was only the emperor's concubine. Stylianos, who is supposed to be the same to whom the *Novellæ* of Leo are addressed, is called Zaoutzes by the Continuator, 220. The name is connected with the Turkish Chiaous.—See Τζαβοτοι in Ducange, *Glossarium med. et. inf. Græcitatis.*

[2] I follow Schafarick, *Slawischce Alterthümer*, ii. 185, in preference to Ducange, *Familiæ Byzantinæ.*

ing the greater part of Germany and Scandinavia with the
necessary commodities from Asia, and with Byzantine manufactures and gold.[1] This extensive and flourishing trade had
gone on increasing ever since a treaty, fixing the amount
of duties to be levied on the Byzantine frontier, had been
concluded in the year 716, during the reign of Theodosius III.
The stipulations of that treaty had always formed the basis on
which the commercial relations between the two states had
been re-established, at the conclusion of every war; but now
two Greek merchants, Stavrakios and Kosmas, bribed Mousi-
kos, a eunuch in the household of Stylianos, to procure an
imperial ordinance for transferring the whole of the Bulgarian
trade to Thessalonica.   These Greeks, having farmed the customs, felt that they could carry on extortions at a distance
which could not be attempted as long as the traders could
bring their goods to Constantinople, and place themselves
under the immediate protection of the central administration.[2]
The monopoly, though it inflicted great losses both on the
Greek and Bulgarian traders, was supported by the favourite
minister of the emperor, who refused to pay any attention
to the reclamations of the Bulgarian government in favour
of its subjects. Simeon, who was not of a disposition to
submit to contemptuous treatment, finding that he had no
hope of obtaining redress by peaceable means, invaded the
empire. The Byzantine army was completely defeated, and
the two generals who commanded were slain in the first battle.
But Simeon tarnished his glory by his cruelty: he ordered the
noses of all the prisoners to be cut off, and sent the Byzantine
soldiers, thus mutilated, to Constantinople. Leo, eager to
revenge this barbarity, sent a patrician, Niketas Skleros, to
urge the Hungarians, a Turkish tribe which had recently
quitted the banks of the Don to occupy the country still
possessed by its descendants, to attack the Bulgarians. They
did so, and defeated them. They sold their prisoners to the
Emperor Leo, who was compelled, shortly after, to deliver
them to Simeon, King of Bulgaria, without ransom, in order
to purchase peace; for the Magyars were defeated in a second
battle, and retired from the contest. Leo, like many absolute
sovereigns, had conceived too high an idea of his power and
prerogatives to pay any respect to his engagements, when

[1] Theophylactus Simocatta says—λέγεται γὰρ ἐν τοῖς ἔθνεσι τοῖς Σκυθικοῖς τὸ
τῶν Ἀβάρων ὑπεῖναι ἐντρεχέστατον ψῦλον, 175. Theophanes, 421.

[2] Continuator, "Leo," 220.

he thought it for his advantage to forget his promises. He took the earliest opportunity of seeking for revenge, and having assembled what he supposed was an invincible army, he sent Leo Katakalon, his best general, to invade Bulgaria. This army was completely destroyed at a place called Bulgarophygos, and after this lesson Leo was glad to conclude peace, A.D. 893.[1]

About the same time the oppressive conduct of the imperial governor at Cherson caused an insurrection of the inhabitants, in which he was murdered.

Leo, in spite of his title of "the Philosopher," was not a man in whose personal history mankind can feel much interest. Though his reign was undisturbed by rebellion or civil war, his life was exposed to frequent dangers. His concubine Zoe discovered a conspiracy against him, and another was revealed by the renegade Samonas, and became the origin of his great favour at court. The prime conspirator was scourged and exiled to Athens. In 902, an attempt was made to murder Leo in the church of St Mokios by a madman, who was armed only with a stick. The blow was broken by the branch of a chandelier, yet the emperor received a severe wound.[2]

Leo died in the year 912, after a reign of twenty-five years and eight months.

SECTION III

ALEXANDER—MINORITY OF CONSTANTINE VII. (PORPHYRO-GENITUS)—ROMANUS I.—LECAPENUS, A.D. 912–944

Reign of Alexander, A.D. 912–913—Minority of Constantine VII., 913–920—Sedition of Constantine Dukas—Byzantine army defeated by Symeon, King of Bulgaria—Intrigues at Constantinople—Romanus I. makes himself emperor, A.D. 920–944—Conspiracies against his government—Dethroned by his son Stephen.

Alexander, who succeeded to the throne, or rather to the government of the empire, on the death of his brother Leo, (for he had long borne the title of Emperor,) was more degraded in his tastes, and more unfit for his station, than Michael the Drunkard. Fortunately for his subjects, he reigned only a year; yet he found time to inflict on the empire a serious wound, by rejecting the offer of Simeon,

---

[1] There is some difficulty in arranging the chronology of the Bulgarian war.—Symeon Mag. 462.   [2] Continuator, "Leo," 222, 274, 225.

king of Bulgaria, to renew the treaty concluded with Leo. Alexander, like his predecessor, had a taste for astrology; and among his other follies he was persuaded that an ancient bronze statue of a boar in the Agora was his own genius. This work of art was consequently treated with the greatest reverence; it was adorned with new tusks and other ornaments, and its reintegration in the hippodrome was celebrated as a public festival, not only with profane games, but even with religious ceremonies, to the scandal of the orthodox.[1]

Leo VI. had undermined the Byzantine system of administration, which Leo III. had modelled on the traditions of imperial Rome. He had used his absolute power to confer offices of the highest trust on court favourites notoriously incapable of performing the duties intrusted to them. The systematic rules of promotion in the service of the government; the administrative usages which were consecrated into laws; the professional education which had preserved the science of government from degenerating with the literature and language of the empire, were for the first time habitually neglected and violated. The administration and the court were confounded in the same mass, and an emperor, called the Philosopher, is characterised in history for having reduced the Eastern Empire to the degraded rule of an Oriental and arbitrary despotism. Alexander carried this abuse to a great extent, by conferring high commands on the companions of his debaucheries, and by elevating men of Sclavonian and Saracen origin to the highest dignities.

The only act of Alexander's reign that it is necessary to particularise, is the nomination of a regency to act during the minority of his nephew Constantine. The Patriarch Nikolaos, who had been reinstated in office, was made one of its members; but Zoe Carbopsina, the young emperor's mother, was excluded from it.

Constantine VII. was only seven years old when he became sole emperor. The regency named by Alexander consisted of six members exclusive of the Patriarch, two of whom, named Basilitzes and Gabrilopulos, were Sclavonians, who had attained the highest employments and accumulated great wealth by the favour of Alexander.[2] The facility with which all foreigners obtained the highest offices at Constantinople, and the rare occurrence of any man of pure Hellenic race in

---

[1] Contin. 234. Στοιχεῖον αὐτοῦ εἴη.—αἰδοῖα καὶ ὀδόντας τῷ χοίρῳ προσανενέωσεν.　　　　　[2] Contin. 233.

power, is a feature of the Byzantine government that requires to be constantly borne in mind, as it is a proof of the tenacity with which the empire clung to Roman traditions, and repudiated any identification with Greek nationality.

It is difficult, in the period now before us, to select facts that convey a correct impression of the condition, both of the government and the people. The calamities and crimes we are compelled to mention tend to create an opinion that the government was worse, and the condition of the inhabitants of the empire more miserable than was really the case. The ravages of war and the incursions of pirates wasted only a small portion of the Byzantine territory, and ample time was afforded by the long intervals of tranquillity to repair the depopulation and desolation caused by foreign enemies. The central government still retained institutions that enabled it to encounter many political storms that ruined neighbouring nations ; yet the weakness of the administration, the vices of the court, and the corruption of the people during the reigns of Constantine Porphyrogenitus and his father-in-law Romanus I., seemed to indicate a rapid decay in the strength of the empire, and they form a heterogeneous combination with the institutions which still guaranteed security for life and property to an extent unknown in every other portion of the world, whether under Christian or Mohammedan sway. The merits and defects of the Byzantine government are not found in combination in any other portion of history, until we approach modern times.

Hereditary succession was never firmly established in the Byzantine empire. The system of centralisation rendered the prime-minister, who carried on the administration for a minor or a weak sovereign, virtually master of the empire. Against this danger Alexander had endeavoured to protect his nephew, by creating a regency of six members, no one of whom could aspire at becoming the colleague of young Constantine. But the arbitrary nature of the imperial power created a feeling of insecurity in the minds of all officials, as long as that power was not vested in a single individual. This feeling inspired every man of influence with the hope of being able to render himself sole regent, and with the desire of assuming the title of Emperor, as the only method of permanently maintaining the post of guardian to the young prince. The most popular man of the time was Constantine Dukas, who had fled to the Saracens with his father Andronikos, in order to escape the anger of Leo VI. His father had embraced Mohammedanism, but Dukas had thrown himself on the mercy of Leo rather than forsake his religion, and had been rewarded by a command on the south-eastern frontier. For three years he served with distinction, and his valour and liberality rendered him popular among the soldiers. The death of Alexander found him commanding a division of the Byzantine army in Asia Minor, with the rank of general of the imperial guard; and a party of the officers of state, knowing his boundless ambition, fixed their eyes on him as the man most likely to overthrow the regency. Even the Patriarch Nikolaos was privy to the schemes of those who urged Dukas to repair secretly to Constantinople, for this ambitious ecclesiastic expected more authority over a young man possessing absolute power, than over six wary statesmen experienced in every department of public business.

As soon as Dukas reached the capital, he was proclaimed emperor by his partisans, who had already prepared the troops and the people for a change; and he marched immediately to the palace of Chalké, where the young emperor resided, and of which he expected to gain possession without difficulty. His attack was so sudden that he rendered himself master of the outer court; but the alarm was soon given, and all the entries into the palace were instantly closed. John Eladas, one of the members of the regency, assumed the command of the guards on duty, and a furious battle was fought in the court. The rebels were repulsed, and the horse of Dukas slipping on the flags of the pavement he was slain. Three thousand men are said to have fallen in this short tumult, in which both parties displayed the most daring courage. The conspirators who fell were more fortunate than those who were taken by the regency, for these latter were put to death with inhuman cruelty; and the Patriarch was justly censured for the apathy he showed when men were tortured, of whose plots he had been cognisant.[1] Several persons of high rank were beheaded, and some were hung on the Asiatic shore opposite the imperial palace. The wife of Constantine Dukas was compelled to take the veil, and banished to her property in Paphlagonia, where she founded a monastery. Stephen, her only surviving son, was made a eunuch, and every other male of the noble house of Dukas perished on this occasion. The family that afterwards bore

[1] Zonaras, ii. 184.

the name, and ascended the throne of Constantinople, was of more modern origin.[1]

The affection of the young emperor for his mother, and the intrigues of the different members of the regency, who expected to increase their influence by her favour, reinstated Zoe Carbopsina in the palace, from which she had been expelled by Alexander. As she had received the imperial crown, she shared the sovereign authority with the regents as a matter of right, and through the influence of John Eladas, she soon became the absolute mistress of the public administration. Zoe thought of little but luxury and amusement. Her administration was unfortunate, and a complete defeat of the Byzantine army by the Bulgarians created a general feeling that the direction of public affairs ought no longer to be intrusted to a woman of her thoughtless disposition.

The evils inflicted on the inhabitants of Thrace by Simeon, king of Bulgaria, after his rupture with Alexander, equalled the sufferings of the empire during the earlier incursions of the Huns and Avars. In the year 913, shortly after Alexander's death, Simeon marched up to the walls of Constantinople almost without opposition; but he found the city too well garrisoned to admit of his remaining long in its vicinity: he retired after an ineffectual attempt to settle the terms of a treaty in a conference with the Patriarch. In 914 he again invaded the empire, and in this campaign Adrianople was betrayed into his hands by its governor, an Armenian named Pankratakas, who, however, as soon as the Bulgarians retired, restored it to the Byzantine government.

A Turkish tribe, called by the Byzantine writers Patzinaks, who had contributed to destroy the flourishing monarchy of the Khazars, had driven the Magyars or Hungarians before them into Europe, and at this period had extended their settlements from the shores of the Sea of Azof and the falls of the Dnieper to the banks of the Danube. They were thus neighbours of the Russians and the Bulgarians, as well as of the Byzantine province of Cherson.[2] They were nomades, and inferior in civilization to the nations in their vicinity, by whom they were dreaded as active and insatiable plunderers,

---

[1] Zonaras, ii. 272. Leo Gramm. 492. Ducange, *Fam. Byz.* 160.

[2] The Patzinaks are called also Petchenegs. The Magyars are called Turks by Constantine Porphyrogenitus, in his curious work, *De Administrando Imperio*, chap. 4, 5. The Patzinaks, Magyars, Uzes, and Kumans, who all made their first appearance in Europe about this time, were Turkish tribes.

always ready for war and eager for rapine. The regency of the Empress Zoe, in order to give the people of Thrace some respite from the ravages of the Bulgarians, concluded an alliance with the Patzinaks, who engaged, on receiving a sum of money, to act in co-operation with the imperial forces. They were to attack the Bulgarians in the rear, the means of crossing the Danube being furnished by the Byzantine government. Zoe, in the mean time, trusting to negotiations she was carrying on at Bagdat for securing tranquillity in Asia Minor, transferred the greater part of the Asiatic army to Europe, and prepared to carry the war into the heart of Bulgaria, and compel Simeon to fight a battle, in order to prevent his country being laid waste by the Patzinaks. A splendid army was reviewed at Constantinople, and placed under the command of Leo Phokas, a man possessing great influence with the aristocracy, and a high military reputation. Before the troops marched northward they received new arms and equipments; liberal advances of pay were made to the soldiers, and numerous promotions were made among the officers. The second in command was Constantine the Libyan, one of the conspirators in the plot of Dukas, who had escaped the search of the regency until he obtained the pardon of Zoe's government. The fleet appointed to enter the mouth of the Danube, in order to transport the Patzinaks over the river, was placed under the command of Romanus the grand admiral.

Leo Phokas pressed forward, confident of success; but Romanus felt no inclination to assist the operation of one whom a successful campaign would render the master of the empire. He is accused of throwing impediments in the way of the Patzinaks, and delaying to transport them over the Danube at the time and place most likely to derange the operations of the Bulgarians. The conduct of Leo was rash, that of Romanus treacherous. Simeon was enabled to concentrate all his forces and fight a battle at a place called Achelous, in which the Byzantine army was defeated, with an immense loss both in officers and men,[1] (20th August 917).

---

[1] Achelous seems to have been the name of both a river and fortress in Bulgaria. River :—Contin. 240. Symeon Mag. 476. Georg. Mon. 569. Leo Gramm. 491. Fortress :—Cedrenus, 613. See Krug, *Chronologie der Byz.* 130, note * * The defeat took place near Anchialus.—Leo Diaconus, 124, edit Bonn. The name Achelous seems to have misled Gibbon into a singular complication of errors. His words are, "On classic ground, on the banks of the Achelous, the Greeks were defeated : their horn was broken by the strength of the barbaric Hercules." He transports the battle into Greece, calls the Asiatic troops of Leo Phokas Greeks ; and grows more poetical than Ovid, whom he quotes.—*Decline and Fall*, vol. x, 201,

Leo escaped to Mesembria, where he attempted to rally the fugitives; but Romanus, as soon as he heard of the disaster, sailed directly to Constantinople without attempting to make any diversion for the relief of his countrymen, or endeavouring to succour the defeated troops as he passed Mesembria. He was accused of treason on his return, and condemned to lose his sight; but he retained possession of the fleet by the support of the sailors; and the empress, who began to perceive her unpopularity, countenanced his disobedience, as she expected to make use of his support.

The partisans of Leo openly urged his claims to be placed at the head of the administration, as the only man capable by his talents of preventing a revolution; and the chamberlain Constantine urged Zoe to appoint him a member of the regency, and invest him with the conduct of public affairs. The empress began to distrust Romanus, from the preponderating power he possessed as long as the fleet remained in the vicinity of the capital. The fleet was therefore ordered into the Black Sea; but Romanus had already received secret encouragement to oppose the designs of Leo from Theodore, the governor of the young emperor, and he delayed sailing, under the pretext that the sailors would not put to sea until their arrears were paid. The crisis was important; so the chamberlain Constantine visited the fleet with the money necessary for paying the sailors, determined to hasten its departure, and perhaps to arrest the grand admiral. This step brought matters to an issue. Romanus seized the money and paid the sailors himself, keeping the chamberlain under arrest. This daring conduct on the part of a man hitherto considered as deficient in ambition as well as capacity, spread alarm in the palace, for it revealed to the empress that there was another pretender to supreme power. Zoe immediately despatched the Patriarch Nikolaos, and some of the principal officers of state, to visit the fleet in order to induce the sailors to return to their allegiance; but the populace, eager for change, and delighted to see the government in a state of embarrassment, attacked the envoys with stones, and drove them back into the palace. The empress, at a loss what measures to adopt, vainly sought for information concerning the causes of this sudden revolution. At last Theodore, the young emperor's governor, declared that the conduct of Leo Phokas and the chamberlain Constantine had caused the popular dissatisfaction, for

Leo had ruined the army and Constantine had corrupted the administration. He suggested that the easiest mode of putting an end to the existing embarrassments would be for the young Emperor Constantine to assume the supreme power into his own hands. This was done, and the young prince, or rather his tutor Theodore in his name, invited the Patriarch and one of the regents named Stephen to consult on the measures to be adopted, though both were known to be hostile to his mother's administration. This produced an immediate revolution at court. The principal officers of state attached to the party of Phokas were dismissed from their employments, which were conferred on men pledged to support the new advisers of the young emperor. Leo, not perceiving that Romanus was directly connected with the new administration, proposed a coalition, but received from that wary intriguer only assurances of friendship and support, while he openly obeyed the orders of the new ministers. Romanus, however, was soon informed by his friend Theodore that the Patriarch and Stephen had resolved to remove him from his command, that they might render him as harmless as Leo: bold measures were therefore rendered necessary, and without hesitation the admiral ranged his fleet in hostile array under the walls of the palace Bukoleon. His friends within, under the direction of the patrician Niketas, invited him to enter and protect the young emperor, and at the same time forced the Patriarch and Stephen to retire.[1] The Emperor Constantine had been already predisposed in favour of Romanus by his tutor, so that he received the insurgent admiral in a friendly manner. The young prince, accompanied by the court, repaired to the chapel in Pharo, where Romanus took an oath of fidelity on the wood of the true cross, and was invested with the offices of grand master and grand heteriarch, or general of the foreign guards, on the 25th of March 919.[2]

Before a month elapsed, the fortunes of Romanus were further advanced by the charms of his daughter Helena.

[1] This Niketas was a Sclavonian landed proprietor in the Peloponnesus, whose daughter was married to Christophoros the eldest son of Romanus. His ass-like Sclavonian visage, to use an expression which amused the courtiers of Constantinople, and has troubled modern scholars, excited the spleen of his imperial relative.—Compare Contin. 243, Constant. Porphyr. De Themat. 25, edit. Banduri, and note at page 284 of this volume.

[2] The date is given by the Continuator, 243; Symeon Mag. 478. But the chronology of this period is reviewed with learning and accuracy by Krug, Kritischer Versuch Zur aufklärung der Byzantinischen Chronologie, mit besonderer Rücksicht auf die frühere Geschichte Russlands; St Petersburg, 1810, p. 133.

Constantine VII. became deeply smitten with her beauty, and the ambition of the father precipitated the marriage in order to secure the title of Basileopater, which gave him precedence over every other officer of state, 27th April 919. He was now even more than prime-minister, and his position excited deeper envy. Leo Phokas took up arms in Bithynia and marched to Chrysopolis, (Scutari), declaring that his object was to deliver the young emperor from restraint; but his movement was so evidently the result of disappointed ambition that he found few to support him, and he was soon taken prisoner and deprived of sight. Another conspiracy, having for its object the assassination of the Basileopater, also failed. The Empress Zoe was accused of attempting to poison him, and immured in a monastery. The governor Theodore, perceiving that he no longer enjoyed the confidence of the friend he had contributed to elevate, began to thwart the ambitious projects of Romanus, and was banished to his property in Opsikion. Romanus, finding that there was now nothing to prevent his indulging his ambition, persuaded his son-in-law to confer on him the title of Cæsar, and shortly after to elevate him to the rank of emperor. He was crowned as the colleague of Constantine Porphyrogenitus by the Patriarch Nikolaos in the Church of St Sophia, on the 17th December 919.[1]

Few men ever possessed the absolute direction of public affairs in the Byzantine empire without assuming the imperial title, even though they had no intention of setting aside the sovereign whose throne they shared. It was well understood that there was no other means of securing their position, for as long as they remained only with the rank of prime-minister or Cæsar, they were exposed to lose their sight, or be put to death by a secret order of the sovereign, obtained through the intrigues of a eunuch or a slave. But as soon as they assumed the rank of emperor of the Romans, their person was sacred, being protected both by the law of high treason and the force of public opinion, which regarded the emperor as the Lord's anointed. Two of the greatest sovereigns who ever sate on the throne of Constantinople, Nicephorus II. (Phokas), and John I. (Zimiskes), shared the throne with Basil II. and Constantine VIII., as Romanus I. did with Constantine VII.

Romanus was a man whose character was too weak to

admit of enlarged views. His vanity was hurt by the fact that he occupied only the second place in the empire, and to gratify his passion for pageantry, and secure the place of honour in the numerous ceremonies of the Byzantine court, he usurped the place of his son-in-law, and conferred the imperial crown on his own wife Theodora, and on his eldest son Christophoros, giving both precedence over the hereditary emperor. Romanus had served in his youth as a marine, and he had risen to the highest rank without rendering himself remarkable either for his valour or ability;[1] the successful career of his family, therefore, naturally excited the dissatisfaction of the aristocracy and the ambition of every enterprising officer. His reign was disturbed by a series of conspiracies, all having for their avowed object the restoration of Constantine Porphyrogenitus to his legitimate rights, though, probably, the real object of the conspirators was to gain possession of the power and position occupied by Romanus. In the year 921, the great officers of the empire—the grandmaster of the palace, the minister of fortifications, and the director-general of charitable institutions—were discovered plotting. Shortly after, a patrician, with the aid of the captain of the guard of Maglabites or mace-bearers,[2] undismayed by the preceding failure, again attempted to dethrone Romanus; and a third conspiracy, planned by the treasurer and keeper of the imperial plate, one of the chamberlains, and the captain of the imperial galley, was organised. All were discovered, and the conspirators were punished. In 924, Boïlas, a patrician, rebelled on the frontiers of Armenia, but his troops were defeated by the celebrated general John Kurkuas, and he was confined in a monastery. Again, in 926, one of the ministers of state and the postmaster-general formed a plot, which proved equally abortive.

As years advanced, the feeble character of Constantine Porphyrogenitus became more apparent. His want of talent, and his devotion to literature and art, warned the ablest statesmen to avoid compromising their fortunes by supporting the cause of one so little qualified to defend his own rights. Romanus, too, having assumed his three sons, Christophoros, Stephanos, and Constantinos, as his colleagues, and placed

---

[1] His son-in-law calls him an illiterate person of no rank.—Ἰδιώτης καὶ ἀγράμματος ἄνθρωπος.—Const. Porphyr. *De. Adm. Imp.* p. 66, edit. Band.

[2] When troops wore plate armour, the iron mace was a more effectual weapon than the sword in single combat.

his son Theophylaktos on the patriarchal throne, considered his power perfectly secure. The spirit of discontent was, nevertheless, very prevalent; the people in the capital and the provinces were as little inclined to favour the usurping family as the nobility. An impostor, born in Macedonia, made his appearance in the theme Opsikion, where he announced himself to be Constantine Dukas; and though taken, and condemned to lose his hand like a common forger, he was enabled to raise a second rebellion after his release. He procured an artificial hand of brass, with which he wielded his sword; the common people flocked round him, and resisted the government with so much determination that he was captured with difficulty, and, to revenge the display he had made of the weakness of Romanus's power, he was burned alive in the Amastrianon at Constantinople.[1]

In early life Romanus had been a votary of pleasure, but when the possession of every wish for three-and-twenty years had tamed his passions, he became a votary of superstition. Feelings of religion began to affect his mind, and at last he allowed it to be discovered that he felt some remorse for having robbed his son-in-law of his birthright, in order to bestow the gift on his own children, who treated him with less respect than their brother-in-law. Christophoros was dead, and Stephanos, impelled either by fear that his father would restore Constantine Porphyrogenitus to the first place in the government, or excited by the usual unprincipled ambition that pervaded the Byzantine court, resolved to secure the possession of supreme authority by deposing his father. Romanus was seized by the agents of his son and carried off to the island of Prote, where he was compelled to embrace the monastic life. Constantinos, his younger son, though he had not been privy to the plot, readily joined in profiting by his father's ill-treatment. Such crimes, however, always excite indignation in the breasts of the people; and in this case the inhabitants of Constantinople, hearing vague rumours of scenes of dethronement, banishment, and murder, in the imperial palace, became alarmed for the life of their lawful sovereign, Constantine Porphyrogenitus. They felt an attachment to the injured prince, whom they saw constantly at all the church ceremonies, degraded from his hereditary place; his habits were known, many spoke in his praise, nobody could tell any evil of him. A mob rushed to the

[1] Contin. 261.

palace, and, filling the courts, insisted on seeing the lawful emperor. His appearance immediately tranquillised the populace, but hopes were awakened in the breasts of many intriguers by this sudden display of his influence. A new vista of intrigue was laid open, and the most sagacious statesmen saw that his establishment on the throne as sole emperor was the only means of maintaining order. Every man in power became a partisan of his long-neglected rights, and a restoration was effected without opposition. The Emperors Stephanos and Constantinos were seized by the order of Constantine VII., while they were sitting at a supper-party, and compelled to adopt the monastic habit, 27th January 945.[1]

SECTION IV.

CONSTANTINE VII. (PORPHYROGENITUS)—ROMANUS II.
945-963.

Character of Constantine VII., A.D. 945-959—Literary works—Death—Conspiracies at court—Pride of Byzantine government—Internal condition of the empire—Sclavonians in the Peloponnesus—Mainates—Saracen war—Bulgarian war—Character of Romanus II., 959-963—Conquest of Crete—Condition of Greece.

We are principally indebted to the writings of the Emperor Constantine Porphyrogenitus, or to works compiled by his order, for our knowledge of Byzantine history during the latter half of the ninth and earlier half of the tenth centuries. His own writings give us a picture of his mind, for he generally communicates his information as it occurs to himself, without hunting for classic and ecclesiastical phrases, and seeking for learned allusions and antiquated words to confuse and astonish his readers, as was the fashion with most of the

---

[1] I may here correct Saulcy, *Essai de Classification des Suites monétaires Byzantines*, 234, and Victor Langlois, in the new edition of *Lettres du Baron Marchant sur la Numismatique*, 89. After all, Marchant was right in attributing the coins usually ascribed to Romanus II. to Romanus I. The *surfrappe* engraved by Langlois is too imperfect to fix any point as incontestably as he supposes. In my own collection I possess three good examples of Constantine VII., with his long visage struck over Romanus. I possess, moreover, a coin of Constantine and Romanus II. struck over Romanus I., which is certainly decisive. I own I had entertained no doubt of the correctness of Marchant's attribution before meeting with these examples, from the great number of the coins I had met with in the Peloponnesus, and which I supposed must have been brought to pay the troops of Romanus I., employed there against the Sclavonians. I possess a Romanus I., also struck over one of the incertains of John Zimiskes, as they are called, but which appear to date from the reign of Basil I. The coins attributed by Saulcy, 201, to Basil I. and Constantine his son, also belong, in some cases at least, to Basil II. and Constantine VIII. I possess a piece in copper, in which the youth of both princes leaves no doubt on the subject.

Byzantine nobles who affected the literary character. Of his person we have a correct description in the writings of his dependants. He was tall and well made, with broad shoulders, a long neck, and a long face. This last feature is represented in caricature on some of the coins of his reign. His skin was extremely fair, his complexion ruddy, his eyes soft and expressive, his nose aquiline, and his carriage straight as a cypress. He was a lover of good cheer, and kept the best of cooks, and a cellar of excellent wine of all the choicest kinds; but he indulged in no excesses, and his morals were pure. He was reserved and mild in his intercourse with his familiars, eloquent and liberal to his dependants, so that we must not wonder that his panegyrists forgot his defects. In a despotic sovereign, such a character could not fail to be popular.[1]

Constantine's long seclusion from public business had been devoted to the cultivation of his taste in art, as well as to serious study. He was a proficient in mathematics, astronomy, architecture, sculpture, painting, and music. The works of his pencil were of course lauded as equal to the pictures by Apelles; his voice was often heard in the solemn festivals of the church. An encyclopedia of historical knowledge—of which a part only has reached our time, but even this part has preserved many valuable fragments of ancient historians—and treatises on agriculture and the veterinary art, were compiled under his inspection.[2]

The historical works written by his order were a chronicle in continuation of the Chronography of Theophanes, embracing the period from the reign of Leo V., (the Armenian,) to the death of Michael III. The name of the writer is said to be Leontios. A second work on the same period, but including the reign of Basil I., was also written by Genesius; and a third work, by an anonymous continuator, carried Byzantine history down to the commencement of the reign of his son Romanus II.[3]

The writings ascribed to Constantine himself are peculiarly

---

[1] Continuator, 292.

[2] The fragments relating to the latter portion of Roman history are collected in the first volume of the edition of the Byzantine historians published at Bonn—*Dexippi, Eunapii, Petri Patricii, Prisci, Malchi, Menandri historiarum quæ supersunt,* 1829, 8vo.

[3] The attention of the Emperor Constantine was naturally directed to continuing the work of Theophanes, as that celebrated annalist was his mother's uncle.—*De Adm. Imp.* chap. xxii. page 76, edit. Bonn. The continuation of Theophanes, and the history of the successors of Basil I., are contained in the volume of the Byzantine historians entitled *Scriptores post Theophanem.* Genesius was first printed in the Venetian edition, but a more correct text is given in the Bonn edition.

valuable, for several relate to subjects treated by no other author. The life of his grandfather, Basil I., tells some truths, from vanity, that an experienced flatterer would have concealed for fear of wounding family pride.[1] A short geographical notice of the themes or administrative divisions of the Byzantine empire gives us the means of connecting medieval with ancient geography. But the emperor's most valuable work is a treatise on the government of the empire, written for the use of his son Romanus, which abounds with contemporary information concerning the geographical limits and political relations of the people on the northern frontier of the empire and of the Black Sea, with notices of the Byzantine power in Italy, and of the condition of the Greeks and Sclavonians in the Peloponnesus, of which we should otherwise know almost nothing.[2] Two essays on military tactics—one relating to naval and military operations with the regular troops of the empire, and the other to the usages of foreigners—contain also much information.[3] The longest work, however, that Constantine wrote, and that on which he prided himself most, was an account of the ceremonies and usages of the Byzantine court. It is probably now the least read of his writings, yet it has been edited with care, though it is published without an index which merited more than a translation.[4]

The government of Constantine was on the whole mild and equitable, and the empire during his reign was rich and flourishing. When he became despotic master of the East, he continued to think and act very much as he had done in his forced seclusion. He displayed the same simplicity of manner and goodness of heart. His weakness prevented him from being a good sovereign, but his humanity and love of justice preserved him from being a bad one, and he continued all his life to be popular with the mass of his subjects. His kind disposition induced him to allow his son, Romanus II., to marry Theophano, a girl of singular beauty, and of the most graceful and fascinating manners, but the daughter of a man in

---

[1] The Life of Basil is contained in *Scriptores post Theophanem*.

[2] The works *De Thematibus* and *De Administrando Imperio* are contained in Banduri's *Imperium Orientale*, and in the Bonn collection. The work *De Adm. Imp.* was terminated in the year 952.—Krug, 266.

[3] The best edition of these treatises is contained in the sixth volume of the works of Meursius.

[4] Part of the work *De Ceremoniis Aulæ Byzantinæ* has been interpolated at a later period, and hence some have conjectured that the whole is the compilation of the Emperor Constantine VIII. The only complete edition of the Notes is that of Bonn.

mean circumstances. The Byzantine historians, who are more frequently the chroniclers of aristocratic scandal than of political history, and whose appetite for popular calumny swallows the greatest improbabilities, have recorded that Theophano repaid the goodness of the emperor by inducing Romanus to poison his father.[1] They pretend that the chief butler was gained, and that Constantine partook of a beverage, in which poison was mingled with medicine prescribed by his physician. Accident prevented him from swallowing enough to terminate his life, but the draught injured a constitution already weak. To recover from the languor into which he fell, he made a tour in Bithynia in order to enjoy the bracing air of Mount Olympus, and visit the principal monasteries and cells of anchorites, with which the mountain was covered. But his malady increased, and he returned to Constantinople to die, 9th Nov. 959.

The picture which we possess of the conduct of Constantine in his own family is so amiable, that we are compelled to reject the accusations brought against Romanus and Theophano ;—we can no more believe that they poisoned Constantine, than we can credit all the calumnies against Justinian recounted by Procopius. To perpetrate such a crime, Romanus would have been one of the worst monsters of whose acts history has preserved a record ; and a character so diabolical would have revealed its inherent wickedness during the four years he governed the empire with absolute power. Yet he appears only as a gay, pleasure-loving, pleasure-hunting prince. His father and his sisters always regarded him with the tenderest affection. Agatha, the youngest, was her father's constant companion in his study, and acted as his favourite secretary. Seated by his side, she read to him all the official reports of the ministers ; and when his health began to fail, it was through her intermediation that he consented to transact public business. That such a proceeding created no alarming abuses, and produced neither serious complaints nor family quarrels, is more honourable to the heart of the princess than her successful performance of her task to her good sense and ability. It proves that affection, and not ambition, prompted her conduct. Historians and novelists may recount that Romanus, who lived in affectionate intercourse with such a father and sister, became a parricide, but the tenor of

[1] Cedrenus 641, and Zonaras, ii. 195, both accuse Theophano and Romanus of parricide.

actual life rejects the possibility of any man acting suddenly, and for once, as a monster of iniquity.[1]

The necessity of a safety-valve for political dissatisfaction, such as is afforded by a free press or a representative assembly, to prevent sedition, is evident, when we find a popular prince like Constantine exposed to numerous conspiracies. Men will not respect laws which appear to their minds to be individual privileges, and not national institutions. Conspiracies then form an ordinary method of gambling for improving a man's fortune, and though few could aspire at the imperial throne, every man could hope for promotion in a change. Hence, we find a plot concocted to place the old Romanus I. again on the throne. Partisans were even found who laboured for the worthless Stephanos, who was successively removed to Proconessus, Rhodes, and Mitylene. Constantinos also, who was transported to Tenedos and then to Samothrace, made several attempts to escape. In the last he killed the captain of his guards, and was slain by the soldiers. The conspirators in all these plots were treated with comparative mildness, for the punishment of death was rarely inflicted either by Romanus I. or Constantine VII.

In spite of the wealth of the empire, and though the government maintained a powerful standing army and regular navy, there were many signs of an inherent weakness in the state. The emperors attempted to make pride serve as a veil for all defects. The court assumed an inordinate degree of pomp in its intercourse with foreigners. This pretension exposed it to envy; and the affectation of contempt assumed by the barbarians, who were galled by Byzantine pride, has been reflected through all succeeding history, so that we find even the philosophic Gibbon sharing the prejudices of Luitprand. Constantine Porphyrogenitus has fortunately left us an unvarnished picture of this senseless presumption, written with the foolish simplicity of an emperor who talks of what a statesman would feel inclined to conceal. He tells of the diplomatic arts and falsehoods to be used in order to prevent foreign princes obtaining a dress or a crown similar to that worn by the emperor of Constantinople; and he seems to consider this not less important than preventing them from obtaining the secret of Greek fire. Foreign ambassadors are to be told that such crowns were not manufactured on earth, but had been brought by an angel to the great Constantine,

1 Contin. 286.

the first Christian emperor; that they have always been deposited in the sacristy of St Sophia's, under the care of the Patriarch, and are only to be used on certain fixed ceremonies. The angel pronounced a malediction on any one who ventured to use them, except on the occasions fixed by immemorial usage; and the Emperor Leo IV., who had neglected this divine order, and placed one on his head, had quickly died of a brain fever. Similar tales and excuses were to be invented, in order to refuse the demands of princes who wished to intermarry with the imperial family; and the bestowal of Greek fire was to be eluded in the same way.[1]

The attachment of the people had once rendered the Patriarch almost equal to the emperor in dignity, but the clergy of the capital were now more closely connected with the court than the people. The power of the emperor to depose as well as to appoint the Patriarch was hardly questioned, and of course the head of the Eastern church occupied a very inferior position to the Pope of Rome. The church of Constantinople, filled with courtly priests, lost its political influence, and both religion and civilisation suffered by this additional centralisation of power in the imperial cabinet. From this period we may date the decline of the Greek church.

The Patriarch Nikolaos, the mystic who had been deposed by Leo VI. for opposing his fourth marriage, (A.D. 908,) was reinstated by Alexander, who acted in opposition to most of his brother's measures, A.D. 912. After Romanus I. was established on the throne, Nikolaos yielded so far to the pre-eminence of the civil power as to consent to a union with the party of his successor, Euthymios, and to own that the marriage of Leo had been sanctified by the act of the Patriarch *de facto*. This was done to avoid what Nikolaos called scandal in the church, but the political experience of the bigoted ecclesiastic having shown him that he must look for support and power to the emperor, and not to the people, he became at last as subservient to the court as the mild Euthymios had ever been. On the death of Nikolaos, (925,) Stephen the eunuch, who was archbishop of Amasia, was appointed his successor, who, after a patriarchate of three years, was succeeded by Tryphon, (A.D. 928.) Tryphon held the office provisionally until Theophylaktos, the son of the Emperor Romanus I., should have attained the full age for ordination;

[1] Constant. Porphyr. *De Adm. Imp.* chap, 13.

but in order to avoid too great scandal in the church, Tryphon was deposed a year before Theophylaktos was appointed. The imperial youth was then only sixteen years of age, but his father obtained a papal confirmation of his election by means of Alberic, consul and patrician of Rome, who kept his own brother, Pope John XI., a prisoner at the time. Legates were sent to Constantinople, who installed Theophylaktos in the patriarchal chair on the 2nd February 933. The highest order of priests in the corporation then called the Church, both in the East and West, insulted Christianity. The crimes and debauchery of the papal court were, however, more offensive than the servility and avarice of the Greek hierarchy. John XI. was appointed Pope at the age of twenty-five, through the influence of his mother Marosia, (A.D. 931.) Marosia and her second husband, Guy of Tuscany, had dethroned, and it is supposed murdered, John X., of the family of Cenci. John XI., as we have mentioned, was imprisoned by his brother Alberic, and died in confinement, a victim to the political intrigues of his brother and his mother. Alberic ruled Rome for about thirty years, and during that time the popes were only the patriarchs of the Latin church. On Alberic's death, his son Octavian succeeded him as patrician, and became Pope at the age of eighteen, under the name of John XII., (A.D. 956.) He is generally considered the greatest criminal that ever occupied the papal throne.[1]

The conduct of the Patriarch Theophylaktos was not much worse than might have been expected from a young man whose father had provided him with a bishopric, merely that he might enjoy a suitable rank and revenue. As long as his father could keep persons about the young man capable of controlling his conduct, outward decency was preserved; but age soon rendered him independent of advice, and he openly indulged tastes extremely unsuitable to his ecclesiastical dignity. He lived like a debauched young prince, and sold ecclesiastical preferments to raise money for his pleasures. He converted the celebration of divine service at St. Sophia's into a musical festival, adorned with rich pageantry. His passion for horses and for hunting exceeded that of the Emperor Basil I., and it caused his death, as it had done that

---

[1] Baronius, *Ann. Eccles.* Bellarmine, according to Daunon. calls him *almost* the worst of the popes.—*De Rom. Pont.* ii. chap. 29. Montor, *Histoire des Souverains Pontifes Romains*, ii. 94, says, "Quant à l'autorité religieuse, il fut sévère, mais, pape legitime, il usait d'un droit reconnu." Historians doubt whether he was murdered on account of his cruelties or his adulteries.

of the imperial groom. The patriarchal stables are said to have contained two thousand ⸀horses. The magnificence of the building, and the manner in which his favourite steeds were fed, bathed, and perfumed, was one of the wonders of Constantinople. On one occasion, as Theophylaktos was officiating at the high altar of St. Sophia's, a slave crept up to him and whispered that his favourite mare had foaled. The congregation was alarmed by the precipitation with which the "most holy" pontiff finished the service. The young Patriarch threw aside his ecclesiastical vestments as quickly as possible, and ran to the stable. After satisfying himself that everything was done for the comfort of the mare and foal, he returned to his cathedral to occupy his place in the procession. The people of Constantinople submitted to receive religious instruction from this festival and hunting loving Patriarch for twenty years; but strange must have been the reports that circulated through the provinces of the empire concerning the impious proceedings, profane songs, indecent dances, and diabolical ceremonies, with which he defiled the Church of the Divine Wisdom, could we look into the secret history of some provincial Procopius. The death of Theophylaktos was in keeping with his life. One of his horses, as self-willed as the Patriarch, and as unfit for its duty, dashed him against a wall. The accident brought on a dropsy, and he died in 956, after having too long disgraced the Greek church, and made St. Sophia's an opera-house.[1] He was succeeded by Polyeuktos, an ecclesiastic whose parents had marked him out for an ecclesiastical life.[2]

It has been said that the general condition of the inhabitants of the Byzantine empire was prosperous; but in a despotic government, any negligence on the part of the central administration is infallibly followed by cruelty and extortion on the part of some of its distant agents, who exercise a power too great to be left uncontrolled without the certainty of abuse. The weakness both of Romanus I. and Constantine VII. allowed considerable disorder to prevail at Constantinople, and the grossest acts of tyranny to be committed in the provinces. Chases, a man of Saracen extraction, was raised to high office by the companions of the debauchery of

[1] These expressions are not stronger than those of Cedrenus, 638, who was scandalised by the remains of the mummeries introduced into the cathedral service by Theophylaktos, and which were perpetuated to his time.

[2] The practice of making children eunuchs to insure their promotion in the church was common at this time in the Byzantine empire.

Alexander, and was governor of the theme of Hellas during the minority of Constantine. His insatiable avarice and infamous profligacy at last drove the inhabitants of Athens to despair, and as he was attending divine service in the great temple of the Acropolis — once dedicated to the Divine Wisdom of the pagans—they rose in tumult, and stoned their oppressor to death at the altar.[1] A governor of Cherson had been murdered for oppression at the end of the reign of Leo the Philosopher. John Muzalon, the governor of Calabria, now shared the same fate. As no attention was paid by such officers to protecting the commercial lines of trade either by sea or land, the navigation of the Archipelago and the Adriatic was infested by pirates, and the great roads of Asia and Europe were dangerous from the bands of brigands, who remained unmolested in their vicinity. Urso Participatio, the seventh doge of Venice, sent his son Petro to Constantinople to announce his election, and concert measures to protect the commerce of the Adriatic against the Saracen and Sclavonian pirates. Petro was honoured with the title of protospatharios, and received many valuable presents from the emperor. But no measures were adopted for protecting trade ; and as the son of the doge of Venice returned home, he was seized by Michael, duke of Sclavonia, and delivered to Simeon, king of Bulgaria. The Sclavonian kept the presents he had received, and the Bulgarian compelled his father to pay a large ransom for his release.[2]

Hugh of Provence, king of Italy, sent an embassy to Romanus I. The Sclavonians in the neighbourhood of Thessalonica attacked the ambassadors, but the Italians of their suite defeated the brigands, and captured several, whom they carried to Constantinople and delivered to the emperor for punishment.[3]

---

[1] Contin. 240. An anecdote recorded by the Byzantine writers deserves notice, though it may be an example of individual wickedness, not general demoralisation. An Athenian named Rendakios (who may have been of Sclavonian descent, as he was a relative of the patrician Niketas), ruined by debauchery and debt, laid a plot to murder his father. The old man quitted Athens to live in tranquillity at Constantinople, but was taken by pirates and carried to Crete. Rendakios pretended that his father was dead, took possession of the family property, sold it, and removed to Constantinople. His attempt to commit parricide became known, and he was compelled to seek an asylum in the precincts of St. Sophia's; but an order was given to arrest him. He contrived to escape, and forged letters of recommendation from the Emperor Romanus to Simeon, king of Bulgaria, but was captured, and condemned to lose his sight.— Contin. 247. [2] Muratori, *Annali d'Italia*, v. 270. Lebeau, xiii. 403.
[3] The stepfather of Luitprand the historian, who was afterwards ambassador from Otho to Nicephorus II., was one of the envoys. Among the presents were two immense boar-hounds. These dogs were so enraged at the appearance the Emperor Romanus made in his imperial robes, that they took him for a wild animal, and were so

Weak, however, as the Byzantine empire may appear to us, it presented a very different aspect to all contemporary governments; for in every other country the administration was worse, and property and life were much more insecure. Its alliance was consequently eagerly sought by every independent state, and the court of Constantinople was visited by ambassadors from distant parts of Europe, Africa, and Asia. The Greeks were then the greatest merchants and capitalists in the world, and their influence was felt not only by all the nations professing Christianity, but by the rival caliphs of Bagdat and Cordova, and the hostile Mohammedan princes of Egypt and Mauritania; it extended even to the Saxon monarchs of England.[1]

The Sclavonians of the Peloponnesus, who had gained a temporary independence during the latter part of the reign of Theophilus, remained tranquil from the time of their subjection by Theodora's regency, until the careless administration of Romanus I. again invited them to rebel. Two tribes, the Melings and Ezerites, who dwelt round Mount Taygetus in a state of partial independence, conceived the hope of delivering themselves from the Byzantine yoke, and boldly refused to pay the usual tribute.[2] Krinites Arotras, the general of the Peloponnesian theme, was ordered to reduce them to obedience, but he was unable to make them lay down their arms until he had laid waste their country from March to November, without allowing them either to reap or sow. On their submission, their tribute was increased, and each tribe was obliged to pay six hundred byzants annually. But disturbances occurring not long afterwards among the Byzantine officers, and a new tribe called the Sclavesians entering the peninsula, the Melings and Ezerites sent deputies to the Emperor Romanus to solicit a reduction of their tribute. The peaceable inhabitants saw their property threatened with plunder and devastation if the Melings and Ezerites should unite with the Sclavesians; the central government was threatened with the loss of the revenues of the province; so the emperor consented to issue a golden bull, or imperial charter with a golden seal, fixing the tribute of the Melings at sixty gold byzants, and that of the Ezerites at three hundred, as it had been before their rebellion.

eager to worry him that they could hardly be held by their keepers from attacking him on his throne.—Luitprand, *De Rebus suo Tempore in Europa gestis,* iii, chap. 5. Muratori v. 422. Lebeau, xiii. 445.   [1] Kemble, ii. introd. x.

[2] The classic name of Taygetus was already forgotten, and the mountain was called as at present, Pentadaktylos.—Const. Porph. *De Adm. Imp.* chap. 50.

The Sclavonian population of the Peloponnesus was not confined to the tributary districts; nor, indeed, were these the only Sclavonians who retained their own local administration. The whole country, from the northern bank of the Alpheus to the sources of the Ladon and Erymanthus, was in their possession, and they governed it according to their national usages until the Crusaders conquered Greece. A considerable body of the Sclavonians had also begun to adopt Byzantine civilisation, and some of the wealthiest contended for the highest places in the administration of the empire. The patrician Niketas took an active share in the intrigues which placed the imperial crown on the head of Romanus. His pride and presumption, as well as his Sclavonian descent, are ridiculed by the Emperor Constantine Porphyrogenitus, though the patrician had formed an alliance with the imperial family.[1]

From this time we hear nothing more of the Sclavonians settled in the Peloponnesus, until the peninsula was invaded by the Crusaders, after they had taken Constantinople, and established the Frank empire of Romania, (A.D. 1204).

The condition of the town of Maina and the district about Cape Tænarus presents us with a picture of the vicissitudes the Greeks had suffered during the decline of the Roman empire. The population of this rugged promontory consisted of the poorer class of agricultural Laconians, and it kept possession of this arid district when the Sclavonians seized the rich plain of the Eurotas, and drove the Greeks out of Sparta. The strangers occupied all the rich pastures on Mount Taygetus, but want of water prevented their advance along the promontory of Tænarus, and the fortified town of Maina enabled the inhabitants to defend their liberty, and support themselves by exporting oil. This secluded country long remained in a state of barbarism, and the rural population soon relapsed into idolatry, from which they were not converted to Christianity until the reign of Basil I. In the time of Constantine Porphyrogenitus, the town of Maina was a place of some commercial importance, and was governed by an officer appointed by the general of the Peloponnesian theme; but the district continued to pay only four hundred pieces of gold to the im-

---

[1] The daughter of Niketas was the wife of the Emperor Christophoros, the eldest son of Romanus I. The verse of a Byzantine poet, which Constantine mentions was applied to Niketas, has caused much learned discussion. The words seem to say that the patrician had an ass-like Sclavonian visage—

$$\gamma\alpha\delta\rho\alpha\sigma\omega\epsilon\iota\delta\eta\varsigma\text{?}\ \delta\psi\iota\varsigma\ \epsilon\sigma\theta\lambda\alpha\beta\omega\mu\epsilon\nu\eta.$$

—De Thematibus, ii. 6. Kopitar, Miscellanea Græcoslavica, p. 63.

perial treasury, which was the amount levied on it in the days of the Roman empire.[1]

It was fortunate for the Byzantine empire that the caliphate of Bagdat had lost its former military power, for if an active enemy on the southern frontier had taken advantage of the embarrassments caused by an enterprising warrior like Simeon, king of Bulgaria, in the north, the empire might have been reduced to the deplorable condition from which it had been raised by the vigour of the Iconoclasts. But repeated rebellions had separated many of the richest provinces from the caliphate, and the tyranny of a religious sway, that enforced unity of faith by persecution, compelled heresy to appeal to the sword on every difference of opinion. This additional cause of ruin and depopulation, added to the administrative anarchy that was constantly on the increase in the caliph's dominions, had greatly weakened the Saracen power. The innumerable discussions which a formal orthodoxy created in the Greek church were trifling in comparison with those which the contemplative tendencies of the Asiatic mind raised in the bosom of Islam.

Several independent dynasties were already founded within the dominions of the caliph of Bagdat, which were disturbed by several sects besides the Karmathians. Yet, amidst all their civil wars, the Mohammedans made continual incursions into Asia Minor, and the Byzantine troops avenged the losses of the Christians by ravaging Syria and Mesopotamia. Slaves and cattle were carried off by both parties, whether victors or vanquished, so that the country became gradually depopulated; and in succeeding generations we find the richest provinces between the Halys, the Euphrates, and the Mediterranean in a state of desolation. The suburbs of the towns were reduced to ashes; valleys, once swarming with inhabitants, and cultivated with the spade, so that they could support millions, were reduced to sheep-walks. During the regency of Zoe, Damian, emir of Tyre, with a powerful fleet under his command, attacked Strobelos in Caria, but he was repulsed;[2] and in the following year the Byzantine army made an irruption into the territories of Germanicia and Samosata, and carried off fifty thousand prisoners, according to the accounts of the Arabian historians. The empress-regent would have willingly concluded

---

[1] *De Adm. Imp.* chap. 50, page 224, edit. Bonn.
[2] Strobelos was the ancient Myndos. It is called an island by the Byzantine writers from its peninsular situation.—Const. Porphyr. *De Them.* p. 15, edit. Bonn.

peace with the Saracens at this time, for she was compelled to transport the greater part of the Asiatic army into Europe to resist Simeon, king of Bulgaria, and it appears that a truce and exchange of prisoners took place. The Byzantine arms had been so much more successful than the Saracen during the preceding campaigns, that when all the Christians had been exchanged, the number of Mohammedans still unredeemed was so great that the caliph had to pay a hundred and twenty thousand pieces of gold for their release, according to the stipulated price fixed by the convention.[1]

Romanus I., who had obtained the throne by means of the support of the navy, appears to have paid more attention to keep it in good order than his predecessors. In the year 926, Leo of Tripolis, who visited the Archipelago, seeking to repeat his exploits at Thessalonica, was encountered in the waters of Lemnos by the imperial squadron under John Radenos, and so completely defeated that it was with difficulty he saved his own ship.

The wars of the Karmathians brought the caliphate into such a disturbed state that the Christians of Armenia again raised their banner, and, uniting their forces with the Byzantine generals, obtained great successes over the Saracens. John, the son of that Kurkuas, who had been deprived of sight for conspiring against Basil I., was appointed commander-in-chief by Romanus, and commenced a career of conquest ably followed up a few years later by the Emperors Nicephorus II. and John I. (Zimiskes.) The military skill of John Kurkuas, the high discipline of his army, and the tide of conquest which flowed with his presence, revived aspirations of military renown long dormant at Constantinople. The learned were pleased to compare him with Trajan and Belisarius, the heroes of the Western and Eastern Empires.

As early as the reign of Leo. VI., the Armenians under Melias had made considerable progress. The territory they delivered from the yoke of the Mohammedans was formed into a small theme, called Lykandos, and Melias was named its general, with the rank of patrician.[2] From the year 920 to 942, John Kurkuas was almost uninterruptedly engaged against the Saracens. In 927 he ravaged the province of Melitene, and took the capital, of which, however, he only retained

---

[1] Weil, *Geschichte der Chalifen*, ii. 635. The Byzantine ambassador was at Bagdat in July, 917.
[2] Constant Porphyr. *De Adm. Imp.* chap. 50, page 228.

possession for a month.[1] Two years after, the Saracen emir of Melitene, finding himself unable to resist the Byzantine armies, engaged to pay tribute to the emperor. In the mean time, the Armenians, with the assistance of a division of Byzantine troops, had pushed their conquests to the lake of Van, and forced the Saracens of Aklat and Betlis not only to pay tribute, but to allow the cross to be elevated in their cities higher than the domes of their mosques. The long series of annual incursions recorded by the Byzantine and Arabian writers may be described in the words plunder, slavery, depopulation. In the campaign of 941, the Byzantine troops are said to have reduced fifteen thousand Saracens to slavery. But the exploit which raised the reputation of John Kurkuas to the highest pitch of glory, was the acquisition of the miraculous handkerchief, with a likeness of our Saviour visibly impressed on its texture ; a relic which the superstition of the age believed had been sent by Christ himself to Abgarus, prince of Edessa. In the year 942, John Kurkuas crossed the Euphrates, plundered Mesopotamia as far as the banks of the Tigris, took Nisibis, and laid siege to Edessa. The inhabitants of the city purchased their safety by surrendering the miraculous handkerchief. The victorious general was removed from his command shortly after, and the relic was transported to Constantinople by others.[2]

The parallel drawn by the people of Constantinople between John Kurkuas and Belisarius, seems imperfectly borne out by the conquests of the later general ; but the acquisition of a relic weighed, in those days, more than that of a kingdom. Yet, perhaps, even the miraculous portrait of Edessa would not have been compared with the conquest of the Vandal and Gothic monarchies, had the two-and-twenty years of John Kurkuas's honourable service not been repaid by courtly ingratitude. In the plenitude of his fame, the veteran was accused of aspiring at the empire, and removed from all his employments. Romanus I., like Justinian, when he examined the accusation, was convinced of its falsity, but he was jealous and mean-spirited.[3]

---

[1] Contin. 257. Weil, ii. 637.

[2] Georg. Mon. 590. Contin. 268. Krug. 225. In this age there was a vehement desire to gain possession of relics.—Chamich, *History of Armenia*, ii. 82.

[3] Manuel, a judge and protospatharios, wrote a work in eight books on the exploits of John Kurkuas. As the holy handkerchief of Edessa was brought to Constantinople after his disgrace, 15th August, 943, his name is not mentioned by the servile historians of the empire in connection with its capture. This fact shows to what extent these writers conceal the truth.—Compare Contin. 265, and Krug. 224.

During the government of Constantine VII., the war was continued with vigour on both sides. Seif Addawalah, the Hamdanite, called by the Greeks Chabdan, who was emir of Aleppo, invaded the empire with powerful armies.[1] Bardas Phokas, the Byzantine general, displayed more avarice than energy; and even when replaced by his son Nicephorus, the future emperor, victory was not immediately restored to the imperial standards. But towards the end of Constantine's reign, Nicephorus, having removed various abuses both in the military and civil service, which had grown out of the gains arising from the traffic in plunder, and slaves captured in the annual forays of the troops, at last prepared an army calculated to prosecute the war with glory. The result of this labour became visible in the reign of Romanus II.

After the conquest of Crete, the whole disposable force of the empire in Asia was placed under the command of Nicephorus, who, according to the Arabians, opened the campaign of 962 at the head of one hundred thousand men.[2] The Saracens were unable to oppose this army in the field; Doliche, Hierapolis, and Anazarba were captured, and Nicephorus advanced to Aleppo, where Seif Addawalah had collected an army to protect his capital. The position of the Hamdanite was turned by the superior tactics of the Byzantine general, his communications with his capital cut off, his army at last defeated, and his palace and the suburbs of Aleppo occupied. A sedition of the Arab troops, and a quarrel between the inhabitants and the garrison, enabled Nicephorus to enter the city, but the citadel defied his attacks. On the approach of a Saracen army from Damascus, Nicephorus abandoned his conquest, carrying away immense booty from the city of Aleppo, and retaining possession of sixty forts along the range of Mount Taurus as the result of his campaign.

The disastrous defeat of the Byzantine army by the Bulgarians at Achelous was the primary cause of the elevation of Romanus I. to the throne; and as emperor, he conducted the war quite as ill as he had directed the operations of the fleet when admiral, though he could now derive no personal advantage from the disasters of his country. In 921, the warlike monarch of the Bulgarians advanced to the walls of Constantinople, after defeating a Byzantine army under John Rector. The imperial palace of the fountains, and many villas about

1 Leo Diaconus, note, page 415, edit. Bonn. D'Herbelot, *Hamadan ben Hamdoun.* Weil, iii. 14.   2 Leo Diaconus, 378, edit. Bonn.

the city, were burned, and Simeon retired unmolested with immense booty. The city of Adrianople was taken in one campaign by treachery, lost and reconquered in another by famine.[1] In the month of September 923, Simeon again encamped before the walls of Constantinople, after having ravaged the greater part of Thrace and Macedonia with extreme barbarity, destroying the fruit-trees and burning the houses of the peasantry. He offered, however, to treat of peace, and proposed a personal interview with Romanus I., who was compelled to meet his proud enemy without the walls, in such a way that the meeting had the appearance of a Roman emperor suing for peace from a victorious barbarian. Romanus, when he approached the ground marked out for the interview, saw the Bulgarian army salute Simeon as an emperor with loud shouts and music, while the body-guard of the Bulgarian king, resplendent with silver armour, astonished the people of Constantinople by its splendour, and the veteran soldiers of the empire by its steady discipline.[2] It seems that the rebellion of the Sclavonians in the Peloponnesus filled Romanus with anxiety; but he affected to solicit peace from motives of religion and humanity, that he might alleviate the sufferings of his subjects. The basis of peace was settled at this conference, and Simeon retired to his own kingdom laden with the plunder of the provinces and the gold of the emperor. The Byzantine writers omit to mention any of the stipulations of this treaty, so that there can be no doubt that it was far from honourable to the empire.[3] It must be remarked, however, that they are always extremely negligent in their notice of treaties, and have not transmitted to us the stipulations of any of those concluded with the Khazars, or other nations through whose territory a great part of the commercial intercourse of the Byzantine empire with India and China was

---

[1] The second capture of Adrianople is placed by all the Byzantine writers in the 10th indiction, A.D. 922; but Krug gives reasons for placing it in the year 923.—*Chron. der Byz.* 155.

[2] Simeon is supposed to have formed an alliance with the Pope, who sent him a royal crown to reward his hostilities against the Byzantine empire and church.—Schafarik, *Slavische Alterthümer,* ii. 187.

[3] There can be no doubt, however, that one of the stipulations of this treaty was the public acknowledgment of the independence of the Bulgarian church, and the official recognition of the archbishop of Dorostylon as Patriarch of Bulgaria, both by the emperor and the Patriarch of Constantinople. The fact is proved by the list of the primates of Bulgaria given by Ducange, *Fam. Aug. Byz.* 175. The patriarchal dignity in Bulgaria was abolished by John I. (Zimiskes), when he conquered the country in 972. The Greek writers err in asserting that the head of the Bulgarian church was ever officially recognised as a patriarch by the church of Constantinople.—Le Quien, *Oriens Christianus,* i. 1227, and ii. 287, and Neale's *History of the Holy Eastern Church,* vol. i. p. 44, afford no information on this curious question.

carried on, and from which the wealth of Constantinople was in a great measure derived.

Simeon then turned his arms against the Servians and Croatians. His cruelty in these hostilities is said to have surpassed anything ever witnessed. The inhabitants were everywhere deliberately murdered, and all Servia was so depopulated that its richest plains remained uncultivated for many years. Every inhabitant not slain was carried into Bulgaria to be sold as a slave; and the capital was so completely destroyed, that, seven years after the retreat of the invaders, only fifty men were found in its vicinity, living as hunters.[1] At last the Bulgarian army was completely defeated by the Croatians, whom the cruelty of Simeon had driven to despair. Simeon died shortly after, and Servia placed itself under the protection of the Byzantine government.

Bulgaria had been formidable at this time by the talents of Simeon rather than its own power. It was now threatened with invasion by the Magyars, who were carrying on plundering incursions into Germany, Italy, and even into France. Peter, who had succeeded his father Simeon, was anxious to secure his southern frontier by forming a closer union with the empire: he married Maria, the daughter of the Emperor Christophoros, and a long peace followed this alliance. But the ties of allegiance were not very powerful among the Bulgarian people, and a rebellion was headed by Michael the brother of Peter. The rebels maintained themselves in a state of independence after Michael's death, and when they were at last compelled to emigrate, they entered the territory of the empire, and, passing through the themes of Strymon, Thessalonica, and Hellas, seized on Nicopolis, and retained possession of that city and the surrounding country for some time. It seems that the incursion of Sclavesians into the Peloponnesus was connected with this inroad of the Bulgarians.[2]

Thrace had not enjoyed sufficient respite from the ravages of the Bulgarians to recover its losses, before it was plundered by the Hungarians, who advanced to the walls of Constantinople in 934.[3] The retreat of these barbarians was purchased by a large sum of money, paid in the Byzantine gold coinage, which was then the most esteemed currency throughout the

---

[1] Servia was ravaged in 927.—Const. Porphyr. *De Adm. Imp.* chap. 32. We may compare the way in which Simeon laid waste and depopulated Servia with that in which William the Conqueror treated Northumberland from policy, and the New Forest for amusement.—Hume, *Hist. of England*, chap. iv.   [2] Cedrenus, 628.

[3] Contin. 262. Symeon Mag. 488. Georg. Mon. 588. Leo Gramm. 506.

known world. In 943, the Hungarians again ravaged Thrace, and their retreat was again purchased with gold.[1] The last year of the reign of Constantine VII. was again marked by an invasion of the Hungarians, who approached Constantinople; but on this occasion they were defeated by the imperial troops, who attacked their camp during the night.[2]

The Byzantine wars in Italy present a series of vicissitudes connected with political intrigues, based on no national object, and leading to no general result. The imperial generals at times united with the Saracens to plunder the Italians, and at times aided the Italians to oppose the Saracens; sometimes occupied to accumulate treasures for themselves, and at others to extend the influence of the emperor. One of the Byzantine governors, named Krinitas, carried his avarice so far as to compel the people of Calabria (Apulia) to sell their grain at a low price, and then, having created a monopoly of the export trade in his own favour, sold it at an exorbitant profit to the Saracens of Africa. Constantine VII., hearing of this extortion, dismissed him from all employment, and confiscated his wealth; but the people who were governed by deputies possessing such powers were sure to be the victims of oppression.[3]

During the regency of Zoe (A.D. 915), Eustathios, the governor of Calabria, concluded a treaty with the caliph of Africa, by which the Byzantine authorities in Italy were bound to pay a yearly tribute of 22,000 gold byzants, and the caliph engaged to restrain the hostilities of the Saracens of Sicily. This tribute was subsequently reduced to 11,000 byzants, but the treaty remained in force until the reign of the Emperor Nicephorus II.[4] Even this distant province in the south of Italy was not safe from the plundering incursions of the Hungarians, who in the year 948 embarked on the Adriatic, and ravaged Apulia under the walls of Otranto. The general interests of Christianity, as well as the extent of Byzantine commerce, induced the Byzantine government to aid Hugh of Provence and the Genoese in destroying the nest of Saracen pirates established at Fraxinet, in the Alps, to the eastward of Nice.[5]

Romanus II. was only twenty-one years of age when he ascended the throne. He bore a strong resemblance to his

---

[1] A Hungarian prince named Bulograd visited Constantinople about 950, and was baptised. He was subsequently taken prisoner while engaged plundering in Germany, and hung by the Emperor Otho.—Cedrenus, 636. Krug, 264.
[2] Cont. 288. Symeon Mag. 496.   [3] Cedrenus, 652.
[4] *Ibid.*, 652.   [5] Muratori, *Annali d'Italia*, v. 319.

father in person, and possessed much of his good-nature and mildness of disposition, but he was of a more active and determined character. Unfortunately, he indulged in every species of pleasure with an eagerness that ruined his health and reputation, though his judicious selection of ministers prevented its injuring the empire. He was blamed for inhumanity, in compelling his sisters to enter a monastery; but as his object was a political one, in order to prevent their marriage, he was satisfied with their taking the veil, though they refused to wear the monastic dress; and he allowed them to live as they thought fit, and dispose of their own private fortunes at will. His own object was obtained if he prevented any of the ambitious nobles from forming an alliance with them, which would have endangered the hereditary right of his own children. His good-nature is avouched by the fact, that when Basilios—called the Bird, a favourite minister of his father—engaged a number of patricians in a conspiracy to seize the throne, he allowed none of the conspirators to be put to death. Though he spent too much of his time surrounded by actors and dancers, both the administration of civil and military affairs was well conducted during his reign. His greatest delight was in hunting, and he spent much of his time in the country surrounded by his gay companions, his horses, and his dogs. His excesses in pleasure and fatigue soon ruined his constitution; but when he died at the age of twenty-four, the people, who remembered his tall well-made figure and smiling countenance, attributed his death to poison. His wife, whose beauty and graceful manner never won the public to pardon a low alliance, which appeared to their prejudices to disgrace the majesty of the purple, was accused of this crime, as well as of having instigated the death of her father-in-law.[1] Romanus on his death-bed did not neglect his duty to the empire. He had observed that his able prime-minister, Joseph Bringas, had begun to manifest too great jealousy of Nicephorus Phokas; he therefore left it as his dying injunction that Nicephorus should not be removed from the command of the army employed against the Saracens.

Joseph Bringas, who conducted the administration during the reign of Romanus II., was a man of talent and integrity. His worst act, in the eyes of his contemporaries, was, that he withdrew a eunuch, named John Cherinas, from a monastery into which he had been exiled by Constantine VII., and con-

---

[1] Leo Diaconus, 31, edit. Bonn.

ferred on him the dignity of patrician, with the command of
the foreign guards. The Patriarch protested in vain against
this act of sacrilege; Bringas wanted a man to command the
guard, over whom he knew the leading nobles could exercise
no influence; so the monk quitted his frock, put on armour,
and became a leading man at court. Sisinios, one of the
ablest and most upright men in the public service, was made
prefect of Constantinople, and rendered the administration of
justice prompt and equitable. A general scarcity tried the
talents and firmness of Bringas, and he met the difficulty by
his great exertions, though it occurred at the very time it was
necessary to make extraordinary preparations to provision the
expedition against Crete. Every measure to alleviate the
public distress was taken in a disinterested spirit. Everything
required for the army was immediately paid for; to prevent
speculation in corn, the exportation of provisions from the
capital was prohibited—a law which may often be rendered
necessary as a temporary measure of police, though it is a
direct violation of the permanent principles of sound commercial policy.

The great event of the reign of Romanus II. was the
conquest of Crete. The injury inflicted on Byzantine commerce by the Saracen corsairs, fitted out in the numerous
ports on the north side of that island, compelled many of the
Greek islands of the Archipelago to purchase protection from
the rulers of Crete by the payment of a regular tribute. The
trade of Constantinople and its supplies of provisions were
constantly interrupted, yet several expeditions against Crete,
fitted out on the largest scale, had been defeated. The overthrow of that undertaken in the reign of Leo. VI. has been
noticed.[1] Romanus I. was unwilling to revive the memory of
his share in that disaster, and left the Cretans undisturbed
during his reign; but Constantine VII., towards the end of
his reign, prepared an expedition on a very grand scale, the
command of which he intrusted to a eunuch named Gongyles.
This expedition was completely defeated; the Byzantine camp
was taken, and the greater part of the force destroyed. Gongyles himself escaped with difficulty.[2]

Romanus was hardly seated on the throne before he
resolved to wipe off the disgrace the empire had suffered.

The only mode of protecting the commerce of the capital and the coasts of Greece was to conquer the island of Crete, and expel all the Saracen population. Romanus determined to fit out an expedition on a scale suitable for this undertaking, and he knew that in Nicephorus Phokas he possessed a general equal to the enterprise. Bringas aided the emperor with zeal and energy, and gave no countenance to the endeavours that some courtiers made to awaken the jealousy of Romanus, that too much glory might accrue to Nicephorus from the successful termination of so great an undertaking.

The expedition was strong in numbers and complete in its equipments. The fleet consisted of dromons and chelands. The dromon was the war-galley, which had taken the place of the triremes of the ancient Greeks and the quinqueremes of the Romans; it had only two tiers of rowers, and the largest carried three hundred men, of whom seventy were marine soldiers. The chelands were smaller and lighter vessels, adapted for rapid movements, and fitted with tubes for launching Greek fire, and their crews seem to have varied from 120 to 160 men. More than three hundred large transports attended the ships of war, freighted with military machines and stores.[1] We are not to suppose that the dromons and chelands were all fitted for war; a few only were required for that purpose, and the rest served as transports for the army, and the provisions necessary for a winter campaign. The land forces consisted of chosen troops from the legions of Asia and Europe, with Armenian, Sclavonian, and Russian auxiliaries. The port of Phygela, near Ephesus, served as the place of rendezvous for the ships collected from the coasts of Greece and the islands of the Egean.[2] Everything was ready in the month of July 960, and Nicephorus disembarked his troops in Crete without sustaining any loss, though the Saracens attempted to oppose the operation. The city of Chandax was prepared to defend itself to the last extremity, and the Mohammedans in the rest of the island took active measures for resisting the progress of the Byzantine troops, and preventing their deriving any supplies from the interior. Chandax was too strongly fortified to be taken with-

---

[1] Symeon Mag. 498, gives us the enumeration of the vessels composing the expedition. He says there were a thousand dromons, two thousand chelandia, and three hundred and sixty transports, and he is an author deserving attention. Our Admiralty built at one time a class of frigates called donkey frigates; perhaps the Byzantine government was no better advised.

[2] Strabo calls it Pygela, xiv. 639. Contin. Romanus 297. Symeon Mag. 498.

out a regular siege, so that the first operation of Nicephorus was to invest it in form. To insure the fall of the place, even at the risk of prolonging the siege, he began his operations by forming a complete circumvallation round his camp and naval station, which he connected with the sea on both sides of the city, and thus cut the enemy off from all communication with the Saracens in the country. The pirates of Chandax had often been at war with all the world, and they had fortified their stronghold in such a way that it could be defended with a small garrison, while the bulk of their forces were cruising in search of plunder. The repeated attacks of the Byzantine emperors had also warned them of the dangers to which they were exposed. Towards the land, a high wall protected the city; it was composed of sun-dried bricks, but the mortar of which they were formed had been kneaded with the hair of goats and swine into a mass almost as hard as stone, and it was so broad that two chariots could drive abreast on its summit. A double ditch of great depth and breadth strengthened the work, and rendered approach difficult.

One of the parties sent out by Nicephorus to complete the conquest of the island having been cut off, he was compelled to take the field in person as soon as he had completed his arrangements for blockading the fortress during the winter. The Saracens, encouraged by their success, had assembled an army, and proposed attempting to relieve the besieged city, when they were attacked in their position, and routed with great loss. The Byzantine general, in order to intimidate the defenders of Chandax, ordered the heads of those slain in the country to be brought to the camp, stimulating the activity of his soldiers in this barbarous service by paying a piece of silver for every head. They were then ranged on spears along the whole line of the circumvallation towards the fortifications of the city; and the number of slain was so great, that many more were cast into the place by means of catapults, in order to let the besieged see the full extent of the loss of their countrymen.

A strict blockade was maintained during the whole winter. When the weather permitted, light galleys cruised before the port, and at all times several of the swiftest dromons and chelands were kept ready to pursue any vessel that might either attempt to enter or quit the port. But though the Saracens were reduced to suffer great privations, they showed no disposition to surrender, and Nicephorus pressed on the siege as spring advanced with mines and battering-rams. At last a practicable breach was effected, and the place was taken by storm on the 7th of May, 961.[1] The accumulated wealth of many years of successful piracy was abandoned to the troops, but a rich booty and numerous slaves were carried to Constantinople, and shown in triumph to the people.

To complete the conquest of the island, it was necessary to exterminate the whole of the Saracen population. To effect this, the fortifications of Chandax were levelled with the ground, and a new fortress called Temenos, situated on a high and rugged hill, about twelve miles inland, was constructed and garrisoned by a body of Byzantine and Armenian troops. Many Saracens, however, remained in the island, but they were reduced to a state approaching servitude. The greater part of the Greek population in some parts of the island had embraced Mohammedanism during the 135 years of Saracen domination. When the island was reconquered, an Armenian monk named Nikon became a missionary to these infidels, and he had the honour of converting numbers of the Cretans back to Christianity.[2] As soon as the conquest of the island was completed, the greater part of the army was ordered to Asia Minor; but Nicephorus was invited by the emperor to visit Constantinople, where he was allowed the honour of a triumph. He brought Kurup, the Saracen emir of Crete, a prisoner in his train.[3]

We may here pause to take a cursory view of the state of Greece during the ninth and tenth centuries. The preceding pages have noticed the few facts concerning the fortunes of this once glorious land that are preserved in the Byzantine annals, but these facts are of themselves insufficient to explain how a people, whose language and literature occupied a predominant position in society, enjoyed neither political power nor moral pre-eminence as a nation. The literary instruction of every child in the empire who received any intellectual culture was thoroughly Greek : its first prayers were uttered in that language : its feelings were refined by the perusal of the choicest passages of the Greek poets and tragedians, and its

---

[1] Leo Diaconus, 11, edit. Bonn. The name Chandax was corrupted into Candia, and extended to the whole island, by the Venetians.

[2] Baronius, *Annal. Eccles.* A.D. 961. F. Cornelius, *Creta Sacra*, i. 206 ; ii. 240.

[3] Leo Diaconus, 28, 420, edit. Bonn. Krug, 314. There is a contemporary poem in five cantos (acroases) on the conquest of Crete, by Theodosius, a deacon, which gives a tolerably correct, though not a very poetical, picture of the war. It was published in the *Creta Sacra* of Cornelius, and is given in the volume of the Byzantine historians that contains Leo Diaconus, printed at Bonn.

opening mind was enlarged by the writings of the Greek historians and philosophers; but here the influence ended, for the moral education of the citizen was purely Roman. The slightest glance into history proves that the educated classes in the Byzantine empire were generally destitute of all sympathy with Greece, and looked down on the Greeks as a provincial and alien race. The fathers of the church and the ecclesiastical historians, whose works were carefully studied, to complete the education of the Byzantine youth, and to prepare them for public life, quickly banished all Hellenic fancies from their minds as mere schoolboy dreams, and turned their attention to the atmosphere of practical existence in church and state. Byzantine society was a development of Roman civilisation, and hence the Byzantine mind was practical and positive : administration and law were to it what liberty and philosophy had been to the Hellenes of old. The imagination and the taste of Hellas had something in their natural superiority that was repulsive to Byzantine pedantry, while their paganism excited the contempt of ecclesiastical bigots. A strong mental difference was therefore the permanent cause of the aversion to Greece and the Greeks that is apparent in Byzantine society, and which only begins to disappear after the commencement of the eleventh century. Its operation is equally visible in the Hellenic race, in whom the spirit of local patriotism has always been powerful, and it kept them aloof from the Byzantine service, so that the native Greeks really occupy a less prominent figure in the social and political history of the empire than they were entitled to claim.

The great social feature of the Hellenic race, during the ninth and tenth centuries, is the stationary condition of society, for the apathy resulting from the secret protestation of the Greek mind against Roman influence was confined to the higher classes. The eighth century was unquestionably a period of great activity, increase, and improvement among the Greeks, as among every other portion of the population of the Eastern Empire. But after the subjection of the Sclavonian colonists in the first years of the ninth century, and the reestablishment of extensive commercial relations over the whole Mediterranean, Greek society again relapsed into a stationary condition. There is no doubt that the general aspect of the country had undergone a total change ; and its condition in the tenth century was as different from its condition in the seventh, as the state of the southern provinces of Russia, in the present century, is from their state in the thirteenth, after the devastations of the Tartars. Numerous new cities had been built.[1]

The legendary history of the Greek monasteries tells us that the country was once utterly deserted, that the rugged limestone mountains were overgrown with forests and thick brushwood, and that into these deserted spots holy hermits retired to avoid the presence of pagan Sclavonians, who occupied the rich plains and pastoral slopes of the lower hills. In these retreats the holy anchorites dreamed that they were dwelling in cells once occupied by saints of an earlier day — men who were supposed to have fled from imaginary persecutions of Roman emperors, who had de-populated whole provinces by their hatred to Christianity, instead of by administrative oppression ; and the hermits saw visions revealing where these predecessors had concealed portraits painted by St. Luke himself, or miraculous pictures, the work of no human hand. Such is perhaps a not unapt representation of a large part of the rural districts of Greece during the seventh century. The immense extent of the private estates of a few rich individuals, from the time of Augustus to that of Leo the Philosopher, left whole provinces depopulated, and fit only to be used as pasture. Landlords, robbers, pirates, and slavery had all conspired to reduce Greece to a state of degradation and depopulation before the Sclavonians colonised her soil.

The vigorous administration of the Iconoclasts restored order, reduced the aristocracy to obedience, subdued the Sclavonians, and revived industry and commerce. The state of Greece was again changed, the Greek population increased as if they had been new colonists settled on a virgin soil, and from the end of the ninth century to the invasion of the Crusaders, Greece was a rich and flourishing province. The material causes of this wealth are as evident as the moral causes of its political insignificance. The great part of the commerce of the Mediterranean was in the hands of the Greeks ; the wealth and laws of the Byzantine empire placed ample capital at their command ; the silk manufacture was to Thebes and Athens what the cotton manufacture now is to Manchester and Glasgow ; Monemvasia was then what Venice

---

[1] Of these some were constructed on ancient sites, like Lacædemon, others replaced neighbouring ancient cities, like Monemvasia, Piada, Nikli, Veligosti, Andravida, and Arkadia.

became at a later period; the slave-trade, though it filled the world with misery, and Christian society with demoralisation, brought wealth to the shores of Greece. The mass of the agricultural population, too, enjoyed as much prosperity as the commercial. The produce of the country was abundant, and labour bore a far higher price than has ever been the case in western Europe. This was a natural result of the state of things in the vicinity of every town and village in Greece. The nature of all the most valuable produce of the land rendered the demand for labour at particular seasons very great; and this labour yielded immense profits, for it fructified olive groves, vineyards, and orchards of the choicest kinds, formed by the accumulated capital of ages. The labour of a few days created an amount of produce which bore no comparison with its cost, and Greece at this time possessed a monopoly of the finer kinds of oil, wine, and fruit. Moreover, the pastoral habits of the Sclavonians, who still occupied large provinces at a distance from the principal towns, prevented the cultivation of corn over a great extent of country; and the ruin of the excellent roads, which in ancient times had admitted of the transport of huge blocks of marble, and the march of armies accompanied by elephants over the roughest mountains, rendered the transport of grain to any considerable distance impossible. All these circumstances rendered labour valuable. The cultivation of grain by spade husbandry was often a matter of necessity, so that the agricultural labourer could easily maintain a position of comparative ease and abundance.

In this state of society, the only chance of improvement lay in the moral advancement of the citizen, which required the union of free local institutions with a well-organised central administration of the state, and a system for distributing justice over which the highest political power could exert no influence. Unfortunately no central government on the continent of Europe, which has possessed strength sufficient to repress local selfishness, and the undue power of privileged classes, has ever yet avoided fiscal oppression; and this was the case in the Byzantine empire. The social condition of the Greeks nourished intense local selfishness; the central operation of the Byzantine government led to severe fiscal exactions. The result of the political and financial, as well as of the moral state of the country, was to produce a stationary condition of society. Taxation absorbed all the annual profits of industry; society offered no invitation to form new plantations, or extend existing manufactures, and the age afforded no openings for new enterprises; each generation moved exactly in the limits of that which had preceded it, so that Greece, though in a state of material prosperity, was standing on the brink of decline. That decline commenced the moment the Italians were enabled to avail themselves of the natural resources of their country. Amalfi, Pisa, Genoa, and Venice, freed from the fiscal oppression of a central government, became first the rivals and then the superiors of the Greeks in commerce, industry, and wealth.

CHAPTER II

PERIOD OF CONQUEST AND MILITARY GLORY,
A.D. 963-1025

SECTION I

REIGNS OF NICEPHORUS II., PHOKAS, AND JOHN I. (ZIMISKES).
A.D. 963-976

Administration of Joseph Bringas—Character of Nicephorus II., 963-969
Public administration—Saracen war—Affairs in Sicily, Italy, and
Bulgaria—Assassination of Nicephorus II.—Character of John I.,
969-976—Coronation—Rebellions of the family of Nicephorus II.
(Phokas)—Russian war—Republic of Cherson—Saracen war—Death
of John I.

THE Empress Theophano was left by Romanus II. regent for
her sons, but as she was brought to bed of a daughter only
two days before her husband's death, the whole direction
of public business remained in the hands of Joseph Bringas,
whose ability was universally acknowledged, but whose severity
and suspicious character rendered him generally unpopular.
His jealousy soon involved him in a contest for power with
Nicephorus Phokas, who, however, did not venture to visit
Constantinople until his personal safety was guaranteed by the
Empress Theophano and the Patriarch Polyeuktes. Nicephorus
was allowed to celebrate his victories in Syria by a triumph, in
which he displayed to a superstitious crowd the relics he had
obtained by his victories over the Mohammedans; and the
piety of the age attached as much importance to these as his
troops did to the booty and slaves with which they were
enriched.[1] Bringas saw that the popularity of Nicephorus and
the powerful influence of his family connections must soon
gain him the title of Emperor, and his jealousy appears to
have precipitated the event he feared. He formed a plot
to have the victorious general seized, in order that his eyes
might be put out. Nicephorus being informed of his danger,
and having secured the support of the Patriarch by his devout
conduct, persuaded Polyeuktes to take prompt measures to

[1] Cedrenus, 646. Zonaras, ii. 198.

protect him from the designs of Bringas. The senate was convoked, and the Patriarch proposed that Nicephorus should be intrusted with the command of the army in Asia, according to the last will of Romanus II.[1] Bringas did not venture to oppose this proposal of the Patriarch, which was eagerly adopted ; and Nicephorus, after taking an oath never to injure the children of Romanus, his lawful sovereigns, proceeded to take the command of all the Byzantine forces in Asia.

Bringas still pursued his schemes ; he wrote to John Zimiskes, the ablest and most popular of the generals under the orders of Nicephorus, offering him the supreme command if he would seize the general-in-chief, and send him to Constantinople as a prisoner. Zimiskes was the nephew of Nicephorus ; but his subsequent conduct shows that conscience would not have arrested him in the execution of any project for his own aggrandisement. On the present occasion, he may have thought that the power of Bringas was not likely to be permanent, and he may have known that he would show little gratitude for any service ; while the popularity of Nicephorus with the troops made fidelity to his general the soundest policy. Zimiskes carried the letter of the prime-minister to Nicephorus, and invited him to assume the imperial title, as the only means of securing his own life and protecting his friends. It is said that John Zimiskes and Romanus Kurkuas were compelled to draw their swords, and threaten to kill their uncle, before he would allow himself to be proclaimed emperor. The same thing had been said of Leo V. (the Armenian), that he was compelled to mount the throne by his murderer and successor, Michael II.[2] Nicephorus at last yielded, and marched immediately from Cæsarea to Chrysopolis, where he encamped. Bringas found little support in the capital. Basilios, the natural son of the Emperor Romanus I., armed his household, in which he had three thousand slaves, and, exciting a sedition of the populace, sallied into the streets of Constantinople, and attacked the houses of the ministers, most of whom were compelled to seek an asylum in the churches.[3] Nicephorus was invited to enter the capital, where he was crowned by the Patriarch Polyeuktes, in St. Sophia's, on the 16th of August, 963.[4]

The family of Phokas was of Cappadocian origin, and had

---

[1] Leo Diaconus, 34.   [2] *Ibid.*, 38. Zonaras, ii. 198.
[3] Basilios was the son of a Sclavonian woman ; like many eminent men of his time, he was a eunuch.—Leo Diaconus, 94.   [4] Leo Diaconus, 48.

now for three generations supplied the empire with distinguished generals.[1]   Nicephorus proved an able emperor, and a faithful guardian of the young emperors; but his personal bearing was tinged with military severity, and his cold phlegmatic temper prevented his using the arts necessary to gain popularity either with the courtiers or the citizens. His conduct was moral, and he was sincerely religious; but he was too enlightened to confound the pretensions of the church with the truth of Christianity, and, consequently, in spite of his real piety, he was calumniated by the clergy as a hypocrite.[2]   Indeed, there was little probability that a strict military disciplinarian, who ascended the throne at the age of fifty-one, should prove a popular prince, when he succeeded a young and gay monarch like Romanus II.

The coronation of Nicephorus was soon followed by his marriage with Theophano, a match which must have been dictated to the beautiful widow by ambition and policy rather than love; though the Byzantine writers accuse her of a previous intrigue with the veteran general, and record that she exerted great authority over him by her persuasive manners. The marriage ceremony was performed by the Patriarch, but shortly after its celebration he forbade the emperor to enter the chancel of St. Sophia's, where the imperial throne was placed, declaring that even the emperor must submit to the penance imposed by the orthodox church on second marriages, which excluded the contracting party from the body of the church for a year.[2]   The hostile feeling, on the part of Polyeuktes, that produced this insolence, also encouraged a report that Nicephorus had acted as godfather to one of the children of Romanus and Theophano—a connection which, according to the Greek church, forms an impediment to marriage.   The Patriarch appears to have adopted this report without consideration, and threatened to declare the marriage he had celebrated null; he had even the boldness to order the emperor to separate from Theophano immediately.   But this difficulty was removed by the chaplain who had officiated at the baptism.

---

1 Luitprand, 347. Cedrenus, 727.
2 Nicephorus sent a hundred pounds' weight of gold from the spoils of Crete to found the monastery of the great Laura on Mount Athos, to which it was said he proposed to retire; and St. Athanasios, a monk whom he charged with this commission, became afterwards indignant when Nicephorus put a crown on his head in place of shaving it. The fanatic thought that he should have preferred the idle life of a cell to the active duties of a palace.—Leo Diaconus, notes, 426. St. Athanasios reorganised the monastic communities of Mount Athos between A.D. 959-969. — Montfaucon, *Palæographia Græca*, 452-454.   2 Zonaras, note of Ducange, ii. 87 ; note 25, edit. Ven.

He came forward, and declared on oath that Nicephorus had not been present, nor had he, the priest, ever said so. The Patriarch found himself compelled to withdraw his opposition, and, to cover his defeat, he allowed Nicephorus to enter the church without remark. This dispute left a feeling of irritation on the mind of the emperor, and was probably the cause of some of his severities to the clergy, while it certainly assisted in rendering him unpopular among his bigoted subjects.

Nicephorus had devoted great attention to improving the discipline of the Byzantine army, and, as it consisted in great part of mercenaries, this could only be done by a liberal expenditure. His chief object was to obtain troops of the best quality, and all the measures of his civil administration were directed to fill the treasury. An efficient army was the chief support of the empire; and it seemed, therefore, to Nicephorus that the first duty of an emperor was to secure the means of maintaining a numerous and well-appointed military force. Perhaps the people of Constantinople would have applauded his maxims and his conduct, had he been more liberal in lavishing the wealth he extorted from the provinces on festivals and shows in the capital. A severe famine, at the commencement of his reign, increased his unpopularity. This scarcity commenced in the reign of Romanus II., and, among the reports circulated against Joseph Bringas, it was related that he had threatened to raise the price of wheat so high, that, for a piece of gold, a man should only purchase as much as he could carry away in his pockets. It is very probable that the measures adopted by Nicephorus tended to increase the evil, though Zonaras, in saying that he allowed each merchant to use his own interest as a law, would lead us to infer that he abolished monopolies and maximums, and left the trade in grain free.[1] The fiscal measures of his reign, however, increased the burden of taxation. He retrenched the annual largesses of the court, and curtailed the pensions granted to courtiers. The worst act of his reign, and one for which the Byzantine historians have justly branded him with merited odium, was his violation of the public faith, and the honour of the Eastern Empire, by adulterating the coin, and issuing a debased coin, called the tetarteron. This debased money

---

[1] Zonaras, ii. 203-206. Cedrenus, 660. The price of a modios of wheat having risen to a nomisma (that is, a bushel for eleven shillings), the emperor sold it from the public granaries at half that price ; yet the people grumbled, because it was said Basil I. had, on some occasion, ordered wheat to be sold at the rate of twelve modioi for a gold nomisma.

he employed to pay the debts of the state, while the taxes continued to be exacted in the old and pure coin of the empire. The standard of the coinage of the Eastern Empire, it must always be borne in mind, remained always the same until the taking of Constantinople by the Crusaders. The gold coins of Leo III. and of Isaac II. are of the same weight and purity; and the few emperors who disgraced their reigns by tampering with the currency have been branded with infamy. Perhaps there is no better proof of the high state of political civilisation in Byzantine society.[1] But the strong grounds of dissatisfaction against Nicephorus were ripened into personal animosity by an accidental tumult in the hippodrome, in which many persons lost their lives. It happened that, while the troops were going through the evolutions of a sham-fight, a report arose that the emperor intended to punish the people, who had thrown stones at him, and insulted him as he passed through the streets. This caused a rush out of the enclosures, and many persons, men, women, and children, perished. The citizens, of course, insisted that the massacre was premeditated.[2]

The whole reign of Nicephorus was disturbed by the ill-will of the clergy, and one of his wisest measures met with the most determined opposition. In order to render the military service more popular among his native subjects, and prevent the veterans from quitting the army under the influence of religious feelings distorted by superstition, he wished the clergy to declare that all Christians who perished in war against the Saracens were martyrs in the cause of religion. But the Patriarch, who was more of a churchman than a patriot, considered it greater gain to the clergy to retain the power of granting absolutions, than to bestow the most liberal donation of martyrs on the church; and he appealed to the canons of St. Basil to prove that all war was contrary to Christian discipline, and that a Christian who killed an enemy, even in war with the Infidels, ought to be excluded from participating in the holy sacrament for three years. With a priesthood supporting such religious opinions, the Byzantine empire had need of an admirable system of administration, and a series of brave and warlike emperors, to perpetuate its long existence.[3] In the first year of his reign, Nicephorus endeavoured to

---

[1] Zonaras, ii. 203. Cedrenus, 658.
[2] Leo Diaconus witnessed the insults Nicephorus bore, and admired his equanimity; but a woman was burnt for throwing a stone at him.—P. 63. Zonaras, ii. 203.
[3] Zonaras, ii. 203. Cedrenus, 658.

restrain the passion for founding monasteries that then reigned almost universally. Many converted their family residences into monastic buildings, in order to terminate their lives as monks, without changing their habits of life. The emperor prohibited the foundation of any new monasteries and hospitals, enacting that only those already in existence should be maintained; and he declared all testamentary donations of landed property in favour of the church void.[1] He also excited the anger of the clergy, by forbidding any ecclesiastical election to be made until the candidate had received the imperial approbation. He was in the habit of leaving the wealthiest sees vacant, and either retained the revenues or compelled the new bishop to pay a large portion of his receipts annually into the imperial treasury.[2]

Nicephorus was so well aware of his unpopularity, that he converted the great palace into a citadel, which he made capable of defence with a small garrison. As the army was devoted to him, he knew that beyond the walls of Constantinople he was in no danger. In estimating the character and conduct of Nicephorus II., we must not forget that his enemies have drawn his portrait, and that, unfortunately for his reputation, modern historians have generally attached more credit to the splenetic account of the Byzantine court by Luitprand, the bishop of Cremona, than diplomatic despatches of that age are entitled to receive. Luitprand visited Constantinople as ambassador from the German emperor, Otho the Great, to negotiate a marriage between young Otho and Theophano, the stepdaughter of Nicephorus. Otho expected that the Byzantine emperor would cede his possessions in southern Italy as the dowry of the princess; Nicephorus expected the German emperor would yield up the suzerainty over Beneventum and Capua for the honour of the alliance. As might be expected, from the pride and rapacity of both parties, the ambassador failed in his mission; but he revenged himself by libelling Nicephorus; and his picture of the pride and suspicious policy of the Byzantine court in its intercourse with foreigners gives his libel some value, and serves as an apology for his virulence.[3]

---

[1] The *Novellæ* of Nicephorus. Leo Diaconus, 309.

[2] Luitprand. Leo Diaconus, 371.

[3] The value of the bishop's evidence as an αὐτόπτης may be estimated from his saying that Bardas, the father of Nicephorus, appeared to be a hundred and fifty years old. Luitprand had visited Constantinople in 943, as ambassador of Berenger, with a present of eunuchs, which Verdun then exported. He then saw the singing tree, the lions of

The darling object of Nicephorus was to break the power of the Saracens, and extend the frontiers of the empire in Syria and Mesopotamia. In the spring of 964, he assembled an army against Tarsus, which was the fortress that covered the Syrian frontier. The river Cydnus flowed through the city, dividing it into two portions, which were united by three bridges. The place was populous, well fortified, and amply supplied with every means of defence, so that the emperor was compelled to raise the siege, and lead his army against Adana, which he took. He then formed the siege of Mopsuestia, and, employing his men to run a subterranean gallery under the walls, he prevented the besieged from observing the operation by throwing the earth taken from the excavation into the Pyramus during the night. When his mine was completed, the beams which supported the walls were burned, and as soon as the rampart fell, the Byzantine army carried the place by storm. Next year (965), Nicephorus again formed the siege of Tarsus with an army of forty thousand men. The place was inadequately supplied with provisions; and though the inhabitants were a warlike race, who had long carried on incursions into the Byzantine territory, they were compelled to abandon their native city, and retire into Syria, carrying with them only their personal clothing. A rich cross, which the Saracens had taken when they destroyed the Byzantine army under Stypiotes in the year 877, was recovered, and placed in the church of St. Sophia at Constantinople. The bronze gates of Tarsus and Mopsuestia, which were of rich workmanship, were also removed, and placed by Nicephorus in the new citadel he had constructed to defend the palace.[1] In the same year Cyprus was reconquered by an expedition under the command of the patrician Niketas.

For two years the emperor was occupied at Constantinople by the civil administration of the empire, by a threatened invasion of the Hungarians, and by disputes with the king of Bulgaria; but in 968 he again resumed the command of the army in the East. Early in spring he marched past Antioch at the head of eighty thousand men, and, without stopping to besiege that city, he rendered himself master of the fortified places in its neighbourhood, in order to cut it off from all relief from the

metal that roared, and the eagle that flapped its wings.—*Luitprandi Hist.* lib. vi. chap. 1. Daru, *Histoire de Venise*, i. 92. The account of Luitprand's embassy to Nicephorus is in Muratori, *Scrip. Rer. Ital.* tom. ii. 479; and in the volume of the Byzantine Collection published at Bonn, which contains Leo Diaconus.
[1] Leo Diaconus, 61, Zonaras, ii, 201,

caliph of Bagdat. He then pushed forward his conquests; Laodicea, Hierapolis, Aleppo, Arca, and Emesa were taken, and Tripolis and Damascus paid tribute to save their territory from being laid waste. In this campaign many relics were surrendered by the Mohammedans.[1] In consequence of the approach of winter, the emperor led his army into winter quarters, and deferred forming the siege of Antioch until the ensuing spring. He left the patrician Burtzes in a fort on the Black Mountain, with orders to watch the city, and prevent the inhabitants from collecting provisions and military stores. The remainder of the army, under the command of Peter, was stationed in Cilicia.[2] As he was anxious to reserve to himself the glory of restoring Antioch to the empire, he ordered his lieutenants not to attack the city during his absence. But one of the spies employed by Burtzes brought him the measure of the height of a tower which it was easy to approach, and the temptation to take the place by surprise was not to be resisted. Accordingly, on a dark winter night, while there was a heavy fall of snow, Burtzes placed himself at the head of three hundred chosen men, and gained possession of two of the towers of Antioch.[3] He immediately sent off a courier to Peter, requesting him to advance and take possession of the city; but Peter, from fear of the emperor's jealousy, delayed moving to the assistance of Burtzes for three days. During this interval, however, Burtzes defended himself against the repeated attacks of the whole population with great difficulty. The Byzantine army at length arrived, and Antioch was annexed to the empire after having remained 328 years in the power of the Saracens. The Emperor Nicephorus, instead of rewarding Burtzes for his energy, dismissed both him and Peter from their commands.

The Fatimite caliph Moëz reigned at Cairowan, and was

[1] The most remarkable of these relics were an old garment and a bloody tress of hair, said to have belonged to John the Baptist, and the tile with the miraculous portrait of our Saviour, which last was taken at Hierapolis.—Cedrenus, 656. Zonaras, ii. 201. This tile was probably an ancient terra-cotta, with a head of Jupiter resembling the received type of the Saviour. The sword of Mahomet was also taken in this campaign, for the Mohammedans were as much votaries of relics in this age as the Christians.

[2] Peter was a eunuch; he distinguished himself in single combat with a Russian champion, whom he killed with his lance.—Leo Diaconus, 109.

[3] The towers of Antioch present very much the appearance they did when they were attacked by Burtzes. "They are about thirty feet square, and project each way so as to defend the interior side, as well as the exterior face of the wall: the latter is from fifty to sixty feet high, and eight or ten feet broad at top, which is covered with cut stones terminated in a cornice. The towers have interior staircases, and three loop-holed stages resting on brick arches, the uppermost having a small platform; and there is a small cistern beneath. Low doors afford a passage along the parapet, so that these structures may be regarded as a chain of small castles connected by a curtain, rather than as simple towers."—Colonel Chesney. The Expedition for the Survey of the rivers Euphrates and Tigris.—Vol. i. p. 426.

already contemplating the conquest of Egypt. Nicephorus not only refused to pay him the tribute of eleven thousand gold byzants, stipulated by Romanus I., but even sent an expedition to wrest Sicily from the Saracens. The chief command was intrusted to Niketas, who had conquered Cyprus; and the army, consisting chiefly of cavalry, was more particularly placed under the orders of Manuel Phokas, the emperor's cousin, a daring officer.[1] The troops were landed on the eastern coast, and Manuel rashly advanced, until he was surrounded by the enemy and slain. Niketas also had made so little preparation to defend his position, that his camp was stormed, and he himself taken prisoner and sent to Africa. Nicephorus, who had a great esteem for Niketas in spite of this defeat, obtained his release by sending to Moëz the sword of Mahomet, which had fallen into his hands in Syria. Niketas consoled himself during his captivity by transcribing the works of St. Basil, and a MS. of his penmanship still exists in the National Library at Paris.[2]

The affairs of Italy were, as usual, embroiled by local causes. Otho, the emperor of the West, appeared at the head of an army in Apulia, and having secured the assistance of Pandulf, prince of Beneventum, called Ironhead, carried on the war with frequent vicissitudes of fortune. Ironhead was taken prisoner by the Byzantine general, and sent captive to Constantinople. But the tyrannical conduct of the Byzantine officials lost all that was gained by the superior discipline of the troops, and favoured the progress of the German arms. Society had fallen into such a state of isolation, that men were more eager to obtain immunity from all taxation than protection for industry and property, and the advantages of the Byzantine administration ceased to be appreciated.

The European provinces of the empire were threatened with invasion both by the Hungarians and Bulgarians. In 966, Nicephorus was apprised of the intention of the Hungarians, and he solicited the assistance of Peter, king of Bulgaria, to prevent their passing the Danube. Peter refused, for he had been compelled to conclude a treaty of peace with

---

[1] He was the son of Leo Phokas, the rival of Romanus I.

[2] Leo Diaconus, 67, 76. Cedrenus seems to consider the conqueror of Cyprus and the prisoner of Sicily different persons; but we can hardly suppose there were too eunuchs of the name of Niketas who were patricians, and held the office of drungarios or admiral.—Pp. 654, 655. The MS. is mentioned by Montfaucon, *Pal. Græca*, 45; and by Hase, in his notes to Leo Diaconus, 443.

the Hungarians, who had invaded Bulgaria a short time before. It is even said that Peter took advantage of the difficulty in which Nicephorus appeared to be placed, by the numerous wars that occupied his troops, to demand payment of the tribute Romanus I. had promised to Simeon.[1] Nicephorus, in order to punish the insolence of one whom he regarded as his inferior, sent Kalokyres, the son of the governor of Cherson, as ambassador to Russia, to invite Swiatoslaff, the Varangian prince of Kieff, to invade Bulgaria, and intrusted him with a sum of fifteen hundred pounds' weight of gold, to pay the expenses of the expedition. Kalokyres proved a traitor : he formed an alliance with Swiatoslaff, proclaimed himself emperor, and involved the empire in a bloody war with the Russians.

Unpopular as Nicephorus II. was in the capital, his reign was unusually free from rebellions of the troops or insurrections in the provinces. His life was terminated in his own palace by domestic treachery. His beautiful wife Theophano, and his valiant nephew John Zimiskes, were his murderers. Theophano was said to have been induced to take part in the conspiracy from love for Zimiskes, whom she expected to marry after he mounted the throne. Zimiskes murdered his friend and relation from motives of ambition.[2] A band of conspirators, selected from the personal enemies of the emperor, among whom was Burtzes, accompanied John Zimiskes at midnight to the palace wall overlooking the pont of Bukoleon, and the female attendants of the empress hoisted them up from their boat in baskets. Other assassins had been concealed in the palace during the day, and all marched to the apartment of the emperor. Nicephorus was sleeping tranquilly on the floor — for he retained the habits of his military life amidst the luxury of the imperial palace. Zimiskes awoke him with a kick, and one of the conspirators gave him a desperate wound on the head, while Zimiskes insulted his uncle with words and blows : the others stabbed him in the most barbarous manner. The veteran, during his sufferings, only exclaimed, "O God ! grant me *thy* mercy." John I. was immediately proclaimed emperor by the mur-

---

[1] Leo Diaconus, 61.
[2] A report was spread that Nicephorus intended to make eunuchs of Basil and Constantine, and declare his brother Leo his successor.—Zonaras, ii. 207. This was probably an invention of Theophano, but it met with little credit, and her crime was ascribed to her warmth of temperament and the coldness of her husband. There was a great fashion of filling monasteries with eunuchs at this time.

derers. The body of Nicephorus was thrown into the court, and left all day on the snow exposed to public view, that everybody might be convinced he was dead. In the evening it was privately interred.

Thus perished Nicephorus Phokas on the 10th December 969—a brave soldier, an able general, and, with all his defects, one of the most virtuous men and conscientious sovereigns that ever occupied the throne of Constantinople. Though born of one of the noblest and wealthiest families of the Eastern Empire, and sure of obtaining the highest offices at a proud and luxurious court, he chose a life of hardship in pursuit of military glory; and a contemporary historian, who wrote after his family had been ruined by proscription, and his name had become odious, observes, that no one had ever seen him indulge in revelry or debauchery even in his youth.[1]

John I. was a daring warrior and an able general.[2] He was thoughtless, generous, and addicted to the pleasures of the table, so that, though he was by no means a better emperor than Nicephorus, he was far more popular at Constantinople: hence we find that his base assassination of his sovereign and relative was easily pardoned and forgotten, while the fiscal severity of his predecessor was never forgiven. The court of Constantinople was so utterly corrupt, that it was relieved from all sense of responsibility; the aristocracy knew no law but fear and private interest, and no crime was so venial as successful ambition. The throne was a stake for which every courtier held it lawful to gamble, who was inclined to risk his eyes or his life to gain an empire. Yet we must observe that both Nicephorus and John were men of nobler minds than the nobles around them, for both respected the rights and persons of their wards and legitimate princes, Basil and Constantine, and contented themselves with the post of prime-minister and the rank of emperor.

The chamberlain Basilios had been rewarded by Nicephorus, for his services in aiding him to mount the throne, with the rank of President of the Council, a dignity created

---

[1] Leo Diaconus, 78.

[2] The name Tzimiskes, an Armenian word, was given to John on account of his short stature.—Leo Diaconus, 92, 454: Lebeau, *Histoire du Bas-Empire*, xiv. 100. The name is written in a fearful manner, and with variations not adapted to render it euphonious, by Avdall in his translation of Chamich.—*History of Armenia*, ii. 77, 91. He calls him Johannes Chimishkik in one passage, and in another, Chumuskik Keurjan. He was born at Hierapolis, on the Euphrates, in the present pashalik of Amida or Diyar-bekr, called by Avdall Chumushkazak, and by Saint Martin, Tchemeschgedzeg.—*Mémoires sur l'Arménie*, i. 95.

on purpose. He was now intrusted by John with the complete direction of the civil administration. The partisans of Nicephorus were removed from all offices of trust, and their places filled by men devoted to Zimiskes, or hostile to the family of Phokas. All political exiles were recalled, and a parade of placing the young emperors, Basil and Constantine, on an equality with their senior colleague was made, as an insinuation that they had hitherto been retained in an unworthy state of inferiority. At the same time, measures were adopted to prevent the rabble of the capital from plundering the houses of the wealthy nobles who had been dismissed from their appointments, which was a usual proceeding at every great political revolution in Constantinople.[1]

The coronation of John I. was delayed by the Patriarch for a few days, for Polyeuktes lost no opportunity of showing his authority. He therefore refused to perform the ceremony until Zimiskes declared that he had not imbued his hands in the blood of his sovereign. He pointed out his fellow-conspirators, Leo Valantes and Atzypotheodoros, as the murderers, and excused himself by throwing the whole blame of the murder on the Empress Theophano. The officers thus sacrificed were exiled, and the empress was removed from the imperial palace.[2] John was then admitted to the favour of the Patriarch, on consenting to abrogate the law of Nicephorus, providing that the candidates for ecclesiastical dignities should receive the emperor's approbation before their election, and promising to bestow all his private fortune in charity. After his coronation, he accordingly distributed one-half of his fortune among the poor peasants round Constantinople, and employed the other in founding an hospital for lepers, in consequence of that disease having greatly increased about this time. He also increased his popularity by remitting the tribute of the Armeniac theme, which was his

[1] Cedrenus, 663. Gold coins, with the effigies of Nicephorus II. and Basil II., attest that Basil preserved all the honours of his rank.—Leo Diaconus, 94.

[2] Theophano was sent to the island of Prote, but escaped, and sought asylum in St. Sophia's. The chamberlain Basilios took her thence by force, and she was exiled to a monastery in the Armeniac theme, founded by her murdered husband. Her indignation on hearing the sentence was so great, that she reviled Zimiskes, and boxed the ears of the chamberlain, whom she called a barbarian and a Scythian woman.—Leo Diaconus, 99. Cedrenus, 664. Gibbon is wrong in saying "she assaulted with words and blows her son Basil;" but Lebeau has committed the same error. Cedrenus says distinctly it was the celebrated eunuch she assaulted, and he was the son of a Scythian woman. There is not a word about her proclaiming the illegitimacy of the young Basil, nor indeed any reason to suppose he was present, from the accounts of Leo Diaconus, Cedrenus, and Zonaras. On the contrary, when Basil became the ruler of the empire, he recalled his mother from banishment.—Cedrenus, 684.

native province, and by adding to the largesses which it was customary for the emperor to distribute.[1]

The Patriarch Polyeuktes died about three months after the coronation, and Zimiskes selected Basilios, a monk of Mount Olympus, as his successor; and without paying any respect to the canons which forbid the interference of the laity in the election of bishops, he ordered him to be installed in his dignity. The monk proved less compliant than the emperor expected. After occupying the patriarchal chair about five years, he was deposed for refusing to appear before the emperor to answer an accusation of treason. The Patriarch declared the emperor incompetent to sit as his judge, asserting that he could only be judged or deposed by a synod or general council of the church. He was nevertheless banished to a monastery he had built on the Scamander, and from which he is called Scamandrinos. Antonios, the abbot of Studion, was appointed Patriarch in his place.

The family of Phokas had so long occupied the highest military commands, and disposed of the patronage of the empire, that it possessed a party too powerful to be immediately reduced to submission. The reign of John was disturbed by more than one rebellion excited by its members. Leo, the brother of Nicephorus, had distinguished himself by gaining a great victory over the Saracens in the defiles of Kylindros, near Andrassos, while his brother was occupied with the conquest of Crete. During the reign of Nicephorus he held the office of curopalates, but had rendered himself hated on account of his rapacity. His second son, Bardas Phokas, held the office of governor of Koloneia and Chaldia when Nicephorus was murdered, and was banished to Amasia. Bardas was one of the best soldiers and boldest champions in the Byzantine army. In the year 970 he escaped from confinement, and rendered himself master of Cæsarea, where he assumed the title of Emperor. In the mean time his father, escaping from Lesbos, and his elder brother Nicephorus from Imbros, attempted to raise a rebellion in Europe. These two were soon captured, and John, satisfied that he had ruined the family when he murdered the Emperor Nicephorus, spared their lives, and allowed the sentence which condemned them to lose their eyes to be executed in such a way that they retained their eyesight. Bardas, however, gave the emperor some trouble, and it was necessary to recall Bardas Skleros

[1] Leo Diaconus, 100.

from the Russian war to take the command against him.[1] Phokas, when deserted by his army, escaped to a castle he had fortified as a place of refuge, where he defended himself until Skleros persuaded him to surrender, on a promise that he should receive no personal injury. Zimiskes, who admired his daring courage, condemned him to reside in the island of Chios, and adopt the monastic robe. His father Leo, who escaped a second time from confinement, and visited Constantinople in the hope of rendering himself master of the palace during the absence of the emperor, was discovered, and dragged from St. Sophia's, in which he sought an asylum. His eyes were then put out, and his immense estates confiscated.

John, in order to connect himself with the Basilian dynasty, married Theodora, one of the daughters of Constantine VII. (Porphyrogenitus.) Another more important marriage is passed unnoticed by the Byzantine writers. Zimiskes, finding that he could ill spare troops to defend the Byzantine possessions in Italy against the attacks of the Western emperor, released Pandulf of Beneventum, after he had remained three years a prisoner at Constantinople, and by his means opened amicable communications with Otho the Great. A treaty of marriage was concluded between young Otho and Theophano, the sister of the Emperors Basil and Constantine. The nuptials were celebrated at Rome on the 14th of April 972; and the talents and beauty of the Byzantine princess enabled her to act a prominent and noble part in the history of her time.[2]

A curious event in the history of the Eastern Empire, which ought not to pass unnoticed, is the transportation of a number of heretics, called by historians Manicheans, from the eastern provinces of Asia Minor, to increase the colonies of Paulicians and other heretics already established round Philippopolis. This is said to have been done by the Emperor John, by advice of a hermit named Theodoros, whom he elevated to the dignity of Patriarch of Antioch. The continual mention of numerous communities of heretics in Byzantine history proves that there is no greater delusion than to speak of the unity of the Christian church. Dissent appears to have been quite as prevalent, both in the Eastern and Western churches, before the time of Luther, as it has been since. Because the Greeks and Italians have been deficient in religious feeling,

---

[1] The family of Skleros is mentioned in the reign of Nicephorus I.—*Incert. Theoph.* 429.
      [2] Muratori, *Annali d'Italia*, v. 435.

and their superior knowledge enabled them to affect contempt for other races, the history of dissent has been neglected, and religious investigation decried under the appellation of heresy.[1]

The Russian war was the great event of the reign of John Zimiskes. The military fame of the Byzantine emperor, who was unquestionably the ablest general of his time, the greatness of the Russian nation, whose power now overshadows Europe, the scene of the contest, destined in our day to be again the battle-field of Russian armies in a more successful campaign, and the political interest which attaches to the first attempt of a Russian prince to march by land to Constantinople, all combine to give a practical as well as a romantic interest to this war.[2]

The first Russian naval expedition against Constantinople in 865 would probably have been followed by a series of plundering excursions, like those carried on by the Danes and Normans on the coasts of England and France, had not the Turkish tribe called the Patzinaks rendered themselves masters of the lower course of the Dnieper, and become instruments in the hands of the emperors to arrest the activity of the bold Varangians. The northern rulers of Kief were the same rude warriors that infested England and France, but the Russian people was then in a more advanced state of society than the mass of the population in Britain and Gaul. The majority of the Russians were freemen; the majority of the inhabitants of Britain and Gaul were serfs. The commerce of the Russians was already so extensive as to influence the conduct of their government, and to modify the military ardour of their Varangian masters. But this commerce, after the fall of the Khazar empire, and the invasion of Europe by the Magyars and Patzinaks, was carried on under obstacles which tended to reduce its extent and diminish its profits, and which it required no common degree of skill and perseverance to overcome. The wealth revealed to the rapacious

---

[1] Cedrenus, 665. It cannot be surprising that dissent was prevalent when we read how the clergy behaved. The Pope or anti-Pope, called Boniface VII., assassinated Benedict VI., and, after despoiling the Vatican, fled to Constantinople, A.D. 974. In 984 he returned to Rome, dethroned the reigning Pope, John XIV., who perished in prison, and occupied the papal throne himself. He died in the following year.

[2] Gibbon observes the singular undeclinable Greek word used to designate the Russians, 'Ῥῶs. It occurs twice in the Septuagint, but our translation makes no mention of the Russians.—Ezek. xxviii. 2; xxix. 1. The Russians appear also to be mentioned twice in the Koran.—Al Fourkan, v. 39; Sale's *Koran*, chap. 25 (the Rass on which Sale has a note is supposed to mean the Russians); and *The Letter "Kaf,"* v. 11.—Sale, chap. 50. See Hammer, *Sur les Origines Russes.*

Varangian chiefs of Kief by the existence of this trade invited them to attack Constantinople, which appeared to be the centre of immeasurable riches.

After the defeat in 865, the Russians induced their rulers to send envoys to Constantinople to renew commercial intercourse, and invite Christian missionaries to visit their country; and no inconsiderable portion of the people embraced Christianity, though it continued long after better known to the Russian merchants than to the Varangian warriors.[1] The commercial relations of the Russians with Cherson and Constantinople were now carried on directly, and numbers of Russian traders took up their residence in these cities. The first commercial treaty between the Russians of Kief and the Byzantine empire was concluded in the reign of Basil I.[2] The intercourse increased from that time. In the year 902, seven hundred Russians are mentioned as serving on board the Byzantine fleet with high pay; in 935, seven Russian vessels, with 415 men, formed part of a Byzantine expedition to Italy; and in 949, six Russian vessels, with 629 men, were engaged in the unsuccessful expedition of Gongyles against Crete.[3] In 966, a corps of Russians accompanied the unfortunate expedition of Niketas to Sicily.[4] There can be no doubt that these were all Varangians, familiar, like the Danes and Normans in the West, with the dangers of the sea, and not native Russians, whose services on board the fleet could have been of little value to the masters of Greece.

But to return to the history of the Byzantine wars with the Russians. In the year 907, Oleg, who was regent of Kief during the minority of Igor the son of Rurik, assembled an army of Varangians, Sclavonians, and Croatians, and, collecting two thousand vessels or boats of the kind then used on the northern shore of the Euxine, advanced to attack Constantinople. The exploits of this army, which pretended to aspire at the conquest of Tzaragrad, or the City of the Cæsars, were confined to plundering the country round Constantinople; and it is not improbable that the expedition was undertaken to obtain indemnity for some commercial losses sustained by imperial negligence, monopoly, or oppression.

---

[1] Continuator, 122. Cedrenus, 551. *Photii Epistolæ*, 58. Compare the observations of Wilken on the conversion of the Russians, with Wilken, *Uber die Verhältnisse der Russen zum Byzantinischen Reich*, 90. Karamsin, *Histoire de la Russie*, i. 148.
[2] Zonaras, ii. 173.
[3] Constant. Porphyr. *De Ceremoniis Aulæ Byz.* i. 652, 660, 664, edit. Bonn.
[4] The Arabian historian Novaïri, quoted by Karamsin.

The subjects of the emperor were murdered, and the Russians amused themselves with torturing their captives in the most barbarous manner. At length Leo purchased their retreat by the payment of a large sum of money. Such is the account transmitted to us by the Russian monk Nestor, for no Byzantine writer notices the expedition, which was doubtless nothing more than a plundering incursion, in which the city of Constantinople was not exposed to any danger.[1] These hostilities were terminated by a commercial treaty in 912, and its conditions are recorded in detail by Nestor.[2]

In the year 941, Igor made an attack on Constantinople, impelled either by the spirit of adventure, which was the charm of existence among all the tribes of Northmen, or else roused to revenge by some violation of the treaty of 912. The Russian flotilla, consisting of innumerable small vessels, made its appearance in the Bosphorus while the Byzantine fleet was absent in the Archipelago.[3] Igor landed at different places on the coast of Thrace and Bithynia, ravaging and plundering the country; the inhabitants were treated with incredible cruelty; some were crucified, others were burned alive, the Greek priests were killed by driving nails into their heads, and the churches were destroyed. Only fifteen ships remained at Constantinople, but these were soon fitted up with additional tubes for shooting Greek fire. This force, trifling as it was in number, gave the Byzantines an immediate superiority at sea, and the patrician Theophanes sailed out of the port to attack the Russians. Igor, seeing the small number of the enemy's ships, surrounded them on all sides, and endeavoured to carry them by boarding; but the Greek fire became only so much more available against boats and men crowded together, and the attack was repulsed with fearful loss. In the mean time, some of the Russians who landed in Bithynia were defeated by Bardas Phokas and John Kurkuas, and those who escaped from the naval defeat were pursued and slaughtered on the coast of Thrace without mercy. The Emperor Romanus ordered all the prisoners brought to Constantinople to be beheaded. Theophanes overtook the fugitive ships in the month of September, and the relics of the ex-

---

[1] If the Russians really on this occasion transported their fleet over some neck of land, in imitation of the exploit of Niketas Oryphas at the isthmus of Corinth, it may have been near Cherson, but not near Constantinople.—*La Chronique de Nestor, traduite en Française par Louis Paris*, i. 36.   [2] Nestor, i. 39.   Krug, 108
[3] The Byzantine writers and Nestor speak of ten thousand boats, but Luitprand, whose stepfather was then at Constantinople as ambassador from Hugh, king of Italy, says there were more than a thousand.—*Luitprandi Hist.* v. 6.

pedition were destroyed, Igor effecting his escape with only
a few boats.[1]   The Russian Chronicle of Nestor says that, in
the year 944, Igor, assisted by other Varangians, and by the
Patzinaks, prepared a second expedition, but that the inhabitants of Cherson so alarmed the Emperor Romanus by their
reports of its magnitude, that he sent ambassadors, who met
Igor at the mouth of the Danube, and sued for peace on terms
to which Igor and his boyards consented.   This is probably
merely a salve applied to the vanity of the people of Kief by
their chronicler; but it is certain that a treaty of peace was
concluded between the emperors of Constantinople and the
princes of Kief in the year 945.[2]   The stipulations of this
treaty prove the importance attached to the commerce carried
on by the Russians with Cherson and Constantinople.   The
two Russo-Byzantine treaties preserved by Nestor are documents of great importance in tracing the history of civilisation
in the east of Europe.   The attention paid to the commercial
interests of the Russian traders visiting Cherson and Constantinople, and the prominence given to questions of practical
utility instead of to points of dynastic ambition, may serve as
a contrast to many modern treaties in the west of Europe.[3]
The trading classes would not have been powerful enough to
command this attention to their interests on the part of the
warlike Varangians, had a numerous body of free citizens not
been closely connected with the commercial prosperity of
Russia.   Unfortunately for the people, the municipal independence of their cities, which had enabled each separate community to acquire wealth and civilisation, was not joined to
any central institutions that insured order and a strict administration of justice, consequently each city fell separately a prey
to the superior military force of the comparatively barbarian
Varangians of Scandinavia.   The Varangian conquest of Russia
had very much the same effect as the Danish and Norman conquests in the West.   Politically, the nation appeared more

[1] Contin. "Romanus Lecapenus," 263.   Leo Gramm. 506.   Symeon Mag. 490.
Nestor, i. 54.   Krug, 186.
[2] The French translation of Nestor gives 945 as the date of the treaty, but Romanus,
Constantine, and Stephen are the emperors named in the text.   Romanus I. was deposed in December 944; Constantine and Stephen, his sons, on the 27th January 945;
and Romanus II., son of Constantine VII. (Porphyrogenitus), was crowned as his father's
colleague on the 6th April 945.   Krug, 210, considers the treaty as concluded by Constantine VII. and Romanus II., and it must have been ratified in the interval before
Igor's death, which happened before the end of 945.
[3] Commerce, as a means of increasing power and population, was beginning to excite
the attention of the barbarians in western Europe.   Athelstan, 925–941, enacted a law
to confer the privileges of a thane on any English merchant who had made three voyages
to a foreign country on his own account.—Wilkins, *Leg. Sax.* 71.

powerful, but the condition of all ranks of the people socially was much deteriorated. It was, however, the Tartar invasion which separates the modern and the medieval history of Russia, and which plunged the country into the state of barbarism and slavery from which Peter the Great first raised it.

The cruelty of the Varangian prince Igor, after his return to Russia, caused him to be murdered by his rebellious subjects.[1] Olga, his widow, became regent for their son Swiatoslaff. She embraced the Christian religion, and visited Constantinople in 957, where she was baptised. The Emperor Constantine Porphyrogenitus has left us an account of the ceremony of her reception at the Byzantine court.[2] A monk has preserved the commercial treaties of the empire, an emperor records the pageantry that amused a Russian princess. The high position occupied by the court of Kief in the tenth century is also attested by the style with which it was addressed by the court of Constantinople. The golden bulls of the Roman emperor of the East, addressed to the prince of Russia, were ornamented with a pendent seal equal in size to a double solidus, like those addressed to the kings of France.[3]

We have seen that the Emperor Nicephorus II. sent the patrician Kalokyres to excite Swiatoslaff to invade Bulgaria, and that the Byzantine ambassador proved a traitor and assumed the purple. Swiatoslaff soon invaded Bulgaria at the head of a powerful army, which the gold brought by Kalokyres assisted him to equip, and defeated the Bulgarian army in a great battle, A.D. 968. Peter, king of Bulgaria, died shortly after, and the country was involved in civil broils; taking advantage of which, Swiatoslaff took Presthlava the capital, and rendered himself master of the whole kingdom. Nicephorus now formed an alliance with the Bulgarians, and was preparing to defend them against the Russians, when Swiatoslaff was compelled to return home, in order to defend his capital against the Patzinaks. Nicephorus assisted Boris and Romanus, the sons of Peter, to recover Bulgaria, and concluded an offensive and defensive alliance with Boris, who occupied the throne. After the assassination of Nicephorus, Swiatoslaff returned to invade Bulgaria with an army of 60,000 men, and his enterprise assumed the character of one of those great invasions which had torn whole provinces from the Western Empire.

---

[1] Leo Diaconus, 106, calls his murderers Germans, meaning doubtless Northmen.
[2] Cedrenus, 636. Const. Porphyr. *De Cer. Aul. Byz.* i. 594, edit Bonn. Krug, 267. [3] Const. Porphyr. *De Cer. Aul. Byz.* i. 690. Krug, 280.

His army was increased by a treaty with the Patzinaks and an alliance with the Hungarians, so that he began to dream of the conquest of Constantinople, and hoped to transfer the empire of the East from the Romans of Byzantium to the Russians. It was fortunate for the Byzantine empire that it was ruled by a soldier who knew how to profit by its superiority in tactics and discipline. The Russian was not ignorant of strategy, and having secured his flank by his alliance with the Hungarians, he entered Thrace by the western passes of Mount Hæmus, then the most frequented road between Germany and Constantinople, and that by which the Hungarians were in the habit of making their plundering incursions into the empire.

John Zimiskes was occupied in the East when Swiatoslaff completed the second conquest of Bulgaria and passed Mount Hæmus, expecting to subdue Thrace during the emperor's absence with equal ease, A.D. 970. The empire was still suffering from famine.[1] Swiatoslaff took Philippopolis, and murdered twenty thousand of the inhabitants. An embassy sent by Zimiskes was dismissed with a demand of tribute, and the Russian army advanced to Arcadiopolis, where one division was defeated by Bardas Skleros, and the remainder retired again behind Mount Hæmus.[2]

In the following spring, 971, the Emperor John took the field at the head of an army of fifteen thousand infantry and thirteen thousand cavalry, besides a bodyguard of chosen troops called the Immortals, and a powerful battery of field and siege engines.[3] A fleet of three hundred galleys, attended by many smaller vessels, was despatched to enter the Danube and cut off the communications of the Russians with their own country.[4]

Military operations for the defence and attack of Constantinople are dependent on some marked physical features of the country between the Danube and Mount Hæmus. The Danube, with its broad and rapid stream, and line of

[1] Leo Diaconus, 103.

[2] Leo Diaconus, 105; see a note at page 472, by Hase, on the chronology of this period. I follow that generally received on the authority of Nestor.

[3] The numbers are given by Leo Diaconus, 130. Cedrenus gives five thousand infantry and four thousand cavalry, 672; Zonaras ii. 211, the same number. The proportion affords some insight into the constitution of Byzantine armies at this period of military glory. The cavalry served as the model for European chivalry, but the sword of the legionary could still gain a battle.

[4] Leo Diaconus, 129, calls the larger vessels triremes, though they certainly had not more than two tiers of oars. Of the smaller he says, συνάμα λέμβοις καὶ ἀκατίοις, ἃ νῦν γαλέας καὶ μονέρια κοινῶς ὀνομάζουσι.

fortresses on its southern bank, would be an impregnable barrier to a military power possessing an active ally in Hungary and Servia; for it is easy to descend the river and concentrate the largest force on any desired point of attack, to cut off the communications or disturb the flanks of the invaders. Even after the line of the Danube is lost, that of Mount Hæmus covers Thrace; and it formed a rampart to Constantinople in many periods of danger under the Byzantine emperors. It was then traversed by three great military roads passable for chariots. The first, which has a double gorge, led from Philippopolis to Sardica by the pass called the Gates of Trajan (now Kapou Dervend), throwing out three branches from the principal trunk to Naissos and Belgrade.[1] The great pass forms the point of communication likewise with the upper valley of the Strymon, from Skupi to Ulpiana, and the northern parts of Macedonia. Two secondary passes communicate with this road to the north-east, affording passage for an army—that of Kezanlik, and that of Isladi; and these form the shortest lines of communication between Philippopolis and the Danube about Nicopolis, through Bulgaria. The second great pass is towards the centre of the range of Hæmus, and has preserved among the Turks its Byzantine name of the Iron Gate.[2] It is situated on the direct line of communication between Adrianople and Roustchouk. Through this pass a good road might easily be constructed. The third great pass is that to the east, forming the great line of communication between Adrianople and the Lower Danube near Silistria (Dorystolon). It is called by the Turks Nadir Dervend. The range of Hæmus has several other passes independent of these, and its parallel ridges present numerous defiles. The celebrated Turkish position at Shoumla is adapted to cover several of these passes, converging on the great eastern road to Adrianople.

The Emperor John marched from Adrianople just before Easter, when it was not expected that a Byzantine emperor would take the field. He knew that the passes on the great eastern road had been left unguarded by the Russians, and he led his army through all the defiles of Mount Hæmus without encountering any difficulty. The Russian troops stationed at Presthlava, who ought to have guarded the passes,

---

[1] Ammianus Marcellinus, xxi. 10. Sozomenes, *Hist. Eccles.* ii. 22. Nicephorus Gregoras, i. 231. Sardica is Triaditza, now Sophia.

[2] Cedrenus, 784, διὰ τῆς λεγομένης Σιδηρᾶς. The Turks call it Demir kapou.

marched out to meet the emperor when they heard he had entered Bulgaria. Their whole army consisted of infantry; but the soldiers were covered with chain armour, and accustomed to resist the light cavalry of the Patzinaks and other Turkish tribes.[1] They proved, however, no match for the heavy-armed lancers of the imperial army; and, after a vigorous resistance, were completely routed by John Zimiskes, leaving eight thousand five hundred men on the field of battle. On the following day Presthlava was taken by escalade, and a body of seven thousand Russians and Bulgarians, who attempted to defend the royal palace, which was fortified as a citadel, were put to the sword after a gallant defence. Sphengelos, who commanded this division of the Russian force, and the traitor Kalokyres, succeeded in escaping to Dorystolon, where Swiatoslaff had concentrated the rest of the army; but Boris, king of Bulgaria, with all his family, was taken prisoner in his capital.

The emperor, after celebrating Easter in Presthlava, advanced by Pliscova and Dinea to Dorystolon, where Swiatoslaff still hoped for victory, though his position was becoming daily more dangerous. The Byzantine fleet entered the Danube and took up its station opposite the city, cutting off all the communications of the Russians by water, at the same time that the emperor encamped before the walls and blockaded them by land. Zimiskes, knowing he had to deal with a desperate enemy, fortified his camp with a ditch and rampart according to the old Roman model, which was traditionally preserved by the Byzantine engineers. The Russians enclosed within the walls of Dorystolon were more numerous than their besiegers, and Swaitoslaff hoped to be able to open his communications with the surrounding country, by bringing on a general engagement in the plain before all the defences of the camp were completed. He hoped to defeat the attacks of the Byzantine cavalry by forming his men in squares, and, as the Russian soldiers were covered by long shields that reached to their feet, he expected to be able, by advancing his squares like moving towers, to clear the plain of the enemy. But while the Byzantine legions met the Russians in front, the heavy-armed cavalry assailed them with their long spears in flank, and the archers and slingers under cover watched coolly to transfix every man where an opening

---

[1] The Russians then wore armour similar to that worn by the Normans in western Europe at a later period.—Leo Diaconus, 108, 144.

allowed their missiles to penetrate. The battle nevertheless lasted all day, but in the evening the Russians were compelled, in spite of their desperate valour, to retire into Dorystolon without having effected anything. The infantry of the north now began to feel its inferiority to the veteran cavalry of Asia sheathed in plate armour, and disciplined by long campaigns against the Saracens. Swiatoslaff, however, continued to defend himself by a series of battles rather than sorties, in which he made desperate efforts to break through the ranks of his besiegers in vain, until at length it became evident that he must either conclude peace, die on the field of battle, or be starved to death in Dorystolon. Before resigning himself to his fate, he made a last effort to cut his way through the Byzantine army ; and on this occasion the Russians fought with such desperation, that contemporaries ascribed the victory of the Byzantine troops, not to the superior tactics of the emperor, nor to the discipline of a veteran army, but to the personal assistance of St. Theodore, who found it necessary to lead the charge of the Roman lancers, and shiver a spear with the Russians himself, before their phalanx could be broken. The victory was complete, and Swiatoslaff sent ambassadors to the emperor to offer terms of peace.

The siege of Dorystolon had now lasted more than two months, and the Russian army, though reduced by repeated losses, still amounted to twenty-two thousand men. The valour and contempt of death which the Varangians had displayed in the contest, convinced the emperor that it would cause the loss of many brave veterans to insist on their laying down their arms ; he was therefore willing to come to terms, and peace was concluded on condition that Swiatoslaff should yield up Dorystolon, with all the plunder, slaves, and prisoners in possession of the Russians, and engage to swear perpetual amity with the empire, and never to invade either the territory of Cherson or the kingdom of Bulgaria ; while, on the other hand, the Emperor John engaged to allow the Russians to descend the Danube in their boats, to supply them with two medimni of wheat for each surviving soldier, to enable them to return home without dispersing to plunder for their subsistence, and to renew the old commercial treaties between Kief and Constantinople,[1] July, 971.

---

[1] Leo Diaconus, 155. I presume the medimnus means here the common measure about a bushel, without any reference to Attic measures. A part of the treaty is given by Nestor, with the date.—Trad. Franc. i. 100.

After the treaty was concluded, Swiatoslaff desired to have a personal interview with his conqueror. John rode down to the bank of the Danube clad in splendid armour, and accompanied by a brilliant suite of guards on horseback. The short figure of the emperor was no disadvantage where he was distinguished by the beauty of his charger and the splendour of his arms, while his fair countenance, light hair, and piercing blue eyes fixed the attention of all on his bold and good-humoured face, which contrasted well with the dark and sombre visages of his attendants. Swiatoslaff arrived by water in a boat, which he steered himself with an oar. His dress was white, differing in no way from that of those under him, except in being cleaner. Sitting in the stern of his boat, he conversed for a short time with the emperor, who remained on horseback close to the beach. The appearance of the bold Varangian excited much curiosity, and is thus described by a historian who was intimate with many of those who were present at the interview : the Russian was of the middle stature, well formed, with strong neck and broad chest. His eyes were blue, his eyebrows thick, his nose flat, and his beard shaved, but his upper lip was shaded with long and thick mustaches. The hair of his head was cropped close, except two long locks which hung down on each side of his face, and were thus worn as a mark of his Scandinavian race. In his ears he wore golden earrings ornamented with a ruby between two pearls, and his expression was stern and fierce.[1]

Swiatoslaff immediately quitted Dorystolon, but he was obliged to winter on the shores of the Euxine, and famine thinned his ranks. In spring he attempted to force his way through the territory of the Patzinaks with his diminished army. He was defeated, and perished near the cataracts of the Dnieper. Kour, prince of the Patzinaks, became the possessor of his skull, which he shaped into a drinking-cup, and adorned with the moral maxim, doubtless not less suitable to his own skull, had it fallen into the hands of others, " He who covets the property of others, oft loses his own." We have already had occasion to record that the skull of the Byzantine emperor, Nicephorus I., had ornamented the festivals of a Bulgarian king ; that of a Russian sovereign now figured in the tents of a Turkish tribe.

The results of the campaign were as advantageous to the Byzantine empire as they were glorious to the Emperor John.

[1] Leo Diaconus, 156.

Bulgaria was conquered, a strong garrison established in Dory-stolon, and the Danube once more became the frontier of the Roman empire. The peace with the Russians was uninterrupted until about the year 988, when, from some unknown cause of quarrel, Vladimir the son of Swiatoslaff attacked and gained possession of Cherson by cutting off the water.

The Greek city of Cherson, situated on the extreme verge of ancient civilisation, escaped for ages from the impoverishment and demoralisation into which the Hellenic race was precipitated by the Roman system of concentrating all power in the capital of the empire.[1] Cherson was governed for centuries by its own elective magistrates, and it was not until towards the middle of the ninth century that the Emperor Theophilus destroyed its independence. The people, however, still retained in their own hands some control over their local administration, though the Byzantine government lost no time in undermining the moral foundation of the free institutions which had defended a single city against many barbarous nations that had made the Roman emperors tremble.[2] The inhabitants of Cherson long looked with indifference on the favour of the Byzantine emperor, cherished the institutions of Hellas, and boasted of their self-government.[3] A thousand years after the rest of the Greek nation was sunk in irremediable slavery, Cherson remained free. Such a phenomenon as the existence of manly feeling in one city, when mankind everywhere else slept contented in a state of political degradation, deserved attentive consideration. Indeed, we may be better able to appreciate correctly the political causes that corrupted the Greeks in the Eastern Empire, if we can ascertain those which enabled Cherson, though surrounded by powerful enemies and barbarous nations, to preserve

> " A Homer's language murmuring in her streets,
>   And in her haven many a mast from Tyre."

The history of mankind in every age shows us that the material improvement of the people, the first great public

---

[1] Cherson replaced the ancient Chersonesos, and Sevastopol now stands near its ruins. Strabo, vii. 308. Scylax, 29. Hudson.

[2] Constantine Porphyrogenitus is very particular in explaining the measures to be adopted in case of insurrections in Cherson. He shows it was in possession of a numerous commercial navy, though it imported wheat, wine, and other necessaries.—*De Adm. Imp.* 53.

[3] There is a very late testimony to these facts in a fragment published by Hase, in his notes to Leo Diaconus, p. 503, edit. Bonn—αὐτονόμων δὲ μάλιστα ἔργων ἀντιποιούμενοι.

works of utility, and the extension of commerce and trade, are effected by the impulsion of local institutions. Such progress is the expression of the popular feeling that excites every man to better the condition of the mass of humanity. Order, unfortunately, too often expresses only the feelings of the class possessing wealth. Its necessity may be felt by all, but the problem of connecting it with equity, and making it dependent on justice, is not easily solved, and hence the pretext of its maintenance serves for the creation of irresponsible power. The government in which the family and the parish occupy the most important part will ever be the best, for it will secure to honesty and truth that deference which a more extended circle attempts to transfer to the conventional virtues of honour and politeness. It is in the family and the parish that the foundation of all virtue is laid, long before the citizen enters the camp, the senate, or the court. The twelve nomes of Egypt doubled the extent and wealth of the country by digging the Canal of Joseph, and forming the lake Moeris, before the Pharaohs became conquerors and builders of pyramids. The energy of municipal institutions filled the Mediterranean and the Euxine with Greek colonies. Rome rose to greatness as a municipality; centralisation arrested her progress and depopulated the world. Great Britain, with her colonies and Indian empire, affords an instance of the superiority of the individual patriotism and self-respect generated by local institutions over the strict obedience and scientific power conferred by the centralisation of authority. But the respective merits of self-government and of central authority, by the weight of scientific power, are in the course of receiving their fullest development under the two mighty empires of the United States of America and of Russia. Both these governments have displayed consummate ability in the conduct of their respective political systems, and the practical decision of the problem, whether local or central government is the basis of the political institutions best adapted to the improvement of man, as a moral and social being, seems by Providence to have been intrusted to the cabinet of the emperor of Russia, and to the people of the United States of America.

In the reign of Diocletian, while Themistos was president of Cherson, Sauromates, king of Bosporos, passing along the eastern shores of the Euxine, invaded the Roman empire. He overran Lazia and Pontus without difficulty, but on the banks of the Halys he found the Roman army assembled under the command of Constantius Chlorus. On hearing of this invasion, Diocletian sent ambassadors to invite the people of Cherson to attack the territories of the king of Bosporus, in order to compel him to return home. Cherson, holding the rank of an allied city, could not avoid conceding that degree of supremacy to the Roman emperor which a small state is compelled to yield to a powerful protector, and the invitation was received as a command. Chrestos had succeeded Themistos in the presidency; he sent an army against Bosporos, and took the city. But the Chersonites, though brave warriors, sought peace, not conquest, and they treated the royal family and all the inhabitants of the places that had fallen into their hands, in a way to conciliate the goodwill of their enemies. Their successes forced Sauromates to conclude peace and evacuate the Roman territory, in order to regain possession of his capital and family. As a reward for their services, Diocletian granted the Chersonites additional security for their trade, and extensive commercial privileges throughout the Roman empire.

In the year 332, when Constantine the Great, in his declining age, had laid aside the warlike energy of his earlier years, the Goths and Sarmatians invaded the Roman empire. The emperor called on the inhabitants of Cherson, who were then presided over by Diogenes, to take up arms. They sent a force well furnished with field-machines to attack the Goths, who had already crossed the Danube, and defeated the barbarians with great slaughter. Constantine, to reward their promptitude in the service of the empire, sent them a golden statue of himself in imperial robes, to be placed in the hall of the senate, accompanied with a charter ratifying every privilege and commercial immunity granted to their city by preceding emperors. He bestowed on them also an annual supply of the materials necessary for constructing the warlike machines of which they had made such good use, and pay for a thousand artillerymen to work these engines.[1] This subsidy continued to be paid in the middle of the tenth century, in the time of Constantine Porphyrogenitus.

Years passed on, and Sauromates, the grandson of him who invaded the empire in the time of Diocletian, determining to

---

[1] Constant. Porphyr. *De Adm. Imp.* chap. 53, tom. iii. p. 251, edit. Bonn. The emperor also sent rings with his portrait engraved, to be used in certain official communications.

efface the memory of his grandfather's disgrace, declared war
with Cherson.　He was defeated by Vyskos, the president of
Cherson, at Kapha, and compelled to conclude a treaty of
peace, by which Kapha was declared the frontier of the territory of Cherson.　Another Sauromates, having succeeded to
the throne of Bosporos, determined to regain possession of
Kapha, when Pharnakes was president of Cherson.　A single
combat between the gigantic king and the patriotic president,
in which Sauromates was slain, terminated this war.　The
dynasty of the Sauromatan family ended, and Bosporos, becoming a free city in alliance with Cherson, raised a statue
to Pharnakes as a testimony of his moderation and philanthropy.

Again, after an interval of years, Lamachos was president
of Cherson, but the people of Bosporos, corrupted by the
memory of a court, and loving pageantry better than liberty,
had elected a king named Asandros.　The Bosporians proposed that the son of Asandros should marry the only daughter
of Lamachos, in order to draw closer the alliance between the
two states; and to this the Chersonites consented, but only
on condition that the young Asander should take up his
residence in Cherson, and engage never to return to Bosporos
—not even to pay the shortest visit to the king his father, or
any of his relations—under pain of death.　The marriage was
celebrated, and Asander dwelt with the young Gycia in the
palace of Lamachos, which was a building of regal splendour,
covering four of the quadrangles marked out by the intersec-
tion of the streets in the quarter of Cherson called Sousa, and
having its own private gate in the city walls.　Two years after
the celebration of this marriage, Lamachos died; his daughter
inherited the whole of his princely fortune, and Zetho was
elected president of Cherson.　At the end of a year, Gycia
went out to decorate her father's tomb, and wishing to honour
his memory with the greatest solemnity, she received permission from the president and senate to entertain the whole
body of the citizens of Cherson, with their wives and children,
at a funeral banquet on the anniversary of her father's death as
long as she lived.　The celebration of this festival suggested
to her husband a plan of rendering himself tyrant of Cherson,
and for two years he collected men and warlike stores secretly
from Bosporos, by means of the ships employed in his commercial affairs.　These he concealed in the immense warehouses enclosed within the walls of his wife's palace.　Three

of his own followers from Bosporos were alone entrusted with the secret of his plot. After a lapse of two years, Asander had collected two hundred Bosporians, with their armour, in the palace of Gycia, and was waiting for the approaching anniversary of the death of Lamachos to destroy the liberty of Cherson.

It happened at this time that a favourite maid of Gycia, offending her mistress, was ordered to be banished from her presence, and confined in a room over the warehouse in which the Bosporians were concealed. As the girl was sitting alone, singing and spinning, her spindle dropped, and rolled along the floor till it fell into a hole near the wall, from which she could only recover it by raising up one of the tiles of the pavement. Leaning down, she saw through the ceiling a crowd of men in the warehouse below, whom she knew by their dress to be Bosporians, and soldiers. She immediately called a servant, and sent him to her mistress, conjuring her to come to see her in her prison. Gycia, curious to see the effect of the punishment on her favourite, visited her immediately, and was shown the strange spectacle of a crowd of foreign soldiers and a magazine of arms concealed in her own palace. The truth flashed on her mind; she saw her husband was plotting to become the tyrant of her native city, and every feeling of her heart was wounded.

She assembled her relations, and by their means communicated secretly with the senate, revealing the plot to a chosen committee, on obtaining a solemn promise that when she died she should be buried within the walls of the city, though such a thing was at variance with the Hellenic usages of Cherson. Whether from the danger of attacking two hundred heavy-armed men, or to avoid war with Bosporos, the president and senate of Cherson determined to destroy the conspiracy by burning the enemy in their place of concealment, and Gycia willingly gave her ancestral palace to the flames to save her country.

When the day of the anniversary of her father's funeral arrived, Gycia ordered the preparations for the annual feast to be made with more than ordinary liberality, and Asander was lavish in his distribution of wine; but due precautions had been taken that the gates of the city should be closed at the usual hour, and all the citizens in their dwellings. At the banquet in her own palace Gycia drank water out of a purple goblet, while the servant who waited on Asander served

him with the richest wines. To the delight of her husband,
Gycia proposed that all should retire to rest at an early hour,
and she took a last melancholy leave of her husband, who
hastened to give his three confidants their instructions, and
then lay down to rest until the midnight should call him to
complete his treachery. The gates, doors, and windows of
the palace were shut up, and the keys, as usual, laid beside
Gycia. Her maids had packed up all her jewels, and when
Asander was plunged in a sound sleep from the wine he had
drank, Gycia rose, locked every door of the palace as she
passed, and hastened out, accompanied by her slaves. Order
was immediately given to set fire to the building on every
side, and thus the liberty of Cherson was saved by the
patriotism of Gycia.

The spot where the palace had stood remained a vacant
square in the time of the Emperor Constantine Porphyrogenitus, and Gycia during her lifetime would never allow
even the ruins to be cleared away. Her countrymen erected
two statues of bronze to honour her patriotism—one in the
public agora, showing her in the flower of youth, dressed in
her native costume, as when she saved her country; the other
clad as a heroine armed to defend the city. On both inscriptions were placed commemorating her services; and no
better deed could be done at Cherson than to keep the bases
of these statues bright and the inscriptions legible, that the
memory of the treachery of the king's son, and the gratitude
due to the patriotism of Gycia, might be ever fresh in the
hearts of the citizens.

Some years after this, when Stratophilos was president,
Gycia, suspecting that the gratitude of her countrymen was
so weakened that they would no longer be inclined to fulfil
their promise of burying her within the walls, pretended to
be dead. The event was as she feared; but when the procession had passed the gates, she rose up from the bier and
exclaimed, "Is this the way the people of Cherson keep their
promise to the preserver of their liberty?" Shame proved
more powerful than gratitude. The Chersonites now swore
again to bury her in the city, if she would pardon their falsehood. A tomb was accordingly built during her lifetime, and
a gilded statue of bronze was erected over it, as an assurance
that the faith of Cherson should not be again violated. In
that tomb Gycia was buried, and it stood uninjured in the
tenth century, when an emperor of Constantinople, impressed

with admiration of her patriotism, so unlike anything he had seen among the Greek inhabitants of his own wide extended empire, transmitted a record of her deeds to posterity.[1]

Cherson retained its position as an independent state until the reign of Theophilus, who compelled it to receive a governor from Constantinople; but, even under the Byzantine government, it continued to defend its municipal institutions, and, instead of slavishly soliciting the imperial favour, and adopting Byzantine manners, it boasted of its constitution and self-government.[2] But it lost gradually its former wealth and extensive trade; and when Vladimir, the sovereign of Russia, attacked it in 988, it yielded almost without a struggle. The great object of ambition of all the princes of the East, from the time of Heraclius to that of the last Comnenos of Trebizond, was to form matrimonial alliances with the imperial family. Vladimir obtained the hand of Anne, the sister of the Emperors Basil II. and Constantine VIII., and was baptised and married in the Church of the Panaghia at Cherson. To soothe the vanity of the empire, he pretended to retain possession of his conquest as the dowry of his wife. Many of the priests who converted the Russians to Christianity, and many of the artists who adorned the earliest Russian churches with paintings and mosaics, were natives of Cherson. The church raised Vladimir to the rank of a saint; the Russians conferred on him the title of the Great.[3]

John Zimiskes, having terminated the Russian war, compelled Boris to resign the crown of Bulgaria, and accept the title of Magister, as a pensioner of the Byzantine court. The frontier of the Eastern Empire was once more extended to the Danube.[4]

The Saracen war had been carried on vigorously on the frontiers of Syria, while the Emperor John was occupied with the Russian campaign. The continued successes of the Byzantine arms had so alarmed the Mohammedan princes, that an extensive confederacy was formed to recover Antioch, and the command of the army of the caliph was intrusted to Zoher, the lieutenant of the Fatimites in Egypt. The imperial army was led by the patrician Nikolaos, a man of great military skill, who had been a eunuch in the household of John

---

[1] Constant. Porphyr. *De Adm. Imp.* chap. 53.
[2] *Fragment*, Leo Diaconus, 503.
[3] Nestor, tr. fr. i. 137.   [4] Cedrenus, 694.

Zimiskes; and he defeated the Saracens in a pitched battle, and saved Antioch for a time.[1] But in the following year (973) the conquest of Nisibis filled the city of Bagdat with such consternation, that a levy of all Mussulmans was ordered to march against the Christians. The Byzantine troops in Mesopotamia were commanded by an Armenian named Temelek Melchi, who was completely routed near Amida. He was himself taken prisoner, and died after a year's confinement.[2]

With all his talents as a general, John does not appear to have possessed the same control over the general administration as Nicephorus; and many of the cities conquered by his predecessor, in which the majority of the inhabitants were Mohammedans, succeeded in throwing off the Byzantine yoke.[3] Even Antioch declared itself independent. A great effort became necessary to regain the ground that had been lost; and, to make this, John Zimiskes took the command of the Byzantine army in person in the year 974. He marched in one campaign from Mount Taurus to the banks of the Tigris, and from the banks of the Tigris back into Syria, as far as Mount Libanon, carrying his victorious arms, according to the vaunting inaccuracy of the Byzantine geographical nomenclature, into Palestine. His last campaign, in the following year, was the most brilliant of his exploits. In Mesopotamia he regained possession of Amida and Martyropolis; but these cities contained so few Christian inhabitants that he was obliged to leave the administration in the hands of Saracen emirs, who were charged with the collection of the tribute and taxes. Nisibis he found deserted, and from it he marched by Edessa to Hierapolis or Membig, where he captured many valuable relics, among which the shoes of our Saviour, and the hair of John the Baptist, are especially enumerated. From Hierapolis John marched to Apamea, Emesa, and Baalbec, without meeting any serious opposition. The emir of Damascus sent valuable presents, and agreed to pay an annual tribute to escape a visit. The emperor then crossed Mount Libanon, storming the fortress of Borzo, which commanded the pass, and, descending to the seacoast, laid siege to Berytus, which soon surrendered, and in which he found an image of the crucifixion that he deemed worthy of being

---

[1] Cedrenus, 666.
[2] Lebeau, xiv. 134. Leo Diaconus, 488 and 389. *Abulfedæ Ann. Muslem.* ii. 513, edit. Reisk.
[3] Zonaras, ii. 215. Glycas, 309.

sent to Constantinople. From Berytus he marched north-ward to Tripolis, which he besieged in vain for forty days. The valour of the garrison and the strength of the fortifications compelled him to raise the siege; but his retreat was ascribed to fear of a comet, which illuminated the sky with a strange brilliancy.[1] As it was now September, he wished to place his worn-out troops in winter-quarters in Antioch; but the inhabitants shut the gates against him. To punish them for their revolt, he had the folly to ravage their territory, and cut down their fruit-trees; forgetting, in his barbarous and impolitic revenge, that he was ruining his own empire. Burtzes was left to reconquer Antioch for the second time; which, however, he did not effect until after the death of the Emperor John.

The army was then placed in winter-quarters on the frontiers of Cilicia, and the emperor hastened to return to Constantinople. On the journey, as he passed the fertile plains of Longias and Dryze, in the vicinity of Anazarba and Podandus, he saw them covered with flocks and herds, with well-fortified farmyards, but no smiling villages. He inquired with wonder to whom the country belonged, in which pasturage was conducted on so grand a scale; and he learned that the greater part of the province had been acquired by the president Basilios in donations from himself and his predecessor, Nicephorus. Amazed at the enormous accumulation of property in the hands of one individual, he exclaimed, "Alas! the wealth of the empire is wasted, the strength of the armies is exhausted, and the Roman emperors toil like mercenaries, to add to the riches of an insatiable eunuch!" This speech was reported to the president. He considered that he had raised both Nicephorus and John to the throne; his interest now required that it should return to its rightful master, and that the young Basil should enjoy his heritage. The Emperor John stopped on his way to Constantinople at the palace of Romanos, a grandson of Romanus I.; and it is said he there drank of a poisoned cup presented to him by a servant gained by the president. Certain it is that John Zimiskes reached the capital in a dying state, and expired on the 10th of January 976, at the age of fifty-one.

[1] Leo Diaconus, 169.

Section II

Reign of Basil II. (Bulgaroktonos),[1] A.D. 976-1025.

Character of Basil II.—Rebellions of Bardas Skleros and of Bardas
Phokas—Wealth of private individuals—Bulgarian war—Defeat of
Basil II.—Samuel, king of Bulgaria, founds the kingdom of Achrida—
Defeats of Samuel—Basil puts out the eyes of his prisoners—Conquest
of the kingdom of Achrida—Basil visits Athens—Conquests in Armenia
—Death of Basil II.

Basil II. was only twenty years of age when he assumed the
direction of public affairs, and for some time he continued to
indulge in the pursuit of pleasure, allowing the president
Basilios to exercise the imperial power to its fullest extent.
Indeed, there can be no doubt that the prime-minister would
have attempted to occupy the place of Nicephorus and Zimiskes, had his condition not effectually excluded him from the
throne. For some time, however, he ventured to exclude Basil
from any active share in the details of administration, and
endeavoured to divert his attention to the pomp of the imperial
court, and to the indulgence of his passions, to which it was
thought the young man was naturally inclined. This conduct
probably awakened suspicions in the mind of Basil, who
possessed a firm and energetic character, and he watched the
proceedings of his powerful minister with attention. His
brother, Constantine VIII., who was seventeen when John
Zimiskes died, enjoyed the rank of his colleague, but was
allowed no share in the public administration, and appeared
well satisfied to be relieved from the duties of his station, as he
was allowed to enjoy all its luxuries. Basil soon gave up all
idle amusements, and devoted his whole time and energy to
military studies and exercises, and to public business. Indefatigable, brave, and stern, his courage degenerated into
ferocity, and his severity into cruelty. Yet, as he reigned the
absolute master of an unprincipled court, and of a people
careless of honour and truth, and as the greater part of his life
was spent in war with barbarous enemies, we may attribute
many of his faults as much to the state of society in his age as
to his own individual character. He believed that he was

---

[1] Gibbon says he enjoyed the title of Augustus sixty-six years, and the reign of the
two brothers (Basil and Constantine) is the longest and most obscure of the Byzantine
history.—*Decline and Fall*, chap. 48, vol. ix. 69. We possess no contemporary
historian except Leo Diaconus, who only supplies a few notices, 169. Cedrenus, however, gives some interesting details concerning the Bulgarian war, 684. The other
Byzantine sources are Zonaras, ii. 215; Manasses, 120; Glycas, 309; Joel, 181;
Ephraemius, 126.

prudent, just, and devout; others considered him severe, rapacious, cruel and bigoted. For Greek learning he cared little, and he was a type of the higher Byzantine moral character, which retained far more of its Roman than its Greek origin, both in its vices and its virtues. In activity, courage, and military skill he had few equals.[1]

Several of the great nobles of the empire considered that their power entitled them to occupy the place left vacant by the death of Zimiskes; and as the great qualities of Basil II. were still unknown, they envied the influence of the president Basilios. Among the leading members of the aristocracy, Bardas Skleros, who commanded the army in Asia, gave the president most umbrage, from his military reputation and great popularity. Skleros was accordingly removed from the command of the army, and appointed duke or governor of Mesopotamia. This step precipitated his rebellion. The two ablest generals in the empire were Bardas Skleros and Bardas Phokas: both were men of illustrious families, and both had filled high offices in the state. As early as the reign of Michael I., a Skleros had been governor of the Peloponnesus;[2] and for four generations the family of Phokas had supplied the empire with a succession of military leaders. Skleros and Phokas had already been opponents in the reign of John I. These two men may be taken as types of the military nobles of the Byzantine empire in the tenth century; and no tale of daring deeds or romantic vicissitudes among the chivalrous adventurers of the West, who had no patrimony but their swords, was more strange than many an episode in the lives of these two nobles, nursed in silken raiment, whose youth was passed in marble palaces on the soft shores of the Bosphorus, who were educated by pedantic grammarians, and trained by Greek theologians, who deemed the shedding even of Saracen blood a sin. Yet these nobles valued themselves as much on their personal skill in arms and headlong daring as any Danish adventurer or Norman knight.[3]

---

[1] Zonaras, ii. 225. Cedrenus, 718, mentions that Basil ordered one of his chamberlains, convicted of a plot to assassinate him, to be thrown to the lions. Several acts of the basest treachery were at least sanctioned by him.—Cedrenus, 714, 717, 718. Though Basil is accused of rapacity, he left the public taxes two years in arrear at the time of his death; now, though this fact may be a confirmation of the accusations brought against him, it seems more probably a proof that the policy which is visible in his laws for the protection of the poor was also the guide of his financial administration: and though he was severe with the rich, he may have been milder with the poor.—Cedrenus, 721, Glycas, 311.   [2] Theophanes, *Scrip. Inc.* 428.

[3] There can be no doubt that for several ages the Byzantine nobles were as regularly instructed in military discipline during their youth as our boys are in their

Bardas Skleros no sooner reached Mesopotamia than he assumed the title of Emperor, and invaded Asia Minor. He had made no preparations for his rebellion; he trusted to his military reputation for collecting a small army, and to his own skill to make the best use of the troops that joined his standard: nor was he wanting to his fame. Some pecuniary assistance from the emirs of Amida and Martyropolis recruited his finances, and a body of three hundred well-armed Saracen horse was considered a valuable addition to his little army. Undismayed by partial defeats and immense difficulties, he at last gained a complete victory over the Byzantine army at Lapara, on the frontiers of Armenia,[1] and a second at Rageas, over a generalissimo of the empire, who had been sent to repair the preceding disaster. Skleros then marched to Abydos, took Nicæa, and sent his son Romanos into Thrace to make preparations for the siege of Constantinople.

The rebellion of Bardas Phokas, and his exile to Chios, have been already mentioned. He was now called from his retreat, and laid aside the monastic dress, which he had worn for six years, to resume his armour. The old rivals again met in arms, and at first fortune continued to favour Skleros, who was a better tactician than Phokas. The imperial army was defeated at Amorium, but the personal valour of Phokas covered the retreat of his soldiers, and preserved their confidence; for when Constantine Gabras pressed too closely on the rear, Phokas, who was watching his movements, suddenly turned his horse, and, galloping up to the gallant chief, struck him lifeless with his mace-at-arms, and rejoined his own rear-guard unhurt. A second battle was fought near Basilika Therma, in the theme Charsiana, and Skleros was again victorious. Phokas retired into Georgia (Iberia), where he received assistance from David, the king of that country, which enabled him to assemble a third army on the banks of the Halys. He found Skleros encamped in the plain of Pankalia. An engagement took place, in which the superior generalship of the rebel emperor was again evident, and Phokas, reduced to despair, sought to terminate the contest by a personal encounter with his rival. They soon met, and their companions suspended the conflict in their immediate vicinity to view the

Latin grammar. Byzantine education seems to have been excellent before entering on public life, and very bad afterwards; ours is better after than before.

[1] The patrician Petros, who commanded the imperial army, had been a eunuch of the household of the Emperor Nicephorus Phokas, and had distinguished himself by his personal valour in the Russian war.—Cedrenus, 685. Leo Diaconus, 81.

combat between two champions, both equally celebrated for their personal prowess. Skleros was armed with the sword, Phokas with the mace-at-arms; the mace glanced from the well-tempered armour, the mace crushed the helmet, and Skleros fell senseless on his horse's neck. The guards rushing to the rescue, Phokas gained an eminence, from which he could already see a portion of his army in full retreat. But the fortune of the day was changed by an accident. As the officers of Skleros were carrying their wounded leader to a neighbouring fountain, his horse escaped and galloped through the ranks of the army, showing the troops the imperial trappings stained with blood. The cry arose that Skleros was slain. The tie that united the rebels was broken, and the soldiers fled in every direction, or laid down their arms. On recovering, Skleros found that nothing was left for him but to escape with his personal attendants into the Saracen territory, where he was thrown into prison by order of the caliph. Several of his partisans prolonged their resistance through the winter.[1]

Bardas Phokas continued to command the imperial army in Asia for eight years, carrying on war with the Saracens, and compelling the emir of Aleppo to pay tribute to Constantinople. But as the Emperor Basil II. advanced in years, his firm character began to excite general dissatisfaction among the Byzantine nobles, who saw that their personal influence, and power of enriching themselves at the public expense, were likely to be greatly curtailed. The attention the emperor paid to public business, and his strict control over the conduct of all officials, began to alarm the president Basilios; while his determination to command the army in person, and to regulate promotions, excited the dissatisfaction of Phokas, who allowed his government to become the refuge of every discontented courtier. The only campaign in which the emperor had yet commanded was one against Samuel, king of Bulgaria, which had proved signally disastrous, so that his interference in military matters did not appear to be authorised by his experience in tactics and strategy. It seems probable that the president excited Phokas to take up arms, as a means of rendering the emperor more dependent on his influence and the support of the aristocracy; but Phokas doubtless required very little prompting to make an attempt to seize the

---

[1] Skleros was defeated in the summer of 979, as the rebellion was suppressed in the 8th indiction, in the fourth year of its duration.—Leo Diaconus, 169. Cedrenus, 694. The 8th indiction commenced on the 1st September 979, and the rebellion continued for some time after the flight of Skleros.

throne.   Assembling the leading men in his government, and
the principal officers of the army under his command, at the
palace of Eustathios Maleïnos, in the theme Charsiana, he
was proclaimed emperor on the 15th of August 987.

Nearly about the same time, Bardas Skleros succeeded in
escaping from the Saracens and entering the empire. He
had been released from his prison at Bagdat, and intrusted
with the command of a legion of Christian refugees, with
which he had distinguished himself in the civil wars of the
Mohammedans.   His adventures in this service were not
unlike those recorded of Manuel in the reign of Theophilus.[1]
His sudden appearance in the empire, and his resumption of
his claim to the imperial throne, brought the two ancient
rivals again into the field, both as rebel emperors, and it
seemed that they must decide by a new war which was to
march as victor against Basil at Constantinople. Phokas
gained the advantage by treachery.   He concluded a treaty
with his rival, by which a division of Asia Minor was agreed
on ; and when Skleros visited his camp to hold a conference,
Phokas detained him a prisoner.[2]   Phokas then devoted all
his energy to dethrone his sovereign ; and during the summer
of 988, he subdued the greater part of Asia Minor ; but at the
commencement of the following year, a division of his army
which he sent to the Bosphorus was defeated by the Emperor
Basil, who had just obtained an auxiliary corps of Varangians
from his brother-in-law Vladimir, the sovereign of Kief.[3]
Phokas was at this time besieging Abydos, which defended
itself with obstinacy until the Emperors Basil and Constantine
arrived with the imperial army to relieve it.   The imperial
troops arrived by sea, and, debarking near Abydos, formed
their camp in the plain.   Phokas, leaving part of his force to
continue the siege, drew out his army to give battle to the
emperors.   When the two armies were taking up their ground,
Phokas rode along the field, seeking for an opportunity to
decide the fate of the war by one of those feats of arms in
which his personal prowess was so distinguished.   His eye
caught a sight of the Emperor Basil engaged in ordering
the movements of his army, and, dashing forward with his
mace-at-arms, he prepared to close in single combat with his

---

[1] Cedrenus, 697.

[2] Skleros was confined at Tyropaion, a place Phokas had fortified as a refuge when
he rebelled against John I. Skleros had secured his personal safety on forcing him to
surrender it.—Leo Diaconus, 126.

[3] The emperor ordered the general of the rebels to be impaled.—Cedrenus, 699.

sovereign. At the very moment when the object of his sudden movement flashed on the minds of all, Phokas wheeled round his horse, galloped to a little eminence, where he dismounted in sight of both armies and lay down on the ground. A long interval of suspense occurred. Then a rumour ran along the ranks of the rebels that their leader was dead, and the troops dispersed without striking a blow. Phokas had drunk a glass of cold water as he mounted his horse, according to his usual custom, and whether he perished by poison or by a stroke of apoplexy was naturally a question not easily settled by the suspicious and vicious Constantinopolitans. Thus ended the career of Bardas Phokas, by a death as strange as the events of his romantic life. He died in the month of April 989.

Bardas Skleros regained his liberty on the death of his rival, but resigned his pretensions to the imperial dignity on receiving the pardon of Basil. The meeting of the emperor and the veteran warrior was remarkable. The eyesight of Skleros had begun to fail, and he had grown extremely corpulent. He had laid aside the imperial costume, but continued to wear purple boots, which were part of the insignia of an emperor. As he advanced to the tent of Basil, leaning on two of his equerries, Basil, surprised at his infirmity, exclaimed to his attendants, "Is this the man we all trembled at yesterday?" But as soon as he perceived the purple boots, he refused to receive the infirm old general until they were changed. Skleros had then a gracious audience, and was requested to sit down. He did not long survive.[1]

The same attention to public business on the part of the emperor which caused the rebellion of Phokas, produced the fall of the president Basilios, whom Basil deprived of all his offices about the same time. His estates were confiscated, his acts annulled, the populace of Constantinople were allowed to plunder his palace, the sacred offerings and dedications he had made were destroyed, and even the monastery he had founded was dissolved. The celebrated minister died in exile, after having attained a degree of wealth and power which marks an unhealthy condition of the body politic in the Byzantine empire. No such accumulation of fortune as Basilios is reported to have possessed, could ever have been obtained by a public servant without the exertion of the grossest oppression, either on the part of the individual or the government. The riches of Basilios must almost have

[1] Cedrenus, 701.

rivalled the wealth of Crassus; at least, he came under the definition of a rich man, according to that wealthy Roman, for he was able to maintain an army. At an early part of his political career, he armed a household of three thousand slaves to aid in placing the imperial crown on the head of Nicephorus II. The aristocracy of Constantinople at this period bore some resemblance, in its social position, to that of Rome at the fall of the Republic, both in wealth and political corruption. The estates of Eustathios Maleïnos, in whose house Phokas raised the standard of revolt, were not less extensive than those of the ambitious president. Maleïnos was fortunate enough to escape punishment for his share in the rebellion, but some years after, as Basil was returning from a campaign in Syria (A.D. 995), he stopped at the palace of Maleïnos in Cappadocia, and was amazed at the strength of the building, and the wealth, power, and splendour of the household. The emperor saw that a man of courage, in possession of so much influence, and commanding such a number of armed servants, could at any moment commence a rebellion as dangerous as that of Skleros or Phokas. Maleïnos received an invitation to accompany the court to the capital, and was never again allowed to visit his estates in Cappadocia. At his death, his immense fortune was confiscated, and most writers ascribed the legislative measures of Basil, to protect the landed property of small proprietors from the encroachments of the wealthy, to the impression produced on his mind by witnessing the power of Maleïnos in Cappadocia; but we must bear in mind that, from the time of Romanus I., the Byzantine emperors had been vainly endeavouring to stem the torrent of aristocratic predominance in the provinces; and both Constantine VII. (Porphyrogenitus) and Nicephorus II., though in general extremely dissimilar in character and policy, agreed in passing laws to protect the poor against the rich.[1] Basil II. fully appreciated all the evils which resulted from the tendency of society to accumulate wealth in the hands of a few individuals, and he endeavoured to aid the middle classes in defending their possessions; but all the power he could exert was unable to prevent the constant diminution that was going on in the

---

[1] Cedrenus, 702. See the laws of Romanus I., *Novels*, 1, 2, 3; Constantine VII., *Novels*, 1, 2; Nicephorus II., *Novels*, 3, 5; and Basil II., *Novels*, 2, 3, 5. Mortreuil, *Histoire du Droit Byzantin*, where references to the texts will be found. The laws of Nicephorus II. are Nos. IV. and VI. in the Collection annexed to Leo Diaconus, p. 320, 322, edit. Bonn.

number of the smaller landed proprietors, the middle classes in the towns, and generally of the civilised races of mankind throughout the greater part of his empire. The task was beyond the power of legislation, and required an improvement in the moral as well as the political constitution of society. The attempts of the emperor to arrest the progress of the evil may have been useless, but they were unquestionably not disadvantageous to the people. It is therefore strange to find the Patriarch, the higher clergy, and the monks opposed to these measures, and engaged in endeavouring to turn him from his purpose, particularly when he wished to render the rich responsible for the taxes of the ruined poor of their district. The Greek church has, however, generally been a servile instrument either of the sovereign power or of the aristocracy, and has contributed little either to enforce equity or civil liberty, when the mass of the lower orders was alone concerned.[1] The evil of increasing wealth in the hands of a few individuals, and of a gradual diminution of the intelligent population in the Byzantine empire, went on augmenting from the time of Basil II. Asia and Europe both lost their civilised races; the immense landed estates of a few Byzantine aristocrats were cultivated by Mohammedan slaves, or Sclavonian, Albanian, and Vallachian serfs; manufactures and trade declined with the population, the towns dwindled into villages, and no class of native inhabitants remained possessing strength and patriotism to fight for their homes when a new race of invaders poured into the empire.

The reign of Basil II. is the culminating point of Byzantine greatness. The eagles of Constantinople flew during his life, in a long career of victory, from the banks of the Danube to those of the Euphrates, and from the mountains of Armenia to the shores of Italy. Basil's indomitable courage, terrific cruelty, indifference to art and literature, and religious superstition, all combine to render him a true type of his empire and age. The great object of his policy was to consolidate the unity of the administration in Europe by the complete subjection of the Bulgarians and Sclavonians, whom similarity of language had almost blended into one nation, and had completely united in hostility to the imperial government.

Four sons of a Bulgarian noble of the highest rank had commenced a revolutionary movement in Bulgaria against the royal family, after the death of Peter and the first victories of

[1] Cedrenus, 706.

the Russians. In order to put an end to these troubles, Nicephorus II. had, on the retreat of Swiatoslaff, replaced Boris, the son of Peter, on the throne of Bulgaria; and when the Russians returned, Boris submitted to their domination.[1] Shortly after the death of John I. (Zimiskes), the Bulgarian leaders again roused the people to a struggle for independence. Boris, who escaped from Constantinople to attempt recovering his paternal throne, was accidentally slain, and the four brothers again became the chiefs of the nation. In a short time three perished, and Samuel alone remained, and assumed the title of King. The forces of the empire were occupied with the rebellion of Skleros, so that the vigour and military talents of Samuel succeeded not only in expelling the Byzantine authorities from Bulgaria, but also in rousing the Sclavonians of Macedonia to throw off the Byzantine yoke. Samuel then invaded Thessaly, and extended his plundering excursions over those parts of Greece and the Peloponnesus still inhabited by the Hellenic race. He carried away the inhabitants of Larissa in order to people the town of Prespa, which he then proposed to make his capital, with intelligent artisans and manufacturers; and, in order to attach them to their new residence by ties of old superstition, he removed to Prespa the body of their protecting martyr, St. Achilles, who some pretended had been a Roman soldier, and others a Greek archbishop. Samuel showed himself, both in ability and courage, a rival worthy of Basil; and the empire of the East seemed for some time in danger of being transferred from the Byzantine Romans to the Sclavonian Bulgarians.

In the year 981, the Emperor Basil made his first campaign against the new Bulgarian monarchy in person. His plan of operations was to secure the great western passes through Mount Hæmus, on the road from Philippopolis to Sardica, and by the conquest of the latter city he hoped to cut off the communication between the Bulgarians north of Mount Hæmus and the Sclavonians in Macedonia. But his military inexperience, and the relaxed discipline of the army, caused this well-conceived plan to fail. Sardica was besieged in vain for twenty days. The negligence of the officers and the disobedience of the soldiers caused several foraging parties to be cut off; the besieged burned the engines of the besiegers in a victorious sortie, and the emperor felt the necessity of commencing his retreat. As his army was passing the defiles

[1] Cedrenus, 646, 666, 694. Leo Diaconus, 81, 136.

of Hæmus, it was assailed by the troops Samuel had collected to watch his operations, and completely routed. The baggage and military chest, the emperor's plate and tents, all fell into the hands of the Bulgarian king, and Basil himself escaped with some difficulty to Philippopolis, where he collected the relics of the fugitives. Leo Diaconus, who accompanied the expedition as one of the clergy of the imperial chapel, and was fortunate enough to escape the pursuit, has left us a short but authentic notice of this first disastrous campaign of Basil, the slayer of the Bulgarians.[1]

The reorganisation of his army, the regulation of the internal administration of the empire, the rebellion of Phokas, and the wars in Italy and on the Asiatic frontier, prevented Basil from attacking Samuel in person for many years. Still a part of the imperial forces carried on this war, and Samuel soon perceived that he was unable to resist the Byzantine generals in the plains of Bulgaria, where the heavy cavalry, military engines, and superior discipline of the imperial armies could all be employed to advantage. He resolved, therefore, to transfer the seat of the Bulgarian government to a more inaccessible position. He first selected Prespa as his future capital, but he subsequently abandoned that intention, and established the central administration of his dominions at Achrida. The site was well adapted for rapid communications with his Sclavonian subjects in Macedonia, who furnished his armies with their best recruits. To Achrida, therefore, he transferred the seat of the Bulgarian patriarchate, and to this day the archbishop of that city, in virtue of the position he received from Samuel, still holds an ecclesiastical jurisdiction over several suffragans independent of the Patriarch of Constantinople. As a military position, also, Achrida had many advantages : it commanded an important point in the Via Egnatia, the great commercial road connecting the Adriatic with Bulgaria, as well as with Thessalonica and Constantinople, and afforded many facilities for enabling Samuel to choose his points of attack on the Byzantine themes of Macedonia, Hellas, Dyrrachium, and Nicopolis. Here, therefore, Samuel established the capital of the Bulgaro-Sclavonian kingdom he founded.

The dominions of Samuel soon became as extensive as the European portion of the dominions of Basil. The possessions of the two monarchs ran into one another in a very irregular

[1] Leo Diaconus, 171.

form, and both were inhabited by a variety of races, in different states of civilisation, bound together by few sympathies, and no common attachment to national institutions. Samuel was master of almost the whole of ancient Bulgaria, the emperor retaining possession of little more than the fortress of Dorystolon, the forts at the mouth of the Danube, and the passes of Mount Hæmus. But the strength of the Bulgarian king lay in his possessions in the upper part of Macedonia, in Epirus, and the southern part of Illyria, in the chain of Pindus, and in mountains that overlook the northern and western slopes of the great plains of Thessalonica and Thessaly. In all these provinces the greater part of the rural population consisted of Sclavonians, who were hostile to the Byzantine government and to the Greek race; and though an Albanian and Vallachian population was scattered over some parts of the territory, they readily united with Samuel in throwing off the Byzantine yoke, and only opposed his government when he attempted to augment his monarchical power at the expense of their habits of local independence. From the nature of his dominions, his only hope of consolidating a regular system of civil government was by holding out allurements to the local chieftains to submit voluntarily to his authority. It was only by continual plundering expeditions into the Byzantine territory, and especially into Greece, that this object could be attained. He was, therefore, indefatigable in forming a large military force, and employing it constantly in ravaging the plain of Thessaly, and attacking the Greek cities.

In the year 990, Basil visited Thessalonica, to take measures for arresting the progress of Samuel, and left Gregory the Taronite with a strong garrison to resist the Bulgarians, until he himself should be able to turn the whole force of the empire against them.[1] For several years Gregory checked the incursions of Samuel, but at last he was slain in a skirmish, and his son Ashot was taken prisoner. This success secured Samuel from all danger on the side of the garrison of Thessalonica, and he resolved to avail himself of the opportunity to complete the conquest of Greece, or at least to plunder the inhabitants, should he meet with opposition. He marched rapidly through Thessaly, Bœotia, and Attica, into the Peloponnesus; but the towns everywhere shut their gates, and

---

[1] Gregory was descended from a branch of the Armenian princes of Taron, long settled in the empire.

prepared for a long defence, so that he could effect nothing beyond plundering and laying waste the open country. In the mean time, the emperor, hearing of the death of Gregory and the invasion of Greece, sent Nicephorus Ouranos with considerable reinforcements to take the command of the garrison of Thessalonica, and march with all the force he should be able to collect in pursuit of Samuel. Ouranos entered Thessaly, and, leaving the heavy baggage of his army at Larissa, pushed rapidly southward to the banks of the Sperchius, where he found Samuel encamped on the other side, hastening home with the plunder of Greece. Heavy rains on Mounts Oeta and Korax had rendered the Sperchius —which at the end of summer is only a brook—an impassable torrent at the time Samuel had reached its banks, and Ouranos encamped for the night in the vicinity of the Bulgarian army, without his arrival causing any alarm. But the people of the country had observed that the river was beginning to fall, and as they were anxious that both armies should quit their territory as fast as possible, they were eager to bring on a battle. In the night they showed Ouranos a ford, by which he passed the river and surprised the Bulgarians in their camp. Samuel and his son Gabriel escaped with the greatest difficulty to the counter-forts of Oeta, from whence they gained Tymphrestas and the range of Pindus. The Bulgarian army was completely annihilated, and all the plunder and slaves made during the expedition fell into the hands of Ouranos, A.D. 996.

This great defeat paralysed the military operations of Samuel for some time, and it was followed by a domestic misfortune which also weakened his resources. He had been induced to allow his daughter to marry Ashot the Taronite, whom he had taken prisoner at Thessalonica, and in order to attach that brave and able young officer to his service, he had intrusted him with the government of Dyrrachium. But Ashot was dissatisfied with his position, and succeeded in persuading the Bulgarian princess to fly with him to Constantinople. Before quitting Dyrrachium, however, he formed a plot with the principal men of the place, by which that valuable fortress was subsequently delivered up to the emperor. This was a serious political, as well as a grievous domestic wound to Samuel; for the loss of Dyrrachium interrupted the commercial relations of his subjects with Italy, and deprived them of the support they might have derived from the enemies of the Byzantine empire beyond the Adriatic

Basil had at length arranged the external relations of the empire in such a way that he was able to assemble a large army for the military operations against the kingdom of Achrida, which he determined to conduct in person. The Sclavonians now formed the most numerous part of the population of the country between the Danube, the Egean, and the Adriatic, and they were in possession of the line of mountains that runs from Dyrrachium, in a variety of chains, to the vicinity of Constantinople.[1] Basil saw many signs that the whole Sclavonic race in these countries was united in opposition to the Byzantine government, so that the existence of his empire demanded the conquest of the Bulgaro-Sclavonian kingdom which Samuel had founded. To this arduous task he devoted himself with his usual energy. In the year 1000, his generals were ordered to enter Bulgaria by the eastern passes of Mount Hæmus; and in this campaign they took the cities of greater and lesser Presthlava and Pliscova, the ancient capitals of Bulgaria. In the following year, the emperor took upon himself the direction of the army destined to act against Samuel. Fixing his headquarters at Thessalonica, he recovered possession of the fortresses of Vodena, Berrhœa, and Servia. By these conquests he became master of the passes leading out of the plain of Thessalonica into the plains of Pelagonia, and over the Cambunian mountains into Thessaly, thus opening the way for an attack on the flank and rear of the forces of the kingdom of Achrida. Vodena or Edessa, the ancient capital of the Macedonian princes, had become, like all the cities of this mountainous district, Sclavonian. Its situation on a rock overhanging the river Lydias, the sublimity of the scenery around, the abundance of water, the command of the fertile valleys below, the salubrity of the spot, and the strength of the position closing up the direct road between Thessalonica and Achrida—all rendered the possession of Vodena an important step to the further operations of the Byzantine arms.

In the following campaign (1002), the emperor changed the field of operations, and, marching from Philippopolis through the western passes of Mount Hæmus, occupied the whole line of road as far as the Danube, and cut Samuel off from all communication with the plains of Bulgaria.[2] He then formed the siege of Vidin, which he kept closely invested

[1] Tzetzes, chil. x. 192.
[2] Cedrenus, 705. The fifteenth indiction extends to 1st September 1002.

during the spring and summer, until at last he took that
important fortress. Samuel formed a bold enterprise, which
he hoped would compel Basil to raise the siege of Vidin, or,
at all events, enable him to inflict a deep wound on the
empire. Assembling an army at Skoupies, on the upper
course of the Vardar, he marched into the valley of the
Stebrus, and by the celerity of his movements surprised the
inhabitants of Adrianople at a great fair which they held
annually on the 15th of August, when the Greek church com-
memorates the death of the Virgin Mary. By this long
march into the heart of the empire, Samuel rendered himself
master of great booty. His success rendered it impossible for
him to return as rapidly as he had advanced, but he succeeded
in passing the garrison of Philoppopolis and crossing the
Strymon and the Vardar in safety, when Basil suddenly overtook him at the head of the Byzantine army. Samuel was
encamped under the walls of Skoupies; Basil crossed the
river and stormed the Bulgarian camp, rendering himself
master of the military chest and stores, and recovering the
plunder of Adrianople. He had thus the satisfaction of
avenging the defeat he had suffered from Samuel, one-and-
twenty years before, in the passes of Mount Hæmus. The
city of Skoupies surrendered after the victory, and its commander Romanus, the younger brother of Boris, the last king of
Bulgaria of the ancient line, whose misfortune prevented his
becoming a rival to Samuel, was honourably treated by the
emperor.[1] Basil then laid siege to Pernikon, a fortress of great
strength, from which he was repulsed by the valour of the Bulgarian governor Krakas. He then withdrew to Philippopolis.

The conquest of Vidin having enabled Basil to deprive
Bulgaria of relief from Samuel and the Sclavonians of Macedonia, the Byzantine generals easily completed the subjection
of the whole of the rich country between Mount Hæmus and
the Danube. The king of Achrida finding himself unable to
encounter the troops of Basil in the field, and seeing his territory constantly circumscribed by the capture of his fortresses,
determined to fortify all the passes in the mountains that lead
into Upper Macedonia. By stationing strong bodies of troops,
and forming magazines behind these intrenchments, he hoped
to present to his assailants the difficulties of a siege in situations where all their supplies would require to be drawn from
a great distance, and exposed to be captured or destroyed on

[1] Romanus had been made a eunuch by order of Joseph Bringas.—Cedrenus, 694.

the way by the Bulgarian light troops and the Sclavonian inhabitants of the mountains. For several years a bloody and indecisive war was carried on, which gradually weakened the resources of the kingdom of Achrida, without affecting the power of the Byzantine empire.

In the year 1014, Basil considered everything ready for a final effort to complete the subjection of the Sclavonian population of the mountainous districts round the upper valley of the Strymon. On reaching the pass of Demirhissar, or the Kleisura, then called Kimbalongo, or Kleidion, he found it strongly fortified. Samuel had placed himself at the head of the Bulgarian army prepared to oppose his progress. The emperor found the pass too strong to be forced; sitting down, therefore, before it, he sent Nicephorus Xiphias, the governor of Philippopolis, with a strong detachment, to make the circuit of a high mountain called Valathista, which lay to the south, that he might gain the rear of the Bulgarian position. This manœuvre was completely successful. On the 29th of July, Nicephorus attacked the enemy's rear, while Basil assailed their front, and the Bulgarians, in spite of all the exertions of Samuel, gave way on every side. It was only in consequence of the gallant resistance of his son Gabriel that the king of Achrida was saved from being taken prisoner, and enabled to gain Prilapos in safety. The emperor is said to have taken fifteen thousand prisoners, and, that he might revenge the sufferings of his subjects from the ravages of the Bulgarians and Sclavonians, he gratified his own cruelty by an act of vengeance, which has most justly entailed infamy on his name. His frightful inhumanity has forced history to turn with disgust from his conduct, and almost buried the records of his military achievements in oblivion. On this occasion he ordered the eyes of all his prisoners to be put out, leaving a single eye to the leader of every hundred, and in this condition he sent the wretched captives forth to seek their king or perish on the way. When they approached Achrida, a rumour that the prisoners had been released induced Samuel to go out to meet them. On learning the full extent of the calamity, he fell senseless to the ground, overpowered with rage and grief, and died two days after. He is said to have murdered his own brother to secure possession of his throne, so that his heart was broken by the first touch of humanity it ever felt.[1]

---

[1] Cruelty similar to that of Basil was perpetrated on a smaller scale by Richard Cœur-de-Lion, though of course it is not necessary to place strict reliance on the num-

After his victory, Basil occupied the fort of Matzoukion, and advanced on Strumpitza, where he ordered Theophylaktos Botaniates, the governor of Thessalonica, who had defeated a large body of Bulgarians, to join him by marching northward, and clearing away the intrenchments constructed by Samuel on the road leading from Thessalonica directly to Strumpitza. In this operation Theophylaktos was surrounded by the Bulgarians and slain, with the greater part of his troops, in the defiles. This check compelled the emperor to retire by the Zagorian mountains to Mosynopolis, having succeeded in gaining possession of the strong fortress of Melenik by negotiation. At Mosynopolis, on the 24th October 1014, he heard of the death of Samuel, and immediately determined to take advantage of an event likely to prove so favourable to the Byzantine arms. Marching with a strong body of troops through Thessalonica and Vodena, he advanced into Pelagonia, carefully protecting that fertile district from ravage, and destroying nothing but a palace of the Bulgarian kings at Boutelion. From thence he sent a division of the army to occupy Prilapos and Stobi, and, crossing the river Tzerna (Erigon) with the main body, he returned by Vodena to Thessalonica, which he reached on the 9th of January 1015.[1]

The cruelty of Basil awakened an energetic resistance on the part of the Sclavonians and Bulgarians, and Gabriel Radomir, the brave son of Samuel, was enabled to offer unexpected obstacles to the progress of the Byzantine armies. Vodena revolted, and expelled the imperial garrison, so that Basil was compelled to open the campaign of 1015 with the siege of that place, which he reduced. The inhabitants were transported to Beleros, to make way for Greek colonists; and two forts, Kardia and St. Elias, were built to command the pass to the westward. After receiving an embassy from Gabriel, with proposals which he did not consider deserving of attention, Basil joined a division of his army engaged in besieging Moglena under the immediate command of Nicephorus Xiphias and Constantine Diogenes, who had succeeded Theophylaktos

bers reported by the Byzantine historians. Richard, to revenge the loss of a body of men, ordered three hundred French knights to be thrown into the Seine, and put out the eyes of fifteen, who were sent home blind, led by one whose right eye had been spared. Philip Augustus, nothing loath, revenged himself by treating fifteen English knights in the same way.—Capefigue, *Philippe Auguste*, ii. 102 ; Vaublanc, *La France au Temps des Croisades*, ii. 4. Putting out men's eyes was, for several centuries, a common practice all over Europe, and not regarded with much horror. As late as the reign of Henry IV., A.D. 1403, an Act of Parliament was passed, making it felony for Englishmen to cut out one another's tongues, or put out their neighbour's eyes.

[1] Cedrenus, 709.

as governor of Thessalonica. By turning the course of the river, the besiegers were enabled to run a mine under the wall, which they supported on wooden props. When the mine was completed, it was filled with combustibles, which reduced the props to ashes, and as soon as the wall fell and opened a breach, Moglena was taken by assault. The whole of the Sclavonian population capable of bearing arms was by the emperor's order transported to Vasparoukan in Armenia. The fort of Notia in the vicinity was also taken and destroyed.

Gabriel, the king of Achrida, though brave, alienated the favour of his subjects by his imprudence, and his cousin, John Ladislas, whose life he had saved in youth, was base enough to become his murderer, in order to gain possession of the throne. Ladislas, in order to gain time, both for strengthening himself on the throne and resisting the Byzantine invasion, sent ambassadors to Basil with favourable offers of peace; but the emperor, satisfied that the struggle between the Sclavonians and Greeks could only be terminated by the conquest of one, rejected all terms but absolute submission, and pushed on his operations with his usual vigour, laying waste the country about Ostrovos and Soskos, and marching unopposed through the fertile plains of Pelagonia.[1] The defeat of a portion of the Byzantine army by Ibatzes, one of the Bulgarian generals, compelled the emperor to march against him in person; and when Ibatzes retreated into the mountains, Basil returned to Thessalonica, and shortly after established himself at Mosynopolis. The conquest of eastern Macedonia was not yet completed: one division of the Byzantine troops was placed under the command of David the Arianite, which besieged and took the fortress of Thermitza on Mount Strumpitza: another, under Nicephorus Xiphias, crossing Mount Hæmus from Philippopolis, took Boion, near Sardica.

The Emperor Basil returned to Constantinople in the month of January 1016, in order to send an expedition to Khazaria, the operations of which had been concerted with Vladimir of Russia, his brother-in-law. He also availed himself of the opportunity to arrange some difficulties relating to the cession of Vasparoukan. When that part of Armenia was annexed to the empire, and the conquest of Khazaria terminated, he again joined the army at Sardica and laid siege to Pernikon, which repulsed his attacks, as it had done fourteen years before. He

---

[1] Zonaras, ii. 226, says Basil took Achrida; but this could not be the case, as the treasures of the Bulgarian kings only fell into his hands in 1018.—Cedrenus, 713.

lost eighty-eight days before the place, but was at last compelled to retire to Mosynopolis.

In the spring of 1017, Basil again turned his arms against Pelagonia. Kastoria, a town situated on a rocky peninsula in a small lake, resisted his attacks, but the booty collected in the open country was considerable; and this he divided into three parts—one he bestowed on the Russian auxiliaries who served in his army, another he divided among the native Byzantine legions, and the third he reserved for the imperial treasury.[1] The operations of Basil in the west were for a time arrested by news he received from the governor of Dorystolon, which threatened to render his presence necessary in Bulgaria. Ladislas was concerting measures with the Patzinaks to induce them to invade the empire; but after a slight delay, Basil was informed the alliance had failed, and he resumed his activity. After laying waste all the country round Ostrovos and Moliskos that was peopled by Sclavonians, and repairing the fortifications of Berrhœa which had fallen to decay, he captured Setaina, where Samuel had formed great magazines of wheat. These magazines were kept well filled by Ladislas, so that Basil became master of so great a store that he divided it among his troops. At last the King of Achrida approached the emperor at the head of a considerable army, and a part of the imperial troops were drawn into an ambuscade. The emperor happened to be himself with the advanced division of the army. He instantly mounted his horse and led the troops about him to the scene of action, sending orders for all the other divisions to hasten forward to support him. His sudden appearance at the head of a strong body of the heavy-armed lancers of the Byzantine army, the fury of his charge, the terror his very name inspired, and the cry, " The emperor is upon us ! " [2] soon spread confusion through the Bulgarian ranks, and changed the fortune of the day. After this victory, Basil, finding the season too far advanced to follow up his success, returned to Constantinople, where he arrived in the month of January 1018.

Ladislas, whose affairs were becoming desperate, made an attempt to restore his credit by laying siege to Dyrrachium,

---

[1] Cedrenus, 711.

[2] Βεζειτε ὁ Τζέαρ are the words as given by Skylitzes.—Cedrenus, 712. Xylander says this is *fugite o Cæsar*. This suggests three questions. Was Latin used as the military language in the Bulgarian army? Do the words represent the language of some remains of the language of the ancient Macedonians, or of the dialect of the modern Albanians? Or were the Vallachians already to be found so far south

which he hoped to take before Basil could relieve it. Its possession would have enabled him to open communications with the enemies of Basil in Italy, and even with the Saracens of Sicily and Africa, but he was slain soon after the commencement of the siege. He reigned two years and five months. As soon as the emperor heard of his death, he visited Adrianople to make preparations for a campaign, which he hoped would end in the complete subjugation of the Bulgarian and Sclavonian population of the kingdom of Achrida. The Bulgarian leaders gave up all hope of resistance. Krakras, the brave chief of Pernikon, who had twice foiled the emperor, surrendered that impregnable fortress and thirty-five castles in the surrounding district. Dragomoutzes delivered up the fortress of Strumpitza, and both he and Krakras were rewarded with the patrician chair. Basil marched by Mosynopolis and Serres to Strumpitza, where he received deputations from most of the cities in Pelagonia, laying their keys at his feet. Even David, the Patriarch of Bulgaria, arrived, bringing letters from the widow of Ladislas, offering to surrender the capital. The emperor continued to advance by Skopia, Stypeia, and Prosakon, and on reaching Achrida he was received rather as the lawful sovereign than as a foreign conqueror. He immediately took possession of all the treasures Samuel had amassed; the gold alone amounted to a hundred centners,[1] and with this he paid all the arrears due to his troops, and rewarded them with a donative for their long and gallant service in this arduous war. Almost the whole of the royal family of Achrida submitted, and received the most generous treatment. Three sons of Ladislas, who escaped to Mount Truoros, and attempted to prolong the contest, were soon captured. The noble Bulgarians hastened to make their submission, and many were honoured with high rank at the imperial court. Nothing, indeed, proves more decidedly the absence of all Greek nationality in the Byzantine administration at this period, than the facility with which all foreigners obtained favour at the court of Constantinople; nor can anything be more conclusive of the fact that the centralisation of power in the person of the emperor, as completed by the Basilian dynasty, had now destroyed the administrative centralisation of the old Roman imperial system, for we have proofs that a considerable Greek population

1 This sum is not quite equal to 480,000 sovereigns.

still occupied the cities of Thrace and Macedonia, though Greek feelings had little influence on the government.[1]

The arrangement of the civil and financial administration of the conquered territory, which had for so many years been separated from the Byzantine empire, occupied the emperor's attention during the remainder of the year. He also ordered two fortresses to be constructed to command the mountain passes leading to Achrida, one in the lake of Prespa, and the other on the road leading to Vodena and Thessalonica. He then visited Diavolis, in order to inspect the passage over the Macedonian mountains that afforded the easiest communication with Northern Epirus.[2] Nicephorus Xiphias was sent at the same time to destroy all the mountain forts still in the possession of Sclavonian chieftains about Servia and Soskos.[3] The taxation of the Sclavonian cultivators of the soil was arranged on the same footing on which it had been placed by Samuel. Each pair of oxen for the plough paid annually a measure of wheat, and one of millet, barley, or maize, and each strema of vineyard paid a jar or barrel of wine to the fisc.[4]

Basil now resolved to re-establish the Byzantine influence on the coast of Dalmatia. A division of the army was sent northward to complete the subjection of the mountainous districts of the theme of Dyrrachium as far as the Dalmatian and Servian frontiers; and an imperial fleet entered the Adriatic to act in co-operation with the authorities on shore. The princes of Servia agreed to acknowledge the supremacy of the emperor, and Constantine Diogenes, the imperial general on the Danube, gained possession of the city of Sirmium by an act of the basest treachery.[5]

After passing the winter in his new conquests, Basil made a progress through Greece. At Zeitounion he visited the field of battle where the power of Samuel had been first broken by the victory of Nicephorus Ouranos, and found the ground still strewed with the bones of the slain. The wall that defended

---

[1] Eustathios, the Byzantine governor of Achrida, addresses the Bulgarian soldiers of the garrison of Pronista thus, Ῥωμαῖος δ᾽ἐγὼ, καὶ Ῥωμαῖος οὐ τῶν ἐπὶ Θράκης καὶ Μακεδονίας οἰκούντων ἀλλ᾽ ἐκ τῆς Μικρᾶς Ἀσίας.—Cedrenus, 715.
[2] The modern pass of Tjangon or Devol—Leake, *Travels in Northern Greece*, i. 335, 339.
[3] For the city of Servia at present, see Leake, *Travels in Northern Greece*, iii. 330.
[4] Modios is the word used.—Cedrenus, 747. Joannis, *Curopalatæ Hist.* (Skylitzes), 850. The modios and medimnos of Byzantine writers seem to be the same measure. Suidas says the medimnos was 108 litras, which shows it had nothing to do with the old Attic medimnos. The ancient medimnos contained 11 gallons (7·1456 pints English); the ancient modios 1 gallon (7·8576 pints).—Smith's *Dictionary of Greek and Roman Antiquities*.   [5] Lucius, *De Regno Dalmatiæ*, 297. Cedrenus, 717.

N

the pass of Thermopylæ retained its antique name, Skelos; and its masonry, which dated from Hellenic days, excited the emperor's admiration. At last Basil arrived within the walls of Athens, and he was the only emperor who for several ages honoured that city with a visit. Many magnificent structures in the town, and the whole of the temples in the Acropolis, had then hardly suffered any rude touches from the hand of time. If the external painting and gilding which had once adorned the Parthenon of Pericles had faded from their original splendour, the Church of the Virgin, into which it was transformed, had gained a new interest from the mural paintings of saints, martyrs, emperors, and empresses that covered the interior of the cella. The mind of Basil, though insensible to Hellenic literature, was deeply sensible of religious impressions, and the glorious combination of the variety of beauty in art and nature that he saw in the Acropolis touched his stern soul. He testified his feelings by splendid gifts to the city, and rich dedications at the shrine of the Virgin in the Parthenon.[1]

From Greece the emperor returned to Constantinople, where he indulged himself in the pomp of a triumph, making his entry into his capital by the Golden Gate, and listening with satisfaction to the cries of the populace, who applauded his cruelty by saluting him with the title of "The Slayer of the Bulgarians."

I have entered into the history of the destruction of the Bulgarian monarchy of Achrida in some detail, because the struggle was national as well as political; and the persevering resistance offered by the Sclavonian population of Macedonia to a warlike sovereign like Basil, proves the density and flourishing condition of that people, and the complete annihilation of all Hellenic influence in extensive provinces, where for ages the civilisation and the language of Greece had been predominant. Against this national energy on the part of the united Bulgarians and Sclavonians, the government of Constantinople had nothing to oppose but a well-disciplined army and a well-organised administration. The Byzantine empire had never less of a national character than at the present period, when its military glory had reached the highest pitch. Its Roman traditions were a mere name, and it had not yet assumed the medieval Greek characteristics it adopted at a later period when it was ruled by the family of Comnenos. No national population followed in the rear of Basil's victories, to colonise

[1] Cedrenus, 717.   Zonaras, ii. 227.

the lands he systematically depopulated by his ravages and cruelty; and hence it appears that extensive districts, instead of being repeopled by Greek settlers, remained in a deserted condition until a nomadic Vallachian population intruded themselves. These new colonists soon multiplied so rapidly that about a century later they were found occupying the mountains round the great plain of Thessaly.[1] The changes which have taken place in the numbers and places of habitation of the different races of mankind, are really as important a branch of historical inquiry as the geographical limits of political governments; and the social laws that regulate the increase and decrease of the various families of the human race, at the same period, and under the same government, are as deserving of study as the actions of princes and the legislation of parliaments, for they exert no inconsiderable influence on the rise and fall of states.

After the conclusion of the Bulgarian war, the attention of Basil was directed to the affairs of Armenia. Great political changes were beginning to take place in Asia, from the decline of the empire of the caliphs of Bagdat; but these revolutions lie beyond the sphere of Byzantine politics at this time, though they began already to exert an influence on the sovereigns of Armenia. Before Basil had taken the command of his armies in the Bulgarian war, he had made a campaign in Armenia (A.D. 991), and gained possession of a considerable portion of Iberia or Georgia. The whole kingdom had been left to him by the will of David, its last sovereign; but George, the brother of the deceased monarch, advancing his claim to the succession, Basil, in order to avoid a war, agreed to leave George in possession of the northern part. It is not necessary to enter into any details concerning the relations of the empire with the different dynasties that then reigned in each of the principalities into which Armenia was divided. Basil, in order to keep some check on the population of Iberia and Armenia, transported colonies of Bulgarians and Sclavonians into the East, while at the same time he removed numbers of Armenians into Bulgaria.

In the year 995, Basil visited the East, in order to re-establish the Byzantine influence in Syria, where it had fallen into discredit in consequence of the defeat of the imperial army on the banks of the Orontes, in the preceding year.[2] The em-

---

[1] Benjamin of Tudela. The Itinerary translated and edited by A. Asher, i. 48.
[2] Nicephorus Ouranos, who defeated Samuel on the banks of the Sperchius in 996

peror soon succeeded in re-establishing his authority. He took Aleppo, Hems, and Sheizar, and laid siege to Tripolis; but that city resisted his attacks, as it had done those of John Zimiskes; and after his return to Constantinople, the lieutenants of the Fatimite caliphs of Egypt recovered possession of Aleppo.

In the year 1021, the emperor was compelled to take the field in person, to make head against a powerful combination of enemies on the Armenian frontier. Senekarim, the prince of Vasparoukan, had been so alarmed by the threatening aspect of the Mohammedan population on his frontiers that he had ceded his dominions to Basil, and received in exchange the city of Sebaste and the adjacent country as far as the Euphrates, where he established himself with many Armenian families who quitted their native seats. Basil undertook to defend Vasparoukan against the Turkish tribes that began to attack it, and Senekarim engaged to govern Sebaste as a Byzantine viceroy.[1] After this cession had been made, George, the sovereign of the northern part of Iberia and Abasgia, in conjunction with Joannes Sembat, the King of Ani, attacked the Byzantine territory, and their operations rendered the presence of the emperor necessary. They had formed secret relations with Nicephorus Xiphias, who, while governor of Philippopolis, had distinguished himself in the Bulgarian war, and with Nicephorus, the son of Bardas Phokas; and these two generals broke out into open rebellion in Cappadocia, and endeavoured to incite all the Armenians to take up arms. Basil was obliged to suppress this rebellion before he engaged a foreign enemy, and he availed himself of the spirit of treachery inherent among men in power in most absolute governments to effect his purpose. He sent letters secretly to each of the rebel chiefs, offering pardon to him who would assassinate his colleague. Phokas, who was bold and daring like his father, immediately communicated the emperor's letter to Xiphias, who, concealing that he had received one of similar import, availed himself of his friend's confidence to assassinate him at a private interview. The rebel army then melted away, and Basil was able to turn all his forces against the sovereign of Iberia. In the first battle the victory

appears to have been taken prisoner by the Saracens in this battle —Cedrenus, 702. For the date of Basil's campaign in Syria, compare Cedrenus 701, and Weil, *Geschichte der Chalifen*, iii. 43; note.

[1] Saint Martin, *Mémoires sur l'Armenie*, i. 368. Chamich, ii. 112.

remained doubtful, but in a second the Iberian and Abasgian troops were completely defeated (11th September 1022). Liparit, the general of the Abasgians, was slain, and the kings of Iberia and Armenia were obliged to sue for peace. A treaty was concluded on the banks of the lake Balagatsis, by which Joannes the King of Armenia, who began to be alarmed at the progress of the Turks, ceded his capital, Ani, to Basil after his death, on condition of retaining the government in his own hands as long as he lived.[1] During this campaign, Basil displayed all his usual foresight and energy: he took measures for putting the fortresses on the eastern frontier of the empire in a state to resist the Turks, who threatened to invade the west of Asia; and some of the military engines he ordered to be constructed were of such power and solidity, that when the Seljouk Turks invaded the Byzantine territory in the reign of Constantine IX. (Monomachos), they found them still well suited for service.

The next object of Basil's ambition was to expel the Saracens from Sicily; and he was engaged in making great preparations for reconquering that island, when he was seized with an illness, which quickly proved fatal. He expired in December 1025, at the age of sixty-eight, after having governed the empire with absolute power for fifty years. He extended the limits of the Byzantine territory on every side by his conquests, and at the end of his reign the Byzantine empire attained its greatest extent and highest power.

The body of Basil was interred in the Church of the Evangelists, in the Hebdomon. Two centuries and a half had nearly passed away. The Byzantine empire had been destroyed by the Crusaders, the Asiatic Greeks were endeavouring to expel the Franks from their conquest, and Michael Paleologos their emperor was besieging Constantinople, when some Greek officers, wandering through the ruins of the church and monastery of the Evangelists, admired the remains of its ancient magnificence, and lamented to see that so splendid a monument of Byzantine piety had been converted into a stable under the ruinous administration of the Frank Cæsars. In a corner of the building, a remarkable tomb that had been recently broken open arrested their attention. A well-embalmed body of an old man lay in the sarcophagus, and in his hand some idle herdsman had placed a shepherd's pipe. An inscription on the wall showed that

the sarcophagus contained the mortal remains of Basil the
Slayer of the Bulgarians.   The Emperor Michael VIII. visited
the spot, and when he found it necessary to retire from before
Constantinople for a time, he ordered the body to be removed
to Selymbria, and interred in the monastery of our Saviour,[1]
A.D. 1260.

1 Cedrenus, 719. Pachymer, i. 80.

CHAPTER III

PERIOD OF CONSERVATISM ON THE EVE OF DECLINE, A.D. 1025–1057

SECTION I

CONSTANTINE VIII., A.D. 1025–1028

Condition of the empire—Character of Constantine VIII.—Government administered by his eunuchs—Oppressive financial administration—Marriage of Zoe with Romanus Arghyros—Death of Constantine VIII.

THE conquest of the Sclavonians in the Thracian, Macedonian, and Illyrian mountains gave a degree of security to the Eastern Empire which it had not enjoyed since the time of Justinian I. If at this period the government had known how to adopt measures for developing the resources of the country, or the Greek people had possessed the energy and moral convictions necessary to force the court to respect their rights as men and citizens, the whole of the provinces lying to the south of Mount Hæmus might have become thickly peopled by the natural increase of the Greek race. Land of the best quality was everywhere ready to receive a better cultivation from new colonists; but improvement was checked, on the part of the government, by exactions similar to those which arrest the progress of society in all arbitrary governments; and the Greeks were now destitute of the sentiment of national patriotism;— they were as selfish as their government was rapacious. Exorbitant taxes, severe fiscal restrictions, and obstructive social trammels, bore heavily on the agricultural classes, and left them, as their share of the fruits of their labour, little more than was sufficient for perpetuating their race, and supplying a due succession of peasants to labour the lands on which their predecessors toiled. Great part of the extensive provinces, depopulated by the destructive system of hostilities pursued by Basil and Samuel, remained long uncultivated, and were gradually invaded by nomadic tribes, who were allowed to pasture their flocks and herds over the richest plains on paying tribute to the Byzantine authorities.

The position of the empire on the death of Basil required a judicious and economical sovereign to organise the civil administration on such a scale, as not to absorb too large a portion of the funds required for the maintenance of the large army with which it was necessary to guard the extensive frontiers, and yet on a footing that would insure an equitable and prompt administration of justice to the subjugated Sclavonians. Unfortunately, Constantine VIII., though he was averse to war and military parade, had no taste for order, and no care for justice. In his personal appearance he bore a strong resemblance to his brother, but any similarity of disposition that ever showed itself was only in defects. His tall robust figure proclaimed the same strength of body and health of constitution, but he was destitute of the activity, fortitude, and courage of Basil. After he assumed the government, he continued to live as he had done while his brother kept him secluded from public business. In the interior of the palace he was surrounded by musicians, singers, dancing-girls, and parasites, and he rarely quitted it except to indulge in the chase, or to celebrate public spectacles in the hippodrome for his own amusement and that of the idle populace of the capital. He left all public business to be transacted by his domestic servants, and he shunned the military pageants in which the emperors usually took an active part. Indeed, he appeared to dread the array of troops as more likely to suggest the idea of internal revolutions than foreign wars. His fears rendered him a suspicious and cruel tyrant ; and his distrust of all men of talent and influence induced him to intrust the principal offices of the state to the eunuchs of his household : men bred up amidst scenes of dissipation, gambling, and hunting, and utterly destitute of all experience in public business, were suddenly charged with the most important duties in the empire.[1]

The dignities of chamberlain,[2] keeper of the wardrobe, and commander of the watch, were intrusted to three eunuchs of the domestic establishment of Constantine, and each received the title of President of the Senate. The command of the foreign mercenaries was conferred on a fourth. The Byzantine emperors, like other despots, preferred intrusting strangers

---

[1] Zonaras, ii. 228.

[2] Cedrenus, 719. Nikolaos was made Παρα κοιμώμενος and Δομέστικος τῶν σχολῶν, or minister-at-war. Nicephorus Πρωτοβεστιάριος, and Simeon Δρουγγάριος τῆς βίγλας.

with the guardianship of their persons.[1]   A fifth, named Spondyles, was appointed duke of Antioch, and intrusted with the command of the troops charged to resist the ambitious projects of the Fatimite caliphs in Syria.   The object of the nomination was to furnish the army with a leader incapable of pretending to the throne, not to supply it with an able general. The sixth of this domestic band, named Niketas, became duke of Iberia.   The Emperor Basil II. must have beaten down the pride of the aristocracy during the latter part of his reign, and effected a great change in the position they had held in the time of Basilios the chamberlain and the rebellions of Skleros and Phokas, or the direction of the government would not have been allowed to remain long in the hands of six eunuchs.   The spirit of conservatism already pervaded society to such a degree as to form a firm support of despotism.   The patience with which Constantine's measures were endured gives us some insight into the social as well as the administrative changes effected by the long reign of his brother.   We see that his policy had proved quite as successful in breaking the power of the great families, and in diminishing the influence of the generals of themes, as in destroying the Bulgarian kingdom and subjugating the Sclavonian people.   All the power the emperor had taken from others was accumulated in his own person ; nothing was done to confer any rights on the people, nor to secure them against injustice on the part of the imperial agents.   The emperor's power was made absolute in practice as in theory, and thus the worthless creatures of Constantine VIII. were enabled to commit acts of greater oppression than the aristocratic officials whose power Basil had curtailed.   Conservatism was now a principle of Byzantine policy, and it is usually a factitious phrase to delude the people from a devotion to order and justice.

Basil II. is accused by the Byzantine historians of fiscal severity.   In this accusation there is reason to suspect that we learn rather the murmurs of the nobles and populace of Constantinople than the deliberate expression of the public opinion of the whole empire.   Basil endeavoured to levy from the rich their due proportion of the public burdens, and to put

---

[1] The title of the commander of the foreign guard was Μέγας ἑταιρειάρχης.   The Varangian corps of the imperial body-guard was formed about this time, and consisted first of Scandinavians and Russians, afterwards of Danes and English.   Cedrenus mentions Varangians at page 735, and their commandant Akoulothos at page 787.—For the German guard of Augustus, see Suetonius, in *Aug.* 49 ; *Taciti Ann.* i . 24 ; and Ernesti's note to *Ann.* 13, 18.   Oberlin, i. 754.

a stop to the absorption of the estates of the poor by the aristocracy, while at the same time he refrained from lavishing immense sums on the shows in the hippodrome. But whatever may have been the extent of his avarice, we see signs of true liberality in his exertions to lighten the burdens of the industrious classes, and real humanity in his endeavours to spare the poor. It has been already noticed that the taxes were two years in arrear when he died. The proceedings of Constantine form a contrast to those of his brother. On one hand, he exacted the arrears of the public taxes with the greatest severity, while, on the other, he lavished the money thus extorted from the provinces in wasteful expenditure in the capital. During his reign of three years he collected and expended the revenue of five. His palace, like that of a Saracen caliph, was filled with foreign slaves and eunuchs, whose strange appearance and barbarous language astonished the natural-born subjects of the empire.[1]

Though no dangerous insurrection broke out, the general discontent could not be mistaken, and it excited the fears of Constantine and his creatures. Many eminent men, representatives of families renowned in the annals of the empire, were seized, and condemned to lose their sight, because the services of their ancestors in past generations appeared to give them too much influence on public opinion. It is difficult to determine, in each case, whether this was a measure of precaution, or a punishment for political imprudence or actual conspiracy. The names of some of the sufferers deserve a record, because they indicate the position of several distinguished families at the time. Nicephorus Comnenos, the governor of Media or Aspourakan, had bravely defended his province against the incursions of the Saracens; but his troops having given him some signs of indiscipline and timidity, he had invited them to take an oath that they would never desert him on the field of battle. This excited the jealousy of the emperor, who recalled Comnenos to Constantinople, where he was condemned to lose his sight for administering unlawful oaths to the army.[2] Constantine, the son of Michael Burtzes, who took Antioch, was also deprived of sight; but in his case it was notorious that the punishment was an act of revenge, as this patrician had informed Basil of some unseemly practices of his brother, in order that

1 Zonaras, ii. 228.
2 Cedrenus, 711. Ducange, *Fam. Byz.* 170.

they might be restrained. The grandsons of the rivals, Bardas Skleros and Bardas Phokas, were united in misfortune. These two patricians lost their sight on some vague accusations brought against them by the eunuchs of the imperial palace. Basilios Skleros had quarrelled with Prusian, the son of Ladislas, the last king of Achrida. Prusian, who held the rank of magister, and was governor of the theme Boukellarion, fought a duel with Skleros; for the pride of the Byzantine military aristocracy displayed itself with as much courage, if not with as much gallantry, as was ever shown by the chivalry of western Europe.[1] The two duellists were exiled to different islands of the Princes' group; but Basilios was soon deprived of his sight, on pretext that he was plotting to escape. Romanos Kurkuas, a member of a distinguished Armenian family, which had supplied the empire with many able generals, and of which the Emperor John Zimiskes was a scion, also lost his sight, as well as several individuals who bear names not unknown in Byzantine history, and others whose barbarous appellations prove that the Bulgarian and Sclavonian aristocracy divided with the Greeks and Armenians a competent share of political influence at the court of Constantinople.[2]

The extent of the disorder caused in the provinces by the creatures sent to govern them by Constantine and his eunuchs, is attested by the notice we possess of some occurrences at Naupactos. The government of that province was intrusted to an officer called, from his violence, Mad George, who, by his tyrannical conduct, drove the people to despair; and in an insurrection which ensued, Mad George was slain, and his palace plundered by the populace. This insurrection was soon quelled; but Constantine took severe vengeance on the inhabitants of Naupactos. Even the archbishop was deprived of his sight, for attempting to protect the people against the exactions of their tyrant.

Foreign nations soon heard how Constantine conducted the government, and hastened to profit by the disorderly state of public affairs. In 1027, the Patzinaks made an irruption into Bulgaria, where they laid waste everything on

[1] Cedrenus, 721. Lebeau, xiv. 234, remarks, that this is the first duel recorded in Byzantine history. Prusianos lost his eyes in the reign of Romanus III., on a suspicion that he was plotting with Theodora, the daughter of Constantine VIII., to mount the throne.—Cedrenus, 723. Zonaras, ii. 230.

[2] Cedrenus, 721. Bogdan, Glabas, and Goudelis. Zacharias, who lost his tongue, was a relation of a personage called Vestas Phevdatos.

their line of march. A Saracen fleet cruised among the Cyclades, visiting the islands one after another, and collecting booty from all. But the spirit infused by Basil into the army and navy was not extinct, though their direction had fallen into unworthy hands. Diogenes, the governor of Sirmium, being created duke of Bulgaria, defeated the Patzinaks, and drove them back beyond the Danube. The governors of Samos and Chios assembled a naval force, with which they attacked the Saracen fleet, and captured twelve of the enemy's ships with all the crews.

Constantine VIII. was suddenly attacked by a disease which was evidently mortal. When he was near his end, he fixed his eyes on Constantine Dalassenos as his successor. The choice was judicious; and a eunuch of the palace was despatched to summon Dalassenos from his residence in the Armeniac theme, when Simeon, the commander of the watch, expecting to find a weaker and more docile sovereign in Romanus Arghyros, who was connected with the imperial family, prevailed on the emperor to recall his first order, and transfer the empire to Romanus. The destined sovereign, on reaching the palace, was informed by Constantine that he was selected to mount the throne, but that he must divorce his wife, and marry one of the imperial princesses. Romanus hesitated to become emperor on this condition; but Constantine, to quicken his decision, informed him that he must either ascend the throne or lose his eyesight, and gave him a few hours to reflect on the choice. The wife of Romanus, learning the alternative, immediately ordered her head to be shaved, and entered a monastery; thus generously relieving her husband from the odium of sacrificing his honour to his timidity or ambition. Constantine had destined Theodora, the youngest of his three daughters, to be the wife of Romanus; but she refused to participate in the throne by marrying the husband of another woman. The emperor was compelled, therefore, to make his second daughter Zoe empress, for the eldest had retired into a monastery.[1] The daughters of Constantine were already of mature age. Their education had been shamefully neglected by their father; and Zoe had taken advantage of the want of all moral restraint in which she lived. She had attained the age of forty-eight when she became a bride; but the posterity of Romanus II. and Theophano were all remarkable for health,

---

[1] A malady, which may have been the smallpox, had disfigured her appearance—Zonaras, ii, 228,

vigour, and longevity.[1]   Her marriage with Romanus III. and
their coronation was celebrated on the 19th November 1028.
On the 21st of the month Constantine VIII. expired.

SECTION II

THE REIGNS OF THE HUSBANDS OF ZOE, A.D. 1028-1054

Personal conduct of Romanus III., 1028-1034—Conspiracies—Saracen
   war—Defeat of Romanus—Exploits of Maniakes—Autograph of Christ
   —Acquisition of Perkrin—Naval operations—Death of Romanus III.—
   Character of Michael IV. (the Paphlagonian), A.D. 1034-1041—John the
   Orphanotroph—Financial oppression — Conspiracies—Saracen war—
   Attempt to surprise Edessa—War in Sicily—Loss of Servia—Rebellion
   of Bulgarians and Sclavonians—Energetic conduct of Michael IV.—
   Death of Michael IV.—Reign of Michael V. (Kalaphates, or the
   Caulker), A.D. 1042—Reign of Zoe and Theodora, 1042—Character of
   Constantine IX. (Monomachus), 1042-1054—Skleraina, the concubine
   of Constantine IX., created empress—Lavish expenditure—Cruelty of
   Theodora—Sedition in Cyprus—Rebellion of Maniakes—Conspiracy of
   the eunuch Stephen—Rebellion of Leo Tornikios—Court plots—Ser-
   vian war—Russian war—Patzinak war—War in Italy—Conquest of
   Armenia—Invasion of the Byzantine empire by the Seljouk Turks—
   Separation of Greek and Latin churches—Deaths of Zoe and Constantine IX.

For twenty-nine years the empire was ruled by a succession
of princes who owed their position on the throne to the
daughters of Constantine VIII.   Under such circumstances,
it is natural that the affairs of the court of Constantinople
attract more than usual attention in a review of Byzantine
history.   Every class of society in the empire appears during
this period to have slumbered in prosperity, consuming its
revenues in a firm conviction that no external power could disturb the internal security of the state.   In no other portion of
the civilised world did the inhabitants enjoy an equal degree
of wealth and security for life and property ; and the military
power and financial resources of every neighbouring government
appeared far inferior to those of the Byzantine empire.   Conservative lethargy was natural under such circumstances.

Romanus III. was sixty years old when accident made him
an emperor.   He was allied to several of the oldest and most
illustrious of the aristocracy, and is a type of the kind of
sovereign a respectable Byzantine noble of conservative ten-

   [1] Zonaras, ii. 232, 260, says Zoe was fifty in the reign of Romanus III., and more
than seventy at her death.   The Chronicle of Lupus, *Bibliotheca Hist. Regni Siciliæ*,
edited by Caiusius, p. 39, says she was seventy at her death, in 1050.

dencies made, during a time when the political horizon was peculiarly tranquil in the East. He enjoyed the reputation of possessing both accomplishments and learning; but his vanity somewhat obscured the lustre of his talents. Feeling that his sudden elevation would excite the ambition of many of the nobility, he adopted measures to conciliate the favour of every class of his subjects. The church was propitiated by bestowing on the clergy of St. Sophia's an annual revenue of eighty pounds' weight of gold, secured as a permanent charge on the imperial treasury. To gain the nobility and the higher ecclesiastical dignitaries, he abolished the Allelengyon, or mutual responsibility of the rich for the taxes due by the poor in their district. It appears that this law, as established by Basil II., had been executed with such severity that several bishops had been reduced to poverty.[1] He also granted a full pardon to all persons who had been persecuted by the jealousy of Constantine VIII. He purchased popularity among the people by releasing all who were confined in the public prisons for debt; and in order to combine justice with charity, he paid their debts to private individuals when he remitted those to the fisc. He redeemed the captives taken by the Patzinaks in their recent invasion of the empire; and, in short, he endeavoured in many ways to render himself so generally popular as to deter any rival from aspiring at the throne. These measures for securing popularity were of themselves well chosen, but their favourable effect was greatly increased by a coincidence beyond the emperor's control. The year of his accession proved one of singular fertility—every species of grain was abundant in the capital, and a rich harvest of olives supplied the people of the provinces both with oil and money.

The piety of Romanus displayed itself in the usual superstition of his age. Considering the failure of his Syrian campaign as a punishment for his sins, and not a consequence of his ignorance of military affairs, he sought to propitiate Heaven by a lavish expenditure on ecclesiastical objects. He founded a new monastery of the Virgin called Semneion, on the church of which he laid out money with profusion. He endowed the monastery with such enormous revenues that even Byzantine ecclesiastics, in recording his liberality, blame the incongruity of placing monks in the position of luxurious nobles, and complain of the emperor seeking to acquire merit with God by exactions that ruined his subjects.[2] Romanus

---

[1] Zonaras, ii. 230.   [2] *Ibid.*, ii. 231.

also covered the capital of the columns in the churches of St. Sophia's and Blachern with gilding, and enriched the buildings with expensive ornaments. He is said likewise to have obtained permission from the Fatimite caliph Daher to rebuild the Church of the Holy Sepulchre at Jerusalem, which had been destroyed by Caliph Hakem in the year 1010. Subsequent disputes with the Egyptian government appear to have delayed the commencement of the work until the reign of Michael IV., and it was not completed until that of Constantine IX. (Monomachus), in the year 1048.[1]

Whenever early education has failed to implant moral feelings in the hearts of men, laws prove ineffectual to supply the want, whether in the case of individuals or nations. The people of the Byzantine empire were now beginning to have the same hankering after hereditary succession which has lately been manifested by the continental nations of Europe for representative government; but in both cases there appears to have been a want of those firm convictions required for attaining any desired end. As usually happens in political matters, the fault lay with the higher and educated classes of society, who allowed themselves to quit the line of duty to pursue any lure held out to their prejudices or passions. Hence we find conspiracies and rebellions continuing to occur in rapid succession in the Byzantine empire, where they were regarded as an unavoidable evil in the lot of man. Conservative tendencies were the most powerless political feeling that ever swayed the counsels of Constantinople. But we must not forget that the Byzantine empire was a government without a nation.

---

[1] The discussion concerning the site of the Holy Sepulchre seems still undecided. The author of this work has endeavoured to show that evidence, and not tradition, must have determined the position in the time of Constantine.—*On the Site of the Holy Sepulchre*, by George Finlay: London, 1847. Mr. Ferguson, in a very able work, entitled *An Essay on the Ancient Topography of Jerusalem*, published in the same year, has maintained that Constantine did not fix on the present site, but that in some later period the present site was imposed on mankind as the site selected by Constantine or Helena. Though the tradition of the church cannot be received as of much value on a topographical question before any site was determined on, it becomes of value from the time a variety of nations and sects began to worship at the same shrine: now, as this has been the case, ever since the time of Constantine, with the Holy Sepulchre, the question arises, At what period was it possible for the priests and pilgrims of many different nations and sects to agree on a fraud so abhorrent to the superstitious feelings of mankind? The authorities relating to the destruction and re-edification of the Church of the Holy Sepulchre at this period, are as follows: The Saracens set fire to the church and burnt the Patriarch of Jerusalem alive, after the victories of Nicephorus II., in 968.—Cedrenus, 661. The caliph Hakem, called by Byzantine writers Aziz, razed the church and demolished the sepulchre in 1010.—Cedrenus, 706. William of Tyre, i. iv. Bongars, 631. Romanus III. obtained permission to rebuild the church.—Cedrenus, 731. William of Tyre, i. vi. Bongars, 632. The new building was completed by Constantine IX. (Monomachus).—William of Tyre, i. vi. Bongars, 632.

The Empress Zoe never forgave her sister Theodora that superiority of character which had induced their father to offer her the empire, if she would accept the husband of his choice; and Romanus III. disliked her for refusing his hand, and feared her on account of her talents. He set a spy over her conduct by drawing from his retreat John, one of the ministers of Basil II., who had deemed it prudent to retire into a monastery on the accession of Constantine VIII. John was now appointed syncellus, and intrusted with the superintendence of Theodora's household. Prusian, the Bulgarian prince who had fought a duel with Romanus Skleros, the brother-in-law of the Emperor Romanus III., was accused of plotting with Theodora to seize the imperial crown. Whether true or false, the jealousy of Zoe and the aversion of Romanus were sure to obtain for this accusation a favourable reception. The emperor had already restored his brother-in-law to his former rank as magistros; he now revenged him by condemning Prusian to lose his sight, and by banishing his mother, the late queen of Bulgaria, to the monastery of Mantineion in the Boukellarian theme. Subsequently, when the court was alarmed at the prospect of a Bulgarian and Sclavonian rebellion under the direction of Constantine Diogenes, Prusian was compelled to embrace the monastic life. It seems strange that the project of transferring the sovereignty of the Byzantine empire to a Bulgarian should be recorded by the Byzantine writers, without the smallest notice that such an event was likely to wound either the Roman pride of the aristocracy of Constantinople, or the national vanity of the Greek race; but we must recollect that the founder of the Basilian dynasty was generally considered to have been a Sclavonian groom.

Another conspiracy, which was formed soon after that of Prusian, was connected with the same interests, and counted on the same feelings for success. Constantine Diogenes, the governor of Sirmium and duke of Bulgaria, had married a niece of the Emperor Romanus III., and had been appointed governor of Thessalonica.[1] While there, it was discovered that he was engaged in frequent communications with the leaders of the Bulgarian and Sclavonian population of the empire, and it was deemed necessary to transfer him to the government of the Thrakesian theme before arresting

[1] Cedrenus, 723; Zonaras, ii. 230; Ducange, *Fam. Byz.* 153, and in his notes to Zonaras, p. 90, edit. Venet., disagree concerning the relationship.

him. He was found guilty of conspiracy against the emperor, and condemned to be incarcerated as a monk in the monastery of Studion. John the syncellus, who seems to have been gained over by Theodora, whom he had been appointed to watch, Eustathios Daphnomeles, the governor of Achrida, two grandchildren of Michael Burtzes, the conqueror of Antioch, and George and Varasvatzes, nephews of the patrician Theudatos, were all condemned for participating in this conspiracy.[1] They were publicly scourged, and then banished. Theodora, who was accused of being privy to their plots, was driven from her palace, and imprisoned in the monastery of Petrion.[2] Some time after, the Empress Zoe visited her sister, and compelled her to assume the monastic habit. Constantine Diogenes was also accused by the archbishop of Thessalonica of plotting to escape into Illyria, in order to assume the title of emperor. To avoid the loss of his eyesight, and the disgrace of being scourged through the streets of the capital, he threw himself from a window, and was killed on the spot. He was buried in the place appropriated to those who committed suicide, A.D. 1032.[3]

The negligence of Constantine VIII. had weakened the military force of the empire. Spondyles, the eunuch intrusted with the government of Antioch, finding that the Saracen emirs who had been rendered tributary by Nicephorus II. and John Zimiskes refused to pay tribute, undertook to re-establish the imperial authority. His rashness and incapacity led to the complete defeat of the Byzantine army on the 31st of October 1029, by which all the imperial possessions of Syria were exposed without defence to the attacks of the emirs of Aleppo and Tripolis, who pushed their incursions up to the walls of Antioch, and rendered themselves masters of the fort of Menik, which had been recently constructed in its immediate vicinity.

Romanus III. resolved to redeem the honour of the empire at the head of his armies. His brother-in-law, Constantine Karantenos, was sent forward to supersede Spondyles. When the emperor reached Philomilion in Pisidia, he was met by an embassy from the emir of Aleppo, who offered to recognise

---

[1] Varasvatzes founded the monastery of the Iberians on Mount Athos.—Cedrenus, 724. The account of Mount Athos, by Comnenos, in Montfaucon's *Paleographia Græca*, omits this fact.

[2] It was situated without the walls, at the head of the port.—Ducange, *Notæ in Zonaræ Ann.* p. 90, edit. Venet. [3] Cedrenus, 729.

the supremacy of the empire, and to pay the same tribute he had paid to Basil II. The wisest councillors of Romanus recommended him to accept these terms, for the season was ill suited for invading Syria, where the heat and want of water rendered great part of the country better adapted for the operations of the light-armed cavalry of the Arabs, than for the military tactics of the Byzantine troops, covered with heavy armour.[1] The emperor was so destitute of military experience, that he believed it would be a matter of little difficulty to rival the exploits of Nicephorus, Zimiskes, and Basil, and he marched forward to take possession of Aleppo. He had arrived at a strong fortress called Azaz, about two days' march from that city, when his outposts were attacked and driven in by the Arabs, who prevented his cavalry from collecting forage, and his troops from approaching the water in the neighbourhood.[2] The position of the Byzantine camp was ill chosen; an attempt to repulse the Arabs led to an unpremeditated engagement, in which a considerable body of troops was defeated, and the fugitives, rushing into the camp, spread disorder far and wide. No measures were adopted for restoring order, and the victorious Arabs advanced up to the intrenchments, and kept the imperial army closely blockaded. The emperor was utterly helpless, and under such a commander there was no choice but to retreat to Antioch. This operation was conducted in the most disgraceful manner. At daylight Romanus abandoned the camp, leaving his own tents and baggage, and the warlike machines, tents, and baggage of the army, a prey to the enemy; and this booty fortunately detained the Arabs so long that a great part of the flying army gained Antioch in safety, August 1030.[3]

Romanus, cured of his passion for military fame, hastened back to Constantinople. The generals he left in command of the army proved as incapable as their sovereign, and Menik, the fort in the vicinity of Antioch, remained in the hands of the Saracens. The emperor, however, at last sent Theok-

---

[1] Cedrenus, 726.

[2] Azaz is about twenty-six miles north by west of Aleppo. The mound on which it stands is nearly circular, and partly of limestone, with a circumference of about two hundred and fifty yards at the base, and ninety yards at the top of the cone, which is about a hundred and twenty feet high; its natural kernel having been increased to this extent, in order that the work might be more defensible.—Colonel Chesney, The Expedition for the Survey of the rivers Euphrates and Tigris, i. 422. This quotation from Colonel Chesney is necessary to prove that Cedrenus is a better authority in the present instance than the Arabian geographer Aboulfeda, though a native of Damascus, who, according to Weil, iii. 71, note, places Azaz only a mile from Aleppo.

[3] Cedrenus, 726. Zonaras, ii. 231.

tistos, the commander of the foreign mercenaries, with a considerable reinforcement of native and foreign troops; and this officer having formed an alliance with the emir of Tripolis, who was alarmed at the progress of the Egyptian power in Syria, succeeded in taking the fort of Menik. Alach, the son of the emir of Tripolis, visited the court of Romanus, and so lax were the political and religious ideas of the Byzantines, in spite of their ecclesiastical bigotry, that he was honoured with the rank of a Roman patrician.[1]

Shortly after the defeat of the Emperor Romanus at Azaz, an incident occurred which deserves notice, principally because it brought into notice an officer who soon took a prominent part in the military affairs of the empire, both in Asia and Europe. George Maniakes was governor of the small province called Telouch.[2] After the flight of the army to Antioch, a body of eight hundred Arabs appeared before the walls of the fortress in which he was residing, announcing the death of the emperor, and the overthrow of the Byzantine power in Syria. They ordered Maniakes to evacuate the place, or they threatened to storm it next day, and put every person within its walls to the sword. Maniakes considered that the nature of their summons indicated either their weakness or their determination to fall on his troops by treachery; he therefore asked to be allowed to remain the night in the fortress, to make preparations for his retreat. The Arab camp was supplied with food and refreshments in abundance, and at midnight Maniakes led out the garrison to attack the enemy, who were found plunged in sleep without a guard. The greater part were slain, and two hundred and eighty camels, laden with the spoil of Romanus's camp, were recaptured. This prize was sent as a present to the emperor, accompanied with the noses and ears of the vanquished.

To reward the valour of Maniakes, he was appointed governor of Lower Media, of which Samosata was the capital.[3] The following year the Saracens invaded Mesopotamia, and plundered the country as far as Melitene; but in 1032, Maniakes contrived to bribe the governor of Edessa, who was subject to the emir of Miarfekin (Martyropolis), to deliver up the town. But as soon as the Byzantine troops got possession of three towers in the wall, they were assailed by the Saracen

[1] Cedrenus, 728. I believe the Grand Mogul was once honoured with the rank of Christian knighthood by an English sovereign.
[2] For the family of Maniakes, compare Cedrenus, 727, 731; Georg. Mon. 533; Leo Gramm. 461.   [3] Cedrenus, 727.

inhabitants, and Maniakes was soon attacked by Apomerman, the emir of Miarfekin, who hastened to expel him from his position. The Saracens, finding it impossible to regain possession of the towers, and learning that fresh troops were marching to the assistance of Maniakes, abandoned Edessa; but before quitting it they burned most of the houses, and destroyed the great church. Though the Saracens had time to carry off the greater part of the wealth of the city, they left behind them what was infinitely more valuable in the eyes of the Christians of that age than the whole wealth of the caliphate. The people of Edessa had long boasted that they possessed a letter written by our Saviour to Abgarus, king of Edessa; this precious relic was now brought to Maniakes, and by him transmitted to Constantinople.[1] It is not known at what period this precious document was fabricated. From the city and territory of Edessa a tribute of 50 lb. of gold was annually remitted to the Byzantine treasury.

The disorganised state of the caliphate of Bagdat, and the power acquired by the Turkish mercenaries, induced several Saracen emirs to solicit the protection of Romanus. The emir of Aleppo, in spite of his victory, became tributary to the empire. Aleim, the emir of Perkrin—a fortress of great importance, on account of its position—delivered up that place to the emperor; and a body of six thousand Byzantine troops, under a Bulgarian patrician, was stationed to defend this advanced post. Aleim was, however, dissatisfied with the reward he received, and opened communications with the Persians, whom he contrived to introduce into Perkrin. The Byzantine garrison was surprised and put to the sword; but a powerful body of native troops and Russian mercenaries soon regained possession of the place, which was taken by assault, and Aleim was put to death.[2]

The Saracens of Africa and Sicily were still in the habit of sending out large fleets to plunder the coasts of the empire. In the year 1031, these pirates laid waste Illyria and the island of Corfu, but they were defeated by the people of Ragusa and the governor of Nauplia, who destroyed the greater part of their fleet. Next year they returned with a large force, and, if we believe the accounts of the Byzantine writers, their fleet

---

[1] Cedrenus, 731. Zonaras, ii. 232. Glycas, 313.

[2] Cedrenus, 732, says Perkrin was near Bagdat; but this must be a mistake, as he evidently alludes to the city of Percri, mentioned by Const. Porphyr. *De Adm. Imp.* chap. 44, as an important fortress in Armenia.—St. Martin, *Mémoires sur l'Arménie*, 1, 137.

consisted of a thousand vessels, and transported ten thousand troops. Two divisions of this great armament were defeated by Nicephorus Karantenos, the governor of Nauplia, and upwards of a thousand prisoners were sent to Constantinople. In 1033, the imperial fleet, under the command of the protospatharios Tekneas, made a descent on the coast of Egypt, and after collecting considerable booty, and carrying off many prisoners, the expedition returned to Constantinople. Every government at this time found it much easier to plunder the territories of its rivals than to defend its own, for most sovereigns had adopted the policy of disarming the great body of their subjects, fearing that, if they possessed arms, they would employ their strength in delivering themselves from the fiscal exactions of their princes.

During the reign of Romanus III., several parts of Asia Minor suffered very severely from earthquakes, locusts, famine, and pestilence; and in a stationary condition of society these calamities often destroy an amount of capital which is never replaced, and become, therefore, an immediate cause of a rapid depopulation.[1]

For two years before his death the emperor was afflicted by a disease which gradually wasted his frame, and caused his hair and beard to fall off. Many ascribed the disorder to the use of aphrodisiacs, which he took to an immoderate extent, in the hope of leaving an heir to the empire; but others believed that the disease originated in a slow poison administered either by the Empress Zoe or by John the orphanotrophos, who expected to raise his brother Michael to the throne. This John was a eunuch and a monk, who had entered the household of Romanus while he was yet in a private station, but who, after he became emperor, received the rank of orphanotrophos, or minister of charitable institutions, an office which proves the existence of a high degree of civilisation in the Byzantine administration. John had several brothers, one of whom, named Michael, commenced life as a goldsmith and money-changer, but while still young, received a place in the imperial household.[2] The face of Michael had the beauty of a perfect statue; his figure was full of grace, and

---

[1] Many of the inhabitants of Asia Minor were reduced to such distress as to sell their children as slaves, to save the lives of both parties.—Cedrenus, 732.

[2] John had two brothers, Constantine and George, who had been educated as doctors, and were, like himself, eunuchs; another Niketas, and a sister named Maria, married to Stephen, who was probably a shipbuilder, though called a caulker.— Cedrenus, 733.

his manners were attractive and dignified, but the young man was liable to sudden and violent attacks of epilepsy. Zoe, though upwards of fifty, is said to have fallen in love with her handsome servant, and to have carried on an intrigue with him by the assistance of his brother John. Romanus, though informed of his wife's conduct, paid no attention to the accusations, which the epilepsy of Michael seemed to render improbable.[1] In the mean time, the health of the emperor rapidly declined, and on the 11th of April 1034 he was taken from the bath in a dying state. While life yet remained, he was visited by Zoe and some of the officers of the court, but he was already speechless, and the empress quitted his side to take measures with the orphanotrophos for placing her epileptic paramour on the throne.

The moment that life was extinct in the body of Romanus III., Zoe assembled the officers of state in the palace, and invested Michael IV. with the imperial robes. He was immediately proclaimed Emperor of the Romans, and seated himself on the vacant throne beside Zoe. The promptitude with which this singular step of raising a domestic to the throne was conceived and executed prevented its encountering the slightest opposition. The Patriarch Alexios was summoned to the palace, where he learned the death of Romanus, and was, to his great astonishment, ordered to crown Michael the Paphlagonian, and celebrate his marriage with the widowed empress. The Patriarch would willingly have delayed making this open display of contempt for decency, but he saw Michael seated on the throne, and he was aware of the power and ability of his brother the orphanotrophos; so, admitting that reasons of state might overrule the dictates of virtue, he celebrated the marriage to avoid greater scandal. Thus a single night saw the aged Zoe the wife of two emperors, a widow and a bride, and Michael a menial and a sovereign. In order to render the sudden elevation of a domestic of the palace less strange in the distant provinces, John, who became his brother's prime-minister, despatched letters to all the governors, announcing that Michael had been selected by the deceased emperor for his successor, and crowned before his death.

The new emperor, though he ascended the throne in the

[1] Zonaras, ii. 233, says that the Emperor Romanus often called Michael to rub his feet when he was in bed with Zoe; and adds, Who can refrain from supposing that the hands of the young valet-de-chambre did not find an opportunity of touching also the feet of the empress?

most disgraceful manner, possessed some good qualities; and his natural good disposition appears neither to have been corrupted by his education as a money-changer, though calumny accused him of having been a fabricator of false coin; nor by his menial service at a corrupt and vicious court, of which he was a depraved member. After he mounted the throne, he soon lost the gaiety of disposition and tranquillity of mind which had increased the beauty of his figure and the grace of his manner. In spite of his constitutional infirmity, he was not destitute of considerable strength of character, and with his vices he united a strong sense of justice. The conduct of Zoe awakened in his mind feelings of distrust for his own safety, and he had spirit enough to dismiss from her service many of the eunuchs of her father's household, who seemed fit agents for new plots. His conscience was soon troubled by his treachery to his benefactor, and during his whole reign he suffered the pangs of remorse. He sought pardon from heaven by praying at the shrines of different saints, and he wasted the revenues of the empire in building monasteries and chapels, and in making lavish donations to priests and monks.[1] But as he continued to enjoy every advantage he had purchased by his crimes, the historians of his reign justly observe that he seemed to trust in the blindness of God for the forgiveness of his sins, as if divine justice could regard good deeds done at the expense of his subjects as any atonement for his private sins, or as any proof of sincere repentance on the part of the imperial sinner.[2] It must be owned that there is more truth in this observation than is agreeable either to the Papal or the Greek church. The anxiety produced by the cares of his situation soon increased the emperor's malady to such a degree that he became liable to sudden attacks; and even at public ceremonies, when he was seated on the throne, it was necessary to have the canopy of state hung round with curtains, which the chamberlains could let fall to hide him from the assembly as soon as his countenance indicated the approach of the terrible convulsions to which he was liable. When his malady seized him, his features were distorted into hideous expressions, his eyes rolled in wild agony, and he often struck his head against the wall until he fell exhausted on the floor. Though his malady was known to be of old

---

[1] He sent two pieces of gold to every priest, and one to every monk in all the provinces and islands of the empire, and he paid a piece of gold and four miliaresia at the baptism of every infant.—Cedrenus, 742.

[2] Cedrenus, 738. Glycas, 315.

date, the people persisted in regarding it as a judgment for his conduct to his benefactor Romanus, and appealed to it as a visible interposition of divine power, which abandoned him from time to time to be tormented by demons as a punishment for his treachery.[1]

Under these circumstances, it appears strange that Michael retained the throne with so little difficulty, and met with no dangerous rival. It is true, he possessed an able prime-minister in his brother, the orphanotrophos, whose interests were completely identified with his own, and who was a statesman competent to relieve him from all the details of administrative labour. Michael could entertain no distrust of his brother John, who could neither supplant him on the throne nor covet it for his posterity. But though the or-phanotroph was a faithful brother and an able minister, he was rapacious and tyrannical, and his administration, though serviceable to Michael, was injurious to the wealth and re-sources of the empire. He is said to have commenced life as a travelling doctor. While Romanus III. was in a private station, he intrusted John with the direction of his household; but after he became emperor, his intendant, with the modest title of Orphanotrophos, and in the humble garb of a monk, directed the whole business in the imperial cabinet. When his brother ascended the throne, he openly assumed the duties of president of the imperial council, and though suffering under the loathsome disease of a cancer in the mouth, the energetic eunuch humbled the aristocracy and ruled the people with a rod of iron.[2]

The administration of John the orphanotrophos deserves attention, not only from forming a principal feature in the reign of Michael IV., but also from marking the era of a mis-chievous change in the financial system of the Byzantine government. The taxes were everywhere augmented, and collected in a more arbitrary manner. An additional charge of from four to twenty byzants was imposed on every landed estate, according to its extent.[3] John's avidity compelled the collectors of the revenue in the provinces to increase their exactions, for when they were regular in their remittances to the treasury, and liberal in their presents to the orphanotro-phos, their oppressive conduct to the provincials was easily overlooked. This system of extortion caused several serious insurrections during the reign of Michael IV. At its com-

---

[1] Zonaras, ii. 239.   [2] *Ibid.*, ii. 235. Cedrenus, 737.   [3] Cedrenus, 742.

mencement the people of Antioch murdered the collector of taxes in that city, and, alarmed at the vengeance John was likely to take for such an offence, shut their gates against his brother Niketas, whom he sent to be their duke.[1] Niketas succeeded in entering the city, where his first act was to put to death a hundred of the inhabitants, and confiscate the wealth of eleven of the richest families. The people of Aleppo also expelled the imperial commissioner sent to reside among them for fiscal purposes, and their position secured them from the vengeance of the Byzantine minister. When Maria, the emperor's sister, and mother of the future emperor, Michael V., visited the city of Ephesus on a pilgrimage to the shrine of St. John the Evangelist, she was struck with compassion at the sight of the excessive misery she beheld in all the country on her road. When she returned to Constantinople, she urged her brother, the orphanotrophos, by every feeling of humanity and religion, to moderate the financial exactions which were rapidly depopulating the empire. The orphanotrophos replied with a smile—"You reason like a woman, ignorant of the necessities of the imperial treasury." His conduct, however, proved in the end unprofitable as a financial operation, for it caused an extensive insurrection of the Bulgarian and Sclavonian population, which cost more to suppress than had been wrung from them. Even the Greeks found their fiscal sufferings so great that they seemed disposed to join the Sclavonians in an attempt to throw off the Byzantine yoke. The collector of the revenues of the theme of Nicopolis was torn in pieces by the people, and the western parts of Greece welcomed the Bulgarian troops.[2]

A government so unpopular as that of Constantinople at this time required not only great talents to direct the central administration, but also a numerous body of firm supporters dispersed through all the provinces, interested to defend the system with all its abuses. This was effected by filling every office with men dependent on the family of Michael IV., and crowding the senate with creatures of the orphanotrophos. On the death of Niketas, Constantine, who was almost as able and active as his brother John, was appointed duke of Antioch, and became afterwards grand domestikos. George was appointed protovestiarios, their brother-in-law Stephen was intrusted with the command of the fleet, and subsequently named commander-in-chief in Sicily; while his son Michael, called, from his father's early profession, Kalaphates, or the caulker, was appointed by his uncle Cæsar, which was almost tantamount to proclaiming him heir-apparent to the Byzantine empire.

John even carried his ambition so far as to make an attempt to place himself at the head of the church as well as the state. Having gained over a party among the bishops to object to the appointment of the Patriarch Alexios as uncanonical, on the ground that he had been intruded on the church by the nomination of Basil II., John proposed to depose Alexios. The Patriarch, however, encountered the attack with courage. He openly discussed the question, and asked what measures were to be taken if all the ordinations which he had made, during the twelve years he had governed the church, were now unexpectedly declared void; and he boldly reminded John, that even the coronation and marriage of the reigning emperor would thus be pronounced null. This boldness alarmed the emperor: and John was compelled to lay aside the hope of becoming Patriarch during the life of Alexios.

Avarice was always a pervading fault of Byzantine society; and the rapacity of the clergy at this period often rivalled the extortions of the fiscal agents of the imperial administration. Two anecdotes, that contrast the moral feelings of a Greek bishop with those of a troop of Varangian soldiers, deserve notice.

Theophanes, the metropolitan of Thessalonica, carried his avarice so far that he held back the payment of the salaries due to the clergy of his chapter; and even during a year of famine refused to pay them their arrears. The Emperor Michael happened to visit Thessalonica, and the starving priests complained to him of the conduct of their bishop; but even the reproof of the emperor failed to obtain justice to the claims of the clergy. Michael then determined to punish the bishop; but, in order to expose his avarice and meanness in a public manner, he sent one of his household to borrow a hundred pounds' weight of gold, promising to repay the money immediately on his arrival at Constantinople. The bishop excused himself on the score of poverty, declaring, with the most solemn oaths, that he had only thirty pounds' weight of gold in his palace. The emperor immediately sent a commission to search the palace, and the sum of three thousand three hundred pounds' weight of gold was found. Theophanes was banished to a country farm, and Prometheos named his successor.[1]

The Varangian guard was dispersed in winter-quarters in the Thrakesian theme, where one of the soldiers, attempting to use violence on the person of a country-woman, she drew his sword and stabbed him. The man died on the spot; but as soon as the foreign troops heard the true history of the affair, instead of insisting on revenge, they applauded the woman's conduct, put her in possession of all the property her assailant had left in his quarters, and exposed his body, without burial, as if he had committed suicide.[2]

The only noble whose great wealth and high character excited the fears of Michael IV., and the jealousy of the orphanotrophos, was Constantine Dalassenos, the man who had been first selected as the husband of Zoe. Dalassenos was residing on his immense estates in the Armeniac theme when he heard of the election and marriage of Michael. The contemptuous words he was said to have uttered sank deep in the mind of the new emperor; and Dalassenos soon received an invitation from the orphanotrophos to visit Constantinople. He, however, declined trusting his person in the capital until he received a solemn assurance of his safety from the emperor. The guarantees he ventured to demand, and which Michael consented to give, afford a curious picture of the proud position of the great nobles, and a sad evidence of the prevalence of falsehood and treachery in the highest ranks of society. A member of the emperor's household, in high office, was sent to Dalassenos with a piece of the holy cross, with the napkin on which the figure of Christ was miraculously imprinted, with the autograph letter of Christ, and with the portrait of the Virgin Mary, painted by the hand of St. Luke; and on these sacred relics this officer swore that he had witnessed the Emperor Michael IV. take an oath that Constantine Dalassenos should suffer no injury if he visited the capital. On this assurance Dalassenos repaired to Constantinople, where he was well received by the emperor, and received the title of Proconsul. But shortly after, Niketas, the emperor's brother, who was duke of Antioch, accused him of being privy to the insurrection in which the imperial tax-gatherers had been slain; and on this improbable charge Dalassenos was confined in the island of Plate. His son-in-law Dukas was thrown into prison, and three nobles of great wealth had their estates confiscated,

[1] A.D. 1038. Cedrenus, 740.   [2] Ibid., 735.

for complaining that this proceeding was a violation of the emperor's oath.

During the Bulgarian rebellion in 1040, a conspiracy was formed to dethrone Michael. Many of the chief men in Constantinople were accused of being privy to the plot; and though they escaped with their lives, the fortunes of the wealthy were confiscated. Among the conspirators was Michael Keroularios, whose guilt compelled him to protect his person by becoming a monk. He afterwards attained the dignity of Patriarch, and displayed the same unquiet intriguing spirit at the head of the church as he had done in a private station.

Some seditious proceedings in the Asiatic army were suppressed by the emperor's brother, Constantine, who put out the eyes of several officers; and not venturing to punish their chief, Gregory the Taronite, who was a patrician, by a local tribunal, sent that dignitary to Constantinople, sewed up in the hide of a newly-slain ox, with only holes cut in it for his eyes, and for breathing.[1]

The military power of the empire was not tarnished by the conduct of Michael IV., though he was sneered at by the aristocracy as a Paphlagonian money-changer. The Saracens vainly endeavoured to recover the possessions which had been conquered by the Christians in Syria and Mesopotamia. The emperor's brother, Constantine, while governor of Antioch, displayed some military talents. He relieved Edessa when attacked by a Saracen army. The possession of Edessa by the Byzantine emperors was a source of continual annoyance to the Mohammedans, and their endeavours to regain it were incessant. In the year 1038, two years after it had been relieved by Constantine, they made use of a stratagem which has obtained immortality as an Eastern tale, though, as a fact, it remains buried in the dulness of Byzantine history. Varasvatzes, a Georgian, commanded in Edessa when twelve Arabians of rank presented themselves before the gates, attended by an escort of five hundred horse, and followed by a train of five hundred camels, declaring that they were going on an embassy to the emperor with rich presents from the caliph.[2] The wary Georgian, however, distrusted their numerous escort; and though he gave the chiefs a hospitable reception, and prepared for them a sumptuous entertainment in his palace, he

---

[1] Cedrenus, 747.
[2] This Varasvatzes, being an Iberian or Georgian, may have been a relation as well as a namesake of the founder of the monastery on Mount Athos.

ordered the escort and the train of camels to be encamped without the walls, and sharply watched. While the banquet was proceeding in the city, a poor Armenian, well versed in the Arabic language, offered his services to the travellers, and was permitted to wander about the encampment. While standing near the wicker baskets with which the camels had been laden, he overheard a man conversing with another, and perceived that a band of armed men, for the purpose of surprising Edessa, was the only present for the emperor which the camels carried. Hastening to the palace of the governor, he succeeded in revealing the secret to the watchful Georgian, who found an excuse for quitting his guests. A body of the garrison was sent to overpower the cavalry, while Varasvatzes, proceeding in person to the encampment, ordered the wicker baskets with the presents for the emperor to be opened, and slew the concealed soldiers as they were found. He then returned to his palace, where he ordered his guests to be seized, and informed them of the issue of their treachery. Eleven were put to death, and the chief, mutilated by the loss of his hands, ears, and nose, was sent to announce the result of the adventure to the court of Bagdat.[1]

The ravages of the Saracen fleets from Africa and Sicily were now more destructive than the incursions of their armies in Asia. Myra in Lycia, and many towns in the Cyclades, were plundered in 1034; but in the following year, when two separate fleets returned to renew these devastations, they were both defeated by the governors of the Thrakesian and Kibyrraiot themes, and the prisoners were treated as pirates, and impaled along the Asiatic coast from Adramytium to Strobilos.

To prevent the recurrence of these plundering expeditions, it was resolved to carry the war into Sicily with the greatest vigour. Maniakes, who had distinguished himself as governor of Vaspourakan, was charged with the task of expelling the Saracens from the island. Abulaphar, the emir of Sicily, having formed an alliance with the empire, received the title of Magistros; but his authority was contested by his brother Abucab, and Sicily was involved in a civil war. In the meantime, the independence of the Sicilian chiefs was so great, that many continued their piratical expeditions against the

---

[1] Compare the story of Ali Baba and the Forty Thieves, in the Arabian Nights, with Cedrenus, 742, and Zonaras, ii. 237. There is a story of armed men introduced into a place, concealed in skins, by a lady, who, in this way, succeeded in avenging the murder of her husband.—*Histoire du Grand Genghizcan*, by Petis de la Croix, 29.

Christians, in spite of the friendly relations established with the emirs. The civil war, however, enabled the Byzantine troops to enter Sicily as allies of Abulaphar, and they met with such success that the two brothers became alarmed, and, forgetting their differences, united to get rid of allies who promised soon to become masters. The moment appeared favourable for expelling the Saracens from the island ; and Michael ordered Maniakes, who commanded the Byzantine forces in Italy, to cross the straits of Messina, and sent a powerful fleet, under his brother-in-law Stephen, to assist the operations of the army. Among the troops that Maniakes had assembled in Calabria were three hundred Norman mercenaries, whose skill in arms had already obtained for them the highest military reputation, A.D. 1038.[1]

Messina was taken by storm, and though a large army of Saracens arrived from Africa to defend their countrymen, the Sicilians were completely defeated by Maniakes at a place called Remata. This victory enabled the Byzantine general to subdue the greater part of the island, and he employed the winter in constructing citadels in the towns he had conquered, in order to keep the inhabitants in check ; for the number of Saracen proprietors settled in the island, and their spirit of local independence, combined with the financial exigencies of the Byzantine administration, threatened the Byzantine government with a violent opposition. The importance of the exploits of Maniakes, and the solidity of his buildings, are attested by the renown of his name and the relics of his works. The thick walls and massive round towers of the citadel he constructed at Syracuse still bear the name of the Castle of Maniakes, and show us how much of the strength and stability of Roman architecture survived in the Byzantine system of fortification in the eleventh century.[2] The site of another of his works retains his name, situated on the roots of Mount Etna ; but all the remains have disappeared in constructing the modern town of Bronte.[3]

In the spring of 1040, another African army arrived in Sicily, to support the Mohammedan domination. Maniakes made his dispositions for a battle with his usual talent, and,

---

[1] Cedrenus, 741. *Saracenicarum Rerum epit. a Carusio.—Biblioth. Hist. Regni Siciliæ*, i. 108.

[2] Two fine antique bronze rams, of the natural size, which adorned the entrance of the castle of Maniakes, are still preserved in the Palazzo Reale at Palermo.

[3] Bronte is inhabited by an Albanian colony.—Gally Knight, *Normans in Sicily*, 166.

confident of success, he ordered Stephen, the admiral of the fleet, to make dispositions for cutting off the retreat of the Africans. The Byzantine army was worthy of its general, and the invaders were completely routed at a place called Draginas; but the incapacity and misconduct of Stephen allowed the beaten troops to escape on board their fleet, and put to sea. Maniakes was indignant at this proof of negligence or cowardice. On meeting Stephen, he lost all command over his temper, and reproached the emperor's brother-in-law with his unfitness for his station; and when the admiral ventured to reply in an insolent manner, the proud Maniakes, re-collecting the caulker, and forgetting the prince, struck him on the head with the seiromast in his hand.[1] This outbreak of passion caused the loss of Sicily. Stephen complained to the orphanotroph of the aristocratic insolence of Maniakes, and accused him of a design to rebel; which appeared no improbable accusation, when brought against a man who dared to strike the emperor's brother-in-law in the presence of many officers of the army.[2] Maniakes was arrested, and sent prisoner to Constantinople, and Stephen was appointed his successor in the government of Sicily. Under a leader so incompetent, the affairs of the Christians soon fell into confusion. Fresh bands of Saracens arrived from Africa; the Byzantine authorities were driven from the towns conquered by Maniakes; the army under the command of Stephen was everywhere worsted; and in a short time Messina alone preserved its allegiance to the government at Constantinople, being preserved by the valour of its governor Katakalon.

The Patzinaks renewed their invasions of the European provinces in the year 1034, when they extended their ravages almost to the walls of Thessalonica. Two years after, they again invaded the empire and wasted Thrace with unusual barbarity, carrying off five imperial officers of high rank as prisoners.

In the year 1040, Servia, which had submitted to the Emperor Basil II., became so discontented with the fiscal

---

[1] The seiromast, according to the classic meaning, was a kind of javelin. But the three weapons which hung at the saddle-bow of every Byzantine officer, at this period, were a battle-axe, a mace-at-arms, and a hooked instrument for catching the enemy's bridle. Such instruments formed the perfect equipment of a Mameluke to the end of the last century, and may still be seen at times exposed for sale at Cairo and Damascus.

[2] The family of Maniakes is mentioned as early as the reign of Michael III.; and the great influence of the commander-in-chief in Sicily is shown by the rivalry that existed between him and Romanos Skleros in Asia Minor.—Georg. Mon. 533. Leo Gramm. 461. Cedrenus, 727, 731.

measures of the orphanotrophos, that the people rose in rebellion and shook off the Byzantine yoke. Stephen Bogislav placed himself at the head of his countrymen and expelled the imperial authorities. The success of his rebellion was promoted by the seizure of a vessel, with a thousand pounds' weight of gold belonging to the imperial treasury, which was driven on the coast of Illyria. The emperor demanded the restitution of this sum, and when it was refused, sent George Provatas with a large army to reduce Stephen to obedience. The Byzantine troops were defeated through the incapacity of their general, and the independence of Servia firmly established and tacitly recognised.[1]

The fiscal exactions of John the orphanotrophos produced another rebellion, which threatened to deprive the empire of the fruits of the long campaigns of Basil II. The land-tax or tribute of the Sclavonian population had been left, by their conqueror, on the footing it had been established by Samuel when he founded the kingdom of Achrida, and consisted of a moderate payment in kind annually for each yoke of oxen and each strema of vineyard.[2] Michael IV., at the advice of his brother, ordered a tax to be levied in money in lieu of the established payments, and the discontent caused by the measure prepared the population for revolt. While everything proclaimed an approaching rebellion, a Bulgarian slave, named Peter Deleanos, fled from his master at Constantinople, and, on reaching Belgrade on the Danube, announced himself to be the grandson of Samuel, king of Achrida. He was soon joined by numbers of discontented Bulgarians, and was proclaimed king. His hopes of being able to resist the power of the Byzantine government lay in the Sclavonian population of Macedonia and Epirus, not in the Bulgarians of the plains between the Danube and Mount Hæmus. He succeeded in making himself master of many strong places in the theme of Dyrrachium, and he commenced the revolution by murdering all the Greeks who fell into his hands. Basil Synnadenos, the governor of Dyrrachium, advanced against him, hoping to extinguish the revolt in its birth; but some intrigues at Constantinople caused him to lose his place, and one of his officers,

---

[1] Cedrenus, 745. Provatas, like many generals in the tenth and eleventh centuries, was a eunuch.
[2] See before, p. 353. Cedrenus, 747. The number of yokes of oxen was a common basis of taxation, and was adopted by the Arabs in Sicily and the Normans in Italy. Robert Guiscard engaged to pay twelve deniers of Pavia to the Pope for each yoke of oxen in his states.—Baronius, *Ann. Eccl.*, A.D. 1059, tom. xvii. 170.

who was named his successor, proved incapable of executing the plan of operations already traced out. The new governor threw everything into confusion; and a large body of troops in the province consisting of Sclavonians, they cast off their allegiance to the emperor, and proclaimed one of their own officers, Teichomeros, king of Bulgaria. Deleanos and Teichomeros agreed to act as allies, and divide the territory from which they might be able to expel the Byzantine officers; but when the two Sclavonian armies formed a junction, Deleanos succeeded in persuading the soldiers to put Teichomeros to death in order to preserve the unity of the kingdom.

The rebels were now sufficiently powerful to advance against Thessalonica, where the Emperor Michael had fixed his residence, in order to pay his devotions at the celebrated shrine of St. Demetrius. Alarmed at the threatening aspect of the revolution, and the unprepared state of the central authorities in Macedonia and Greece, he hastened to Constantinople to expedite warlike preparations, leaving a Bulgarian named Ibatzes in charge of his baggage, with orders to follow him to the capital. Ibatzes fled to Deleanos, and delivered all the treasure intrusted to his care to the new monarch. In the mean time, Alusianos, the younger brother of Ladislas, the last king of Achrida, witnessing the rapid progress of the rebellion, and disgusted with the avarice and injustice of the orphanotrophos, quitted Theodosiopolis, of which he was governor, and joined Deleanos in his camp at Ostrovos. He was intrusted with the command of a division of the Bulgarian army, and ordered to undertake the siege of Thessalonica, where he conducted his military operations so ill, that he was very soon defeated by the imperial troops, and lost about 15,000 men. The splendour of the victory was of course attributed to St. Demetrius, who was reported to have taken the command of the Greeks in person. The failure before Thessalonica was in some degree compensated by the capture of Dyrrachium, which had already fallen into the hands of Kaukanos, one of the Bulgarian generals.

While these operations were going on in the north, a Sclavonian army under Anthimos invaded Greece, and endeavoured to rouse their countrymen in the Peloponnesus to take up arms. The inhabitants of Thebes, which was then a wealthy and populous manufacturing city, boldly took the field to defend the cause of the Greek population, but were defeated

o

with great loss.[1] The oppressive conduct of the Byzantine fiscal agents had been so general, that the Greeks were in some places more inclined to favour the Bulgarian revolution than to support the central government of Constantinople. The people in the theme of Nicopolis murdered Koutzomytes, the tax-collector of the province, and invited the Bulgarians to their assistance, who easily rendered themselves masters of all western Greece. The city of Naupaktos (Lepanto) was alone preserved in its allegiance by the presence of its garrison.

It was fortunate for the Byzantine empire that the political government of the rebels was directed by men destitute of talent and honesty, for the minds of the Greek population were in general so alienated, and the amount of the imperial forces in Greece was so trifling, that it would not have been a difficult matter to have subdued the whole country. But in place of attending to the public cause, Deleanos and Alusianos turned all their attention to intrigue. The first felt that, if he could not destroy his rival, he should lose his throne; and the other feared that his royal blood and his recent defeat would cost him his life. At last Alusianos found an opportunity of seizing the king by treachery, and, putting out his sovereign's eyes, he assumed the vacant crown. But bred up amidst the luxuries of Byzantine civilisation, and caring little for Sclavonian nationality, he preferred enduring the insolence of the orphano-trophos to encountering the hardships of a revolutionary war. He deserted his countrymen, resigned the title of king, and made his peace with the court of Constantinople.

The Emperor Michael IV. was now suffering under a severe attack of dropsy, in addition to repeated paroxysms of his old malady; but he displayed the greatest energy from the moment that the Bulgarian rebellion broke out. He was well aware that he could not hope to survive for any length of time, but his mind seemed to gain vigour from his anxiety to transmit the sceptre he held without degradation to his successor. He assembled an army at Thessalonica, and accompanied its movements, though his disease had made such progress that he was lifted from his horse every evening utterly exhausted. The Bulgarian army, left without a leader by the treachery

---

[1] Cedrenus, 747. The great wealth, commercial enterprise, and high state of culture at Thebes, during this flourishing period of the Byzantine empire, may be estimated from the description Benjamin of Tudela gives us of the city subsequently, in a declining period. It had even then 2000 Jewish inhabitants, who were eminent manufacturers of silk and purple cloth : and scholars, whose equal was only to be found at Constantinople. —j. 47, edit. Asher.

of Alusianos, was defeated and destroyed. The blind Deleanos and the deserter Ibatzes were both taken prisoners, and in one campaign the dying emperor reduced all the Bulgarians and Sclavonians who had taken arms to submission, and restored tranquillity in Macedonia, Epirus, and Greece. This vigorous and noble conduct closed the reign of Michael. He returned to Constantinople to die.

The people, who looked on his original malady as a divine judgment, were confirmed in this superstition by the prodigies they witnessed during his reign. Hailstones fell which killed men at their work; earthquakes followed one another with fearful rapidity; meteors blazed in the sky so bright, that the stars were rendered invisible at midnight; and a pestilence visited various parts of the empire with such terrible mortality that the living found it difficult to bury the dead.[1] Taxation also began to press with increasing severity on a stationary society, so that, in spite of Michael's charitable works—his building churches, monasteries, and hospitals—his death was awaited with impatience by his subjects, in the hope that it would deliver the empire from the effects of divine wrath. Michael himself participated in the superstition of the people, and when he felt his end approaching, he retired from the imperial palace to the monastery of St. Anarghyros, where he assumed the habit of a monk. He died a few days after, on the 10th of December 1041, having reigned seven years and eight months.[2]

The Empress Zoe now assumed the direction of the administration as the lawful heiress of the empire, and in virtue of the will of her deceased husband, and she attempted to carry on her government with the assistance of the eunuchs of her household. But a few days' experience of the toils which were imposed on the sovereign by the Byzantine system of administration soon showed her both the inconveniences and dangers of her position. Though the Athenian Irene had ruled the empire as absolute mistress for some years, and several female regents had presided over the government at different times, still the traditional aversion of the Roman

---

[1] Cedrenus, 735. Walsh, *Residence at Constantinople*, ii. 332, describes a similar hail-storm in modern times. The hailstones perforated the tiles of the roof, and were solid lumps of ice about five inches in circumference.

[2] Cedrenus, 749. It was during the reign of Michael IV. that Robert the Devil, duke of Normandy, visited Constantinople on his pilgrimage to Jerusalem, and rebuked the pride and insolence of the Byzantine court. The anecdote is given by Ducange, *Gloss. med. et inf. Latinitatis*, v. "*Bancus.*" *Medieval Greece and Trebizond*, 83.

state to female sway was not entirely extinct.[1] Zoe, therefore, immediately perceived the necessity of giving the empire a male sovereign, and she took only three days to choose between adopting a son or marrying a husband. Michael the son of Stephen, the unlucky governor of Sicily, had been raised to the rank of Cæsar by his uncle Michael IV., and he had the reputation of being a man of capacity and energy; but his uncle, who seems to have formed a more correct judgment of his disposition than the world at large, had seen so much to distrust in his character that he had excluded him from all share of public business, and given him no hope of mounting the throne as his successor. Zoe, too, displayed more confidence in his talents than in his principles; for before placing the crown on his head, she required him to swear in the most solemn manner that he would ever regard her as his benefactress, and treat her as his mother. She also required him to banish the orphanotrophos, Constantine the domestikos, and George the protovestiarios. Michael promised everything and obtained the crown.

But as soon as he felt himself firmly established in power, he revealed his meanness of soul, and treated his benefactress with insolence as well as ingratitude. He recalled the orphanotrophos to his counsels, and conferred on him the high dignity of despot; but he soon neglected his advice, and placed all his confidence in Constantine, whom he honoured with the rank of nobilissimus.[2] He then began to intrigue against the Patriarch Alexios. After receiving the Patriarch with honour, and bestowing on him a donation of four lb. of gold, he appointed a meeting with him at a monastery on the Bosphorus, intending to exclude him from the city, and get a new Patriarch elected during his absence. At last he carried his presumption so far as to send the Empress Zoe to Prince's Island, and compel her to adopt the monastic habit. But when the people heard of this last instance of his ingratitude, which he had the insolence to announce in a public proclamation, their fury burst through every restraint. They assailed the imperial heralds and paraded the city, exclaiming that "the caulker" had ceased to reign, and that they would scatter his bones abroad like dust. An assembly was held in the Church of St. Sophia, to which Theodora was brought from the monastery of Petrion, and proclaimed empress with her sister.

---

[1] The aversion to female succession is mentioned in the fifth century, on the death of Theodosius II.—Priscus, 151, edit. Bonn.   [2] Zonaras, ii. 243.

In the mean time the emperor, alarmed at the progress of the sedition, brought Zoe back to the palace, and attempted to pacify the people by persuading her to appear at a balcony overlooking the hippodrome. The sight of Michael, however, who endeavoured to address the assembly, revived the popular fury, and preparations were made to storm the palace. The emperor now showed himself a coward as well as a tyrant, and wished to fly to the monastery of Studion. His uncle Constantine, however, made him understand that his only hope of life was in preserving the throne, and roused him to take measures for defending the palace.

The attack was made on the following day, and after a long defence the people, who assaulted it in three divisions from the hippodrome, the court of guard, and the tchukanisterion, stormed the palace.[1] Katakalon, who saved Messina, had just returned from Sicily, and happening to be at the palace, directed the defensive arrangements, while Constantine the nobilissimus, assembling all his household in arms, added to the strength of the guards.[2] The fury of the people overcame all resistance; but it is said that three thousand were slain before they forced their entrance into the interior of the building.[3] Everything was then plundered, and the public registers were destroyed. Michael V. and his uncle Constantine succeeded in escaping to the monastery of Studion during the confusion. Zoe immediately assumed the ensigns of the imperial power, and endeavoured to force her sister Theodora back into retirement, but the senate and people insisted that the two sisters should reign conjointly. Though Zoe was eager to tyrannise over her sister, she showed a disposition to spare her own tyrant Michael. She was, however, compelled by Theodora and the senate to join in his condemnation, for the populace shouted incessantly, " Let him be impaled, let him be crucified, let his eyes be put out!" Officers were therefore sent to drag him from his asylum and

---

[1] The tzukan was the favourite game of Byzantine gentlemen. Every city had its tchukanisterion.—Ducange, *Glossarium med. et inf. Græcitatis;* and *Medieval Greece and Trebizond,* 391.

[2] Cedrenus, 751. The wealth accumulated by Constantine in the public service, which could enable him to arm a numerous household, shows us how much the Roman aristocratical organisation of society still existed in the Byzantine empire.

[3] It may be remarked that the Byzantine historians generally report "that it is said three thousand persons perished" in every sedition. The number alludes to the three thousand Israelites slain by the Levites, who rushed through the camp with drawn swords to avenge the idolatry of the golden calf.—Exodus, xxxii. 28. The *Septuagint* and the *Iliad* were the principal sources of literary inspiration at Constantinople for some centuries.

put out his eyes. When placed beside his uncle in the Sigma to suffer his sentence, he meanly entreated the executioners to put out the eyes of Constantine first; and that daring eunuch submitted to the punishment with the greatest firmness, while the dethroned emperor excited the contempt of the people by his cries and moans. They were then sent to pass the remainder of their lives as monks in the monastery of Elegmos. Michael the Caulker sate on the imperial throne four months and five days.[1]

The joint government of Zoe and Theodora lasted less than two months. We need not wonder, therefore, that it is praised by all historians, for the salutary effects of a violent display of popular indignation were sure to extend over the whole period. Byzantine officials moderated their exactions in alarm, and the two empresses were reminded by the empty chambers of their palace that public opinion was not always to be despised with impunity. In order to secure the support of the imperial council of state, and of the municipality of Constantinople—or of the Roman senate and people, as these bodies proudly styled themselves—numerous promotions were made and large donations lavished. An ordinance was published prohibiting the sale of official situations, for this species of traffic had been rendered an ordinary source of revenue by the eunuchs of the imperial household, who had possessed themselves of most of the highest offices of the state. At the same time strict orders were issued to enforce the administration of justice with impartiality, and to restrain oppressive conduct on the part of the fiscal agents of government.

The unprincipled manner in which the adventurers and eunuchs, who had been introduced into the public service since the death of Basil II., appropriated the funds in the imperial treasury to their own use, deserves particular notice. Great deficiencies were detected in the accounts of the short financial administration of the nobilissimus Constantine; and the ministers of Zoe and Theodora found it necessary to examine him personally, in order to discover how the money had been employed. The blind monk, knowing that he had no chance of ever quitting the monastery in which he was confined, candidly informed the new ministers that he had abstracted the sum of 5300 lb. of gold from the treasury for his own use, and deposited it in a vaulted cistern attached to his palace, near the Church of the Holy Apostles.[2]

---

[1] Cedrenus, 751. Zonaras, ii. 246.   [2] Cedrenus, 753.

The two sisters appeared always together at the meetings of the senate, and when they held courts of justice, or gave public audiences; but it was evident their union would not prove of long duration. Zoe was jealous of her sister, and though she was eager to be relieved of the burden of public business, she was determined not to allow Theodora to conduct it alone —probably the more so, because Theodora showed great aptitude in state affairs, and took great pleasure in performing her administrative duties. Zoe, therefore, bethought herself of looking out for a third husband, to whom she might resign the throne, and thus deprive her sister of the influence she was rapidly acquiring. Zoe was now sixty-two years old, and, the age of passion having passed away, her memory reverted to the merits of Constantine Dalassenos, who had been destined by her father to be her first husband. She invited that proud noble to an interview in the imperial palace, in order to judge of his character before revealing her purpose. But in place of the splendid and gallant nobleman of her imagination, she met a stern old man, who expressed strongly his disapprobation of the whole system of the imperial administration since the death of Basil II.; who openly blamed the vices of the court, and hardly concealed his contempt for her own conduct. Such a husband might have infused new vigour into the lethargic system of government, but Zoe was not inclined to submit her actions to the control of so severe a master.[1]

She turned, therefore, to one of her former lovers, Constantine Artoklinas; but when his wife heard of the honour to which he was destined, she displayed none of the meekness of the wife of Romanus III. Artoklinas suddenly sickened and died, and his wife was supposed to have poisoned him, either from jealousy, or from her aversion to be immured in a convent. Zoe was easily consoled. She again selected an old admirer, Constantine Monomachos, who had been banished to Mitylene by the jealousy of Michael IV., but recalled on the accession of Zoe and Theodora, and named Judge of Greece.[2] A swift-rowing galley was despatched to convey him to the capital, where, on his arrival, he was invested with the

---

[1] Zonaras, ii. 246.

[2] Ducange, *Notæ in Cedrenum*, 52, edit. Venet. Codinus, *De Off.* 52. Gibbon says, "The epithet of Monomachus (the single combatant) must have been expressive of his valour and victory in some public or private quarrel;" but it was merely a hereditary surname, and had no more relation to the qualities of the individual than the surnames of Skleros, Kekaumenos, and many others of the same period, or than Champion or Boxer in the present day.

imperial robes. His marriage with Zoe was celebrated by one
of the clergy, for the Patriarch Alexios declined officiating at
a third marriage of the empress, which was doubly uncanonical,
since both the bridegroom and the bride had been twice married. Nevertheless, on the day after the marriage ceremony,
the Patriarch crowned the emperor with the usual solemnities.

The reign of Constantine IX. demands more attention from
the historian of the Byzantine empire than the worthless character of the man or the feeble policy of his cabinet appears
at first glance to require. It typifies the moral degradation
into which Byzantine society had fallen, for his vices were
tolerated, if not approved of, by a large portion of his subjects. His open profligacy expresses the immorality of the
age; his profusion indicated the general manner of living
among all classes of his subjects; and while he destroyed
the civil organisation of the government, and undermined
the discipline of the Roman armies, they wasted the national
capital and diminished the resources of the empire.

The domestic profligacy of Zoe had been concealed from
the public by the household of eunuchs that surrounded her,
and by whom the inhabitants of the palace were kept completely separated from the world without its walls. But her
third husband, Constantine Monomachos, was so indifferent to
all feelings of self-respect as to make an open parade of his
vices at the public ceremonies of the court. After he had
buried two wives, he obtained the favour of a beautiful young
widow belonging to the powerful and wealthy family of Skleros.
She was the granddaughter of that celebrated Bardas, who
had disputed the empire with Basil II., and the daughter
of Romanos Skleros, the brother-in-law of the Emperor
Romanus III. The eminence of her family eclipsed the name
of her husband, and she was called Skleraina. Infatuated by
love for Constantine Monomachos, she openly assumed the
position of his mistress, and shared his banishment at Mitylene.
It is, however, only justice to the character of the fair Skleraina
to observe that, in the opinion of the bigoted members of
the Greek church, her position of mistress, as being less uncanonical, was more respectable than it would have been had
she become the third wife of her lover. When Zoe raised
Constantine to the throne, he bargained to retain his mistress,
and the people of Constantinople were treated to the singular
spectacle of an emperor of the Romans making his public
appearance with two female companions dignified with the title

of empress, one as his wife and the other as his mistress.
Skleraina was regularly saluted with the title of Augusta, and
installed in apartments in the palace, with a separate court as
empress, and a rank equal to that held by Theodora. Zoe and
she lived together on the best terms, and the want of jealousy
of the aged wife is less surprising than her want of self-respect.
The disposition of the beautiful Skleraina was extremely
amiable, and she was respected to a certain degree for the
constancy of her attachment to her lover in his misfortunes,
which contrasted with the behaviour of Zoe, who had never
allowed any passion, however violent, to retain permanent hold
of her heart. She soon lost whatever popularity she enjoyed
with the people, on account of the lavish expenditure of the
emperor. She had possessed an ample fortune when Constantine was an impoverished exile, and her wealth had
been consumed to gratify her lover's luxurious habits. The
good-natured sensualist now strove to repay Skleraina with unbounded liberality. Her apartments were rendered more
splendid than any Constantinople had yet seen; her elegant
manners created round her a graceful court, which seemed
more brilliant from its contrast with the dull ceremony that
reigned in the apartments of Zoe and Theodora. As the
populace can rarely be so completely corrupted in their moral
feelings as their superiors, the extravagant expenditure of the
emperor on his concubine awakened the public indignation.
They felt the financial oppression more grievous when they
saw their money employed to insult their feelings, and they
began to fancy that the lives of Zoe and Theodora might be in
danger in a palace where vice was honoured, and where secret
murder was supposed to be an ordinary occurrence.

Constantine IX. had pursued his career of voluptuous
extravagance for two years, without a thought of his duties
either to God or to his subjects, when he was suddenly
awakened to a sense of the danger of his situation by a furious
sedition of the people. On the feast of the Forty Martyrs it
was usual for the emperor to walk in solemn procession to the
Church of our Saviour in Chalke, from whence he proceeded
on horseback to the Church of the Martyrs. But as the procession was about to move from the palace, a cry was raised,
"Down with Skleraina; we will not have her for empress!
Zoe and Theodora are our mothers—we will not allow them to
be murdered!" The fury of the populace was ungovernable,
and they made an attempt to lay hands on the emperor, to

tear him to pieces. Many persons were trodden to death in the tumult, and Constantine was in imminent danger of his life, when the sudden appearance of Zoe and Theodora at a balcony drew off the attention of the crowd, and allowed the emperor to escape. The sisters assured the people that they were not in the smallest danger, and as no leaders stepped forward to direct the populace, tranquillity was easily restored; but the emperor did not accompany the procession to the Church of the Forty Martyrs in the year 1044.[1]

There are some articles in the expenditure of Constantine IX. which indicate that he lived in an enlightened age, and reigned over a civilised people. To solace his conscience, he constructed houses of refuge for the aged and hospitals for the poor, as well as monasteries and churches for the clergy. He also raised the most distinguished literary men of his time to high offices.[2] He completed the rebuilding the Church of the Holy Sepulchre at Jerusalem, and augmented the endowments of the clergy of St. Sophia's, in order that service might be performed with due pomp every day.[3]

In order to fill the treasury, when he had drained it by his lavish expenditure, he adopted a measure which proved ruinous to the empire, and was an immediate cause of the success of the Seljouk Turks in Asia Minor. The frontier provinces of the East had been exempted from the payment of direct taxes to the central government, and the dependent states in alliance with the empire in that quarter had been relieved from tribute, on the condition of maintaining bodies of regular militia constantly under arms, to defend their territories. Constantine IX. consented to relieve them from these obligations, on their paying a sum of money into his exhausted treasury. By this unpolitic proceeding, an army of fifty thousand men on the Iberian and Armenian frontiers was disbanded, and the Asiatic provinces left open to the invasion of the Seljouk Turks, whose power was rapidly increasing. The money remitted to Constantinople was quickly despatched in luxury and vice.[4]

The death of the Patriarch Alexios, who died in the year 1043, after having ruled the Byzantine church upwards of

---

[1] Cedrenus, 761.—9th March.

[2] Michael Constantine Psellos, who for his much scribbling was called πολο-γραφώτατος, and who was really the last man of superior learning Constantinople produced, was raised to office by Constantine IX. and took a considerable part in public affairs until the death of Michael VII.—Schoell, *Geschichte der Griech. Litteratur von Pinder*, iii. 269, 419.

[3] The friendly relations that existed between Constantine IX. and the court of the Fatimite caliph is noticed by Cedrenus, 789.   [4] Cedrenus, 790. Zonaras, ii. 260

seventeen years with some reputation, afforded a sad confirmation of the depraved state of society, and the frightful extent to which avarice had corrupted the Eastern clergy. The emperor, who knew that the Patriarch had heaped up considerable sums of money in a monastery he had constructed, sent and seized this treasure, which was found to amount to the sum of 2500 lb. of gold.[1] Michael Keroularios, who had been compelled to enter a monastery on account of the part he had taken in a conspiracy against Michael IV., was appointed Patriarch, and distinguished himself by his violent proceedings in the disagreement between the sees of Rome and Constantinople.

Theodora, though by her sister's marriage she was deprived of all direct influence over the administration, still possessed the power of violating the law with impunity. John the orphanotrophos was seized by her order while living tranquilly in banishment at Marykatos, and deprived of sight. It was said by some that this cruel deed was executed without the emperor's permission, but others attributed it to revenge on the part of Constantine, who ascribed his long exile at Mitylene to the malice of the orphanotrophos. We must recollect, however, that Theodora was of a sterner and more unforgiving temper than her brother-in-law, and that she had probably good reason for complaining of the conduct of the orphanotrophos, even when he was minister of Romanus III. In any case, it is a sufficient proof of the disorganisation of the administration that the act is ascribed to Theodora by Zonaras, who was himself a minister, and that it was inflicted without even the formality of a legal sentence.[2]

A weak and lavish court, surrounded by a proud and wealthy aristocracy, under the government of an absolute sovereign, is the hotbed of rebellion. Constantine IX. had ascended the throne, without any merit of his own, by the shameless preference of a worthless old woman. It is not surprising, therefore, that many nobles should have attempted to wrench the sceptre from his hand; but it is a strong proof of the original excellence of the organisation of the Byzantine system of administration that all these attempts proved unsuccessful. The conservative tendencies of society, which had grown out of the system of government, presented a

---

[1] Cedrenus, 758. Zonaras, ii. 250. It is important to notice these large sums accumulated in private hands, in the Byzantine empire, at a time when the wealthiest sovereign of Western Europe could with difficulty extort from his subjects the smallest sums. [2] Zonaras, ii. 251. Cedrenus, 758.

passive resistance to all revolutionary endeavours to disturb the established order of things. A sedition in Cyprus, however, occurred even before Constantine IX. mounted the throne. No sooner was it known throughout the empire that Michael V. had been dethroned by a popular insurrection, and that the government of Zoe and Theodora was not likely to prove of long duration, than Theophilos Erotikos, the governor of Cyprus, formed the project of gaining possession of that rich island for himself during the threatened confusion. Theophilos was a turbulent and presumptuous man, of ability far inferior to his ambition. Two years previous to his rebellion in Cyprus he had been driven from Servia, which he then governed, by Stephen Bogislav; he now incited the people to attack Theophylaktos, the intendant of finance, on the ground that this officer collected the taxes with undue rigour. Theophylaktos was slain, and the governor expected that, in removing a check on his plot, he had succeeded in compromising the inhabitants so far as to secure their support to his ambitious project. Constantine IX., however, immediately on assuming the government, despatched a force to suppress the revolt, and as the Cypriots had no idea of waging war against the central government at Constantinople, or of aiding Theophilos to assume the imperial crown, they offered no resistance, and the governor was arrested and sent a prisoner to the capital. The insurrection was considered so contemptible that Theophilos was exhibited to the people at the public games in a female dress, and escaped with the confiscation of his estates.

The rebellion of Maniakes, which occurred in the first year of the reign of Constantine IX., would in all probability have deprived him of the throne, had it not been suddenly terminated by one of those strokes of fortune by which Heaven deranges the wisest plans and destroys the most powerful expeditions. Maniakes was released from confinement at the death of Michael IV., and reappointed to the command of the Byzantine possessions in Italy. He found the Italians everywhere in rebellion, and the chief military power in the hands of the Norman mercenaries, who had formed themselves into an independent community: the cities of Bari, Brindisi, Otranto, and Tarento were alone occupied by Byzantine garrisons. The moment Maniakes landed, he commenced his military operations with the vigour and skill for which he was so remarkable. He defeated the Normans in a well-contested battle between Monopoli and Matera; and as these two towns had shown a hostile disposition, he allowed them to be plundered by his troops, and even ordered two hundred of the principal inhabitants of the latter to be decapitated for favouring the Normans. The animosity between the Greeks and Italians was now so violent that the success of the Normans and the separation of the two churches were produced rather by the hatred of the parties than by the superior valour of the Normans, or by any religious arguments of the clergy. Though the Italians were destitute of the virtue and endurance necessary to gain their independence, they possessed at this time an able and active leader, Arghyros, the son of Mel, and it was in moral far more than in military qualities that they were inferior to the northern mercenaries.

The progress of Maniakes was suddenly arrested by the news that Constantine Monomachos, the lover of Skleraina, was named emperor, for Maniakes was engaged in violent contests with her brother, Romanos Skleros, concerning the limits of their hereditary estates in Asia Minor. Romanos, who had the courage to contend personally with the fiery Maniakes, as his father had contended with Prusianos, the Bulgarian prince, had received some deep insults, for which he now avenged himself by seducing his enemy's wife and seizing the disputed property. Maniakes knew that there was no hope of obtaining justice from the emperor, over whom Skleraina exercised unbounded influence; he resolved, therefore, to administer justice in his own cause. He immediately recruited his army with all the Norman and other mercenaries he was able to collect in Italy, and proclaimed himself emperor. Constantine IX., the moment he heard of the rebellion, sent an officer with a body of troops to arrest Maniakes, expecting that it would be as easy to do so on this occasion as it had proved in Sicily. But Maniakes fell on the Byzantine troops at the moment of their arrival, routed them, and, gaining possession of the treasure they had brought, embarked his own army at Otranto, and landed at Dyrrachium, in the month of February, 1043. The emperor sent an army, under the command of one of Zoe's eunuchs, named Stephen, to arrest the progress of the rebel. Maniakes, despising the unwarlike character of his opponent, attacked the imperial army near Ostrovos. His charge bore down everything, and victory seemed assured to his standard, when an arrow from an unknown hand pierced him to the heart.

His death left his followers without a cause, as well as without a leader, and they instantly retired from the field of battle. The Norman, Frank, and Italian mercenaries in the rebel army entered the Byzantine service, and continued for many years to make a prominent figure in the wars of the empire.[1] The victorious eunuch made his public entry into Constantinople mounted on a white charger, with the head of Maniakes borne before him on a lance.

Stephen's accidental success awakened his ambition, and when he found, on his return to the capital, that the emperor did not estimate his services as highly as he considered was their due, he began to plot against him. He selected Leo, the governor of Melitene, as the future emperor, but his intrigues were discovered. Leo and his son Lampros were deprived of sight, but Stephen was only immured in a monastery after his estates were confiscated.

In the year 1047, Constantine IX. was again in danger of losing his throne by the rebellion of his own relation, Leo Tornikios. The character of Leo rendered him extremely popular at Adrianople, where he resided. To remove him from the seat of his influence, the emperor named him governor of Iberia, where he was soon accused of aspiring to the throne. Constantine IX., jealous of his talents and popularity, ordered him to resign his governorship and adopt the monastic life; but the friends of Tornikios put him on his guard in time to enable him to escape to Adrianople, where he was immediately proclaimed emperor. At the head of the garrison of that city, and such motley forces as he could assemble on the spur of the occasion, he marched to Constantinople. He hoped to render himself master of the capital by the favour of the citizens, counting more on their aversion to the emperor's conduct than on the military force under his own orders. But the inhabitants feared a military revolution far more than they hated their sovereign. Constantine also, on receiving the first information of the revolt, despatched orders to a Saracen eunuch, who commanded a corps of Byzantine troops in Iberia, to march rapidly to the capital, with all the forces he could concentrate on the way.

Tornikios encamped before the walls in the month of September, and being unable to invest the line of the forti-

---

[1] These mercenaries formed at first a corps called Maniakatoi.—*J. Skylitzæ Curopalatæ Historia*, at the end of Cedrenus, 854. Their numbers were considerable in the army of Nicephorus Briennius, defeated by the Emperor Alexius, during the reign of Nicephorus III. (Botaneiates) in the year 1078.—Anna Comnena, 11.

fications from the port to the Sea of Marmora, established himself before the gate of Blachern. The emperor, who, in spite of his warlike surname, was utterly ignorant of military affairs, ordered a party of a thousand men to intrench themselves outside this gate. The operation was undertaken against the advice of his military counsellors; and, to see the result of his own tactics, the emperor placed himself in a balcony overhanging the walls, in full view of the position of his advanced guard. Tornikios immediately took advantage of the imperial folly; he stormed the intrenchment, and the rebel archers, sending a flight of arrows at the balcony, compelled the emperor and his court to abandon their position with ludicrous celerity, amidst the derisive cheers of the citizens as well as of the enemy. But Tornikios, proud of the day's exploit, and trusting always to the delusive hope that the inhabitants would open the gates, delayed pressing the assault as the fugitives were entering within the walls. Next day, when he found the people would hold no communication with him, he ordered a general assault. The garrison had employed the whole night in making preparations to meet it; and as the defence was intrusted to experienced officers, and the citizens supported the regular troops, to save their property from the danger to which it would be exposed if a victorious enemy entered the city, Tornikios was defeated with considerable loss. He now found it necessary to raise the siege and retire to Arcadiopolis. Shortly after, he attacked the city of Rhedestos, and, the bishop keeping the inhabitants firm in their allegiance, he was again defeated. His cause now became desperate; for the news reaching his camp that the Asiatic troops had arrived at Constantinople, his followers quitted his standard, and he was forced to seek refuge in a church, from which he was taken by force, and sent to the emperor in chains. On Christmas eve he was deprived of his sight.

In the year 1050, several nobles of distinction were accused of conspiring to dethrone the emperor. The accusation may have been nothing more than a court intrigue or a fiscal measure, for only one was punished by the confiscation of his estates.[1]

Another plot shows the contemptible condition to which the imperial power had fallen in the estimation of the courtiers. Boïlas, a man of low birth, had gained the favour of Con-

[1] Cedrenus, 786.

stantine IX. by his talents for buffoonery and his capacity for business. He amused the emperor by his wit, and relieved him from much embarrassment by his application. Boïlas being utterly destitute of all principle, and possessing little judgment with a daring character, conceived the preposterous idea of making himself emperor. He knew that he was fitter to fill the throne than the reigning emperor, and he thought the court so worthless that he expected to succeed in his design. He applied to several persons in high office to secure their assistance, and found intriguers and malcontents who were willing to make him an instrument in their hands, while he believed he was using them as the servants of his own ambition. The conspiracy was revealed on the very night it had been resolved to assassinate Constantine; but it seems the emperor was never persuaded that his favourite was really guilty, for he soon restored him to his office, in order to enjoy his buffoonery.[1]

The reign of Basil II. marks the summit of the military power of the Byzantine empire. In the reign of Constantine IX. the first traces of decay are visible in the military system, which, for three centuries and a half, had upheld a standing army equal to the Saracen forces in the East, and superior to any troops the nations of Europe had been able to maintain permanently in the field. The alliance of the Servians and Armenians was now lost; the Normans were allowed to acquire an independent existence in Italy; and though the Russians and Patzinaks were defeated, the Seljouk Turks began to undermine the whole fabric of the Byzantine power in Asia.

The disorders which attended the dethronement of Michael V. induced Stephen Bogislav, the sovereign of Servia, to invade Illyria and Macedonia, from which he carried off immense booty, ravaging the country like a wild beast rather than a man.[2] Constantine IX., in order to prevent his repeating his depredations, ordered the governor of Dyrrachium to march into Servia with a large body of troops—the garrisons of all the neighbouring themes that could be immediately concentrated; and it was pretended that the army consisted of sixty thousand men.[3] The general, ignorant of military science, trusted entirely to his numbers, which the Servians were unable to resist in the open field. He pushed carelessly

---

[1] A patrician named Boïlas attempted to mount the throne in the reign of Romanus I. See page 272.　　　[2] Zonaras, ii. 248.　　　[3] Cedrenus, 757.

forward into the heart of the country, ravaging everything around, and collecting booty, until he involved himself in the mountainous district, full of narrow defiles and rugged roads. As no enemy was to be found, he here gave the order to return to Dyrrachium; but no sooner was the retreat commenced than the Servians resumed their activity, and Stephen suddenly beset the passes with his army. The head and rear of the Byzantine columns were assailed at the same time, the march was delayed, and the booty lost. The Byzantine general, incapable of combining the movements of his different divisions for their mutual support, and his lieutenants, ignorant of one another's movements, were thrown into inextricable confusion. A general attack of the Servians in one of the mountain passes completed the rout of the army, and, if we believe the Byzantine writers, seven generals and forty thousand men perished in this expedition.[1]

We have already seen that the social condition of the inhabitants of Russia in the preceding century was considerably more advanced than that of the people in western Europe. Their commerce with the Byzantine empire, which had been one of the causes of their progress in wealth and civilisation, was greatly extended during the present century; and after the conquest of Cherson, and the decay of that flourishing city, a considerable number of Russian merchants established themselves at Constantinople. The influence of these traders soon became very great, for, besides the regular trade they carried on between the north and south, they also acted as bankers for the Varangian and Russian mercenaries in the Byzantine service, and as agents for many Bulgarian and Sclavonian landed proprietors, whose produce they purchased. About the commencement of the year 1043, it happened that a Russian of rank was slain in a tumult, and the sovereign of Kief, Yaroslaf, deemed it a favourable occasion for making conquests in the Byzantine territory, as the Normans had done in France, and the Danes in England. The Emperor Constantine in vain offered all reasonable satisfaction; the Northmen and the Russians were determined to try the fortune of war, for they wanted to obtain something very different from indemnity for the consequences of a tumult in the streets of Constantinople. An expedition, composed of Varangians

---

[1] The Servians are sometimes called Triballi, and sometimes mentioned in conjunction with the Triballi, that name being applied to the Sclavonians generally.—Cedrenus, 754. Zonaras, ii. 248. Laon. Chalcocondylas, 17.

and Russians, under the command of Vladimir, son of Yaroslaf, who had been elected prince of Novgorod by his father's influence, and Viuchata, as his counsellor and lieutenant-general, crossed the Black Sea. The commerce of Russia was a matter of so much importance to the capital, the Varangians and Russian mercenaries formed so valuable a part of the imperial land-forces, and the indolent Constantine was so averse to war, that he made a sacrifice of the punctilio of Byzantine diplomacy, and again demanded peace when the hostile armament appeared off the entrance of the Bosphorus. But the Russians, bent on plunder and conquest, rejected peace, unless the emperor would engage to pay three pounds' weight of gold to each soldier in the expedition.

Constantine now made active preparations for repulsing the attack on his capital. He had already arrested all the Russian merchants and soldiers in the empire, and sent them into distant themes, to be guarded as prisoners until the war should be terminated. The greater part of the Byzantine fleet was either absent in the Archipelago or employed on the coast of Italy; but the ships in the port of Constantinople were prepared for sea; and their size, as well as the use of Greek fire, gave them such a superiority over the boats of the Russians that the sailors were eager for a battle. The first naval engagement proved indecisive, and the Russians contrived to destroy a part of the Greek fleet which separated from the main squadron; but in another action the Russians suffered great loss, and a storm shortly after completed the ruin of their enterprise. In landing to plunder, their troops were also defeated. On their retreat, a second storm overtook them in passing Varna, and their losses were so great that, according to the accounts of their own historians, fifteen thousand men perished. Three years elapsed before peace was re-established, but a treaty was then concluded, and the trade at Constantinople placed on the old footing.[1] From this period the alliance of the Russians with the Byzantine empire was long uninterrupted; and as the Greeks became more deeply imbued with ecclesiastical prejudices, and more hostile to the Latin nations, the Eastern church became, in their eyes, the symbol of their nationality, and the bigoted attachment of the Russians to the same religious formalities obtained for them from the Byzantine Greeks the appellation of the most Christian nation.[2]

[1] Cedrenus, 758. Zonaras, ii. 253. *Chronique de Nestor*, par Paris, i. 178.
[2] Nicetas, 337.

The Patzinaks, who still occupied the whole country from the Dnieper to the Danube, had not repeated the ravages they committed in the year 1036. They were occupied by wars with the Russians and with the Uzes, a nomadic nation of Turkish race like themselves, but who proved their irreconcilable enemies.[1] Tyrach was at this time king of the Patzinaks, and Keghenes, a man whose merits as a soldier had raised him to rank, commanded the army. The fame of the general excited the envy of the king, and Keghenes was forced to seek shelter in the Byzantine empire, to which he retired with a numerous body of followers.[2] From an island in the Danube, near Dorystolon, in which he had intrenched himself, the Patzinak general solicited permission to enter the empire, and Constantine IX., well pleased to gain the services of so distinguished a warrior, gave orders that he should be honourably received. Keghenes embraced the Christian religion, and received the title of a Roman patrician. His followers were established in forts on the banks of the Danube, where they employed themselves in plundering the country they had quitted. Tyrach called on the emperor to restrain these forays, but, finding his reclamations neglected, he took advantage of the severe winter of 1048 to cross the Danube on the ice, and invade the empire with a numerous army.[3] Bulgaria was ravaged, but the sudden changes of plenty and privation to which the invaders were compelled to submit spread disease through their ranks. The followers of Keghenes and the Byzantine troops concentrated round them, their numbers were thinned by disease, famine, and incessant attacks, until Tyrach and his whole surviving army were compelled to surrender at discretion. Keghenes urged the Byzantine generals to put all their prisoners to death, observing that it was wise to kill the viper when he was benumbed, lest the returning warmth of the sun should enable him to escape and use his venom; but the Byzantine empire was too civilised for such an act of wholesale inhumanity, and the captive soldiers were

1 The Uzes, Uzu, or Uzi, seem to be a cognate nation of the Kumans. Little is known of the race and language of the Patzinaks. Cedrenus calls them royal Scythians, and says they were divided into thirteen tribes.—775.
2 Cedrenus, 776. Twenty thousand men are reported to have accompanied Keghenes.
3 Cedrenus says there was a Byzantine fleet of a hundred triremes, as he pedantically terms river-craft, stationed on the Danube, to prevent the passage of the barbarians.—777. Keghenes had derived his greatest profits from the sale of the young women and children he captured as slaves in the Byzantine empire. This shows the great extent of the slave-trade at this period ; and it is not improbable that nearly all domestic servants throughout the cities were slaves.

established as agricultural colonists on waste lands near Sardica and Naissos. It had always been one of the problems in the Roman empire how to find the means of filling up the drain of the native population that time seemed perpetually to sweep away with unsparing activity. The king and many of the Patzinak nobles were sent to Constantinople, where they embraced Christianity, and were well treated by the emperor.

In the mean time fifteen thousand of the ablest soldiers were selected from among the prisoners, enrolled in the Byzantine army, and sent to join the troops on the Armenian frontier, where an army was preparing to encounter a threatened attack of the Seljouk Turks under Togrulbeg. This body of Patzinaks was placed under the command of the patrician Constantine Artovalan, but was formed into four divisions under native officers. On reaching Damatrys, Kataleim, one of the Patzinak generals, persuaded his countrymen to attempt forcing their way home. A rapid march enabled them to reach the Bosphorus, but when they arrived at the monastery of St. Tarasios, on the narrowest part of the straits, they found no boats to cross into Europe. Kataleim immediately arranged a body of cavalry in order, and plunged into the stream at their head. A sufficiency of boats was easily secured on the European side, and the whole army transported over. Without any delay they pushed on to Sardica and Naissos, where they were joined by their countrymen, who had been established in that country as agricultural colonists, and then, hastening to the banks of the Danube, they occupied a strong position near the mouth of the river Osmos. They also formed a second camp at a place called the Hundred Hills, and from these stations plundered the districts in their vicinity.

On hearing of this daring movement, the emperor summoned Keghenes and his followers to Constantinople. As these troops lay encamped without the walls waiting for orders, three Patzinaks attempted to assassinate Keghenes, but were secured after inflicting on him some severe wounds. When brought before the emperor, they accused Keghenes of treasonable correspondence with the fugitives, and Constantine, with suspicious timidity, gave credit to their improbable story, and ordered Keghenes to be put under arrest. The immediate consequence of this false step was, that the followers of the arrested general fled and joined their countrymen, who had advanced to the neighbourhood of Adrianople. The emperor in his alarm released Tyrach, the Patzinak king, on receiving his oath to reduce his countrymen to obedience; but that monarch, on regaining his liberty, laid aside his Christianity, repudiated his promises, and placed himself at the head of a powerful army, eager to avenge his former defeat. Two Byzantine armies were routed with great slaughter.

Great exertions were used to assemble another army in order to repress the ravages of the Patzinaks, who were devastating all the country between the Danube and Adrianople. Nicephorus Bryennios took the command at the head of the Frank and Varangian mercenaries, and the Asiatic cavalry from Telouch, Cilicia, and Mesopotamia. Keghenes was restored to favour, and sent to negotiate terms of peace with his countrymen. The military operations circumscribed the forays of the enemy, and the Byzantine army surprised and destroyed a number of the Patzinaks at Chariopolis; but Keghenes, trusting himself among his countrymen, was treacherously murdered. After many vicissitudes, the Patzinaks were forced to retreat, and concluded a truce for thirty years.[1]

In Italy the affairs of the empire went to ruin after the departure of Maniakes. Constantine IX. favoured Arghyros because he had opposed Maniakes, and that chief rendered himself virtually independent, and assumed the title of Prince of Bari and Duke of Apulia. The Normans, taking advantage of the intrigues and dissensions that prevailed, quitted their profession of mercenaries for that of feudal chieftains, and by taking such a part in the wars between Arghyros and Guaimar, prince of Salerno, as their own interests dictated, they succeeded in forming their captains into a confederation of territorial barons, under a leader, who became count of Apulia. Their progress excited the alarm of the emperor of Constantinople, the emperor of Germany, and the Pope; but their services were so often in requisition by powerful rivals, and their conduct was so prudent, that they prevented any coalition of their enemies which might have crushed them in their early career. The Byzantine troops were defeated, the intrigues of the emperor of Germany were baffled, Pope Leo IX., who ventured to appeal to arms, was beaten and taken prisoner; while the victors, as pious as politic, purchased the support of the See of Rome from their captive by offering to hold all their conquests as a fief of St. Peter's chair. The schism of the Greek and Latin churches, which broke out with great animosity about this

[1] Cedrenus, 790.

time, increased the aversion of the Italians to Byzantine domination, and tended quite as much as the military superiority of the Norman troops to give stability to their government.

The capture of Otranto by the Normans under Robert Guiscard, in the year 1055, may be considered as the termination of the Greek power in Italy.

While the Byzantine empire was beginning to exhibit symptoms of decline in the West, Constantine IX. added to its territories in the East by destroying the Armenian kingdom of the Bagratians, which had long acted a brilliant part in the military history of Asia.[1] No act, however, could have been more unnecessary or imprudent than the annexation of the city of Ani, the last capital of Armenian independence, to the empire, for the whole of the Byzantine frontier was thus thrown open to the invasion of the Seljouk Turks, without the barrier of independent Christian mountaineers that had hung on the flank of previous invaders. It has been mentioned that the Emperor Basil II., during his campaign against the Iberians in 1022, compelled Joannes Sembat to sign a treaty ceding, at his death, Ani and his whole kingdom to the emperor.[2] Constantine IX. considered the moment favourable for calling on Gagik, the nephew of Joannes, to fulfil the obligations of this treaty; and when the Armenian objected, he formed an alliance with Aboulsewar, the Saracen emir of Tibium (Tovin), and sent a Byzantine army to attack Ani. The treachery of the Armenian nobles aided the progress of the Byzantine and Saracen arms. Gagik, a prince of some ability, finding it useless to struggle with so powerful a combination, consulted the interests of his subjects by submitting to the Christians. On receiving a safe-conduct for his person, he repaired to plead his cause before the emperor at Constantinople, and the city of Ani surrendered to the Byzantine troops, A.D. 1045. Gagik, finding there was no hope of preserving his ancestral kingdom, accepted the rank of magistros, and received extensive estates in Cappadocia. Thus the oldest Christian kingdom was erased from the list of independent states by a Christian emperor. The only Armenian district which continued to preserve its independence between the Byzantines and Saracens was Kars, where Gagik Abas, a member of the family of the Bagratians, ruled as prince. The Byzantine government

---

[1] At this time Armenian princes governed Sebaste, Karuz, the Gurgars, Iberia, and Abasgia. [2] See page 357.

carried its jealousy of the Armenians so far as to compel their Patriarch, Peter, to quit the city of Ani and take up his residence at Arzen, from whence they subsequently transferred him to Constantinople.[1]

In the year 1048 the Seljouk Turks attacked the empire. They were one of the hordes which formed itself out of the fragments of that great Turkish empire, whose commercial connection with Constantinople occupied the attention of Roman statesmen in the time of Justinian.[2] Togrulbeg, called by the Byzantine historians Tangrolipix, was its chief. The Turkish tribes of central Asia were now acting the part, in the empire of the caliphs of Bagdat, which the Goths formerly acted in the Roman empire. Under Mahmoud the Gaznevid, the Turkish hordes which furnished mercenaries to the caliphs founded for themselves an empire, but the son of the Gasnevid was defeated by new hordes, who elected Togrulbeg as their chief. This new sovereign, after destroying the dynasty of the Bowides, became sultan of Persia, and the limits of his dominions touched the frontiers of the Byzantine conquests in Armenia. Togrulbeg visited Bagdat, assumed the title of Defender of the Faith and Protector of the Caliph ; and when he had rendered himself completely master of the temporal power at Bagdat, he compelled the haughty caliph to receive him as a son-in-law, by showing the representative of the Prophet that he possessed the power of starving him on his sacred throne.

Eight years before Togrulbeg succeeded in establishing himself as a sovereign in Bagdat, he sent his cousin Koutoulmish to attack the emir of Diarbekir.[3] Koutoulmish was defeated, and compelled to retreat to the Armenian frontier of Vasparoukan, where he solicited permission to pass through the Byzantine territory, promising to maintain the strictest discipline in his march. The governor of Vasparoukan refused the request of the defeated general, and prepared to oppose

---

1 Gagik, the last king of Armenia, was murdered at Cybestra in 1079. The Patriarch at last obtained permission to reside at Sebaste, where he died in 1060.—Chamich, *History of Armenia*, by Avdall, ii. 161. Saint Martin, *Mémoires sur l'Arménie*, i. 421.   2 *Greece under the Romans*, 331.
3 The Byzantine historians, Cedrenus, 769 ; Zonaras, ii. 256, erroneously place the taking of Bagdat by Togrulbeg before the invasion of the empire, but it happened eight years later, in 1050.—Weil, *Geschichte der Chalifen*, iii. 87, 94. Nassir ed Dulah, son of Merwan, was prince of Diarbekir ; and, though a Mahommedan, was a tributary of the empire.—St. Martin, ii. 216. Koutoulmish was the grandson of Seljouk, and the ancestor of the Seljouk sultans of Roum or Iconium. He and his eldest son perished in attempts to render themselves independent. Souleïman, his second son, was appointed by Malek-shah to a command in Asia Minor, with authority to found a feudatory principality, in 1074.—Nicephorus Bryennius, 24.

the Turks, should they venture to pass the frontier. Koutoul-mish, who saw that only prompt and vigorous measures could save him from being surrounded, attacked the Byzantine governor, routed his army, and, carrying him away as a prisoner, sold him as a slave in Tabreez. On his return, he vaunted so loudly the fertility of Vasparoukan, and spoke with such contempt of the Byzantine troops, that Togrulbeg determined to invade the empire. Hassan the Deaf was in-trusted with the vanguard, amounting to twenty thousand men, but was completely defeated near the river Stragna by Aaron the son of Ladislas, the last king of Bulgaria, who was governor of Vasparoukan, and Katakalon the governor of Ani. The main body of the Turkish army, however, under Ibrahim Inal, the nephew of Togrulbeg, avenged the defeat. It was composed of Turks, Kaberoi, and Limnites.[1] Katakalon, an experienced general, wished to meet this army in the field, as it was composed chiefly of infantry, or cavalry whose horses were unshod; but his Bulgarian colleague appealed to the emperor's instructions, which ordered his army to await the arrival of Liparites the prince of Abasgia. The Turkish general, finding the greater part of the wealth of the country secured in strong fortresses, advanced to attack the populous city of Arzen, which was unfortified. The inhabitants, trust-ing to their numbers and valour, had neglected to convey their valuable effects into the impregnable fortress of Theo-dosiopolis, in their neighbourhood. Arzen was at this time one of the principal centres of Asiatic commerce, and was filled with warehouses belonging to Syrian and Armenian merchants. The inhabitants defended themselves against the Turks with courage for six days, by barricading the streets and assailing the enemy from the roofs of the houses. Kata-kalon in vain urged his colleague to march to the relief of the place. Ibrahim, however, felt the danger of an attack on his rear, and, abandoning the hope of securing booty by the taking of the place, thought only of destroying the resources it fur-nished to the Byzantine government. He set fire to the place and reduced the whole of this great commercial city to ashes. Never was so great a conflagration witnessed before, and it has only since been rivalled by the burning of Moscow. One hundred and forty thousand persons are said to have perished by fire and sword, yet the Turks captured so many prisoners

[1] Cedrenus, 771. St. Martin, *Mém. sur l'Armenie*, ii. 204, conjectures that the Kaberoi were Curds, and the Limnites Dilimites.

that the slave-markets of Asia were filled with ladies and children from Arzen. The Armenian historians dwell with deep feeling on this terrible calamity, for it commenced a long series of woes which gradually destroyed all the capital accumulated by ages of industry in the mountains of Armenia, rendering them one of the richest and most populous districts in the East. Indeed, the ruin of Arzen was the first step to the dispersion of the Armenian Christians and the desolation of Asia Minor.[1]

As soon as Liparites effected the junction of the Iberian and Abasgian troops with the Byzantine army, a battle was fought with the Turks near Kapetron, on the 18th September 1048.[2] The loss on both sides was great and the results indecisive, but Liparites was taken prisoner, and the Byzantine troops retired. Ibrahim, however, found himself unable to continue the campaign, and returned to Rey. Togrulbeg released Liparites without ransom, or rather he bestowed the ransom sent by the Byzantine emperor on the Abasgian prince, recommending him to be always a friend to the Turks. It is said by Arabian historians that Constantine IX., in order to equal the generosity of Togrul, repaired the Mohammedan mosque at Constantinople.[3]

Negotiations were commenced between Constantine and Togrul, but they led to no result, and Togrul invaded the Byzantine empire in person. His first attack was directed against the independent principality of Kars, and the Armenians were defeated in battle, and their general, Thatoul, taken prisoner. Thatoul was said to have wounded Arsouran, the son of the favourite minister of Togrul, and when the captive general was led before his conqueror, the sultan told him that if the young man died he should be put to death. To this Thatoul calmly replied, "Sultan, if the wound was inflicted by my hand, your warrior will certainly die." This proved true, and Togrul had the barbarity to execute the brave Armenian, and send his head to the minister whose son had died, as a proof that it could not slay another.[4]

Togrul then directed his forces against the city of Manzikert, employing in the siege an immense ballista which had been constructed by the Emperor Basil II., which he had

---

[1] St. Martin, ii. 201. Chamich, ii. 138, says Arzen contained three hundred thousand inhabitants, and eight hundred churches.

[2] St. Martin places the battle in 1049, but the second indiction commenced on the 1st September 1048.—Cedrenus, 773.

[3] St. Martin, ii. 217.   [4] Chamich, *History of Armenia*, ii. 143.

taken in the town of Bitlis. This immense engine required four hundred men to drag it along, yet it proved of little use to the Turks, for a Gaul in the Byzantine service destroyed it by breaking over it three bottles of an inflammable mixture, while he was approaching the camp of the besiegers as the bearer of a letter to the sultan. The loss of this engine, however, did not abate the courage of the troops, and Alkan, the general of the Khorasmians, promised the sultan to carry the place by assault. The governor of Manzikert made preparations for giving the storming party a desperate reception. The walls were garnished with engines, and the artillery was well supplied with ponderous stones, gigantic arrows, and beams shod with iron, to launch on the assailants. The defenders were ordered to remain carefully concealed behind the battlements, and Alkan, after commencing the attack with volleys of missiles, advanced to the foot of the wall, satisfied that he had silenced the enemy. But when his men began to plant their ladders, a tempest of stones, arrows, beams, boiling pitch, and smoke-balls overwhelmed the bravest, and the rest shrunk back. Their hesitation was the signal for a furious sally, in which Alkan was taken prisoner, and immediately beheaded on the city walls, in sight of the sultan. Togrul, finding that he could not take Manzikert, gave up all hope of breaking through the barrier of fortresses that defended the frontier of the empire, and retired into Persia, A.D. 1050.

He again invaded the empire in 1052, but the Byzantine army having received a strong reinforcement of Frank and Varangian mercenaries, showed itself so superior to that of the Seljouk sultan in military discipline, that Togrul thought it prudent to retire without hazarding a battle.[1] The military system established by Leo III. and Constantine V., and perfected by Nicephorus II., John I., and Basil II., still upheld the glory of the Byzantine arms.

In looking back from modern times at the history of the Byzantine empire, the separation of the Greek and Latin churches appears the most important event in the reign of Constantine IX.; but its prominency is owing, on the one hand, to the circumstance that a closer connection began shortly after to exist between the Eastern and Western nations; and, on the other, to the decline in the power of the Byzantine empire, which gave ecclesiastical affairs greater import-

[1] Cedrenus, 780, 788. Chamich, ii. 142. The chronology of the Byzantine historian is entitled to more credit than the Armenian. For this period, indeed, Cedrenus is a valuable authority.

ance than they would otherwise have merited. Had the successors of Constantine IX. continued to possess the power and resources of the successors of Leo III. or Basil I., the schism would never have acquired the political importance it actually attained; for as it related to points of opinion on secondary questions, and details of ecclesiastical practice, the people would have abandoned the subject to the clergy and the church, as one not affecting the welfare of Christians, nor the interests of Christianity. The Emperor Basil II., who was bigoted as well as pious, had still good sense to view the question as a political rather than a religious one. He knew that it would be impossible to reunite the two churches; he saw the disposition of the Greek clergy to commence a quarrel, to avoid which he endeavoured to negotiate the amicable separation of the Byzantine ecclesiastical establishment from the papal supremacy. He proposed that the Pope should be honoured as the first Christian bishop in rank, but that he should receive a pecuniary indemnity, and admit the right of the Eastern church to govern its own affairs according to its own constitution and local usages, and acknowledge the Patriarch of Constantinople as its head. This plan, reasonable as it might appear to statesmen, had little chance of success. The claim of the Bishop of Rome to be the agent of the theocracy which ruled the Christian church, was too generally admitted to allow any limits to be put to his authority. The propositions of Basil II. were rejected, but the open rupture with Rome did not take place until 1053, when it was caused by the violent and unjust conduct of the Greek patriarch, Michael Keroularios. He ordered all the Latin churches in the Byzantine empire, in which mass was celebrated according to the rites of the Western church, to be closed; and, in conjunction with Leo, bishop of Achrida, the Patriarch of Bulgaria addressed a controversial letter to the bishop of Trani, which revived all the old disputes with the papal church, adding the question about the use of unleavened bread in the holy communion. The people on both sides, who understood little of the points contested by the clergy, adopted the simple rule, that it was their duty to hate the members of the other church; and the Greeks, having their nationality condensed in their ecclesiastical establishment, far exceeded the Western nations in ecclesiastical bigotry, for the people in the western nations of Europe were often not very friendly to papal pretensions. The extreme bigotry of the Greeks soon tended to make the people of the Byzantine empire averse to all intercourse with the Latins, as equals, and they assumed a superiority over nations rapidly advancing in activity, wealth, power, and intelligence, merely because they deemed them heretics. The separation of the two churches proved, consequently, more injurious to the Greeks, in their stationary condition of society, than to the Western Christians, who were eagerly pressing forward in many paths of social improvement.

The Empress Zoe died in the year 1050, at the age of seventy.[1] Constantine IX. survived to the year 1054.[2] When the emperor felt his end approaching, he ordered himself, according to the superstitious fashion of the time, to be transported to the monastery of Mangana, which he had constructed. His ministers, and especially his prime-minister, John the logothetes, and president of the senate,[3] urged him to name Nicephorus Bryennios, who commanded the Macedonian troops, his successor. The forms of the imperial constitution rendered it necessary that the sovereign should be crowned in Constantinople, and a courier was despatched to summon Bryennios to the capital. But as soon as Theodora heard of this attempt of her brother-in-law to deprive her of the throne she had been compelled to cede to him, she hastened to the imperial palace, convoked the senate, ordered the guards to be drawn out, and, presenting herself as the lawful empress, was proclaimed sovereign of the empire with universal acclamations. The news of this event embittered the last moments of the dying voluptuary, who hated Theodora for the respect her conduct inspired.

SECTION III

REIGNS OF THEODORA AND MICHAEL VI. (STRATIOTIKOS, OR THE WARLIKE), A.D. 1054–1057

Character and administration of Theodora, 1054–1056 — Incapacity of Michael VI., 1056–1057 — Administration of the empire transferred to the eunuchs of the imperial household — Conspiracy of the great nobles in Asia Minor — Michael VI. dethroned.

Theodora, with a good deal of masculine vigour of character, possessed the confined views and acrimonious passions of a

---

[1] Zonaras, ii. 260. Lupus in *Bibliotheca Hist. Regni Siciliæ*, i. 39.
[2] Zonaras, ii. 262.
[3] Zonaras, ii. 261. John was a eunuch of great literary pretensions, but of scanty classical and no great political knowledge.

recluse. Her first act was to revenge on Bryennios the attempt which her brother-in-law had made to deprive her of the throne. He and his partisans were banished, and his estates confiscated. Her personal attention to the duties of a sovereign, and the strictness with which she overlooked the general administration, proved that, unlike her predecessor, she acted according to the dictates of her own conscience in public affairs, and not as the passive instrument of those who were willing, for their own ends, to relieve her from exertion. Yet she followed the system by which the members of her family, in establishing their despotic power, had undermined the fabric of the Byzantine administration. Instead of selecting the ablest native senators to act as ministers and judges, she intrusted the direction of every department of government to eunuchs of her household, and her prime-minister was Leo Strabospondyles, an ecclesiastic, synkellos of the Patriarch of Constantinople. She even sent one of her eunuchs to supersede Isaac Comnenos as commander-in-chief of the army placed on the frontier to watch the movements of the Turks.[1] Isaac belonged to one of those great aristocratic families in Asia Minor whose wealth and power had long excited the jealousy of the emperors; and Theodora now displayed much too openly the distrust with which they were regarded by the central administration. To preserve all power as much as possible in her own hands, she presided in person in the cabinet and the senate, and even heard appeals as supreme judge in civil cases. The performance of this last duty, though little in harmony with the executive power, was in her age looked upon by her subjects as a most laudable act.

Fortune favoured Theodora in the circumstances of her short reign, and her popularity was in a great measure derived from events over which she exercised no control. She was the last scion of a family which had upheld with glory the institutions of the empire for nearly two centuries, which had secured to its subjects a degree of internal tranquillity and commercial prosperity far greater than had been enjoyed during the same period by any equal portion of the human race, and the memory of which in succeeding years excited deep regret in the breasts of the Greeks themselves, though the Greeks were the body of their subjects treated with greatest neglect. During her reign, the empire was disturbed by no civil war, nor desolated

[1] Cedrenus, 791.

by any foreign invasion. The seasons were temperate, the fertility of the earth enabled the people to enjoy the blessings of peace, and a pestilence which had previously ravaged the principal cities of the empire suddenly ceased.

At the advanced age of seventy-six, Theodora felt herself so robust that she looked forward to a long life; and the monks who swarmed in her palace, observing her infatuated confidence in the vigour of her frame, flattered her with prophecies that she was destined to reign for many years. The superstitious feelings of the time, as well as the personal vanity of Theodora, caused her to place implicit confidence in these ecclesiastical soothsayers; but in the midst of her projects she was suddenly attacked by an intestine disorder that brought her to the grave. To prevent the government falling into the hands of the territorial aristocracy, she, with her dying breath, named Michael Stratiotikos as her successor.[1] He had been a general of some reputation, and an efficient member of the official establishment; but advanced age had converted him into a decrepit general and doting senator. The prime-minister and the eunuchs of Theodora had nevertheless suggested his nomination, as it promised to place on the throne one who could not avoid being an instrument in their hands. Theodora, hoping to recover her health, compelled the new emperor to swear with the most tremendous imprecations that he would always remain obedient to her orders, but she survived his nomination only a few hours; and with her expired the race of Basil the Sclavonian groom, and the administrative glory of the Byzantine empire, on the 30th of August, 1057.[2]

The accession of Michael VI. was no sooner known than the president of the senate, Theodosios Monomachos, nephew of Constantine IX., attempted to mount the throne, pretending a hereditary claim to the imperial succession. To enforce his ridiculous pretension, he armed his household slaves, who formed a numerous body, collected assistance from his friends, assembled a mob, and, proceeding through the streets of Constantinople at the head of this band, broke open the public prisons and talked of revolution. His plan was to storm the palace; but the moment his movements were made known to the officers of the native and Varangian companies of guards on duty, they marched against him, and he was immediately

---

[1] Stratiotikos is really an epithet, and not, like Monomachos, a surname. Had Michael VI. left posterity, his children might have converted it into a surname.
[2] Zonaras, ii. 262. Cedrenus, 792.

abandoned by all his followers. When he sought an asylum in St. Sophia's, he found the doors of the church closed against him, and was taken with his son sitting on the steps. This sedition was so contemptible that the people ridiculed the affair in a lampoon, and the emperor only banished its leader to Pergamus.[1]

Michael VI. was a man of a limited capacity, and his faculties were now dulled by age; yet accident intrusted him with the direction of the government at a delicate crisis. He was called upon to maintain the integrity of the Roman administrative system against the assaults of a territorial aristocracy, on whom the manners of the age and the altered relations of society had conferred powers at variance with the strict centralisation of the empire. Yet the incapacity of Michael must be regarded as having only accelerated a change which it would have required the genius and energy of a great administrative reformer like Leo III. to avert, and which could only have been averted by remodelling the constitution of the empire.

The administrative vigour of the government was diminished; its legal supremacy had vanished; the connection between the provinces and the capital was weakened; the people at a distance no longer respected the emperor as the centre of social order and the fountain of impartial justice; ruined roads had broken up the administrative unity of empire; great nobles governed their immense estates as sovereign princes; and frontier communities, being often compelled to defend themselves against foreign invaders by their own resources, began to consider how far those resources could be rendered available to lessen the fiscal extortions of the central government. The territorial aristocracy of the Byzantine empire had also at this time become warriors like the barons of the feudal states, and as they joined learning to their military qualities, they were able to perform the duties of judges and magistrates on their estates. Jealousy of their power, and the corruption of society in the capital, had led the emperors to intrust not only the direction of the civil administration, but even the highest military commands, to eunuchs of the imperial household, and a gradual hostility had grown up between this class and the territorial aristocracy. This employment of slaves and domestics as generals and statesmen seems strange to those who judge of the past by the actual condition of society; but no feature in Eastern manners has been more permanent than

[1] Zonaras, ii. 264.

the high social position acquired by slaves in their masters' families. Their education was often as carefully attended to, their character and abilities more impartially estimated, and their faults more judiciously eradicated, than those of the children of the house. The oldest records of society show us the slave as superior to the hired servant ; and the administration of the Ottoman empire, even in modern times, has been of easier access to the slave than to the citizen.[1] Despotism is also compelled to seek rather for personal devotion than systematic service, and no stronger proof can be adduced of the progress which the Byzantine government had made towards pure despotism, than the power the emperors had acquired of ruling their subjects by the members of their household.

Michael VI. was not blind to the hostile feelings of a powerful class of his subjects, but he relied on the permanence of the established order of things. The support of the senate, the obedience of the municipality of Constantinople, the conservative feelings of the clubs of the hippodrome, and of the corporations of the traders, seemed a complete guarantee against the success of any revolution ; and the emperor treated all these classes with liberality.[2] He felt, likewise, so confident in the attachment of the soldiers to their military organisation, that he imprudently wounded the pride and self-interest of the principal officers of the army and the official nobility, by holding back from them the promotions and donatives they were accustomed to receive at Easter. Other measures, equally ill-judged, were adopted about the same time. Katakalon, the most popular general in the empire, was deprived of the command at Antioch on a charge of fraudulently enriching himself by diminishing the number of soldiers in his government, and extorting money from the inhabitants. The justice of the act was, however, suspected, as he was replaced by Michael Ouranos, a nephew of the emperor.[3] Michael VI. likewise, on re-establishing Nicephorus Bryennios to the rank of which he had been deprived by Theodora, refused to restore his private fortune, which had been unjustly sequestrated ;

---

[1] Leviticus, chap. xxii. 10, 11 :—"There shall no stranger eat of the holy thing : a sojourner of the priest, or an hired servant, shall not eat of the holy thing. But if the priest buy any soul with his money, he shall eat of it, and he that is born in his house : they shall eat of his meat."

[2] He was accused, however, after his fall, of promoting clerks from the public offices, instead of senators, to be collectors of the revenue in the provinces.—Cedrenus, 793.

[3] This Michael assumed the name of Ouranos, and did not belong to the distinguished family of that Ouranos who defeated Samuel, king of Achrida, on the banks of the Sperchias.—Cedrenus, 793. Zonaras, ii. 263.

and when Bryennios urged his claim in person, the old emperor cut short his solicitations by saying, " Finished work alone merits wages." He had already ordered the restored general to lead a division of three thousand men to reinforce the army in Cappadocia, and Bryennios now left the capital inflamed with anger. Several of the most powerful nobles of Asia Minor had already formed a plot to overthrow the existing government, and they availed themselves of the offence given to Katakalon and Bryennios to establish secret communications with these officers and engage them in the conspiracy. Isaac Comnenus, Romanos Skleros, Michael Burtzes, and Nicephorus Botaneiates, who resided at Constantinople in princely state, directed the plot and arranged the plan of rebellion.[1]

The attention of government was diverted from these conspirators by the conduct of an officer with whom they had no connection. Hervé, a Norman general, who had distinguished himself under Maniakes, had subsequently served the empire with zeal and fidelity. On soliciting the rank of magistros, his claim was treated by the emperor in a way which irritated the pride of the Norman to such a degree that he quitted Constantinople, and hastened to an estate he possessed at Dabarme in Armenia. Collecting three hundred of his countrymen from the garrisons in the neighbourhood, he deserted to the Turks. He found, however, that the Infidels were less inclined to tolerate the proud spirit of independence that characterised the Normans than the Byzantines, and, separating from Samouch, the Seljouk leader, with whom he quarrelled, he led his little band to the city of Aklat, where he was surprised and made prisoner by the emir Aponasar.[2]

The rashness of Bryennios was even greater than that of Hervé; and as he was one of the conspirators, his conduct might have ruined their enterprise. The chiefs at Constantinople, having settled their plans, decided that Isaac Comnenus was to be the future emperor; and after plighting their mutual faith, with all the religious ceremonies and horrid imprecations which were then considered necessary to bind the conscience, retired to their estates to collect troops. Bryennios

---

[1] Manasses, *Chron.* 129.
[2] The adventures of Hervé are recorded by Cedrenus, 794. The importance of the Norman race is a curious instance of moral superiority, without any superiority of civilisation. In the Byzantine empire, and in Scotland, where they were not conquerors, they attained nearly as high a position as in Russia, France, England, and Naples, which they subdued with the sword.

P

had, in the mean time, reached Cappadocia, where he ordered the paymaster of the army to make an advance of pay to the soldiers under his command. This was refused, as being at variance with the emperor's orders. John Opsaras, who held the office of paymaster, was a patrician; yet, when he visited Bryennios in his tent, that officer so completely lost all command over his temper, that he struck him on the face, pulled his beard, threw him on the ground, and then ordered him to be dragged to prison. Another patrician, Lykanthos, who commanded the troops of Pisidia and Lycaonia in a separate camp, convinced that the conduct of Bryennios announced an intention to rebel, hastened with his guards to the spot, delivered Opsaras from confinement, and arrested Bryennios, whose eyes Opsaras ordered to be put out, and then sent him a prisoner to Constantinople.

The principal conspirators, fearing that their plot was discovered, repaired to Kastamona in Paphlagonia, where Isaac Comnenus was waiting, at his family seat, until the preparations for the rebellion were completed. The assembly of the conspirators having put an end to concealment, Isaac Comnenus was conducted by his partisans to the plain of Gounavia, and proclaimed emperor, on the 8th June 1057. Katakalon, finding some difficulty in joining his companions, forged an imperial order, giving him the command of five legions, which he concentrated in the plain of Nicopolis, pretending that he was to lead them against Samouch, a Turkish chief who had invaded the empire.[1] By promises and threats, he succeeded in engaging the officers of this force to join the rebellion; and, effecting a junction with the troops Isaac had already assembled, the rebels crossed the Sangarius, and gained possession of Nice.[2]

The Emperor Michael placed the imperial army under the command of Theodore, a eunuch whom he had raised to the rank of Domestikos of the East, and the Bulgarian prince, Aaron, who, though a brother-in-law of Isaac, was his personal enemy. The imperial generals broke down the bridges over the Sangarius, in order to cut off the communications of the rebels with the provinces in which their family influence lay, and then approached Nice. Isaac Comnenus was en-

---

[1] Two of these legions were composed of western Europeans, one of Russians, besides the native legions of Koloneia and Chaldia.—Cedrenus, 799.

[2] Isaac placed his treasures and his wife, who was a daughter of Ladislas, the last Bulgarian king of Achrida, in the castle of Pemolissa, in the castle of the Halys.— Cedrenus, 799.

camped about twelve stades to the north of the city, and the foragers of the two armies were soon in constant communication; the leaders on both sides overlooking the intercourse, in the expectation of gaining deserters. The imperialists urged their opponents not to sacrifice their lives for an ambitious rebel, who exposed their lives and fortunes for his own profit; while the rebels laughed at the idea of serving an old dotard, who intrusted the command of his armies to eunuchs. Isaac, seeing that nothing was to be gained by these conversations, gave strict orders to break off all communication; and Theodore, attributing the measure to fear, advanced to Petroa, only fifteen stades from the rebel camp.

A battle was thus inevitable. Isaac Comnenus drew out his army, which was composed of veteran troops, at a place called Hades. Katakalon commanded the left wing, and was opposed to Basil Tarchaniotes, the general of the European troops, the ablest and most distinguished of the Macedonian nobility. Romanos Skleros, at the head of the right wing, was opposed to Aaron, who had under his orders the patrician Lykanthos and the Norman Randolph. Isaac and Theodore directed their respective centres. The battle was not severely contested. Aaron routed the right wing of the rebels, but his success led to no result; for Katakalon, having defeated the Macedonian troops, stormed the imperial camp, while Isaac overthrew their centre. The aristocratic constitution of society displays itself in the incidents of this battle. The superior temper of the arms of the chiefs gave their exploits as much importance as in the Homeric battles. When the victorious troops of Isaac and Katakalon assailed the troops of Aaron, Randolph found himself borne away among a crowd of fugitives. Disengaging himself, he perceived Nicephorus Botaneiates leading the pursuers. Shouting his war-cry, the Norman knight met the Asiatic noble; but his sword was broken on the well-tempered helmet of his enemy, and he was led a prisoner to the rebel camp.[1] Several officers of rank were slain in the imperial army, and many made prisoners. The victors lost only one man of rank.

Isaac Comnenus advanced to Nicomedia, where he was met by envoys from the Emperor Michael, who offered him the title of Cæsar for himself, and a general amnesty for his partisans, if they would lay aside their arms. Isaac knew that he had no safety but as emperor, and Katakalon boldly opposed

[1] Cedrenus, 802.

all terms of arrangement. Michael Psellos, called the Prince of Philosophers, was one of the envoys, and seeing how matters were likely to end, he deserted the cause of his old master with more promptitude than might have been expected from a learned pedant. The emperor, finding he had nothing to expect from negotiation, attempted to fortify himself in Constantinople. He compelled the senators to take an oath, and subscribe a declaration, that they would never acknowledge Isaac Comnenus as emperor; and he lavished money, places, promotions, and privileges, on the people and the municipality. Yet the moment the victors reached the palace of Damatrys, the senators rushed to St. Sophia's, and begged the Patriarch to absolve them from the oath they had just taken. The stern Patriarch, Michael Keroularios, affected to resist, but consented to be himself the medium of communication with the new emperor. The cause of Michael VI. was now hopeless; Isaac was proclaimed emperor, and his predecessor was ordered to quit the imperial palace, that it might be prepared for the reception of the new sovereign. It is said the old man, before departing, sent to ask the Patriarch what he would give him for his resignation; the intriguing pontiff replied, with sarcastic humility, "The kingdom of heaven." On the 31st of August, Michael VI. returned as a private individual to his own house, where he lived undisturbed, dying two years after. On the 2nd of September, Isaac I. received the imperial crown in the Church of St. Sophia.

To contemporaries, this revolution presented nothing to distinguish it from the changes of sovereign, which had been an ordinary event in the Byzantine empire, and which were ascribed by the wisest statesmen of the time to the decree of Heaven, and not to the working of political and moral causes, which the will of God allows the intelligence of man to employ for effecting the improvement or decline of human affairs. It would be an error to ascribe the success of this rebellion to the weakness of the reigning emperor, and to the defects of his administration, or to the ability of bold and rapacious conspirators, without taking into account the apathy of the inhabitants of the empire to a mere change in the name of their emperor. Perhaps no man then living perceived that this event was destined to change the whole system of government, destroy the fabric of the central administration, deliver up the provinces of Asia an easy conquest to the Seljouk Turks, and the capital a prey to a band of crusaders.

We have now traced the progress of the Eastern Roman Empire through an eventful period of three centuries and a half. We have contemplated the rare spectacle of a great empire reviving from a state of political anarchy and social disorganisation; we have seen it reinvigorated by the establishment of a high degree of order and security for life and property; and we have recorded its progress to the attainment of great military power. We have endeavoured to trace the causes that led to this change, as well as to record the events which accompanied it. It would now be an instructive task to compare the condition of the population living under this reformed Roman Empire with that of the inhabitants of the countries which had once constituted the Empire of the West; but scholars have not yet performed the preliminary work necessary for such an inquiry, so that even a superficial examination of the subject would run into discussions on vague details. Each student of history, therefore, who may happen to turn over the pages of this volume, must institute the comparison for himself in that branch of historical or antiquarian research with which he is most familiar. Unfortunately the records of the Eastern Empire are deprived of one great source of historical interest—they tell us very little concerning the condition of the mass of the population; and while they enable us to study the actions and the policy of the emperors, and even to observe the political consequences of their respective administrations, they leave us in ignorance concerning many important questions relating to the composition of the mass of society; they supply few facts for discriminating its separate elements, or for forming a classification of its social ranks. We know that freemen, serfs, and slaves were mingled together in every city and province; and over the whole surface of the Byzantine dominions, heterogeneous races of mankind were compressed into apparent unity by the powerful government that ruled at Constantinople. But we are without the means of assigning to each class of society, and to each discordant nationality, its exact share and influence in the mass that composed the empire. We perceive that there was no real unity among the people, and yet the unity created by the government was so imposing, that both contemporary and modern historians have treated the history of the Byzantine empire as if it represented the feelings and interests of a Byzantine nation, and almost overlooked the indelible distinctions of the Greek, Armenian, and Sclavonian races, which, while forced into simultaneous action by the great administrative power that ruled them, constantly retained their own national peculiarities.

Two grand social distinctions illuminate the obscurities of Byzantine history during the period comprised in this volume. A regular administration of justice, that secured a high degree of security for life and property, gave the people an immeasurable superiority over the subjects of all contemporary governments, and bound the various nations within the limits of the Eastern Empire in willing submission to the central power.

Through all the darkness of the Byzantine annals, we perceive that a middle class exerted some influence on society, and that it formed an element of the population, independent of the heterogeneous national races from which it was composed. But the nature of its composition explains sufficiently why its political influence proved extremely insignificant when compared with its numbers, wealth, and social importance. Local institutions were reduced to such a state of subordination to the central authority, that they wanted the power to train the different nations of which the middle class was composed to similar political sentiments. All attempts of the people to reform their own condition proved fruitless, and demands for redress of public grievances could only prove successful by a revolution. Perhaps this evil may be inherent in the nature of all governments which carry centralisation so far as to suppress the expression of public opinion in municipal bodies. In such governments, whether monarchical or republican, the central authority becomes so powerful, that public opinion is rendered inefficacious to effect reform, and the people soon learn to regard revolutions as the only chance of improvement.

The middle class through the Byzantine empire was a remnant of ancient society—an element that had survived from the days of municipal liberty and national independence. Many free citizens still continued to till their lands—many were occupied in manufactures and commerce. It was the existence of this class which filled the treasury of the emperors —(taxation yields comparatively little in a state peopled by great nobles and impoverished serfs);—and it was the wealth of the Byzantine government which gave it an ultimate superiority over all its contemporaries for several centuries. Military excellence was at that time as much the effect of individual strength and activity in the soldier, as of discipline in the army or talent in the general. The wealth of the Byzantine emperors enabled them to fill their armies with the best soldiers in Europe; in their mercenary legions, knights and nobles fought in the ranks, and the captains of their guards were kings and princes.[1] Nor were the native troops inferior to the foreign mercenaries. The lance of the Byzantine officer was famous in personal encounters long before the aristocracy of western Europe sought military renown by imitating an exercise in which sleight-of-hand rather than valour secured the victory.[2]

It is not difficult to point out generally the causes which supplied the Byzantine treasury with large revenues, at a period when the precious metals were extremely rare in the west of Europe. A curious comparison might be made between the riches and luxury of the court of Constantinople during the reign of Theophilus, and the poverty and rudeness that prevailed at the court of Winchester under his contemporary, Egbert. The difference of the value of the precious metals is peculiarly striking. Theophilus gave two pounds' weight of gold, or a hundred and forty-four byzants, for a fine horse, of which the market value appears to have been a hundred byzants; yet, among the Saxons, about the same time, the price of a common horse was two-thirds of a pound weight of silver.[3] It is difficult to explain the rarity of the precious metals in the West, when we remember that the tin of Egbert's dominions found its way to Constantinople, and that the byzants of the Eastern emperors were the current gold coin throughout England. The subjects of the Byzantine empire supplied the greater part of western and the whole of northern Europe with Indian produce, spices, precious stones, silk, fine woollen cloth, carpets, cotton, what we now call morocco leather,[4] dye-stuffs, gums, oil, wine, and fruits; besides most manufactured articles, and all luxuries. Yet, from the poverty of the Western nations, their consumption

---

[1] For the exploits of Harold Hardrada, king of Norway, who was slain at Stamford Bridge, see Mallet's *Northern Antiquities*, 168, 194—Bohn's Antiquarian Library.

[2] See the account of the death of a Russian chief by the lance of Peter the Eunuch. —Leo Diaconus, 107, edit. Bonn.

[3] Leo Gramm. 454, edit. Par. Henry, in his *History of England*, quoting Wilkins' *Leges Saxonicæ*, gives the value of a horse at only £1. 15s. 2d. in modern money. There is a curious law of Isaac I., reviving older regulations concerning fees to be paid to bishops, which gives some idea of the value of money in the Byzantine empire under the Basilian dynasty.—Bonefidius, *Jus Orientale*, 36. Leunclavius and Freher, *Jus Græco-Romanum*, i. 120.

[4] Among the presents Alaric received to raise the siege of Rome, were three thousand skins of red leather.—Zosimus, lib. v. chap. 41, page 306, edit Bonn.

must have been comparatively small. The profits of the trade, however exorbitant they might have been on particular transactions, would not have formed an important article of national wealth, unless a constant profit had been realised by the difference of value of the precious metals in the various countries with which dealings were carried on. Few of the Western nations worked any mines, and yet they were constantly consuming a considerable amount of gold and silver; the Byzantine empire possessed considerable mines of silver, and we know that gold was always abundant in the treasury.[1] Gold and silver coin and slaves were consequently commodities on which a sure profit was always realised. But in the eleventh century a great change took place in society in western Europe, coincident with the stationary condition of the Byzantine empire. In the West, the spirit of social reform infused a sentiment of justice into the counsels of kings; in the East, a spirit of conservation, pervading the imperial administration, withered the energies of society.

---

[1] Byzantine gold coins are still common. We learn from many passages that silver was abundant in the Byzantine treasury; and several silver mines are still worked in Turkey, though at present to little purpose.

THE END

INDEX

W. BRENDON AND SON, LTD., PRINTERS, PLYMOUTH

Thessalonike   248

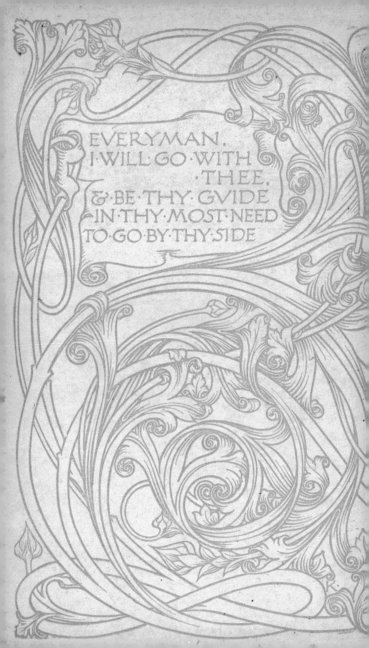

EVERYMAN,
I·WILL·GO·WITH
THEE,
&·BE·THY·GVIDE
IN·THY·MOST·NEED
TO·GO·BY·THY·SIDE